Managerial finance
a systems approach

Managerial Finance

a systems approach

EUGENE M. LERNER

Northwestern University

HARCOURT BRACE JOVANOVICH, INC.

New York / Chicago / San Francisco / Atlanta

This book is dedicated to my students, who, over the years, have given me some pain and much pleasure.

C

ISBN: 0-15-554705-4

Library of Congress Catalog Card Number: 73-153746

Printed in the United States of America

Preface

This book draws heavily upon my experiences in teaching Finance at the City College of the City University of New York, New York University, the University of California at Los Angeles, and Northwestern University. At each of these schools, I found the students to be capable and willing. And, I discovered what must be true at all schools: a subject treated as a vital and intellectually stimulating discipline engages students. But when issues are handled in a superficial manner, when excessive detail clouds the major theme, and when technique is displayed for its own sake, students simply "tune out" the professor and let him carry on with his monologue. This textbook was written with this knowledge clearly in mind. Hard issues in managerial finance are tackled, for this is where the intellectual action is to be found. Picayune details, technique for its own sake, and jargon (both verbal and mathematical) are omitted.

Financial management is built upon a series of relationships that link the integral parts of a firm together. Actions taken with respect to one activity have an impact upon other activities, and these, in turn, influence the first activity. The particular activities and relationships stressed in this book are the information flows that a manager receives, the cash flows through the firm, the growth of the enterprise, the market valuation placed upon the firm, and the environment within which the system as a whole operates.

Managerial Finance: A Systems Approach is designed for the first course in finance. With the perspective and material of this textbook as background, students can quickly and effectively move through more advanced topics presented in such courses as Investments, Portfolio Management, Money and Capital Markets, Financial Institutions, and various case courses in financial management. It can also serve as the basis of a terminal course in the field if a student does not elect to take further courses in finance.

Several colleagues have contributed greatly to this book, and, although I cannot identify here all those who helped, the special debt I owe to some must be acknowledged.

The work on systems in Chapter 1, the material on public utility information requirements in Chapter 12, the linear programming models of the firm as a system in Chapter 14, and the analysis of banks in Chapter 23, all draw heavily on the ideas and insights articulated by Joseph S. Moag. Many of the ideas on financial disclosure (Chapter 4) and linear programming (Chapter 13) were first proposed by Alfred Rappaport, a scholar deeply interested in the relationship between accounting statements and financial activities. The material on risk in Chapters 15 and 20 was strongly influenced by the work of Robert Machol, a systems analyst of great ability. Chapter 17 presents a security valuation framework developed in collaboration with Willard Carleton, my coauthor of *A Theory of Financial Analysis* (Harcourt, 1966).

Special thanks must be given to my good friend Donald P. Jacobs, who provided constructive criticisms of the ideas in every chapter and stressed the need for clarity and precision in thinking about financial matters.

Professors Dallas R. Blevins, Roger Upson, and Sidney Jones read drafts of this manuscript and made many helpful comments.

I am also indebted to the administration of the Graduate School of Management at Northwestern University, for the school was generous in rendering computer support and in allowing me to use early drafts of the manuscript in the classroom for the past two years.

Thanks are due to Eva Vincent and Naomi Schapira, who patiently typed draft after draft.

All authors know how much time is spent in writing a book. They know that during this period family life tends to come to a halt. If Susan, Laura, and Dean had not been willing to let their father devote almost all his attention to writing and if my wife, Janet, had not been willing to permit her husband to neglect her hour after hour, *Managerial Finance: A Systems Approach* could not have been completed.

EUGENE M. LERNER

Contents

Introduction

What does the financial manager of a corporation do which is so differ-ent from what other managers do that it warrants a special course of study? This section, which consists of a single chapter, formulates an answer to this question. By examining the finance function in a systems context, it shows the impact of decisions by the financial manager upon the entire firm.

The finance function
in a systems context

1

Financial managers realize that when a firm makes a major decision, the effect of the action will be felt throughout the enterprise. An increase in plant and equipment expenditures, for example, will affect the firm's cash position, its borrowing ability, and its dividend payments. Once the new plant begins operating the firm's production function may change; the volume of goods and services it can produce may increase, while the number of employees it hires may fall. Moreover, if the new equipment embodies a change in technology, the level of skill that is required of the firm's employees may increase.

Capital expenditures have such widespread ramifications because the activities of a firm are systematically interrelated. Consider the relationship between expenditures and their financing. Should the funds for a proposed expansion come from a reduction in dividend payments, from borrowing, from a cutback of other activities, or from some other source? The choice of financing depends on what the management of the firm believes the effect of that decision will be. If funds are raised by lowering dividends, the price of the company's stock may fall. If funds are raised through borrowing, the firm may find itself in a difficult position when the time comes to repay the loan. If other corporate activities are cut back in order to raise funds, the company's competitive position may deteriorate. Of course, not all these adverse effects may occur. The facts will vary from situation to situation. The point is, however, that the possible effects of capital-expenditure outlays on other corporate activities are important and must be considered in reaching a decision.

Some of the questions that capital-expenditure plans give rise to are social. For example, the construction of a new plant in a new location may result in lower costs, lower product prices, and higher profits for the company. The closing of the old plant, however, may cause an increase in unemployment in the area where it is located. Under these conditions, should the new investment be made?

Who determines the course the firm is to follow? Who controls the system? Who redesigns the system when the environment changes and new challenges arise to be met? In the pages and chapters that follow, the argument will be made that the financial manager's role is crucial in designing and controlling the complex system called a firm.

A traditional approach to the finance function

In the past, the duties and responsibilities of financial managers were considered to consist of a number of specific and unrelated tasks, many of which could be enumerated. For example:

(1) CREDIT AND PAYMENTS POLICY.

Receivables were to be collected in good order and bills were to be paid on time. To accomplish this task, the financial manager was to establish and supervise a credit and collection policy, and a payable policy. These policies would indicate the amount of credit to be extended to customers, the procedures to be followed when accounts became delinquent, and the priority to be followed in meeting payables.

(2) BANK RELATIONS.

When the company needed funds, the financial manager was to negotiate with various bankers to secure the money. This meant he had to maintain good relationships with bankers, holding regular meetings with them and reporting to them on favorable company activities.

(3) INVESTING EXCESS FUNDS.

Periodically, the firm might have an excess of cash in its bank account. The financial manager was to invest the excess in some short-term instrument, such as a Treasury bill, so that all the firm's assets would be contributing to total corporate profits.

(4) CAPITAL BUDGETING.

The financial manager was to review the proposals submitted by other operating departments for new plants and equipment with an eye to their financial feasibility. He was to alert the president if the profit potential of a proposal was too low for it to warrant serious consideration or if it would require more money than it was practical to raise.

(5) STOCKHOLDER RELATIONS.

Security analysts from various brokerage firms periodically visit companies to inquire about their potential profit opportunities. The financial manager was to meet with the analysts and inform them of the general prospects of the firm. In addition, he was to answer correspondence from shareholders about the annual report, dividend payments that might have been lost, and so forth.

(6) PENSION AND PROFIT-SHARING FUNDS.

The financial manager was to supervise the administration of the firm's profit-sharing and pension funds. He might be charged with actually selecting the investments that the fund makes or perhaps only with the more limited task of acting as an advisor to the trustees of the fund.

This listing of tasks and duties could be continued for several more pages without completely covering the wide range of financial activities and the diversity of skills demanded of a financial manager. The listing itself, however, reflects a style of thinking about the finance function that is no longer operative. It suggests that the function consists of performing effectively a series of specific, isolated, well-defined tasks. Today, no intellectually respectable executive would define the finance function in this way. *The job of the finance manager in a modern firm centers on the design and control of systems.* Some illustrations will help to clarify this distinction.

Credit policy, for example, is extremely important to a firm. But once a policy as to when credit will be extended is set and the procedures for executing the policy are defined, the activity itself can be carried on by a well-programmed computer. Each credit request that the company receives can be evaluated by the computer and a line of credit established or denied. When a change in the creditor's position warrants a change in the amount of credit extended, the computer can update and revise the credit line. When a payment is late, a collection letter can be automatically sent to the customer. If the payment is not received within a specified period, a notice can be sent to a collection agency, as well as to the customer.

From time to time, however, the entire credit and collection procedure may have to be revamped. New competitors may enter the scene, new products may be added to the line, and new commission structures may have to be established for the company's salesmen. These and other changes in the operation of the business itself may make the old credit system obsolete. Designing the changes that will go into the new credit and collection system is a finance problem. Once the new system is operative, extending credit and collecting receivables again becomes routine.

Investing excess funds is another important financial activity. These funds represent a potentially important source of earning power, but their investment is a task that can be performed automatically, once an effective cash-management system is established. For example, a company can arrange to have its customers pay their bills to a conveniently located collection bank, rather than to the firm itself. This may immediately cut down on the amount of time it takes the firm to invest its funds, since the length of time that a customer's check will be in the mail is reduced. The collection bank that receives the check simply photostats it, credits the money to the firm's account, and sends a copy of the check to the company for internal processing. Thus, instead of first updating its internal records and then depositing the customer's check, the company with an effective cash-management system will first deposit the check and then complete its records with a copy of the document.

When the company's deposit balance in the various local collection banks exceeds a specified amount, the excess funds can be sent by wire-transfer to a larger regional bank. The regional bank will then either forward the funds to the company's disbursement banks or automatically invest them in appropriate short-term, interest-paying investments.

Designing the firm's total cash-management system is an important finance problem; once the system is established, the actual orders to transfer funds and invest excessive balances are routine.

Capital budgeting, or the selection of the capital projects that a firm will undertake, is still a third design and control problem. For each investment project proposed, the financial manager may regularly collect data on such topics as:

(1) the market potential in the area where the investment is to be made;

(2) the degree of market penetration expected;

(3) the expected competitive response to the investment;

(4) the resources required to sustain the activity, i.e., the combinations of labor, machinery and materials that will be required to achieve different sales levels;

(5) technological dependencies implicit in the project, i.e., whether the project is feasible given the present level of technology or depends on some new development; and

(6) technological exposure, i.e., the vulnerability of the project to change.

Armed with these data and a working model of the entire firm, the financial manager can evaluate the project in terms of its impact on the firm as a whole. By simulating the outcomes, in this case the financial position of the firm with and without the project, its effect on the firm's future earnings, future cash flows, debt structure, ability to pay dividends, and so forth can be estimated. Once again, the financial manager's task is not to perform the calculations that demonstrate, say, the profitability of specific projects. Rather, it is the design and control of the system that will be used to evaluate all the capital projects that the firm will consider.

To summarize, financial management is no longer the simple performance of various well-defined tasks. Rather, *financial managers today design and control systems*—credit systems, cash-management systems, capital-budgeting systems, and so forth. But the manager's task does not end with the construction of these models alone. The subsystem models he creates must be combined and integrated into a global, or overall, model of the firm. By experimenting with the global model, he can evaluate the consequences of actions taken in one part of the firm in terms of their impact on other parts of the system.

The firm as a system

What are the components of a system? How does a financial manager go about designing and controlling a system? How does he proceed to modify it when it is no longer adequate?

All of us are familiar with the heating system of a home. It consists of three elements: a furnace, a thermostat, and the temperature in the room. When the room temperature falls below a certain point, the thermostat starts the furnace; when the room temperature exceeds an upper control point, the thermostat shuts off the furnace.

A business firm can be thought of in terms of the same three elements that describe the heating system.

(1) AN OPERATING SYSTEM.

The operating system is to a firm what the furnace is to the heating system. A firm's operating system consists of all the physical flows that go on inside the company. The actual inputs, such as the number of people who come to work each day and the amount of materials used to produce the actual outputs, are components of the operating system. Other components include the amount of goods stored as inventory, the number of plants the company maintains, and the physical machinery it has available.

(2) A STRATEGIC DESIGN SYSTEM.

The strategic design system plays a role comparable to the thermostat in the heating system. It effectively directs the firm's operating system in much the same way as the thermostat controls the furnace.

A firm's strategic design system consists of four elements:

(a) The goals or preferences that the management holds as to where the firm "ought to be" or what the firm "ought to look like" at a future date.

(b) The information that the management has about the firm's environment. This information consists of data about how the firm is currently performing, as well as data about new developments that are taking place outside the firm, in the industry and in the economy.

(c) Models indicating the relationships that link the elements in the operating system. These models can range from relatively simple statements about the physical inputs that are required to produce a unit of output to complex relationships that link potential investment opportunities to the funds that will be available to pay, say, the firm's creditors.

(d) A set of performance measures and standards, such as accounting budgets, quality-control standards, and work-force standards.

A firm's strategic design system will guide management in making decisions. It will help the manager to forecast the outcomes of various actions. From these forecasts, he can determine which action he should take to reach the goals that he has established efficiently.

For example, consider the cash-management system described in the preceding section. Management has certain preferences, or goals. In this case, it was to earn as much as possible on its excess cash balances. Management also knows certain things about the environment in which it operates: that it receives checks from a large number of sending points; that it can earn more money by collecting its checks faster; that it takes time for the mails to carry checks. The set of relevant models specify the relationships that link the collection-bank, regional-bank, disbursement-bank complex to the time that elapses between a customer's mailing his check in payment for goods and a banker's investing the funds in interest-bearing instruments. These models result in forecasts ("A dollar can be invested two days after the customer makes payment"), and they lead to a set of decisions (open collection banks in San Francisco, Chicago, and Dallas; use a New York bank as a regional bank; make disbursements from Chicago, New York, and Boston).

(3) AN ENVIRONMENT.

The third component of the firm, when it is viewed in a systems context, is its environment. This factor plays a role similar to that of the room temperature in the heating system: changes in the environment of the firm will trigger certain responses in the strategic design system, which in turn will result in a change in operations. For example, an automobile company's sales can be proceeding at a satisfactory pace when signs develop of a change in customer tastes. Market research indicates that smaller, more powerful, but less costly cars are growing in popularity. New operating systems, based on this intelligence concerning the change in the environment, may have to be constructed if the firm is to continue to grow and expand.

In addition to an operating system, a strategic design system, and an environment, a business firm also has a control system. These controls compare the firm's planned and realized outputs and generate feedback to the management when discrepancies arise between the two. For example, the strategic design system in the cash-management illustration forecast how long it would take to invest the funds once a customer deposited a check in the mail. Suppose that the model forecast that the process could be completed in two days, but that five days actually passed between the time a customer wrote a check and the money was invested. Obviously, something is wrong: Either the models that gave rise to the forecast are in error and must be revised; or one of the banks in the operating system is not functioning as it should and should be changed; or the environment itself has changed, e.g., the postal system now takes longer to deliver a letter than when the system was established. Once the firm is alerted to the discrepancy between expected and actual results, plans for making a change can be undertaken.

A firm's cash-budgeting procedure can be used to illustrate the continuous nature of the process of model-building, checking the results, and then modifying the model. Let us assume that the decision has been made that the firm's cash balance is not to fall below a certain level and that bank borrowings are not to exceed a pre-set amount. The financial officer can estimate what expenses are likely to be incurred and when the firm is likely to collect funds from its customers. By simulating the cash budget, i.e., by experimenting with different payable and collection policies, the change in the firm's cash position through time can be estimated. Then, by comparing the actual change that occurs with the figure forecast by the model, the financial manager can determine whether the budget as a whole, or any part of it (such as the collection of receivables or the disbursements for materials) is "in control."

Minor deviations from the budget may be ignored. Deviations lying a little further from the forecast value may be programmed to initiate a particular course of action, such as referral to the department head. If still larger discrepancies occur between the planned and realized outcomes, the system is "out of control." Did the environment change, so that assumptions made in the model are no longer accurate? Is there a flaw in the thinking that went into the construction of the model? Did part of the operating system fail? Once again the entire system must be evaluated. Meetings must be held between the several interested parties to determine the source of the discrepancy and to plan a remedial tactic. Once this is done, a new model for estimating the firm's cash balance through time will be developed that can accurately simulate the firm's cash position. The two tasks of designing the strategic system and controlling the operating system are therefore intimately related.

To summarize, the components of a firm are the strategic design system, the operating system, and the environment. In addition, a control system compares the planned and actual outputs of the firm. This latter system contains a series of important feedback loops that modify either the strategic design system or the operating system as needed. It takes both skill

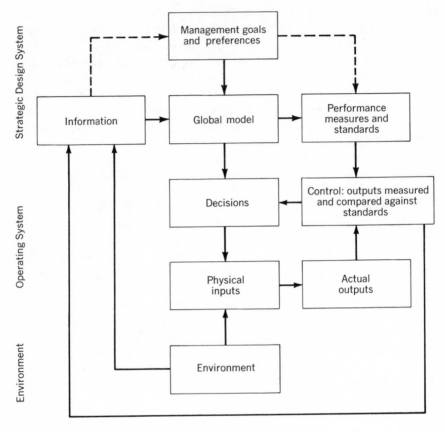

FIGURE 1.1

The Firm as a System.

and art to develop the ability to "read" the environment and select from it the strategic variables that affect a firm's range of options. And it takes technical competence to design a model of a firm's operating system and to update and revise it as the facts warrant. It is precisely these talents that characterize the successful modern financial officer.

The modern financial manager typically operates at the corporation's strategic design system level. He gathers information, reads the preferences of the firm's shareholders, and designs models that lead to decision guidelines for the operating system. The actual physical processes take place at the operating level. Extending credit, collecting receivables, and producing goods on a production line are operating-system activities.

The concept of a financial manager as one who executes a series of tasks places him at the operating-system level. In this view, the finance man "talks to analysts, negotiates with bankers, extends credit to cus-

The finance function in a systems context

tomers, supervises pension funds," and so forth. These are important tasks, and subordinates in the chief financial officer's department typically perform them. The difficulty with the concept of the finance function as being only, or primarily, concerned with the performance of a series of specified tasks is that it leaves unanswered such questions as: What decision rules guide the officer's conduct? Are they to be established by custom or conventions of the trade, or are they to be rational in the sense that they move the firm toward stated objectives? Furthermore, if the chief financial officer spends his time on operating-system activities, who does the corporate planning? Who monitors the environment to determine the impact of changes that are occurring in the environment? Who controls the firm by comparing planned outputs to actual results? Finally, if the financial officer is exclusively concerned with operating details, important as they may be, whose strategic design model dominates the firm's style? If a goal of the firm is to increase the price of the company's stock, which executive has the skill and training to advise on how this objective can best be met?

Considerations such as these dictated the change in the definition of the finance function over the years. The financial executive was driven by the complexity of events to rise above his daily routine and to impose a certain structure on the duties of his office. Operating at the strategic design system level, however, is not easy; we shall examine some of the difficulties in the next section.

Problems in model-making

At least three major problems confront a financial officer as he attempts to operate at the strategic design level. First, there are many possible models to build; second, the criteria of a successful model may not be met; and third, because a firm is more than a rational technical organization, since its actions have political and legal aspects as well as economic and technical ones, the models that are built may not be all-inclusive.

CHOOSING A MODEL

Any firm is a complex mechanism affording opportunities for an enormous set of models. Ideally, a single global model will be developed that organizes all other supportive, or subsystem, models. To date, however, no such global models have been made fully operational. The few that exist are still theoretical statements and work is now underway in many different quarters to improve them.

In lieu of global models, managers must work with models that are operational for only a narrow band of the firm's activities. What the financial officer does is assume that certain variables are fixed. He thereby closes off the model that he is working with to various sectors of the firm's behavior. For example, a model of short-term borrowing may assume that the interest rates which the firm pays to different types of lenders are fixed. In another context, however, the financial officer will work with a model that attempts to determine how much interest rates will change as the firm's total borrowing increases. In developing this model, he may have assumed that a constant relationship exists between the country's monetary policy and the availability of funds. At still another time, the financial officer might try to ascertain when lenders such as banks will have more funds available to loan out. Strictly speaking, closing off the model to sectors of the firm's activities results in suboptimal solutions. However, the significance of such suboptimization will vary from situation to situation. At some times it may be critical; at others it may be ignored.

CRITERIA FOR SUCCESS

A second problem in model-building is the question of inclusiveness. The firm encompasses countless relationships. Which of these should the financial officer or manager recognize and which should he ignore? How shall he incorporate the large number of relationships he does recognize into his model of the system? The way he answers these questions will determine how he closes what is in fact an open system.

There are two requirements of any model of a system. The first is that it must be internally consistent and adequately predictive. The second is a behavioral requirement—it must be both realistic and operational These criteria are frequently difficult to meet. Although it is useful to think of the firm as a fixed system fully reflected in the models of its strategic design system, the realities of economic and business activity seldom permit models to be designed which fully account for all the significant activities of the firm. Information is either partial or unreliable, or both. People change their preferences, new technologies evolve, and environments change radically and quickly. As a result, the models the manager works with are often ad hoc and subject to frequent change. As information develops or is corrected, the strategic design itself must change.

SOCIAL AND POLITICAL CONSIDERATIONS

Difficulties arise in model-building because the firm is an open system, and one reason for this open system is that the firm is a social as well as an economic entity. Its decisions are not purely technical and economic; it makes legal, political, and social decisions as well. None of these decisions can currently be handled by the same rational structure used to tackle technical-economic decisions.

Unlike the technical-economic decisions, which involve arguments about effectiveness and efficiency, legal decisions involve precedent, intention, authority, and adjudication. Legal problems can arise from a number of sources: from the responsibilities that the firm has to its stockholders, from the contractual relationships established through collective bargaining with unions, from transactions with lenders for funds, and from the environment. Conflicts in these areas are frequently settled by appeals to precedent or authority and may hinge on the question of intent.

Political and social decisions involve choices among goals. Conflicts arise in this area for a number of reasons. Even if there is agreement as to what the ultimate corporate end is, the goal cannot always be readily translated into operational terms. As a consequence, various paths to these goals become themselves rival ends of organizational behavior. Firms often seek intermediate goals such as an expanding market share or technological superiority as ends in themselves, even though their real goal is to achieve maximum profits. Since the payoff from these various activities is not or cannot be known, they are difficult to rank in terms of their contribution to the larger corporate goal. There can also be discrepancies between the firm's goals and those of its employees or the community. When any such conflict arises, either a political or a social solution must be found. Political solutions (the allocation of values) are achieved by bargaining, voting, or the exercise of power. Social solutions (the integration of values) are achieved by persuasion.

The implications of these considerations for a model maker seem clear. In lieu of global models, top corporate management must supervise the entire strategic design system, the control systems and the operating systems which support it. Furthermore, there are operational and nonoperational models. The suppression of socio-behavioral considerations can result in a model which either is too rigid to be truly operational or has to be altered too frequently for its user to have any confidence in its results. The act of building a successful model, which the financial officer is continuously called upon to do, is to close an open system in such a way that it describes the firm accurately and yet remains operational.

The work ahead

Designing a firm's strategic planning system and controlling its operating system is not an easy task. It is, however, the function of a modern financial officer, and it is the purpose of this book to help him perform this task.

Part Two describes the structure of one source of information about the firm, its financial statements. This section is important because many of the firm's goals, as well as many of the controls that are placed on the operating system, are financial.

Part Three discusses some operating and financing problems. A number of submodels are presented that are relevant for the specific classes of assets and liabilities. Short-term financial planning systems are discussed in terms of the insights that arise from the use of these models.

Part Four explores some of the considerations that enter into planning the growth strategies of the firm. Specifically, capital budgeting and the cost of funds are discussed. Once more, stress is placed on developing the strategic planning models that can help the firm move closer to its objectives.

Parts Five and Six concentrate on the changing environment of the modern firm. Part Five stresses the market for corporate equities and various stock-valuation and portfolio models; Part Six stresses the economic and banking environment within which the modern firm operates.

Throughout the book, the emphasis is not so much on particular models as on the thought process that gives rise to them, the environment from which they are drawn, and the uses to which they can be put. The common theme of all the chapters is that the firm is a system and that the ability to influence and control the corporate system is a requirement of a successful financial manager.

Questions for discussion and problems

1. Prepare a list of possible consequences within a corporation as a result of:
   (a) A change in interest rates,
   (b) A change in wage rates,
   (c) A change in credit policy.
   Indicate the linkages that give rise to these effects and evaluate which of the possible consequences are in fact likely to occur.

2. The way that a corporate financial manager closes what is in fact an open system depends on what factors he holds constant. Suppose that you were asked to simulate the effects of a merger upon a corporation. What factors might you hold constant in developing a model? How would the model change if you dropped the assumption that these factors were constant?

3. The chief financial officer of a corporation is charged with designing strategic planning models and controlling operations. What functions do the chief marketing manager and the chief production manager perform?

4. How important do you think mathematical modeling can be to a financial officer with respect to strategic planning models? Will mathematical modeling be more or less important to him than to one of his subordinates who functions at the operating level?

5. What are some of the limitations of the analogy that a corporate system is like a heating system?

6. If you were a chief financial officer, how would you allocate your time between planning strategic systems and controlling operations? How many employees do you think that most large firms need to carry out each of these two activities?

REFERENCES AND SUGGESTED READINGS

Articles

Boulden, James B., and Buffa, Elwood S., "Corporate Models: On Line, Real Time Systems," *Harvard Business Review* (July–August 1970), pp. 65–83.

Donaldson, G., "Financial Management in an Affluent Society," *Financial Executive,* vol. XXXV (April 1967), pp. 52–69.

Drucker, P. F., "Business Objectives and Survival Needs," *Journal of Business,* vol. 31 (April 1958), pp. 81–90.

Gershefski, George, "Building a Corporate Financial Model," *Harvard Business Review* (July–August 1969), pp. 61–72.

Moag, Joseph S., Carleton, Willard T., and Lerner, Eugene M., "Defining the Finance Function: A Model Systems Approach," *Journal of Finance,* vol. XXII, no. 1 (December 1967), pp. 543–57.

Moore, John R., "The Financial Executive in the 1970's," *Financial Executive,* vol. XXXV (January 1967), pp. 28–36.

Searby, Frederick, "Using Your Hidden Cash Resources," *Harvard Business Review* (March–April 1968), pp.71–80.

Weston, J. Fred, "The Finance Function," *Journal of Finance,* vol. IX (September 1954), pp. 265–82.

Books

Ansoff, H. Igor, *Corporate Strategy* (New York: McGraw-Hill, 1965).

Chamberlain, Neil, *Enterprise and Environment* (New York: McGraw-Hill, 1968).

Guthmann, H. G., and Dougall, H. E., *Corporate Finance Policy,* 4th ed. (Englewood Cliffs, N. J.: Prentice-Hall, 1952).

Solomon, Ezra, *The Theory of Financial Management* (New York: Columbia Univ. Press, 1963).

Van Horne, James C., *Financial Management and Policy* (Englewood Cliffs, N. J.: Prentice-Hall, 1968).

Vickers, Douglas, *The Theory of the Firm: Production, Capital and Finance* (New York: McGraw-Hill, 1968).

Weston, J. Fred, and Brigham, Eugene F., *Managerial Finance,* 2nd ed. (New York: Columbia Univ. Press, 1963).

Basic information about the system: the analysis of financial statements

Since the financial manager is concerned with the design of the firm as a whole, he must be knowledgeable concerning all the activities and operations of the firm. One way in which he monitors these activities is through financial statements. Part Two focuses on the construction, interpretation, and application of these statements.

Chapter 2 describes how a financial statement is constructed. It therefore covers some of the same ground traditionally covered by accounting courses. Chapter 3 discusses how financial statements are read and interpreted. With these chapters as background, two specific problems are raised: First, can financial statements be designed that are more relevant to their readers' needs than those now in use? And second, what kind of information could be obtained if a financial statement were constructed for the economy as a whole? Answers to these questions are discussed in Chapters 4 and 5.

The development of
financial statements

2

The financial officer of a corporation generally performs a number of activities during any one day. However, his basic function, as we have seen, centers on two tasks, the first of which is the design and construction of the analytical models that enable a firm to progress from where it is now to where it wishes to be. These models must specify not only which variables are strategic in a particular situation but what relationships are important between them.

The second task of the financial officer is to control the system he designs. This requires that he know not only how the system *should* perform but how it *is* performing. The firm's financial statements are an important source of data on its actual performance, since they capture the dollar flows through time, transaction by transaction. By structuring these transactions one way, the financial officer can determine the amount of profit made by the firm during any one period; by structuring them another way, he can measure the change in the company's liquidity during that period. It is important, therefore, to understand how financial statements are constructed and how they are to be read and interpreted. In this chapter we shall discuss the firm's three most important financial statements: the *income statement,* the *balance sheet,* and the *sources-and-uses-of-funds statement.*

Developing an income statement and a balance sheet

Over a period of time, company X had a number of different cash transactions. In Table 2.1, the period during which these transactions took place, A to F, is measured along the vertical arrow.

TABLE 2.1
A Series of Transactions of Company X
During the Period A to F

Time	
A.	Sells $1,000 in equity for cash.
B.	Spends $750 in cash to build a plant.
C.	Receives first order for $500.
D.	Purchases $300 in inputs on credit.
E.	Sells and delivers the product.
F.	Receives $500 in payment for the goods sold; pays $300 for the inputs purchased at time D.

A firm's balance sheet shows the stated value of the firm's assets, liabilities, and equity at a moment in time. At the end of period B, for example, the balance sheet of company X will read:

Balance Sheet of Company X, Period B

Cash	$ 250	Liabilities	$ 0
Building	750	Equity	1,000
	$1,000		$1,000

A firm's income statement indicates the amount by which the revenue realized from sales exceeds the costs incurred to produce the sales. Assume that company X simply marks up and resells the inputs it buys. For the period B through F, its income statement will be:

Income Statement of Company X, Period B Through F

Sales	$500
Less cost of goods sold	300
Gross profits	$200
Depreciation	75
Profits before taxes	$125

In this example, the $750 plant is depreciated at the rate of 10 percent per annum, or $75 each year. The wear and tear, or depreciation, of the plant is a cost of doing business, just as are the outlays for the raw materials and labor used to produce the product. The income statement recognizes this fact. However, the exact amount of wear and tear that occurred is a matter of judgment and tax law.

The balance sheet of the company at the end of period F will show:

Balance Sheet of Company X at Time F

Cash	$ 450	Liabilities	$ 0
($250		Equity	1,125
+ $75 depreciation		($1,000	
+ $125 net income)		+ $125 net income)	
Building	675		
($750 − $75			
depreciation)			
Total assets	$1,125		$1,125

During the period B to F, the company's working capital, i.e., its current assets (in this case cash only) less current liabilities (zero), rose by $200. Since the volume of working capital can be a measure of the firm's liquidity (its ability to meet payments as they fall due), company X's position has improved substantially.

This increase in working capital arose through the operations of the firm and can be calculated in two ways. First, it can be calculated directly from the operations of the firm:

Increase in Working Capital, Period B Through F

Sales	$500
Less cost of goods sold	300
Increase in working capital from operations	$200

Alternatively, the change in working capital can be calculated from the firm's income statement:

Increase in Working Capital, Period B Through F

Profits before taxes, per income statement	$125
Depreciation expenses	75
Increase in working capital from operations	$200

Several comments are in order concerning these financial statements. First, the firm's income statement is not an accurate indicator of its liquidity. The income of the firm from C through F was $125, but the increase in working capital during that period was $200. Since both profitability and liquidity are of concern to the financial manager, both the income statement and the changes in working capital must be studied. An analysis of the firm's income statement alone is an incomplete measure of the firm's progress during the period.

Second, changes in working capital arise from the operations of the firm. If depreciation charges were higher, working capital would not increase because reported income would be lowered by the amount of the rise in depreciation.

The influence of tax payments

When the income taxes that company X must pay are taken into account, however, the statement that working capital is unaffected by the size of the depreciation charge is no longer accurate. This can be seen by comparing the two statements below. In case 1, company X continues to depreciate its assets at a rate of 10 percent; in case 2, however, it uses a 5 percent depreciation rate. In both cases, the corporate income tax rate is 50 percent.

Case 1—Income Statement of Company X When the
Depreciation Rate Is 10 Percent

Sales	$500.00
Cost of goods sold	300.00
Depreciation	75.00
Income before taxes	$125.00
Taxes	62.50
Net income after taxes	$ 62.50

Case 2—Income Statement of Company X When the
Depreciation Rate Is 5 Percent

Sales	$500.00
Cost of goods sold	300.00
Depreciation	37.50
Income before taxes	$162.50
Taxes	81.25
Net income after taxes	$ 81.25

If the taxes that company X owes are paid during the period in which they are incurred, the working capital statements become:

Change in Working Capital of Company X

	Case 1	Case 2
Sales	$500.00	$500.00
Less cost of goods sold	300.00	300.00
Less taxes paid	62.50	81.25
Increase in working capital	$137.50	$118.75

This same finding, that the change in working capital is higher as depreciation charges increase, is reached by analyzing the income statements.

Income Statement of Company X

	Case 1	Case 2
Net income after taxes	$ 62.50	$ 81.25
Depreciation	75.00	37.50
Increase in working capital	$137.50	$118.75

The balance sheets of company X, using the different depreciation schedules, are:

Balance Sheet of Company X at End of Period F, Case 1

Cash

($250 + $75 depreciation + $62.50 net income)	$ 387.50
Building ($750 − $75 depreciation)	675.00
Total assets	$1,062.50
Liabilities	$ 0.00
Equity ($1,000 + $62.50 net income)	1,062.50
	$1,062.50

Balance Sheet of Company X at End of Period F, Case 2

Cash

($250 + $37.50 depreciation + $81.25 net income)	$ 368.75
Building ($750 − $37.50 depreciation)	712.50
Total assets	$1,081.25
Liabilities	$ 0.00
Equity ($1,000 + $81.25 net income)	1,081.25
	$1,081.25

The $37.50 reduction in depreciation charges from case 1 to case 2 raises company X's income before taxes by the full amount of the reduction. The firm's net income after taxes, however, increases by only one-half this amount, or $18.75, because of the 50-percent tax rate applied to corporate profits.

Even though the firm reported a higher net income after taxes when it depreciated its assets at a rate of 5 percent than when it depreciated them at a rate of 10 percent, the working capital statements show that company X generates $18.75 more in funds when it depreciates its assets at the faster rate. This is because the payment of some operating expenses, such as taxes, decreases both working capital and operating income. However, other operating expenses, such as depreciation charges, do not require the use of cash. These expenses decrease operating income and fixed assets, but not working capital. Because depreciation charges were higher in case 1, only $62.50 in taxes had to be paid, while in case 2 the taxes paid were $81.25. The difference between the taxes paid in case 1 and case 2, $18.75, represents the greater increase in working capital that occurred in case 1.

Suppose that the taxes company X incurred during period B through F were not paid during this period, but at a later date. In this case, the actual cash position would not be affected by different depreciation schedules. However, both the company's balance sheets and its working capital position would be affected.

Balance Sheet of Company X at End of Period F, Case 1

Cash	
($250 + $75 depreciation + $62.50 accrued taxes + $62.50 net income)	$ 450.00
Building ($750 − $75 depreciation)	675.00
Total assets	$1,125.00
Liabilities	
Accrued taxes	$ 62.50
Equity ($1,000 + $62.50 net income)	1,062.50
Total liabilities and equity	$1,125.00

Change in Working Capital of Company X over Period B to F, Case 1

Current assets	$450.00
Current liabilities	62.50
Ending working capital	$387.50
Initial working capital	250.00
Change in working capital	$137.50

Balance Sheet of Company X at End of Period F, Case 2

Cash	
($250 + $37.50 depreciation + $81.25 net income + $81.25 accrued taxes)	$ 450.00
Building	
($750 − $37.50 depreciation)	712.50
Total assets	$1,162.50
Liabilities	
Accrued taxes	$ 81.25
Equity	
($1,000 + $81.25 net income)	1,081.25
Total liabilities and equity	$1,162.50

Change in Working Capital of Company X over Period B to F, Case 2

Current assets	$450.00
Current liabilities	81.25
Ending working capital	$368.75
Initial working capital	250.00
Change in working capital	$118.75

To summarize, tax considerations will influence how fast a company will want to write off, or depreciate, its assets. If the firm's depreciation charges are high, its reported income will be reduced but its working capital will increase by the amount of the tax savings. In the example given here, working capital increased by one-half the amount of the rise in depreciation charges since the firm paid 50 percent of its income in taxes.

The income statement

TIMING COSTS

In case 1 in the preceding section, the plant was depreciated over a 10-year period. In case 2, the firm would continue to incur depreciation charges for twenty years. These judgments as to when the expenses occurred had an important effect on the reported flow of income and working capital. What guidelines can a financial officer use in determining when to recognize depreciation costs?

Many assets, such as buildings or machines, generate a stream of productive services over several income periods. To which of these several periods should the expense of depreciation be charged, and how large should the charges be in the various periods? One answer to this question is simply that depreciation should be charged over the useful life of the asset in proportion to the wear and tear that actually occurs. The difficulty with this answer is that the financial officer cannot be certain what the productive life of the asset will be. Technological change is constantly occurring, and changes in consumer tastes may render the products produced by a machine unprofitable. Both these events, technological changes and shifts in market factors, are likely to occur long before the machine physically wears out. When they do, a machine may be uneconomical to operate even though it is still durable enough to function.

When a financial officer fixes a depreciation schedule, he makes an implicit forecast of the useful economic life of the firm's assets. If his forecast is incorrect, the firm will report an inaccurate figure both for its net income for the period and for the owner's equity.

Income, as accountants use the term, *is the difference between earned revenues and incurred costs.* These costs are calculated so that the owner's equity remains intact. If depreciation charges are too low, reported income will be overstated and capital will not remain intact. In other words, if an amount of funds equal to the depreciation charges were reinvested in the firm's physical assets, it would not be sufficient to replace the equipment that wore out during the period. If depreciation charges are too high, reported income will be understated. Capital will also be understated, since if an amount of funds equal to the depreciation charges were reinvested, more equipment could be purchased than actually wore out.

There is, then, no single correct answer to the question, How fast should an asset be depreciated? The most the financial manager can do is recognize the limitations and consequences of the decision he makes.

To illustrate the problem of timing when a cost occurs repeatedly, suppose company X spends $100 for research and development at time D':

TABLE 2.2
Transactions at Various Time Periods,
Including an Outlay for R & D

Time	
C.	Receives an order for $500.
D.	Purchases inputs for $300 on credit.
D'.	Spends $100 for research and development.
E.	Sells and delivers the product.
F.	Receives $500 in payment for goods sold; pays $300 for the inputs purchased at time D.

Assume that the research expenditure is for the creation of a new product, not heretofore produced. How should this outlay be treated?

At least two possibilities are open to the firm. First, it can consider the entire outlay as an expense and charge it off against the income earned during period CF. The income statement and balance sheet of the firm would then read:

Income Statement of Company X During CF
(Expensing R & D)

Sales	$500
Cost of goods sold	300
	$200
Depreciation	75
R & D expenses	100
Income before taxes	$ 25

Balance Sheet of Company at Time F

Cash	$ 350	Liabilities	$ 0
Building	675	Equity	1,025
	$1,025		$1,025

Alternatively, it could consider the research and development expenditures as a long-lived asset and capitalize the expense, just as it would if it had made an outlay for a new building. In the future, as revenues from the new product are received, the capitalized R and D expenditure would be charged to operations. The corresponding statements would then be:

Income Statement of Company X During CF
(Capitalizing R & D)

Sales	$500
Cost of goods sold	300
	$200
Depreciation	75
Income before taxes	$125

Balance Sheet of Company X at Time F

Cash	$ 350	Liabilities	$ 0
Building	675	Equity	1,125
R & D	100		
	$1,125		$1,125

Both methods involve problems. Charging off the R and D outlays against current income is misleading because the benefits of the expenditures, that is, the revenues that will result from the research, will come in a future period. Treating the outlays as current operating expenses will therefore lead to an overstatement of the future profit figures.

Capitalizing the expenses, however, also causes problems. First, R and D expenditures are unlike physical assets, which have a well-defined resale value. They tend to be payments for wages and consumable materials. Second, the revenues that the firm hopes will result from the outlay are not now in hand. Indeed, there is no assurance that they will ever be forthcoming, since no new product may be discovered and, if it is, it may not find a market. Should this happen, and the R and D outlay is carried as an asset on the firm's balance sheet, the owner's equity will be overstated. Here, once again, the problem of recognizing when costs are incurred has no single "correct" answer.

In short, the problem of determining when a cost occurs becomes increasingly complex (1) as the length of time over which the asset can perform a valuable service increases and (2) as the length of time between the cash outlay and the benefit to be obtained increases. How this problem is resolved clearly influences the firm's reported income. In the absence of taxes, however, it does not alter the firm's working-capital position. This can be seen by comparing the balance sheets of company X when it expensed the R and D outlays and when it capitalized them. In both cases, working capital was $350 at the end of period F. When taxes are considered, the treatment of R and D outlays will influence both the firm's income statement and its working-capital statement. When R and D outlays are expensed, reported income is reduced and the company's tax bill is smaller. Thus, working capital increases by the amount of the tax saving.

MEASURING COSTS

Financial officers encounter still another problem in ascertaining their costs. In addition to the problem of timing, the chief financial officer encounters the problem of measuring the costs of production when the prices of inputs change.

In Table 2.3, company X receives two orders, each for $500, and makes one delivery. The price of the material used for producing the product rises by $100 between D' and D''. How should the firm measure its production costs for the period CF? What income should it report to its shareholders?

The cost of goods sold during a period can be measured as the sum of the firm's initial inventory and the purchases made during the period, less the ending value of the inventory. Since the beginning inventory was zero and two purchases, for a total of $700, were made, the problem that must be answered to determine the cost of the goods sold is, What is the value of the ending inventory?

TABLE 2.3

Transactions of Company X at Various
Times During Period CF When the Price
of Materials Changes

Time		
C.		Receives an order for $500.
D.		Purchases inputs for $300.
D'.		Receives a second order for $500.
D''.		Purchases inputs for $400.
E.		Sells and delivers the first order.
F.		Receives the first payment of $500.

If the firm adopts the *FIFO* (first-in-first-out) method of inventory valuation, it will value its ending inventory at $400. The cost of the goods sold will then be $300, and the firm will report an income before taxes of $125.

Determination of Cost of Goods Sold, FIFO Method

Beginning inventory	$ 0
Purchases	700
	$700
Less ending inventory	400
Cost of goods sold	$300

Income Statement of Company X Using FIFO Method
of Valuing Inventories

Sales	$500
Cost of goods sold	300
	$200
Less depreciation	75
Income before taxes	$125

On the other hand, if it adopts the *LIFO* (last-in-first-out) method of inventory valuation, the corresponding statements are:

Determination of Cost of Goods Sold, LIFO Method

Beginning inventory	$ 0
Purchases	700
	$700
Less ending inventory	300
Cost of goods sold	$400

Income Statement of Company X Using LIFO Method of Valuing Inventories

Sales	$500
Cost of goods sold	400
	$100
Less depreciation	75
Income before taxes	$ 25

The logic of measuring inventories under LIFO rather than FIFO when prices are rising is readily apparent from a comparison of these financial statements. LIFO is simply a device to avoid confusing operating profits and capital gains. Under FIFO, company X's net income was reported as $125. If the owners of the company, thinking this to be their real operating income, withdrew the profits in the form of dividends, they would seriously jeopardize their cash position. At current costs, the firm must pay $400 for its inventory. If it sells this inventory for $500, it will realize $100 in profits; but if it distributes $125 in cash dividends to its shareholders, it weakens its cash position.

Using the LIFO method of inventory valuation, it is clear that the $125 in reported earnings has two components: $25, which represents the operating profits for the period, and $100, which represents the capital gains stemming from the inventory price rise. However, although it serves to distinguish between operating income and capital gains during periods of rising prices and hence reduces reported income for tax purposes, the LIFO method, introduces difficulties of its own. If prices continue to rise for a long time, the stated values of inventories can become seriously misleading.

The balance sheets of the firm at the end of period F under the two methods of valuing inventory are:

Balance Sheet of Company X Using FIFO Method of Valuing Inventories

Cash	$ 250	Accounts payable	$ 700
Accounts receivable	500		
Inventory	400	Equity (original)	1,000
	$1,150	+ Net income	125
Building	675		$1,125
		Total liabilities and	
Total assets	$1,825	equity	$1,825

The development of financial statements

Balance Sheet of Company X Using LIFO
Method of Valuing Inventories

Cash	$ 250	Accounts payable	$ 700
Accounts receivable	500		
Inventory	300	Equity (original)	1,000
	$1,050	+ Net income	25
Building	675		$1,025
		Total liabilities and	
Total assets	$1,725	equity	$1,725

Note that the LIFO-valued inventories could not be replaced for $300. Should inventories become depleted, the cost of goods sold would reflect these lower costs and profits would rise dramatically.

To summarize, it is difficult to measure costs when prices that firms must pay for inputs change. If the FIFO method of valuing inventory is used, the reported profit figure will be overstated during periods of rising prices, since it will include a capital gain as well as an operating profit. If the LIFO method is used, the value of the inventory on the balance sheet will be understated. Should the stock of inventory ever be depleted, reported profits will rise sharply since the reported profit figure will then also include a capital gain.

The timing and measurement of revenues

We have seen that the timing and measurement of costs produce a number of intractable problems. The measurement and timing of revenues produce a similar set of problems. In general, revenues are recognized at the time of sale, since it is at this time that an objective measure of the revenues received can be determined. The more appropriate time to recognize revenues, however, is when they are earned. For example, suppose company X begins to make a product that will be completed and delivered in a period which is later than that covered by the current income statement. A portion of the revenues that will be received in this future accounting period can properly be considered to have been earned in the present period, and the accounting statement should reflect this. One way of handling this problem is to allocate the revenues that will be realized from the sale according to the percentage of the work completed in each period. Thus, if 50 percent of the product were completed at the end of the current period, 50 percent of the revenue would be included in this period's income. The difficulty with this procedure, however, is that the sale may not be made at the time or at the price that is now contemplated. Hence the current earnings figure could turn out to be misleading.

Sources and uses of funds

Through our analysis of the income statement, we have studied how the operations of company X influence its working capital. Operations, however, are only one source of change in working capital. For example, if the company realized cash through the sale of long-term debt or equity, or by disposing of a long-term asset, its working capital would rise.

In general, any increase in liabilities or equity or any reduction in assets can be thought of as a source of funds; any increase in assets or reduction in liabilities or equity can be thought of as a use of funds.

To make these remarks more concrete, let us examine the actual financial statements of a specific firm, the Ford Motor Company, for 1968 and 1969.

TABLE 2.4
Balance Sheet of Ford Motor Company, 1968 and 1969
(in millions)

		1968		1969	Change
Current assets		$4,128.3		$4,087.1	−41.2
Investments		580.8		721.8	+141.0
Property, plant, and equipment	$6,360.9		$6,776.1		
Less accumulated depreciation	2,963.2		3,237.9		
Plus unamortized special tools	567.2		573.0		
Net property, plant, and equipment		3,964.9		4,111.2	+146.3
Investment in subsidiaries		279.2		279.2	0
Total assets		$8,953.2		$9,199.3	+246.1
Current liabilities		$2,994.0		$2,979.4	−14.6
Long-term debt		341.8		304.6	−37.2
Other liabilities and reserves		564.1		588.5	+24.4
Minority interest in net assets of consolidated companies		106.7		104.8	−1.9
Stockholders' equity		4,946.6		5,222.0	+275.4
Total liabilities and equity		$8,953.2		$9,199.3	+246.1

SOURCE: Ford Motor Company, *1969 Annual Report*, pp. 40–41.

All the items on this balance sheet are self-explanatory, with the exception of "minority interest." This item arises when a company, such as Ford, owns a substantial proportion of, but not all, the equity of another company. Ford reports all the income of the company in its own income statement, even though some of the income belongs to the minority shareholders. The size of the claim that these shareholders have in the various consolidated subsidiaries of Ford is indicated on the liability side of the balance sheet.

The development of financial statements

In Table 2.5, the changes in balance-sheet items are rearranged so that they can be used for a sources and uses of funds statement.

TABLE 2.5
Changes in the Balance Sheet of
Ford Motor Company, 1968—1969

Sources of Funds	
Stockholders' equity	$275.4
Other liabilities and reserves	24.4
	$299.8
Uses of Funds	
Investments	$141.0
Property, plant, and equipment	146.3
Retirement of long-term debt	37.2
Reduction of minority interests	1.9
	$326.4
Decrease in working capital	$ 26.6
Memo:	
Reduction in current assets	$ 41.2
Reduction in current liabilities	14.6
Change in working capital	$ 26.6

SOURCE: Ford Motor Company, *1969 Annual Report*, pp. 40–41.

These data show that, during 1969, the major use of Ford Motor Company funds was for plant and other investments, while the major source of funds was stockholders' equity. Since the uses of funds were greater than the sources, the firm had to reduce its working capital by $26.6 million.

The changes in balance-sheet items, however, indicate only very gross flows of funds. Most financial analysts require more details before they can evaluate the performance of the firm. Balance-sheet data alone do not answer such important questions as whether the firm paid dividends, whether it sold any additional stock, and, if so, how much. Moreover, a statement that is based solely on changes in balance-sheet items does not permit the chief financial officer to identify the funds raised through operations and those acquired from other sources.

To develop a better perspective on the flow of funds through the corporation, the balance-sheet figures must be adjusted by values given in other financial statements, such as the income statement in Table 2.6.

Let us now combine the information from these two statements (Tables 2.5 and 2.6) with some other supplementary financial data supplied by the company.

TABLE 2.6
Income Statement of Ford Motor Company, 1969

(in millions)

Sales	$14,755.6
Costs (excluding items listed below)	$11,743.5
Depreciation	385.2
Amortization of special tools	418.5
Selling and administrative costs	903.8
Employee retirement plans	158.1
Provision for supplemental compensation	36.5
Total	$13,645.6
Operating income	$ 1,110.0
Other income	5.1
Income before taxes	1,115.1
Provision for taxes	554.4
Income before minority interests	560.7
Minority interests	14.2
Net income	546.5

SOURCE: Ford Motor Company, *1969 Annual Report,* p. 39.

Adjusting the equity

The change in stockholders' equity reported in Ford's balance sheet for the year was $275.4 million. The net income reported, however, was $546.5 million. How can the difference of $271.1 million be accounted for?

The answer is twofold. First, during the year, Ford paid $260.8 million in dividends. Second, it purchased some of its own stock back from shareholders in order to reissue the shares at a later date to its employees in the form of supplemental compensation. Finally, it received some funds from the issuance of shares to executives who exercised their stock options.

The change in stockholders' equity of $275.4 million thus arose as follows:

Change in Equity of Ford Motor Company, 1969

(in millions)

Net income from operations	$546.5
Sale of stock to employees	2.5
Total	$549.0
Dividends paid	$260.8
Repurchase of stock for treasury	12.8
Total	$273.6
Net change in equity	$275.4

Adjusting plant and equipment

The analysis of the balance sheet shows that the net plant of Ford Motor Company rose by $146.3 million in 1969. How can we obtain additional information on this figure? Specifically, how can we obtain an estimate of the total new plant and equipment expenditures?

One way of estimating this is to work with the reported gross plant and equipment and gross depreciation charges on the balance sheet. The change in gross plant and equipment (in millions) was $415.2.

1969 gross plant and equipment	$6,776.1
1968 gross plant and equipment	6,360.9
Increase in gross plant and equipment	$ 415.2

An estimate can also be made of the amount of property retired during the year. Thus:

1968 gross-depreciation charges	$2,963.2
Additional depreciation charges (per income statement)	385.2
Expected 1969 gross-depreciation charges	$3,348.4
Actual 1969 gross-depreciation charges	3,237.9
Difference	$ 110.5

The difference of $110.5 million between the actual and expected depreciation figure can be assumed to arise largely because of retirements. When a property is fully depreciated, both the gross depreciation charges and the total value of the property account are reduced. Since the reported figure for gross plant and equipment in 1969 is less than the reported figure for 1968 by the amount of retirements, an estimate of the new plant and equipment outlays during 1969 is therefore:

Additional plant and equipment outlays (per changes in gross plant and equipment accounts)	$415.2
Estimated value of retirements	110.5
Estimated new expenditures	$525.7

The text and financial statements presented in Ford Motor's annual report are quite complete. As a result, it can be ascertained from these statements that the actual expenditures for expansion, modernization, and replacement of facilities were $534 million. There are a number of possible reasons for the difference between this actual figure and our estimate of $525.7. For example, our assumption that all the property that was disposed of was fully depreciated is probably incorrect. Moreover, some of the expenditures may have been expensed rather than capitalized. Such estimating errors, however, are usually small, as indeed is the case here.

All the automotive companies spend large amounts for special tools that are used only to make a particular model. Since these tools are of value only for the life of the model, their costs are amortized, or written off the books, in a relatively short time. The amortization charges, like depreciation charges, are a non-cash expenditure. Since they lead to a reduction in assets, they can be thought of as a source of funds.

The balance sheet and income statement of the Ford Motor Company in Tables 2.4 and 2.6 do not give enough information for us to determine the extent of the outlays for tools or the extent of the amortization charges in 1969. The text of the company's annual report does, however, furnish this data. In 1969, Ford amortized $418.5 million of tools and spent $424.3 million for new tooling. The balance-sheet totals that were presented for this item in Table 2.4 can therefore be reconciled as follows:

Reconciliation of Special Tooling Account
(in millions)

Unamortized special tools at end of 1968	$567.2
Expenditures on tools in 1969	424.3
Total	$991.5
Less amortization charges	418.5
Unamortized special tools at end of 1969	$573.0

Sources and uses of funds

The more detailed information we now have on the changes in equity, plant and equipment, and tooling allows us to recast the sources-and-uses-of-funds statement as in Table 2.7.

This statement gives the chief financial officer a great deal more information than could be gleaned from the changes in balance-sheet figures alone. It indicates that during the year substantially all Ford's funds came from operations. These funds were used primarily to build new plant and equipment, purchase new tools, pay dividends, and increase the company's investments in other companies.

The data also show that during the year Ford's working capital fell by $26.6 million. Phrased differently, the total uses of funds exceeded the sources generated by the company. As a result, the firm's liquidity was reduced. Determining whether this reduction is a cause for concern would require further analysis.

TABLE 2.7
Statement of Sources and Uses of Funds
for Ford Motor Company in 1969
(in millions)

Sources	
Net income	$ 346.8
Depreciation	385.2
Amortization of special tools	418.5
Other liabilities and reserves	24.4
Proceeds from issuance of stock	2.5
Total sources	$1,377.4
Uses	
Cash dividends paid	$ 260.8
Additions to plant and equipment	525.7
Tooling expenditures	424.3
Increase in investments	141.0
Retirement of long-term debt	37.2
Repurchase of stock for treasury	12.8
Reduction of minority interests	1.9
Total uses	$1,403.7
Decrease in working capital	$ 26.6

To summarize: The sources-and-uses-of-funds statement indicates the volume of funds that the company was able to generate from its internal operations and the volume that arose from external sources. By also specifying how the funds were used, the statement permits the two flows to be compared. When the uses of funds are greater than the sources, the firm's working capital will be reduced; when the reverse is true, its liquidity will be improved.

Financial officers find this information useful not only for analyzing past data, but also as an aid in estimating their future requirements of funds. For example, a firm may estimate that it can generate $1,000,000 from internal sources over the next three years and that it can borrow an additional $2,000,000 from an insurance company. If it wants to undertake a major expansion program that will require $3,000,000 and still continue its dividend payments of, say, $100,000 each year, it can expect its working capital to fall by $300,000 over this period. Should it curtail its capital expenditures? seek to borrow additional funds? reduce its dividend payments? permit its liquidity to be impaired? Armed with this information, the chief financial officer can form an intelligent opinion as to the course of action the firm should adopt. While no analytical tool, by itself, can tell him which alternative to choose, it can help him identify the range of alternatives open to the firm.

Summary

A firm's financial statements are an important source of data on its performance. From the actual transactions of the firm, three statements can be prepared: an income statement, a balance sheet, and a sources-and-uses-of-funds statement.

Each of these statements describes a different aspect of the firm's activities. The income statement shows the difference between the flow of revenues and costs for a stated period. The balance sheet indicates the value of the stock of assets, liabilities, and equity at a moment in time. The sources-and-uses-of-funds statement indicates how the cash flows of the company originated and were allocated.

A firm's income statement does not reveal all the data that is of interest to the firm's financial officer. While it does measure the profits that were generated over a given period, it does not reflect the change in liquidity that may have occurred during the period.

Taxes influence a corporation's choice of a depreciation rate. If assets are depreciated quickly, the firm will report a lower level of income than it would if its assets were depreciated more slowly. However, the firm's cash position will be improved.

Problems arise in determining when a cost is actually incurred if an asset is long-lived or if a long span of time elapses between the time an outlay is made and the time the revenues from that outlay are received.

If the prices of the input factors change during the accounting period, it is difficult to measure the cost of the product. These measurement problems are reflected in the inventory valuation process.

The sources-and-uses-of-funds statement brings together changes in the accounts listed on the firm's balance sheet, its income statement, and other supporting data. These statements help the financial officer to develop a perspective on the major financial flows within the system.

Questions for discussion and problems

1. What are the consequences of failing to match the period in which revenue is earned with the period in which the cost of production occurs?

2. What kinds of problems are introduced into the analysis of financial statements when the price of the products that are produced or the price of raw materials that are purchased changes?

3. Under what conditions will the LIFO method of inventory valuation result in a higher reported-earning figure? Under what conditions will it result in a lower reported-earnings figure?

4. The financial statements of a firm are prepared at discrete intervals, either every quarter or every year. Some financial theorists have suggested that a more appropriate period for reporting on a particular project is the life of the project itself. Evaluate the merits and difficulties of this approach.

5. The change in a firm's working capital can be calculated directly from its balance sheet. Why is a sources and uses of funds statement, which shows the same change in working capital, a useful analytical tool?

[Answers to problems 6-8 follow references and suggested readings.]

6. Condor Container Corporation owns a new $150,000 corrugating machine that it could depreciate in either 10 or 15 years. During the coming year, Condor projects gross sales of $250,000 and a cost of goods sold of $150,000 from the operation of this one machine. The company is in the 50-percent tax bracket.
   (a) Determine net income after depreciation and taxes from the operation of the corrugating machine for both depreciation schedules. Assume that a straight-line method of depreciation is used.
   (b) What is the change in working capital from operations each year under the two depreciation schedules?

7. A New Hampshire canning concern's December 31, 19x2, balance sheet is as follows:

Current assets		
Cash	$ 80,000	
Fixed assets		
Plant and equipment	400,000	
Total assets		$480,000
Liabilities		0
Equity		$480,000
Total liabilities and equity		$480,000

In 19x3, gross sales are $210,000, and the cost of goods sold is $120,000. Depreciation on plant and equipment is $40,000. The firm is in the 50-percent tax bracket but is not required to actually pay its taxes during 19x3.

   (a) Show the company's balance sheet as of December, 31, 19x3, and the change in its working-capital position.
   (b) If the $40,000 of depreciation represented 10 percent on a straight-line basis, what effect would reducing the rate to 5

percent have on the 19x3 balance sheet and working-capital position?

8. (a) Fleegle Lumber Company handled an inventory of 290,000 board-feet of lumber last year in the following lots, at the following purchase prices:

		Bd. Ft.	Avg. Price/ Bd. Ft.	Total
Jan. 1	Beginning inventory	100,000	$2.00	$200,000
Apr. 24	Purchases	80,000	2.15	172,000
July 17	Purchases	45,000	2.18	98,100
Oct. 12	Purchases	65,000	2.20	143,000
				$613,100

Ending inventory for the year was 80,000 board-feet of lumber. Calculate Fleegle's ending inventory valuation and cost of goods sold for the year using the FIFO method. Recalculate, using the LIFO method.

(b) Fleegle recorded $600,000 in lumber sales last year and depreciation of $75,000. Using your cost-of-goods-sold figures, calculate the company's income before taxes using the FIFO and LIFO methods of inventory valuation.

(c) If the FIFO method is used to report operating income, what amount of Fleegle's income before taxes represents capital gains resulting from the inventory price rise?

REFERENCES AND SUGGESTED READINGS

Articles

Arnett, Harold, "Taxable Income vs. Financial Income: How Much Uniformity Can We Stand?" *Accounting Review* (July 1966), pp. 479–86.

Bierman, Harold, Jr., "Measurement and Accounting," *Accounting Review* (July 1963), pp. 501–10.

Goldschmidt, Y., and Smidt, S., "Valuing the Firm's Durable Assets for Managerial Information," *Accounting Review* (April 1969), pp. 317–29.

Green, David, Jr., and Sorter, George H., "Accounting for Obsolescence—A Proposal," *Accounting Review* (July 1959), pp. 433–41.

Horngren, Charles T., "The Funds Statement and Its Use by Analysts," *Journal of Accountancy,* vol. XCIX (January 1956), pp. 55–59.

Vatter, William, "Fund Flows and Fund Statements" *Journal of Business,* vol. XXVI (January 1953), pp. 15–25.

Wright, F. K., "Depreciation and Obsolescence in Current Value Accounting," *Journal of Accounting Research* (Autumn 1965), pp. 167–81.

Books

Anton, Hector, *Accounting for the Flow of Funds* (Boston: Houghton Mifflin, 1962).

Bierman, Harold, Jr., and Drebin, Allan R., *Financial Accounting* (New York: Macmillan, 1968).

Dyckman, Thomas R., *Investment Analysis and General Price Level Adjustments: A Behavioral Study* (Evanston, Ill.: American Accounting Assn., 1970).

Hendricksen, Eldon S., *Price Level Adjustments of Financial Statements—An Evaluation and Cost Study of Two Public Utility Firms* (Pullman, Wash.: Washington State Univ. Press, 1961).

Jaedicke Robert K., and Sprouse, Robert T., *Accounting Flows: Income, Funds, and Cash* (Englewood Cliffs, N. J.: Prentice-Hall, 1966).

Mason, Perry, *Price Level Changes and Financial Statements, Basic Concepts and Methods* (Evanston, Ill.: American Accounting Assn., 1968).

ANSWERS TO PROBLEMS 6–8

6. (a) *Income Statement*

	15-year life	10-year life
Gross sales	$250,000	$250,000
Cost of goods sold	150,000	150,000
Depreciation	10,000 (6.6%)	15,000 (10%)
Net income	90,000	85,000
Taxes (50%)	45,000	42,500
Net income after taxes	$ 45,000	$ 42,500

(b) *Change in working capital:*

Net income after taxes	$ 45,000	$ 42,500
Depreciation	10,000	15,000
Increase in working capital	$ 55,000	$ 57,000

The 10-year life generates $2,500 less net income after taxes. The faster depreciation (10%) generates $2,500 more working capital.

7. (a)

Balance Sheet as of December 31, 19x3

Current assets		
Cash ($80,000 original + $40,000 depreciation + $25,000 accrued tax + $25,000 net income)	$170,000	
Fixed assets		
Plant and equipment ($400,000 − $40,000 depreciation)	360,000	
Total assets		$530,000
Current liabilities		
Accrued tax	$ 25,000	
Equity	505,000	
Total liabilities and equity		$530,000

Change in working capital:

Current assets	$170,000
Current liabilities	25,000
Ending working capital	145,000
Beginning working capital	80,000
Decrease in working capital	$ 65,000

(b) Balance Sheet as of December 31, 19x3

Current assets
  Cash ($80,000 original + $20,000 depreciation +
        $35,000 accrued tax + $35,000 net income) $170,000
Fixed assets
  Plant and equipment
  ($400,000 − $20,000 depreciation)   380,000
      Total Assets $550,000

Current liabilities
  Accrued tax $ 35,000
Equity ($480,000 + $35,000 net income)   515,000
      Total liabilities and equity $550,000

Change in working capital:
  Current assets $170,000
  Current liabilities   35,000
  Ending working capital   135,000
  Beginning working capital   80,000
  Decrease in working capital $ 55,000

8. (a)
FIFO
Ending inventory:
  65,000 bd. ft. @ $2.20 $143,000
  15,000 bd. ft. @ $2.18   32,700
                                  $175,700

Cost of goods sold:
  100,000 bd. ft. @ $2.00 $200,000
   80,000 "   " @ 2.15   172,000
   30,000 "   " @ 2.18   65,400
                                  $437,400

LIFO
Ending inventory:
  80,000 bd. ft. @ $2.00 $160,000
Cost of goods sold:
  65,000 bd. ft. @ $2.20 $143,000
  45,000 "   " @ 2.18   98,100
  80,000 "   " @ 2.15   172,000
  20,000 "   " @ 2.00   40,000
                                  $453,100

(b)
	FIFO	*LIFO*
Gross sales	$600,000	$600,000
Less: Cost of goods sold	437,400	453,100
	$162,600	$146,900
Less: Depreciation	75,000	75,000
Income before taxes	$ 87,600	$ 71,900

(c) Capital gains on inventory are $15,700

The analysis of financial
relationships

3

Different people use different performance standards to judge corporations. The community may use a social or political standard. Their concern may focus on such issues as whether the firm offers steady and meaningful employment to the people living in the area, whether it contributes financial and other resources to local and civic projects, and whether it encourages its employees to take an active role in local affairs. Even within the firm, technicians specializing in different functional areas may use different standards. The marketing staff may measure corporate performance by the sales trend of specific products or the share of the national or regional market the firm controls. Production people may be interested in the quality of the firm's products or their degree of technical excellence.

None of these various performance standards are monitored directly by the firm's financial statements. Even so, these statements are probably the most important documents that the firm prepares. There are several reasons why they are so significant. First, many of the immediate, or short-run, goals of the firm are stated in financial terms, and the progress that is made toward reaching them is revealed by the firm's financial statements. For example, one short-term goal may be to earn a higher rate of return on assets. By bringing together data from the income statement and the balance sheet, the actual rate of return that the system as a whole earned can be calculated and compared to the target value. A second short-term financial goal may be to maintain a high degree of liquidity to meet contingencies. One way of measuring the progress the firm is making toward achieving this goal is to examine its working-capital position.

However, financial statements do more than measure the progress that the firm makes toward specific financial goals. They are also important for control purposes and often alert the firm to changes in the factor or the product market. For example, if recorded sales fall, the firm may be reminded forcefully of the presence of a new competitor in the market or of a change in customer tastes. A drop in the ratio of profits to sales may alert the firm to heretofore unnoticed changes in material costs or a change in the efficiency of the production process. In short, by monitoring various financial output measures and comparing them to the plans that were made at the start of the period, the manager can measure the performance of the operating system and ensure its continued relevance to the long-range corporate goal. Once he ascertains why the discrepancies between the planned and actual results occurred, the financial manager can determine what corrective action to take.

Third, financial statements help the firm plan for the future. By providing information about financial relationships that have existed in the past, they enable the financial manager to draw inferences concerning these relationships in the future. In this way, the analysis of financial statements helps to place bounds on the range of expected results. Suppose that a company's records show that in the past it took $1 in assets to generate $3 in sales. The firm's marketing forecasts now indicate that a substantial increase in sales can take place in the next few years. If the firm is operating at capacity and wants to exploit this potential demand, plans must be made for an expansion of assets by roughly one-third the size of the predicted increase in sales.

Both skill and training are required to use financial statements effectively. Here and in Chapter 4, we shall make several suggestions about what to look for in reading the statements and how to interpret the data they reveal.

Financial relationships

Valid conclusions about the operations of the firm as a whole cannot be gained by examining only a single financial measure, such as the trend in sales or profits. These trends, important as they are, will not, for example, answer such questions as, How effectively is the firm utilizing its resources? How has its past growth been financed? Where are funds for future growth likely to come from? How well can the firm meet its current obligations? How soon can it collect its receivables, and how rapidly can it convert its inventory into cash?

One technique that is widely used in interpreting financial statements is *ratio analysis*. Ratios are used to bring together data from various financial statements. Four frequently used ratios are:

(1) profitability ratios, which measure overall operating performance;

(2) financing ratios, which indicate the relationships that exist among the various sources of funds;

(3) liquidity ratios, which measure the ability of the firm to meet short-term obligations; and

(4) activity ratios, which measure the turnover of various classes of assets.

In discussing these ratios, frequent reference will be made to the income statement and balance sheet of the hypothetical company A, presented in Tables 3.1 and 3.2.

TABLE 3.1
Income Statement of Company A

Sales	$300
Cost of goods sold	200
Gross profit	$100
Selling, general, and administrative expenses	20.50
Depreciation	35.50
Earnings before interest and taxes	$ 44.00
Interest	9.00
Net operating income	$ 35.00
Taxes	17.50
Net profit after taxes	$ 17.50
Memo:	
Dividends to shareholders	9.17
Retained earnings	8.33
Net profits after taxes	$17.50

TABLE 3.2
Balance Sheet of Company A

Cash	$ 55
Accounts receivable	40
Inventory	50
Total current assets	$145
Gross plant	355
Less accumulated depreciation	100
Net plant	$255
Total assets	$400
Accounts payable	20
Accruals	5
Bank loan	25
Total current liabilities	$ 50
Long-term debt	150
Common stock	75
Retained earnings	125
Total liabilities and equity	$400

Financial relationships

Profitability ratios

The gross profits of company A were $100, and its net profits after taxes were $17.50. What standard of comparison can both the financial manager, who is inside the firm, and interested observers outside the firm use to evaluate whether these figures are high or low or whether the firm is doing well or poorly?

One test that the financial manager can use has already been mentioned. He can compare the firm's realized profits to the level of profits the firm expected to earn. If actual profits are higher or lower than planned, he can then proceed systematically to determine how the discrepancy arose and take action to bring the planned and realized profits closer in succeeding income periods.

Outsiders, however, are not likely to know what level of profits the firm had expected to realize. They must look elsewhere for a standard of comparison, and an obvious place to look is the financial statements of a competing firm. With these data in hand, an outsider can ask, Did company A make more or less money than its competitor? Or, Did it operate more efficiently?

To make comparisons with other firms, however, it is necessary to express the profits of both firms in comparable units. One method of doing this is to express profits as a percentage of sales. The various ratios of profits to sales are called *operating margins*. Thus, the *net-profit margin* for company A is:

$$\text{Net-profit margin} = \frac{\text{net profits}}{\text{sales}} = \frac{17.50}{300} = .058$$

The *gross-profit margin* is:

$$\text{Gross-profit margin} = \frac{\text{gross profits}}{\text{sales}} = \frac{100}{300} = .333$$

While the various operating margins show how well the firm performs given a particular level of sales, it does not show how well the firm uses the resources at its command. Two other measures of profitability are particularly relevant in this regard: the *rate of return on assets,* which is the ratio of profits before interest and taxes to total assets, and the *return on equity,* which is the ratio of profits after interest and taxes to common equity. The latter measure is sometimes called the *return on book value*.

Using the financial statements of the hypothetical company A, we can easily calculate its rate of return on assets:

$$\text{Rate of return on assets} = \frac{\text{earnings before interest and taxes}}{\text{total assets}}$$

$$= \frac{44}{400}$$

$$= 11 \text{ percent}$$

The return on equity is:

$$\text{Return on equity} = \frac{\text{net profits after taxes}}{\text{total equity}}$$

$$= \frac{17.50}{200}$$

$$= 8.75 \text{ percent}$$

Since the rate of return on assets is an overall measure of a firm's effectiveness, it is frequently used to compare the operating performance of two or more firms. If these firms follow similar accounting practices with respect to depreciation, research and development outlays, and so forth, the ranking is unambiguous. If their accounting practices differ, if, say, one firm depreciates its assets more quickly than the other, or if business practices vary, if one firm rents its plant while the other owns its facilities the comparison is less meaningful.

THE IMPORTANCE OF THE RATE OF RETURN

Despite the accounting problems that make the rate of return a difficult measure to interpret, it remains a very useful statistic. If we lived in a world of perfect certainty and all resources were mobile, economic theory suggests that the rate of return on assets would tend to be the same for all firms in the economy. Firms would seize upon every opportunity for extraordinary gains and step up their volume of investment in the most profitable areas. They would avoid every loss and contract their resources in unprofitable areas. In short, funds would flow from assets with low expected yields to the assets with high expected yields. As a consequence of these flows, the yields of all assets would tend to approach one another until an equilibrium point was reached.

On the other hand, if we lived in a world where changes in demand and cost conditions could not be forecast and resources were not mobile, the initial impact of every change in economic conditions would be reflected in the rate of return. In such a world, every increase in demand would find industry unprepared, and as a result prices and profits would immediately rise; similarly, every fall in demand would cause prices to drop and lower rates of return. Of course, neither of these extremes describes the world in which we do live.

George Stigler,[1] an economist with the National Bureau of Economic Research, who investigated the rates of return that different firms earn over a sustained period of time, found that in 1955 the rate of return in 98 industries ranged from −2 percent to +14 percent. This indicates that not all resources are completely mobile. Stigler also found that the investment outlays in the different industries varied; from 1954 to 1955, changes in the stock of capital ranged from a drop of 13 percent in one industry to an increase of 28 percent in another. In general, capital left the industries with a low rate of return and was attracted to the industries with a high rate of return. Had these large capital flows not occurred, i.e., were capital less mobile, the range in the rate of return for different industries would have been even wider. Since the flow of capital continues to be relatively sticky, similar results would no doubt be found if a study were made of industries today.

The rate of return, then, performs the critically important function in our economy of guiding resources from one sector to another. For, if an industry has a high rate of return, it can afford to pay high wages to its employees and so both hold and expand its labor force; and it can afford to purchase new plant and equipment and thereby increase its output. If an industry's return is not competitive, however, it will lose the financial capacity to attract resources; its growth will cease and the industry may decline.

SOME RELATIONSHIPS BETWEEN THE RATE OF RETURN AND OTHER FINANCIAL RATIOS

The return on shareholders' equity is closely linked to the return on assets. To see the relationship between the two measures, recall that the rate of return on assets, r, was defined as:

$$r = \frac{\text{earnings before interest and taxes}}{\text{total assets}}$$

The interest payments that the firm makes can be thought of as the product of the interest rate, i, it pays on borrowed funds and the volume of its total liabilities, L.[2] Profits after interest payments, therefore, equal $rA - iL$, where A is total assets.

---

[1] "Capital and Rates of Return in Manufacturing" (Princeton, N. J.: Princeton Univ. Press, 1963).

[2] This is a convenient simplification. In practice, however, some short-term liabilities do not carry an explicit interest rate. Accounts payable, for example, do not usually require interest payments.

If T is the effective tax rate a company pays, then,

(3–1) $$\text{Profits after taxes} = (1 - T)(rA - iL)$$

The total assets of a firm, A, equal the sum of its liabilities, L, and equity, E.

(3–2) $$A = L + E$$

Substituting the right-hand side of equation 3–2 for A in equation 3–1,

$$\begin{aligned}\text{Profits after taxes} &= (1 - T)[rE + rL - iL)] \\ &= (1 - T)[rE + (r - i)L]\end{aligned}$$

To find the rate of return on equity, we divide both sides of this equation by the firm's total equity:

(3–3) $$\text{Return on equity} = \frac{\text{profits after taxes}}{\text{equity}} = (1 - T)\left[r + (r - i)\frac{L}{E} \right]$$

Substituting the arithmetic values of the hypothetical company A in equation 3–3 we find that the company's return on equity is 8.75 percent.

$$\begin{aligned}\text{Return on equity} &= (1 - .5)\left[.11 + (.11 - .045)\frac{200}{200} \right] \\ &= (.5)(.175) \\ &= .0875\end{aligned}$$

This value could, of course, be found directly:

$$\text{Return on equity} = \frac{\text{profits after taxes}}{\text{total equity}} = \frac{17.50}{200} = .0875$$

The advantage of equation 3–3, however, is that it shows clearly the relationship that exists between the return on a firm's equity and other important financial variables: the rate of return on assets, the ratio of debt to equity, the interest paid for borrowed funds, and the effective tax rate.

Equation 3–3 shows that a fall in tax rates or a rise in r will always lead to a higher return on equity. More important, it shows that if the firm's rate of return on assets is greater than the interest rate it pays for borrowed funds, an increase in the ratio of debt to equity, i.e., a greater reliance on debt to finance assets, will lead to an increase in the return on equity.

Figure 3.1 shows the relationship between the rate of return on equity and the firm's ratio of debt to equity for three different situations. When $r > i$, an increase in the ratio L/E leads to a higher r. However, when $r < i$, an increase in the debt-equity ratio leads to a reduction in r. Only when $r = i$ is the rate of return unaffected by changes in the debt-equity ratio.

These observations give rise to a series of problems. It appears that when r is greater than i, the return on equity can be raised simply by increasing the ratio of debt to equity. Under these conditions, would not the management of the hypothetical company A, and every real firm in the economy, finance 90 or 95 or even 99 percent of its assets by borrowing? Alternatively, when r is less than i, would not a firm cut back drastically on its use of debt? In short, should we not expect to find that all firms have either a great deal of debt or very little debt in their financial structure?

In practice, however, most firms tend to finance their assets with roughly equal amounts of debt and equity. Either businessmen seeking a high rate of return on equity are extremely foolish, or we have omitted something from the analysis. A little investigation shows that the latter is indeed the case.

An examination of equation 3–3 shows that no bounds were placed on the values of r, i, or L/E. But is it reasonable to expect L/E to rise without limit? Will creditors furnish funds to a firm as its shareholders withdraw their money? The answer is surely No. To develop more useful models, we must go on to ask, What factors influence the supply of credit to a firm? And how much debt will the firm want to acquire? To answer these questions, we must go behind the balance sheet

FIGURE 3.1

The Relationship Between the Ratio of Liabilities to Equity, the Rate of Return of Equity, and the Interest Rate.

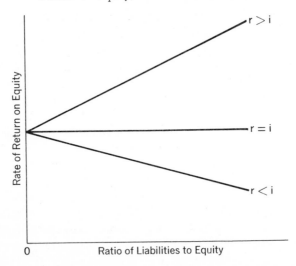

The analysis of financial relationships

and income statements and examine the actual economic conditions prevailing in the capital market. This we shall do in later chapters.

Continued examination of equation 3–3 reveals a second deficiency of the analysis. None of the linkages between the variables in the equation were stated. Even if limitless credit is available, will the price of this credit, the interest rate, remain the same, or will it rise as more debt is used? Moreover, as the firm expands its debt and adds to its assets, will the rate of return it can earn on investment projects remain the same? May not the return fall as the firm takes on less and less attractive projects? Again the investigator must go behind the balance sheet to the underlying economic reality for his answers.

These remarks suggest a third limitation of equation 3–3. The financial variables r, i, and L/E are obviously related to one another in different ways. For example, a rise in L/E will lead to a rise in i; and a rise in L/E may lead to a fall in r. Before equation 3–3 can effectively be used by a financial manager, he must combine all the relationships that exist among the variables into an integrated model that reflects the firm as an integrated system.

Equation 3–3 raises still a fourth problem. The price that a firm pays for its borrowed funds appears to be measured by the interest rate, i. Since shareholders also supply funds to the corporation, is it not logical to believe that the firm must also pay them for the use of their funds? If the answer is Yes, what is the payment? How is the cost of equity to be measured? We shall deal with this question also in later chapters, since there is a great deal of controversy among financial analysts as to the answer. Some analysts believe that the cost of equity can be calculated only by incorporating into the analysis factors outside the firm's control, such as the price of its common stock. Other financial writers believe that both dividends and the expected growth of dividends must be considered in the calculation. Still others contend that the cost of equity capital can be given only by a set of equations that describe the economic conditions in the firm's product market, factor market, and production process.

To summarize, a firm's profitability ratios bring together data that measure its overall efficiency. The rate of return on assets and the rate of return on equity are two such measures.

The rate of return on assets is particularly important because it is the signal that guides the flow of resources from one sector of the economy to another. From the point of view of the individual firm, the rate of return is a measure of its ability to hold and attract additional resources.

The rate of return on equity can be expressed in terms of other financial variables. Before it can be properly evaluated, however, a systems approach that brings together all the variables of concern to the financial manager must be developed.

Financing ratios

A second group of ratios focuses on the way the firm finances its assets. The two most important of these are the *retention rate* and the *debt-equity ratio*.

The retention rate is the ratio of retained earnings to profits after taxes. The debt-equity ratio is the ratio of total liabilities to total equity. Using the data for company A, we can calculate its retention rate as:

$$\text{Retention rate} = \frac{\text{retained earnings}}{\text{profits after taxes}} = \frac{8.33}{17.50} = .476$$

The debt-equity ratio of company A is:

$$\text{Debt-equity ratio} = \frac{\text{total liabilities}}{\text{total equity}} = \frac{200}{200} = 1$$

Let us discuss each in turn.

THE RETENTION RATE

A firm can raise equity in two ways: it can sell additional shares of its stock to the public, or it can retain a portion of its profits each year. In the past, American corporations have increased their equity primarily through retention of earnings. A study by economist Arnold Sametz[3] shows that from 1901 to 1929 the total equity of all nonfinancial corporations in the United States increased by $138 billion. Of this amount, $115 billion, or 83 percent, came from retained earnings and only 17 percent from the sale of new shares of common stock. Furthermore, from 1930 to 1958, total equity increased by $406 billion. Retained earnings accounted for an even larger fraction than in the earlier period: $371, or 92 percent. New flotations of equity accounted for $34 billion, or only 8 percent.

When a corporation earns a profit, it has the choice of distributing its earnings to its shareholders as dividends, retaining them to expand its assets, or some combination of the two. What factors will influence the firm in making its decision? We can gain an important insight into this question by first asking a slightly different one: What factors will lead a firm to change its present dividend payments to either a higher or lower level? This question has been studied in great depth; both interviews and empirical studies indicate that most managers believe that unless there are compelling reasons to the contrary, their fiduciary responsibility, as well as their sense of fairness, requires them to distribute

[3] Arnold Sametz, "Trends in the Volume and Composition of Equity Finance," *Journal of Finance*, vol. XIX, no. 3 (September 1964), pp. 450–69.

a portion of any substantial increase in earnings to shareholders.[4] On the other hand, no corporate manager wants to be placed in a position where he would be forced to retrench and cut back on dividend payments once shareholders have come to expect that a certain level of payments will be maintained. Other factors, such as the legal restrictions on dividend payments that may be imposed on the firm by long-term-bond holders or changes in interest rates that marginally influence the cost of borrowed funds, are less important in the eyes of management than the concept of letting shareholders participate in the growth of earnings of the company.

These considerations are incorporated in the following equation, first formulated by Lintner,[5] used to describe the change in dividend payments:

$$(3\text{-}4) \qquad \Delta D_t = c(D_t' - D_{t-1}) + u_t$$

where ΔD is the change in dividends in period t, D_t' is the target dividend payment in period t, D_{t-1} is the dividend payment in the preceding period, c is a measure of the speed of adjustment to the new dividend level, and u_t is an error term.

The target dividend payment is given by:

$$(3\text{-}5) \qquad D_t' = (1 - b)\pi_t$$

where b is a target retention rate and π_t is the profit earned in period t.

To illustrate this model, suppose that the target payout rate, $1 - b$, is .5, i.e., the firm wishes to pay out to its shareholders one-half of its current earnings. Earnings have been stable for several years at $4 a share, with dividend payments of $2 a share. If earnings now rise to a new level, say $6 a share, the new target dividend payment, D', will be $3, since $D' = (1 - b)\pi_t$. Let c, the speed-of-adjustment factor, be .5. In the first year of higher reported earnings, dividends will rise by 50 cents:

$$\Delta D = .5(3 - 2)$$
$$= .50$$

In the second year, dividends will increase by 25 cents:

$$\Delta D = .5(3 - 2.50)$$
$$= .25$$

Dividends will continue to rise each year until they reach the $3 level. At this point D' will be equal to D_{t-1}, and no further adjustment will be made.

[4] John Lintner, "Distribution of Incomes of Corporations Among Dividends, Retained Earnings and Taxes, *American Economic Review* (May 1956), pp. 97–113.
[5] *Ibid.* See also J. A. Brittain, *Corporate Dividend Policy* (Washington, D. C.: Brookings Institute, 1966).

Financing ratios

The speed-of-adjustment factor, c, depends on the conviction of management about the permanence of its new earnings plateau, its need for internally generated funds, and similar considerations. Empirical studies indicate that c is usually about .3 and that $1 - b$ is roughly .5.

While managers recognize their responsibility to pay dividends to shareholders, they are also aware that retaining earnings will enable them to expand their assets and grow. To see this more clearly, recall that the rate of return on equity could be expressed as:

$$\frac{\text{profits}}{\text{equity}} = (1 - T)[r + (r - i)L/E]$$

Let b represent the percentage of profits that are retained and $1 - b$ the dividend-payout ratio. If both sides of the equation are multiplied by the retention rate:

(3–6)
$$\frac{\text{retention rate} \cdot \text{profits}}{\text{equity}} = b(1 - T)[r + (r - i)L/E]$$

The retention rate times profits is nothing more than the change in equity that will result in the next period. Thus the left-hand side of the equation can be rewritten as:

$$\frac{\text{change in equity}}{\text{equity}} = \text{growth in equity} = g_E$$

The growth of a corporation's equity can now be seen to depend on a number of factors: the retention rate, the tax rate, the rate of return on assets, the interest rate, and the ratio of debt to equity. What considerations impel a firm to choose one particular target level for these variables over another? What consequences flow from adopting one retention rate policy rather than another? What relationship is there between corporate growth and the price of the company's shares? Is there an "optimum" retention-rate policy for any particular financial manager?

THE DEBT-EQUITY RATIO

The retention rate–dividend-payout rate question is intimately linked to the second financing ratio described above, the debt-equity ratio. The arithmetical linkage is obvious: *For a given level of assets and a given level of profits, a rise in the retention rate will increase the firm's equity and lower the debt-equity ratio.* The economic linkage between the two, however, is more subtle. We can explore this linkage by studying the factors that influence the supply and demand of debt.

How much debt are firms willing to incur? This depends on such factors as the regularity of the cash flow and the earning streams of the firm and on the willingness of the company management to assume risk. Debt must be repaid. Failure to meet a claim as it falls due will force the firm into bankruptcy. As a firm increases its debt, it increases its commitment to make larger cash outlays in the future. As long as the economy is prosperous and the cash flows generated by the firm are reasonably stable, it will have no particular difficulty in meeting the interest or the amortization payments on its debt. However, when the economy is less prosperous and competition intensifies, a firm with a heavy debt burden may find it difficult to meet these payments.

The tradeoff that the manager faces in planning the financing of a new capital expenditure is clear: If he relies heavily on debt and the expected return on the investment is greater than the interest rate he pays for the funds, he will raise the expected return on equity; however, he runs the risk that in adverse times the company may not be able to meet all its commitments or, if enough funds can be raised to meet them, that other activities important to the firm will have to be sacrificed. Different firms will, of course, be willing to expose themselves to different amounts of risk.

If considerations such as these influence the *supply* of corporate debt, what factors affect the *demand* for debt? In general, bonds are held by institutions that have to meet fixed claims or by individuals who want to receive stable, regular cash payments. In recent years, dramatic changes have occurred that have influenced the amount of bonds that both these groups want to hold. One of these changes is the rise in interest rates that took place in the 1960's. Interest rates rose during the 1960's for a number of reasons. First, the supply of bonds increased sharply because firms expanded rapidly and financed their new plant and equipment expenditures with debt. This increase in supply tended to raise interest rates. More important, the consumer price index rose sharply during the latter half of the decade, reducing the purchasing power of the money investors received in interest payments. As a result of this inflation, investors demanded higher rates. High-quality long-term corporate bonds, for example, yielded 4.5 percent interest in 1960 and 7.0 percent in 1969. This rise in rates, however, meant that all the purchasers of long-term bonds in the earlier years suffered substantial capital losses by the end of the period. The bonds purchased in 1960 with a yield of 4.5 percent fell in price, for, were they to be sold in 1969, they would have to yield the higher rates that were available on comparable later instruments.

Who bought the bonds that corporations issued in the 1950's and 1960's, and who thereby sustained the capital losses that resulted from the rise in interest rates? The Federal Reserve Bank of Cleveland, which studied this question,[6] found that the composition of ownership of cor-

[6] "Corporate Bonds: 1960–1968," Federal Reserve Bank of Cleveland, *Economic Review* (September 1969), p. 14.

TABLE 3.3

Distribution of Ownership of Outstanding Corporate and Foreign Bonds

Year-end Levels 1960–1968

Amount (in billions of dollars)

Owners	1960	1961	1962	1963	1964	1965	1966	1967	1968
State and local governments	$ 10.2	$ 12.6	$ 15.3	$ 18.4	$ 21.7	$ 24.8	$ 29.2	$ 36.0	$ 35.4
Commercial banks	1.0	0.9	0.8	0.8	0.9	0.8	0.9	1.6	1.8
Mutual savings banks	3.8	3.6	3.5	3.2	3.1	2.9	3.2	5.2	6.6
Life insurance companies	48.2	50.7	53.2	56.0	58.3	61.1	63.3	67.1	71.2
Other insurance companies	1.7	1.7	1.8	2.0	2.4	3.4	3.6	3.9	4.1
Private pension funds	15.7	16.9	18.1	19.6	21.2	22.7	24.6	25.6	26.5
Households	6.7	6.5	5.8	4.8	4.4	4.6	5.7	6.8	9.2
Others	2.8	2.2	2.3	2.5	3.0	3.5	4.9	5.8	11.8
Total	$ 90.1	$ 95.8	$101.6	$108.1	$115.7	$124.7	$136.1	$152.0	$166.6

Percent Distribution

Owners	1960	1961	1962	1963	1964	1965	1966	1967	1968
State and local governments	11.3%	13.2%	15.1%	17.0%	18.8%	19.9%	21.5%	23.7%	21.2%
Commercial banks	1.1	0.9	0.8	0.7	0.8	0.6	0.6	1.1	1.1
Mutual savings banks	4.2	3.8	3.4	3.0	2.7	2.3	2.4	3.4	4.0
Life insurance companies	53.5	52.9	52.4	51.8	50.4	49.0	46.5	44.1	42.7
Other insurance companies	1.9	1.8	1.8	1.9	2.1	2.7	2.6	2.6	2.5
Private pension funds	17.4	17.6	17.8	18.1	18.3	18.2	18.1	16.8	15.9
Households	7.4	6.8	5.7	4.4	3.8	3.7	4.2	4.5	5.5
Others	2.0	2.3	2.3	2.3	1.6	2.8	2.6	3.8	7.1
Total	100.0%	100.0%	100.0%	100.0%	100.0%	100.0%	100.0%	100.0%	100.0%

NOTE: Details may not add to totals because of rounding.
SOURCE: Board of Governors of the Federal Reserve System, Flow-of-Funds Accounts.

porate bonds changed considerably between 1960 and 1968. While the identity of purchasers of new bond issues is not known, an analysis can be made of the ownership of the total outstanding bonds in the economy.

The data in Table 3.3 show that the bulk of corporate bonds is held by institutional investors which either have legal restrictions that limit their investment alternatives or institutions that, for legal reasons, prefer securities with fixed coupons. Life insurance companies, which must meet fixed dollar claims, held the largest dollar volume of corporate and foreign bonds. However, life insurance companies usually have more investment freedom than the retirement systems of state and local governments. Thus, it is not surprising to find that insurance companies reduced their share of total outstanding corporate and foreign bonds from more than 53 to less than 43 percent over this period.

From 1960 to 1968, the dollar amount of corporate and foreign bonds held by state and local governments increased more than threefold. Moreover, the proportion of total outstanding bonds held by these groups increased from a little over 11 to a little over 21 percent. The strong demand for corporate bonds on the part of state and local governments stems from the rapid growth of state retirement systems and the fact that most states require their retirement systems to invest a large proportion of their assets in bonds.

No investor wants to tie up his funds in corporate bonds that decline in price year after year. To protect their capital, an increasing number of institutional investors are fighting for the right to expand their investment opportunities. This fact has great significance for corporate treasurers who rely heavily on debt instruments to finance the expansion of their assets. Should the laws be changed so that at some future date state retirement systems, insurance companies, and other financial institutions are no longer required to confine the bulk of their investments to bonds it is highly probable that, if inflation persists, these traditional buyers will find more attractive investment outlets for their funds and the number of buyers of long-term corporate debt will be drastically reduced.

To summarize, we have seen that two ratios, the retention rate and the debt-equity ratio are of critical importance in financing the expansion of assets. The retention rate indicates the percent of profit that the firm will retain. Subtracting the retention rate from one gives us the dividend payout rate of a firm. The amount of dividends a company will pay depends on both the target level of dividends that it establishes for itself and the speed with which it moves from its current dividend level to the target level.

Because dividends tend to move slowly from one level to another, the fluctuations in profits that occur as a result of changes in underlying economic conditions are absorbed chiefly by the firm's retained earnings.

Financing ratios

The retention rate that a firm actually experiences can, therefore, fluctuate over a wide range from year to year.

Assets can be financed through borrowed funds as well as through equity. One measure of the relative importance of these two sources for a firm is the ratio of debt to equity. If the rate of return that a project earns is greater than the interest cost of the borrowed funds used to finance it, the financial manager can raise the firm's return on equity. However, as the firm increases its fixed commitments, it also increases the risk of bankruptcy.

In recent years, interest rates have risen, partly because of an increase in the supply of bonds and partly as a result of general inflationary pressures. As a result of the rise in rates, bondholders have suffered substantial capital losses. Many buyers of long-term debt, such as state retirement systems, continue to purchase these instruments in part because of legal restrictions on the kinds of assets they can hold. Insurance companies, which have more alternatives, have already cut back appreciably their commitment to these instruments. Should the law regarding state funds be changed, and should interest rates and prices continue to rise, a dramatic decrease in the availability of funds for purchasing bonds can be expected.

Liquidity ratios

Both financial analysts, who study firms from the outside, and financial managers, who operate within them, are concerned with other facts about the corporation than just its profitability or its sources of long-term funds. They are also concerned, for example, with such issues as, How much liquidity should the firm hold? and What kind of credit policy is most appropriate for the firm? Within these two broad problem areas, specific managerial problems arise: How can the firm manage its cash most efficiently? How can receivables best be monitored? What percentage of the receivables now outstanding are likely to become delinquent?

MEASURES OF LIQUIDITY

Perhaps the most widely used measure of a corporation's liquidity is the *current ratio,* the ratio of the firm's current assets to its current liabilities. The value of this ratio for company A, whose financial statements appear as Tables 3.1 and 3.2, is 2.9:

$$\text{Current ratio} = \frac{\text{current assets}}{\text{current liabilities}} = \frac{145}{50} = 2.9$$

The current ratio is important because all liabilities are ultimately paid with funds generated by the liquidation of assets. When receivables are collected, the cash that is generated will enable the firm to pay the bills that fall due.

If a firm's current assets are large, relative to the volume of current liabilities, there is a high probability that the liabilities can be paid as they fall due, i.e., that the company will be able to generate a sufficient volume of cash to meet its commitments. But a high current ratio by itself does not guarantee that this will be the case. Current assets include cash, marketable securities, accounts receivable, and inventory. Suppose that the bulk of a firm's current assets are its inventories. To get cash, the inventories must be sold and the receivables produced by the sale collected. If too long a period elapses before all the receivables are collected, bills may fall due for which the firm has inadequate funds. As a result, some financial experts feel that the current ratio is not an adequate measure of a firm's ability to meet its current obligations.[7] They prefer to use what is called the *quick ratio,* or the "acid test," to measure the firm's ability to meet its current commitments. This ratio ignores inventories, since they are the least liquid of a firm's current assets. The quick ratio for company A is:

$$\text{Quick ratio} = \frac{\text{cash} + \text{securities} + \text{receivables}}{\text{current liabilities}} = \frac{95}{50} = 1.9$$

However, both measures, the current and quick ratio, are more likely to be used by a person who wants to make a rough appraisal of a firm's liquid position than by a financial manager who has the specific responsibility of paying bills as they fall due. This is because current assets, like any other asset, have to be financed, and the funds that are tied up in them are costly. The firm must either pay an explicit interest charge for the funds it has invested in current assets or forego an investment opportunity elsewhere in the firm. As a consequence, the financial manager will want to prepare specific estimates of the dollar value of the liabilities that will fall due each day, when the outstanding receivables are likely to be collected, and when its holdings of short-term securities will mature. Armed with this greater detail, the financial manager can plan his liquidity position more carefully than by the use of ratios alone.

Let us consider how a financial manager might look at his accounts receivable. Receivables arise in the normal course of business: a seller extends credit to a buyer when a sale is made and, usually, receives payment at the end of the month or on some other specified date. These assets are of particular interest to the financial manager because, by skillfully extending credit, the firm can add to its profits. On the other hand,

[7] Altman, Edward "Financial Ratios, Discriminant Analysis, and the Production of Corporate Bankruptcy," *Journal of Finance,* vol. XXIII (September 1968), pp. 589–609.

receivables, like any other asset, must be financed, and holding them represents a cost to the firm.

It is relevant to this discussion to measure how current the firm's receivables are. One measure of this is the *receivable turnover,* the ratio of total sales to outstanding receivables. If a firm has level sales throughout the year and collects its receivables at the end of each month, its receivable turnover will be 12 times per annum. Company A's receivable turnover, on the other hand, is 7.5 times:

$$\text{Receivable turnover} = \frac{\text{total sales}}{\text{outstanding receivables}} = \frac{300}{40} = 7.5$$

Another way of expressing this relationship is to say that the receivables of company A represent 49 days of sales receipts. To arrive at this figure, note that the average daily sales of company A are $.82.

$$\text{Average daily sales} = \frac{\text{total sales}}{\text{days in the year}} = \frac{300}{365} = .82$$

The days' sales outstanding in receivables is then:

$$\text{Days' sales outstanding in receivables} = \frac{\text{outstanding receivables}}{\text{average daily sales}} = \frac{40}{.82} = 49$$

Values such as 7.5 times per annum, or 49 days, have little meaning in themselves, but they can be informative when they are contrasted with the industry practice or the company's own prior history. Suppose that over the past three years, the days' sales outstanding of company A fell steadily from 62 to 54 to 49 days. One could infer from this that the firm had changed its credit policy and that it was policing its receivables more carefully now than in the past.

A more accurate measure of receivable policy can be found by calculating the "age" of the receivables. This is done by tabulating the receivables that were generated by sales made prior to two weeks ago, four weeks ago, and so forth. Thus, the schedule for company A might be:

Sales Made	Outstanding Receivables
1–15 days ago	$10
16–30 " "	15
31–45 " "	10
46–60 " "	4
over 60 " "	1
	$40

These figures indicate that $25 of the $40 in receivables came from sales made in the last month. Only $1 in receivables remains outstanding from sales made two months ago. In short, most of company A's receivables are "current," and there is no indication that its customers have trouble paying their bills.

To summarize, then, corporations measure their liquidity in a number of ways: by the current ratio, by the quick ratio, and by the turnover of different liquid assets. However, these financial measures do not reveal all the facts that are important to a corporate financial manager. To reach a more accurate conclusion about the firm's liquidity, he will generally seek additional data, such as the age of the firm's receivables. This allows him to assess how current his receivables really are and to determine, within reasonable limits, the volume of cash flows that he will receive in the coming months. We shall turn now to get another type of relationship that is of interest to users of financial statements, activity ratios.

Activity ratios

Activity ratios compare sales or cost of goods sold to some asset, such as inventory or total plant, or total assets. For example, a straightforward calculation shows that the inventory turnover of company A is four times per year. This is an activity ratio.

$$\text{Inventory turnover} = \frac{\text{total cost of goods sold}}{\text{inventory}} = \frac{200}{50} = 4$$

Since the turnover ratio is 4, company A carries its inventory for an average period of three months. Whether this is a long or short time depends on the kind of business that company A is in. The ratio can be interpreted only in terms of what other companies in the industry are doing and the past experience of the company itself.

If company A's inventory-turnover figure for the past three years declined from, say, 5.5 to 5 to 4, a detailed analysis of the situation may be necessary. Investigation may show that the firm's stock of finished goods contains a number of obsolete items; it may reveal a breakdown in the production process so that goods can no longer flow smoothly through the plant; or it may bring to light a decision made by the production department to carry more raw-material inventories to permit longer and more efficient production runs.

Other turnover ratios are also frequently calculated. For example, the turnover of net plant and equipment is often cited as a measure of the firm's operating efficiency. In the case of company A, this ratio is approximately 1.2.

$$\text{Plant and equipment turnover} = \frac{\text{sales}}{\text{net plant}} = \frac{300}{255} = 1.18$$

The turnover of net plant and equipment can be relatively high for two reasons. A new plant may improve the quality of the product, leading to a high and rising sales volume. In this case, the high ratio would be coveted by all. On the other hand, a heavily depreciated plant can also lead to a high turnover ratio, even when the firm's sales are low and falling, a condition that would not be envied. To determine which of these two possibilities is actually the case, other facts must be considered. For example, did the profit margin per item change? What is the trend in sales? What is the firm's depreciation policy?

The inventory-turnover rate is a useful overall measure of how effectively one of the firm's major assets is being utilized. It is also an important part of the firm's control system. However, since a number of factors can bring a change in the rate of inventory turnover or the plant and equipment turnover, no single remedial act is automatically called for when the ratio moves outside the established limits or norms. Rather, changes in the ratio should lead to detailed studies of various aspects of the company's operations.

Summary

Four types of ratios have been presented in this chapter: profitability, financing, liquidity, and activity ratios. These ratios can be combined in various ways. For example, one profitability ratio, the return on assets, can be broken down into two separate measures, the profit-margin measure, and the turnover of total assets. Thus:

$$r = \frac{\text{earnings before interest and taxes}}{\text{assets}}$$

$$= \frac{\text{earnings before interest and taxes}}{\text{sales}} \cdot \frac{\text{sales}}{\text{assets}}$$

Similarly, the rate of return on equity can be expressed in terms of a financing ratio, the return on assets, the tax rate, and the interest rate:

$$\frac{\text{profits after taxes}}{\text{equity}} = (1 - T)\left(r + (r - i)\frac{L}{E}\right)$$

These ratios are helpful for many purposes, although they seldom measure subtle economic and financial considerations. To describe fully the complex relationships that link production processes to marketing considerations and both of these, in turn, to conditions in the money market, a full system of equations describing the firm must be stated and evaluated.

Questions for discussion and problems

1. What conditions must hold to make the following statement true: When allowances are made for risk, the rate of return will tend to be the same in every industry. Do these conditions hold in our economy today? If not, is the statement relevant for analyses of economic activity?

2. The rate of return on equity can be higher or lower than the rate of return on assets. Under what conditions will each event occur? Should a firm strive for a high rate of return on assets or a high rate of return on equity?

3. Shareholders pay income taxes on the dividends they receive. Why do they want to receive dividends when they could avoid the tax payment by allowing the firm to retain the funds and reinvest them, thereby adding to the value of their shares?

4. Growth, in the sense of becoming larger, can take place in several ways. What are some of the ways in which a firm can grow, and are they all equally desirable?

5. How does inflation affect the lending policies of the major financial institutions of the country? If financial institutions protect themselves from inflation by designing new debt instruments, will the widely held view that debtors gain and creditors lose during an inflation continue to be valid?

6. Why should a corporation strive to hold liquid balances, since it can earn a profit by drawing down its liquid balances and investing the funds that it frees?

[*Answers to problems 7–16 follow references and suggested readings.*]

7. A company has the following income statement and balance sheet:

Income Statement

Gross sales	$1,000
Cost of goods sold	600
Gross profits	400
Depreciation	20
Interest payments	10
Profit before taxes	370
Taxes	185
Profit after taxes	$ 185

Balance Sheet

Cash	$100	Liabilities	$100
Plant and equipment	200	Equity	200
	$300		$300

From these data, compute its:
(a) gross profit margin.
(b) net profit margin.
(c) return on assets.
(d) return on equity.
(e) average interest rate.
(f) average tax rate.
(g) How did the difference between the return on equity and the rate of return on assets arise?

8. Consider the following equation:

$$\text{Return on equity} = (1 - T)[r + (r - i)L/E]$$

Suppose that the relationship between the firm's ratio of debt to equity and the interest rate it pays for borrowed funds is $i = .1(L/E)$. If $T = .5$ and $r = .18$, what is the return on equity when (a) $L/E = 1$? (b) $L/E = 2$? (c) $L/E = \frac{1}{2}$? What ratio of debt to equity will maximize the firm's return on equity?

9. You are given the equations

$$\Delta D_t = c(D' - D_{t-1})$$

and

$$D' = (1 - b)\pi_t$$

(a) Calculate the equilibrium level of dividends if $\pi_t = \$3$ and $b = \frac{2}{3}$
(b) Calculate the new equilibrium level of dividends if π_t rises to $6.
(c) If $c = .8$, how large will dividends be at the end of the first period?

10. If $T = .4$, $b = .6$, $r = .10$, $i = .05$, and $L/E = 1$, what is the growth rate of the company's equity? How is the growth rate affected if b falls to .4? if it rises to .8?

11. (a) If an investor wants to earn a real return of 5 percent and he anticipates a 5-percent inflation, what interest rate will he demand?
(b) If he owns a bond that has a maturity date in the far future and pays $5 a year in interest, what will its market price be?

12. Suppose that a firm has an inventory-turnover ratio of 4 and a receivable turnover of 6. How long will it take the firm, on the average, to convert its inventory into cash?

The analysis of financial relationships

13. If a company has an inventory-turnover ratio of 7, gross sales of $550,000, and gross profits of $200,000, what is the value of its inventory?

14. Dazzle Fireworks Company has $5,000 in cash, $85,000 in accounts receivables, and $36,000 worth of pinwheels and rockets in stock. It owes the printer $17,000 and its gunpowder supplier $28,000. Using only the information given, compute Dazzle's current and quick ratios.

15. A furniture firm has been experiencing a rate of return on its assets of 10 percent. The owner has $50,000 of equity in the business and has borrowed another $25,000 of long-term debt at a rate of 5 percent. Last year the company paid 40 percent of its earning in taxes. What is the owner's return on equity?

16. A firm with current assets of $75,000 has a current ratio of 2.5/1. Indicate the effect, if any, the following transactions will have on its current ratio and working-capital position. Handle each item separately.
   (a) The purchase of $5,000 worth of merchandise on account.
   (b) The collection of $2,500 on accounts receivable.
   (c) The repayment of a note currently payable to the bank with $10,000 cash.
   (d) The payment of $6,000 in wages, $1,500 of which has accrued.
   (e) The sale for $5,000 of a machine that originally cost $30,000 but had been depreciated to $10,000.

REFERENCES AND SUGGESTED READINGS

Articles

Altman, Edward, "Financial Ratios, Discriminant Analysis, and the Production of Corporate Bankruptcy," *Journal of Finance,* vol. XXIII (September 1968), pp. 589–609.

Baumol, William J., and Malkiel, Burton G., "The Firm's Optimal Debt-Equity Combination and the Cost of Capital," *Quarterly Journal of Economics,* vol. LXXXI, no. 4 (November 1967), pp. 547–79.

Ben-Shahar, Haim, "The Capital Structure and Cost of Capital: A Suggested Exposition," *Journal of Finance,* vol. XXIII, no. 4 (September 1968), pp. 639–54.

Bowlin, O. D., "The Current Ratio in Current Position Analysis," *Financial Analysts Journal* (March–April, 1963), pp. 67–75.

Davidson, Sidney, Sorter, George, and Kalle, Hemu, "Measuring the Defensive Posture of a Firm," *Financial Analysts Journal* (January–February 1964), pp. 23–29.

Dearden, John, "The Case Against ROI," *Harvard Business Review* (May–June 1969), pp. 124–36.

Donaldson, Gordon, "Strategies for Financial Emergencies," *Harvard Business Review* (November–December 1969), pp. 67–80.

Henderson, Bruce, and Dearden, John, "New System for Divisional Control," *Harvard Business Review* (September–October 1966), pp. 144–60.

Lintner, John, "Distribution of Incomes of Corporations Among Dividends, Retained Earnings, and Taxes," *American Economic Review* (May 1956), pp. 97–113.

Mausiel, John, and Anthony, Robert, "Misevaluation of Investment Center Performance," *Harvard Business Review* (March–April 1966), pp. 98–106.

McCloud, B. G., "Pitfalls in Statement Analysis," *Bulletin of The Robert Morris Associates,* vol. 39 (January 1957), pp. 143–48.

Miller, Merton, and Modigliani, Franco, "Dividend Policy, Growth, and the Valuation of Shares," *Journal of Business,* vol. XXXIV, no. 4 (October 1961), pp. 411–33.

Modigliani, Franco, and Miller, Merton, "The Cost of Capital, Corporation Finance, and the Theory of Investment," *American Economic Review,* vol. LXVIII, no. 3 (June 1958), pp. 261–97.

Sametz, Arnold, "Trends in the Volume and Composition of Equity Finance," *Journal of Finance,* vol. XIX, no. 3 (September 1946), pp. 450–69.

Schwartz, Eli, "Theory of the Capital Structure of the Firm," *Journal of Finance,* vol. XIV, no. 1 (March 1959), pp. 18–39.

Solomon, Ezra, "Return on Investment: The Relation of Book Yield to True Yield," in *Research in Accounting Measurement* (Evanston, Ill.: American Accounting Assn., Collected Papers, 1966), pp. 232–45.

Sorter, George, and Benston, George, "Appraising the Defensive Position of a Firm: The Internal Measure," *Accounting Review,* vol. XXXV (October 1960), pp. 633–40.

Walter, James E., "Dividend Policy: Its Influence on the Value of the Enterprise," *Journal of Finance,* vol. XVIII, no. 2 (May 1963), pp. 280–91.

Books

Beranek, W., *Working Capital Management* (Belmont, Calif.: Wadsworth, 1966).

Brittain, J. A., *Corporate Dividend Policy* (Washington, D. C.: Brookings Institute, 1966).

Donaldson, Gordon, *Corporate Debt Capacity* (Cambridge, Mass.: Harvard Univ. Press, 1961).

Foulke, Roy A., *Practical Financial Statement Analysis,* 5th ed. (New York: McGraw-Hill, 1961).

Gordon, Myron, *The Investment, Financing and Valuation of the Corporation,* (Homewood, Ill.: Irwin, 1962).

Lerner, Eugene, and Carleton, Willard T., *A Theory of Financial Analysis* (New York: Harcourt Brace Jovanovich, 1966).

Stigler, George, *Capital and Rates of Return in Manufacturing* (Princeton, N. J.: Princeton Univ. Press, 1963).

Vickers, Douglas, *The Theory of the Firm: Production, Capital, and Finance* (New York: McGraw-Hill, 1968).

ANSWERS TO PROBLEMS 7–16

7. (a) $\dfrac{400}{1,000} = 40$ percent

    (b) $\dfrac{185}{1,000} = 18.5$ percent

(c) Rate of return on assets = $\dfrac{\text{profits before interest and taxes}}{\text{assets}}$ = $\dfrac{380}{300}$ = 127 percent

(d) Return on equity = $\dfrac{\text{profits after taxes}}{\text{equity}}$ = $\dfrac{185}{200}$ = 92.5 percent

(e) 10 percent

(f) 50 percent

(g) Return on equity = $(1 - T)[r + (r - i)L/E]$
$$= (.5)[1.27 + (1.27 - .10)\tfrac{1}{2}]$$
$$= .927$$

8. (a) .13

(b) .07

(c) .122

The firm's return on equity will be maximized when the ratio of debt to equity is .9.

9. (a) \$1.00

(b) \$2.00

(c) \$1.80

10. $g = b(1 - T)[r + (r - i)L/E]$

When $b = .6$, $g = 5.4$ percent; when $b = .4$, $g = 3.6$ percent; when $b = .8$, $g = 7.2$ percent.

11. (a) 10 percent

(b) \$50

12. Since it takes 90 days to sell an item after it enters the firm's inventory and it takes another 60 days to collect the receivables, it takes 150 days to convert an item into cash after it enters inventory.

13. Gross sales $\quad$ \$550,000
Gross profits $\quad$ $-200,000$
Total cost of goods sold $\quad$ \$350,000

$$\dfrac{\$350,000}{x} = 7$$

$$x = \$50,000 \text{ inventory}$$

14. Current ratio = $\dfrac{5 + 85 + 36}{17 + 28}$ = $\dfrac{126}{45}$ = 2.8

Quick ratio = $\dfrac{5 + 85}{17 + 28}$ = $\dfrac{90}{45}$ = 2

15. Return on equity = $(1 - .4)\left[.10 + (.10 - .05)\dfrac{25,000}{50,000}\right]$
$$= (.6)(.10 + .025)$$
$$= .075$$

16. (a) The current ratio will be lower; working capital will remain the same.

(b) The current ratio and working capital will remain the same.

(c) The current ratio will be higher; working capital will not change.

(d) The current ratio will be lower; working capital will decrease by \$4,500.

(e) The current ratio will be higher; working capital will increase by \$5,000.

Financial disclosure by diversified firms

4

An income statement, a balance sheet, and a sources-and-uses-of-funds statement were developed in Chapter 2 for a hypothetical company. This company produced only a single product and sold the product in only a single market. While problems arose over such questions as, When should costs be recognized? or, How should costs be calculated if factor prices change? there was no ambiguity over what activities gave rise to the entries on the financial statements. In such cases, the methods and techniques for analyzing financial statements we have discussed yield results that are relatively easy to interpret.

This state of affairs does not hold when a corporation produces more than one product or sells its products in more than one market. This is, of course precisely what most companies do. They strive to produce a "full line" of products and to sell them in a number of different markets, both foreign and domestic. Moreover, many companies have diversified into a number of unrelated businesses. General Motors makes automobiles and refrigerators; Eastman Kodak makes film and carpets; General Electric makes atomic power plants, toasters, and several hundred, if not several thousand, other products.

When these companies publish their consolidated income statements and balance sheets, it is impossible for a reader to determine which product or which market gave rise to the entries. This does not mean that the published financial statements are without value, but the fact of corporate diversification does raise the question of whether a financial officer could design a system of reports that would be more valuable to its users than the statements now available.

General- versus special-purpose statements

The three financial statements discussed in Chapter 2 are general-purpose statements. They are designed to convey data about the firm that can be used in different ways by a large number of people. Any particular user, however, is likely to want more data than the general-purpose statements provide. For example, suppose we adopt the perspective of a shareholder who wants to use the company's published reports as a basis for estimating the probable profits of the company in some future year. Suppose, further, that the company has two divisions, which produce more or less unrelated products. The combined profits of the two divisions for the past four years, as shown on the consolidated income statement, are $4,200, $3,400, $2,800 and $2,600 respectively. A forecast of earnings for the next year, based on a simple extrapolation of this data, would probably be below $2,600.

Suppose now, that more-detailed information is disclosed about the company's activities. For example, suppose that the earnings of each division are reported, as in Table 4.1.

TABLE 4.1
Divisional Earnings

	Year 1	Year 2	Year 3	Year 4
Division A	$4,000	$3,000	$2,000	$1,000
Division B	200	400	800	1,600
Total	$4,200	$3,400	$2,800	$2,600

It is now apparent that if past trends continue, earnings for the company need not fall in the next year. Indeed, they might even rise to $3,200 if division B continues to double its profits every year. When a corporation has two or more divisions that are growing at sharply different rates and each contributes materially to the performance of the total enterprise, an investor really needs information about each segment before he can form a reasonable estimate of the company's future earnings.

Other users of the firm's general-purpose statements may also want more detailed data than are currently available. A banker may want a special expense statement indicating how much the firm spends for rental and lease payments. A supplier might like to have a special schedule prepared indicating the maturity of the firm's payables, so that he could assess when he is likely to get paid. A manager may want special financial reports on the performance of a single division or on a specific activity within a division. A labor union may want wage and profit figures on a plant-by-plant basis for bargaining purposes. The Federal Trade Commission or the Justice Department may want sales figures broken down by product so that it can calculate the market shares of each product that are held by any one firm.[1]

[1] Hearings Before the Subcommittee on Anti-Trust and Monopoly, Committee on the Judiciary, U. S. Senate, Eighty-ninth Congress, 1st session.

General- versus special-purpose statements

No firm can, of course, fulfill all these special-purpose requests. Not only does the cost of preparing a large number of special-purpose reports rise as the amount of detail increases but the value to the firm of many of these reports is questionable. Moreover, the cost and profit figures themselves become increasingly arbitrary as the amount of detail increases.

One reason for this arbitrariness is that some costs are imposed on the firm by the mix of products, rather than by the level of production. Suppose that a firm can produce ten widgets an hour at a cost of $1 a unit under "normal" circumstances. If the orders for a second product that the firm makes increase, the firm may begin to produce the widgets on an overtime basis. Under these conditions, how is the unit cost of widgets to be calculated? Should the widgets bear the higher overtime costs because more orders were received for another product? Should the product whose sales rose be allocated the increase in widget costs? Should the overtime expenses be allocated equally between the two products? There are obvious difficulties with each of these "solutions."

A second factor that makes detailed statements of costs and profits arbitrary has to do with the way fixed costs are allocated. Suppose that a plant produces more than one product. The question then arises, How should the depreciation costs of the plant be allocated among the various products? Should they be allocated according to the amount of space that each product takes? according to the number of man-hours spent on it? or according to the revenue it generates?

Both these problems—the allocation of costs that arise from the actual product mix and the allocation of fixed costs—involve what is ultimately an arbitrary decision. How they are resolved is of little concern if only a general-purpose financial statement is prepared but may be very important if a special-purpose statement is prepared for each activity, since the decision can make the accounting profits that are reported for a product either positive or negative. A corporate financial officer is thus faced with an important design problem: general-purpose statements may not be specific enough to be of substantive value to other corporate managers or to the firm's shareholders. Extremely detailed statements will also be unsatisfactory. Not only will they be costly to prepare and tedious to read, but they are likely to be arbitrary at best and perhaps even misleading.[2] How can this issue be resolved?

Corporate disclosure to shareholders

How should the activities of a corporation be aggregated to disclose data that is meaningful to its user? Before such a question can be answered,

[2] A. A. Sommer, Jr., "Conglomerate Disclosure: Friend or Foe?" in Alfred Rappaport, Peter A. Firmin, and Stephen Zeff, *Public Reporting by Conglomerates: The Issues, The Problems and Some Possible Solutions* (Englewood Cliffs, N. J.: Prentice-Hall, 1968).

Financial disclosure by diversified firms

the model, or analytical framework, that the user employs to structure the data he receives must be known. The ratio of debt to equity or the difference between current assets and current liabilities has meaning to financial analysts as an input of their models of corporate liquidity. Similarly, the ratio of earnings to assets has meaning to investors because it is part of a larger framework that helps them estimate how efficiently a corporation is run. Other users of financial statements, such as corporate managers, shareholders, or bankers, employ different models. Their goals and aspirations are different and their responsibilities to the company are certainly different. Thus there is no reason to believe that the accounting reports which are suitable for one group will meet all the requirements of the other.

Throughout this chapter, the perspective of a corporate shareholder will be adopted. The answer to the question, What reports are most meaningful to the investor? depends on which model he uses to determine the value of a share of the company's stock. If a corporation's published statements do not specifically address themselves to the analytical framework the shareholder employs, the financial data that are reported are likely to be deficient in two respects: First, the statements may include numbers that are irrelevant to the user; and second, the statements may omit data that are required as inputs to the user's analytical framework.

In later chapters, stock-valuation models will be studied in depth. At this point, it is sufficient to note that two factors are critical in determining how much a shareholder will pay for a security: the expected level of earnings that the company will report and the expected rate of growth of its earnings through time. The greater the earnings and the higher the expected growth rate, the higher the price an investor will pay for the securities.

These are not the only factors of importance in determining the price of a share of stock. Some investors may use a valuation model that emphasizes the company's expected dividend payments or its ratio of debt to equity. However, the expected level of earnings and the expected rate of growth of earnings are of such overwhelming concern in most valuation models that most investors would want diversified companies to disclose data that enable them to estimate these values more accurately.

The expected level of earnings and expected growth rate can be estimated in a number of ways. Two common methods are described below.

Forecasting returns through industry analysis

One method of forecasting a company's future earnings is to study the industry to which it belongs. A forecast of the industry performance may be obtained in several ways. Specific demand and cost factors affecting the industry can be studied and a qualitative determination made of how they are likely to change over time. Alternatively, a statistical analysis can be made of the relationship between the industry and such gross macroeconomic variables as consumer spending or industrial production. Then, once the gross macroeconomic measures are estimated, relevant industry statistics such as industrywide sales or output can be computed.

After the estimate is prepared of what conditions in the industry are likely to be, the investor must determine the company's relationship to the industry as a whole, e.g., the share of the market it will have. However, neither a firm's market share nor its ability to translate growth in sales into increased earnings remains constant over the years. Investors therefore require data about the company itself, as well as data about the industry, to make their forecast. These data may be financial, such as the firm's proposed expenditures on new facilities or its intended outlays for research and development. Frequently, however, the most important data required is nonfinancial. For example, an investor may want to know if the company is planning to change its distribution system or whether its middle management is being trained to take over when the present top management retires.

The earnings-estimation problem associated with this kind of analysis is in reality even more complicated than these remarks indicate, since most companies sell in more than one market and operate in more than one industry. Thus, a manufacturer may sell a single product to three markets within an industry: government, wholesale, and retail markets. Moreover, the company may be, simultaneously, in the glass business, the chemical business and several other industries far removed from the technology associated with its major product line.

For an investor to use an industry framework effectively, some knowledge of the different products the company makes and the markets in which it operates is essential. The contribution each segment makes to the firm's overall performance must also be known, since different segments of an industry offer different opportunities for future growth. Finally, ancillary data such as the investment outlays that are being made in each segment must be determined. These data give the investor an indication of the company's intention to participate in the future of the various industries and the markets it serves.

In short, one way an investor might develop an estimate of the future growth in a company's earnings is to start with an estimate of the future sales growth of the several industries in which the company operates. Its ability to continue to participate in the growth of each industry must then be determined. The immediate implication of this estimating procedure for corporate-disclosure practices is that income-statement figures should be broken down by industry. However, industries are not homogeneous. Some markets within an industry may be growing at a different rate than others. When this occurs, some further breakdown of corporate activities is required for adequate disclosure. In addition, segmented source and application of funds data are required to give the investor an indication of the probable future importance of the various segments to the company, since these outlays will indicate the management's financial commitment to each segment.[3]

Forecasting earnings from company data

A second, less-involved method of forecasting a company's future earnings is to study only the data on the company's past performance and extrapolate this performance into the future. For example, if earnings per share have been falling at the rate of 20 cents a year for the past three or four years, an investor using this method would expect earnings to drop by another 20 cents in the next year.

The difficulties inherent in extrapolating the past performance of the firm as a whole into the future are well known. With no understanding of what factors gave rise to a particular trend, an investor cannot determine what conditions will lead to its reversal. However, if sufficient detail is available about the past performance of the company's various segments, estimates of the firm's overall earnings that are prepared by extrapolating the past trends of these various segments may be a valid procedure. If this method of forecasting is adopted, two or more segments that have had a similar earnings growth in the past and are likely to show a similar trend in the future can be combined and considered as a single segment.

An illustration will help to clarify the distinction between the two methods of classifying the earnings of a firm.[4] Imagine a hypothetical company that sells a number of products in each of three industries: leisure time, agribusiness, and education. The earnings contributions, that is, revenues less traceable expenses, for each activity within an industry, as well as the recent growth rates of each activity, are indicated in Table 4.2. In addition, the expenses that are common to all the activities within an industry and total corporate expenses not traceable to any industry are indicated. These data can also be arranged in a matrix format. Thus, in Table 4.3, the earnings contribution for each industry appear as a row total, while the earnings contribution for each growth-rate segment appears as a column total.

In the leisure-time industry, the earnings contributions of camp equipment and boats were aggregated and only a single profit figure of $172

[3] R. K. Mautz and Fred Skousen, "Some Problems in Empirical Research in Accounting," *Accounting Review* (July 1969), pp. 447–57.
[4] This illustration, as well as much other material in this chapter, draws heavily upon Alfred Rappaport and Eugene M. Lerner's *Framework for Financial Reporting by Diversified Companies* (New York: National Association of Accountants, 1969).

TABLE 4.2
Segmented Earnings and Growth Rates of a Hypothetical Company

Earnings Contributions by Industry	Thousands of Dollars	Growth Rate of Earnings Contribution Over the Past 3 Years
Leisure time		
Camp equipment	$100	11%
Fishing equipment	50	2%
Boats	72	15%
Sporting goods	12	3%
	$234	
Agribusiness:		
Milk processing	85	2%
Canning	72	8%
Chicken farming	12	15%
	$169	
Education:		
Textbook publishing	40	3%
Papers and supplies	17	6%
	$ 57	
Total Earnings Contribution	$460	
Less expenses common to more than one activity but traceable to an industry:		
Leisure-time industry	$106	
Agribusiness	90	
Education	28	
	$224	
Less overall corporate expenses	74	
	$298	
Net income after taxes	$162	

TABLE 4.3
Segmented Earnings Contribution Matrix

Industry	Growth Rate 0–5%	Growth Rate 5–10%	Growth Rate 10–15%	Industry Earnings Contributions	Expenses Common to an Industry	Net Earnings Contribution by Industry
Leisure time	$ 62	$ 0	$172	$234	$106	$128
Agribusiness	85	72	12	169	90	79
Education	40	17	0	57	28	29
Total	$187	$89	$184	$460	$224	$236
Corporate expenses						74
Net income after taxes						$162

TABLE 4.4
Basic Activities Index

Industry	0–5%	Growth Rate 5–10%	10–15%
Leisure Time	Fishing equipment Sporting goods		Camping equipment Boats
Agribusiness	Milk processing	Canning	Chicken farming
Education	Textbook publishing	Paper and supplies	

was reported in Table 4.3 because both segments of the industry grew at a rate of 10–15 percent. Similarly, fishing equipment and sporting goods were aggregated and a figure of $62 was reported because both these activities grew at a rate of 0–5 percent.

If an investor uses an industry approach to estimate the earnings of the company and its expected growth rate, he will use the total of each row in Table 4.3. On the other hand, if he estimates the company's earnings by extrapolating the earnings of different segments, he will use the column totals in Table 4.3. Thus: 41 percent ($187/$460) of the firm's reported earnings came from activities that grew at a rate of less than 5 percent, another 19 percent from activities that grew at a 5–10-percent rate, and the remaining 40 percent from sectors that grew at a rate between 10 and 15 percent. Combining these figures, we see that if the activities that make up the growth-rate segments continue to perform in the future as they have in the past, next year's aggregate earnings will be 9 percent higher than the current year's figure.

Using the midpoint of the growth-rate intervals,

$$.41(1.025) + .19(1.075) + .40(1.125) = 1.09$$

and

$$\$460(1.09) = \$505$$

Thus earnings will rise to $505.

In short, for an investor to make an accurate estimate of future earnings growth based on the past performance of the firm when different segments of the company are growing at different rates, he needs financial statements that indicate the proportion of current earnings that are growing at various rates. These growth-rate segments, which cut across industry lines, are different aggregations than have heretofore been reported.

Segmented funds statements

In the preceding section, a corporation's income statement was segmented to enable investors to estimate the future growth of company earnings.

The sources-and-uses-of funds statement is also a potentially valuable source of data to the investor in a diversified firm. The traditional funds statement, like the traditional income statement, does not provide the investor in a diversified firm with any information on the "basic activities" for which the funds are expended. Thus, the traditional statement would reveal that total capital outalys were x dollars. However, no information would be given, except perhaps in the text of the annual report, as to whether the funds were expended to support activities in industry A or industry B. Moreover, the traditional statement does not reveal which activities were net suppliers of funds and which were net users.[5]

Investors interested in the growth of earnings and dividends of a company should ask the following questions:

(1) Is the company committing its funds primarily to high-growth potential activities, or are the funds being deployed to support low-growth activities?

(2) Are there major low-growth activities that constitute a significant drain on corporate funds?

(3) What is the productivity of the funds that are invested in the various segments?

(4) Assuming that present estimates of sources and uses of funds during the next year or two are accurate, will the company need to seek external financing?

(5) What changes in dividend rates can be expected, given present estimates of earnings and capital requirements during the next few years?

These questions are not answered by the traditional funds statement; however, they could be determined from a segmented funds statement such as that presented in Table 4.5.

Table 4.5 uses the earnings-contribution growth-rate intervals established in the preceding section. Thus, the column headings 0–5%, 5–10%, and 10–15% correspond with those in Table 4.3. The basic activities within each growth-rate segment are those given in Table 4.4. Thus the basic-activity components of the 0–5 percent growth rate are fishing equipment, sporting goods, milk processing, and textbook publishing.

The "Corporate Office" column of the segmented funds statement includes all funds changes not traceable to individual basic activities. Thus the company's financing, business-acquisition program, dividends, and operating costs not traceable to basic activities would ordinarily be included in this classification. Note, for example, that the $298,000 of operating costs not traceable to basic activities appearing on the funds statement is equal to the sum of the $224,000 in expenses common to three industries and the $74,000 of corporate expenses in Table 4.2.

[5] Hector R. Anton, *Accounting for the Flow of Funds* (Boston: Houghton Mifflin, 1962).

TABLE 4.5
Segmented Statement of Sources and Uses of Funds
(in thousands)

	Growth Rate			Corporate Office	Total
	0–5%	5–10%	10–15%		
Funds were provided by:					
Earnings contribution of "basic activities" by growth-rate segment	$187	$ 89	$184		$ 460
Charges against earnings not requiring funds—					
Depreciation, depletion, and amortization	50	40	65	$ 58	213
Deferred federal income taxes	20	10	30	10	70
Disposals of property, plant, and equipment	10		25		35
Increase in long-term debt				2,240	2,240
Proceeds from sale of common stock				1,300	1,300
Proceeds from exercise of stock options				200	200
Common stock exchanged in business acquisitions				2,000	2,000
	$267	$139	$304	$5,808	$6,518
Funds were used for:					
Cash dividends				$ 100	$ 100
Operating costs not traceable to "basic activities"				298	298
Acquisitions of other companies				3,800	3,800
Increase in working capital	$ 20	$ 10	$ 30	400	460
Capital expenditures[1]	600	110	750	400	1,860
Intra-company cash transfers	(353)	19	(476)	810	—
	$267	$139	$304	$5,808	$6,518

[1] Expensed development costs not included in capital expenditures figures are $150, $100, $200, and $250, respectively.

We can now attempt to answer our investors' questions.

(1) WHERE IS THE COMPANY COMMITTING ITS FUNDS?
    The amount of funds used for capital expenditures is a prime indication of management's commitment to the future of the basic activities within a growth-rate segment. In addition to capital expenditures, most firms spend significant sums on development projects which will generate earnings in the future but which are expensed for accounting purposes in the current period. In evaluating the extent of management's commitment

Segmented funds statements

to an activity, consideration should be given not only to capital expenditures but to expensed development costs as well. (Note that the expensed development outlays are disclosed, by growth-rate segments, as a footnote to the funds statement.) The company resources committed to intermediate and long-range benefits may be summarized as follows:

	Growth-Rate Segment		
	0–5%	*5–10%*	*10–15%*
Capital expenditures	$600	$110	$750
Expensed development costs	150	100	200
	$750	$210	$950

Whether the data is analyzed in absolute terms or relative to the earnings contribution or sales of each segment, it is apparent that a greater emphasis is being placed by the company on the slower (0–5%) growth-rate segment than on the faster (5–10%) segment.

Assuming that the reported growth rates of the firm's various basic activities will continue, we would expect the segments with higher growth rates to receive the bulk of the firm's investment dollars. This is obviously not the case here. The disparity between the historical growth rate of the various activities and the firm's allocation of resources may be an indication that management believes that the firm's basic activities will be distributed differently among the growth-rate segments in the future; i.e., the commitment of funds to low-growth-rate areas may mean that management expects these segments to grow more rapidly in the future. On the other hand, it may mean that management is making significant errors in judgment in its resource allocation. In either case, the funds statement provides the investor with some information as to the future direction and emphasis of the firm.

(2) WHICH SEGMENTS ARE SOURCES, AND WHICH ARE USERS, OF FUNDS?

Intra-company cash transfers are closely linked to the problem of how the company deploys its resources. These transfers may be viewed as a residual account; that is, they are what is left of the funds provided by operations after capital expenditures and required expansions of working capital are subtracted. Note that, in the illustration, the slowest and fastest growth-rate segments were net users, while the 5–10 percent growth-rate segment was a modest provider, of funds. An analysis of intra-company cash transfers will give the investor some hints as to whether cash flows generated by established activities can be relied on to finance the investment opportunities likely to provide significant earnings contributions in the years ahead.

(3) WHAT IS THE PRODUCTIVITY OF CAPITAL?

The precise rate of return on investment earned in different segments cannot be estimated directly from the income and flow of funds statements. However, an investor can judge the productivity of capital in the various segments by comparing the financial statements of the firm over time. Suppose an investor finds that for several years the company has continued to invest substantial sums in a low-growth area. Suppose, further, that the number of basic activities in the segment has remained constant and that the level of profits has not risen by an amount comparable to the increase in investment. An obvious inference can be drawn about the returns in that sector.

This kind of calculation cannot, however, be made using the traditional statements now furnished by firms in their annual reports. Since these statements aggregate all the corporation's activities, no estimation can be made of the performance of the various segments.

(4) AND (5) WILL THE COMPANY REQUIRE ADDITIONAL FINANCING IN THE FUTURE, AND WILL DIVIDEND PAYMENTS BE INCREASED?

Table 4.5, like the traditional sources and uses of funds statement, provides some basis for assessing the future financing requirements of the firm. No financial statement by itself, however, can provide enough information for the investor to make a definitive assessment in this area. Some information is needed on the company's plans for entering new areas or expanding its present operations. Table 4.5 does, however, like traditional sources and uses of funds statements, provide enough data to let the investor determine whether the funds generated from operations are sufficient to support the dividends being paid. The hypothetical company whose data make up the table did not generate sufficient funds to cover the $100,000 outlays for dividends.

Table 4.6 shows that funds to support business acquisitions, capital expenditures, and increased working capital during the year were obtained

TABLE 4.6
Funds Generated by Company Operations
(in thousands)

Earnings contributions		$460
Depreciation, depletion, and amortization		213
Deferred federal income tax		70
Disposals of property, plant, and equipment		35
		$778
Less:		
Operating costs not traceable to basic activities	$298	
Increased working capital required for operations	460	758
Net funds generated by operations		$ 20

via increases in long-term debt and common shares. It is left for the investor to estimate the extent to which these financing sources will be utilized in the years to come.

The analysis of the company's requirements for funds and sources of financing also gives the investor a basis for estimating probable changes in dividend rates, since dividends, in large measure, depend on earnings, cash generated by operations, capital-expenditure levels, business-acquisition plans, and choices among alternative financing plans, as well as on the management's dividend policy.

Determining basic activities

While corporate disclosure by growth-rate segments would be valuable for investors, the method of disclosure raises a number of technical problems. Among these are: What are the components of the growth-rate segments of a company? How can these components be determined? What problems arise in the construction of growth-rate segments?

The earnings-contribution entries reported in Table 4.3 are the sum of the earnings contributions of various basic activities within each industry. (See Table 4.4.) *A basic activity is any product line or market area that generates material revenues and expenses for the firm.* Table 4.2 shows nine basic activities. The earnings contributions of two basic activities in the leisure-time industry, fishing equipment and sporting goods, were added to make up the industry entry reported in the 0–5 percent growth column in Table 4.3. Camping equipment and boats were similarly aggregated in the 10–15 percent column.

Transactions giving rise to revenues and expenses can be aggregated in a number of ways. As a result, different observers of the corporation could aggregate its transaction data in ways that give rise to different basic activities. Several economic guidelines help a firm in determining what a basic activity is and the number of basic activities that it can meaningfully report to investors. Among these guidelines are (1) the way data from outside the firm on products or markets are structured, (2) the revenue and expense patterns characteristic of various activities, and (3) the materiality, or size, of the basic activity itself.

EXTERNAL DATA

To prepare an earnings forecast, an investor may wish to combine corporate data with data from such varied sources as the press, trade associations, and government bulletins. These are, of course, only three of many potential "outside" sources of information valuable to investors.

Information about corporate developments prepared by external sources tends to be structured in one of two ways: by product line or by market. For the investor to be able to integrate corporate reports with external data, the reporting of a firm's basic activities could be in terms of either of these concepts. The actual earnings contribution the firm will report for its basic activities will depend on which definition is employed.

To illustrate how reports can differ when different definitions of basic activities are used, let us suppose that a corporation makes two products, X and Y, in a single plant. Some of the machines in the plant are used to make both products, and some are unique to each. Furthermore, we shall assume that both products are marketed through the same set of dealers, some of whom are domestic and some foreign.

If the corporation defines a basic activity as a product line, it would report the earnings contributions of X and Y as in Table 4.7.

TABLE 4.7
Earnings-Contribution Statement When Basic Activities Are Products

	Products		Common Expenses	Total
	X	Y		
Sales	$1,300	$1,500		$2,800
Less traceable expenses				
Manufacturing costs	750	850		1,600
Selling and administrative costs	130	150		280
	$ 880	$1,000		$1,880
Earnings contribution by product lines	$ 420	$ 500		920
Expenses common to product lines X and Y			$620	620
Earnings contribution X and Y combined				$ 300

Suppose, however, that the firm defined its basic activities by the different markets it served. It would then report the earnings contributions of its basic activities as in Table 4.8.

While the revenues and earnings contributions of the two activities combined are the same in both cases, the contributions of the basic activities are quite different since the method of segmentation affects the relative proportions of traceable and common expenses. The entries that would appear in an earnings-contribution matrix would also differ, for this reason. Which of the two possible definitions of a basic activity, a product or a market, is appropriate clearly depends on the nature of the corporation. However, the criterion that should be met in selecting from among these and other alternatives is clear: *The financial report that will ultimately be disclosed should be the one that enables the investor to estimate the future state of affairs of the firm most accurately.* If there is an abun-

TABLE 4.8
Earnings-Contribution Statement When Basic Activities Are Markets

| | Markets | | Common | |
	Domestic	Foreign	Expenses	Total
Sales	$2,000	$800		$2,800
Less traceable expenses				
Manufacturing costs	600	240		840
Selling and administrative costs	500	300		800
	$1,100	$540		1,640
Earnings contribution by markets	$ 900	$260		$1,160
Expenses common to domestic and foreign markets			$860	860
Earnings contribution of domestic and foreign markets combined				$ 300

dance of information readily available to investors about foreign and domestic market conditions, a market-oriented definition of a basic activity may be appropriate. If the available external data is accumulated primarily by product line, a product-line definition may be more useful. Whatever definition is selected, it should be used consistently, so that succeeding statements can be compared, consistently, unless a basic change in the firm or its environment warrants a revised definition.[6]

REVENUE AND EXPENSE PATTERNS

Differences in the pattern of the revenue stream and the expense stream generated by a product or market are also important in forecasting the future earnings contribution of a basic activity. A fall in the price of a product will lead to an increase in gross revenues if the demand for it is elastic and to a decrease in gross revenue if the demand is inelastic. Similarly, an increase in national income will lead to a large increase in the gross revenues of a product whose demand curve is income elastic, but to a small increase in the revenues of one whose demand curve is income inelastic. Products will therefore have different patterns of revenue flows through time if their demand schedules have different price and income elasticities. If two products have similar demand elasticities, they can be considered as a single activity in forecasting. If their demand elasticities are different, however, they should be treated as separate activities since the revenue stream of each will differ over time.

[6] R. K. Mautz, *Financial Reporting by Diversified Companies* (New York: Financial Executives Research Foundation, 1968).

Financial disclosure by diversified firms

Similar considerations apply to the costs associated with a product. If the costs of one product are stable through time, while those of another are rising rapidly, the earnings contribution of the two products will exhibit different patterns through time. Combining the activities will reduce the value of the report to the investor.

Two products are likely to have different cost trends if their production functions are different. If one product is heavily labor-intensive while another is heavily capital-intensive, it is probable that each will have a different pattern of costs through time and should be considered as a separate basic activity. However, if two products have a similar production function, they are likely to exhibit a similar trend in costs and may be considered as a single basic activity. Note also that aggregating activities with a common production function into a single basic activity tends to reduce the magnitude of common expenses.

MATERIALITY

If the earnings contribution of one product, or activity, is substantially larger than that of another and the two are combined into a single basic activity, the trends developing in the market for the smaller product will be concealed. Thus, an investor who is concerned with the progress of the smaller product will be denied information that is of concern to him. Moreover, if the earnings of the smaller product are growing at a different rate than those of the larger product, combining the two can be misleading.

Most businesses which produce a number of different products are aware that many of their products make only nominal contributions to common expenses and corporate earnings. To consider each of these products as a basic activity would place an undue burden on both the investor and the corporation. Thus, *in determining the number of basic activities in which it is engaged, the corporation must keep in mind the materiality of the contribution of each product.* No hard-and-fast rules can be given as to when an activity makes a material contribution. Even so, it seems reasonable to suggest that investors could use data on activities that contribute 10 percent or more of each industry's total earnings. Moreover, an enlightened management will consider not only the current materiality of an activity but the expected change in its materiality over the next few years.

Summary

The financial statements used by modern corporations are highly aggregative. Hence any user who has a specific requirement in mind generally needs more data than they provide. One important group of users of financial statements are the corporation's shareholders, who read the statements with a view to estimating both current earnings and the growth rate of future earnings.

Most modern corporations have diversified. They make a number of products, some of which are closely related to one another and others which are wholly unrelated. Thus an investor needs data on the behavior of earnings in each of the major segments of the corporation in order to ascertain the company's future earning power.

It is difficult for a financial officer to design an effectively segmented financial statement. If the segments are defined narrowly, the profit and cost figures will be arbitrary. If the segments are defined too broadly, they may fail to disclose the relevant earning trends that are developing.

Investors would also find it valuable if a corporation prepared and disclosed a segmented sources-and-uses-of-funds statement. Such a statement clearly shows whether a diversified firm is making investment commitments in high- or low-growth areas and whether these areas are suppliers or users of funds. Moreover, by comparing these statements over time, estimates can be developed of the productivity of capital in various sectors. Based on these data, investors can obtain better estimates of future growth rates than is now possible.

Some criteria that a financial officer could use in determining what constitutes a firm's "basic activities" are:

(1) Basic activities are activities that generate both revenue and expense streams. They can be structured either by product or by market.

(2) The decision to classify activities by product or market should take into account the dominant classification system used by other sources of information available to the investor.

(3) If two or more products or product markets have a common demand elasticity, they should be treated as a single activity.

(4) If two or more activities have a common production function and similar cost trends, they should be considered as a single activity.

(5) Basic activities should be of sufficient materiality to warrant separate disclosure.

Questions for discussion and problems

1. What kind of financial data that might be important to a labor union or to a commercial banker would not be of real value to a corporate shareholder? In what data is a shareholder interested that is not of major concern to these groups?

2. Interest in segmented financial statements has grown in recent years. Why do you think such groups as (a) the Justice Department, (b) the Securities and Exchange Commission, and (c) the Accounting Principles Board have developed this interest?

3. Use the data in Table 4.2.
    (a) If a change in the definition of a basic activity occurred, would the statistics in each row change?
    (b) Would these changes affect the usefulness of the data for shareholders?

4. Use the data in Table 4.3.
    (a) Would the statistics in each cell change if 2-year or 5-year growth rates had been used instead of 3-year figures?
    (b) Would these changes affect the usefulness of the data for shareholders?

5. Is estimating the future performance of a company from past growth rates a valid statistical procedure? What alternatives are available to the investor?

6. If a company reports a segmented flow-of-funds statement, do you think that corporate managers will become more or less willing to take on projects that do not "pay off" for the first few years?

[Answers to problems 7–10 follow references and suggested readings.]

7. A firm with two operating divisions has shown a consolidated income during the past four years of $5,050, $4,100, $3,400, and $3,200, respectively. Division B produced $250 in profits four years ago and has been doubling them each year since. What can be said about division A? What should next year's consolidated income be?

8. The Omniwit Corporation, a diversified firm, has been engaged in the following pursuits in recent years:

Activity	Recent Average Growth Rate of Earnings Contribution
Communications satellite manufacture	15%
Textile manufacture	13
Railroad operation	1
Women's ready-to-wear retailing	9
Knitwear manufacture	6
Broadcast operations	8
Inland-waterway ferries	3
Recording studios	4

The current year's total earnings contributions of $37.5 million were distributed among the communications, apparel, and transportation industries. Activities in the 0–5 percent growth rate segment accounted for 23 percent of the total earnings figure, those in the 5–10 percent segment for 42 percent, and those in the 10–15 percent segment for 35 percent of the total.

(a) Construct a basic-activities index.

(b) Project an average-expected-earnings figure for the coming year.

9. During the current year, Omniwit Corporation (see problem 8) has expensed the following sums for development of its basic activities:

	(in millions)
Communications satellite manufacture	$25.0
Textile manufacture	5.0
Railroad operation	1.5
Women's ready-to-wear retailing	2.0
Knitwear manufacture	1.0
Broadcast operations	15.0
Inland-waterway ferries	.5
Recording studios	7.0

In addition, capital expenditures in the three growth-rate segments, were $50 million, $75 million, and $105 million, respectively. Show how the company's resources are being committed to intermediate and long-range benefits.

10. The Melcamp Company markets two products worldwide. Total sales during the preceding year were $30,000, 60 percent of which was sales of product A. Of the total, Melcamp had $16,000 in foreign sales. Manufacturing costs traceable to the products totaled $15,000, 40 percent of which was attributable to product B. Foreign and domestic traceable manufacturing expenses for A and B were $5,000 and $9,000, respectively. Selling and administrative costs totaled $8,000, of which 35 percent was attributable to product A. However, expenses for foreign sales and administration were $4,500, and similar domestic expenses were another $4,000. Expenses common to A and B were $3,500. Expenses common to both foreign and domestic markets were $2,000. Prepare earnings contribution statements for both product and market definitions of basic activities and compare the results.

REFERENCES AND SUGGESTED READINGS

Articles

Cramer, Joe, Jr., "Income Reporting by Conglomerates—Views of American Businessmen," *Abacus,* vol. 4, no. 1 (August 1968).

"Disclosure of Supplemental Financial Information by Diversified Companies," Statement of The Accounting Principles Board, September 1967 (New York: American Institute of Certified Public Accountants), pp. 1–5.

Mautz, R. K., and Skousen, K. Fred, "Some Problems in Empirical Research in Accounting," *Accounting Review* (July 1969), pp. 447–57.

"Reporting the Results of Operations," Opinion Number 9 of the Accounting Principles Board, December 1966 (New York: American Institute of Certified Public Accountants).

Sommer, A. A., Jr., "Conglomerate Disclosure: Friend or Foe?" in Alfred Rappaport, Peter A. Firmin, and Stephen A. Zeff, *Public Reporting by Conglomerates: The Issues, The Problems and Some Possible Solutions* (Englewood Cliffs, N. J.: Prentice-Hall, 1968), pp. 1–16.

Sorter, George H., "An 'Events' Approach to Basic Accounting Theory," *Accounting Review*, vol. XLIV, no. 1 (January 1969), pp. 12–19.

Books

Anton, Hector R., *Accounting for the Flow of Funds,* (Boston: Houghton Mifflin, 1962).

Backer, Morton, and McFarland, Walter, *External Reporting for Segments of a Business* (New York: National Association of Accountants, 1968).

Mason, Perry, *"Cash Flow" Analysis and the Funds Statement,* Accounting Research Study 2 (New York: American Institute of Certified Public Accountants, 1961).

Mautz, R. K., *Financial Reporting by Diversified Companies,* (New York: Financial Executives Research Foundation, 1968).

Rappaport, Alfred, and Lerner, Eugene M., *A Framework for Financial Reporting by Diversified Companies* (New York: National Association of Accountants, 1969).

ANSWERS TO PROBLEMS 7–10

7.

			Year		
	1	*2*	*3*	*4*	*5*
Division A	$4,800	$3,600	$2,400	$1,200	$ 0
Division B	250	500	1,000	2,000	4,000
Consolidated income	$5,050	$4,100	$3,400	$3,200	$4,000

Division A's operations are being phased out; earnings are falling at a rate of $1,200 a year. Next year's consolidated operations should produce at least $4,000 of income.

8. (a)

	Basic Activities Index		
	0–5%	5–10%	10–15%
Communications	Recording studios	Broadcasting	Satellites
Apparel		Women's ready-to-wear and knitwear	Textiles
Transportation	Railroads and ferries		

(b) $.23(1.025) + .42(1.075) + .35(1.125) = 1.081$
$1.081(37.5) = \$40,537,500.$

9.

	Growth Rate Segments		
	0–5%	5–10%	10–15%
Expensed development cost (in millions)	$ 9	$18	$ 30
Capital expenditures (in millions)	50	75	105
Total	$59	$93	$135

10.

Earnings Contribution Statement for Basic Activities

	Products		Total	Markets		Total
	A	B		Domestic	Foreign	
Sales	$18,000	$12,000	$30,000	$14,000	$16,000	$30,000
Less traceable expenses						
Manufacturing	9,000	6,000	15,000	9,000	5,000	14,000
Sales and Administration	2,800	5,200	8,000	4,000	5,500	9,500
	$11,800	$11,200	$23,000	$13,000	$10,500	$23,500
Earnings contribution	6,200	800	7,000	1,000	5,500	6,500
Common expenses			3,500			2,000
Earnings contribution of combined activities			$ 4,500			$ 4,500

The flow of funds

5

We have seen how financial statements provide information about the performance of the firm. However, balance sheets and income statements can be constructed not only for a single firm but for a combination of firms. For example, composite statements could be prepared for all the firms in the steel industry, the oil industry, or the chemical industry. If such statements were published, the sources and uses of funds in each industry over time could be identified. Statements from the late nineteenth century, would reveal, for example, that railroads were heavy demanders of funds, spending large amounts for rolling stock, roadbeds, and supporting physical facilities. Statements from the first half of the twentieth century would show public utilities as major users of funds, as the demand for electricity, gas, and telephone service spread across the land. Statements from more recent years would show outlays of manufacturing companies for plant, equipment, and working capital as dominating the movement of funds in the capital market.

While the composite sources and uses of funds statements of industries would reveal a great deal of American economic history, they would also raise a number of questions. How much of the investment that was made was financed through funds generated by the industries themselves, and how much was borrowed from other sectors of the economy? If both individuals and financial intermediaries (such as banks and insurance companies) advanced credit to various industries, what proportion of the total funds came from each source?

Questions about the sources of funds available to individuals and governments, and the uses to which they are put, can also be asked. If financial statements were developed for these sectors of the economy, answers to such questions, too, could be found.

In the early 1950's, under the direction of Morris Copeland, the National Bureau of Economic Research began a study of financial flows in different sectors of the American economy. When this work was completed, its value was so apparent that the Board of Governors of the Federal Reserve System took on the responsibility of updating the Bureau's estimates of the flow of funds between sectors at regular intervals. These updated estimates are important to financial managers for the insights they provide into the environment of the corporate system.

In this chapter, we shall sketch out the framework for, and discuss, the data the Federal Reserve now prepares.

The flow-of-funds format

A corporation can generate funds by increasing its liabilities, increasing its equity, or reducing its assets. It can use the funds it raises to expand its assets, reduce its liabilities, or lower its equity through the payment of dividends or the repurchase of outstanding shares. The total sources of funds that the corporation raises must, of course, from an accounting viewpoint, equal its total uses of funds.

A firm's sources and uses of funds can be arranged in a number of ways to study different problems. For example, suppose a financial analyst wants to study the volume of a firm's investment outlays or the size and relative importance of its sources of funds. Let the data in Table 5.1 describe the change in balance-sheet entries over a period of time for a hypothetical company Y. These data can then be arranged as in format I, to emphasize the firm's two sources of funds (internal and external) and its two uses of funds (capital expenditures and other uses.)

TABLE 5.1
Change in Balance-Sheet Entries for Company Y

Change in liquid assets		$ 7	Change in liabilities	$10
Change in plant and equipment	$10		Change in equity	2
Change in depreciation	5			
Net change in capital assets		5	Change in liabilities and equity	$12
Change in total assets		$12		

If the data for different years are arranged as in format I, the effect of changes in credit-market conditions on the firm's ability to raise and employ funds can be traced. Other formats, stressing other relationships, can also be designed. For example, suppose a financial manager wants to emphasize the change in the firm's liquidity over time. He might prefer to arrange the data in Table 5.1 according to format II.

Format I

Sources of funds of Company Y
Internally generated funds:

Change in equity	$2
Depreciation charges	5
Total	$ 7

Externally generated funds:

Change in liabilities	10
Total sources	$17

Uses of funds of Company Y

Capital expenditures	$10
Other uses (change in liquid assets)	7
Total uses	$17

Format II

Funds generated through operations:

Change in equity	$ 2
Depreciation charges	5
Total	7
Less capital expenditures	10
Change in working capital	−$ 3

Memo:

Change in liquid assets	$ 7
Less change in liabilities	10
Change in working capital	−$ 3

Format III

Savings of Company Y

Change in equity	$ 2
Depreciation charges	5
Gross savings	$ 7

Investment of Company Y

Capital investment		$10
Financial investment		
Change in liquid assets	$ 7	
Less change in liabilities	10	
Net financial investment		−$ 3
Gross investment		$ 7

The flow-of-funds format

When the data are arranged this way, they show that during the year the capital expenditures of company Y exceeded the funds it raised through operations. Thus the firm's net working capital decreased.

The data in Table 5.1 can be arranged in still a third way. Corporate savings can be defined as revenues from sales of goods and services less cash outlays for the cost of goods sold and taxes. Corporate investment can be divided into financial investments such as cash, accounts receivable, and bonds, and real investments such as buildings, inventories, and machinery. The relationship between savings and investment can then be traced.

Format III highlights the fact that the gross savings of the company equals its total investment. The total savings of the firm, that is, its profits plus depreciation charges, are $7. The $3 decline in working capital can be thought of as a negative financial investment. This negative financial investment, combined with the $10 outlay for real investment, gives us the firm's net investment figure of $7.

Company Y acquired $7 in liquid assets; these could take various forms. For example, the firm could have purchased a short-term security issued by the federal government or increased its receivables by advancing credit to a customer. Similarly, the $10 increase in liabilities could have been a payable owed to suppliers or a debt instrument of some kind. It is important, in analyzing these data, to remember that *the financial assets of company Y are liabilities of another party* and that *the financial liabilities of company Y are considered to be financial assets by the individuals and institutions that hold them.*

To summarize, corporate data can be arranged in a number of different formats to emphasize a variety of points. One such format focuses on the savings and investments of the firm. These two flows must always be equal. Thus, company Y's savings in the example were $7; it made a real investment of $10 and a financial investment of —$3. From the point of view of the economy as a whole, net financial investment will always equal zero, since the financial assets of one sector are the financial liabilities of another. Further, since total savings equal total investment, for the economy as a whole savings must be equal to real investment.

The flow-of-funds matrix

Let us simplify things for a moment by supposing that the economy consists of only three entities; company Y, discussed above, Mr. Doe, an individual, and a government body. Consider a flow-of-funds statement, similar to that presented in format III, for Doe. Let Doe's income during the year be $40 and his outlays for consumption and taxes be $31. His cash available for investment is therefore $9. Suppose, further, that Doe owns some durable goods such as an automobile and a refrigerator, which depreciate through time. Let the depreciation charges be $5. Doe's net savings will then be $4. Gross savings for Doe, as for a firm, are equal to net savings plus depreciation charges, or $9.

The money that Doe saved can be invested in either real or financial assets. Suppose he spends part of his savings, say, $7, to purchase a durable good and invests the remainder in government securities. Since Doe had the money, he could pay for the good in full and invest his remaining $2 in bonds. To make the transaction more realistic, however, let us suppose that he paid only $5 down for the $7 good and borrowed the remaining $2 from the seller. Under these conditions, Doe's cash outlay *from savings* for the good is only $5. Since he had $9 in cash, he has $4 left with which to acquire financial assets such as government bonds or securities issued by company Y. However, since he incurred $2 in debt, his net financial investment will be only $2. His sources-and-uses-of-funds statement will thus be:

Sources and Uses of Funds for Mr. Doe

Savings

Depreciation charges		$5
Net savings		4
Gross savings		$9

Investment

Capital expenditures		$7
Financial investment		
Change in financial assets	$4	
Less change in financial liabilities	2	
Net financial investment		2
Gross investment		$9

Let us now investigate the third sector of our economy, the government. The government receives revenues from tax collections and makes expenditures for goods and services. The difference between the funds it receives and those it expends are the government saving. Let the revenue and expenditure figures be $10 and $9 respectively. Government saving will then be $1.

Suppose, further, that the government issues $5 in bonds to raise funds for an expenditure it plans to make at a later date. It invests the $5 from the sale of the bonds, as well as its $1 in current savings, in short-term securities issued by company Y. The sources-and-uses-of-funds statement of the government will then be:

The flow-of-funds matrix

93

Sources and Uses of Funds of Government

Savings of government

Total receipts	$10	
Less total expenditures	9	
Net savings of government		$1

Investment of government

Financial investment

Change in assets	$6	
Less change in liabilities	5	
Net financial investment		$1

Let us now combine the flow of funds for the three sectors of the economy into single matrix, as in Table 5.2.

TABLE 5.2
Flow-of-Funds Matrix for a Three-Sector Economy

	Company Y Use	Company Y Source	Mr. Doe Use	Mr. Doe Source	Government Use	Government Source	Total Use	Total Source
Gross savings		7		9		1		17
Capital consumption		5		5		0		10
Net savings		2		4		1		7
Gross investment	7		9		1		17	
Capital expenditure	10		7		0		17	
Net financial investment	−3		2		1		0	
Total	7	7	9	9	1	1	17	17
Memo:								
Financial uses	7		4		6		17	
Financial sources		10		2		5		17

Several comments can be made about the flow-of-funds matrix in Table 5.2:

(1) For each sector of the economy, the total sources of funds equals the total uses of funds.

(2) The capital expenditures of company Y exceed its savings. As a result, the firm is a net borrower of $3. It was a net borrower from Mr. Doe of $2 and a net borrower from the government of $1.

(3) Company Y actually expanded its liabilities by $10, and to finance its borrowings it sold $4 of securities to Doe and $6 of securities to the government. However, it also increased its financial assets by $7, since it purchased the debt instruments issued by the other sectors of the economy. The combined effect of company Y's purchase and sale of securities is a net financial investment of —$3. Similarly, the combined effect of the purchase and sale of securities by each of the other sectors is their net financial investment.

(4) For the economy as a whole, the row totals of gross savings and investment are equal.

(5) For the economy as a whole, financial investment is equal to zero. Since gross savings equal gross investment, the volume of capital expenditures in the economy as a whole equals the gross savings in the economy as a whole.

In the real world, of course, an individual would be unlikely to both borrow from, and lend to, the same firm, and a government would be unlikely to invest its excess funds in securities of a private corporation. The sectors, can, however, be made more inclusive. Instead of the data for company Y, we can imagine the data for all nonfinancial business in the economy aggregated; instead of Mr. Doe, we can imagine a composite of all households. When this extension is made, it is no longer unreasonable to think of a sector as both incurring financial liabilities and purchasing financial assets from another sector. Moreover, the example can be expanded to incorporate other sectors of the economy. Banks and insurance companies, for example, can be added. None of these changes, however, would alter the basic logic of the flow-of-funds matrix developed above: sources and uses of funds must still be equal for each sector; net financial investment must equal zero for the economy as a whole; and the gross savings of all sectors must equal the gross investment of all sectors.

How many sectors, then, does the Federal Reserve monitor? How large are the actual flows through these sectors? We shall examine these questions in the next section.

The flow of funds for 1969

The flow-of-funds data published by the Federal Reserve System highlight four major sectors of the economy: (1) the private domestic nonfinancial sector, (2) the U.S. government, (3) the financial sector, and (4) the rest of the world. Two of these sectors are further divided. The private nonfinancial sector has three parts: households, business, and state and

TABLE 5.3

Sources-and-Uses-of-Funds Accounts for 1969

(Seasonally adjusted annual rates; in billions of dollars)

		Private domestic nonfinancial sectors								
Sector	House-holds		Business		State and local govts.		Total		U. S. Govt.	
Transaction category	U	S	U	S	U	S	U	S	U	S
1 **Gross saving**	—	**146.6**	—	**81.8**	—	**−5.6**	—	**222.8**	—	7.
2 Capital consumption	—	82.7	—	66.5	—	—	—	149.2	—	—
3 Net saving (1-2)	—	63.9	—	15.2	—	−5.6	—	73.6	—	7.
4 **Gross investment (5 + 10)**	**137.3**	—	**74.7**	—	**−7.5**	—	**204.4**	—	**8.6**	—
5 Private capital expenditures	116.8	—	111.1	—	—	—	227.9	—	—	—
6 Consumer durables	89.8	—	—	—	—	—	89.8	—	—	—
7 Residential construction	22.0	—	10.2	—	—	—	32.2	—	—	—
8 Plant and equipment	5.0	—	92.8	—	—	—	97.8	—	—	—
9 Inventory change	—	—	8.0	—	—	—	8.0	—	—	—
10 **Net financial investment (11-12)**	**20.5**	—	**−36.4**	—	**−7.5**	—	**−23.4**	—	**8.6**	—
11 **Financial uses**	**50.2**	—	**25.5**	—	**1.9**	—	**77.7**	—	**7.0**	—
12 **Financial sources**	—	**29.8**	—	**62.0**	—	**9.4**	—	**101.1**	—	**−1.**
13 Gold & official foreign exchange	—	—	—	—	—	—	—	—	1.4	—
14 Treasury currency	—	—	—	—	—	—	—	—	—	.
15 Demand deposits and currency	—	—	—	—	—	—	—	—	—	—
16 Private domestic	3.4	—	.5	—	2.2	—	6.0	—	—	—
17 U. S. Government	—	—	—	—	—	—	—	—	1.1	—
18 Foreign	—	—	—	—	—	—	—	—	—	—
19 Time and savings accounts	11.3	—	—	—	—	—	−4.1	—	—	—
20 At commercial banks	3.3	—	−7.8	—	−7.5	—	−12.0	—	−.1	—
21 At savings institutions	8.0	—	—	—	—	—	8.0	—	—	—
22 Life insurance reserves	4.5	—	—	—	—	—	4.5	—	—	—
23 Pension fund reserves	15.8	—	—	—	—	—	15.8	—	—	1.
24 Interbank items	—	—	—	—	—	—	—	—	—	—
25 Credit market instruments	18.7	31.4	11.4	48.1	7.2	8.9	37.3	88.3	2.6	−3.
26 Corporate shares	−4.3	—	—	4.3	—	—	−4.3	4.3	—	—
27 U. S. Government securities	13.1	—	−1.4	—	4.2	—	15.8	—	−1.3	−3.
28 State and local obligations	3.8	—	2.3	—	.1	8.5	6.1	8.5	—	—
29 Corporate and foreign bonds	4.9	—	—	12.1	2.8	—	7.7	12.1	—	—
30 Home mortgages	−.5	16.0	—	−.5	.2	—	−.3	15.5	.1	−.
31 Other mortgages	1.8	1.1	—	10.8	—	—	1.8	11.9	.6	—
32 Consumer credit	—	9.3	1.8	—	—	—	1.8	9.3	—	—
33 Bank loans n.e.c.	—	2.0	—	12.5	—	—	—	14.5	—	—
34 Other loans	—	2.9	8.7	8.9	—	.4	8.7	12.3	3.2	—
35 Security credit	−.8	−2.4	—	—	—	—	−.8	−2.4	—	—
36 To brokers and dealers	−.8	—	—	—	—	—	−.8	—	—	—
37 To others	—	−2.4	—	—	—	—	—	−2.4	—	—
38 Taxes payable	—	—	—	.8	—	—	—	.8	1.0	—
39 Trade credit	—	.4	17.3	11.4	—	.5	17.3	12.3	.9	—.
40 Equity in noncorporate business	−4.8	—	—	−4.8	—	—	−4.8	−4.8	—	—
41 Miscellaneous claims	2.1	.3	4.2	6.5	—	—	6.3	6.8	.1	
42 Sector discrepancies (1-4)	9.4	—	7.1	—	1.9	—	18.4	—	−.8	—

SOURCE: *Federal Reserve Bulletin* (May 1970), p. 470.

The flow of funds

	Financial sectors										Rest of the world		All sectors		Discrepancy	Natl. savings and investment	
Total		Sponsored credit agencies		Monetary auth.		Coml. banks		Pvt. nonbank finance									
U	S	U	S	U	S	U	S	U	S	U	S	U	S	U	U	
—	3.9	—	.1	—	*	—	3.7	—	.1	—	.6	—	235.1	—	234.5 —	1
—	1.4	—	—	—	—	—	.7	—	.6	—	—	—	150.6	—	150.6 —	2
—	2.6	—	.1	—	*	—	.9	—	—.5	—	.6	—	84.5	—	83.9 —	3
2.2	—	*	—	*	—	2.7	—	—.5	—	3.7	—	218.9	—	16.3	225.6 —	4
1.4	—	—	—	—	—	.6	—	.8	—	—	—	229.2	—	5.9	229.2 —	5
—	—	—	—	—	—	—	—	—	—	—	—	89.8	—	—	89.8 —	6
—	—	—	—	—	—	—	—	—	—	—	—	32.2	—	—	32.2 —	7
1.4	—	—	—	—	—	.6	—	.8	—	—	—	99.2	—	—	99.2 —	8
—	—	—	—	—	—	—	—	—	—	—	—	8.0	—	—	8.0 —	9
.8	—	*	—	*	—	2.1	—	—1.3	—	3.7	—	—10.4	—	10.4	—3.7 —	10
78.2	—	9.2	—	4.1	—	16.9	—	48.0	—	10.1	—	173.0	—	—	6.5 —	11
—	77.4	—	9.1	—	4.1	—	14.9	—	49.3	—	6.5	—	183.4	—	10.1 —	12
—.1	—	—	—	—.1	—	—	—	—	—	—1.0	.3	.3	.3	—	— —	13
*	—	—	—	*	—	—	—	—	—	—	—	*	.3	.2	— —	14
—	6.6	—	—	—	3.3	—	3.3	—	—	—	—	7.7	6.6	—	— —	15
.4	5.9	*	—	—	2.8	—	3.1	.3	—	—	—	6.4	5.9	—.6	— —	16
—	.5	—	—	—	.6	—	—.1	—	—	—	—	1.1	.5	—.6	— —	17
—	.2	—	—	—	—.1	—	.3	—	—	.2	—	—	.2	—	— —	18
—.1	—3.0	—	—	—	—	—	—	—.1	—	—	—	—3.0	—3.0	—	— —	19
—.1	—11.0	—	—	—	—	—	—11.0	—.1	—	1.2	—	—11.0	—11.0	—	— —	20
*	8.0	—	—	—	—	—	—	*	8.0	—	—	8.0	8.0	—	— —	21
—	4.5	—	—	—	—	—	—	—	4.5	—	—	4.5	4.5	—	— —	22
—	14.2	—	—	—	—	—	—	—	1.42	—	—	15.8	15.8	—	— —	23
.9	.9	—	—	*	.4	1.0	.5	—	—	—	—	.9	.9	—	— —	24
77.3	31.0	8.9	8.8	4.2	—	14.9	4.3	49.3	17.9	1.9	3.5	119.2	119.2	—	— —	25
12.8	5.5	—	—	—	—	—	*	12.8	5.6	1.5	.2	10.0	10.0	—	— —	26
—8.0	9.1	—.4	9.1	4.2	—	—11.2	—	—.5	—	—1.1	—	5.5	5.5	—	— —	27
2.4	—	—	—	—	—	1.4	—	1.0	—	—	—	8.5	8.5	—	— —	28
6.8	1.7	—	—	—	—	—.4	.1	7.2	1.6	.5	1.2	14.9	14.9	—	— —	29
15.6	*	3.9	—	—	—	2.6	—	9.2	*	—	—	15.4	15.4	—	— —	30
9.5	—	.6	—	—	—	2.3	—	6.5	—	—	—	11.9	11.9	—	— —	31
7.5	—	—	—	—	—	3.3	—	4.2	—	—	—	9.3	9.3	—	— —	32
16.4	2.1	—	—	—	—	16.4	—	—	2.1	—	—.3	10.4	16.4	—	— —	33
14.3	12.5	4.8	—.3	*	—	.5	4.2	9.0	8.6	1.0	2.4	27.2	27.2	—	— —	34
—3.8	—2.2	—	—	—	—	—1.2	—	—2.6	—2.2	—.2	—.2	—4.8	—4.8	—	— —	35
—1.2	—2.2	—	—	—	—	—1.2	—	—	—2.2	—.2	—	—2.2	—2.2	—	— —	36
—2.6	—	—	—	—	—	—	*	—2.6	—	—	—.2	—2.6	—2.6	—	— —	37
—	.3	—	—	—	*	—	.2	—	.1	—	—	1.0	1.1	.1	— —	38
.3	—	—	—	—	—	—	—	.3	—	1.0	.4	19.5	12.4	—7.1	— —	39
—	—	—	—	—	—	—	—	—	—	—	—	—4.8	—4.8	—	— —	40
3.2	25.1	.3	.5	—	.4	2.3	17.5	.7	6.9	7.0	2.5	16.6	34.9	18.3	— —	41
1.7	—	—	—	—	—	1.0	—	.6	—	—3.1	—	16.3	—	16.3	8.9 —	42

local governments. The financial sector is divided into sponsored credit agencies, the monetary authority, commercial banks, and private nonbank financial institutions.

It would be helpful for some purposes if more sectors of the economy or more subdivisions of the existing sectors were recognized. Because only the net flows between sectors are reported, the flows within a sector are lost. If the steel industry, for example, extended credit to the automobile industry and the auto industry increased its outstanding credit to other industries in the nonfinancial sector by the same amount, the net flow out of the sector as a whole could be zero. Reporting only the change in financial assets and liabilities of *all* businesses obviously conceals a great deal of data that would be uncovered by a finer breakdown.

A second criticism of the flow-of-funds data reported by the Federal Reserve is that it combines both new cash flows and changes in the value of capital assets in a single measure. This happens because the estimates of the flows are prepared from changes in balance-sheet data. During a year, an asset can increase in value for two reasons: because more of the asset is acquired or because the original asset is revalued upward. Similarly, an asset can decline in value from one balance-sheet date to another either because a portion of it was sold or because it was revalued downward.

In spite of these limitations of the data (which could only be remedied at a substantial cost to the agency that prepares the estimates), the figures on the flow of funds through the sectors of the economy that are recognized are most revealing. The data in Table 5.3 indicate the flow of funds in the American economy in 1969. (To prepare these figures, the Federal Reserve uses a number of different sources. Not all these sources are equally accurate, and, as a consequence, minor statistical discrepancies may arise between the sources and uses of funds within a sector.)

During 1969, households saved almost $147 billion and business firms saved roughly $82 billion. Depreciation charges were more important than net savings in both the business and household sectors. In the business sector, depreciation charges were roughly 4 times as large as net savings.

Households made capital expenditures of $117 billion. These funds were used for products such as consumer durables and homes. Since their savings were $147 billion, households increased their net financial assets by over $20 billion. This net financial investment of households resulted from an increase in financial assets of almost $50.2 billion and an increase in liabilities of $29.8 billion. The financial assets acquired included demand deposits, time deposits, and pension-fund reserves. Liabilities arose from home mortgages, consumer credit, and bank loans.

Business firms, on the other hand, spent substantially more on capital expenditures than they generated through internal sources. They were *net borrowers* from other sectors of the economy, primarily households, of over $36 billion. As in the case of households, the net-financial-investment figure conceals several important developments. In 1969, business firms actually expanded their financial assets by over $25 billion. This included increases in demand deposits and savings certificates, the extension of consumer and trade credit (receivables), and the purchase of the securities issued directly by other firms. Business borrowings increased by almost $62 billion. Firms issued substantial amounts of bonds and mortgages to help finance new plant; they borrowed heavily from banks and other businesses, both through the direct sale of commercial paper and through trade credit (payables); and by allowing their accrued taxes to rise, firms borrowed funds, so to speak, from the federal government.

The volume of savings by firms in the financial sector is insignificant compared to that of households and nonfinancial businesses. However, these institutions marshall the savings of the households and business and invest them in the debt obligations issued by these sectors. The liabilities of commercial banks—demand deposits and time and savings deposits—increased by almost $15 billion. These funds were invested in government securities, mortgages, business loans, and consumer credit. Similarly, private nonbank financial firms, such as insurance companies, savings and loan associations, and financial companies increased their liabilities by over $49 billion. They received their funds through the sale of shares to the public, through issuing savings deposits and through the build-up of pension fund reserves. They employed the funds they acquired by purchasing mortgages, government securities, debt instruments of corporations and extending consumer credit.

A detailed sector statement

The flow-of-funds statistics prepared by the Federal Reserve are actually based on more detailed figures than those in Table 5.3. The sector statement for nonfinancial corporate business for 1955–1969 in Table 5.4 is typical.

The capital expenditures of *nonfinancial business corporations* were greater than the volume of gross internal funds or gross savings in every year. In 1955, for example, business firms were net borrowers of $6.5 billion; in 1969, of $32 billion. (The difference between the recorded savings of $62.7 billion in 1969 and the recorded expenditures of $87.5 billion is $24.8 billion. Adding the statistical discrepancy of $7.1 billion to this figure and adjusting for rounding gives us a net financial investment of −$32 billion.)

The two major components of gross savings are undistributed profits, or retained earnings, and capital consumption, or depreciation, charges. These two components differ both in magnitude and in the way they behave over time. Capital-consumption charges increased steadily from 1955 to 1969 while undistributed profits followed a more cyclical path. From 1966 to 1969, undistributed profits actually declined.

The major component of business capital expenditures is plant and equipment outlays. Except for modest declines in 1958 and 1961, this series expanded rapidly and in 1969 had reached $77 billion. These outlays stemmed from the new opportunities generated by such factors as automation, expanding markets, and population movements, and probably, to some degree, from the belief that a postponement of expenditures would only mean higher construction costs and higher interest costs in the future. Moreover, as one firm in an industry modernized its plant, other firms were driven to follow its lead to remain competitive.

This sustained high level of expenditures has had far-reaching effects. For example, it has led to steady employment and relatively high wages in the construction and machine-tool industry; these used to be considered "feast and famine" industries, in which good years were followed by bad ones. For the past decade, however, this has no longer been the case. Good years have been followed by better ones, and employment has continued steady.

For the past several years, also, business capital expenditures have exceeded gross corporate savings by substantial amounts. To finance these outlays, business firms had to compete aggressively in the funds market. The intensive search for funds by financial managers undoubtedly contributed to high interest rates in the late 1960's. It also spurred companies to seek new ways of conserving cash and to develop new financial instruments that would be attractive to firms and individuals with excess funds.

The search for funds has driven many firms into a position where they are now financing a portion of their long-term assets—plant and equipment outlays—with short-term liabilities, i.e., with liabilities that fall due in a relatively short period such as 30, 60, or 90 days. Unless the firms can refinance these assets as they fall due, they are likely to encounter severe cash problems.

The second major component of corporate capital expenditures is the outlays for inventory. These investments are made both to assure customers rapid delivery of merchandise and to guarantee uninterrupted production runs within the firm itself. The investment in inventory, however, is quite volatile. Between 1966 and 1969, for example, inventory investment fell by over $7 billion. Although fluctuations in inventory investment have in the past contributed to recessions, the economy continued to operate at a high level from 1955 to 1968. This fact is testimony to the changes that have occurred in the structure of our economic system. For example, in previous years, the volume of inventory investment was a major component of total corporate investment; in 1968, plant and equipment outlays were ten times as large as the investment in inventory.

Plant and equipment expenditures and inventory outlays exceeded gross corporate savings every year from 1955 to 1969. Nonfinancial corporations were therefore compelled to increase their financial liabilities more than their financial assets. What financial assets did firms acquire, and how were they able to borrow the funds to finance this growth in assets?

The data in Table 5.4 show that the composition of liquid assets changed sharply over the period covered, although trade credit (accounts receivable) remained the most important. In 1969, receivables increased by over $17 billions.

A second liquid-asset investment important in 1969, commercial paper (open-market paper) was relatively unimportant in earlier years. This asset arises when a firm, such as a finance company, sells its debt securities directly to a corporation that has a temporary excess of funds. In 1969, the interest rates paid by companies selling commercial paper were quite high, and, as a consequence, astute financial managers preferred these assets to government securities or time deposits in commercial banks. In 1969, the commercial paper held by corporations increased by $8.7 billion, while other liquid assets rose by lesser amounts.

Financial liabilities rose by $56.2 billion in 1969. The single most important source of funds for corporations was the flotation of bonds. Almost $12 billion was raised by this method alone. The second most important source of funds was bank loans, which amounted to almost $11 billion. Mortgages accounted for another $4.5 billion. Trade debt (accounts payable) and other liabilities, i.e., various accruals, contributed $10.9 and $6.5 billion respectively. Still another source of funds was "other loans," commercial paper issued by nonfinancial corporations. Despite high interest rates, over $6.2 billion of these instruments were sold in 1969.

To summarize, the flow-of-funds data provide detailed statements of the sources and uses of funds in major segments of the economy. A study of one of the segments, nonfinancial corporate business, indicates the dimensions of the financial problems of a modern corporate financial executive. Capital expenditures must be made, and the amount of these expenditures generally exceeds the funds internally generated by the firm. In addition, financial assets must be acquired to sustain a constantly higher level of activity. To finance these outlays, funds must be raised through various short- and long-term instruments or the sale of equity. Detailed statements of other sectors are also prepared by the Federal Reserve, and the reader is encouraged to examine them.

TABLE 5.4

Sources and Uses of Funds of Nonfinancial Corporate Business
(in billions of dollars)

Category	1955	1956	1957	1958	1959	1960	1961	1962	1963	1964	1965	1966	1967	1968	1969
1 Profits before tax	42.0	41.8	39.8	33.7	43.2	40.1	40.2	44.6	49.1	55.7	65.7	71.1	66.2	75.6	76.6
2 Less: Profits tax accruals	19.8	19.7	18.9	16.2	20.7	19.5	19.7	20.8	22.8	24.2	27.5	30.0	28.1	35.6	36.7
3 Net dividends paid	9.4	10.1	10.4	10.2	10.9	11.6	11.6	12.7	14.2	14.9	16.8	18.1	19.0	20.3	21.6
4 Equals: Undistributed profits	12.8	12.0	10.6	7.3	11.6	9.0	8.9	11.0	12.0	16.5	21.3	22.9	19.1	19.7	18.4
5 Plus: Fgn. branch profits, net	1.1	1.2	1.3	1.0	1.0	1.0	1.3	1.3	1.5	1.8	1.8	1.8	2.1	2.4	2.5
6 Inv. valuation adj.	-1.7	-2.7	-1.5	-.3	-.5	.2	-.1	.3	-.5	-.5	-1.7	-1.8	-1.1	-3.2	-5.6
7 Capital consumption	17.0	18.4	20.3	21.4	22.9	24.2	25.4	29.2	30.8	32.8	35.2	38.2	41.2	44.3	47.4
8 Equals: Gross internal funds	29.2	28.9	30.6	29.5	35.0	34.4	35.6	41.8	43.9	50.5	56.6	61.2	61.2	63.1	62.7
9 Gross investment (10 + 15)	25.0	23.7	27.9	25.8	30.2	30.0	31.2	36.9	40.0	43.6	49.4	53.1	53.0	56.2	55.6
10 Capital expenditures	*31.5*	*35.9*	*34.7*	*27.3*	*36.9*	*39.0*	*36.7*	*44.0*	*45.6*	*52.1*	*62.8*	*77.1*	*72.5*	*76.9*	*87.5*
11 Fixed investment	26.6	31.0	34.1	29.8	32.8	36.0	35.1	39.3	41.2	46.2	54.9	62.7	66.0	70.3	80.0
12 Plant and equipment	25.8	30.7	33.4	28.4	31.1	34.9	33.2	37.0	38.6	44.1	52.8	61.6	63.8	68.0	77.2
13 Residential construction	.8	.4	.7	1.4	1.7	1.1	1.9	2.3	2.6	2.1	2.0	1.1	2.2	2.3	2.9
14 Change in inventories	4.9	4.9	.6	-2.5	4.1	3.0	1.5	4.7	4.3	5.9	7.9	14.4	6.4	6.5	7.4
15 Net financial investment	**-6.5**	**-12.2**	**-6.8**	**-1.5**	**-6.8**	**-9.0**	**-5.4**	**-7.1**	**-5.5**	**-8.5**	**-13.4**	**-24.0**	**-19.5**	**-20.7**	**-31.9**
16 Net acquis. of finan. assets	*18.6*	*6.3*	*6.0*	*13.2*	*16.2*	*4.7*	*15.6*	*16.0*	*17.7*	*12.8*	*23.1*	*15.5*	*13.5*	*26.6*	*24.2*
17 Liquid assets	5.5	-4.1	-.2	2.6	5.6	-3.3	3.7	3.5	4.7	1.2	1.7	1.9	*	10.1	2.3
18 Demand dep. and curr.	1.0	.1	*	1.5	-1.0	-.5	1.7	-.9	-.8	-2.3	-1.5	.7	-2.2	1.3	.5
19 Time deposits	-.1	—	—	.9	-.4	1.3	1.9	3.7	3.9	3.2	3.9	-.7	4.1	2.2	-7.8
20 U.S. Govt. securities	4.2	-4.5	-.4	*	6.6	-5.4	-.2	.5	.5	-1.5	-1.6	-1.2	-3.1	1.8	-1.4
21 Open mkt. paper	.1	.1	.1	.3	-.2	1.6	.3	.3	.9	1.6	.5	2.0	1.5	4.5	8.7
22 State and local oblig.	.2	.1	.1	.5	.7	-.2	*	-.3	.2	.2	.5	1.0	-.4	.4	2.3

The flow of funds

23 Consumer credit	.7	.5	.3	.6	.8	.4	.2	.7	1.0	1.3	1.2	1.2	.9	1.7	1.3
24 Trade credit	11.4	7.5	2.8	8.3	7.7	5.3	9.5	8.5	8.1	8.1	15.1	11.3	8.8	14.8	17.3
25 Other financial assets	1.0	2.4	3.1	1.8	2.0	2.3	2.2	3.2	3.9	2.2	5.1	1.0	3.8	.1	3.4
26 *Net increase in liabilities*	*25.0*	*18.5*	*12.8*	*14.7*	*23.0*	*13.7*	*21.0*	*23.1*	*23.2*	*21.3*	*36.5*	*39.4*	*33.0*	*47.3*	*56.2*
27 Credit mkt. instruments	10.6	12.9	12.1	10.1	11.5	11.3	12.4	12.7	12.4	13.7	20.5	24.9	29.3	31.0	38.0
28 Corporate bonds	2.8	3.6	6.3	5.7	3.0	3.5	4.6	4.6	3.9	4.0	5.4	10.2	14.7	12.9	12.1
29 Corporate stock	1.9	2.3	2.4	2.1	2.2	1.6	2.5	.6	−.3	1.4	*	1.2	2.3	−.8	4.3
30 Mortgages	1.8	1.6	1.6	2.9	3.0	2.5	4.0	4.5	4.9	3.6	3.9	4.2	4.5	5.8	4.5
31 Bank loans n.e.c.	4.0	5.3	1.2	−.4	3.5	1.8	.7	3.0	3.7	3.8	10.6	7.9	6.4	9.6	10.9
32 Other loans	*	.1	.5	−.2	−.3	1.9	.6	*	.2	.9	.6	1.4	1.4	3.6	6.2
33 Profit tax liability	4.1	−2.0	−2.1	−2.6	2.4	−2.2	1.4	.6	1.9	.5	2.2	.2	−4.1	3.7	.8
34 Trade debt	7.9	4.7	.6	4.8	5.5	.7	5.5	4.6	5.3	3.6	9.1	7.8	2.6	5.7	10.9
35 Other liabilities	2.5	2.9	2.2	2.4	3.6	4.0	1.7	5.2	3.7	3.5	4.6	6.5	5.2	6.9	6.5
36 Discrepancy (8–9)	4.1	5.3	2.7	3.7	4.8	4.4	4.4	5.0	3.8	6.9	7.2	8.0	8.2	6.9	7.1
37 *Memo: Net trade credit*	3.5	2.8	2.2	3.5	2.2	4.6	4.0	3.9	2.8	4.5	5.9	3.5	6.2	9.2	6.4
38 Profits tax payments	17.0	22.1	21.3	18.7	18.2	21.6	18.0	20.4	20.4	23.6	25.8	30.5	32.7	32.0	36.0

SOURCE: *Federal Reserve Bulletin* (November 1969 and May 1970), p. A71.4.

A detailed sector statement

TABLE 5.5

Statements of Financial Assets and Liabilities by Sector:
Nonfinancial Corporate Business

(Amounts outstanding at end of year; in billions of dollars)

Category	1955	1956	1957	1958	1959	1960	1961	1962	1963	1964	1965	1966	1967	1968	
Total financial assets	155.4	162.6	169.2	183.3	200.5	206.6	221.3	238.2	257.3	271.5	296.1	313.3	329.4	358.2	1
Liquid assets	58.7	54.6	54.4	57.0	62.7	59.4	63.0	66.4	71.1	72.3	74.0	75.9	77.4	86.9	2
Demand deposits and currency	32.0	32.2	32.1	33.6	32.6	32.1	33.8	32.8	32.0	29.8	28.2	28.9	27.8	29.1	3
Time deposits	1.0	1.0	1.0	1.9	1.5	2.8	4.6	8.3	12.2	15.4	19.2	18.6	22.7	24.8	4
U.S. Govt. securities	23.3	18.8	18.4	18.4	25.0	19.5	19.2	19.6	20.2	18.6	17.0	15.8	13.4	14.5	5
Open market paper	1.2	1.3	1.4	1.2	1.1	2.7	3.0	3.5	4.4	6.0	6.5	8.5	9.9	14.5	6
State and local obligations	1.2	1.3	1.5	2.0	2.6	2.4	2.4	2.1	2.3	2.5	3.0	4.0	3.6	4.0	7
Consumer credit	7.1	7.5	7.9	8.4	9.3	9.7	9.9	10.6	11.6	12.9	14.1	15.3	16.3	17.9	8
Trade credit	67.6	75.1	77.9	86.2	93.9	99.2	106.2	114.8	122.8	130.9	146.0	157.3	166.1	180.9	9
Miscellaneous financial assets	22.0	25.3	29.0	31.6	34.6	38.2	42.2	46.4	51.8	55.4	62.1	64.8	69.7	72.6	10
Total liabilities	200.7	217.1	227.6	240.5	261.5	273.8	277.3	299.9	324.1	344.1	381.0	419.4	451.0	499.1	11
Credit market instruments	100.8	111.4	121.0	129.1	138.6	148.3	158.2	170.3	183.3	195.4	215.9	239.5	266.9	298.2	12
Corporate bonds	53.3	56.9	63.2	68.9	71.9	75.3	80.0	84.5	88.4	92.4	97.8	108.0	123.0	135.9	13
Mortgages	20.3	21.9	23.6	26.5	29.5	32.0	36.0	40.5	45.4	49.0	52.8	57.1	61.6	67.3	14
Bank loans n.e.c.	24.9	30.2	31.4	31.1	34.8	36.6	37.3	40.3	44.4	47.9	58.6	66.4	72.9	82.5	15
Other loans	2.3	2.3	2.8	2.7	2.5	4.3	5.0	5.0	5.1	6.0	6.7	8.0	9.5	12.4	16
Profit taxes payable	20.1	18.1	16.0	13.4	15.8	13.6	15.1	15.7	17.6	18.5	20.7	20.9	16.8	20.5	17
Trade debt	49.2	54.0	54.6	59.4	64.6	65.3	68.0	72.6	77.9	81.5	90.6	93.4	101.0	106.7	18
Miscellaneous liabilities	30.6	33.7	35.9	38.6	42.5	46.6	36.0	41.3	45.3	48.8	53.8	60.5	66.3	73.8	19

SOURCE: *Federal Reserve Bulletin*, (November 1969) page A71.15.

Sector statements of financial assets and liabilities

The flow-of-funds data include still other material, in addition to that described above. For example, they also show the stock of financial assets and financial liabilities of the various sectors. Table 5.5 reproduces this data for nonfinancial corporate businesses for the period 1955–1968. This table shows how carefully financial managers have managed their short-term liquid assets. Note that over the entire period 1955–1968, the amount of demand deposits held by firms changed very little. This stability did not occur by chance; in Chapter 6, we shall discuss some of the techniques of cash management that have been developed to ensure this stability.

The data also show that the holdings of government securities fell, while the growth of time deposits and open-market paper was rapid. These shifts occurred because of the difference in the interest yields offered by the securities. Finally, Table 5.5 also shows that corporate liabilities have risen more rapidly than corporate liquid assets. While it would be incorrect to draw inferences about the ability of firms to meet the claims of creditors as they fall due from these data alone, the statistics do suggest that corporate financial officers must plan the timing of their receipts and disbursements carefully to avoid the possibility of not meeting claims when they fall due.

Summary

The financial transactions of different sectors of the economy can be aggregated. In each sector, the total sources of funds must equal the total uses of funds.

The sources-and-uses-of-funds statement can be structured to show the gross savings, the real capital expenditures, and the net financial investment of the sector. For the economy as a whole, net financial investment must equal zero, since every change in financial assets is offset somewhere else in the economy by a change in financial liabilities. As a result, gross corporate savings equal gross capital formation. Empirical estimates of these various flows, however, may not show these precise results because of the way in which the data that make up the estimates are collected.

In the American economy households and businesses dominate the savings and capital-expenditures flows. Historically, the business sector has spent more on capital expenditures than it has saved. The reverse is true of households.

Business firms and households increased both their financial assets and their financial liabilities in absolute terms from 1955 to 1969. Corporations increased their financial liabilities by a greater amount than their financial assets and used the additional funds they borrowed to finance capital expenditures.

The single largest class of financial assets that firms hold is accounts receivable; the largest liability of corporations is the bonds that they may have outstanding.

Questions for discussion and problems

1. The changes that occur in a corporation's balance sheet can be structured to show that corporate savings equal corporate investment. What are some advantages of taking this perspective?

2. How do you reconcile the fact that one sector of the economy can have real investment outlays that exceed its savings year after year with the fact that, for the economy as a whole, savings must equal real investment?

3. Capital gains and losses are combined with net cash flows to obtain estimates of sector flows. What difficulties might this estimating technique cause in interpreting the data?

4. How do you account for the large financial flows through financial intermediaries, in view of the relatively small amount of savings and real investment that takes place?

[*Answers to problems 5–7 follow references and suggested readings.*]

5. The Standard Company's 19x1 and 19x2 balance sheets appear below:

	19x2		19x1	
Liquid assets		$44		$40
Fixed assets	$99		$87	
Less depreciation	62		56	
		37		31
Total assets		$81		$71
Liabilities		$30		$24
Equity		51		47
Total liabilities and equity		$81		$71

From this information, construct a statement showing the relationship between the company's savings and investments during 19x2.

6. Examine Table 5.3.
   (a) What were the major financial uses of funds by households in 1969?

(b) What were the major financial sources of funds for households in 1969?

(c) Businesses spent almost $101 billion for plant, equipment, and inventory in 1969. How was this financed?

7. Look at the figures for 1955 and 1969 in Table 5.4.

(a) How much did profits before taxes increase?

(b) How much did undistributed profits increase?

(c) What two factors account for the difference between answers (a) and (b)?

(d) How much did gross internal funds increase between these two dates?

REFERENCES AND SUGGESTED READINGS

Articles

Freund, William C., and Zinbarg, Edward D., "Application of Flow of Funds to Interest Rate Forecasting, *Journal of Finance,* vol. XVIII (May 1963), pp. 231–48.

Ritter, Laurence, "The Flow of Funds Accounts: A Framework for Financial Analysis," Bulletin no. 52 (New York: New York Univ. Institute of Finance, 1968).

Robinson, Roland I., "Discussion of the Flow-of-Funds Accounts," *Journal of Finance,* vol. XVIII, no. 2 (May 1963), 262–63.

Taylor, Stephen, "Uses of Flow-of-Funds Accounts in the Federal Reserve System," *Journal of Finance,* vol. XVIII (May 1963), pp. 249–58.

Books

Copeland, Morris, *A Study of Money Flows in the United States* (New York: Bureau of Economic Research, 1952).

Flow of Funds in the United States, 1939–1953, (Washington, D. C.: Board of Governors of the Federal Reserve System, 1955).

Goldsmith, Raymond W., *The Flow of Capital Funds in the Postwar Economy* (New York: National Bureau of Economic Research, 1965).

Van Horne, James C., *The Function and Analysis of Capital Market Rates* (Englewood Cliffs, N. J.: Prentice-Hall, 1970).

ANSWERS TO PROBLEMS 5–7

5.

Savings			*Investment*		
Change in equity	$4		Capital investment		$12
Depreciation charges	6		Financial investment		
Gross savings		$10	Change in liquid assets	$4	
			Less change in liabilities	6	
					−$ 2
			Gross Investment		$10

6. (a) Increasing time and savings accounts was the most important; increasing demand deposits was the second most important.
    (b) Mortgage credit and consumer credit.
    (c) Approximately $82 billion came from operations (i.e., savings plus depreciation). The rest was borrowed from outside sources.

7. (a) $34.6 billion
    (b) $5.6 billion
    (c) Taxes and dividends
    (d) $33.5 billion

Financial operations of the system: short-term assets and liabilities

The various activities of a firm determine its cash flows. Chapter 6 describes several methods of forecasting a company's future cash position. Chapter 7 presents a number of techniques that have been developed to manage cash.

The level of inventory a firm holds, like the level of its cash and receivables, has important consequences for the financial position of the firm. Under some circumstances, profits may rise if the level of inventory is reduced. Chapter 8 describes some of the considerations that arise in designing inventory systems.

Finally, since all the short-term assets of the firm must be financed, Chapter 9 focuses on the various sources of funds and the considerations a financial manager must bear in mind in choosing among them.

Short-term financial planning

6

The design of new systems and the periodic reevaluation of old ones are the central finance function in a modern firm. One critically important system focuses on the firm's short-term liquidity position. Short-range financial planning to achieve a target cash position is essential, simply because the cost of holding either too low or too high a cash balance is great. If bills are not paid because the firm is short of cash, its suppliers will be reluctant to ship it additional merchandise and its production process may be interrupted. Customers, hearing rumors of production difficulties, or perhaps receiving their orders late, may question the ability of the firm to continue servicing them and turn to a competitor. Employees, seeing the company curtail or eliminate certain activities in a frantic effort to conserve cash, may question the ability of the firm to continue in business and seek employment elsewhere. Any one of these developments, all of which are possible consequences of a cash shortage, can push the firm into bankruptcy.

Even if such drastic events do not occur, the cost of an unanticipated cash shortage will still be high. Lenders are reluctant to extend credit on an emergency basis. Should the firm suddenly seek a large sum of cash, it will be forced to pay a higher interest rate and accept more stringent credit terms than if it had planned ahead and foreseen that it was likely to have a cash problem at a future date.

Holding too much cash is also costly, though perhaps less so. Firms have investment alternatives. If the average rate of return the firm earns on its non-cash assets is 7 percent and the firm holds $100,000 in excess cash, it is forgoing $7,000 annually in potential income. To understand how large this sum is, consider a firm whose net profits are 4 percent of its gross sales. To earn an additional $7,000 in gross profits through operations, it would have to increase its sales by *twenty-five times $7,000,* or $175,000.

A firm therefore suffers a loss if it holds too small or too large a cash balance. How can it estimate its cash needs so as to avoid both these conditions? The most popular analytical tool used by firms to anticipate their short-run cash requirements is the *cash budget*. Two variations of cash budgeting are (1) the receipts-and-disbursements method and (2) the adjusted-net-income method. Each will be discussed in turn.

Receipts-and-disbursements method

To illustrate the receipts-and-disbursements method of cash budgeting, suppose company X estimates that sales for each of the next several months will be as follows:

Estimated Sales of Company X	
January	$ 500
February	1,000
March	1,000
April	1,500
May	1,500
June	1,000
July	1,000
August	750

In practice, of course, the actual sales will deviate from these estimates. For the moment, however, we shall ignore the forecasting error and treat the sales estimates as if they were precise. We shall also make the following assumptions:

(1) Ten percent of each month's sales are for cash and the remaining 90 percent are for credit. The receivables that originate from these sales are all collected during the month following the sales. For example, $50 of the $500 in sales in January are made for cash. The receivables generated by the remaining $450 in sales are collected in February.

(2) The inventories required to produce the goods sold in any month must be purchased two months in advance. These materials cost 50 percent of the final sale price. Thus, $250 in inventory must be purchased in November to support January sales of $500.

(3) The accounts payable that arise from the purchase of inventory are paid in the month following the purchase; i.e., November's purchases are paid for in December.

(4) Company X has regular cash outlays of $250 per month for salaries, rent, fuel, and similar operating costs.

(5) The company plans to pay a $50 dividend in March and June. In addition, it will pay $200 in taxes on March 15 and June 15.

The balance sheet of the company on December 31 is as follows:

Balance Sheet of Company X, December 31

Cash	$ 200	Accounts payable	$ 500
Accounts receivable	300		
Inventory	750	Equity	1,250
Current assets	1,250	Total liabilities	
Plant and equipment	500	and equity	$1,750
Total assets	$1,750		

Given this information, a cash budget, or a statement showing the change in costs during each time period, can be prepared for company X. The total sales of the company are divided into cash and credit components according to assumption (1) above:

Analysis of Sales of Company X

	J	F	M	A	M	J	Total
Cash sales	$ 50	$ 100	$ 100	$ 150	$ 150	$ 100	$ 650
Credit sales	450	900	900	1,350	1,350	900	5,850
Total sales	$500	$1,000	$1,000	$1,500	$1,500	$1,000	$6,500

Since there is a one-month lag in collecting receivables, the total cash inflow of company X in January will be the sum of cash sales in January ($50) plus the receivables that were outstanding at the end of the preceding year.

Cash Receipts of Company X

	J	F	M	A	M	J	Total
Cash sales	$ 50	$100	$ 100	$ 150	$ 150	$ 100	$ 650
Collections of receivables	300	450	900	900	1,350	1,350	5,250
Total receipts	$350	$550	$1,000	$1,050	$1,500	$1,450	$5,900

Assumption (2) is that the total inventory purchased each month is equal to 50 percent of the expected sales two months in the future. Thus:

Inventory Purchases of Company X

J	F	M	A	M	J	Total
$500	$750	$750	$500	$500	$375	$3,375

The cash outlays for these purchases, however, will not occur until one month after each purchase order is placed. Thus the purchases made in December, and carried as accounts payable on a balance sheet, will be paid for in January.

The firm's total cash outlays can be calculated by adding to the cash outlays incurred each month the outlays for inventory purchases. According to assumptions (4) and (5), these are as follows:

Cash Outlays of Company X

	J	F	M	A	M	J	Total
Payment of payables	$500	$500	$ 750	$ 750	$500	$ 500	$3,500
Labor and other cash charges	250	250	250	250	250	250	1,500
Taxes	—	—	200	—	—	200	400
Dividends	—	—	50	—	—	50	100
Total outlays	$750	$750	$1,250	$1,000	$750	$1,000	$5,500

Comparing the total cash receipts with the total cash disbursements gives us the monthly change in the firm's cash position:

Change in Cash Position of Company X

	J	F	M	A	M	J	Total
Cash receipts	$350	$550	$1,000	$1,050	$1,500	$1,450	$5,900
Cash outlays	750	750	1,250	1,000	750	1,000	5,500
Change in cash position	−$400	−$200	−$250	+$ 50	+$750	+$450	+$400
Cumulative change in cash position	−$400	−$600	−$850	−$800	−$ 50	+$400	

For the six-month period as a whole, company X will generate $400 in cash. During the first five months, however, it will experience a net cash outflow. Since the initial balance sheet shows that the firm has only $200 in cash, it must obtain some additional cash if it is to continue operations during this period.

The firm has several options. It could try to borrow the money it needs from a bank, using statements such as those developed above to demonstrate to the bank how much money it will need and when the loan can be repaid. Thus, if the firm wants to maintain a $200 cash balance at all times, the statement shows that it must borrow $400 in January and increase its loans to $850 by March. It can begin to repay the money in April, and it will complete its repayment in June.

As an alternative to borrowing from a bank, the firm might postpone payment to some of its suppliers and, in effect, rely more heavily on trade credit. Some suppliers, recognizing that their customers may have difficulty in paying their bills until the merchandise that they bought is sold, use a system of "seasonal dating"; i.e., if a customer places a large order at the start of a selling season, the supplier will not ask for payment until the end of the season.

Another option for a firm that wishes to improve its cash position is to try to accelerate the flow of payments from its creditors. For example, firms in the aircraft industry make it a practice to ask for "progress" payments as work is completed. Some government contracts call for the payment of substantial sums to the seller even before a production run is undertaken. If none of these options are attractive to the firm, it may still be able to raise additional cash by selling stock or long-term bonds or by leasing some of its assets.

A cash budget, then, does not tell the financial officer which option he should choose. (Pinpointing an optimum course of action would require a broader framework of analysis than has so far been presented.) Its purpose is simply to indicate what the firm's cash position will be in the future as a result of current mode of operation.

The format of the cash budget varies with the circumstances of the firm. Many firms find that the account classifications in the illustration above are too broad and conceal particular cash inflows and outflows that are of special interest. A more detailed format is presented in Table 6.1. However, even this more detailed format might be inadequate for some firms.

To summarize, one method of estimating the future cash position of a firm is to estimate when each disbursement, and each collection, will be made. By tabulating these estimates, a forecast can be prepared of the cash position of the firm for the next several weeks, months, or quarters.

The most difficult figure to estimate is the sales figure. Moreover, an error in this figure may throw off many of the other entries, such as collections from receivables, outlays for materials, and shipping expenses. One way of guarding against this is to prepare several forecasts utilizing different "optimistic" and "pessimistic" sales estimates. The number of possible combinations of events that can arise, however, is very large. For example, sales can be high, low, or fair; the receivable collection and payable policies can be fast or slow; dividend payments can be high, low, or medium. Without the use of a computer, it is seldom feasible to explore more than one or two of these combinations.

While the receipts-and-disbursements method of cash forecasting shows which factors give rise to changes in the firm's cash position, it does not take into account changes in other balance-sheet items. For example,

TABLE 6.1
Format for Receipts-and-Disbursements Method of Cash Budgeting

	January	February	March	April	May
I. Beginning balance					
Cash					
Marketable securities					
Total					
II. Cash receipts					
Cash sales					
Collection of receivables					
Sale of fixed assets					
Repayment from subsidiaries					
Interest and dividend income					
Bank loans					
Sale of stock or bonds					
Total receipts					
III. Cash disbursements					
Payroll					
Taxes					
Material purchases					
Freight					
Operating expenses					
Advertising expenses					
Pension fund					
Insurance					
Dividends					
Interest payments					
Repayment of bank loans					
Capital expenditures					
Miscellaneous expenses					
Total disbursements					
IV. Ending balance					
Cash					
Marketable securities					

Is inventory being accumulated too rapidly? Is the ratio of sales to out-standing receivables being maintained at a reasonable level? Is the bank loan needed to maintain the firm's cash position too large relative to the firm's equity? To answer questions such as these, a different method of cash forecasting, the *adjusted-net-income method* must be used.

Adjusted-net-income method

The adjusted-net-income method of cash forecasting does not require the preparation of a detailed listing of each cash receipt and disbursement month by month. Instead, the financial manager begins by projecting sales and expenses over some specified period, such as a quarter or six months. From these data, he calculates the operating profits; adjustments are then made to convert this estimate into a cash income or loss figure, which is then further adjusted for cash transactions not recorded on the income statement. (These adjustments include changes in working capital, capital expenditures, financing developments, and so forth.) The resulting estimate indicates the change in the firm's cash position over the period as a whole. An analysis of the associated balance sheet and income statement allows the manager to ascertain whether the firm has maintained the relationships between items it desires over the period.

To illustrate this method, suppose that the financial officer prepares an income statement and ending balance sheet for the same six months that were considered in the earlier receipts-and-disbursements example. Assume that the firm depreciates its beginning plant-and-equipment account of $500 at a rate of 10 percent per year.

Income Statement for Company X
for Six Months Ending June 30

Sales		$6,500
Cost of sales		
($3,250 of material costs + $1,500 for labor, rent, etc.)		4,750
		$1,750
Depreciation		$ 50
Taxes		400
Net income		1,300
Memo:		
Dividends		100
Increase in retained earnings		$1,200

The cost-of-sales, or cost-of-goods-sold, figure has two components. The first, material costs of $3,250, includes a beginning inventory of $750 and purchases during the period of $3,375. Since two months' purchases of materials are carried over to the next period, the firm's ending inventory is $875. The materials component of the cost of goods sold is then calculated as follows:

Beginning inventory	$ 750
Plus purchases	3,375
Total inventory	$4,125
Less ending inventory	875
Material cost of goods sold	$3,250

Balance Sheet of Company X, June 30

Cash	$ 600	Accounts payable	$ 375
Accounts receivable	900	Equity ($1,250 +	
Inventory	875	$1,300 income −	
	2,375	$100 of dividends)	2,450
Plant and equipment	450	Total liabilities	
Total assets	$2,825	and equity	$2,825

From these data, the change in cash as calculated by the adjusted-net-income method would be as follows:

Funds provided through operations		
Net income	$1,300	(These values are derived from
Depreciation charges	50	the income statement.)
Change in receivables	−600	(These values are derived from
Change in inventories	−125	the beginning and ending bal-
Change in payables	−125	ance sheets.)
Total	+$ 500	
Less dividend payments	−100	(This is a memo item from
		the income statement.)
Change in cash position	+$ 400	

Note that the estimated change in cash over the period as a whole is $400, the same figure given by the receipts-and-disbursements method. However, even though both methods give the same result, there are important differences between them. The adjusted-net-income method of estimating cash requirements gave no indication of the sharp cash problems that arose in the months between the beginning and ending balance-sheet dates. Recall that in March the accumulated cash shortage was $850. On the other hand, the receipts-and-disbursements method, which highlighted the intraperiod cash problem, did not show the sharp rise in working capital that occurs over the period as a whole. At the start of the period, the firm's current assets less its current liabilities was $750; at the end, the figure stood at $2,400. Each technique of cash budgeting, then, has a weakness when it is used by itself. When both methods are used together, the financial manager has a useful analytical tool that can help him plan his short-term financial strategy.

A final comment about the adjusted-net-income method is in order. Just as the original format used in the receipts-and-disbursements illustration may have been inadequate for some firms, so too more detailed formats for the adjusted-net-income method may be required. One such format is presented in Table 6.2.

TABLE 6.2
Format for Adjusted-Net-Income Method of Cash Budgeting

	December	March	June

I. Beginning balance
  Cash
  Marketable securities
II. Funds provided through total operations
  Pre-tax income
  Depreciation charges
  Other non-cash income
  Less federal-income-tax payments
  Change in inventories
  Change in customers' receivables
  Changes in accounts payable
  Change in prepaid expenses
    Total
III. Capital expenditures
  Fixed-asset retirements
  Less depreciation reserves on these assets
  Facilities and equipment
  Leased machinery
  Development outlays
    Total
IV. Financing
  Change in bank loans
  Change in long-term debt
  Change in preferred stock
  Change in common stock
V. Dividend payments
  Common stock
  Preferred stock
    Total
VI. Investments in other companies
  Company A
  Company B
    Total
VII. Ending balance
  Cash
  Marketable securities

Simulating a cash budget

It is important, in preparing a cash budget, to estimate expected cash outflows and inflows with accuracy. Realism, however, demands that the financial manager treat his receipts-and-disbursements estimates as estimates, subject to a margin of error. Simulation, a method of experimenting by assigning different value to the parameters of a problem, is therefore an appropriate tool for this aspect of financial management.

Simulation is a valuable tool of financial analysis because it permits the financial manager to incorporate in his planning both the most likely value of an activity and the margin of error associated with that estimate. The advantage of simulating the cash budget is threefold: First, the financial manager can determine the size of the buffer stock of cash, liquidity, or line of credit he will need to meet contingencies. Second, he can ascertain the effect of changes in company policies—for example, the effect of a change in receivable or payable policy or in the timing of purchases of production materials—on its cash position. Finally, he can determine which corporate activities have the greatest influence on cash balances. He can then concentrate on sharpening his estimates of strategic activities and ignore those that have only a minor impact.

To illustrate how simulation can help the financial manager prepare his cash budget, let us make the following assumptions about a hypothetical company:

(1) The number of units that the firm sells has a marked seasonal pattern. Using the average monthly sales as a base, the financial manager has developed the following seasonal index:

January	.75	July	1.00
February	.75	August	1.00
March	.50	September	1.10
April	.85	October	1.15
May	.90	November	1.50
June	1.00	December	1.50

(2) No trend is forecast in the number of units sold, and, were it not for the seasonal pattern, 500 units would be sold each month.

(3) The *expected* number of items that will be sold each month is found by multiplying 500 units times the seasonal factor. The *actual* number of units that will be sold fluctuates around this level. Sales are assumed to be normally distributed, with a standard deviation of 20 units. This means, for example, that if the number of units expected to be sold in January is 375, actual sales will be between 355 and 395 units (between the mean and plus or minus one standard deviation) roughly two-thirds of the time. We shall also assume, to keep our example from becoming too complicated, that sales is the only variable not known with certainty. In practice, of course, many other variables that enter into the calculation of the cash budget are also uncertain. For example, the selling price of the product could change with fluctuations in demand; similarly, the cost of goods sold could vary with changes in the labor market.

(4) The selling price of each item is $10.

(5) Ten percent of each month's sales are for cash; the remaining 90 percent are for credit.

(6) The receivables generated by the credit sales are collected at the following rates: 70 percent the first month after sale, 20 percent the second month after sale, and 10 percent the third month after sale.

(7) Inventories are purchased two months in advance. Thus inventories expected to be sold in March will be purchased in January, and so on.

(8) Only enough inventory is ordered each month to cover the expected volume of sales two months later.

(9) The purchase price of the inventories is $3 per unit.

(10) Payments are made to suppliers by the 10th of the following month, enabling the firm to take a 2-percent discount on the purchase.

(11) Other monthly cash outlays are $1,000 for labor, $500 for other manufacturing expenses and $1,250 for administrative expenses.

(12) Dividends and taxes of $375 and $750, respectively, are paid quarterly in March, June, September, and December.

A computer program based on these assumptions can now be written to estimate the firm's cash budget. For each month, a particular sales level is selected from the distribution of possible levels. The inventories required to support this level of sales, the receivables that would result from this volume of sales, and similar values are then determined. In this way, a cash budget for each month is calculated. The entire procedure is then repeated, a large number of times. The data in Table 6.3 show the firm's average monthly cash balances and the standard deviation about these means.

TABLE 6.3
Simulated Cash Balance
(standard deviation of units sold = 20)

	Average Cash Balance	Standard Deviation
January	$3,104	$334
February	1,258	375
March	− 1,221	353
April	− 1,104	402
May	− 363	403
June	− 1,068	372
July	591	421
August	566	387
September	− 570	339
October	452	383
November	909	369
December	+ 2,109	345

Analyzing the simulation

The simulation shows that the firm will experience its largest cash inflow, $3,104, in January and its most severe cash drain, $1,221, in March. However, because sales are not known with certainty, the actual cash balances will not be known with certainty. Thus in January the standard deviation of the cash balance about its mean is $334. The firm will have a cash inflow between $2,770 and $3,438 (the expected value of $3,104 plus and minus one standard deviation) roughly two-thirds of the time.

How can the financial manager use the results of this simulation? One way is traditional: For example, in three of the four months in which the firm normally pays a dividend, i.e., in March, June and September, it can expect a net cash drain. The financial manager can avoid sharp fluctuations in the company's cash balance by changing the quarterly dividend periods to, say, February, May, August, and November. *The simulated cash budget enables management to anticipate periods of sharp change in its cash balances and suggests various options for coping with these fluctuations.*

The results of the simulation, however, can also be used in other ways. Consider, for example, the change in cash during the month of March. We saw that the firm can expect a cash deficit in March of $1,221. Hence it must carry a buffer stock of cash or make arrangements for a bank loan at the end of February equal to at least this amount. However, the $1,221 deficit is only an expected value; at least half the time, the cash deficit in March will exceed this amount.

Suppose the firm decides that it does not want the probability that it will be caught short of cash in March to be larger than 1 in 1,000. To guard against this, it will have to carry enough cash, or secure a line of credit, to protect it from events that lie as far as 3.3 standard deviations from the mean. Since the standard deviation about the March cash balance is $353, it will have to secure funds equal to 3.3 times $353, or $1,165. When this value is added to its expected shortage of $1,221, we see that a cash balance or line of credit of $2,386 is needed at the end of February to provide for March's contingencies.

Cash deficits also can be expected in April, May, and June. Moreover, in each month, the deficit may be smaller or larger than the expected, or average, value. How large a buffer stock of liquidity must the firm hold to protect itself from possible adverse random outflows of cash throughout the entire period?

The problem is further complicated because an assumption must be made about how the cash deficit in March is related to the deficit in April. If the deficit in March exceeds the expected value, will it automatically be above the expected value in April and, if so, by how much? More precisely, what is the *covariance* of the cash deficit between successive months?

The variance of a distribution is defined as the square of its standard deviation. The variance of the sum of four variables is given by the expression:

$$\text{Var}(A + B + C + D) = \text{Var}(A) + \text{Var}(B) + \text{Var}(C) + \text{Var}(D) \\ + 2\,\text{Cov}(AB) + 2\,\text{Cov}(AC) + 2\,\text{Cov}(AD) + 2\,\text{Cov}(BC) \\ + 2\,\text{Cov}(BD) + 2\,\text{Cov}(CD)$$

This formidable-looking expression is simplified if the monthly cash balances are independent, since then all the covariance terms will be zero. In other words, if the cash deficit in March is above its expected level, the deficit in April is as likely to be above as it is to be below its expected level. This is the case in the illustration: the fact that March's cash balance may be above its expected value tells us nothing about whether April's cash balance will be above or below its expected value. The variance of the cash balance over the four months will be, therefore, simply the sum of the four variances. The standard deviation for the four-month period as a whole is the square root of this value, or $778 in the illustration. Let us now apply these results.

Suppose the firm does not want the probability that it will run out of cash over the whole period March through June to be larger than 1 in 1,000. Again it must hold enough cash so that it can handle events as far as 3.3 standard deviations from the mean. Thus, it will want to hold a buffer stock of cash or secure a line of credit equal to 3.3 times $778, or $2,567. Adding this buffer stock to its anticipated needs of $3,756 (the sum of the four months' deficits) gives us a cash requirement for March through June of $6,323.

To summarize our findings to this point:

(1) The financial officer of a modern corporation prepares a cash budget to anticipate the company's cash needs and to ensure that profits will not be depressed by holding a suboptimum cash balance.

(2) Preparing the cash-expenditures-and-receipts estimates can be difficult. A financial manager should, however, be able to estimate a most likely value for each variable in his budget and the probable variation about that value.

(3) Using these figures, he can simulate his cash budget to determine both the expected change in cash during each month and the variation about this value. It then becomes a simple task to determine the buffer stock of cash, or liquidity, that the company will need for the period.

Extending the simulation

The simulations presented above were based on an assumption as to how fast receivables would be collected and payables would be met. Suppose now that the firm changes its policies in these areas. How would this affect the firm's cash position? While any number of alternative policies can be considered using computer simulation, we shall limit the discussion here to the four shown below.

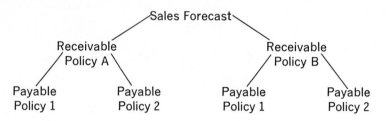

Receivable policy A is the one described earlier, in assumption (6); i.e., the percentages of bills collected in the first three months after sale are .70, .20, and .10, respectively,

Receivable policy B is a more liberal policy. The percentages of receivables collected in the three months following a sale are .50, .30, and .18, respectively. (Note that the more liberal policy assumes that only 98 percent of the bills are collected.) Were such a policy enacted, sales would be likely to rise. However, to make the policies directly comparable, we assume that no change in sales takes place.

FIGURE 6.1

Mean Cash Balances: Receivable Policy A

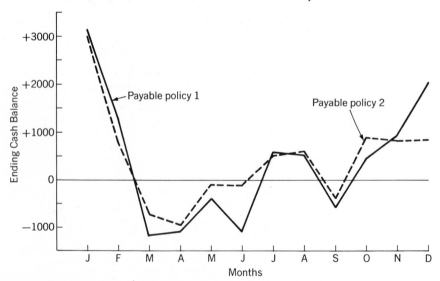

SOURCE: Eugene M. Lerner, "Simulating a Cash Budget," *California Management Review* (Winter 1968), pp. 78–87.

Short-term financial planning

FIGURE 6.2
Mean Cash Balances: Receivable Policy B

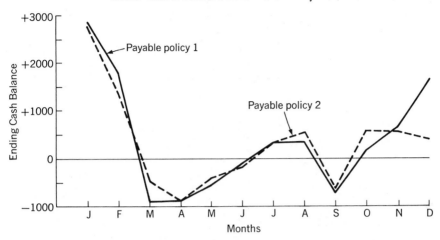

SOURCE: Eugene M. Lerner, "Simulating a Cash Budget," *California Management Review* (Winter 1968), pp. 78–87.

Payable policy 1 is the same as in the earlier example: a 2-percent discount is taken since payment is made by the 10th of the following month. Under payable policy 2, all purchases are paid for two months after they are made and no cash discount is taken.

The results of the simulation are shown in Figures 6.1 and 6.2. If receivable policy A is followed, then the two payable policies produce a marked difference in the cash position of the firm in the months of June and December. If receivable policy B is followed, the effect of the two payable policies is different only in December.

Through simulation, then, the financial manager can ascertain the impact of a change in corporate policy on the firm's cash position. Instead of adopting a course of action intuitively and hoping for the best, the financial manager can experiment with various alternative policies and choose the most satisfactory.

Accuracy in forecasting simulation

In the simulations just described, the financial manager had to develop information about both the expected value and the variation of elements in the cash budget. The question naturally arises, What benefit will accrue from spending extra time and effort to improve these forecasts? To answer this question, let us examine a second set of simulations, using a less accurate forecasting equation for the number of units sold each month.

Accuracy in forecasting simulation

125

All the assumptions made earlier hold, except the standard deviation of the error term, which is now 50 rather than 20. The results of this second set of simulations are shown in Table 6.4.

TABLE 6.4
Simulated Cash Balance
(standard deviation of units sold = 50)

	Average Cash Balance	Standard Deviation
January	$3,098	$469
February	1,284	475
March	− 1,160	500
April	− 1,070	502
May	− 344	454
June	− 1,032	484
July	582	485
August	573	438
September	− 533	458
October	422	447
November	817	459
December	1,986	507

The expected monthly values of the cash balances are approximately equal for both simulations. The standard deviations of the two distributions, however, are markedly different. The standard deviations in the second simulation are larger than the first forecast by approximately one-third. Substantially larger buffer stocks of cash must therefore be kept on hand to provide an equal amount of protection. For example, to ensure a probability of running out of cash in March of no more than 1 in 1,000, 3.3 times 500, or $1,650 must be held at the end of February as the buffer stock of cash. Previously, only $1,165 was needed.

The loss in potential revenue from the increased amount of funds that must be kept on hand is, then, one measurable cost of a poor forecasting model. Of course, it is only one component of the total loss caused by large forecasting errors: larger inventories must also be kept on hand, and production costs are likely to be higher.

Simulation thus helps the financial manager determine the value of information. Specifically, he can see how results would be changed if better estimates of particular inputs to the cash-budget model were available. If the results are only marginally improved and the data are expensive to collect, the financial manager can afford to work with less precise estimates than if the improved data cause marked changes in his results.

Summary

Short-term financial planning is an important operating problem. If the firm runs short of cash, costs can rise dramatically. On the other hand, if the firm is holding too large a cash balance, it forgoes the benefits it could have obtained by investing the excess funds.

Two methods are commonly used to forecast the short-term cash requirements of a firm: the receipts-and-disbursements method and the adjusted-net-income method.

The receipts-and-disbursements method attempts to estimate specific cash receipt-and-disbursement items. By combining these items through time, the major factors contributing to the firm's cash position can be readily identified and the periods when cash will be short or abundant determined.

The adjusted-net-income method estimates the change in cash that will occur over a given period by first estimating the firm's net operating income and then adjusting the figure for non-cash expenses and revenues. This method highlights the changes likely to occur in the firm's balance sheet over the period under study, rather than the intraperiod cash flows.

Because many of the firm's receipts and disbursements are hard to estimate accurately, simulation techniques are often used in forecasting. Simulation also enables the financial manager to experiment with different financial policies quickly and efficiently. Finally, it helps him determine the degree of precision needed in estimating values for the cash-budget model.

Questions for discussion and problems

1. Construct an example, using a hypothetical set of data, of both the receipts-and-disbursements method and the adjusted-net-income method of estimating the change in a company's cash position.

2. How would a financial analyst use the adjusted-net-income method of cash forecasting to calculate the effect on funds of a change in inventory policy or a change in receivable policy?

3. If a wholesaler uses seasonal dating as a marketing strategy, should a retailer be given a discount if he pays for the goods immediately? What would be a reasonable discount?

4. A cash budget cannot tell the financial officer what specific course of action to follow to alter the firm's cash flows. What kinds of considerations are involved in this decision?

5. When would it be helpful for a firm to use simulation to estimate its cash position, rather than preparing only a single estimate? Is the extra information that can be gained from the simulation likely to be worth the additional cost that it imposes on the firm?

   [*Answers to problems 6–8 follow references and suggested readings.*]

6. What will be the probable effect on a firm's cash position of:
   (a) rapidly rising sales?
   (b) a more liberal credit policy?
   (c) holding larger inventories?
   (d) delaying paying payables?
   (e) a fall in sales after a sharp rise in sales?

7. The XMA Corporation must pay off a loan on July 31. At the start of the year, the president of XMA asked his financial manager to estimate whether funds would be available to repay the loan. Prepare an answer for the president based on the following data.

   XMA purchases its raw materials at 50 percent of their final sale price. It makes these purchases two months in advance of its sales and it pays its supplier one month after it receives delivery.

   Ten percent of XMA's output is sold for cash, another 60 percent is paid for within 30 days and another 25 percent is paid for within 60 days. The remaining 5 percent of the bills are uncollectable. Based on its sales in November and December, XMA estimates that it will collect $1,140 in January and $350 in February.

   The firm's projected sales for the first eight months of the year are:

January	$600	April	$1,600	July	$1,500
February	800	May	2,000	August	1,000
March	900	June	1,800		

   XMA has other monthly expenditures of $200 and pays $150 in taxes every quarter, beginning in March.

8. Reufus Construction Company begins the new year with the following balance sheet:

Cash	$1,300	Accounts payable	$1,800
Accounts receivable	2,400	Equity	5,750
Materials inventory	3,100	Total liabilities	
	$6,800	and equity	$7,550
Equipment	750		
Total assets	$7,550		

   During the first six months of operation Reufus takes $50 of depreciation and pays $500 in taxes and $100 in dividends. Its gross sales are $5,600. It makes materials purchases worth $2,200 and ends the period with $400 less in inventory than when it began. It pays other sales expenses of $1,750. In addition, Reufus owes suppliers $2,100 and is due to receive $3,000 from customers as of June 30. How much has Reufus changed its cash position during this six-month period?

REFERENCES AND SUGGESTED READINGS

Articles

Churchman, C. West, "An Analysis of the Concept of Simulation," in Austin C. Hoggatt and Frederick E. Balderston, eds., *Symposium and Simulation Models* (Cincinnati: South Western, 1963), pp. 1–12.

Horn, F. E., "Managing Cash," *Journal of Accounting*, vol. 117 (April 1964).

Lerner, Eugene M., "Simulating a Cash Budget," *California Management Review* (Winter 1968), pp. 78–87.

Pflomm, Norman E., "Managing Company Cash," National Industrial Conference Board Studies in Business Policy No. 99, (1961), pp. 1–123.

Weston, J. Fred, "Forecasting Financial Requirements," *Accounting Review*, vol. XXXIII (July 1958), pp. 427–40.

Books

Cash Flow Analysis for Managerial Control, Research Report No. 38 (New York: National Association of Accountants, October 1961).

Guetzkow, Harold, ed., *Simulation in Social Science* (Englewood Cliffs, N. J.: Prentice-Hall, 1962).

Hamburg, Morris, *Statistical Analysis for Decision Making* (New York: Harcourt Brace Jovanovich, 1970).

Helfert, Erich, *Techniques of Financial Analysis* (Homewood, Ill.: Irwin, 1967).

Jaedicke, Robert K., and Sprouse, Robert T., *Accounting Flows: Income, Funds and Cash* (Englewood Cliffs, N. J.: Prentice-Hall, 1965).

McKinney, James L., *Simulation Gaming for Management Development* (Cambridge, Mass., Harvard Univ. Press, 1967).

ANSWERS TO PROBLEMS 6–8.

6.
(a) Cash will fall.
(b) Cash will fall.
(c) Cash will fall.
(d) Cash will rise.
(e) Cash will rise.

7.

Receipts	Jan.	Feb.	Mar.	Apr.	May	June
Cash	$ 60	$ 80	$ 90	$ 160	$ 200	$ 180
30-day receivables	840	360	480	540	960	1200
2-month receivables	300	350	150	200	225	400
Total	$1,200	$790	$ 720	$ 900	$1,385	$1,780

Purchases	$ 400	$450	$ 800	$1,000	$ 900	$ 700
Other expenses	200	200	200	200	200	200
Taxes			150			150
Total	$ 600	$650	$1,150	$1,200	$1,100	$1,050
Changes in cash position	+$600	+$140	−$430	−$300	+$285	+$ 730
Cumulative change	+$600	+$740	+$310	+$ 10	+$295	+$1,025

XMA will be able to repay the loan and will not require additional short-term financing during this period of operations.

8.

Cost of Goods Sold

Beginning inventory	$3,100
Purchases	2,200
	$5,300
Less ending inventory	2,700
Materials cost of goods sold	$2,600

Income Statement

Gross sales	$5,600
Cost of sales	4,350
Gross margin	$1,250
Depreciation	50
Taxes	500
Net income	$ 700
Less dividends	100
Increase in retained earnings	$ 600

Change in Cash Position

Net income	$ 700
Depreciation	50
Change in receivables	− 600
Change in inventory	+ 400
Change in payables	+ 300
	$ 850
Less dividends	100
Change in cash	$ 750

The management of liquid
assets: cash, securities, and
accounts receivable

7

Some of the tools a financial manager uses to estimate his firm's future cash needs were discussed in the last chapter. Once these estimates are prepared, he faces a second problem: how to manage his firm's liquid balances. What proportion of these funds should he hold in cash, in short-term interest-bearing securities, and in receivables? When should these proportions change?

Even though a firm's cash inflows and outflows may be equal over a period of time, such as a month, managers cannot normally synchronize daily cash inflows and outflows. They must, therefore, hold liquid balances as a buffer against unforeseen outflows. Should a period of sustained cash outflows occur, the firm can then continue to meet its bills as they fall due by drawing down its liquid balances.

Firms also hold cash so that they will be in a position to take advantage of favorable business opportunities as they arise. Whenever a supplier is willing to sell merchandise or equipment at a deep discount, for example, corporations want to be able to take advantage of the situation. Holding cash gives them this flexibility.

Third, firms hold cash to facilitate normal business transactions. A manager wants to be able to pay for the items his firm buys without having to go to a bank and borrow money each time a purchase is made. Moreover, when a firm makes a sale, it may not want to immediately purchase more inventory or add to its plant and equipment.

These three motives for holding cash can be loosely categorized as *precautionary, speculative,* and *transactions* motives. They are not, however, the only reasons firms carry cash, nor do they adequately explain the fact, discussed in Chapter 5, that manufacturing firms in the aggregate have held a constant amount of deposits, roughly $30 billion, since 1955.

Consider the first two of these motives: cash is a buffer against contingencies, and it gives a firm the flexibility to take advantage of new opportunities. Both these goals could also be satisfied by a line of credit from a bank. If a corporation had a line of credit that it could draw down and pay off at will, it would be protected from adverse cash outflows. Similarly, a line of credit would enable it to take advantage of unforeseen investment opportunities as they arise. *A line of credit is thus a substitute for holding cash.*

Alternatively, a firm could hold highly liquid balances, such as short-term government securities or commercial paper, instead of cash. These assets could be sold when the need to make expenditures arose. Moreover, since interest can be earned on these short-term investments, corporate profits can rise so long as the earnings on the invested funds exceed the purchase and sale costs.

Most firms have a line-of-credit relationship with a bank. Some have an explicit contract with a bank specifying the amount they can borrow and the interest rate that will be charged. Others have an implicit contract that arises from their long-standing relationship with their bank. The question then arises: Is the third reason, the transactions motive, enough to account for the bulk of the $30 billion that the flow-of-funds data indicate corporate businesses hold in the form of currency and demand deposits?

Recent studies indicate that the answer to this question is No. Most large firms carry 50 to 100 times the amount of cash that they need to satisfy their transactions demand.[1]

How can this fact be explained? Why do financial managers hold such large excess balances and forgo the opportunity to invest the funds in an earning asset? To understand why firms hold the amount of cash that they do, it is necessary to explore the relationship that a firm has with its commercial bank.

Banks perform a number of services for a firm. Perhaps the two most important of these are processing checks and extending credit. Banks collect the funds when a firm deposits a check, and banks pay out funds when a firm writes a check drawn against its deposit. In addition, banks stand ready to make loans to firms that need funds.

To compensate the banks for these and other services, firms both pay fees and maintain deposits with them. The size of the deposit balances are often explicitly negotiated and are called *compensating balances.* The reason banks want compensation in the form of deposit balances as well as fees is that *these deposits are the raw material a bank needs to extend*

[1] Case M. Sprenkle, "The Uselessness of Transaction Demand Models," *Journal of Finance*, vol. XXIV, no. 5 (December 1969), pp. 835–49.

loans. Thus, if five firms each maintain a $100,000 balance at all times in a particular bank, any one of them could borrow up to roughly $500,000 at one time.

Thus the fourth reason firms hold the amount of deposit balances they do is that they use these deposit balances as partial payment for the financial services they receive from commercial banks. The subject of commercial banking will be covered in greater detail in a later chapter. At that time, the total relationship that a customer has with his commercial bank will be considered, and the logic of requiring deposit balances as compensation for services rendered will be investigated more fully.

The flow-of-funds data in Chapter 5 show that, since 1965, the level of demand deposits and currency held by business firms has remained highly stable; between 1955 and 1962, these balances ranged between $32.0 billion and $33.8 billion; between 1963 and 1968, they ranged between $27.8 and $29.8 billion. Even though firms are prepared to compensate banks for the services they perform, it is evident from these statistics that financial managers exercise great care in managing their cash, for the amount of cash that they hold fluctuates within very narrow limits. How is the result achieved?

Cash management

Many medium-sized companies, and almost all large firms today, have cash-management systems that carefully monitor all receipts and disbursements, both those that appear on the firm's balance sheet and those that do not. As a result of these systems, firms have been able to free substantial sums of money. There are examples in the literature of an oil company that reduced the cash in its system by 75 percent, providing over $25 million in new funds; of a railroad that reported only $9 million in cash but drew $17 million out of its cash system; and of an insurance company that showed only $8 million in cash on its books but was able to mobilize $18 million in additional funds from its cash system. How were these results achieved?

One key to understanding modern cash management lies in the fact that there is usually a discrepancy between the records that the firm keeps and the records that the bank keeps of the amount of cash that the firm has on deposit. When a firm makes a deposit, it records the transaction as a credit to its cash account at the bank. In fact, however, the bank does not consider the deposit "good money" until funds are collected from the bank on which the check was drawn. This may take one, two, or three days, depending on the time of day the check is deposited and the location of the paying bank. On the other hand, when a firm writes a check to make a payment, it immediately debits its record of the amount of cash that it has at the bank. However, the check may not be presented for payment at the bank until several days later. Thus the bank's records will show a larger balance for the firm than the firm's own records indicate.

The records that count, so to speak, are the bank's, not those of the firm. The bank does not know how many checks the firm is about to deposit with it, or how many checks the firm has drawn against its account. It knows only the size of the deposit that the firm now has. Moreover, a bank will honor a check only if there are "good funds," i.e., collected balances, in the account.

Once a deposit level is agreed on by both the firm and the bank as adequate compensation for the services that the bank is performing, there is no reason for the firm to keep a larger balance in the account. Indeed, if it does, it is only forgoing the opportunity to earn a return on the excess funds.

A large firm may have more than one bank account—indeed, most firms selling in a national market will have a bank account in every city where they have a plant or a sales office. A good corporate-cash-management system lets the firm know the amount of collected balances it has on each bank's books each day. Moreover, it enables the firm to collect promptly all the funds that are due it; to invest the balances that are over an agreed-upon minimum, and to hold on to the funds it must disburse for as long as possible.

To analyze a modern firm's cash-management system and to see how the oil company, the railroad, and the insurance company referred to earlier were able to realize so much money from their systems, it is useful to divide the cash management problem into two parts: the cash-gathering process and the cash-disbursement process.

CASH GATHERING

One obvious, but easily overlooked, method of raising more funds is to send out bills on time. For example, if sales are made from branch offices but bills are sent from central headquarters, the invoices must first be forwarded to headquarters. The branch office may delay sending the invoices, causing bills to go out late. A simple improvement in internal operating procedures can result in faster cash collection through a reduction of outstanding receivables.

The opportunity for imaginative management of cash-gathering systems, however, occurs once a customer pays for his purchases by putting a check in the mail. Contrast the following two systems: In the first system, the customer mails the check directly to the headquarters of the firm. Depending on where the customer is located, the mail time required for the check to reach corporate headquarters is from one to five days. Once the check is received, the internal processing begins. The check is compared to the invoice to see if the correct amount of money is enclosed; discrepancies are noted, and appropriate actions taken; receivables are credited, and the check is prepared for deposit. In some firms, this internal processing may take as long as ten days. Moreover, once the check is deposited, it may take the bank as long as three days to collect the funds from the bank on which the check is drawn. In this system, then, as many as eighteen days may pass between the time the customer mails the check and the firm collects the money.

In the second system, the customer mails the check and invoice to a post-office box (called a *lock box*) in a nearby city. The maximum amount of time that the check is in the mails is one or two days. Under an agreement with the firm, a bank in the city is authorized to have access to the post-office box. Each day, and sometimes more than once a day, a bank messenger empties the lock box. The bank opens the customer's envelope for the firm, photostats the check, and attaches the photostatic copy of the check to the invoice. It then deposits the check in the firm's account and mails the photostat and the invoice to corporate headquarters for internal processing.

Since the lock box is located in a city close to the customer, the bank that empties the lock box can usually collect the money from the bank on which the check is drawn in one or two days. Once the funds are collected, the bank wires the money to a central collection bank where the funds will be invested for the corporation. In this way, the firm will have the use of its funds in two to four days instead of eighteen days. The savings to the firm from the second cash-management system are the interest it can earn on the funds for roughly fourteen to sixteen days.

A slightly different problem arises when deposits are made in local banks by agents of the company. Here the problem is not the time the checks spend in the mails or in the internal-processing system. Rather, it is the time it takes for a check to be processed by the banking system and the funds sent to the central collection bank for investment. Instead of transferring the funds by wire from the local bank to the central collection bank at a cost of roughly $1.50, a *depository transfer draft* can be used. Under this system, the local agent makes his deposit in the local bank and mails a depository transfer draft for the amount of the deposit to the headquarters bank. The transfer draft is drawn on the local bank and will be processed by the central collection bank in exactly the same way as any other check. The central collection bank will present the check to the local bank for payment at approximately the same time the local bank collects on the agents' check. Since the cost of transfer drafts is nominal, the headquarters bank can gather all the funds deposited in local banks throughout the system each day rather than, say, once a week.

CASH DISBURSING

Firms save substantial sums by gathering their funds efficiently. A similar saving can arise from planning disbursements. One obvious method of saving is not to pay bills until they are due. For example, if bills must be paid by the 10th of the month for the firm to be eligible for a discount, there is little point in paying them on, say, the first of the month. The difference between paying on the first and the 10th, for the firm, is the interest that can be earned on the funds for 10 days. For example, an oil company, after analyzing its disbursements policy, found that it was sending out $10 million each month in royalty payments 12 days ahead of the legally required time. Simply by delaying the mailings, it saved $237,000. The recurring savings were calculated as follows:

$$\$10,000,000 \cdot \frac{12}{365} \cdot 12 \cdot .06 = \$237,000$$

The first 12 is the number of days saved; the second 12 is the number of months in which the savings occurred. Six percent is the rate at which these short-term funds could be invested.

A second and more subtle way of saving money through disbursing funds is to take advantage of the fact that not all checks are cashed immediately. Suppose a firm makes a $20-million dividend disbursement, and, through a careful study, finds that $5 million are cashed in the first three days, $5 million between the fourth and the tenth day, and the remaining $10 million are cashed at the rate of $1 million a day for the next 10 days. Clearly, the firm need not hold $20 million in its account on the day the checks are mailed. What it could do is invest $15 million of this amount for three days, $10 million for ten days, and so forth. That is, it could invest the funds until the dividend checks will be presented to the bank for payment.

To avoid the problem of writing checks when there are no balances in the account, the firm could use *payable-through drafts* to pay its dividends. These instruments look like checks, and are accepted as such, but they are payable only through a designated bank and with the consent of the payer. The consent for payment will be issued only when the draft is actually presented for payment. This allows the firm to retain the use of its funds while the draft is in the process of collection. This item is so important that many firms use payable-through drafts to meet even their regular weekly and monthly payrolls.

It is now apparent how the railroad and insurance company could extract more cash from the system than they showed on their balance sheet. They were able to collect funds faster and invest them for longer periods using special-purpose devices such as lock boxes, wire-transfers, and depository transfer drafts. Frequently, the firm began to earn interest on cash received from the customer before their internal records showed that the bill had been paid or that they had the funds. Moreover, by using payable-through drafts, the firms were able to continue to earn interest on funds after their internal records showed that they no longer had control of the money. Through the use of techniques such as these, then, firms can improve their liquidity position by freeing funds that previously were lost in the system.

Other liquid assets

Even though firms in the aggregate have not increased their cash holdings, they have increased the amount of highly liquid assets (assets that can be converted into cash quickly and without loss) that they hold. The data in Table 7.1, taken from the flow-of-funds data published by the Federal Reserve, show that liquid balances of nonfinancial corporate businesses increased by over $30 billion between 1955 and 1968. The composition of their liquid-asset portfolios also changed radically during these years.

TABLE 7.1
Short-Term Liquid Assets of Nonfinancial Corporate
Businesses on Selected Dates
(in billions of dollars)

	1955	1960	1965	1968
Certificates of deposit	$ 1.0	$ 2.8	$19.2	$24.8
U. S. Government securities	23.3	19.5	17.0	14.5
Commercial paper	1.2	2.7	6.5	14.5
State and municipal obligations	1.2	2.4	3.0	4.0
Total	$26.7	$27.4	$45.7	$57.8

Certificates of deposit, or CD's, are interest-bearing instruments issued by banks. They must be held for a specified period, and they are issued only in relatively large denominations. The maximum interest rate that banks can pay on these deposits is determined by the Federal Reserve System under Regulation Q.

Commercial paper is a short-term debt instrument issued by a firm of unquestioned credit standing. From the point of view of the issuer, say, a firm such as General Motors Acceptance Corporation, the commercial-paper market is a vehicle for borrowing funds. From the point of view of the purchaser, perhaps a pension fund or another corporation, the instrument is a profitable liquid investment.

Most of the U. S. Government securities that firms hold are Treasury bills. These bills usually mature in six months, but the market for them is so broad and deep that any firm can buy and sell them quickly at a nominal commission. State and municipal obligations are tax-exempt. However, they are usually not as liquid as the other instruments that firms hold.

The growth in the liquid-asset holdings of corporations over the past decade and a half is best understood by comparing it to another corporate series, total sales. (See Table 7.2.)

TABLE 7.2
Corporate Sales and Liquid Balances on Selected Dates
(in billions of dollars)

	Liquid Assets Held by Nonfinancial Corporations	Total Sales of All Manufacturing Corporations	Liquid Assets as a Percentage of Total Sales
1955	$26.7	$278.4	9.6
1960	27.4	345.7	8.0
1965	45.7	492.2	9.3
1968	57.8	630.0	9.2

Note that, except for 1960, when it fell to 8 percent, the ratio of liquid assets to sales remained relatively stable at a fraction over 9 percent. These data suggest that the corporate need for precautionary and speculative balances has not altered very much over the years.

The change in the composition of corporate liquid assets, however, is striking. In 1955, the dominant liquid asset held by firms was U. S. government securities. From 1955 to 1965, when the yield on certificates of deposit was above that of Treasury Bills, holdings of U. S. Government securities declined, and holdings of certificates of deposit increased dramatically. Investors saw little difference in the credit standing of the nation's major banks and the federal government, and the instruments were convenient to buy and sell.

In 1965, however, a second shift in the makeup of corporate liquid-asset portfolios began to unfold as the yield on both U. S. Treasury securities and certificates of deposit fell relative to that of commercial paper. For example, in October 1969, the yields of these three types of instruments were as follows:

Prime commercial paper	8.57 percent
U. S. Government securities	6.99 percent
Certificates of deposit	6.00 percent

Once these yield patterns were recognized, corporate financial officers reacted quickly. Charts prepared by the Federal Reserve Bank of St. Louis (see Figures 7.1 and 7.2) show that when the yield on commercial paper and certificates of deposit was roughly comparable, the amount of each of these two assets that firms were willing to hold increased at roughly the same rate. When the difference in yields between the two instruments began to widen, the demand for commercial paper increased sharply, while the demand for certificates of deposit fell sharply. This rate differential emerged because banks at this time were not permitted by the Federal Reserve to pay more than 6 percent on certificates of deposit. The rate that firms selling commercial paper offer fluctuates freely in response to market forces.

One consequence of the decrease in demand for certificates of deposit for individual banks was a decline in the supply of their most important raw material for loans—money. As a result, new sources of funds had to be developed, and the amount of funds that banks borrowed in foreign capital markets and from other banks in the United States increased during this period. Despite these borrowings, banks were unable to meet all the loan demands of their customers. Corporations, therefore, had to find new sources of credit, and they turned in increasing numbers to the commercial-paper market.

To summarize, efficient cash-management has enabled many firms to reduce their holdings of cash to the minimum level required by commercial banks as compensation for their services. The reduction in cash balances, however, is not a reflection of any reduction in the overall corporate need for liquidity. Firms have simply shifted their holdings of liquid assets from cash to interest bearing instruments.

As corporate treasurers became more familiar with the wide variety of short-term liquid instruments available, they gradually moved toward the purchases that offered the highest yield. Thus, in 1955, corporations held primarily U. S. Government securities. By 1965, holdings of these assets had declined substantially, and certificates of deposit and commercial paper emerged as the dominant investment vehicles. When rates on CD's became no longer competitive (in mid–1968), holdings of these instruments declined and holdings of commercial paper increased rapidly.

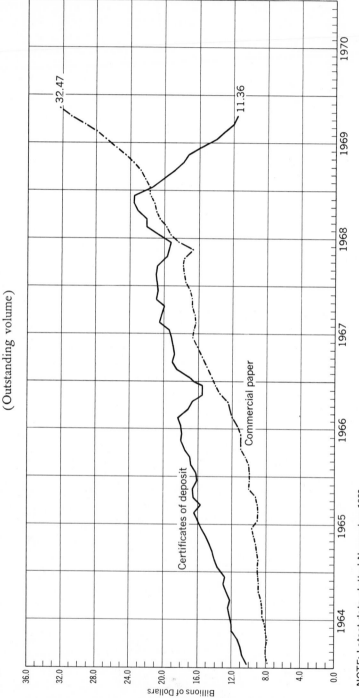

FIGURE 7.1

Certificates of Deposit and Commercial Paper

(Outstanding volume)

32.47

11.36

Certificates of deposit

Commercial paper

Billions of Dollars

36.0
32.0
28.0
24.0
20.0
16.0
12.0
8.0
4.0
0.0

1964   1965   1966   1967   1968   1969   1970

NOTE: Latest data plotted November 1969.

SOURCE: Federal Reserve Bank of St. Louis.

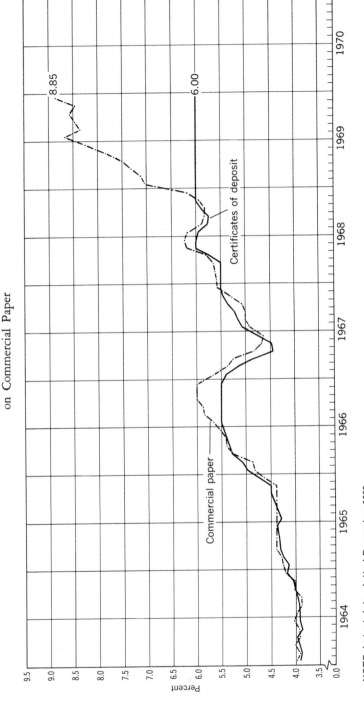

FIGURE 7.2

New Issue Rate on Certificates of Deposit and Dealers' Offering Rate on Commercial Paper

NOTE: Latest data plotted December 1969.

SOURCE: Federal Reserve Bank of St. Louis.

Other liquid assets

141

Accounts receivable

Receivables are the largest component of current assets. The flow-of-funds data of the Federal Reserve show that, in 1968, manufacturing firms had $181 billion in outstanding receivables. Why do firms extend trade credit to their customers instead of selling for cash? The answer is that *trade credit is advantageous to both the buyer and the seller.*

A vendor usually knows more about his customers than do other suppliers of funds. In the normal course of business, the vendor develops information about the volume of business a customer can do, how quickly he pays his bills, his ability as a business manager, and so forth. Because he can usually appraise his customers' creditworthiness more accurately and at a lower cost than a third party, a vendor is often the only person who will extend credit to a customer.

Of course, firms that sell on credit risk a loss if the firm receiving the credit is unable to pay its bills when they fall due. While no financial manager welcomes such a loss, a firm with no delinquent receivables probably has such a stringent credit policy that it is forgoing some profits. To illustrate how a firm can sometimes raise its profits by relaxing its credit standards, suppose that a company sells a product for $20 and that its gross profit margin is $5. If it normally sells 10 units on the first of every month, to customers who pay their bills on the first of the following month, the firm will always have $200 in outstanding receivables, and it will report $600 in gross profits for the year. Let the firm now relax its credit standards, and, by attracting new customers, increase its sales to 15 units a month. In the unlikely event that all the firm's customers now pay in 60 days rather than 30, receivables will rise to $600, an increase of $400. The firm's gross profits, however, will rise to $900, an increase of $300.

The firm will also experience some extra costs as a result of its more liberal credit policy. For example, if it has to pay 10 percent for borrowed funds, it will have to incur an additional interest charge of $40 to finance the receivables. Even so, it can sustain substantial credit losses without falling back to its original level of profits.

Whether extending trade credit is profitable depends on change in sales that will result from a change in credit policy, the firm's profit margins, the amount of credit extended, and the cost of funds that are invested in receivables. If credit conditions are tight, i.e., if customers have a difficult time financing their inventory purchases, suppliers are likely to increase their profits by extending credit. On the other hand, it is precisely during these periods that the suppliers' cost of funds is likely to be highest.

The data in Table 7.3 indicates the status of receivables of different-sized firms. Column 2 shows the dollar volume of sales in the third quarter of 1969 for manufacturing firms of various sizes. Column 3 shows the outstanding receivables of these firms. By assuming that sales were level throughout the year and that receivables remained at their third-quarter level, we can estimate the annual turnover rate of receivables (column 5) and the day's sales outstanding in receivables (column 6).

TABLE 7.3
Analysis of Receivables of Manufacturing Firms
(Third Quarter, 1969)

Asset-Size of Firm (in millions)	3rd-Quarter Sales (in millions)	Total Receivables (in millions)	Sales ÷ Receivables	Annual Turnover Rate	Number of Days Sales Outstanding in Receivables
Less than $1	$18,536	$7,993	2.32	9.28	39.3
$1–$5	15,003	7,477	2.01	8.04	45.4
5–10	5,827	3,187	1.83	7.32	49.9
10–25	8,569	4,536	1.88	7.52	48.5
25–50	7,105	4,091	1.74	6.96	52.4
50–100	8,396	5,133	1.64	6.56	55.6
100–250	14,946	8,778	1.70	6.80	53.7
250–1,000	34,627	19,808	1.75	7.00	52.1
Over 1,000	59,410	36,076	1.64	6.56	55.6

SOURCE: *Quarterly Financial Report, SEC-FTC,* (3rd quarter 1969).

Table 7.3 indicates that small firms generally have less liberal credit policies than large firms. Whereas the smallest firms turn over their receivables 9.28 times a year (i.e., they have 39.3 days sales outstanding in receivables), the largest firms turn over their receivables only 6.56 times a year (i.e., they have 55.6 days sales outstanding in receivables).

There are several reasons for the pattern of credit extension in Table 7.3. Many small manufacturing firms do not have enough equity to finance their internal operations. As a result, they rely on their large suppliers to finance activities. The payables of these small firms are, of course, the receivables of the larger firms. If small firms pay their bills slowly this is reflected in a slow turnover rate of receivables of large firms. In addition, because large firms tend to have relatively more equity than small firms, they can assume a greater degree of risk in their credit policy. Thus they are in a better position than small firms to advance funds to a customer who is a marginal credit risk and who will pay his bills slowly.

Payment habits also differ among industries. For example, firms selling perishable goods, such as food, extend less credit than do firms selling durable goods. Thus, the annual turnover rate of receivables in the food industry is 12, while the turnover rate in the electric-utility industry is 6, only half as large.

To summarize, receivables are the largest component of current assets. The financial manager is responsible for setting the credit terms and policing the collection policy of the firm. Extending credit can be profitable for a firm, but since receivables must be financed, they also give rise to costs. An analysis of the financial statements of manufacturing firms indicates that larger firms generally extend more credit than smaller firms, in part because they have relatively more equity than small firms. Payment habits also differ by industry.

Summary

The cash holdings of all firms have remained relatively stable at a level of roughly $30 billion for a number of years. This stability reflects careful cash management. It also raises the issue of why the level of balances is what it is. Why do firms in the aggregate not manage their funds so as to hold a lower level of cash?

Most corporate cash balances are at the level that they are because banks require firms to hold a specified amount of funds in order to compensate the banks for their services to the firm. Corporations use sophisticated cash-gathering and disbursement techniques to maintain their balances at the levels set by the banks and to ensure that any funds in excess of the agreed amount are promptly invested.

Although the amount of cash that firms maintain has been stable for the last several years, corporate holdings of other liquid assets have risen in proportion to sales. The data suggest that while firms recognize the need to maintain liquid balances, they prefer holdings in the forms of interest-bearing instruments of cash. Managers have been astute in making these financial investments, and they have responded quickly to changes in the interest rate of different instruments.

Accounts receivable, like cash and short-term securities, are also liquid assets. The policies of different-sized manufacturing corporations with respect to this asset, however, are quite different. In general, larger firms extend more credit than smaller firms.

APPENDIX

Estimating outstanding receivables

Corporate financial analysts spend a great deal of time trying to answer such questions as, Does the additional profit that would be realized from a change in credit policy warrant the additional costs that will be incurred? Before they can be answered, the analyst must know how large the outstanding receivables will be at any moment, what percentage of the accounts will be paid in full, and how large the bad-debt losses as a result of the change in credit policy will be.

Suppose that each customer of a firm who is now current with respect to his receivables has three options. He can (1) keep his account current by paying regularly and making additional purchases, (2) pay off his debt completely, or (3) carry his outstanding receivables for another period.

Let us assume that the probabilities of these events are .4, .4, and .2, respectively. Thus:

Probabilities

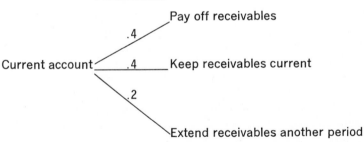

A customer who has an account that is one period old can be thought of as having four options: (1) he can pay off his debt completely at the end of the period; (2) he can pay the old debt and make a new purchase, so that the account becomes current; (3) he can make a partial payment, so that the account is still one period old; or (4) he can let the account become two periods old. If (4) happens, the firm considers the receivable delinquent. Let the probabilities of these events be .2,

.3, .4, and .1, respectively. Thus:

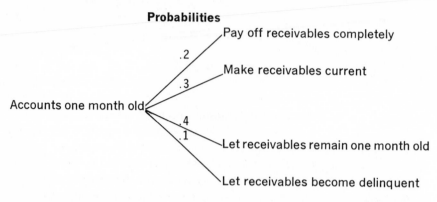

Probabilities

Accounts one month old

.2 — Pay off receivables completely

.3 — Make receivables current

.4 — Let receivables remain one month old

.1 — Let receivables become delinquent

Finally, we introduce two artificial cases that assist in the computation of the total amount of outstanding receivables. First, if an account is paid in full at the beginning of a period, we assume that it remains paid; and, second, if an account is delinquent at the beginning of a period, we assume that it stays delinquent. These two cases are called *absorbing states*, since once an account enters one of these states, it cannot leave it.

The probabilities associated with these various states can be arranged in a transition matrix, as follows:

| Present Status | Status Next Period | | | |
	Paid in Full	Delinquent	Current	One Month Old
Paid in Full	1	0	0	0
Delinquent	0	1	0	0
Current	.4	0	.4	.2
One Month Old	.2	.1	.3	.4

Each of the rows add to 1, since only four possibilities exist for a receivable starting in any state. The theory of absorbing Markov chains can be used to determine the volume of outstanding receivables, the percentage of receivables that will ultimately become delinquent, and the percentage of receivables that will be collected each month.

The matrix above can be partitioned as follows:

$$P = \left(\begin{array}{c|c} I & \emptyset \\ \hline R & Q \end{array} \right)$$

Each of the four partitions is itself a 2×2 matrix. I is an identity matrix, and $\emptyset$ is the null set. The R matrix indicates the probability that a receivable which starts in any state will become absorbed by being either paid in full or becoming delinquent. The Q matrix indicates that a receivable starting in any state will either become current or become one period old.

A receivable that is current can become one month old in the next period. Starting from that point, it can become current again. Finally, in the fourth period, it can be paid in full. A receivable can therefore pass through the state of being current or being one month old several times before it is finally absorbed. To estimate the volume of outstanding receivables, we must know how long, on the average, a receivable starting in any particular state will remain outstanding before it is absorbed.

Here we must introduce a new concept, the N matrix, which is equal to the inverse of $(I - Q)$. Thus: $N = (I - Q)^{-1}$

The N matrix is the fundamental matrix of an absorbing chain. The elements of N indicate the average number of times that a receivable starting in a particular state will pass through that state before it finally is either paid in full or becomes delinquent. For example, since

$$Q = \begin{pmatrix} .4 & .2 \\ .3 & .4 \end{pmatrix}$$

N, the fundamental matrix, equals:

$$N = (I - Q)^{-1} = \left[\begin{pmatrix} 1 & 0 \\ 0 & 1 \end{pmatrix} - \begin{pmatrix} .4 & .2 \\ .3 & .4 \end{pmatrix} \right]^{-1} = \begin{bmatrix} .6 & -.2 \\ -.3 & .6 \end{bmatrix}^{-1}$$
$$= \begin{bmatrix} 2 & \frac{2}{3} \\ 1 & 2 \end{bmatrix}$$

The values in this matrix are interpreted as follows:

(1) A receivable that is current at the start will, on the average, pass through the state of being current two times before it is absorbed.

(2) A receivable that is current at the start will, on the average, pass through the state of being one month old $\frac{2}{3}$ times before it is absorbed.

(3) A receivable that is one month old at the start will, on the average, pass through the state of being current once before it is absorbed.

(4) A receivable that is one month old at the start will, on the average, pass through the state of being one month old twice before it is absorbed.

Adding the elements in the rows of the N matrix shows that, on the average, a receivable that is now current will remain on the books for $2\frac{2}{3}$ months before it is absorbed. A receivable that is now one month old will, on the average, stay on the books for an additional three months.

How can this information be used? Since the N matrix indicates the average number of times that a receivable will be in a particular state, and the R matrix shows the probability of passing from that state to one of the absorbing states, the probability that a receivable will either be paid in full or declared delinquent can be found by multiplying the N and R matrices. Thus:

$$B = NR = \begin{pmatrix} 2 & \frac{2}{3} \\ 1 & 2 \end{pmatrix} \begin{pmatrix} .4 & 0 \\ .2 & .1 \end{pmatrix} = \overset{\text{Paid} \quad \text{Delinquent}}{\begin{pmatrix} .933 & .066 \\ .80 & .20 \end{pmatrix}}$$

The probability that an account which is now current will ultimately be paid is therefore .933, and the probability that it will become delinquent is .066. Similarly, the probability that a receivable which is one month old will be paid is .8, and the probability that it will become delinquent is .2.

Suppose the firm plans to sell the same volume of merchandise to 500 new accounts each period. What will be the distribution of its receivables at some future date when this market has been developed and a "steady state" emerges? Since there are 500 new accounts each period (i.e., none are one month old), multiplying the row vector (500, 0) by the N matrix will give us the result we seek. Thus:

$$(500, 0) \begin{pmatrix} 2 & \frac{2}{3} \\ 1 & 2 \end{pmatrix} = (1000, 333)$$

The financial officer can therefore expect that when the new sales program is fully established, the receivables of 1,000 of the new accounts will be current and those of 333 will be one month old.

If the average size of both the current accounts and those that are one month old is $40, the total value of the firm's outstanding receivables will be:

$$(1,000, 333) \begin{pmatrix} \$40 \\ \$40 \end{pmatrix} = \$53,320$$

The average length of time that a current receivable is on the books is $2\frac{2}{3}$ months. Sales from new accounts are $20,000 per month ($500 \cdot \$40$). $2\frac{2}{3}$ times $20,000 is the result we find, $53,320.

Of the $53,320 in outstanding receivables, $40,000 are current and $13,320 are one month old. The monthly cash collections, as well as the monthly bad-debt losses, can be estimated by multiplying this vector by the R matrix:

$$(40,000, 13,320) \begin{pmatrix} .4 & 0 \\ .2 & .1 \end{pmatrix} = (18,664, 1,320)$$

Thus, each month, approximately $18,664 of the outstanding receivables will be collected and $1,320 will be charged off as bad debts. (The total of these two values, $19,984, differs from the monthly sales volume of $20,000 because of rounding errors.)

Questions for discussion and problems

1. If a firm had only a marginal need for bank services, how large a compensating balance would it be expected to have? As firms turn to the commercial-paper market as a source of funds, are their deposit balances likely to rise or fall? What is the implication of this for bankers who want to expand their deposit balances?

2. When one firm collects its cash faster, another firm loses cash more rapidly. This is clearly a zero-sum game for the system as a whole. If there is no gain to business as a whole, why do firms try to streamline their collection systems?

3. Firms generally invest their excess funds in the highest yielding short-term security. What does this imply for regulated industries that may have ceilings imposed from without on the amount of interest that they can pay?

4. If commercial paper rates are higher than the yield on government bonds, does this mean that the government cannot borrow money? Why?

5. If both government and private industry compete for funds by paying higher and higher interest rates, why do interest rates not rise indefinitely?

6. Under what conditions will it *not* pay a firm to relax its credit terms? Is it true that a customer that pays its bills in 6 months is as good as one who pays in 30 days? How can you calculate the difference in the profitability of the two customers?

7. Does a tightening of credit conditions, that is, an increase in the cost of funds, affect large and small firms equally? If not, what alternatives does the sector that is most affected have?

   [*Answers to problems 8–10 follow references and suggested readings*]

8. Last month Feather Bay I-Beam Corporation, a huge manufacturer of structural steel, placed large orders for safety shoes, safety glasses, and hard hats, all of which are distributed to new employees in the mill. The bills, totalling $73,000, arrived on the first of this month and are payable on the 10th. The money to pay these bills is currently invested in short-term securities that yield 8 percent interest a year. How much can the firm save by not paying the bills until the due date? (Assume a normal 365-day calendar year.)

9. A certain firm maintains a compensating balance of $50,000 at the bank serving its corporate headquarters and half that amount at each of 10 other banks around the country. If these institutions can earn an average rate of 8.5 percent a year on these balances, how much is the firm paying the banks for their annual services?

10. Firm A, with average daily sales of $37,500, has $625,000 worth of receivables outstanding during the month of April. It also has an annual turnover rate of 8.25. What is the company's ratio of sales to receivables and how many days, on the average, do its receivables stay outstanding, based on its turnover rate?

REFERENCES AND SUGGESTED READINGS

Articles

Anderson, P. F., and Harman, R. D. B., "The Management of Excess Corporate Cash," *Financial Executive,* vol. 32 (October 1964), pp. 26–30, 51.

Archer, Stephen H., "A Model for the Determination of a Firm's Cash Balances," *Journal of Financial and Quantitative Analysis,* vol. 1, no. 1 (March 1966), pp. 1–11.

Baumol, William J., "Transaction Demand for Cash—An Inventory Theoretic Approach," *Quarterly Journal of Economics,* vol. LXVI, no. 4 (November 1952), pp. 545–56.

Benishay, Haskel, "A Stochastic Model of Credit Sales Debt," *Journal of the American Statistical Association,* vol. LXI (December 1966), pp. 1010–28.

————, "Managerial Control of Accounts Receivable—A Deterministic Approach," *Journal of Accounting Research,* vol. III (Spring 1965), pp. 114–33.

Cyert, R. M., Davidson, J. J., and Thompson, G. L., "Estimation of the Allowance for Doubtful Accounts by Markov Chains," *Management Science,* vol. VII (April 1962), pp. 287–303.

Gibson, W. E., "Compensating Balance Requirements," *National Banking Review,* vol. 2, no. 3 (March 1965), pp. 387–95.

Greer, Carl C., "The Optimal Credit Acceptance Policy," *Journal of Financial Analysis and Quantitative Methods* (December 1967), pp. 399–417.

Heston, Alan W., "An Empirical Study of Cash, Securities, and Other Current Accounts of Large Corporations," *Yale Economic Essays,* vol. 2, no. 1 (Spring 1962), pp. 117–68.

Jacobs, Donald P., "The Marketable Security Portfolio of Nonfinancial Corporations; Investment Practices and Trends," *Journal of Finance,* vol. XV, no. 3 (September 1960), pp. 341–52.

Jeffers, James R., and Kwon, Jene, "A Portfolio Approach to Corporate Demands for Government Securities," *Journal of Finance,* vol. XXIV (December 1969), pp. 905–21.

Johnson, Robert, "More Scope for Credit Managers," *Harvard Business Review,* vol. 39 (November–December 1961), pp. 109–20.

Law, W. A., and Crum, M. C., "New Trend in Finance: The Negotiable C.D.," *Harvard Business Review,* vol. 41 (January–February 1963), pp. 115–26.

Meltzer, Alan H., "The Demand for Money: A Cross Section Study of Business Firms," *Quarterly Journal of Economics,* vol. LXXVII, no. 3 (August 1963), pp. 405–22.

Smith, Paul F., "Measuring Risk on Consumer Installment Credit," *Management Science,* vol. 11, no. 2 (November 1964), pp. 327–40.

Soldofsky, Robert M., "A Model for Accounts Receivable Management," *NAA Bulletin* (January 1966), pp. 55–58.

Sprenkle, Case, "The Uselessness of Transaction Demand Models," *Journal of Finance,* vol. XXIV, no. 5 (December 1969), pp. 835–49.

———, "Is the Precautionary Demand for Money Negative?" *Journal of Finance,* vol. XXII no. 1 (March 1967), pp. 77–82.

Tobin, James, "The Interest Elasticity of the Transactions Demand for Cash," *Review of Economics and Statistics,* vol. XXXVIII, no. 3 (August 1956), pp. 241–47.

Books

Bierman, Harold, Jr., and McAdams, Alan K., *Management Decisions for Cash and Marketable Securities* (Ithaca, N. Y.: Cornell Univ. Graduate School of Business, 1962).

Orgler, Yair E., *Cash Management—Methods and Models* (Belmont, Calif.: Wadsworth, 1970).

ANSWERS TO PROBLEMS 8–10

8. $(\$73,000) \left(\dfrac{10}{365}\right) (.08) = \$160$

9. $\$50,000 + \$250,000 = \$300,000$
$(\$300,000)(.085) = \$25,500$

10. $(\$37,500)(30) = \$1,125,000.$

Sales-to-receivables ratio $= \dfrac{\$1,125,000}{\$\ \ 625,000}$

$= 1.80$

Days receivables are outstanding $= \dfrac{365}{8.25}$

$= 44.2$

The management of
physical materials

8

The production process of many firms can be divided into three parts: the acquisition of raw materials, the conversion of raw materials into finished products, and the sale of the finished product. Many firms are organized in terms of these three aspects of production; when this occurs, each of the three groups has an incentive to carry a large amount of inventory.

Usually, two groups within the firm are directly involved with raw materials. The first group is the purchasing department, which is responsible for selecting suppliers who will furnish the materials the firm needs at the lowest price. Since the price per unit frequently falls as the size of the order increases, purchasing departments have a built-in incentive to order large quantities. However, as the size of the orders placed with suppliers increases, fewer orders per year need be placed, and the average amount of inventory that the firm carries during the year increases.

The second group within a firm that is concerned with raw materials is production control. This group is responsible for assembling all the materials needed to ensure continuous production runs. If some materials or parts are not available, the start of a production run will be delayed, and this in turn may lead to increased costs. Consequently, even though production control is usually charged with the responsibility of maintaining a satisfactory level of inventory turnover, the department has a strong incentive to maintain large stocks of materials at all times.

The manufacturing manager is primarily concerned with production itself—with the processes and methods that will enable the firm to convert raw materials into finished goods at the lowest cost. Unit-production costs will fall, however, if long production runs can be achieved, since the *set-up cost,* i.e., the cost of changing the configuration of the machines so that the output conforms to certain specifications as to size and shape, is usually significant. The drive for low unit costs thus encourages long runs, which in turn means that the firm will carry high inventories of both raw materials and finished goods.

The marketing manager, who has a number of customer-related tasks, is usually responsible for the delivery of orders his sales force generates. If orders can be filled from stocks, deliveries can be made with a minimum of delay. Fast deliveries build customer satisfaction and enhance the general reputation of the firm. Thus the marketing department like the purchasing, production-control, and manufacturing staffs, tends to favor large inventories.

While large inventories may lead to higher profits, inventory investment also imposes costs on the firm. The raw materials and goods in process may be bulky and require extra warehouse space. The finished-goods inventories may become obsolete, damaged, or stolen if they are not sold quickly. Moreover, the entire stock of inventories must be financed.

The cost of financing inventories is not insignificant. Estimates of the dollar volume of raw-material, goods-in-process, and finished-goods inventories prepared by the Securities and Exchange Commission indicate that American corporations, in the aggregate, carry over $170 billion of inventories. Moreover, while the incremental investment in inventories varies from year to year, the flow-of-funds data show that, in the past, inventories have risen by roughly $7 billion a year. If sales continue to rise, as seems likely, there is every reason to believe that this rate of increase will be maintained.

How does a firm balance the benefits that will accrue from additional inventories against the cost of holding them? Obviously, benefits will be maximized and costs minimized by coordinating the efforts of finance, marketing, and production. All three groups want materials to be purchased at the best possible price, production costs to be at a minimum, and the firm's customers to be satisfied with both the quality of the product and the delivery schedule. Moreover, all three groups understand that the funds invested in inventories have a high opportunity cost. (In the last chapter we saw that when funds are "freed up" and invested in short-term highly liquid assets, they produce a yield in excess of 8 percent.) Good communications between groups, and goodwill among corporate managers, however, is seldom enough.

How can the financial costs of carrying inventories be compared to the other costs associated with the management of physical materials so as to achieve the lowest overall cost? How can the savings from lower levels of inventories be compared to the savings from larger orders to suppliers, longer production runs, or additional sales? How can purchasing determine the optimum size order; or production, the optimum size batch;

or marketing the optimum number of different items the firm should carry in finished-goods inventories? Only after these technical economic, or financial, problems are solved and a minimum-cost solution found can bargaining begin between the departments over whether it is desirable to operate at this level or some other point.

A framework for inventory decisions

To cope with the technical aspects of determining optimum inventory levels, managers follow a three-step procedure. The first and most difficult task is to identify and quantify the various costs involved in a particular inventory problem. These costs are then combined into *a single total cost function*. Finally, the inventory policy that minimizes this total cost function must be found.

Three kinds of costs are typically associated with inventories:

(1) C_c, the cost of carrying the inventory, includes direct outlays such as warehouse and handling charges, shrinkage charges, and the cost of the funds that are invested in the inventories.

While accurate estimates can be prepared of some of these charges, there is substantial disagreement as to how the cost of funds should be determined. The issues that arise here are closely linked to those raised in Chapter 1, where the concept of the cost of capital was first introduced. Suppose inventories are financed through trade credit, and that the terms the seller offers are "2/10, net 30" (a 2 percent discount can be taken if payment is made in 10 days; otherwise, the full amount of the bill is due in 30 days). If the firm buys inventory and pays its bills within 10 days, should it consider the cost of the funds invested in inventory to be zero? If it borrows from a bank at a 10-percent rate of interest to pay for the inventory, should this be the cost of the funds? In order to secure the bank loan, the firm had to have some equity. How should the cost of this equity be computed? And, once the cost of the equity is determined, should it be combined with the cost of the borrowed funds to obtain an overall figure for the cost of the funds invested in inventory?

We shall return to these problems in a later chapter. However, it is apparent even now that if the cost of capital is calculated at a low rate, say, 5 percent, a firm will tend to carry a higher average level of inventories than if a high rate, say, 36 percent, is used.

(2) C_s, the cost of shortages, includes the loss in profits and goodwill when a customer orders merchandise and the order cannot be met from stocks. To avoid such losses, some mail-order houses have adopted a policy of, where possible, immediately filling orders for out-of-stock items with higher-priced merchandise. Other firms will delay the shipment, risking

the loss of goodwill and perhaps losing the sale. In either case, the costs of a shortage are real.

Like the cost of capital, the cost of a shortage is difficult to fix precisely. Some firms have established such policies as "no more than 1 percent of the orders received are to be returned stamped 'out of stock,'" or "no more than 2 percent of the items we carry must be out of stock at any time."

(3) C_r, the cost of ordering inventories, includes the time corporate officers spend talking to salesmen, the paperwork involved in ordering and paying for goods, and so forth.

Order costs are difficult to estimate accurately because they are distributed among different departments. Moreover, there is a great difference between the marginal cost of one additional order and the average ordering cost. Once a firm has a purchasing department, for example, the cost of ordering one more item is nominal; and once a procedure has been established for checking invoices and paying bills, the expense of processing one more item is negligible. The *marginal* cost of placing an order may therefore be close to zero. The *average* cost of an order, however, may be quite high, including as it does the entire operating cost of the purchasing department and much of the accounting department's costs as well.

Putting aside for a moment these empirical problems in reaching cost estimates, it is clear that the total costs associated with inventory can be stated as the sum of C_c, C_s, and C_r. Thus:

$$TC = C_c + C_s + C_r$$

If a firm carries a large inventory, the cost of a shortage will approach zero, since an item is not likely to be out of stock. C_c, the carrying costs of the inventory, however, will be high. Similarly, the firm can minimize its carrying costs if it is willing to reorder frequently and be short an item on occasion. That is, C_c can be kept small by permitting C_r and C_s to rise.

The problem for the firm, however, is not to minimize any single component of inventory costs, but rather to keep total costs, the sum of these three components, as low as possible. How can the financial officer accomplish this task?

Economic order quantity

In developing an approach to the problem of minimizing total inventory costs, it is helpful to make a number of simplifying assumptions. Once a solution is found, the assumptions can be dropped, one by one, and more operational results can be reached. The assumptions we shall make are:

(1) When a firm places an order, the supplier fills it immediately. No lead time, therefore, is required between placing an order and receiving merchandise.

This assumption implies that C_s, the cost of a shortage, is zero, since out of stock items can be replaced immediately. The firm's total inventory costs are thus: $TC = C_c + 0 + C_r$.

In practice, of course, some lead time is usually needed before a supplier can ship an order. To avoid running out of an item, many firms carry a buffer stock of inventory at all times. The size of this buffer stock will depend on the rate at which sales are made and the length of time it takes to receive goods from the supplier.

(2) Inventory carrying costs are directly proportional to the dollar value of the inventory. For example, let the warehouse, handling, insurance and cost of funds equal 10 percent of the value of the inventory. Thus, if a firm has $1,000 in inventory, the carrying costs will be $100. Similarly, if the value of the firm's inventory is $2,000, carrying costs will be $200.

In practice, only the cost of the funds that are tied up in inventory is likely to be proportional to the dollar value of the stock. Warehousing and handling charges are more likely to be related to the weight and volume of a commodity than to its dollar value. Just how restrictive the assumption of proportionality is, however, depends on the kind of business the firm is in.

(3) Reorder costs are a constant dollar amount per transaction. For example, each time the firm places an order, the ordering costs might be $5.

(4) No quantity discounts are given by the firm's suppliers. That is, the price charged per unit is the same regardless of the quantity of the goods ordered. For example, the price that the firm must pay for each unit might be $20, regardless of the number of items purchased.

Were we to drop this assumption, we would then have to grapple directly with the problem of quantity discounts. When they are offered, the firm must determine whether the savings offered by the discounts and the reduction in ordering costs are large enough to offset the higher carrying costs associated with larger inventory holdings. The answer will depend on such factors as the availability of warehouse space and, most importantly, on the cost assigned to the funds that are tied up in inventories.

(5) The demand for the final product is known with certainty. For example, it is known that exactly 1,200 items will be sold during the year.

In practice, demand is not known with certainty and must be treated as a variable that takes on different values with different probabilities.

Under these conditions the cost of shortages becomes a real consideration, for if demand should reach an unlikely high the firm may encounter shortages. If it guards against this possibility by carrying a large stock of inventory, its carrying costs may be excessive.

(6) The rate of demand is uniform throughout the year. For example, if 1,200 items are purchased during the year, exactly 100 units will be purchased each month, and within the month, 25 units per week.

This assumption is also unrealistic in many instances. Items such as Christmas trees or lawn-mowers, for example, have a strong seasonal sales pattern. In such cases, it is not helpful to assume a level sales pattern over a long period. Other items are subject to style changes. For example, a retailer of high-fashion women's clothing cannot carry over items from one season to the next; the demand for these items is not uniform even within a single season.

Nevertheless, the six assumptions made above approximate the conditions a firm often faces. When this happens, the average amount of funds invested in inventory, the optimum quantity to order at any one time, and the number of orders to place each year can be readily found. If the assumptions do not hold for a particular firm, the value of the analysis is, of course, reduced for that firm.

Suppose the assumptions do hold. How, then, shall we proceed? Note that the ordering costs over any given period will fall as the size of the order increases. If demand is known to be 1,200 units, twenty-four orders of 50 units or sixteen orders of 75 units or twelve orders of 100 units will satisfy the demand equally well. If the cost of placing an order is $5, the annual ordering costs for these various quantities will fall from $120 to $80 to $60, respectively. Figure 8.1 illustrates the change in ordering costs as the order size increases.

FIGURE 8.1
Ordering Costs.

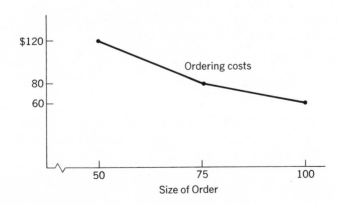

The carrying costs over a period, however, will rise as the order size increases. The rate of demand is assumed to be uniform throughout the year. If only a single order for 1,200 items is placed on the first day of the year, the average amount of inventory carried throughout the year will be 600 units, since by December 31 the stock on hand will fall to zero. Similarly, if 100 units are ordered twelve times a year, the average stock of inventory will be 50 units; if 50 units are ordered 24 times a year, the average stock of inventory will be 25 units. Since each item is assumed to cost $20, the average dollar value of the inventory would be $12,000, $1,000 and $500 respectively under the three ordering policies.

Carrying costs are assumed to equal 10 percent of the dollar value of the inventory. The costs of the three different ordering policies will, therefore, be $1,200, $100, and $50 respectively. Figure 8.2 illustrates how carrying costs increase with the average size order.

Let us now combine Figures 8.1 and 8.2 to obtain a picture of total inventory costs.

The total cost of a firm's inventory policy is the sum of its ordering costs and its carrying costs. Ordering costs fall, but carrying costs rise, as the size of the order increases. Thus the firm's total-inventory-cost curve first falls and then rises as the order size increases, as in Figure 8.3. Total inventory costs are at a *minimum* when carrying costs and ordering costs are equal. The order size 0A, associated with the minimum point on the total cost curve, is the *economic order quantity*. From the graph, we see that this quantity is roughly 77 units.

FIGURE 8.2

Carrying Costs.

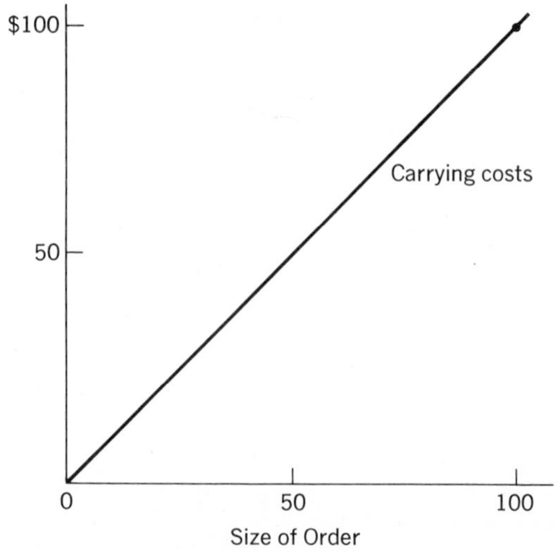

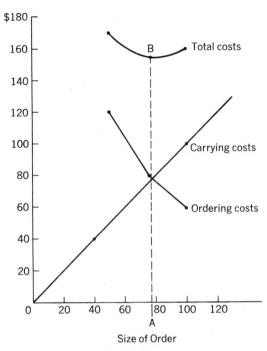

FIGURE 8.3
Total Inventory Costs.

This result, an economic order cost of 77 units, can also be derived by analyzing the total cost function, which in this case is:

$$TC = C_c + C_r$$

Consider first C_c, the cost of carrying the inventory. Since demand is assumed to be uniform throughout the period, the average number of units that the firm carries is $Q/2$, where Q is the number of items ordered each time. The total value of the inventory is found by multiplying this quantity times the cost per unit, C_u. Thus:

$$\text{Value of inventory} = (\text{number of items}) \cdot (\text{unit cost}) = \frac{Q}{2}(C_u)$$

The carrying cost is a fixed percentage, i, of the total dollar value of the inventory:

$$\text{Carrying cost} = C_c = (\text{value of inventory}) \cdot (\text{percentage carrying cost})$$
$$= \frac{Q}{2}(C_u)(i)$$

The second term in the total cost function, the total ordering cost, C_r, is reached by multiplying the cost of placing an order times the number of orders placed. If D is the total demand during the year and Q is the amount ordered during each time period, D/Q must equal the number of orders placed during the year. If C_o is the dollar cost per order, the ordering costs for the year are:

$$C_r = \text{(number of orders placed)} \cdot \text{(costs per order)} = \frac{D}{Q}(C_o)$$

Thus the firm's total costs are:

$$TC = C_c + C_r$$

(8–1)
$$= \frac{QC_ui}{2} + \frac{DC_o}{Q}$$

The value of Q that will minimize inventory costs[1] is:

(8–2)
$$Q = \sqrt{\frac{2DC_o}{C_ui}}$$

Note that the economic order quantity will rise as the demand for the product increases and the cost of placing an order rises. It will fall as the price of the product rises and as carrying costs increase.

In our example, $D = 1,200$, $C_o = \$5$; $C_u = \$20$, and $i = .10$. Thus,

$$Q = \sqrt{\frac{2(1,200)(5)}{(20)(.10)}}$$
$$= 77.4$$

To minimize its inventory costs, the firm should order approximately 77 units at a time. Since demand is 1,200 units, the firm will place approximately 16 orders a year $(1,200/77 = 15.6)$, or roughly every three weeks. The average value of the inventory that the firm will carry is $770:

$$\frac{77 \cdot \$20}{2} = \$770$$

---

[1] To find the minimum costs, we find the derivative of total costs with respect to Q and set it equal to 0. Thus:

$$\frac{dTC}{dQ} = \frac{C_ui}{2} - \frac{DC_o}{Q^2} = 0$$

or
$$Q^2C_ui - 2DC_o = 0$$

and
$$Q = \sqrt{\frac{2DC_o}{C_ui}}$$

The management of physical materials

The total costs of this inventory policy are:

$$TC = C_c + C_r$$
$$= \frac{QC_u i}{2} + \frac{DC_o}{Q}$$
$$= \frac{77}{2}(20)(.10) + \frac{1,200}{77}(5)$$
$$= 77 + 78$$
$$= \$155$$

Inventory costs are minimum when the carrying costs equal the ordering costs. The $1 difference between the two values in the example arose because of rounding errors.

Inventory policy when certain costs are unknown

Two costs that enter the calculation of the economic order quantity are particularly difficult to determine: i, the percent of the outstanding dollar value of the inventory that represents carrying costs, and C_o, the dollar cost of placing an order. If estimates of these values are wide of the mark, will this seriously reduce the value of the analysis presented above, or will the model that was developed remain a useful guide for inventory management? To explore this question, it is helpful to use a numerical example. Suppose that the firm must maintain inventories of three items. The price and yearly demand for these items are shown in the first two columns of Table 8.1.

TABLE 8.1
Conventional Ordering Pattern

Item	Annual Demand (units)	Price (C_u)	Number of Orders Per Year	Dollars of Inventory Purchased Per Order	Average Investment in Inventory
A	10,000	$4	10	$ 4,000	$ 2,000
B	30,000	3	10	9,000	4,500
C	40,000	4	10	16,000	8,000
					$14,500

Because it is convenient to do so, the firm orders each item 10 times during the year. This policy results in an average inventory investment for the three items combined of $14,500. Can the firm reduce this figure without changing the total number of orders? Can it place 30 orders, the same number it is now placing and, by changing the number of orders for the different items, reduce its investment in inventory? The answer is Yes.

The total cost of a firm's inventory with respect to any given item is:

$$TC = \frac{QC_u i}{2} + \frac{DC_o}{Q}$$

The economic order quantity for that item is given by:

$$Q = \sqrt{\frac{2DC_o}{C_u i}}$$

Substituting the right-hand side of this equation, the economic order quantity, for Q in the total-cost equation gives us the minimum total inventory cost for each product:

$$
\begin{aligned}
TC &= \left(\frac{C_u i}{2}\right)\left(\sqrt{\frac{2DC_o}{C_u i}}\right) + \frac{DC_o}{\sqrt{\dfrac{2DC_o}{C_u i}}} \\[2mm]
&= \sqrt{\frac{DC_o C_u i}{2}} + \sqrt{\frac{DC_o C_u i}{2}} \\[2mm]
&= \sqrt{2DC_o C_u i} \\[2mm]
&= (\sqrt{2C_o i})(\sqrt{DC_u})
\end{aligned}
$$

(8-3)

The minimum total inventory cost for all three items is simply:

$$TC_m = (\sqrt{2C_o i}\,\sqrt{DC_u})_A + (\sqrt{2C_o i}\,\sqrt{DC_u})_B + (\sqrt{2C_o i}\,\sqrt{DC_u})_C$$

where A, B, and C are the three products.

Suppose that the ordering costs, C_o, and the carrying cost percentage, i, is the same for all three items. The minimum total inventory cost for all three items is then:

(8-4) $$TC_m = \sqrt{2C_o i}\,[(\sqrt{DC_u})_A + (\sqrt{DC_u})_B + (\sqrt{DC_u})_C]$$

The value of the three terms in the square bracket can be readily calculated:

Item	Demand	Price	$\sqrt{DC_u}$
A	10,000	$4	200
B	30,000	3	300
C	40,000	4	400
			900

If 30 orders are placed each year and the sum of the three $\sqrt{DC_u}$ terms is 900, the number of times that each item should be ordered to preserve proportionality between the three products is:

Item	Weight	Total Annual Orders		Number of Orders Per Year
A	$\dfrac{200}{900}$	· 30	=	6.7
B	$\dfrac{300}{900}$	· 30	=	10.0
C	$\dfrac{400}{900}$	· 30	=	13.3
				30.0

Once the number of orders per year for each item is known, finding the average level of inventory for all three products for the year is simple. The optimum ordering pattern for items *A, B,* and *C* is shown in Table 8.2.

TABLE 8.2
Optimum Ordering Pattern

Item	Total Demand	Number of Orders Per Year	Quantity Ordered Each Time	Price	Order Size in Dollars	Average Value of Inventory
A	10,000	6.7	1,500	$4	$ 6,000	$ 3,000
B	30,000	10.0	3,000	3	9,000	4,500
C	40,000	13.3	3,000	4	12,000	6,000
						$13,500

The last column of Table 8.2 shows that by changing its inventory policy, the firm can reduce its average investment in inventory of $14,500 in Table 8.1 to $13,500. The $1,000 that was formerly tied up in inventory can now be used to support another corporate activity, thus raising the firm's overall level of earnings.

The economic-order-quantity approach to inventory management also has other financial implications. The economic order quantity can be written as follows:

$$Q = \sqrt{\frac{2DC_o}{C_u i}}$$

$$= \sqrt{\frac{2D}{C_u}} \cdot \sqrt{\frac{C_o}{i}}$$

or,

$$Q^2 = \frac{2D}{C_u} \cdot \frac{C_o}{i}$$

and

$$\frac{C_o}{i} = \frac{Q^2 C_u}{2D}$$

If the ordering and carrying costs of items A, B, and C are roughly comparable, the ratio C_o/i for each item should be comparable. Here, when 10 orders a year are placed for each item, they are not, and the ratios are far apart, as Table 8.3 indicates.

TABLE 8.3
The Values of C_o/i When 10 Orders Are Placed Each Year for Each Item

Item	Orders Per Year	Annual Demand	Quantity Ordered	Price	$\frac{Q^2 C_u}{2D} = \frac{C_o}{i}$
A	10	10,000	1,000	$4	$2,000
B	10	30,000	3,000	3	4,500
C	10	40,000	4,000	4	800

When the optimum ordering procedure is followed, however, the ratio of C_o/i for each item is exactly $450. (This figure is calculated in the same way as the ratios in Table 8.3.) So long as the firm places 30 orders per year, no further economies can be achieved.

The appeal of this approach to a financial manager is apparent: It offers a rough check on whether funds can be "freed up" by reducing inventories. It is simplest to study one segment of inventories, such as raw materials, at a time. The average inventory investment in different raw materials should be roughly proportional to the square root of the demand for each item times its unit cost. By comparing the actual levels of inventory carried with the optimum standard, the financial manager can identify the areas where excess funds are invested. A similar procedure can then be applied to finished-goods inventories.

To summarize, the economic-order-quantity framework of inventory analysis can be used by a financial manager to determine whether the firm's investment in inventory is excessive. Moreover, if demand is uniform through the year, he can ascertain this fact without knowing explicitly either his carrying costs or his ordering costs. This is because an optimum policy requires an ordering frequency proportional to $\sqrt{DC_u}$. Placing orders in this way ensures that the inventory investment of each item will also be proportional to its $\sqrt{DC_u}$. Under these conditions, each item's C_o/i ratio will be identical, and no further economies can be obtained by a change in ordering policy.

Quantity discounts

How can the economic-order-quantity framework be used to determine whether a firm should take advantage of quantity discounts? Once again, a numerical example is helpful to illustrate the central points of the analysis.

Let D, once again, $= 1,200$, $C_o = \$5$, $C_u = \$20$, and $i = .10$. The economic order quantity under these conditions, as we have seen earlier, is 77 units. Suppose a supplier now offers a 1 percent discount if the buyer orders twice his normal amount, or 154 units. Should the firm accept the offer?

To measure the impact of quantity discounts, all the effects on the inventory must be considered. The direct savings from the discount are:

$$\text{Direct savings in purchase price} = DdC_u$$

where d is the size of the discount. Since $d = .01$, and the firm buys 1,200 units during the year, the total savings from the reduction in the purchase price will be:

$$\text{Savings} = 1,200(.01)(\$20) = \$240$$

Moreover, because a larger quantity will be ordered at any one time to secure the discount, fewer orders per year need be placed. The savings in ordering costs will be:

$$\text{Savings in ordering costs} = \frac{DC_o}{Q} - \frac{DC_o}{kQ} = \frac{DC_o}{Q}\left(1 - \frac{1}{k}\right)$$

where Q is the economic order quantity, and k is the percentage by which this quantity must be raised. In our example, $k = 200$ percent.

The total savings in ordering costs in the example are:

$$\text{Savings} = \frac{1,200(5)}{77}\left(1 - \frac{1}{2}\right)$$

$$= \$39$$

The total savings if the firm takes advantage of the discount will, therefore, be the sum of the price savings and the ordering savings, or $\$279$ ($\$240 + \$39$).

These savings will be offset, however, to some extent by an increase in carrying costs. Carrying costs will rise because the investment in inventory is larger now than it was before. The average order size if the discount is taken is kQ, or 154 units. Since demand is uniform throughout the year, the firm will have an average inventory of $kQ/2$ or 77 units, with the discount; without the discount, it carries only $Q/2$, or 38.5 units.

The value of the inventory investment will be

$$77 \cdot \$19.80 = \$1,534.60$$

since each item will cost the firm \$19.80. If carrying costs remain 10 percent of the value of the investment, the carrying costs will be \$153.46. If the discount is not taken, the average investment in inventory is

$$38.5 \cdot \$20 = \$770$$

and the carrying cost is \$77. The increase in carrying costs is therefore \$76.46(\$153.46 — \$77). The savings that result from the discount, \$279, are thus greater than the extra costs imposed on the firm, and the discount should be taken.

The problem of quantity discounts, in practice, is often complicated by changes in the parameters of the model. For example, carrying costs may not remain at 10 percent. With more supplies about, warehouse charges may rise, shrinkage costs may increase, and handling charges may be greater than before. Moreover, purchasing a large quantity of goods may reduce the flexibility of management. If another supplier offers a better price in the future, the firm, having no need for further merchandise, may not be able to take advantage of it.

While these limitations are important, they hardly invalidate the economic-order-quantity approach to inventory management. Indeed, the framework is often more valuable as a list of checkpoints to be reviewed before the firm takes an action than as a definitive indicator of the correct course of action.

Lead times

A supplier seldom fills an order immediately. Instead, some time is likely to pass before the goods that are ordered are received. This delay may arise because the supplier first had to produce the item, or, if he carried it in stock, because of delays in shipping schedules.

When demand is uniform throughout the year and the lead time is known exactly, no special problem in inventory management is posed. Consider again our example where $D = 1,200$, $C_o = \$5$, $C_u = \$20$, and

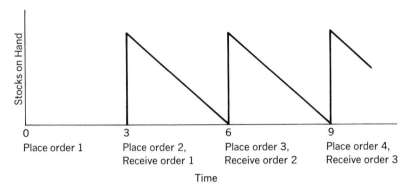

FIGURE 8.4
Stocks on Hand Over Time.

$i = .10$. The economic order quantity is 77 units, and orders are placed every three weeks. Suppose it takes exactly three weeks for the supplier to fill an order. Since orders are placed every three weeks even when they are filled immediately, the only adjustment that the firm needs to make is to place its orders one cycle in advance. That is, at the time it receives its first shipment, it places its second order. This will arrive just as the stock on hand from the first order is depleted. The firm can continue to operate in this way without running out of inventory, without incurring any shortage costs, and without carrying a buffer stock. This situation is illustrated in Figure 8.4.

In practice, of course, the problem cannot be handled so mechanically. Usually only an approximate lead time is known and demand for the product varies. As a result, firms find it convenient to carry buffer stocks to tide them over the period it takes to fill an order.

To analyze this problem effectively, we must first drop the concept of demand as certain and substitute a concept of demand as a series that takes on varying values. We have assumed, until now, in our example that the demand for the product was 1,200 units per year, or 100 units per month. Suppose now that 100 units per month is still the mean value of the demand for the product, but that there is some probability that the actual number of units sold will fall short of this value and some probability that the actual number of units sold will exceed it. Let the standard deviation of the monthly distribution be 10 units. The distribution of the demand for the product in a single month is shown in Table 8.4 and Figure 8.5. Sales will exceed 70 units in every month; sales will exceed 110 units in 16 percent of the months; and sales will be in excess of 120 units in 3 percent of the months.

Assume that the demand for the product in consecutive months is inde-

Lead times   **167**

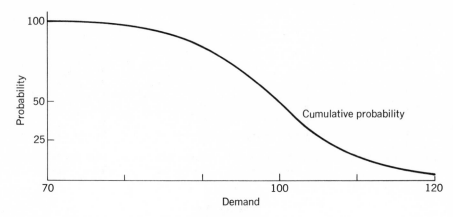

FIGURE 8.5

Cumulative Probability Distribution of Demand.

pendent. By this we mean that the sales made in one month do not influence the expected values of the sales in the succeeding month. Suppose, further, that suppliers require a six-week lead time, that is, six weeks must pass between the time the firm places an order and the time the shipment is received. If sales are unusually high in two successive months and the firm places only its regular order of 77 units every three weeks, it may find its stocks depleted. On the other hand, if orders are slow in two successive months, it will find its stock of inventory excessive. How can the firm ensure that it will have ample but not excessive stocks when deliveries will not arrive for six weeks and demand is uncertain?

TABLE 8.4

Units Demanded	Probability	Probability That Sales Will Exceed the Lower Limit of Column I
70–80	.03	1.00
80–90	.13	.97
90–100	.34	.84
100–110	.34	.50
110–120	.13	.16
120–130	.03	.03

Consider the distribution of demand over a two-month period. The expected level of sales is 200 units. But what will be the standard deviation of this distribution? We know that the standard deviation of each period's demand is 10 units and that the variance of the demand distribution (i.e., the square of the standard deviation), is 100 units. For two

The management of physical materials

consecutive months, 1 and 2, the variance in demand is given by the expression:

$$\text{Var}(1 + 2) = \text{Var}(1) + \text{Var}(2) + 2\,\text{Cov}(1,2)$$

The covariance of demand between the two periods is zero because we have assumed that the demand in each period is independent of the demand in the preceding period. Therefore:

$$\text{Var}(1 + 2) = 100 + 100 = 200$$

The standard deviation of demand over the two-month period is $\sqrt{200}$, or $10\sqrt{2}$. How can this information be used?

Suppose the company decides that it does not want the probability that it will run out of stock to be more than five in 1,000. The size of the buffer stock that it must hold can be readily calculated. An event that occurs five times in a thousand lies 2.55 standard deviations away from the mean. To be protected from such an event, the firm must hold a buffer stock equal to $(2.55)(10)(\sqrt{2})$, or 36 units.

The firm can, therefore, adopt the following inventory procedure: Place an order for 113 units (i.e., 77 required units plus 36 units of buffer stock) approximately six weeks before it begins operations. Place a second order for 77 units three weeks later. Place orders for 77 units each time the stock on hand from a particular order falls to 36 units.

Thus, six weeks after the initial order is placed, 113 units arrive. Thirty-six of these units are designated as buffer stock, and all incoming orders are filled from the remaining 77 units. Whenever the level of regular stock falls to 36, an order for 77 more units is placed.

The second order of 77 units that was placed three weeks after the initial order will arrive at approximately the same time that the firm exhausts its working stock of 77 units and is starting to fill orders from the 36 units that it held in reserve. The new shipment will bring the number of units on hand back up to approximately 113. If any of the buffer stock was used, it is replenished (i.e., brought back up to its level of 36 units) from this shipment, and all new orders are filled from the new shipment. When the stock on hand from this shipment falls to 36 units, a third order is placed and the entire procedure is repeated.

What is the cost of such an inventory system? The carrying costs for the buffer stock equal i times the value of the stock. Thus,

$$\text{Carrying costs}_{(\text{buffer stock})} = 36(20)(.10) = \$72$$

The carrying costs for the regular 77 units are found as before:

$$\text{Carrying costs}_{(\text{regular inventory})} = \frac{77}{2}(20)(.10) = \$77$$

The total carrying costs of the inventory, therefore, are:

$$TC = 77 + 72 = \$149$$

Adding the ordering costs to this figure will give us the total cost of the inventory system.

In conclusion, several comments can be made about the problem of inventory management when demand is a variable and a lead time between ordering and receiving inventory is required. First, many firms now use an inventory system called the *two-bin system,* similar to the one described above. The buffer stock is placed in a separate bin (or has a string tied around it). When the inventory in the regular bin is used up, the 36 items are moved from their bin into the regular-stock bin (or the string is untied) and a new order is placed immediately. The arguments developed above indicate the considerations that enter into such a two-bin system.

Second, the size of the buffer stock of inventory will increase (1) as the required lead time increases, because a greater allowance must be made for the variations in demand; and (2) as the firm's willingness to tolerate a shortage decreases. Had the firm in our illustration been willing to be out of stock only one time in 10,000, it would have had to increase its buffer stock to $(3.7)(10)(\sqrt{2})$, or 52 units. On the other hand, if it was willing to be out of stock 10 percent of the time, it need only have carried $(1.28)(10)(\sqrt{2})$, or 18 units.

To summarize, the problem of lead time and uncertain demand for a product can be incorporated into the economic-order-quantity framework through the expedient of a buffer stock. The size of this buffer stock will depend on the degree of variability of demand and the willingness of the firm to risk being caught short. It may also be costly to carry a buffer stock. In our illustration, the cost of carrying the buffer stock was almost as great as the cost of carrying the regular inventory. In some industries, especially those with long lead times and a highly variable demand, the cost of the buffer stock may exceed that of the regular inventory; in other industries, the cost of the buffer stock may be nominal.

Summary

Different departments within a firm have an interest in the size of the firm's inventory. Purchasing, production control, manufacturing, and marketing staffs tend to favor large inventories, but carrying inventory has a cost. Funds tied up in raw materials, goods and services, and finished goods have a high opportunity cost. Corporations therefore strive to minimize their commitment to inventories, and to carry only the amount of goods that are needed to maintain operations at a high level of performance.

One way a firm can minimize the funds invested in inventory is to order the amount of goods it needs in a way that minimizes overall inventory costs. This quantity is called the economic order quantity (EOQ).

The EOQ method of ordering inventory, however, rests on several assumptions, among them, that both ordering costs and the costs of carrying inventory are known. Even if these costs are not known, and often they are not, the financial manager can still use the analytical framework to determine whether the inventory of the various items that he is carrying is well balanced. The minimum investment in inventory for a given number of orders can be determined, and the minimum number of orders to place for a given investment can be found.

The EOQ approach can also be used as a framework for determining whether to accept quantity discounts and the amount of buffer stock to carry if the demand for a product is uncertain or varies over a period of time.

Questions for discussion and problems

1. Many firms are organized by function (i.e., marketing, production, manufacturing, R and D, finance, etc.). If a different organizational structure were designed, would the problems associated with inventory be eliminated?

2. What are the principal components of the analytical framework that gives rise to the economic-order-quantity framework?

3. If ordering costs (C_o) and the cost of funds (i) are the same for all a firm's products, why does the EOQ method of inventory purchasing lead to an optimum investment in inventory?

4. How can the EOQ model be modified if demand is not uniform over time?

5. What factors must a firm consider in deciding how large a buffer stock of inventory to hold?

[Answers to problems 6–9 follow references and suggested readings]

6. The Wynter Sportswear Company sells 750 ski parkas each year, which it purchases for $25 each. It costs Wynter $6 to place an order for parkas and 10 percent to carry them in inventory.
(a) What is Wynter's economic order quantity for parkas, and how many orders should it place each year?
(b) What is the value of Wynter's average parka inventory?
(c) What is the total cost of this inventory policy?

7. A firm carries four products, whose annual demands and unit prices are:

Product	Annual Demand	Unit Price
A	900	$4
B	600	6
C	500	5
D	300	3

The ordering costs and carrying costs for the four products are the same. Normally, each item is ordered 10 times each year. What is the optimum ordering pattern and total average inventory for the firm?

8. A fairly uniform demand requires John Bell, a grocery buyer for Sideway, Inc., to purchase 6,000 cases of coffee 12 times a year. He has an opportunity to triple the size of his order and reduce by 1 percent the present purchase price per case of $8.50. Sideway has sufficient warehouse space for the new volume and believes that carrying costs will remain 10 percent of inventory value. Knowing that the administrative costs of each purchase of coffee are $10, should Bell take advantage of this purchase discount?

9. Korn Brothers, Inc., a home-appliance distributor, sells 120 Model 1434E refrigerators each month and has recorded a standard deviation in that sales average of 12 refrigerators. The company is reviewing its inventory requirements and has decided that its buffer stock for this item should be enlarged. With a lead time of five weeks, Korn will need to plan for at least a two-month period. If sales in any month are not affected by sales in any other month and Korn wants the probablity that it will run out of stock to be only 2 percent (2.05 standard deviations from the mean), what should the new buffer stock be?

REFERENCES AND SUGGESTED READINGS

Articles

Ammer, Dean S., "Materials Management as a Profit Center," *Harvard Business Review,* vol. 47 (January–February 1969), pp. 72–89.

Beranek, William, "Financial Implications of Lot Size Inventory Models," *Management Science,* vol. XIII (April 1967), pp. 401–408.

Gomersall, Earl R., "The Backlog Syndrome: It is Better to Run with Downtime and Overtime Than to Build Dangerous Inventories," *Harvard Business Review,* vol. 42 (September–October 1964), no. 5, 105–15.

Silver, E. A., "Bayesian Determination of the Reorder Point of a Slow Moving Item," *Operations Research,* vol. 13 (November–December 1965), pp. 989–97.

Snyder, Arthur, "Principles of Inventory Management," *Financial Executive,* vol. XXXII, no. 4 (April 1964), pp. 13–21.

Books

Baumol, William J., *Economic Theory and Operations Analysis,* 2nd ed. (Englewood Cliffs, N.J.: Prentice-Hall, 1965).

Churchman, C. W., Ackoff, Russell L., and Arnoff, E. Leonard, *Introduction to Operations Research* (New York: Wiley, 1957).

Felter, Robert B., and Dalleck, Winston C., *Decision Models for Inventory Management* (Homewood, Ill.: Irwin, 1961).

Hadley, G., and Whitin, T. M., *Analysis of Inventory Systems* (Englewood Cliffs, N. J.: Prentice-Hall, 1963).

Inventory Management in Industry, Studies in Business Policy No. 88 (New York: National Industrial Conference Board, 1958).

Starr, Martin K., and Miller, David; *Inventory Control: Theory and Practice,* (Englewood Cliffs, N. J.: Prentice-Hall, 1962).

Stockton, R. S., *Basic Inventory Systems: Concepts and Analysis* (Boston: Allyn and Bacon, 1965).

ANSWERS TO PROBLEMS 6–9

6. (a) $D = 750$
$C_o = \$6$
$C_u = \$25$
$i = .10$

$$\text{EOQ} = \sqrt{\frac{2(750)(6)}{(25)(10)}} = 60$$

It should place $\frac{750}{60} = 12.5$, or 13 orders.

(b) Average inventory value $= \dfrac{(60)(\$25)}{2} = \$750$

(c) Total cost $= \frac{60}{2}(25)(.10) + \frac{750}{60}(6)$

$= 75 + 75$
$= \$150$

7.

Product	$\sqrt{DC_u}$	Weight		Total Annual Orders	Optimum Number of Orders Per Year
A	60	$\frac{60}{200}$	$\times$	40	12
B	60	$\frac{60}{200}$	$\times$	40	10
C	50	$\frac{50}{200}$	$\times$	40	6
D	30	$\frac{30}{200}$	$\times$	40	6
	200				40

Optimum Ordering Pattern

Product	Demand		Orders		Optimum Qty.		Price		$ Quantity	Avg. $ Value
A	900	$\div$	12	$=$	75	$\times$	$4	$=$	$300	$150
B	600	$\div$	12	$=$	50	$\times$	6	$=$	300	150
C	500	$\div$	10	$=$	50	$\times$	5	$=$	250	125
D	300	$\div$	6	$=$	50	$\times$	3	$=$	150	75
										$500

All C_o/i ratios of the optimum pattern are 1.25.

8. $D = 72,000 \quad d = .01 \quad C_o = \$10. \quad k = 3 \quad Q = 6,000 \quad C_u = \$8.50 \quad C_c = 10\%$

Purchase price savings $= Dd(C_u) = 72,000(.01)(\$8.50) = \$6,120$

Order cost savings $= \dfrac{DC_o}{Q}\left(1 - \dfrac{1}{k}\right) = \dfrac{72,000(\$10)}{6,000}(1 - \tfrac{1}{3}) = \$80.$

Total savings $= \$6,200$

New carrying costs $= \left(\dfrac{kQ}{2}\right)[(1 - d)C_u](C_c)$

$\qquad\qquad\qquad = (9,000)(\$8.415)(.10) = \$7573.50$

Old carrying costs $= \left(\dfrac{Q}{2}\right)(C_u)(C_c)$

$\qquad\qquad\qquad = \left(\dfrac{6,000}{2}\right)(\$8.50)(.10) = \$2,550$

Increase in carrying costs $= \$7,573.50 - \$2,550 = \$5,023.50$

The incremental cost is less than the incremental savings, and the opportunity should be accepted.

9. Var(month 1 + month 2) $= 144 + 144 = 288$

$\sqrt{288} = 17$

$(17)(2.05) = 35$

The management of
liabilities

9

The flow-of-funds data in Chapter 5 revealed that the outstanding debt of American nonfinancial corporations at the end of 1968 was approximately $500 billion. Of this amount, 40 percent was long-term debt and the remaining 60 percent was short-term.

The largest percentage of short-term debt arose through trade credit (accounts payable). In 1968, firms borrowed over $106 billion from their suppliers. Bank loans gave rise to another $82 billion of debt, while accrued taxes and miscellaneous liabilities accounted for almost $95 billion. Bonds and mortgages accounted for $135 and $67 billion respectively.

What principles should guide corporate financial officers in the management of their liabilities? When should long-term debt be issued, and when is the use of short-term debt appropriate? What are the effects on the firm's financial system when one source of funds is used rather than another? What are the costs of the various instruments that firms can use?

In Chapter 9 we come to grips with questions such as these. We shall first describe some of the more important debt instruments, and then go on to questions of financial policy.

Debt instruments

TRADE CREDIT

Trade credit represents the largest source of borrowed funds for all nonfinancial corporations. These funds originate in the normal course of business. When one firm sells a product to another on credit, the selling firm records an increase in accounts receivable on its ledger, while the buying firm records an increase in accounts payable.

If the buyer pays promptly, a discount from the purchase price is usually given. If payment is delayed, the discount is lost. For example, if a product is sold on the terms "2/10, net 30," the buyer can subtract a discount of 2 percent of the purchase price of the article if payment is made within 10 days; otherwise the full purchase price is to be remitted in 30 days. Failure to take advantage of the discount means that the seller extends credit to the buyer at a rate up to 36 percent interest. (In effect, the buyer pays an extra 2 percent for borrowing money for 20 additional days, and, since there are 18 such 20-day periods in a year, the effective rate is 36 percent. If the terms are changed to, say, "2/10, net 60," the effective interest rate falls to 14 percent.)

The Federal Trade Commission and the Securities Exchange Commission publish detailed quarterly financial statements for all manufacturing corporations. While this is a smaller universe of firms than that covered by the flow of funds (a disadvantage), the data are classified according to the asset size of the firm (an advantage). The data in Table 9.1, taken from the FTC-SEC report, provide a basis for assessing the relative importance of trade credit to firms of different sizes.

TABLE 9.1
The Importance of Trade Credit as a Source of Funds for
Manufacturing Firms with Different Asset Sizes
(Third Quarter, 1969)

Asset Size of Firm (in millions)	Trade Credit (in millions) (1)	Total Liabilities (in millions) (2)	Total Liabilities Plus Equity (in millions) (3)	(1) ÷ (2)	(1) ÷ (3)
Less than $1	$ 4,860	$ 14,187	$ 28,615	34.2%	17.0%
$1–$5	4,013	13,225	29,819	30.3	13.4
5–10	1,665	5,928	13,284	28.1	12.5
10–25	1,897	9,137	21,019	20.8	9.0
25–50	1,573	8,467	19,387	18.6	8.1
50–100	1,902	11,534	24,824	16.5	7.7
100–250	3,283	19,963	44,412	16.4	7.4
250–1,000	7,508	49,292	106,828	15.2	7.0
Over 1,000	16,755	106,645	243,213	15.7	6.9

SOURCE: *Quarterly Financial Report, SEC-FTC* (3rd qtr. 1969).

These data indicate that trade credit is substantially more important to small firms. Over 34 percent of the total current liabilities of firms under $1 million in asset size arise from trade credit, while only 16 percent of the current liabilities of the largest firms originate from this source. A similar pattern emerges when trade credit is expressed as a percentage of total liabilities and equity. Trade credit accounts for 17 percent of the total liabilities and equity of the smallest firms, but for less than 7 percent of the liabilities and equity of the largest firms.

Both large and small firms extend credit to customers and borrow from their suppliers. The data in Table 9.2 show that in 1969 and in an arbitrarily selected earlier year, 1966, the amount of credit advanced by manufacturing firms of all sizes exceeded the amount of credit that they received. Over the period as a whole, the largest firms increased their net investment in trade credit by more than $9 billion, while all the firms under $100 million in asset size together increased their net investment in trade credit by less than $600 million. The smallest firms, those whose assets are under $1 million, increased their investment in net trade credit by a larger amount than slightly larger firms, perhaps because a larger percentage of the sales of small firms are to retailers and consumers, rather than to other manufacturing firms.

Combining the data in Tables 9.1 and 9.2 gives us a clear picture of the financing pattern that characterizes American manufacturing corporations. Both large and small firms advance credit to other manufacturing firms, as well as to wholesalers, retailers, and consumers. The larger manufacturing firms, however, tend to advance relatively more credit to the smaller firms than they receive from them. Moreover, in recent years, the rate at which the larger firms advanced credit exceeded the rate at which smaller firms advanced credit. In the three-year period between 1966 and 1969, the net investment in trade credit of the largest firms roughly doubled, while the increase in the net investment in trade credit by smaller firms (those whose assets ranged from $1 to $100 million) was less than 5 percent. How can this difference be explained?

During the period 1966–1969, interest rates rose, and a "tight money" condition characterized the economy. Later in the chapter we shall see that while firms of all sizes increased their bank borrowings during this period, substantially more credit was extended to larger firms. One reason banks responded to the tight-money conditions in this way is that the larger firms held substantially more deposits at the start of the period. They, therefore, had a stronger claim on the credit that the banks could extend as the economy continued to prosper.

The data presented in Tables 9.1 and 9.2 indicate that the larger firms used some of the funds they borrowed to increase their investment in trade credit. This phenomenon, a sharp expansion in the amount of trade credit larger firms extend to smaller firms during peak economic periods, is not a new development. During other peak periods in business conditions, both large and small firms responded similarly. The full implications of this behavioral pattern for the economic system as a whole, however, still remain to be studied by financial analysts and economists. Such questions must be answered, as: Does the credit relationship strengthen or weaken the competitive thrust of the economy as a whole? Does the relationship frustrate or further the ability of the government to control inflation? Is it a desirable social policy to have smaller firms depend

TABLE 9.2

Net Trade Credit Extended by Manufacturing Firms in 1966 and 1969, by Size of Firm

(in millions of dollars)

Asset Size of Firm (in millions)		3rd Quarter, 1969	3rd Quarter, 1966	Change in Net Between 1966 and 1969
Less than $1	Total receivables	7,993	7,596	
	Trade accounts	4,860	4,868	
	Net	3,133	2,728	+405
$1–$5	Total receivables	7,477	7,086	
	Trade accounts	4,013	3,650	
	Net	3,464	3,436	+28
5–10	Total receivables	3,187	2,858	
	Trade accounts	1,665	1,258	
	Net	1,522	1,600	−78
10–25	Total receivables	4,536	4,199	
	Trade accounts	1,897	1,687	
	Net	2,639	2,512	+127
25–50	Total receivables	4,091	4,039	
	Trade accounts	1,573	1,413	
	Net	2,518	2,626	−108
50–100	Total receivables	5,133	4,410	
	Trade accounts	1,902	1,383	
	Net	3,231	3,027	+204
100–250	Total receivables	8,778	8,133	
	Trade accounts	3,283	2,793	
	Net	5,495	5,340	+155
250–1000	Total receivables	19,808	15,598	
	Trade accounts	7,508	5,490	
	Net	12,300	10,108	+2,192
Over $1,000	Total receivables	36,076	18,938	
	Trade accounts	16,755	8,981	
	Net	19,321	9,957	+9,364

SOURCE: *Quarterly Financial Report, SEC-FTC* (3rd qtr. 1966, 1969).

The management of liabilities

on the credit policy of larger firms during a period of prosperity, or should some alternative system be designed?

The fact that large firms advance substantial sums to small firms in the form of trade credit suggests that small firms find this method of financing to be relatively inexpensive, while large firms find it a relatively attractive outlet for their funds. This could happen only if the cost of capital for the two classes of firms were different. Specifically, the cost of capital for large firms must be less than the corresponding cost for small firms. After we have examined other debt instruments that corporations use, we shall pursue this line of reasoning further.

BANK CREDIT

Bank borrowings are a second source of funds for firms. The data in Table 9.3 show that borrowings account for 12 to 13 percent of the total liabilities and equity of manufacturing firms under $100 million in asset size. As firms increase in size beyond this level, the importance of bank borrowings falls.

The statistic "bank loans as a percentage of total liabilities and equity" does not capture the change in borrowing patterns that has occurred over the past several years. The difference between bank loans and the asset item "cash on hand and in the bank" shows the net contribution that banks have made toward financing the assets of firms in a particular size class. Thus, the data in Table 9.4 show that, in 1970, firms with under· $1 million in assets were net borrowers of $511 million, while the largest firms, those whose assets exceeded $1 billion, were net borrowers of $6.3 billion. Table 9.4 also shows the net position for firms three years earlier, in the third quarter of 1966. A comparison of these two statistics reveals that, over this period, the largest firms increased their net borrowing dramatically, while the smaller firms increased theirs at a more moderate rate. In other words, over this period, banks increased their loans to the largest firms at a substantially faster rate than they increased their loans to the smaller firms.

The important conclusion to be drawn from Tables 9.3 and 9.4, for purposes of corporate liability management, is that banks do not stand ready to advance credit during a period of sustained prosperity to all firms at the same rate. A banking relationship is likely to extend over many years. If the firm is profitable to the bank over the period as a whole, i.e., if it maintains large cash balances and uses the bank's services often, the bank, in turn, is likely to look favorably on a request for credit. On the other hand, if the firm is only a marginally profitable customer over the period, the bank may be less willing to advance a large amount of credit to it when other lending alternatives are available.

The interest rate a firm pays for borrowed funds also depends on its

TABLE 9.3

The Importance of Bank Credit as a Source of Funds for
Manufacturing Firms with Different Asset Sizes
(Third Quarter, 1969)

Asset Size of Firm (in millions)		Bank Credit (in millions) (1)	Total Liabilities (in millions) (2)	Total Liabilities Plus Equity (in millions) (3)	(1) ÷ (2)	(1) ÷ (3)
Less than $1	Short-term loans	$1,751				
	Installments on long-term bank loans due in 1 year	387				
	Long-term loans	1,323				
	Total	3,461	$14,187	$28,615	24.4%	12.1%
$1–$5	Short-term loans	2,340				
	Installments on long-term bank loans due in 1 year	320				
	Long-term loans	1,137				
	Total	3,797	13,225	29,819	28.7	12.7
5–10	Short-term loans	937				
	Installments on long-term bank loans due in 1 year	119				
	Long-term loans	585				
	Total	1,641	5,928	13,284	27.7	12.3
10–25	Short-term loans	1,480				
	Installments on long-term bank loans due in 1 year	222				
	Long-term loans	1,060				
	Total	2,762	9,137	21,019	30.2	13.1
25–50	Short-term loans	1,296				
	Installments on long-term bank loans due in 1 year	156				
	Long-term loans	992				
	Total	2,444	8,467	19,387	28.9	12.6

relationship with its bank. Under the *prime-rate convention,* the best customers of the bank, those whose credit ranking is unquestioned and who maintain large deposit balances, pay a prime rate for funds. In early 1970, this rate was 8.5 percent. As the credit rating of the firm falls or as its deposit balances drop, the interest rate that the bank will charge

The management of liabilities

TABLE 9.3 (Continued)

Asset Size of Firm (in millions)		Bank Credit (in millions) (1)	Total Liabilities (in millions) (2)	Total Liabilities Plus Equity (in millions) (3)	(1) ÷ (2)	(1) ÷ (3)
50–100	Short-term loans	$1,444				
	Installments on long-term bank loans due in 1 year	233				
	Long-term loans	1,328				
	Total	3,005	$11,534	$24,824	26.0	12.1
100–250	Short-term loans	2,892				
	Installments on long-term bank loans due in 1 year	259				
	Long-term loans	1,970				
	Total	5,121	19,963	44,412	25.6	11.5
250–1,000	Short-term loans	5,270				
	Installments on long-term bank loans due in 1 year	395				
	Long-term loans	4,386				
	Total	10,051	49,292	106,828	20.4	9.4
Over $1,000	Short-term loans	6,793				
	Installments on long-term bank loans due in 1 year	745				
	Long-term loans	6,224				
	Total	13,762	106,645	243,213	12.9	5.6

SOURCE: *Quarterly Financial Report, SEC-FTC* (3rd qtr. 1969).

rises. Some firms will pay "¼ over prime," or 8.75 percent, others will pay "½ over prime," or 9 percent, and so forth. When the prime rate itself changes, all the rates charged all the customers will move in unison. Not only is the prime rate the base on which other rates are built, but the bank will often advance credit to its "old-line" customers even during periods when it could earn a higher interest rate from another investment.

In addition to charging interest, however, a bank will also ask firms to keep a "compensating balance" with it when they borrow funds. This compensating balance will vary from firm to firm and may be as high as 20 percent. Thus, if a prime-rate customer borrowed $100, it would have to pay $8.50 in interest. If a compensating balance of 20 percent were charged, however, the firm could draw down its account,

Debt instruments

TABLE 9.4

Net Bank Credit Extended to Manufacturing Firms in 1966 and 1968, by Size of Firm

(in millions of dollars)

Asset Size of Firm (in millions)		3rd Quarter, 1969	3rd Quarter, 1966	Change in Net Between 1966 and 1969
Less than $1	Short-term loans	1,751	1,621	
	Installments on long-term loans due in 1 year	387	299	
	Long-term loans	1,323	1,154	
	Total	3,461	3,074	
	Less cash on hand in deposit	2,950	2,815	
	Net borrowings	511	259	+252
$1–$5	Short-term loans	2,340	1,973	
	Installments on long-term loans due in 1 year	320	206	
	Long-term loans	1,137	948	
	Total	3,797	3,127	
	Less cash on hand in deposit	2,098	2,071	
	Net borrowings	1,699	1,056	+643
5–10	Short-term loans	937	889	
	Installments on long-term loans due in 1 year	119	77	
	Long-term loans	585	404	
	Total	1,641	1,361	
	Less cash on hand in deposit	749	756	
	Net borrowings	892	605	+287
10–25	Short-term loans	1,480	1,296	
	Installments on long-term loans due in 1 year	222	106	
	Long-term loans	1,060	722	
	Total	2,762	2,124	
	Less cash on hand in deposit	1,152	1,127	
	Net borrowings	1,610	997	+613
25–50	Short-term loans	1,296	1,101	
	Installments on long-term loans due in 1 year	156	89	
	Long-term loans	992	690	
	Total	2,444	1,880	
	Less cash on hand in deposit	1,018	1,101	
	Net borrowings	1,426	779	+647

or use, only $80. The effective interest cost of the loan is then $8.50/$80, or 10.6 percent.

The size of the compensating balance required of a firm will depend on several factors, such as the other business the firm transacts with the

The management of liabilities

TABLE 9.4 (Continued)

Asset Size of Firm (in millions)		3rd Quarter, 1969	3rd Quarter, 1966	Change in Net Between 1966 and 1969
50–100	Short-term loans	1,444	1,000	
	Installments on long-term loans due in 1 year	233	137	
	Long-term loans	1,328	851	
	Total	3,005	1,988	
	Less cash on hand in deposit	1,235	1,169	
	Net borrowings	1,770	919	+851
100–250	Short-term loans	2,892	2,146	
	Installments on long-term loans due in 1 year	259	112	
	Long-term loans	1,970	1,255	
	Total	5,121	3,513	
	Less cash on hand in deposit	1,951	1,925	
	Net borrowings	3,170	1,588	+1,582
250–1,000	Short-term loans	5,270	3,552	
	Installments on long-term loans due in 1 year	395	168	
	Long-term loans	4,386	2,029	
	Total	10,051	5,749	
	Less cash on hand in deposit	4,482	3,572	
	Net borrowings	5,569	2,177	+3,392
Over $1,000	Short-term loans	6,793	1,867	
	Installments on long-term loans due in 1 year	745	127	
	Long-term loans	6,224	2,329	
	Total	13,762	4,323	
	Less cash on hand in deposit	7,444	5,172	
	Net borrowings	6,318	−849	+7,167

SOURCE: *Quarterly Financial Report, SEC-FTC* (3rd qtr. 1966, 1969).

bank, as well as the history of the bank-customer relationship. If the customer does no other business with the bank, the balance requirement is likely to be strictly enforced. On the other hand, if the customer has had a relationship with the bank for a long time and has held large balances in the past, the compensating-balance rule may be less strictly enforced.

In managing the firm's liabilities, then, the financial manager must consider more than a single time period. For just as past events influence the borrowing alternatives available in the present period, so the actions the firm takes today will influence the alternatives available to it tomorrow.

A third, rapidly growing source of funds for corporations is commercial paper. Although financial history of this instrument goes as far back as the early 1800's, commercial paper in its present form came into use early in the twentieth century. Then, as now, business firms that had high credit ratings and were well known could obtain short-term funds by selling unsecured notes on a discounted basis to banks, pension funds, wealthy individuals, and other buyers with temporary excess funds. The maturities of these unsecured notes have usually ranged from four to six months, although some mature in as little as five days and others not for nine months. The denominations of the notes vary, but for the most part are multiples of $5,000.

Specialized firms, called commercial-paper dealers, have arisen to bring the buyers and sellers in this market together. At present, some 500 firms issue commercial paper through dealers. In the latter half of the 1960's, this market was particularly active, and in 1969, roughly $12 billion in commercial paper was sold through it.

During the 1930's, finance companies such as General Motors Acceptance Corporation (GMAC) bypassed dealers and sold their commercial paper directly to the ultimate buyers (the corporations with excess funds, pension funds, banks, and wealthy individuals mentioned earlier). Direct placement has remained an effective sales method, as the data in Table 9.5 show. In 1969, over $19 billion of funds were raised in this way.

TABLE 9.5
Outstanding Volume of Commercial Paper,
1963–1969
(in millions of dollars)

	Total	Placed Through Dealers	Placed Directly
1963	6,747	1,928	4,819
1964	8,361	2,223	6,138
1965	9,058	1,903	7,155
1966	13,279	3,089	10,190
1967	16,635	4,901	11,634
1968	20,497	7,201	13,296
1969	31,624	11,817	19,807

Firms resort to issuing commercial paper because the funds raised in this way are less costly than funds borrowed from banks. Between May and December of 1969, the prime rate that banks charged for loans was

8.5 percent, and the 20-percent compensating-balance requirement raised the effective rate to 10.6 percent. During this same period, the commercial-paper rate ranged from a low of 8.25 percent to a high of 9 percent. Since no compensating balances are required to obtain these funds, the savings in interest payments are substantial.

A firm that issues commercial paper usually secures a line of credit from a bank so that it can obtain a loan if it encounters some temporary problem. The importance of having such a line of credit was brought home to financial managers in mid-June of 1970, when the Penn Central Railroad declared bankruptcy and defaulted on the payment of $87 million outstanding in commercial paper. Following the railroad failure, buyers of commercial paper began to check the credit of all the issuing corporations more carefully. Rumors began to spread that the Chrysler Corporation was in some type of financial difficulty, and buyers became reluctant to hold the commercial paper of Chrysler Financial, a wholly owned subsidiary. They tried to sell the paper they had purchased back to the company, and, as the notes they still held matured, refused to purchase more. As a result, Chrysler Financial began to lose cash at the rate of $60 million per day! To meet this crisis, the company drew down all its $650 million in bank lines and tried to borrow substantial sums in addition. Had not a consortium of bankers been formed immediately that was willing to extend an additional $400 million in credit to Chrysler Financial, the Chrysler Corporation itself could have been forced out of business.

The Chrysler Financial episode is so important to the commercial-paper market that portions of the story as reported in the *New York Times* on July 7, 1970 are worth reproducing here:

> The story really began late in the afternoon on Friday, June 19, when the Nixon Administration shocked Wall Street by backing down on its pledge to guarantee $200 million in loans for the Penn Central Transportation Company.
>
> The following Monday—with big headlines about the Penn Central's filing for reorganization under the bankruptcy laws splashed across the morning newspapers—Chrysler Financial experienced no difficulties in doing a completely normal business in the commercial paper market.
>
> All told, Chrysler Financial had more than $1.5 billion in commercial paper (the shorthand term for unsecured corporate i.o.u.'s that are sold to investors in the open market) outstanding at that time, a large part of very short maturity—say, three to five days—and substantial additional amounts due to mature on June 30.
>
> The next day, Tuesday, the 23rd, was also a normal day—the company not only got all the money it wanted, but got more besides. That evening, it had $14 million in temporarily surplus funds that it reinvested in overnight loans in the money market. Furthermore, Chrysler Financial had no bank debt that day.

SOURCE: © 1970 by The New York Times Company. Reprinted by permission.

But trouble was brewing. On Tuesday morning, shares of the parent Chrysler Corporation did not begin trading on the New York Exchange at the normal 10 A.M. opening because a large block of stock had been dumped on the market without a buyer.

In the glare of attention that always accompanies such situations, rumors about Chrysler began to circulate in a market that was already hypersensitive from the Penn Central failure. On Wednesday morning, with several negative brokerage house letters on Chrysler already in circulation, investors began to pull away from Chrysler Financial commercial paper.

According to Gordon E. Areen, president of Chrysler Financial, the company's commercial-paper sales dropped to about 40 percent of what might be considered a "normal" average for the company. In an interview Mr. Areen declined to specify what "normal" was, but he said that in May sales ran about $100 million a day—mostly, of course, involving the rolling over of three- to five-day paper.

On Thursday, the trouble continued and Mr. Areen was on the phone to Manufacturers Hanover to tell the bank about it. On Friday, there was more trouble, and more long-distance telephoning. The decision was made to wait over the weekend to see whether the negative trend would reverse itself the next week.

But on Monday, June 29, according to Mr. McGillicuddy, "it was obvious that the trend was not going to reverse itself without additional action." Furthermore, by this time, Chrysler Financial has used the bulk of its existing bank credit lines of $650 million to pay off maturing commercial paper.

On Tuesday morning Lynn Townsend, chairman of Chrysler, flew to New York with Mr. Areen, Walter J. Simons (Vice president and treasurer of Chrysler) and several other company officials, for a meeting at Manufacturers Hanover.

By noon the basic outlines of the deal were set, and Mr. McGillicuddy and Mr. Woodruff were on the phone to other major New York City banks, calling them together for a meeting in the Manufacturers Hanover boardroom that afternoon.

MORE BANKS CALLED

On Wednesday, while Mr. Woodruff stayed behind in New York to telephone banks outside the major centers (among them banks in Boston and Cleveland and on the West Coast). Mr. Townsend, Mr. Areen, and Mr. McGillicuddy flew to Chicago and then, late in the afternoon, to Detroit for a 6 P.M. session with the major banks there.

Meanwhile, Manufacturers Hanover's lawyers were busy grinding out a complex legal document required to complete the deal—A task that was not finally completed until 1 A.M. Friday.

* * *

OTHER TRANSACTIONS

Over and above this financing package, which totals $410 million altogether, Chrysler Financial has also received another $100-million shot in the arm from its parent and affiliated companies in separate transactions in the last few weeks. Under a plan agreed to in May, the parent company increased its investment in Chrysler Financial by $45 million (bringing the company's total capital to $280 million) and Chrysler Leasing took over another $54 million in lease paper that Chrysler Financial had been holding.

According to Mr. McGillicuddy, Federal banking laws forced state-chartered banks—among them, in addition to Manufacturers, Morgan Guaranty, Chemical, Bankers and Irving in New York, Cleveland Trust, United California in Los Angeles, Detroit Bank, and the Northern and the Harris in Chicago—to carry a heavy part of the burden in the financing.

*   *   *

At this point, all the bankers can do is hope that they have done enough to quiet the jittery market. "We were worried about the money market atmosphere and having to correct it," said Mr. Woodruff. "If it [panicky rejection of Chrysler paper] had extended to many other companies, we would have been deluged. We didn't want it to deteriorate to the point where it would spread."

"The magnitude of the effort here," Mr. McGillicuddy said, "exceeded a half billion dollars. If a half billion dollars can't make an impression on the money market," he said, "then we have a problem."

On July 9th, two days later, the *Times* tried to tone down the excitement engendered by the original report:

The full story on what has happened to the paper market since the Penn Central debacle jolted Wall Street confidence, is still a matter of conjecture.

*   *   *

Most participants in the commercial paper market seem to agree that the total of dealer paper outstanding has behaved in reasonably normal fashion—notwithstanding the fact that $87 million in commercial paper on which the Penn Central defaulted had been placed in this market.

Rather, the problems seem to have been concentrated among a small number of major finance companies, that have been the target of erroneous, and perhaps even irrational rumors that have been sweeping through the market.

The Chrysler Financial Corporation, whose operations have been shored up by more than $400 million in new bank-credit facilities, apparently suffered an attrition in its outstanding paper of more than $600 million, while the Commercial Credit Company of Baltimore had a runoff of almost $700 million.

The last line of this apparent attempt to soothe nerves and calm fears, however, is somewhat at variance with the rest of the story. The fact remains that events in 1970 showed commercial paper to be more vulnerable to runoffs than financial managers had believed up to that time.

To summarize, commercial paper, like accounts payable or bank loans, is another short-term instrument a firm can use to finance its assets. The cost of raising funds in the commercial-paper market is less than the cost of a bank loan, and the size of this market has expanded rapidly in the past several years. At present, the principal firms using this market are large and well-known, with an unquestioned credit standing. Even these firms, however, have found it necessary to support their commercial-paper with bank lines to guarantee the availability of operating funds should they encounter problems in selling paper.

BONDS

The flow-of-funds data presented earlier (see Table 5.5) show that corporate bonds and mortgages account for over $200 billion of outstanding corporate liabilities. These statistics, however, are highly aggregative. The data in Table 9.6 provide a better perspective on the bond market by indicating (1) which sectors of the economy issue bonds and (2) the value of the funds raised in this way by each sector.

TABLE 9.6
Gross Proceeds of New Corporate Bond Issues[1]
by Industrial Sectors, 1960–1968
(in billions of dollars)

	Total	Manu-facturing	Com-mercial and Other	Trans-portation	Public Utilities	Com-munica-tion	Financial and Real Estate[2]
1960	$ 8.1	$1.5	$0.6	$0.7	$2.3	$1.0	$2.0
1961	9.4	3.4	0.8	0.7	2.3	0.7	1.5
1962	9.1	2.9	0.6	0.6	2.3	1.3	1.4
1963	10.8	3.2	0.7	1.0	2.2	0.9	2.8
1964	10.8	2.8	0.9	0.9	2.1	0.7	3.4
1965	13.8	4.7	1.2	1.0	2.3	0.8	3.8
1966	15.6	5.9	1.2	1.9	3.1	1.8	1.7
1967	22.0	9.9	1.9	2.0	4.2	1.8	2.2
1968	17.4	5.7	1.7	1.8	4.4	1.7	2.2

[1] Offered for cash in the United States.
[2] Excludes investment companies.
SOURCE: Securities and Exchange Commission.

The data in Table 9.6 show that, from 1960 to 1968, the great bulk of bonds were issued by manufacturing firms. In 1967, for example, manufacturing corporations accounted for 45 percent of the total bond offerings. The strong demand for funds by manufacturing firms stemmed from both new plant and equipment outlays and the need to build working capital. In addition, many of these borrowers, anticipating a continued

The management of liabilities

TABLE 9.7
The Importance of Long-Term Funds to Manufacturing Firms of
Different Asset Sizes in 1966 and 1969
(in millions of dollars)

Asset Size of Firm (in millions)		3rd Quarter, 1969	3rd Quarter, 1966
Less than $1	Long-term debt from banks	1,323	1,154
	Other long-term debt	2,601	2,456
	Other noncurrent liabilities	185	192
	Total	4,109	3,802
	Total liabilities and equity	28,615	26,737
	Long-term debt as a percentage of total liabilities and equity	14.4%	14.2%
$1–$5	Long-term debt from banks	1,137	948
	Other long-term debt	2,366	2,143
	Other noncurrent liabilities	282	293
	Total	3,785	3,384
	Total liabilities and equity	29,819	27,719
	Long-term debt as a percentage of total liabilities and equity	12.7%	12.2%
5–10	Long-term debt from banks	585	404
	Other long-term debt	1,243	975
	Other noncurrent liabilities	186	159
	Total	2,014	1,538
	Total liabilities and equity	13,284	12,108
	Long-term debt as a percentage of total liabilities and equity	15.1%	12.7%
10–25	Long-term debt from banks	1,060	722
	Other long-term debt	2,199	1,777
	Other noncurrent liabilities	381	279
	Total	3,640	2,778
	Total liabilities and equity	21,019	18,321
	Long-term debt as a percentage of total liabilities and equity	17.3%	15.1%
25–50	Long-term debt from banks	992	690
	Other long-term debt	2,264	1,871
	Other noncurrent liabilities	423	396
	Total	3,679	2,957
	Total liabilities and equity	19,387	18,602
	Long-term debt as a percentage of total liabilities and equity	19.0%	15.9%
50–100	Long-term debt from banks	1,328	851
	Other long-term debt	3,513	2,687
	Other noncurrent liabilities	731	515
	Total	5,572	4,053
	Total liabilities and equity	24,824	21,577
	Long-term debt as a percentage of total liabilities and equity	22.4%	18.8%

Debt instruments

TABLE 9.7 (Continued)

Asset Size of Firm (in millions)		3rd Quarter, 1969	3rd Quarter, 1966
100–250	Long-term debt from banks	1,970	1,255
	Other long-term debt	6,195	4,631
	Other noncurrent liabilities	1,288	1,101
	Total	9,453	6,987
	Total liabilities and equity	44,412	40,774
	Long-term debt as a percentage of total liabilities and equity	21.3%	17.1%
250–1,000	Long-term debt from banks	4,386	2,029
	Other long-term debt	15,986	12,159
	Other noncurrent liabilities	3,927	2,828
	Total	24,299	17,016
	Total liabilities and equity	106,828	87,768
	Long-term debt as a percentage of total liabilities and equity	22.7%	19.3%
Over $1,000	Long-term debt from banks	6,224	2,329
	Other long-term debt	32,996	15,020
	Other noncurrent liabilities	12,290	4,937
	Total	51,510	22,286
	Long-term debt as a percentage of total liabilities and equity	21.1%	16.2%

rise in borrowing costs, wanted to obtain long-term funds at what they correctly believed would be favorable terms.

However, as Table 9.7 shows, not all segments of manufacturing participate equally in the long-term bond market. In 1966, long-term debt represented 17 to 19 percent of the capital structure of the larger manufacturing corporations and only 12 to 14 percent of the capital structure of the smaller corporations. Furthermore, although long-term debt has increased in importance as a source of funds for all manufacturing corporations between 1966 and 1969, the percentage increase was greater for larger firms. Smaller firms increased their debt from 12 to 15 percent of their capital structure, while larger firms increased their debt to 21 or 22 percent.

What are the costs associated with long-term bond issues, and how do these costs compare with those of short-term instruments? To answer this question, we must analyze the relationships captured in the *yield curve*. This curve indicates the effective yield of bonds of comparable quality on different dates. Three yield curves for U. S. government bonds are presented in Figures 9.1, 9.2, and 9.3. Figure 9.1 shows the yields prevalent on October 30, 1964; note that long-term bonds offered the investor a higher rate of return than short-term bonds. Figure 9.2 shows

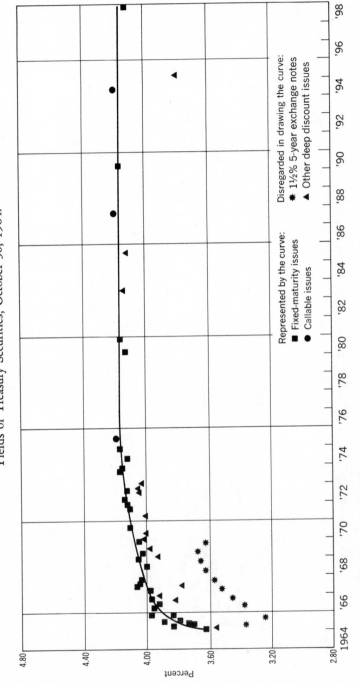

FIGURE 9.1

Yields of Treasury Securities, October 30, 1964.

Represented by the curve:
■ Fixed-maturity issues
● Callable issues

Disregarded in drawing the curve:
✳ 1½% 5-year exchange notes
▲ Other deep discount issues

SOURCE: Office of the Secretary of the Treasury

FIGURE 9.2

Yields of Treasury Securities, October 31, 1968.

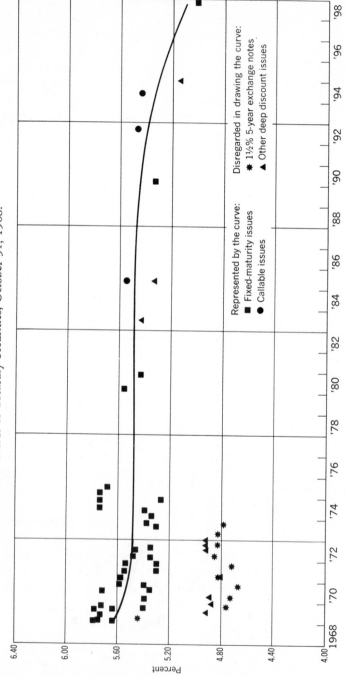

SOURCE: Office of the Secretary of the Treasury

the yields prevalent on October 31, 1968. At that time, the yield on bonds was roughly comparable over a broad range of maturities. On November 28, 1969, when Figure 9.3 was constructed, the yield of long-term bonds was markedly lower than the yield of short-term securities.

Long-term bonds, then, can yield an investor (and cost the issuer) either more or less than short-term bonds. The relationship between long- and short-term yields, however, is not random, for the yield curve changes systematically in relation to the business cycle. For example, suppose that the economy is now experiencing a period of prosperity, but that investors believe a recession to be near. Moreover, investors expect interest rates to fall when the recession comes. Under these conditions, the yield curve will slope downward, for investors will be attracted to long-term bonds and bid their prices up. This is because when the interest rate falls during the recession, investors will be able to sell these long-term bonds at a capital gain. To attract buyers away from long-term bonds, the current yields on short-term securities would have to be higher than the current yields on long bonds.

The opposite state of affairs occurs during a recession, when investors expect an upturn in the economy and rising interest rates. A rise in rates would force the prices of long-term bonds down and lead to capital losses for the bondholders. Consequently, investors will try to avoid holding long-term bonds and will fill their portfolios with more short-term securities. This will drive short-term rates down and long-term rates up, leading to an upward-sloping yield curve.

The problem of interest rates, however, is more complicated than this analysis of the yield curve suggests. The level of all rates, as well as the slope of the yield curve, must be considered. During a period of prosperity, the yield curve may slope downward, but the *entire level* of the curve is likely to be higher than during a period of recession. One reason for this is that the nominal level of interest rates reflects two factors. The first is the *real productivity of capital,* and the second is the *expected change in the price level.* Thus, suppose a firm is considering an investment that will yield a return of 5 percent if prices remain constant. If the firm expects that the profits on the investment will rise by 3 percent because of inflation, it will be willing to pay up to 8 percent to borrow funds to make the investment. Similarly, if the purchaser of a bond wants a real return of 5 percent and expects prices to rise 3 percent, he will demand an 8 percent return.

These remarks indicate that there is no simple answer to the question, Is it less expensive to borrow long-term money than short-term money? During some periods of the business cycle, long rates will be lower than short rates, and during others the opposite will be true. Moreover, during some periods the entire level of interest rates will be higher than during other periods.

FIGURE 9.3

Yields of Treasury Securities, November 28, 1969.

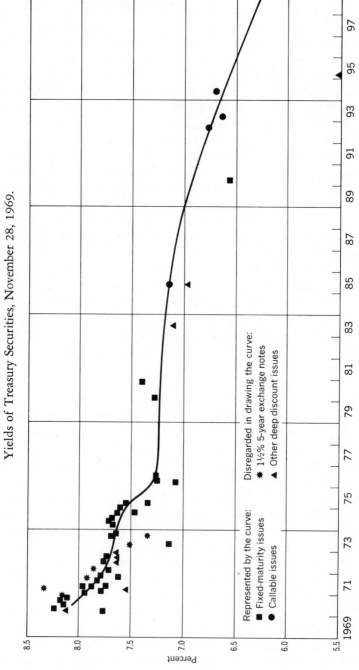

Represented by the curve:
■ Fixed-maturity issues
● Callable issues

Disregarded in drawing the curve:
✳ 1½% 5-year exchange notes
▲ Other deep discount issues

SOURCE: Office of the Secretary of the Treasury

The management of liabilities

CONVERTIBLE BONDS

Corporations issue different kinds of bonds, each of which afford the buyer a different yield and impose a different out-of-pocket cost on the corporation. For example, one type of bond that has gained in popularity is the *convertible bond,* which can be converted into a fixed number of shares of common stock at the option of the holder.

Suppose the price of a firm's common stock is $50 a share. To raise funds, it issues a $100 bond at par that pays $6 a year in interest and is convertible into two shares of common stock. If the price of the common stock appreciates to $60, the price of the bond will rise to at least $120, for the owner always has the option of exchanging the bond for two shares of stock and selling them for $120. On the other hand, if the price of the common stock falls to $40, the price of the bond may not fall to $80. If the $6 interest payment is comparable to the yield on other bonds of similar quality, the price may remain at $100.

A convertible bond, then, is really two things: a bond and an option to purchase stock at a fixed price. By selling the two things together, i.e., by issuing a convertible bond, the firm cuts its out-of-pocket interest cost. Suppose the prevailing interest rate is 8 percent. The yield on the convertible bond described in the preceding paragraph is 6 percent. Without the conversion feature, the bond would sell for $75, since investors would demand an 8 percent yield. In paying par, or $100, for this 6-percent bond, investors are paying $25 for the option to purchase the common stock at a fixed price.

Convertible bonds can be considered in a different light. If a convertible bond selling at par can be exchanged for two shares of common stock, the conversion price is $50 a share. Suppose the market price of the firm's common stock is $45, i.e., the bond's value as stock is $90. Investors are then paying a $10 premium for the bond over its value as common stock. They are prepared to pay this premium to enjoy the relative safety of owning a bond and, at the same time, have the opportunity of participating in any price appreciation of the stock.

To illustrate the implications of the conversion feature further, suppose that the value of a company's stock is $25. The value of a bond convertible into two shares of common stock, considered as a stock, is then $50. If the bond sells at par, the price of the stock must double before the conversion privilege will become operative. If the prospects of such a doubling are dim, the option will have little value and the bond will sell on a straight-yield basis like any other bond. As the price of the common stock approaches $50, however, the conversion privilege takes on value. The market price of the bond will begin to reflect the movements of the common stock, and, once the price of the stock passes $50, the price of the bond will move in unison with the price of the stock.

Debt instruments

A convertible bond, then, is an instrument that enables a firm to raise money at a little lower interest rate than it would otherwise have to pay. The convertible bond yields a lower rate because it offers the purchaser the opportunity to participate in the future growth of the company's equity. A convertible bond has a limited amount of downside risk, for if the price of the company's stock falls, the bond will sell on a straight-yield basis. On the other hand, if the price of the stock rises, the bond will rise in value.

OFF-BALANCE-SHEET FINANCING

The various short and long-term debt instruments described above are not the only alternatives open to a manager for raising funds. There are other important vehicles for controlling the use of a physical asset that do not appear on a firm's balance sheet.

For example, suppose a business firm rents, instead of buying, a building. When it rents, its balance sheet does not show the building as an asset, nor does it indicate the corresponding liability, even though the firm has obligated itself to continue its rental payments for the life of the lease. The only financial report which will indicate that the firm has the use of an important asset will be the income statement, which will report the size of the rental payments. Had the company purchased the building and financed the purchase with a mortgage, its balance sheet would reflect both an asset and a liability, and its income statement would report the size of the depreciation and interest charges, rather than rental payments.

Like other special-purpose instruments that enable the firm to command resources, leases have certain advantages. Specifically, they shift the risk of loss should the asset become worthless for the purpose for which it was intended from the firm to the owner of the property. A lease limits the length of time that a firm has command over a resource. Thus, if a supermarket chain wants to open a store in a certain location, it may be more advantageous for it to lease the property than to own it. If the neighborhood changes over time and becomes less attractive the supermarket is free to move at the end of its lease. Finding another use for the asset is then the owner's problem.

Leases are commonly used by businesses in areas where there is a slow but steady technological change in the physical asset. Stores are a common example: supermarkets are now larger and have more parking areas then they formerly did. Gasoline stations have wider driveways than formerly. The design of drive-in restaurants has changed to accommodate the changing tastes of consumers. All these facilities are usually leased by firms rather than bought outright. Some kinds of equipment, such as computers, are also subject to rapid technological change. A computer generation lasts roughly five years; as a result, many firms find it cheaper to lease computers than to own them.

The important financial consideration in deciding between a lease and a purchase, aside from the possible change in the value of the asset, is the cost of the funds required to gain use of it. If a firm leases a building or a machine, it pays rent; if it borrows the funds directly and buys the asset, it pays interest on the borrowed funds but uses some of its annual cash flow to retire the debt. Under some circumstances, it may be less costly for a firm to lease equipment than to own it; under other circumstances, the reverse may be true.

Debt management

The preceding discussion of various debt instruments indicates that the management of corporate liabilities involves a number of issues. Among the questions to be considered are:

(1) How long will the funds be needed? If the assets that are acquired are held for only a brief period, for example, if inventories are accumulated to satisfy a seasonal peak in sales, it may be desirable to borrow funds only for a short period. If long-term funds were used, interest would still have to be paid on the borrowed funds throughout the life of the instrument, even though the funds are no longer needed for their original purpose and may not be profitably invested at all times. On the other hand, if a long-term asset is to be acquired, it may be appropriate to borrow the funds for a long period. Not only will the financing of the project be assured throughout its entire life, but the borrower will know exactly what his interest costs will be throughout the life of the instrument.

(2) What will interest rates be in the future? Obviously, if interest rates are expected to rise, long-term financing is preferable, whereas if rates are expected to fall, short-term funds should be borrowed and the asset refinanced when lower rates prevail. Determining what interest rates will prevail in the future, however, is not always easy.

(3) What is the supply of funds available through various instruments? A small firm, for example, may find that during a period of high interest rates, its only sources of funds are trade credit and leases; bank loans or long-term debt may be unobtainable. Large firms, on the other hand, may find the commercial-paper market and long-term debt instruments such as convertible bonds a good source of funds even during periods of high interest rates.

(4) What are the operational consequences of issuing one type of instrument rather than another? Bondholders may place restrictions on

the amount of dividends the firm can pay, what it can do with its assets, the businesses it can enter, and so forth. Similar restrictions may not be imposed by banks or vendors that advance trade credit. Similarly, a lease may give a firm more flexibility than a bond if the asset that is to be acquired is subject to technological change.

(5) What will the firm's cash position be in the foreseeable future? If the firm expects a cash shortage in the near future, it would be better off if it held long-term debt, since it would have to pay only the interest and not the entire principal of the debt in any single year. However, if the firm expects to generate a great deal of cash in the foreseeable future, it may be less concerned about the due date of its debt.

It is apparent that no hard-and-fast rules can be established as to the proper ratio of short- to long-term debt, since it varies it with the circumstances of the firm. Moreover, none of the questions raised about liability management can be adequately answered without considering the firm as a total system, i.e., without simultaneously considering its asset requirements. Only when both the demand for assets and the supply of funds are considered can an answer be found to the question of how to structure the liabilities of the firm. Not all firms have the same investment or the same borrowing alternatives. Consequently, the cost of capital to various firms will be different. These costs will make it attractive for some firms to lend funds to others; for some to borrow short-term funds and others to lease assets; for some to rely on bank loans and others on commercial paper.

Summary

The management of liabilities requires that a firm recognize the length of time it will need command over resources. In addition, estimates must be prepared of both the future level of interest rates and of the yield curve that will prevail in the future. Only then can the financial manager decide which instruments are appropriate for the firm. Not all instruments are equally suitable, nor is their cost to the firm the same.

Among the more common short-term instruments used by firms to obtain funds are trade credit, bank loans, and commercial paper. Among the more common long-term sources of funds are bonds, mortgages, and leases.

It is one of the tasks of financial management to combine these various borrowing alternatives in the way that will best satisfy the goals and aspirations of the firm.

Questions for discussion and problems

1. What are the most important developments that have taken place in recent years with respect to trade credit? What factors account for this trend?

2. Is it prudent for a bank to treat customers differently depending on their long-term relationship with it? Would it be more profitable for banks to treat each transaction with each customer as an isolated event?

3. What factors are responsible for the growth of commercial paper as a short-term debt instrument? What bearing does the material covered in Chapter 7 have on your answer?

4. What is the significance of a rising, a falling, and a flat yield curve?

5. What considerations dominate a corporate manager's deliberations over the relative merits of using short- and long-term funds to finance assets?

6. A convertible bond typically pays an investor a lower interest rate than a "straight" bond. By this standard, it is an inferior instrument. Moreover, when the bond is issued, the price at which it can be exchanged for shares is usually above the market price of the stock. Thus, if an investor wanted to purchase stock in the company, it would be less expensive for him to buy the stock directly. If a convertible bond is inferior both as a bond and as a stock, why has it grown in popularity?

   [Answers to problems 7–9 follow references and suggested readings]

7. Valley Hardware Co. had the opportunity to purchase similar quality hand tools from two suppliers. The first offered terms of 4/15, net 60, and the second offered terms of 2/10, net 30. What is the effective interest rate at which each supplier is willing to extend credit?

8. During the past year, a firm increased its monthly gross sales an average of $30,000 over the preceding year's $120,000 figure. However, instead of half the gross sales being paid within the 2/10 discount period, as occurred in previous years, about 70 percent were paid on a net/30-day basis. What change took place in the dollar volume of discounts extended?

9. The yield on three government bonds, all selling at $100, is as follows:

Bond maturing in 1 year	5.00 percent
Bond maturing in 2 years	5.50 percent
Bond maturing in 3 years	5.75 percent

(a) If an investor purchased the two-year bond, what would his total dollar income be?

(b) Suppose the investor purchases the one-year bond and plans, when it matures, to buy another one-year bond. How much must he earn on the second one-year bond to be as well off as if he had purchased the two-year bond today?

(c) If he buys the two-year bond now instead of the three-year bond, how much must be earned on a one-year bond two years from now to be as well off?

(d) What does the fact that a yield curve is rising imply about the future trend in short-term interest rates?

REFERENCES AND SUGGESTED READINGS

Articles

Agemian, Charles A., "Maintaining an Effective Bank Relationship," *Financial Executive,* vol. XXXII (January 1964), pp. 24–28.

Andrews, Victor L. "Captive Finance Companies," *Harvard Business Review,* vol. 42 (July–August 1964), pp. 80–92.

Baxter, Nevins D., and Shapiro, Harold T., "Compensating Balance Requirements: The Results of a Survey," *Journal of Finance,* vol. XIX, no. 3 (September 1964), pp. 483–96.

Baumol, William J., Malkiel, Burton G., and Quandt, Richard E., "The Valuation of Convertible Securities," *Quarterly Journal of Economics,* vol. LXXX (February 1966), pp. 48–59.

Bierman, Harold, Jr., "The Bond Issue Size Decision," *Journal of Financial and Quantitative Analysis* (December 1966), pp. 1–15.

————, "Risk and the Addition of Debt to the Capital Structure," *Journal of Financial and Quantitative Analysis* (December 1968), pp. 415–27.

Borman, Keith L., "The Use of Convertible Subordinated Debentures by Industrial Firms, 1949–1959," *Quarterly Review of Economics and Business,* vol. III (Spring 1963), pp. 65–75.

Bower, Richard S., Herringer, Frank C., and Williamson, J. Peter, "Lease Evaluation," *Accounting Review,* vol. XLI, no. 2 (April 1966), pp. 257–65.

Brigham, Eugene F., "Analysis of Convertible Debentures: Theory and Some Empirical Evidence," *Journal of Finance,* vol. XXI (March 1966), pp. 35–54.

————, "The Impact of Bank Entry on Market Conditions in the Equipment Leasing Industry," *National Banking Review,* vol. II (September 1964), pp. 11–26.

"Commercial Paper," in *Money Market Instruments,* (Cleveland: Federal Reserve Bank of Cleveland, 1965), pp. 41–48.

Culbertson, John M., "The Term Structure of Interest Rates," *Quarterly Journal of Economics,* vol. LXXI (November 1957), pp. 485–517.

Donaldson, Gordon, "New Framework for Corporate Debt Policy," *Harvard Business Review,* vol. 40 (March–April 1962), pp. 117–31.

The management of liabilities

Heston, Alan W., "An Empirical Study of Cash, Securities, and Other Current Accounts of Large Corporations," *Yale Economic Essays,* vol. 2, no. 1 (Spring 1962), pp. 117–68.

Mayer, Thomas, "Trade Credit and the Discriminating Effects of Monetary Policy," *National Banking Review,* vol. III (June 1966), pp. 543–45.

Meltzer, Alan H., "Mercantile Credit, Monetary Policy, and Size of Firms," *Review of Economics and Statistics,* vol. XLII, no. 4 (November 1960), pp. 429–37.

Poensgen, Otto H., "The Valuation of Convertible Bonds," Part I and II, *Industrial Management Review* (Fall 1965, Spring 1966), pp. 77–92 and 83–98.

Robichek, A. A., Teichroew, D., and Jones, J. M., "Optimal Short Term Financing Decisions," *Management Science,* vol. XII (September 1965), pp. 1–36.

Van Horne, James C., "Interest Rate Expectations, the Shape of the Yield Curve, and Monetary Policy," *Review of Economics and Statistics,* vol. XLVIII, no. 2 (May 1966), pp. 211–15.

Weil, Roman L., Jr., Segall, Joel E., and Green, David, Jr., "Premiums on Convertible Bonds," *Journal of Finance* (June 1968), pp. 445–64.

Wood, John H., "Expectations, Error, and the Term Structure of Interest Rates," *Journal of Political Economy,* vol. LXXI (April 1963), pp. 160–71.

Books

Baxter, Nevins D., and Shapiro, Harold T., *The Commercial Paper Market* (Princeton, N. J.: Princeton Univ. Press, 1964).

Cagan, Philip, *Changes in the Cyclical Behavior of Interest Rates* (New York: National Bureau of Economic Research, 1966).

Donaldson, Gordon, *Corporate Debt Capacity* (Cambridge, Mass.: Harvard Univ. Press, 1961).

Kaufman, Henry, *The Changing Dimensions of the Corporate Bond Market* (New York: Solomon and Hutzler, 1967).

Kessel, Reuben H., *The Cyclical Behavior of the Term Structure of Interest Rates,* (New York: National Bureau of Economic Research, 1966).

Malkiel, Burton G., *The Term Structure of Interest Rates* (Princeton, N. J.: Princeton Univ. Press, 1966).

Meiselman, David, *The Term Structure of Interest Rates* (Englewood Cliffs, N. J.: Prentice-Hall, 1962).

Robinson, Roland I., *The Management of Bank Funds* (New York: McGraw-Hill, 1962).

Selden, Richard, *Trends and Cycles in the Commercial Paper Market* (New York: National Bureau of Economic Research, 1963).

Van Horne, James C., *Function and Analysis of Capital Market Rates* (Englewood Cliffs, N. J.: Prentice-Hall, 1970).

ANSWERS TO PROBLEMS 7–9

7. Since there are, eight 45-day periods per year, supplier 1's effective rate is $(8)(4\%)$ or 32%. Since there are eighteen 20-day periods per year, supplier 2's effective rate is $(18)(2\%)$, or 36%. Thus supplier 1 would be the least expensive.

8. *Previous Years*

$60,000   (50% gross)
  ×.02   (discount)
$ 1,200.00   (total discount)

Last Year

$150,000   (gross sales)
   ×.30   (discount)
$ 45,000.00
       ×.02 (discount)
    $900.00 (total discount)

There was a $300 difference in the amount of credit extended.

9. (a) $11
    (b) $6
    (c) $6.25
    (d) It implies that they will rise.

Managing and planning the growth of the system: the cost of capital and capital budgeting

The decisions of the firm with respect to its plant and equipment outlays are among the most important decisions it makes. For these decisions determine how effectively the firm will be able to meet many of the challenges that face it in the future.

Chapter 10 discusses how projects can be ranked in terms of profitability and liquidity. Chapter 11 discusses how the cost of funds committed to projects can be estimated. The problems that arise both in ordering projects and in estimating their costs highlight the need for the systems approach to investment decisions presented in Chapter 12. The material in these chapters is heavily descriptive. Chapter 13 and 14 therefore present a more formal approach to capital budgeting. However, not even the powerful tools described in these chapters meet all the needs of the financial manager when uncertainty exists as to the outcome of an investment decision. Chapter 15 comes to grips with the problem of uncertainty in capital budgeting and points out some of the alternatives open to the financial manager.

Selecting investment projects

10

One of the most important financial decisions that a firm makes is determining which investments it should make and which it should reject. Is it wiser for a firm to build a new plant or modernize its old one? Should a new machine that will let the firm compete in new markets be purchased, or can the firm's resources be deployed more profitably elsewhere? If the correct equipment is purchased, and the right productive processes adopted, the firm can grow and become a more competitive force than it now is. Still other opportunities will then present themselves and in turn pose challenges for management. However, if the firm makes a wrong capital-expenditure decision, it may gradually lose the markets it now has and the profits it now enjoys.

Given then the importance of the capital-investment decision, how does the financial manager approach the problem of which investment projects to adopt and which to reject? What models does he use to structure the data that are relevant for the decision? What is the objective function, or goal, in these models, and what are the constraints that limit his actions? All these questions must be answered.

First we need to review some of the terms financial managers use and some of the concepts that structure their thinking about investment decisions. We shall use a single numerical example throughout the discussion to make the analysis more concrete.

To capture the most important considerations that enter into the investment decision, the problem must ultimately be cast in a systems framework. Only then can we see how changes in the demand for the firm's product, the production function it uses, and the supply schedule of its factor inputs interact to influence the firm's dollar outlay for equipment, the dividends it pays to shareholders, and the volume of funds it borrows in the open market.

Suppose a firm must choose between two investments. The revenues and costs associated with each are known. Hence the cash flow associated with each project each year in the future is also known. Furthermore, the two projects are independent; the purchase of one will not influence the cash flows associated with the other.

Machine A, the first investment proposal, costs $10,000, and if purchased will function for five years. During each year of its life, it will produce a profit of $1,000. At the end of the fifth year, it will have only a nominal scrap value. The firm will use the straight-line method of depreciation to write off the asset; hence depreciation charges will be $2,000 per year.

Machine B, the second investment proposal, costs $8,240 and has an expected life of ten years. During each year of its life, it will generate a profit of $1,166, and, since the straight-line method of depreciation will be used once again, depreciation charges will be $824 per annum. Its scrap value at the end of ten years will be nominal.

Which project should the firm undertake?

Payback method

Some method is needed to rank the various projects that a firm has under consideration before a choice can be made between them. One ranking technique that is widely used is to order each project according to the length of time it takes to recover the original investment. This is called the *payback method*.

Project A generates $2,000 a year in cash from depreciation charges and $1,000 a year in profits. Its total cash throw-off is, therefore, $3,000. The project will therefore pay for itself (i.e., the $10,000 outlay for the machine will be recovered) in $3\frac{1}{3}$ years. A corresponding set of calculations for project B shows that its payback period is 4.14 years. By this test, then, project A is preferable to project B and should be adopted.

There are, however, some obvious difficulties with the payback method of ranking projects. If the length of time it takes to recover the cash outlay for a project is the only criterion used and no regard is given to the cash stream generated beyond the payback period, then the most desirable projects for a firm to invest in are inventories, receivables, commercial paper, and other short-term assets. Inventories may turn over four times a year, and hence have a payback period of three months. Receivables may have an even shorter payback period, and short-term government bonds can have a payback period of a week or less. Indeed, if the payback period were the only criterion used to select investments, a firm might never purchase long-lived assets.

The payback method of ranking projects, then, places no value on the stream of revenues generated by the project after the initial costs are recovered or on the timing of these flows. Yet this stream is clearly important, for no project would be seriously considered if the total projected revenues merely equaled the original cash outlay. Some other method of ranking projects, one that incorporates all the cash flows generated by the project over its entire life and the timing of these flows, is clearly desirable.

Given the serious drawbacks of the payback method, why do firms still use it in investment analysis? One reason for calculating the payback is that it can be used in a different way than that described above. Instead of being used alone to rank projects, a fixed payback period may be just one of many constraints that a project must meet before it will be accepted. For example, the firm may be willing to consider only projects in the same industry in which the firm now operates, projects that will not require an expansion of its labor force by more than a certain number of men, or projects that do not require technological pioneering. Not all projects that meet the payback criterion are, therefore, automatically purchased.

A second reason the payback is widely used as a measure of a project's feasibility is that the assumption underlying our example, that the cash flows of a project are known, does not always hold. If the cash flows are highly variable, as is often the case, then the uncertainty of a project will be reduced if it pays for itself quickly; i.e., the firm will not have to wait for events that will not occur for many years before it knows whether it will recover the outlays that it has made. Moreover, many investment projects are flexible in the sense that they may require greater or lesser amounts of funds in later years. This flexibility requires that the decision-maker have information of a certain type, and, in the absence of other data about the markets that the project serves, payback information may be helpful.

To summarize, under conditions of certainty, payback is a poor method of ordering the attractiveness of projects. Under conditions of uncertainty, however, the measure may have some value as one of the constraints that limit a firm's range of options. More important, it can be a rough guide to reduce the degree of uncertainty associated with a project, since if a project has a quick payback, the decision-maker is left only with the problem of whether the useful life of the project beyond the payback period is long enough to make it attractive. If a project has a long payback period, the firm may not even recover its costs, let alone earn a return on its investment.

Return on average book value

One measure that has been proposed to meet the criticisms leveled against the payback method of ranking projects is the *return on average book value*. Under this method, we would begin by observing that even though project A costs $10,000, the company's average investment over the lifetime of the project will be only $5,000, since $2,000 are recovered each year in depreciation charges. The corresponding average investment in project B is $4,120. Since project A generates a profit of $1,000 per year, its return on average investment is 20 percent. Project B, which generates a profit of $1,166, has an average return of 28.3 percent. By this measure, project B is the preferable investment.

Like the payback method, however, this method of ranking projects has some obvious drawbacks. The cash flow of a project is defined as the sum of profits and depreciation. The two components of the cash flow, however, are not treated the same. The depreciation portion is used to reduce the denominator of the return measure, while the profit portion is used as the numerator of the expression. Even though the sum of the two remains the same, a change in the proportion of profits to depreciation will influence the reported return; yet in practice the distinction between depreciation charges and profits may be quite arbitrary, as we have seen in earlier chapters.

A second difficulty also plagues users of this method. The illustration assumed that the project produced the same amount of profit each year. A more realistic assumption is that the profits differ from year to year. If this is the case, then the average profit earned over a period by one project may be equal to that of another, but the timing of the actual profit flows of the two projects may be different. How, then, are such projects to be ranked? Clearly, if it is desirable to have funds available early, the two rankings should not be equal. Finally, the two projects have different lives. Project A runs for only five years while project B lasts ten. How can the projects even be compared when funds must be committed to one project twice as long as to the other?

To answer these questions effectively, the frame of reference for the investment decision must be expanded to include still another dimension: the timing of the cash flows. If the investment opportunities that will be open to the firm when A's cash flows are received are more attractive, it may be the preferable investment; if those that will be available when B's flows are received are more attractive then perhaps B should be the project adopted. Both the size of the cash flows generated by a project and when the flows will occur must, therefore, be considered before projects can be okayed. Before the problem of timing is discussed, however, the concept of *present value* must be introduced.

The present value of a future stream

Assume that a person has an opportunity to invest his funds in government bonds with a 5 percent rate of return. If he invests $1 in this asset, he will, by the end of the year, have $1.05 (or 105 percent of his original funds). If P_e is his ending balance and P_b is his beginning balance, then $P_e = P_b (1.05)$.

Similarly, if he invests all his funds for a second year at the same 5 percent rate, his ending balance will be $1.1025 since:

$$P_e = P_b(1.05)(1.05)$$

If he invests his funds for n years at a rate of return r, his ending balance will be given by the expression:

0–1) $$P_e = P_b(1 + r)^n$$

This process of continuously reinvesting funds is called *compounding*.

The relationships described above can be turned around. Instead of the ending value, the beginning amount can be determined. This process is called *discounting*. The beginning value is *the present value* of the ending amount of money, and the rate that equates the ending value and the beginning value is the *discount rate*.

For example, if at the end of one year a person will receive $1.05, and he discounts this amount at a 5 percent rate, the present value of the funds he will receive is $1:

$$PV = \frac{\$1.05}{1 + .05} = \$1.00$$

If a person will receive $1.1025 two years from now and discounts this amount at a 5 percent rate, the present value is:

$$PV = \frac{\$1.1025}{(1.05)^2}$$
$$= \$1$$

In general,

0–2) $$PV = \frac{CF_n}{(1 + k)^n}$$

where CF_n is the amount of funds that will be received in period n, and k is the discount rate. (Note the similarity between equations 10–1 and 10–2.)

Assume now that a person will receive a cash flow of $1 in both years 1 and 2. What is the present value of the entire stream if he uses a 10-percent rate of discount? The value of the dollar received in the first year is

$$PV = \frac{1}{(1.10)} = .909$$

and the value of the dollar received in the second year is

$$PV = \frac{1}{(1.10)^2} = .826$$

The total stream is worth

(10–3)
$$PV = \sum_{i=1}^{2} \frac{CF_i}{(1 + k)^i}$$

where Σ is the sum of the values in i periods and $i = 2$. In this example, therefore,

$$PV = .909 + .826$$
$$= 1.74$$

Note that we started with both a known cash flow and a known discount rate. Using these values, we found the present value of a future stream of funds. Equation 10–3 can also be used to find the value of k, the discount rate, when both the cash flows generated by the asset through time and its purchase price are known. Suppose a project costs $1.74 and will produce a cash flow of $1 in each of the next two years. What rate of discount will make the funds that the purchaser of this asset will receive equal its present value of $1.74?

Using the present-value formula, equation 10–3,

$$1.74 = \frac{1}{(1 + k)} + \frac{1}{(1 + k)^2}$$

By trial and error we find that $k = 10$ percent, the answer we expected. In general, there are as many possible values for k as there are periods, i. In the example above, the value of $-.52$ would also satisfy the equation. Since a negative discount rate has no economic meaning, it can be ignored. If the cash flow extends for three periods, the flow in the third year is discounted at the rate $(1 + k)^3$, and three values of k (not necessarily all different) will then satisfy the present-value formula. However, if, as sometimes occurs, more than one of these values is positive, complications will arise in interpreting the results.

Discounting cash flows

We now return to the problem posed at the beginning of the chapter—whether project A or B is the preferable investment. We have seen that ranking projects according to the return on average book value is superior to the payback method because it considers all the flows generated over the lifetime of the project. It is deficient, however, in that it values the flows received in each time period equally. Would it not, then, be an obvious improvement in the ranking technology to order projects according to the discounted value of their lifetime flows?

We can do this in two ways. The present value of a future stream was defined as

$$PV = \sum_{i=1}^{n} \frac{CF_i}{(1 + k)^i}$$

Since we know the purchase price of each asset and the stream of cash that each project generates each year, we can find the rate of discount, k, that equals the sum of the future cash flows to its purchase price. The projects can then be ordered according to the size of their discount rate, or *internal rate of return*. The project with the highest discount rate is the preferable investment.

We could also proceed by selecting an arbitrary discount rate, such as the rate at which the firm can secure additional funds. Using this rate, we compute the present value of the project's cash flow and compare the present-value figure to the actual purchase price of the asset. If the present-value figure is greater than the purchase price, the difference is called the *excess present value*, and projects can be ranked according to this standard. Alternatively, the present-value figure can be divided by the purchase price to obtain an *index of profitability*, and projects ranked by the value of this ratio. The project that has the highest index is, of course, the more desirable investment. We shall discuss each method in detail below.

The internal rate of return

To find the internal rate of return for projects A and B, we proceed by trial and error.[1] That is, we first arbitrarily select a discount rate and substitute it in our equation to see whether it does in fact convert the cash

[1] Precise algorithms for finding the internal rate of return have been developed. One such procedure is discussed by Seymour Kaplan in "Computer Algorithims for Finding Exact Rates of Return," *Journal of Business*, vol. 40 (Oct. 1967) pp. 389–93.

flows into their present value. If the present values of the flows exceed the purchase price, the discount rate is raised; if the present value of the flow is less than the purchase price the discount rate is lowered.

Consider project A, which cost $10,000 and generates a stream of cash of $3,000 for each of five years. When 10 percent is selected as the discount rate, the present value of the flow is $11,370 (see Table 10.1). Since this sum is greater than the cost of the project, 10 percent is too low a rate of discount. If we raise the rate to 20 percent, the present value of the flows is $8,970, an amount less than $10,000. Hence the internal rate of return, or the discount rate that will make the sum of the present value of the project's future cash flows equal to the purchase price of the asset, lies somewhere between 10 and 20 percent. A third and, if need be, a fourth, rate can be chosen until the precise internal rate of return is found.

A similar set of computations can be made for project B. The data in Table 10.1 show that both the 10 percent and the 20 percent figure are too low for this project. Additional rates, higher than 20 percent, must be substituted until the correct discount rate is found.

The internal rate of return of project B is thus greater than 20 percent, while that of project A is substantially less than this amount. Hence if projects are ranked by this criterion, B is the preferable investment.

In this example, the two projects being compared have different life times. Project B has a longer life, and, since it also has a higher internal rate of return, no special problem seems to emerge. What if the ordering were reversed, and A, the shorter lived project, had the higher return? How would we proceed?

The logic of the internal rate of return method implies that the funds generated in each period can be reinvested to yield a return equal to the internal rate of return. To compare two projects, one of which ceases to exist at the end of five years while the other continues to produce funds for ten years, the rate at which the funds can be invested in the fifth year must also be known. Whether it is better to invest money at 20 percent for five years or at 18 percent for 10 years clearly depends on the alternatives available in year 5. If another 20 percent project can be found in year 5, the first project is obviously preferable. If the best alternative that is available in year 5, however, is a project yielding 15 percent, the second project may be more satisfactory.

Is the internal rate of return, then, the measure for ranking projects that we have been seeking? It does take into consideration all the project's cash flows, as well as the matter of timing. Moreover, it can be used to structure the relevant data when the projects being compared have different lifetimes. Unfortunately, however, it leads to ambiguous results in certain cases.

TABLE 10.1
A Comparison of Two Investment Projects

Year	Present Value of $1 Received in the Year Discounted at 10%	Cash Flow of Project A	Present Value of A's Cash Flow	Cash Flow of Project B	Present Value of B's Cash Flow
1	.909	$3,000	$ 2,727	$1,990	$ 1,808.91
2	.826	3,000	2,478	1,990	1,643.74
3	.751	3,000	2,253	1,990	1,494.49
4	.683	3,000	2,049	1,990	1,359.17
5	.621	3,000	1,863	1,990	1,235.79
6	.564			1,990	1,122.36
7	.513			1,990	1,020.87
8	.467			1,990	929.33
9	.424			1,990	843.76
10	.386			1,990	768.14
Total			$11,370		$12,226.56

Year	Present Value of $1 Received in the Year Discounted at 20%	Cash Flow of Project A	Present Value of A's Cash Flow	Cash Flow of Project B	Present Value of B's Cash Flow
1	.833	$3,000	$2,499	$1,990	$1,657.67
2	.694	3,000	2,082	1,990	1,381.06
3	.579	3,000	1,737	1,990	1,152.21
4	.482	3,000	1,446	1,990	959.18
5	.402	3,000	1,206	1,990	799.98
6	.335			1,990	666.65
7	.279			1,990	555.21
8	.233			1,990	463.67
9	.194			1,990	386.06
10	.162			1,990	322.38
Total			$8,970		$8,344.07

Consider an investment project with the following three properties:

(1) a cost of $1,

(2) a life of 2 years, and

(3) a cash flow of $5 during the first year and a flow of −$6 during the second year.

What is the internal rate of return on this project? That is, what value of k will satisfy the following expression?

$$1 = \frac{5}{(1 + k)} - \frac{6}{(1 + k)^2}$$

The internal rate of return

Applying the method of analysis used earlier, we find that two positive values of k, 100 and 200 percent, will satisfy the equation. If $k = 200$ percent, the expression becomes:

$$1 = \frac{5}{(1 + 2)} - \frac{6}{(1 + 2)^2}$$
$$= \tfrac{5}{3} - \tfrac{6}{9}$$
$$= 1$$

Similarly, if k equals 100 percent, the expression becomes:

$$1 = \frac{5}{(1 + 1)} - \frac{6}{(1 + 1)^2}$$
$$= \tfrac{5}{2} - \tfrac{6}{4}$$
$$= 1$$

Which figure, 100 percent or 200 percent, is the correct answer? The answer is, both, since certain projects can have more than one positive internal rate of return. But if a project has multiple internal rates of return, then different projects may not be ranked consistently. One person, looking at one of the two rates, may rank one project as preferable to another, while a second person, looking at the other rate, could reverse the ordering of the two projects. The internal rate of return, therefore, does not appear to be the general method for ordering projects we have been seeking.

To summarize, the internal rate of return is the rate of discount that equates a project's expected cash flow and its purchase price. The internal rate of return is found by trial and error: If the present value of the cash flows exceeds the purchase price, the discount rate is too low; if the present value of the cash flows is less than the purchase price, the discount rate is too high.

Ranking projects according to their internal rate of return appears to dispose of the criticisms leveled against both the payback and average rate of return methods. All the cash flows generated by a project are included in the analysis, and flows that will be received in the distant future are less highly valued than those that will be received in the near future.

There is, however, one practical difficulty with the measure. More than one positive internal rate of return may exist. In general, for each time the cash flow changes signs from positive to negative and back, there will be another and different value of k that will satisfy the requirements of the present-value formula. Thus whenever the cash flows fluctuate from positive to negative, an ambiguity in ranking projects will arise.

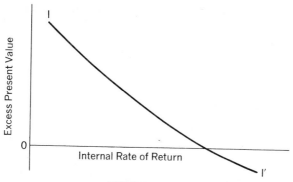

FIGURE 10.1

Excess Present Value of an Investment Project with Positive Cash Flows.

The point that is being made can be readily diagrammed. Figure 10.1 shows an investment project that has only positive cash flows. As a result, there is only a single internal rate of return which satisfies the condition that there be no excess present value, i.e., that the purchase price be equal to the present value. If the cash flows of a project are not always positive, there is more than one internal rate of return that will equate the purchase price of the asset to its present value. Two such rates, r_1 and r_2, are illustrated in Figure 10.2.

The index of profitability

Is the second measure that was mentioned earlier, the index of profitability, the measure we want to use to rank projects? Recall that the present-

FIGURE 10.2

Excess Present Value of an Investment Project with Positive and Negative Cash Flows.

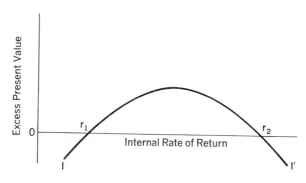

value approach assumes that the firm knows the value of k and CF in the formula:

$$PV = \sum_{k=1}^{n} \frac{CF_i}{(1 + k)^i}$$

The present value of the flows is then divided by the purchase price of the asset to determine the index of profitability.[2]

This technique can be illustrated by referring to Table 10.1. If the firm wanted to earn only 10 percent on its investment, it would have been prepared to pay as much as \$11,370 for project A and as much as \$12,226 for project B. Expressing these sums as percentages of the actual price of the investment projects gives us their profitability indexes. Thus,

Index of profitability of A = 11,370/10,000 = 1.14
Index of profitability of B = 12,226/8,240 = 1.48

Since B has the higher index, it is the preferable investment. Were a 20-percent rate of discount applied, the indexes would be:

Index of profitability of A = 8,970/10,000 = .89
Index of profitability of B = 8,344/8,240 = 1.02

Again, project B is more attractive.

Once a rate for discounting the cash flow generated in each period by each project is determined, the present value of the project's entire stream of cash can be readily calculated, and, as we have seen, various projects can be ranked. Moreover, the discount rate that is used in different periods can be changed to reflect the different investment opportunities that may arise for the firm. This technique thus has great appeal for financial managers. However, complications can also arise when investment projects are ordered by the index of profitability.

Consider the following two investment projects:

(1) both projects cost \$1;

(2) both have a two-year life;

(3) project 1 generates an aggregate flow of \$2.25 over the two years, \$1 in the first year and \$1.25 in the second; project 2 generates an aggregate flow of \$2.20 over the two years, \$1.20 during the first year and \$1 during the second.

---

[2] If the purchase price is subtracted from the calculated present-value figure, the difference is called the excess present value. The difficulty with using this measure to order projects is that it does not consider the actual amount of funds that are committed to a project. Thus, a project that costs \$10,000 may have an excess present value of \$1,000. It is not necessarily preferable to a project that costs \$5,000 and has an excess present value of \$900. The index of profitability measure eliminates this ambiguity.

Given a discount rate, which project, 1 or 2, yields the higher index of profitability?

Suppose that the discount rate is 10 percent. The following table can then be used to decide which project is preferable.

Year	Present Value of $1 at 10%	Cash Flow of Project 1	Cash Flow of Project 2	Present Value of Cash Flow of Project: 1	Present Value of Cash Flow of Project: 2
1	.91	1.00	1.20	.91	1.09
2	.83	1.25	1.00	1.04	.83
				Total 1.95	1.92

The present value of project 1 is $1.95. The present value of project 2 is $1.92. Since both projects cost $1, the index of profitability of project 1 is the greater, and it is the preferable project.

Suppose, however, that the discount rate that is applied to the stream of cash is not 10 but 30 percent, as in the following table.

Year	Present Value of $1 at 10%	Cash Flow of Project 1	Cash Flow of Project 2	Present Value of Cash Flow of Project: 1	Present Value of Cash Flow of Project: 2
1	.77	1.00	1.20	.77	.92
2	.59	1.25	1.00	.74	.59
				Total 1.51	1.51

Both projects now have the same present value, $1.51. Their index of profitability scores are equal. Moreover, at all discount rates greater than 30 percent, project 2 is the preferable investment. The choice of the discount rate can thus alter the ranking of different projects.

It is easy to understand why at one discount rate one project is preferable to another while at another rate the reverse is true. The rate of discount can be thought of as the rate at which a firm can invest its funds. It reflects the other investment opportunities of the firm. If the outlook for other investments is good, it will prefer a stream of revenues such as $1.20 and $1.00 to a stream such as $1.00 and $1.25, since it can invest the $1.20 that is received in the first period at a high rate. On the other hand, if the other opportunities for investment are unattractive, the project that yields a total flow of $2.25 will be preferred to the one that yields only $2.20.

To summarize, a financial manager can discount a project's cash flows at a known rate and determine their present value. He can then express this present-value figure as a percentage of the project's purchase price to calculate an index of profitability. Projects with a high index are preferable to those with a low index.

This method of ranking projects has neither the drawbacks of the payback method nor those of the average rate of return. All the cash flows are included in the analysis, and current flows are more highly valued than distant flows. Moreover, once a discount rate is chosen, the index produces an unambiguous ranking, even if some flows are positive and some negative.

There is, however, an underlying difficulty with this method of ranking: The choice of the discount rate itself can change the ordering of two projects. Two investments whose cash flows differ in size and timing can be ranked differently when different discount rates are used.

Further complications

All four methods for ranking investment projects described above rested on two assumptions—that the precise cash flows generated by each product in each period were known and that the projects were independent (the adoption of one project did not influence the returns of the second). In practice, of course, these assumptions seldom hold true. The cash flows that a project will earn at a future date can only be estimated, and the estimates can vary over a wide range. Moreover, the projects that are under consideration are frequently related. The purchase of one machine may make a second more productive, or it may make it obsolete. It will be helpful, therefore, to describe, briefly, some of the methods financial managers use to cope with the two problems of uncertainty and interdependence.

Uncertainty in capital budgeting

The problem of uncertainty in capital budget can arise for a number of reasons. The gross sales that will arise from a project can more properly be thought of as a probability distribution than as a fixed, or point, value. Similarly, the material and labor costs that will be associated with producing these values are uncertain. As a consequence, estimates of the profits and gross-cash flow that will be generated by an investment can span a wide range of values.

Suppose that the distribution of the index of profitability of two projects under consideration is as plotted in Figure 10.3. Both projects have the same expected value, but project B has a larger standard deviation than project A. Are the two projects equally attractive?

Most financial analysts would argue that the two projects are not equally desirable. Rather, because of the greater dispersion associated with the estimated return of project B, it is a more uncertain and, therefore, less

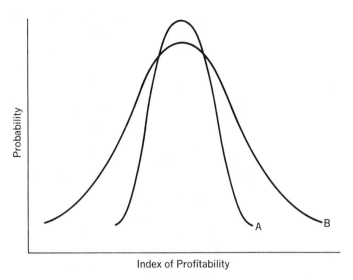

FIGURE 10.3

The Distribution of the Index of Profitability for Two Projects.

attractive investment opportunity than project A. Two methods have been proposed for incorporating this fact into the ranking system.

LOWERING THE CASH-FLOW VALUES

One method that has been proposed to cope with the problem of uncertainty in selecting investment projects is to penalize a project's cash flows when they are highly variable. The effect of such an adjustment is to lower the value of the numerator in the present-value formula. When the project's index of profitability is computed, the project will therefore receive a lower ranking than it would have had its flows been less volatile.

For example, if the cash flow of a project is equally likely to be $10 or $20, the numerator used in calculating the present value might be only $14, $1 less than the expected return of $15. If the return is even less certain, if, say, cash flows of $5 or $25 are equally likely, the numerator might be assigned a value substantially below the $15 expected value, such as $12.50.

Let the curve U in Figure 10.4 represent the utility curve of a financial manager, that is, the satisfaction he will receive as the project earns higher returns. Notice that the curve is both *monotonically increasing* and *concave downward*. This means that while additional returns raise the *total* utility of the financial manager, *equal increments of return afford diminishing increments of satisfaction.*

Uncertainty in capital budgeting   **219**

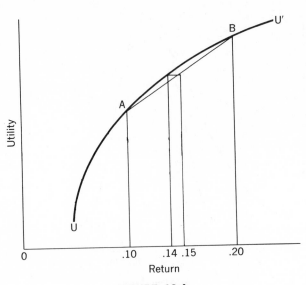

FIGURE 10.4
The Utility Schedule of a Financial Manager.

Consider now a project that can produce two returns, $10 and $20, with equal probability. The expected return of the project is $15. However, the utility that the financial manager will derive from this return is less than the amount he would receive if he could earn $15 with certainty. The utility he will receive from the uncertain project is found by combining the utility of a certain $10 return and the utility of a certain $20 return, with each return given equal weight. The satisfaction the financial manager will receive from the uncertain project can be represented graphically by the height of the chord connecting points *A* and *B* at $15. This height is equal to the level of satisfaction that he would have received had he been able to earn $14 with certainty. In other words, a certain return of $14 is equivalent in terms of satisfaction, to a return of $10 with a probability of .5 and a return of $20 with a probability of .5. One way, therefore, to compute the present value of a project's cash flows when the return may vary is to substitute the equivalent certain return ($14) for the expected return ($15).

It is apparent from the graph that if the range of expected returns is $5 and $25, rather than $10 and $20, a still lower certain return, say $12.50, will satisfy the financial manager. This smaller value can then be used in the calculation of that project's present value. The result of this procedure, then, is to systematically lower the index of profitability of projects as their cash streams become more uncertain.

This method of handling uncertainty has a number of advantages. It is flexible enough to be used by managers who exhibit different degrees of risk aversion. The analysis is applicable if the utility function of the manager is almost a 45-degree line (if all incremental returns are valued equally) or if it is relatively flat (if incremental returns beyond some amount increase his satisfaction only a little). Moreover, it incorporates all the information that is developed about a project, not just a single expected return value.

However, this method does not tell the manager what the slope of the utility schedule should be. One manager, with one type of utility schedule may reject a project that a second manager with a different utility schedule will adopt.

RAISING THE DISCOUNT RATE

A second method of reducing the attractiveness of a project when its returns are variable is to raise the discount rate applied to the estimated cash flow, rather than lowering the cash-flow figure.

Consider the examples cited above. If a project generates a certain $15 flow each year, the firm may discount the flow at 10 percent. If the project is equally likely to generate returns of $10 and $20, the firm may discount the project's expected $15 return at 15 percent. If returns of $5 and $25 are equally likely, the firm might discount the $15 average return at a still higher rate of, say, 20 percent. Increasing the discount rate, again, lowers the index of profitability. As a result, projects whose returns are more uncertain will be less highly valued than those whose returns are more certain, other things being equal.

Financial managers frequently use this strategy in ranking projects proposed by different divisions. Suppose one division of a company proposes an investment project that calls for replacing an old machine with one that is technologically superior, while a second division proposes an investment that will take the firm into a new industry. The estimated cash flows from the replacement project are likely to be close to the actual levels, since the estimates will be based on the firm's experience with the original equipment. The flows that will arise from the second project are highly uncertain. Thus the financial manager may be content with an expected return of 12 percent on the replacement project but refuse to approve the second project, involving the new activity, unless the estimated return exceeds 25 percent.

The difficulty with coping with uncertainty by raising the discount rate is that not all the information that is developed about a project is used in the final ranking procedure. Only the expected value of the cash flow generated by the project is employed. Moreover, no procedure for determining how much to raise the discount rate for increasing degrees of uncertainty is specified. In spite of these technical criticisms, however, the method has a wide appeal.

Interdependence

Problems other than uncertain returns also plague the financial manager when he tries to determine which projects to adopt and which to reject. In the analysis presented above, all the projects that were considered were independent. The purchase of one asset did not influence the return earned on the other. In practice, this assumption is not likely to hold.

Projects can be related in a number of ways. In an extreme case, two projects would be directly complementary. For example, suppose that the project under review is an attachment to a new machine. The attachment will generate a cash flow only if the machine itself is purchased.

Frequently, the production costs of one investment project are influenced by the adoption or rejection of a second project. For example, two projects may draw on the same labor pool. As the output of one project expands, the wage costs associated with the other will rise. If the output of the two projects is shipped to the same warehouse, the storage and handling costs of the goods produced by one machine will be affected by the production schedule of the other. Moreover, since both projects draw financial resources from a common pool of funds, the adoption of one may influence the interest costs that must be paid for the other.

When projects are related, one obvious strategy is to consider the two projects as one and compare their combined payoff to still a third project, thus concealing the effect of the interdependence. A second strategy is to estimate the return of one project and assign all the additional costs that would arise if a second project were adopted to that second project. The difficulty with this approach is that it presupposes that the order in which projects should be adopted is known, the very problem we set out to solve. Moreover, suppose the first, fifth, and eighth projects out of a potential list of fifteen were considered attractive. What assurance is there that all the costs that each of these impose on the other and all the revenues that each might contribute to the other have been properly evaluated.

It seems clear, then, that some method must be developed for considering simultaneously all the projects a firm has under review. Moreover, the effect of the supply of funds, as well as other resources such as labor, space, and managerial talent, must also be brought into the calculation. In short, treating the capital-budgeting problem as one of choosing between well-defined, independent projects is likely to result in suboptimum solutions. Here too, a systems point of view must be adopted before an answer to the problem can be found.

Summary

Four popular methods of ranking projects were discussed. None of the four, however, is wholly satisfactory. The payback method is inadequate because it does not consider the cash flows generated by a project after the initial outlay is recovered. The average-rate-of-return method does take into consideration all the cash flows generated by a project, but it does not consider when the flows are received; hence it is of limited value.

The internal-rate-of-return method makes use of all the flows and incorporates the time value of funds by valuing dollars received in the distant future at a lower rate than those received in the near future. Unfortunately, this method of ranking projects breaks down when the pattern of the cash flows alternates over time, being negative (outflows) one year and positive (inflows) the next, since more than one internal rate of return can then equate the project's cash flows to its purchase price. Under these conditions, this method will not provide a unique ordering of investment projects.

The index-of-profitability method also considered all the cash flows generated by a project and the time value of money. Moreover, once a discount rate is selected, the present-value formula provides an unambiguous ranking. However, when one project's cash flow starts from a low level and rises through time and a second project's cash flow is level or starts from a high level and declines through time, the ranking of these two projects will depend on the discount rate used.

The ranking problem is further complicated when the cash flows of various projects are uncertain. Two projects that have the same expected returns may not be equally attractive if the standard deviations of the returns differ. While uncertainty can be compensated for by adjusting either the numerator or the denominator in the present value calculations, both methods have limitations.

Finally, the various projects that a firm has under consideration may be interdependent. When the adoption of one project will influence the returns or costs of a second project, an approach that allows the firm to consider its various options simultaneously must be developed. To come to grips with this aspect of capital budgeting, a systems approach must be developed.

Questions for discussion and problems

1. Create a hypothetical project, and calculate its payback, average rate of return, internal rate of return, and index of profitability.

2. The internal rate of return implies that the flows generated by a project each year can be reinvested at that rate. If this condition does not hold, is the measure still a valid way of ranking projects?

3. Given that it is difficult to rank projects, why don't firms simply give the available funds to the most powerful divisional manager and let him spend them as he sees fit?

4. Suppose a firm adopted a project because it expected a 20 percent rate of return and a survey taken two years later indicates that the project is earning only 5 percent. Should the firm stop trying to forecast cash flows?

5. Is it always true that a dollar received in the future is worth less than a dollar received today? What does this imply about the trade-off that any generation will make between its current consumption and that of as-yet-unborn future generations?

6. If a financial manager's utility curve was concave upward, what kind of investment decisions would he make?

7. Are all investment projects interdependent? Suggest some projects that are relatively independent. What kind of firm is most likely to have independent projects?

8. Suppose a firm decides that the difficulties arising from uncertain returns and interdependent projects are so severe that it can use only the payback method to rank projects. What discount rate has the firm, in effect, assigned to funds generated after the payback period?

[*Answers to problems 9–12 follow references and suggested readings.*]

9. Catalyst Chemical Company is considering two alternative methods of processing a chemical byproduct for further commercial use. Equipment costs for both methods will be fully and evenly depreciated over a 20-year period.

	Initial Cost	Estimated Annual Income
Method A	$1,200	$ 90
Method B	1,500	$135

If they are ranked by their average-rate-of-return, which method is preferable?

10. A project's net cash flows are computed each December 31 as:

Year	Net Cash Flow
1	−$1,600
2	$ 300
3	$ 700
4	$ 825
5	$1,575
6	$1,300

If a return of 5 percent per annum is expected from this project, what is the maximum amount the firm should invest in it at the present time?

11. A firm plans to invest in one of the following projects.

Project	Cost	Annual Cash Inflow	Project Life (in years)
A	$23,000	$3,750	10
B	$26,500	$4,250	9
C	$30,800	$4,800	13

The annual cash inflows include depreciation charges. Rank the projects by their internal rates of return.

12. Grayside, Inc. in considering two investments, each of which requires an initial investment of $180,000. The total cash inflows, that is, profits after taxes and depreciation charges, for each project are:

Year	A	B
1	$30,000	$ 60,000
2	50,000	100,000
3	60,000	65,000
4	65,000	45,000
5	40,000	
6	30,000	
7	16,000	

Grayside's cost of capital is 8 percent. Rank these investments by their excess present values. Which is the most profitable?

REFERENCES AND SUGGESTED READINGS

Articles

Alchian, A. A., "The Rate of Interest, Fisher's Rate of Return Over Cost, and Keynes' Internal Rate of Return," *American Economic Review* (December 1955), p. 938.

English, J. Morley, "The Rate of Return and Assessment of Risk," *Engineering Economist,* vol. XI (Spring, 1966) pp. 1–12.

Gordon, Myron, "The Payoff Period and the Rate of Profit," *Journal of Business* (October 1955), pp. 253–60.

Jean, William H., "On Multiple Rates of Return," *Journal of Finance,* vol. XXIII, no. 1 (March 1968), pp. 187–92.

Levy, Haim, "A Note on the Payback Method," *Journal of Financial and Quantitative Analysis,* vol. III, no. 4 (December 1968), pp. 433–45.

Mao, James C. T., "The Internal Rate of Return as a Ranking Criterion," *Engineering Economist* (Winter 1966), pp. 1–13.

———, "Survey of Capital Budgeting: Theory and Practice," *Journal of Finance,* vol. XXV (May 1970), pp. 349–61.

Meckling, William H., "Relevant Thinking for Investment Decisions," *Management Accounting,* vol. XLVII (February 1966), pp. 8–11.

Näslund, Bertil, "A Model of Capital Budgeting Under Risk," *Journal of Business,* vol. XXXIX, no. 2 (April 1966), pp. 257–72.

Robichek, Alexander A., and Van Horne, James C., "Abandonment Value and Capital Budgeting," *Journal of Finance,* vol. XXII (December 1967), pp. 577–90.

Sarnat, Marshall, and Levy, Haim, "The Relationship of Rules of Thumb to the Internal Rate of Return: A Restatement and Generalization," *Journal of Finance,* vol. XXIV, no. 3 (June 1969), pp. 479–91.

Schwab, Bernhard, and Lusztig, Peter, "A Comparative Analysis of the Net Present Value and the Benefit Cost Ratios Measures of the Economic Desirability of Investment," *Journal of Finance,* vol. XXIV, no. 3 (June 1969), pp. 507–17.

Solomon, Ezra, "The Arithmetic of Capital Budgeting Decisions," *Journal of Business,* vol. XXIX, no. 2 (April 1956), 124–29.

Van Horne, James C., "The Analysis of Uncertainty Resolution in Capital Budgeting for New Products," *Management Science,* vol. 15, no. 8 (April 1969), pp. 376–87.

Weingartner, H. Martin, "Capital Budgeting of Interrelated Projects: Survey and Synthesis," *Management Science,* vol. XII (March 1966), pp. 485–516.

————, "The Excess Present Value Index—A Theoretical Basis and Critique," *Journal of Accounting Research* (Fall 1963), pp. 213–24.

————, "The Generalized Rate of Return," *Journal of Financial and Quantitative Analysis,* vol. IV, no. 3 (September 1969), pp. 1–29.

————, "Some New Views on the Payback Period and Capital Budgeting Decisions," *Management Science,* vol. XV (August 1969), pp. B594–B607.

Books

Ben Shahar, H. and Sarnat, M., *Capital Investment Decisions in Industry* (Jerusalem: Hebrew University Department of Business Administration, 1966).

Bierman, Harold, Jr. and Schmidt, Seymour, *The Capital Budgeting Decision* New York: Macmillan, 1966).

Dean, Joel, *Capital Budgeting* (New York: Columbia Univ. Press, 1951).

Hirshleifer, J., *Investment, Interest and Capital* (Englewood Cliffs, N. J.: Prentice-Hall, 1970).

Hunt, Pearson, *Financial Analysis in Capital Budgeting* (Cambridge, Mass. Harvard Univ. Press, 1964).

Quirin, G. David, *The Capital Budgeting Expenditure Decision* (Homewood, Ill.: Irwin, 1967).

Solomon, Ezra, *The Management of Corporate Capital* (Glencoe, Ill.: Free Press, 1959).

————, *The Theory of Financial Management* (New York: Columbia Univ. Press, 1963).

ANSWERS TO PROBLEMS 9–12

9.   *Method A*   *Method B*

$$\frac{90 \text{ (average profit)}}{600 \text{ (average investment)}} = 15\% \qquad \frac{135 \text{ (average profit)}}{750 \text{ (average investment)}} = 18\%$$

B is therefore the preferable investment.

10. $PV = \sum_{i=1}^{6} \dfrac{CF_i}{(1 + k)^i}$

       $= .952(-1,600.) + .907(300) + .864(700) + .823(825) + .784(1,575)$
       $+ .746(1,300)$

       $= \$2235.72$

11. | Rank | Internal Rate of Return |
|------|-------------------------|
| C | 12% |
| A | 10% |
| B | 8% |

12.

Year	P.V. Factor	A	B
1	.926	$ 27,777	$ 55,554
2	.857	42,865	85,730
3	.794	47,628	51,597
4	.735	47,775	33,075
5	.681	27,224	$225,956
6	.630	18,906	
7	.583	9,336	
		$221,511	
Excess Present Value		$ 41,511	$ 45,956

Project B is the most profitable.

The cost of capital

11

Chapter 10 discussed several difficulties a financial manager encounters when he tries to rank projects in order of their profitability—possible multiple rates of return, the lack of guidelines for selecting discount rates, uncertainty about cash flows, and interdependence among investment projects. Even if all these problems could be resolved, however, one important decision would still remain: Which projects should the firm adopt, and which should it reject? Once the financial manager constructs a schedule of projects ranked according to their profitability, how far down this list should the firm go in appropriating funds for their purchase?

Perhaps the firm should continue to adopt projects until it runs out of funds. But most companies have the option of going to a bank or to the capital market to obtain additional funds. Are these potentially available dollars to be included in the pool of funds that the firm has to invest, or shall only funds generated internally be counted? If borrowed funds are included, how large an amount should be considered to be "available?" Moreover, firms have other uses for their funds than making new investments. They can distribute dividends to shareholders, or they can repay some of their past borrowings. Since the rule that a firm should continue to invest in capital projects until all its available funds are exhausted does not consider these options, it cannot be an appropriate guide for financial managers.

Should the firm simply choose a target rate of return? All projects with a return greater than this target rate can then be adopted, and all those with a lower return rejected. The difficulty with this rule, of course, is that it begs the question we started out to answer, and introduces further problems. How should the target rate be determined? Should it be the average rate that the firm now earns on its assets? Should it be set at a desirable level, such as 30 or 50 percent? Should the rate be a constant or depend on other variables? If the latter, what variables should be considered? Arbitrarily selecting a rate and buying all projects whose return exceeds this rate appears to be an unsatisfactory solution also.

However, there is a third alternative, one which recognizes that the funds invested in various projects have a cost. If a project's return is greater than the cost of the funds needed to finance it, it should be adopted; if the return is not high enough to cover the cost, the project should be rejected. For example, suppose that the investment schedule *II'* in Figure 11.1 was derived by ranking several independent investment projects according to their internal rate of return. All the projects had positive cash flows, so no ambiguity in the ranking occurred. Suppose the cost of the funds needed to finance these projects is k percent. The firm can then invest up to $0A$ amount of money and acquire projects that have a return greater than k.

If the cost of capital were known, it could also be used as the discount rate that is applied to each project's cash flows. Any project whose present value is greater than its purchase price will have a return that is greater than k and should be adopted. Any project whose present value is less than its purchase price will have a return less than k and should be rejected.

In Figure 11.2, alternative investments are ranked according to their ratio of present value to purchase price, the index of profitability described in Chapter 10. Investment outlays equal to $0A$ are needed to finance all the projects with a ratio greater than 1.

Before either of these approaches can be used, however, the cost of capital for the firm must be determined. Some financial theorists suggest that the firm average the cost estimates of different sources of funds

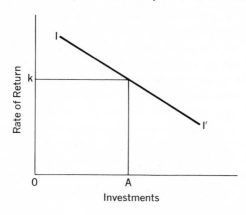

FIGURE 11.1
Investment Schedule of Projects Ordered by Their Internal Rate of Return.

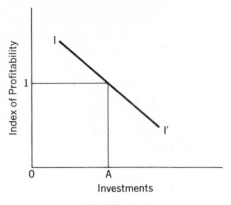

FIGURE 11.2

Investment Schedule of Projects Ordered by Their Index of Profitability.

to obtain a "weighted average cost of capital." There are, however, a number of difficulties in constructing and using such a weighted average. We shall first discuss these difficulties and then go on to develop the beginnings of an alternative framework that can meet the criticisms of this measure.

Formulating the weighted average cost of capital

The cost of any project can be thought of as the opportunity that the firm forgoes to use its resources elsewhere. For example, if a public utility uses its financial resources to build a coal-burning plant in one area, the cost of the plant can be thought of as the opportunity that the utility forgoes to spend those resources on a nuclear plant located elsewhere.

The concept of an *opportunity cost* can be extended to a firm's shareholders as well. The opportunity cost of purchasing a share in a particular company is the rate of return the shareholder forgoes by not putting his funds elsewhere. If management has the shareholders' interests in mind when it makes its investment decisions, it should, theoretically, use this opportunity-cost figure to determine the cutoff point along its investment-opportunity schedule.

While the concept of forgone opportunities, or opportunity costs, is quite precise, it is difficult, if not impossible, to determine these costs exactly. A shareholder has the option not only of investing his funds in the securities of many different companies but of spending his money on consumption goods. Even if the rate of return that a shareholder expected to earn on other investments could be determined, how can

The cost of capital

the satisfaction that he forgoes by giving up consumption expenditures be calculated? The measurement problem is further complicated by the number of shareholders a firm has. The goals and aspirations of different individuals must somehow or other be combined before the financial manager can use the opportunity cost of shareholders as a basis for the firm's investment decisions.

Because of the severe practical problems posed by this approach, another method of determining the cost of capital has been developed. This method rests on the proposition that a firm should earn a sufficiently high rate of return on projects so that its shareholders are no worse off after a project has been adopted than they were before it was adopted. *That rate of return which leaves shareholders indifferent to a project's acceptance or rejection is the value of the firm's cost of capital.*

How are we to measure when shareholders are better or worse off? If we use current corporate profit as the criterion by which to measure the condition of shareholders, then any project that will not lower current profits is acceptable. However, if a steady rate of growth of earnings is the criterion, then any project that lowers this growth rate will make shareholders worse off and should be rejected. These measures, current profits and the rate of growth of earnings, can, and frequently do, produce conflicting results: A project acceptable under one measure is often unacceptable under the other.

A more direct measure of how a shareholder is affected by an investment project is provided by the price of the company's shares. If the return of a project is greater than the firm's cost of capital, shareholders are better off as a result of the firm's having undertaken the project, and the price of the company's shares should appreciate. On the other hand, if the cost of the capital invested in a project is greater than the return generated by the project, shareholders will be worse off as a result of the firm's undertaking the activity, and the price of the company's shares can be expected to decline. *That rate of return on projects which will keep share prices constant is,* therefore, *the firm's cost of capital.*

The problem of measuring a firm's cost of capital in this way is intimately linked to the problem of measuring how shareholders value the companies in which they invest. The relationship between share prices and corporate earnings can be expressed as

$$P = m\pi$$

where P is the price of the company's shares, π is the earnings per share, and m is the multiple that shareholders use to relate current earnings to the price of the stock. In this valuation equation $1/m$, or π/P, is the cost of the capital that shareholders supply to the firm (the cost of equity capital).

If a firm earns $3 per share and the market price of its stock is $30, shareholders can be said to expect a return of 10 percent on their invest-ment. If the firm is in a 50-percent tax bracket, projects that yield a return greater than 20 percent before taxes will be beneficial to the com-pany's shareholders, since they will produce an after-tax return greater than 10 percent. Projects financed by equity capital that earn less than 20 percent before taxes will be detrimental to the shareholders interests, since they yield a return that is less than the firm's cost of equity capital.

However, not all the funds a firm uses to finance its assets come from equity. Some proportion of its assets are financed through debt. Suppose that a firm can borrow money at 6 percent interest, and that these bor-rowed funds do not affect the price of its stock. The cost of debt and the cost of equity can now be combined to obtain the weighted average cost of capital. Thus, if a firm has a capital structure of 40 percent debt and 60 percent equity, the weighted average cost of capital will be:

Weighted average cost of capital
$$= .40 \cdot (\text{cost of debt}) + .60 \cdot (\text{cost of equity})$$
$$= (.40)(.06) + (.60)(.20)$$
$$= .144$$

This measure, the weighted average cost of capital, can be used as the discount rate when projects are ranked according to their index of profitability and as the cutoff point for investment projects when they are ranked according to their internal rate of return.

To summarize, if a financial manager keeps the interest of the firm's shareholders in mind when he makes investment decisions, he will adopt only those projects which yield a return that is greater than the share-holders' funds could earn elsewhere. The concept of an opportunity cost, however, is not operational. Consequently, some financial analysts have modified the concept by suggesting that firms should not invest in projects that will reduce the welfare of their shareholders. If the measure of share-holder welfare is the price of the company's stock, the cost of capital is the rate of return that a project must earn for share prices to remain constant.

The cost of capital is, therefore, intimately linked to the problem of stock-valuation models. One widely used model states that the price of a share of stock is a multiple, m, of its earnings. The cost of equity capital is then equal to $1/m$, or earnings per share divided by the price of the stock.

Since projects are financed by debt as well as equity, the cost of debt must also be considered. If the amount of debt a firm uses does not influence the price of a company's shares, the cost of debt is the interest rate the firm pays for borrowed funds. The weighted average cost of capital is simply the average of the cost of equity and the cost of debt when each component is weighted according to the proportion of debt and equity in the firm's capital structure.

There are three rather obvious difficulties with this formulation of the cost of capital. The first involves the stock-valuation model. Suppose that the price of the shares of a company with a high growth is fifty times its current earnings, while the price of another firm's shares is only ten times its current earnings. Does this mean that the cost of equity of the company with the high growth rate is two percent, while the cost of equity of the other company is 10 percent? Would the shareholders of the first company really be better off if the firm sold new shares (at an alleged cost of two percent) and invested the funds in a six percent government bond? The answer is clearly No. Indeed, the return that the company with the high growth rate must earn on its equity to keep the price of its stock from falling is likely to be higher than the return that the company with the low price-earnings ratio must earn.

The second difficulty has to do with the measurement of the cost of debt. The assumption that changes in the cost of debt do not influence the cost of equity is questionable. In fact, there is substantial theoretical and empirical evidence that the two costs are highly correlated. The valuation model $P = m\pi$ ignores this relationship, since it assumes that the value of m is known and constant. A more sophisticated valuation model would show that the multiple applied to corporate earnings depends on the amount of debt that the firm uses.

The third difficulty involves the relative cost of debt and equity. Ideally, the cost of the two sources at the margin should be equal. After all, if debt were cheaper than equity, firms would maximize their profit by expanding their use of debt and cutting back their use of equity. Conversely, if equity were cheaper than debt, firms would raise funds from equity whenever possible. The weighted-average-cost-of-capital framework ignores the problem of the relative cost of acquiring new funds from different sources.

The failure to take into consideration either the relationship between the cost of debt and the cost of equity or the possibility that different sources of funds will cost different amounts at the margin can be expected to cause severe problems. When the weighted-average-cost-of-capital framework is applied, it may even lead to "wrong" answers.

Computing the weighted average cost of capital

How can the weighted average cost of capital be used? Assume that a company has an opportunity to invest in a project that costs $60. The project can be financed through debt or equity or some combination of the two. The equity can be raised by retaining earnings or floating new shares. Assume further that the company has $1,000 in assets at present and that these assets are financed with $400 in debt bearing 6 percent interest and $600 in equity. The company is in a 50 percent tax bracket, and aggregate profits after taxes are $90. Thirty shares of stock are outstanding; hence earnings per share are $3. The multiple assigned by the market to these earnings is 10, making the price of each share $30.

What rate of return must the $60 investment yield to equal the firm's cost of capital? That is, what rate of return on assets must it earn to keep the price of the stock from falling? Four methods of financing the project are considered below: (1) financing the $60 investment entirely with equity raised throughout the flotation of new shares; (2) financing the project entirely through debt; (3) financing through a combination of debt and equity, and (4) financing the project with funds generated by the operations of the firm itself.

CASE 1—ALL EQUITY, NEW SHARES

The market price of the stock is $30 a share. Ignoring underwriting expenses, the $60 in new equity needed to finance the project can be raised by the flotation of two additional shares. These new shares will bring the total number of shares outstanding to 32.

If the multiple remains 10, for the price of the stock not to fall, earnings per share must remain at $3 and total earnings after taxes must rise from $90 to $96. Profits before taxes must, therefore, rise by $12. The data in column 2 of Table 11.1 show that if interest payments remain at $24, earnings before interest and taxes must rise from $204 to $216, $12 more than they were before the $60 project was undertaken. Thus the rate of return, measured before interest and taxes, that the firm must earn on the new project for the shareholder to be as well off after its adoption as before is 20 percent ($12/60 = .2$). This is equivalent to 10 percent after taxes, or the value given by π/P ($3/30 = .10$).

CASE 2—FLOATING NEW DEBT

Suppose that the firm borrows the $60 it needs to finance the project at the 6 percent interest rate it is currently paying for its outstanding debt. To keep earnings at $3 per share, revenues must rise to meet the added interest payments. Column 3 of Table 11.1 shows that if the firm boosts its revenues to $207.60, or earns 6 percent on the new funds it invests, the earnings per share will remain constant. The cost of debt capital in this illustration, then, is 6 percent.

CASE 3—MAINTAINING THE SAME RATIO OF DEBT TO EQUITY

Suppose that the $60 to finance the new project is raised in such a way that the ratio of debt to equity remains unchanged after the financing. Then 40 percent of the $60, or $24, will be borrowed, and 60 percent, or $36, will be raised from equity. Assuming that fractional shares can

Contrast this finding with the situation when the $60 investment is financed through selling new shares and the investment generates enough earnings to keep the price of the stock constant. When new equity is floated, none of the firm's earnings are needed to finance the investment, and the full $90 in profits can be distributed to the shareholders. The shareholders, however, commit $60 to the venture by purchasing the shares themselves. The change in wealth over the period, for the shareholders, is then:

Ending wealth (32 shares · $30 per share)	$ 960
+ dividends received	90
	$1,050
Less: Cost of newly issued shares	60
+ beginning wealth	900
	$ 960
Equals: Change in wealth over period	$ 90

Here then lies the answer to the paradox of why the required rate of return was greater when new shares were issued than when retained earnings were used. *When new shares were issued, shareholder wealth increased by more than it did when retained earnings were used.* It is apparent, then, that our original formulation of the cost-of-equity problem was not correct. We used share prices alone as a measure of shareholders welfare when we should have cast our net wider and considered both the dividends the shareholders received and the change that took place in the market value of the stock.

To follow this lead, let us assume that the $60 investment yielded a 20 percent return before tax and interest payments. If retained earnings were used to finance the project, total corporate earnings after taxes and interest would rise to $96 and, since the number of shares remained constant at 30, earnings per share would rise to $3.20.

If the multiplier of 10 still holds, share prices will rise to $32. The change in wealth can be readily calculated:

Ending wealth (30 shares · $32 per share)	$960
+ dividends received	30
	$990
Less: Cost of newly issued shares	0
+ beginning wealth	900
	$900
Equals: Change in wealth over period	$ 90

Thus, when the investment yields a 20 percent return before interest and taxes and the multiplier remains constant at 10, shareholder wealth will rise by $90 whether the project is financed through retained earnings or through new shares.

Note also that if no investment had taken place, the firm could have distributed the entire $90 in profits as dividends. If the assets continued to generate profits of $3 per share and the price of the securities remained $30, the wealth of shareholders would have increased by $90. This is the same change that arises when new funds are invested to yield 20 percent. Therefore, for shareholders to be at least as well off after an investment financed with equity as before, the corporation must invest in projects that earn a 20 percent return.

To summarize, the cost of equity raised through retained earnings appears to be less than the cost of equity raised through issuing new stock when shareholder wealth is measured by the price of the company's shares alone. When the concept of wealth is broadened to include both the dividends received during the period and the change in the market value of the company's shares, the cost of equity is the same whether the equity originates from retained earnings or the sale of new shares of stock.

This conclusion, that all forms of equity have the same cost, depends on the assumption that the multiple assigned to the earnings-per-share figure in the valuation equation remains constant. Suppose that the firm invested in a project which did produce a 20 percent return and that the project was financed through internally generated funds. Earnings per share would then rise from $3 to $3.20. If m now rises from 10 to 11, shareholder wealth will rise dramatically. The multiplier could rise if rising earnings lead the market to believe that the company will achieve a higher permanent growth rate of earnings. If m equals 11, the per-share price of the stock becomes $35.20 ($11 \cdot \$3.20$), and the total value of the firm rises to $1,056 ($30 \cdot \$35.20$), an increase of $156 over its original value of $900. When the $30 in dividends are added to this figure, the increase in total shareholder wealth over the period is $186. If the multiple is not a constant, then, but depends on the change in per-share earnings that results from the new investments, shareholders are not likely to be indifferent to the method of equity financing. They will definitely prefer expansion through retained earnings.

In the example presented above, a project financed by debt needed to return only 6 percent for shareholders to be as well off after the investment is made as before. When the same investment was financed by equity, it had to return 20 percent. Why is the cost of debt less than the cost of equity?

Surely, if debt cost less than equity, firms would use debt rather than equity to finance any expansion of assets. Over time, we would expect to find that the ratio of debt to equity in most corporations had risen.

There is, however, no empirical evidence of such a development. Obviously, we have overlooked something in our analysis.

We have assumed, up to now, that the out-of-pocket interest costs are the entire cost of debt. Suppose, however, that a change in the ratio of debt to equity has an impact on the valuation equation itself as well as on earnings. For example, suppose that the multiple m, which the market assigns to a company's earnings is a function of the ratio of liability to equity, L/E, and that b_0 and b_1 are parameters of the equation

$$m = b_0 - b_1 L/E$$

If this is the case, then changes in the debt-equity ratio will not only raise interest costs but lower share prices.

The reason an increase in the ratio of debt to equity may lead to a lower multiple and lower share prices is that *as the ratio of debt to equity rises, the income stream that accrues to shareholders becomes more variable.* For example, suppose a company reports earnings before interest and taxes of $10, $20, and $30 in three periods. If the firm pays $2 in interest charges and is in a 50-percent tax bracket, its earnings after taxes for these three periods will be $4, $9, and $14. Suppose, now, that the firm substitutes debt for equity, so that its interest payments rise to $6. Before-tax earnings are now $4, $14, and $24, and after-tax earnings are $2, $7, and $12. The average after-tax return over the three years is $9 in the first case, and the range of the reported returns (the maximum amount by which they differ) is $10; the average earnings in the second case are only $7, although the range is again $10. The variation of the return, compared to its average value, is, therefore, higher when more debt is used. Since large variation in returns are usually undesirable, the market will assign a lower multiple to the earnings of a company that is financed largely with debt, other things being equal, than to one that is financed more heavily with equity.

"Increased variability of return" is not the only reason m may fall as the ratio of debt to equity rises. Shareholders know that lenders look upon a firm's equity as providing the ultimate protection in the event of default. If the equity base is relatively small, any major shrinkage in the value of the firm's assets will leave lenders unprotected. Hence, they are reluctant to advance additional funds to firms that, in their eyes, have inadequate equity. With their sources of funds thus restricted, the ability of a firm to take advantage of new investment opportunities is more limited.

Suppose that the value of b_0 in the equation $m = b_0 - b_1 L/E$ is 12.4 and that the value of b_1 is 3.6. If the $60 project is financed with debt, what rate of return must be earned for shareholders to be as well off after the investment is made as they were before?

Before the new project was undertaken, the ratio of debt to equity was 400/600, and the value of the multiplier was:

$$m = 12.4 - 3.6(400/600)$$
$$= 12.4 - 2.4$$
$$= 10$$

After the investment, the multiplier will fall to:

$$m = 12.4 - 3.6(460/600)$$
$$= 12.4 - 2.7$$
$$= 9.7$$

If $P = m\pi$, then, to keep share prices at $30, earnings per share must rise to approximately $3.14 ($9.7 \cdot \$3.14 = \$30$). The income statement of the company will then be as follows:

Earnings before interest and taxes	$216.00
Less interest	27.60
Earnings before taxes	$188.40
Less taxes	94.20
Earnings after taxes	$ 94.20
Memo:	
Number of shares	30
Earnings per share	$ 3.14

Before the $60 investment was made, earnings were $204. (See Table 11.1) If the multiplier is a function of the debt-equity ratio, earnings must rise to $216, an increase of $12. These values imply that the cost of debt is 20 percent ($12/60 = .2$).

What happens to the wealth of the shareholders if the firm adopts a $60 project that does yield 20 percent and finances it entirely with debt sold to third parties? The data below show that wealth will rise by $90.

Ending wealth (30 shares · $30 price)		$900
+ dividends received		90
		$990
Less:	Value of debt instruments	0
	+ beginning wealth	900
		$900
Equals:	Change in wealth over the period	$ 90

This is precisely the same increase that resulted when an equity issue was floated and the multiple applied to earnings was constant at 10.

The cost of capital

If the $60 in debt is sold to the present shareholders, the change in wealth will still be $90:

Ending wealth (30 shares · $30 price)	$ 900
+ bonds held	60
+ dividends received	90
	$1,050
Less: Value of debt instruments	$ 60
+ beginning wealth	900
	$ 960
Equals: Change in wealth over the period	$ 90

The finding in this example, that the cost of debt is 20 percent, obviously depends on the values of the parameters b_0 and b_1 and the valuation equation used. Clearly, if these values were different, the cost of debt would be more or less than 20 percent. The analysis demonstrates, however, that the answer to the question of what is the cost of funds depends on the particular model used to express share prices and the relationships that are posited between the variables.

To summarize, the cost of debt is less than the cost of equity if (1) the valuation equation $P = m\pi$ is used, (2) the interest rate is less than $1/m$, and (3) m is not functionally related to either the interest rate or the firm's capital structure.

If debt were in fact cheaper than equity, corporate financial officers could be expected to move toward raising their ratio of debt to equity. That there is little evidence of such a movement indicates that debt is not a cheaper source of funds.

If a corporation's debt ratio is one determinant of m, that is, if the debt-equity ratio is included in the valuation equation, changes in debt may lower the market price of the company's shares. As a consequence, the cost of debt, from the shareholder's point of view, is not simply the interest rate the firm pays for funds. Rather, the effect of the change in the price of the stock must also be included in calculating the cost of debt.

Summary

We began this chapter by looking for a way to determine the value of the cost of capital, which then could be used as the cutoff point for investment projects or as the discount rate in calculating the present value of the cash flows of projects under consideration. We discussed the weighted average cost of capital as a measure of this value and found it wanting. The underlying reason for this failure was that the weighted average cost of capital did not consider the firm as a financial system whose parts are interrelated. Rather, it considered each component of the firm's financial structure as independent.

As our analysis of the weighted average cost progressed, it became obvious that the cost of retained earnings could not be measured without giving consideration to the dividends that the corporation could pay. Moreover, if the multiplier applied to the firm's per-share earnings is related to the growth rate of per-share earnings, then the cost of retained earnings may not be the same as the cost of equity raised through new stock flotations. Since equity raised through retained earnings does not increase the number of shares outstanding, projects financed internally can lead to higher per-share growth rates than projects financed by issuing new shares. It also became evident from the analysis that the cost of debt could not be discussed meaningfully without considering how share prices are determined. For if the multiple in the valuation equation is linked to the debt-equity ratio, then the price of the company's securities depends on the method of the financing used.

Where do these remarks lead us?

First, the valuation equation $P = m\pi$ is incomplete. The multiple m is not a constant; it depends on a number of factors such as the growth rate of the company's earnings and the method of financing employed. Moreover, the dividends that a company pays must also be incorporated in the analysis to capture fully the change in the shareholders' wealth that will occur as a result of the corporation's activities.

Second, the choice of financing, the growth of earnings, and the level of dividends that the firm will pay are all affected by the attractiveness of the company's investment opportunities. If a project has a high rate of return, perhaps it can be financed with new equity, even though this will lower the per-share growth rate. Or, perhaps it can be financed with debt, even though this will lower the multiplier applied to the firm's earnings. In short, a full system of equations that describe the firm must be developed and all parameters specified before the cost of capital can be determined.

Questions for discussion and problems

1. Why is it important for a firm to determine a cutoff point along its investment-opportunity schedule? What are the consequences of choosing too high or too low a value?

2. If the concept of opportunity costs is nonoperational, or at least difficult to apply in practice, why has it not been abandoned?

3. Why is the stock-valuation equation a firm uses critical in determining the cost of equity?

4. The weighted-average-cost-of-capital concept uses both the cost of equity and the cost of debt as inputs. If a firm is not publicly traded

and its shares do not have a market price, can the concept still be used in decision-making?

5. Why do funds generated by retained earnings appear "free" when the weighted-average-cost-of-capital approach is used?

6. A firm can generate funds from depreciation charges as well as profits. What is the cost of funds generated in this way?

7. In calculating the weighted average cost of capital, many financial theorists recommend that a "package" of instruments, i.e., both debt and equity, be sold. If this is done, the ratio of debt to equity will be the same both before and after the new investment project is undertaken. What is the logic behind this approach?

8. Why must dividend payments be included in the analysis in order to calculate a firm's cost of capital?

9. What complications arise in calculating the cost of equity if the multiplier applied to corporate earnings depends on the firm's debt-equity ratio?

[*Answers to problems 10–13 follow references and suggested readings.*]

10. Elliston Manufacturing Company has assets of $1,600, which are financed with $520 of debt and $1,080 of equity. The firm's total profits after taxes for the year just ended were $135. It pays 8 percent interest on borrowed funds and is in the 50-percent tax bracket. It has 90 shares of stock outstanding, selling at a market price of $12 per share.
    (a) What is Elliston's stock valuation multiplier?
    (b) What is its weighted average cost of capital?

11. Magna Corporation presently has $5,000 of debt, on which it pays 8 percent interest, and $15,000 in equity. It has 1,000 shares of common stock outstanding at the current price of $24 per share. Magna pays 50 percent of its income in taxes. The most recent profits after taxes figure was $2,400.

    The firm has chosen to finance a new $1,800 project entirely through the sale of additional shares of stock to current stockholders, with no underwriting cost involved. Its goal is to maintain earnings per share of $2.40. What is the project's required rate of return?

12. Magna Corporation, described in problem 11, changes its mind and decides to finance its new $1,800 project completely from retained earnings. This amount would be subtracted from the firm's most recent profits after taxes and would be unavailable for distribution as dividends to stockholders. Evaluate the change in shareholder wealth under this method of financing, assuming that the project has a 20 percent rate of return, that the stock-valuation multiple remains constant at 10, and that Magna's cost of debt remains the same.

13. A firm has assets of $168,000, financed with a total debt of $56,000, and equity of $112,000. Its common stock is presently valued at $36 a share. The values of $b_0 = 10.2$ and $b_1 = 2.4$ are currently being used to compute the firm's stock-valuation multiplier, $m = b_0 - b_1(L/E)$. A $14,000 project is being contemplated that would be financed entirely with additional debt. If the project is undertaken, how much must earnings per share increase to maintain the current price per share of the common stock?

REFERENCES AND SUGGESTED READINGS

Articles

Baxter, Nevins D., "Leverage, Risk of Ruin and the Cost of Capital," *Journal of Finance*, vol. XXII, no. 3 (September 1967), pp. 395–404.

Baumol, W., and Malkiel, B., "The Firm's Optimal Debt-Equity Combination and the Cost of Capital," *Quarterly Journal of Economics* (November 1967), pp. 547–78.

Ben-Shahar, Haim, "The Capital Structure and the Cost of Capital: A Suggested Exposition," *Journal of Finance*, vol. XXIII, no. 4 (September 1968), pp. 639–53.

Boness, A. James, "A Pedagogic Note on the Cost of Capital," *Journal of Finance*, vol. XIX, no. 1 (March 1964), pp. 96–106:

Bower, Richard S., "Leverage and the Cost of Capital," *Engineering Economist*, vol. X, no. 2 (Winter 1965), pp. 15–36.

Brewer, D. E., and Michaelson, J., "The Cost of Capital, Corporation Finance, and the Theory of Investment: Comment," *American Economic Review*, vol. LV (June 1965), pp. 516–24.

Brigham, Eugene F., and Gordon, Myron, "Leverage, Dividend Policy, and the Cost of Capital," *Journal of Finance*, vol. XXIII, no. 1 (March 1968), pp. 85–103.

Durand, David, "The Cost of Debt and Equity Funds for Business," in Ezra Solomon, ed., *The Management of Corporate Capital* (Glencoe, Ill.: Free Press, 1959), pp. 91–116.

Johnson, Robert W., "An Integration of Cost Capital Theories," in *Fourth Summer Symposium of the Engineering Economy Division of the American Society for Engineering Education* (1966), pp. 11–17.

Lerner, Eugene M., and Carleton, Willard T., "Financing Decisions of the Firm," *Journal of Finance*, vol. XXI, no. 2 (May 1966), pp. 202–14.

————, "The Integration of Capital Budgeting and Stock Valuation," *American Economic Review*, vol. LIV (September 1964), pp. 683–702.

Lintner, John, "The Cost of Capital and Optimal Financing of Corporate Growth," *Journal of Finance*, vol. XVIII, no. 2 (May 1963), pp. 292–310.

Miller, Merton, and Modigliani, Franco, "The Cost of Capital to the Electric Utility Industry," *American Economic Review*, vol. LVI (June 1966), pp. 333–91.

Modigliani, Franco, and Miller, Merton, "The Cost of Capital, Corporation Finance, and the Theory of Investment," *American Economic Review*, vol. XLVIII (June 1958), pp. 261–97.

Robichek, Alexander A., "Problems in the Theory of Optimal Capital Structure," *Journal of Financial and Quantitative Analysis*, vol. I (June 1966), pp. 1–35.

Robichek, Alexander A., and McDonald, John G., "The Cost of Capital Concept: Potential Use and Misuse," *Financial Executive,* vol. 33 (June 1965), pp. 2–8.

Vickers, Douglas, "Elasticity of Capital Supply, Monopsonistic Discrimination, and Optimum Capital Structure," *Journal of Finance,* vol. XXII, no. 1 (March 1967), pp. 1–10.

———, "The Cost of Capital and the Structure of the Firm," *Journal of Finance,* vol. XXV, no. 1 (March 1970), pp. 35–47.

Weston, J. Fred, "A Test of Cost of Capital Proportions," *Southern Economic Journal,* vol. XXX (October 1963), pp. 105–12.

Wippern, Ronald F., "Financial Structure and the Value of the Firm," *Journal of Finance,* vol. XXI, no. 4 (December 1966), pp. 615–34.

———, "A Note on the Equivalent Risk Class Assumption," *Engineering Economist,* vol. XI (Spring 1966), pp. 13–32.

Books

Barges, Alexander, *The Effect of Capital Structure on the Cost of Capital* (Englewood Cliffs, N. J.: Prentice-Hall, 1963).

Gordon, Myron J., *The Investment, Financing and Valuation of the Corporation* (Homewood, Ill.: Irwin, 1962).

Lerner, Eugene M., and Carleton, Willard T., *A Theory of Financial Analysis* (New York: Harcourt Brace Jovanovich, 1966).

Robichek, Alexander A., and Meyers, Stuart C., *Optimal Financing Decisions* (Englewood Cliffs, N. J.: Prentice-Hall, 1965).

Vickers, Douglas, *The Theory of the Firm: Production, Capital and Finance* (New York: McGraw-Hill, 1968).

ANSWERS TO PROBLEMS 10–13

10. (a) Earnings per share $= \$135/90 = \$1.50$

$P = m$ (earnings per share)
$12 = m(1.50)$
$m = 8$

(b) Since m is 8, $\frac{1}{m}$ is 12.5% and the cost of equity before taxes is 25 percent.

Since the proportion of debt and equity is .325 and .675, respectively, then:
Weighted average cost of capital $= .325(.08) + .675(.25)$
$= .195$

11.

	Original Position	Floating New Shares
EBIT	$5,200	$5,560
Interest	400	400
PBT	4,800	5,160
Taxes	2,400	2,580
PAT	2,400	2,580
Memo:		
Number of shares	1,000	1,075
Earnings per share	$2.40	$2.40
Change in EBIT	—	$360
Required Return on $1,800 investment	—	20%

Questions for discussion and problems **245**

12. $\dfrac{\$2,580 \text{ (profits after taxes)}}{1,000 \text{ (shares)}} = \$2.58$

$10(\$2.58)(\text{price per share}) = \$25.80$

Ending wealth (1,000 shares) · ($25.80 per share)	$25,800
+ dividends received	600
	$26,400
Less new shares purchased	0
+ beginning wealth	$24,000
Change in wealth over the period	$ 2,400

13. Before investment,

$m = 10.2 - 2.4(\tfrac{5.6}{11.2})$

$m = 9.0$

$\$36 = 9(x)$

$x = \$4.$

After investment,

$m = 10.2 - 2.4(\tfrac{7.0}{11.2})$

$m = 8.7$

$\$36 = 8.7(x)$

$x = \$4.138, \text{ or } \$4.14$

Hence, earnings per share must increase to $4.14.

The cost of capital and its application to a regulated public utility

12

Before a financial manager can estimate his firm's average cost of capital, a measure described in the last chapter, he must first determine the cost of the funds raised through debt and through equity. How these two costs are determined depends on the stock-valuation model he uses.

In this chapter, a valuation model will be developed that brings together the firm's dividend-payout rate, the price-earnings ratio, a discount rate, and the corporation's growth rate. Such a model is used by public-utility regulators to help them decide the rate of return on assets a public utility should earn.

Any single-equation model used to describe the relationship among a number of variables has inherent defects. The model that will be presented here is no exception, even though it is widely used in financial circles and by regulatory bodies. The critical defect of single-equation models is that the linkages which exist among the variables in the equation are not specified. Before this defect can be overcome, a more powerful framework must be fashioned, one which captures the strategic relationships that characterize the entire system under consideration.

Earnings models once again

The valuation equation $P = m\pi$ was introduced in Chapter 11. P was defined as the price of a company's shares, π as the earnings per share, and m as the multiple that is applied to the earnings to bring both sides of the equation into equality.

What is the rationalization for such an expression? What assumptions lie behind the view that the price of a share of stock is a linear function of the company's earnings? Why, for example, was the expression

$$P = m\pi^2$$

or

$$P = m\pi^3$$

not postulated as the valuation equation?

Again, it is helpful to use an example. Suppose that the earnings per share of a company are expected to be $3 per year for an indefinite period. If the shareholder discounts these earnings at a rate of 10 percent, what will be the price of the security? In other words, how much will investors be willing to pay for the security?

The answer can be found by taking the sum of the terms

(12–1) $$P = \frac{\pi}{(1 + k)} + \frac{\pi}{(1 + k)^2} + \cdots + \frac{\pi}{(1 + k)^n}$$

where $\pi = \$3$ and $k = .10$.

To find the sum of this infinite series, we multiply both sides of equation 12–1 by $1 + k$:

(12–2) $$P(1 + k) = \pi + \frac{\pi}{(1 + k)} + \cdots + \frac{\pi}{(1 + k)^{n-1}}$$

Subtracting equation 12–1 from equation 12–2 yields:

(12–3) $$P(1 + k) - P = \pi + \left[\frac{\pi}{(1 + k)} - \frac{\pi}{(1 + k)} \right] + \cdots$$

$$+ \left[\frac{\pi}{(1 + k)^{n-1}} - \frac{\pi}{(1 + k)^{n-1}} \right] - \frac{\pi}{(1 + k)^n}$$

Note that all the terms on the right-hand side of equation 12–3 disappear, except for two: the first term, π, and the last $\pi/(1 + k)^n$. If n is large, i.e., if we are considering an indefinitely long period, the term $\pi/(1 + k)^n$ will approach zero and can be disregarded. Dropping this term, we have:

$$P + Pk - P = \pi$$
$$Pk = \pi$$

and

(12–4) $$P = \frac{\pi}{k}$$

If $\pi = \$3$ and $k = .10$, the price of the security is $30. Had shareholders used a lower discount rate, say 5 percent, the value of the future stream of earnings would be $60.

$$P = \frac{\$3}{.05} = \$60$$

The expression $P = \pi/k$ can also be written $P = m\pi$, where $m = 1/k$.

The stock-price model $P = m\pi$, then, is based on nothing more than the concept of the present value of a future stream of earnings. To develop this expression, three assumptions were made. The first is that k, the discount rate applied to the future earnings of the firm, will remain constant in the future. The second is that the company's earnings will remain constant in all future periods. The third assumption is that the shareholders receive the earnings that are generated. Probably, all three assumptions are unwarranted.

The discount rate is likely to change as the corporation's activities change or as the investment alternatives for the corporation's shareholders elsewhere in the economy change. The earnings of most companies change over time. Moreover, the shareholder does not receive in cash all the earnings a company generates. He receives only a portion of these earnings in dividends. The undistributed earnings are reinvested in the company and will, it is hoped, give rise to higher earnings in the future. For example, suppose that a company earns $3 a share and distributes two-thirds of its earnings, or $2, in dividends. The remaining $1 will be retained and reinvested, leading to a rise in earnings and dividends in future years. The question that we must now ask is, Can a valuation model be constructed that incorporates both current dividends and the expected growth in dividends through time?

Dividend models

To come to grips with the problem of both dividend payments and growth, let us define the price of a security as the present value of future stream of dividends, where the dividends are expected to grow at a steady rate of g percent per annum and are discounted at k percent. Thus,

12-5) $$P = \frac{D}{(1 + k)} + \frac{D(1 + g)}{(1 + k)^2} + \frac{D(1 + g)^2}{(1 + k)^3} + \cdots + \frac{D(1 + g)^{n-1}}{(1 + k)^n}$$

where D is the dividends the shareholder receives, g is the expected growth rate, and k is the discount rate. The solution to this equation is readily found by multiplying both sides by $(1 + k)/(1 + g)$:

12-6) $$\frac{P(1 + k)}{(1 + g)} = \frac{D}{(1 + g)} + \frac{D}{(1 + k)} + \frac{D(1 + g)}{(1 + k)^2} + \cdots + \frac{D(1 + g)^{n-2}}{(1 + k)^{n-1}}$$

Dividend models

Subtracting equation 12–5 from equation 12–6 yields:

$$(12\text{–}7) \quad \frac{P(1+k)}{(1+g)} - P = \frac{D}{(1+g)} + \left[\frac{D}{(1+k)} - \frac{D}{(1+k)}\right] + \cdots - \frac{D(1+g)^{n-1}}{(1+k)^n}$$

Again, all the terms on the right-hand side of the equation disappear, with the exception of two: $D/(1+g)$ and $D(1+g)^{n-1}/(1+k)^n$.

Consider the last term. If g is greater than k, then the price of the stock given by equation 12–5 rapidly approaches infinity. This is unreasonable; no security sells at an infinite price. *The relationship between the growth rate and the discount rate must be such that k is always greater than g.* If a company is expected to grow at a steady rate of 5 percent per annum, the discount rate that shareholders apply to the firm's growing stream of revenues must be greater than 5 percent. When k is greater than g, however, and n is large (i.e., as the time under consideration becomes long), the term

$$\frac{D(1+g)^{n-1}}{(1+k)^n}$$

approaches zero. Setting this term equal to zero yields:

$$\frac{P(1+k) - P(1+g)}{(1+g)} = \frac{D}{(1+g)}$$

$$P + Pk - P - Pg = D$$

$$(12\text{–}8) \qquad\qquad\qquad P = \frac{D}{k - g}$$

To apply this expression to security valuation, suppose that dividends are $2, the expected growth rate is .033 percent per annum, and a 10 percent discount rate is applied to the growing stream of dividends. The price of the security will then be:

$$P = \frac{\$2.00}{(.10 - .033)} = \frac{\$2.00}{.066} = \$30.30$$

If the expected growth rate rises to 6 percent, the price of the security will be:

$$P = \frac{\$2.00}{(.10 - .06)} = \frac{\$2.00}{.04} = \$50.00$$

Similarly, if the dividend increases to $2.50, while k and g remain constant at 10 and 6 percent respectively, the price of the security will rise to $62.50.

Dividends plus capital gains

The dividend model above assumed that the shareholder's return is given by the stream of dividends he receives as long as he holds the stock. However, many people buy a security with the intention not of keeping it indefinitely but of reselling it at a later date to realize a capital gain. Is not a more realistic valuation equation, then, one that states that the price an investor is willing to pay for a security is the present value of both the dividends he expects to receive and the price he expects to get when he sells it?

Suppose an investor expects to sell the security at a price of P_1 one year from now. The price he is prepared to pay today would then be given by:

$$12\text{-}9) \qquad P_0 = \frac{D_1}{(1+k)} + \frac{P_1}{(1+k)}$$

This valuation equation can be shown to be equivalent to equation 12-8. The critical problem in equation 12-9 is determining the price of the security one year from now. It is reasonable to expect that, one year from now, prospective investors will try to estimate the future growth of the stream of dividends they will receive, much the same as they do today. Suppose, then, that the price of a security one year from now is the present value of the future stream of dividends from that time forward. That is,

$$12\text{-}10) \qquad P_1 = \frac{D_2}{(1+k)^1} + \frac{D_2(1+g)}{(1+k)^2} + \cdots + \frac{D_2(1+g)^{n-1}}{(1+k)^n}$$

Note that D_2, the dividend that will be paid a year from now, is simply $D_1(1+g)$. Hence we can write:

$$12\text{-}11) \qquad P_1 = \frac{D_1(1+g)}{(1+k)} + \frac{D_1(1+g)^2}{(1+k)^2} + \cdots + \frac{D_1(1+g)^n}{(1+k)^n}$$

Substituting the right-hand side of equation 12-11 for P_1 in equation 12-9 gives us:

$$12\text{-}12) \qquad P_0 = \frac{D_1}{(1+k)^1} + \frac{D_1(1+g)}{(1+k)^2} + \cdots + \frac{D_1(1+g)^n}{(1+k)^{n+1}}$$

Equation 12-12, however, is identical to equation 12-5, which led directly to the valuation equation:

$$P = \frac{D}{k-g}$$

We have discussed three valuation equations, all based on the present value of a future stream of revenues. The first model stated that the price of a share of stock was equal to the present value of a future stream of stable earnings; the second, that it was equal to the present value of a growing stream of dividends; and the third, that it was equal to the present value of the future dividends and future resale price of the security.

When the original earnings model was used to describe stock prices, the cost of equity capital was given by the expression π/P. The difficulties associated with this measure were described in Chapter 11. One problem was that the model seemed to suggest that if a company's earnings grew rapidly and the market price of its shares was high relative to its current earnings, the company's cost of capital was low. How is this difficulty overcome by using equation 12–8, $P = D/(k - g)$?

The cost of capital in the dividend model

The valuation equation $P = D/(k - g)$ can be rewritten as:

$$Pk - Pg = D$$
$$Pk = D + gP$$
$$k = \frac{D}{P} + g$$

Thus k, the discount rate used in the share-price model, can be thought of as having two components: the current dividend yield and the expected growth rate. In the example used in the last section, the dividend yield was $\$2.00/\$30.30 = .066$, and the expected growth rate was .033. The return that a shareholder receives is the sum of these two terms, or 10 percent.

The expression $k = D/P + g$ can also be rewritten to show the relationship between the price of the company's stock and its earnings. The dividends a company pays can be thought of as the product of two things, the payout rate and earnings. Thus,

$$\text{Dividends} = \text{payout rate} \cdot \text{earnings}$$

Substituting the right-hand side of this equation in the valuation equation, we have

$$k = \frac{\text{payout rate} \cdot \text{earnings}}{P} + g$$

(12–13)
$$k = \frac{\text{payout rate}}{P/\pi} + g$$

where π is the earnings per share.

Using the data in our example, earnings per share are $3, the payout rate is two-thirds of earnings, the price-earnings ratio is 10, and the expected growth rate is .033. Thus,

$$k = \frac{.666}{10} + .033$$

$$= .10$$

the value we found above.

Consider equation 12–13. A firm's cost of capital falls as the price-earnings ratio rises (the result we found when the earnings model was used). However, it rises as the expected growth rate rises and as the dividend-payout ratio increases, a fact that was not apparent before.

An analysis based on equation 12–13 was used in a recent regulatory hearing to determine the rate of return that a major public utility should be permitted to earn on its assets. A witness, citing a number of Supreme Court rulings, argued that the utility should be permitted to earn a rate of return on its assets equal to its cost of capital, for this rate would enable the firm to continue to attract funds, grow, and provide needed services. If the regulatory commission granted a return that was less than this amount, he asserted, the firm would not be competitive in the capital market.

The witness went on to suggest a way of finding what the firm's cost of capital was. Using the valuation model presented in equation 12–13, he argued that reasonable men expected the utility under discussion to grow at a 5-percent rate. The firm's current price-earnings ratio was 18, and its payout rate was .65. Based on these facts, he recommended that the company be permitted to earn an 8.6 percent rate of return on their assets, since

$$k = \frac{.65}{18} + .05$$

$$= .086$$

What can be said about this formulation of the cost of capital, and how appropriate were the witness's remarks? The first and most obvious question raised by the model is, How is g determined? How did the witness know that "reasonable men" expected the firm's dividends to continue to grow at a 5-percent rate?

Several methods of arriving at this 5-percent growth-rate figure were offered. First, the company's past record could be examined, and the historic growth rate projected forward. However, dividend growth rates are notoriously unstable. Dividends frequently rise abruptly to a new level and then remain at this plateau or increase slowly until a new breakthrough in profits occurs. The projections therefore depend greatly on the choice of the base year.

A second method of finding the expected growth rate is to poll informed people about their expectations as to the company's future. Security analysts who make their living analyzing the relative attractiveness of different utility stocks may be considered to constitute such an informed group, and their opinions on this matter could be taken as the basis for determining what reasonable men believe.

Still a third method of estimating the growth prospects of the company would be to study the demand-and-supply conditions in the various markets that the company serves and prepare estimates of what progress it is likely to make in each. An easy way of doing this is to use the estimates that the management of the firm prepares for itself. These estimates, however, may be biased by the enthusiasm of management about its own ability.

Even if the expected value of g were determined to the satisfaction of all, however, a second difficulty with the model would remain because the relationships that exist among the variables in the equation have not been fully specified. For example, in the testimony submitted in the utility case, k was given as .086 and g as .05. Suppose that reasonable men had expected the growth rate to be 10 percent instead of 5 percent. Is it reasonable then to expect the payout rate to remain .65 and P/π to remain 18? That is, should the rate of return that the company can earn on its assets be allowed to rise to 13.6 percent, if this is the value of k?

$$k = \frac{\text{payout}}{P/\pi} + g$$

$$= \frac{.65}{18} + .10$$

$$= .136$$

The answer, most assuredly, is No, for there is a relationship between g and P/π that has not been captured by the model. For example, suppose that the relationship between the growth rate and P/π is given by the function:

$$P/\pi = 10 + 160g$$

Then, if the expected growth rate is zero, P/π will be 10; and if, as in the rate case, g is given as 5 percent, P/π will be 18. If the expected growth rate now changes to 10 percent, P/π rises to 26. The cost of capital is then given by:

$$k = \frac{.66}{26} + .10$$

$$= .025 + .10$$

$$= .125$$

This value is substantially less than 13.6 percent, the value suggested when the relationship between P/π and g was ignored.

Still other functional relationships link the variables in the stock-valuation model. For example, there is a relationship between the expected growth rate and the dividend-payout function. Presumably, if a company has the opportunity to invest in projects that will enable it to grow rapidly, it will retain a larger share of its earnings to finance this growth than if it did not have these opportunities. Other things being equal, the higher the firm's expected growth rate is, the lower its dividend-payout ratio will be. Similarly, there may be a relationship between the firm's use of debt and its growth rate. If the firm has a number of attractive investment opportunities, it may finance the projects with debt. Hence companies with high growth rates may have a higher ratio of debt to equity than companies that are not growing as rapidly. Until all the relationships that link the variables in the valuation equation are specified, the model for determining the cost of capital is incomplete.

A third criticism leveled at this model is that it ignores the problem of variability in the growth rate. Yet, it seems reasonable to believe that a firm's cost of capital will be higher if it is in a high-risk industry than if it is in a low-risk one. There are several ways in which the problem of variability in the growth rate, can be handled. All the techniques lead to a higher value for k in highly variable industries and a lower value in industries with a more stable pattern of growth. For example, suppose that the P/π ratio depends on both the growth rate, g, itself, and variations in the growth rate. Thus:

$$P/\pi = a_0 + a_1(g) - a_2 \, Var(g)$$

where $Var(g)$ is a measure of the variability of the growth rate and a_0, a_1 and a_2 are parameters. If this equation accurately reflects the marketplace in which shares are traded, a firm in a highly variable industry will have a lower P/π ratio than one with the same growth rate that operates in a more stable industry. As a consequence, the ratio of the dividend-payout rate to P/π will be higher for the more volatile firm. Thus for a given value of g, the firm with the more variable growth rate will have a higher cost of capital; i.e., the value of k will be larger for such a firm.

A second alternative for handling variability is not to alter the cost-of-capital measure at all, but to allow for the uncertainty of the returns of specific projects in constructing the firm's investment opportunity schedule. (One method of lowering the present value of a project's cash flows when returns are unstable was described in Chapter 10.) The cost of capital can then be treated as a minimum that the returns on projects must exceed. Once the returns of all the projects are adjusted for variability, they can all be evaluated using the same cost-of-capital figure.

The cost of capital in the dividend model

To summarize, an equation can be developed for the cost of capital that reflects both the dividends a company pays and its expected growth rate. Thus,

$$k = \frac{D}{P} + g$$

The dividends a firm pays can be broken down into a payout rate and an earnings-per-share figure. The value of k can then be written as:

$$k = \frac{\text{payout rate}}{P / \pi} + g$$

While this formula for estimating the cost of capital is very popular it is not without defects. For one thing, it is difficult to estimate a company's growth rate. Another, more serious criticism is that not all relationships are fully specified. There is, for example, a relationship between the price-earnings ratio and the expected growth rate and between the dividend-payout rate and the growth rate. Both these relationships must be considered before the cost of capital can be determined. Furthermore, until these relationships are specified, the effect of a change in growth on the cost of capital cannot be determined. A third criticism involves the variability of the growth rate. Shareholders will tend to apply a higher value of k to the returns of a firm in a volatile industry than to the returns of one in a stable industry. A financial manager using this framework to select investment projects can proceed in two ways: He can use a high value of k to discount the returns of projects when they are variable, or he can adjust the returns of each project for variability and use the same value of k throughout.

These remarks have an important implication for the weighted-average-cost-of-capital framework described in Chapter 11. If the cost of equity is considered to be $D/P + g$ and g depends on the amount of debt the firm uses to finance projects, then the cost of debt cannot be considered to be independent of the cost of equity. Rather, the cost of both debt and equity must be found simultaneously.

If this is true, then a framework different from the one outlined above may be more appropriate for determining the optimum volume of capital expenditures for a firm. To sketch out such a framework, let us return to the problem of permissible rates of return for public utilities.

The accounting model

Much of the data-collecting done by regulatory agencies to help them assess the rate of return requirements of a utility is motivated by two accounting equations. The first states:

(12–14)
$$R = O + (V - D)r$$

where R is the total return, O is the operating costs, $(V - D)r$ is a return-to-capital measure in which r is the rate of return, V is the original value of the plant and equipment, and D is accumulated depreciation.

This model suggests a *mark-up-over-cost* framework, in which the regulatory agency lets the firm charge prices that allow it to cover operating costs and obtain a return on the *rate base, V − D*. The size of the rate base is determined by the cost of the company's physical facilities. The critical question, therefore, is, How large should the allowable rate of return be?

The second equation, which recognizes that the return is distributed to bondholders and shareholders, is:

(12–15)
$$r(V - D) = iL + kE$$

where i is the interest rate that is actually paid on liabilities, L, that the company has incurred and k is the return earned on equity, E. The variables i, L, and E are readily determined from financial statements. Some of the strategies for finding k, and the limitations of these methods, were discussed in the last section. If k were known, however, all the terms on the right-hand side of the equation would be known, and the rate of return that the company should earn on its rate base to satisfy this model could easily be calculated.

These two accounting equations, however, do not give the regulatory agency all the data it needs to determine the rate of return. This is because the choice of a rate of return has repercussions that go beyond accounting relationships. The rate that is selected may enable the firm to generate the funds it needs to combine resources more efficiently, or it may allow inefficient production processes to be continued. It may lead to windfall gains by shareholders or frustrate their legitimate expectations. It may encourage the growth of communities serviced by the utility or impose so high a cost on these areas that their future growth is limited.

A framework must therefore be constructed that goes behind the accounting equations to economic processes. Let us assume that the regulators know the level of output the utility must achieve each year for the next several years to meet the forecast requirements of the community it serves. We shall also assume that the regulatory commission wants the utility to sell its output at the lowest price consistent with the constraints that bind the firm. Prices higher than this level will force the community to spend too much for the utility's services; prices lower than this level violate economic constraints.

Given that the regulators know the state of affairs they wish to see realized, rational decision-making procedures require them to develop information about the functional relationships that characterize the firm. From the viewpoint of the information requirements of the regulators, the accounting framework has several deficiencies:

(1) The accounting equations do not explicitly incorporate all the major variables that are of interest to the regulatory commission. For example, the level of output, both now and in the future, does not appear as a formal target variable in the equations. Because of this omission, there is a real risk that the commission, by basing the price at which services are sold on the rate of return alone, may unknowingly fix the output of some services at undesirable levels.

(2) The variables in the accounting identities are related to one another in ways other than those made explicit in the equations. For example, the interest rate, i, is linked to the proportion of debt in the capital structure; as the proportion of debt increases, the rate of interest that the utility must pay for the funds it borrows increases. Operating costs, O, are a function of the level of output, Q, which in turn is one component of the total revenue function. In general, then, there is a systematic relationship among events in the utility and between the utility and its environment that are not reflected by the accounting framework.

(3) There is no decision technology for choosing among alternative states of affairs. Whenever a regulator chooses a certain level of revenues, a certain price, a certain rate of return, or a certain capital structure, that choice will have effects on the environment of the firm as well as on the firm itself. Some of the effects will occur in the current period, others will occur in future periods. In choosing one rate of return over another, the regulator is, in effect, choosing one rather complex state of affairs over another. However, the accounting framework does not allow him to predict or evaluate the state of affairs that will result from a decision.

Given these deficiencies of the accounting framework for decision-making, is there another way for the regulatory agency to proceed? The underlying problem is to ensure that the utility produces a level of services that is equal to or exceeds the minimum requirements of the community at the lowest possible price.

Considerations in developing a model

To build a model that can handle this problem, the regulator must specify the constraints that bind the firm and estimate the value of the parameters that affect each constraint. The information needed to do this may be difficult to obtain because of the interdependencies between the variables. In addition, the constraints themselves, the value of the parameters, and the actual output of the utility can change as a. result of technological developments. The extent to which it is practical to obtain information therefore depends in large part on the value of the data.

When a regulator knows his output preferences and the functional relationships that constitute the utility, he can make decisions with respect to the variables directly within his control that will enable the firm to achieve the goals that have been set. The functional relationships that describe the aspects of the firm we are interested in, and the ways in which the various parts of the system interact, are described below.

THE DEMAND CURVE

The demand curve of a utility is usually highly elastic with respect to income and highly inelastic with respect to price. This means that, as income increases through time, the consumption of the utility's service will increase. The demand curve will shift to the right, as in Figure 12.1. However, changes in prices will not effectively curtail or boost demand. To raise its output, the utility must expand its plant or change its production function.

THE PRODUCTION FUNCTION

The production function links the utility's output to inputs such as labor and materials. In Figure 12.2, the production function, holding

FIGURE 12.1
Demand Curves.

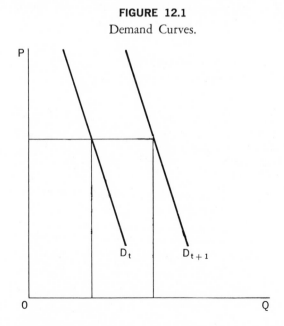

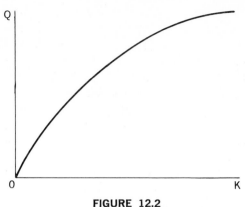

FIGURE 12.2
The Production Function.

labor and materials constant, shows diminishing returns with respect to capital. By this we mean that additional increments of capital tend to raise output, but at an ever-decreasing rate. Like those of the demand curve, the parameters of the production function are empirically determined. If the function drawn were a straight line through the origin, it would indicate constant returns to scale; a concave upward function would indicate increasing returns to scale.

Let us now combine Figures 12.1 and 12.2. We assume that the production function is stable through time, but that the utility's demand curve shifts upward because of a change in income (note the left-hand side of Figure 12.3). If the price of the utility's services remains fixed at

FIGURE 12.3
The Production Function and the Demand Curves for a Utility.

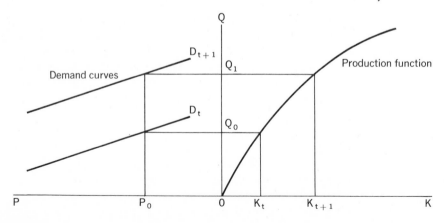

The cost of capital and its application to a regulated public utility

P_0, the demand for them will rise from Q_0 to Q_1. To achieve this much of an increase in output, capital must increase from K_t to K_{t+1}. The question then becomes, Can this volume of capital be financed by the utility if it continues to charge a price of P_0?

Since the demand for the utility's output is price inelastic at any moment in time, a rise in price will not discourage the demand for the product. However, if the price increase granted by the regulatory agency is too large, the public will be paying to support a larger volume of output than it requires; in this sense, it will be overpaying for the utility's services. If the price increase authorized is too small, the firm will be unable to finance the stock of capital needed to raise output to the new level demanded by the community. The public interest will not be served, and the shareholders will not be compensated.

What must be uncovered, then, is the linkage that exists between the prices a utility charges for the services it sells and the volume of funds that will be available to finance its plant and equipment outlays.

Prices and available funds

The funds a corporation uses to pay dividends to shareholders, and to expand plant and equipment can be realized through either current operations or borrowings. The volume of funds generated internally depends on the firm's gross revenues, cost of operations, and past financing decisions. The production function of a public utility is such that fixed interest payments and overhead charges constitute a high percentage of the firm's total outlays. Once revenues are large enough to cover these fixed charges, an increasing proportion of each additional dollar of revenues can be used for new equipment outlays and dividend payments. The function linking the prices a utility charges and the funds it generates internally therefore rises steadily and is concave upward.

The volume of funds a utility can borrow from outside lenders will also increase as the prices it charges rise. This is because the volume of funds a firm can borrow from outside lenders depends on the interest rate it is prepared to pay and the size and stability of the revenue stream it generates. The higher the rate of interest the firm is prepared to pay, the greater the volume of funds it can raise, and the more money it earns, the more interest it can afford to pay. The larger and the more stable the flow of internally generated funds, therefore, the greater the volume of funds that the firm can secure from outside lenders, since the chance of loss to those who advance credit to the utility declines. Because of these considerations, the function linking the funds a utility can raise from internal and external sources to the prices it can charge

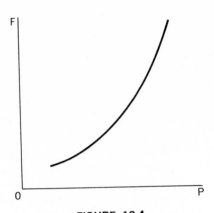

FIGURE 12.4

The Supply of Funds Schedule.

for its output rises at an increasing rate if other things remain constant.[1]
Figure 12.4 shows this relationship.

Suppose we now combine the analysis of the output needs of the community (Figure 12.1), the production function (Figure 12.2), and the funds available to the utility (Figure 12.4) in a single graph, as in Figure 12.5. The demand curve is located in quadrant II. To focus directly on the increment to output needed to meet the increase in demand and the additional plant required to produce it, we shall ignore the existing output and capacity of the utility. The additional output needed for the next period is Q'. The production function in quadrant I shows the increment of capital needed to produce the additional output. The financial relationship that links the increase in the corporation's available funds to the price it charges is shown in quadrant III. Finally, the transform in quadrant IV relates the funds generated by the corporation to the increments of capital needed to produce additional output. The slope of the transform will be determined by the price of capital goods.[2]

To illustrate how the framework of analysis presented in Figure 12.5 is used, suppose that the demand curve facing the utility is completely inelastic in the relevant range. The regulator can then determine the minimum price that the public must pay for the level of service it requires.

[1] A more complete model would show that funds depend on the price, output, outside borrowings, L, and outside parameters, O. Thus, $F = f(P,Q,L,O)$. Outside borrowings in turn depend on the interest rate, i, price, quantity, and the variability of revenues, v. Thus, $L = l(P,Q,i,v)$. Substituting in the two equations, we find that $F = h(P,Q,i,v,O)$. Thus, the other things that are equal are Q, i, v, and O.

[2] To be strictly accurate, we should note that the funds transform also includes the labor and materials costs associated with the new physical capital. Thus, if one new machine costs $100, and using it requires $50 in labor and $50 in material, the funds transform will show that $200 must be raised if a new machine is purchased.

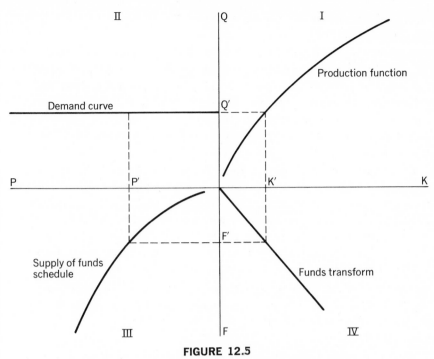

FIGURE 12.5

A Systems Approach to Public Utility Financing.

Thus, if Q' is the minimum desirable level of output, P' is the price that will generate this level of output. For P' will generate a quantity of funds, F', which is the amount needed to purchase the increment of physical capital, K', necessary to sustain an output of Q'. Of course, a change in interest rates may shift the available-funds schedule, and a change in the production function will alter the relationship between output and capital. When this happens, the price needed to ensure the desired level of output will also change. Once the economic constraints that bind the utility are incorporated into the analysis, mathematical models can be developed that will aid the decision-making process of the regulator.

Regulatory implications

The analysis above sketched the functions that link the firm's physical output to its financial resources. Several comments are now in order.

(1) Determining the parameters of the functions described is the first task of the regulatory body. To secure this information is not easy: changes in technology, for example, will change the production function;

changes in money-market conditions will bring about shifts in the finance function, and so forth.

(2) The performance of the public utility is properly measured by its total impact on the community it serves. The relevant parameters for the regulatory commission are thus the utility's physical output and the prices the public pays for the services received. Alternative measures, such as the ratio of one financial flow to another, may lead to ambiguous empirical results since any particular ratio can be achieved in more than one way.

(3) One regulatory goal is to find the lowest price the utility can charge that will be consistent with its ability to meet the output requirements imposed on it through time. Once this goal is adopted, achieving it becomes a technical problem, in which the objective function, or goal, is to minimize the cost of the utility's services to the public and the constraints are the relationships that link the various facets of the firm.

(4) If a framework such as that described above were adopted, it would transfer the locus of decision-making information from an accounting or a legal framework to an economic one, and the degree to which the goals set by the regulatory agency were being met could be monitored more effectively.

(5) This framework can be readily extended to apply to a firm that makes many different products. To make this extension, however, we would have to develop information about the parameters of each product's demand, production, and supply-of-inputs schedules and specify the relationships between them.

To summarize, by adopting a systems approach, a regulatory agency can determine the rate of return a public utility needs to be able to produce the quality and quantity of services the community requires. However, it must be able to develop estimates of the funds that will be required to purchase the capital needed to produce the amount of goods and services the community wants. These funds can originate from both internal and external sources. That rate of return which allows a level of revenues consistent with the growth of output the community desires and the production function of the utility is the appropriate target return.

Summary

In this chapter, valuation models were developed to find the cost of capital that a firm could apply to its investment schedule. Several models were constructed that brought together in a single equation the relationships between dividends, growth, and price-earning ratios. However, no single-equation model can capture all the relationships that exist between these variables; a more complex model is required.

To indicate the dimensions of a full financial model, the perspective of a regulatory commission charged with setting prices for a public utility was adopted. It was shown that by combining the demand curves, the production function, and the supply-of-funds schedule, revenue decisions could be made that would lead to an output level consistent with the public interest.

The task of developing the data required to make such a systems model operational is severe. However, the difficult problems discussed in the systems framework will not be resolved by adopting a simpler approach, just ignored.

Questions for discussion and problems

1. Several valuation models were presented in this chapter that make use of the present-value framework. Is it a valid procedure to consider a security as an asset that generates a stream of cash and the price of the stock as the present value of this flow?

2. If both an earnings model and a dividend model are based on the present-value framework of analysis, in what sense can one be said to be better than the other?

3. Three men are discussing the question of the cost of capital. One says that if the price of the company's stock rises, the cost of capital falls, since $D/P + g$ will be reduced. The second says that the value of k will rise because the reason P rose is that g rose, and the rise in g will be greater than the decline in D/P. The third claims that the cost of capital is determined outside the firm. Changes in g will therefore offset exactly the decline in D/P.
Which of the three positions, if any, is correct?

4. Why are public-utility commissions concerned with the cost of a utility's capital? Why are corporate executives interested in the topic?

5. What is the rationale for going beyond accounting identities in public-utility rate-making hearings?

6. Can the model described in Figure 12.5 be applied to a nonregulated corporation? What problems arise in applying it? What alternatives to this model are open to the financial officer of the firm?

[Answers to problems 7–11 follow references and suggested readings.]

7. Figstrom Candlestick Company has current per share earnings of $4.72 and a cost of capital of .0775. What is the present value of Figstrom's future stream of earnings?

8. Monstrose Corporation has been paying a $3.28 dividend per share and expects to grow at a rate of 3 percent each year. If the best return that can be earned on funds elsewhere is 7 percent, what will investors be willing to pay for its shares?

9. An investment analyst is evaluating a list of securities and is eliminating from further consideration all firms with discount rates (k) below 8 percent. Which of the following will escape elimination?

Firm	Available Information
A	Share price, $20; total shares outstanding, 10,000; last-period earnings, $40,000; last-period dividends, $10,000; expected growth rate, 4 percent.
B	Price-earnings ratio, 8; last-period earnings $200,000; last-period dividends $48,000; expected growth rate, 3 percent.
C	Last-period total dividends, $37,500; total market value of outstanding shares, $937,500; expected growth rate, .035.
D	Last-period total dividends, $96,000; total shares outstanding, 30,000; price per share, $80; expected growth rate, .05.
E	Expected growth rate, 4 percent; last-period earnings per share, $3.40; share price, $34; last-period dividends per share, $2.04.

10. The $26.25 price per share of Crocker Plate Glass Corporation's common stock is 15 times its most recent per-share earnings. The firm's investors expect a return of 8.25 percent on their money.
   (a) If the firm's per share dividend is $1.05, what is Crocker's projected rate of growth?
   (b) If Crocker's growth-rate projection is increased by .0075 and its discount-rate, dividend, and earnings-per-share figures remain stable, how much will the price of its stock change?

11. A regulated firm has annual operating expenses of $425,000. It pays .095 in interest on liabilities of $6.8 million and has a cost of equity capital of .085. It has total assets of $15 million and equity of $8.2 million. Using the accounting model presented in this chapter, calculate the operating revenues required by the firm.

REFERENCES AND SUGGESTED READINGS

Articles

Averch, Harvey, and Johnson, Leland, "Behavior of the Firm Under Regulatory Constraints," *American Economic Review,* vol. LII (December 1962), pp. 1052–69.

Benishay, Haskel, "Variability in Earnings Price Ratios of Corporate Equities," *American Economic Review,* vol. LI (March 1969), pp. 81–94.

Bosland, Chelcie C., "The Valuation of Public Utility Enterprises by the Securities and Exchange Commission," *Journal of Finance,* vol. XVI (March 1961), pp. 52–64.

Brigham, Eugene F., and Pappas, James L., "Duration of Growth, Change in Growth Rates, and Corporate Share Prices," *Financial Analysts Journal* (May–June 1966), pp. 157–162.

Brigham, Eugene, and Gordon, Myron J., "Leverage, Dividend Policy, and the Cost of Capital," *Journal of Finance,* vol. XXIII (March 1968), pp. 85–103.

Crockett, Jean, and Friend, Irwin, "Capital Budgeting and Stock Valuation," *American Economic Review,* vol. LVII (March 1967), pp. 214–20.

Friend, Irwin, and Puckett, Marshall, "Dividends and Stock Prices," *American Economic Review,* vol. LIV (September 1964), pp. 656–82.

Gordon, Myron J., "The Rate of Return AT&T Should Be Allowed to Earn," FCC Docket No. 16,258, Federal Communications Commission, 1967.

———, "Rate of Return on Equity Capital Under Regulation," in Harry M. Trebing and R. Hayden Howard, eds., *Rate of Return Under Regulation* (East Lansing, Mich.: Institute of Public Utilities, Michigan State Univ. Graduate School of Business Administration, 1969), pp. 195–204.

Holt, Charles C., "The Influence of Growth Duration on Share Prices," *Journal of Finance,* vol. XVII (September 1962), pp. 465–75.

Lerner, Eugene M., "Capital Budgeting and Financial Management," in Alexander A. Robichek, ed., *Financial Research and Managerial Decisions* (New York: Wiley, 1967), pp. 72–89.

Lerner, Eugene M., and Moag, Joseph S., "Toward an Improved Decision Framework for Public Utility Regulation," *Land Economics,* vol. XLIV, no. 3 (August 1968), pp. 403–09.

———, "Information Requirements for Regulatory Decisions," in Harry M. Trebing and R. Hayden Howard eds., *Rate of Return Under Regulation* (East Lansing, Mich.: Institute of Public Utilities, Michigan State Univ. Graduate School of Business Administration, 1969), pp. 195–204.

Lintner, John, "Optional Dividends and Corporate Growth Under Uncertainty," *Quarterly Journal of Economics,* vol. LXXXVIII (February, 1964), pp. 49–95.

Miller, Merton, and Modigliani, Franco, "Dividend Policy Growth, and the Valuation of Shares," *Journal of Business,* vol. XXIV (October 1961), pp. 411–33.

Modigliani, Franco, and Miller, Merton, "The Cost of Capital, Corporation Finance, and The Theory of Investment," *American Economic Review* (June 1958) pp. 261–97.

Morton, Walter A., "Rate of Return and the Value of Money in Public Utilities," *Land Economics,* vol. 28, no. 2 (May, 1952), pp. 91–131.

Porterfield, James T. S., "Dividends, Dilution and Delusion," *Harvard Business Review,* vol. 37 (November–December 1959), pp. 156–61.

Wendt, Paul F., "Current Growth Stock Valuation Models," *Financial Analysts Journal,* vol. XXXIII (March–April 1965), pp. 3–15.

Books

Bonbright, James C., *Principles of Public Utilities Rates* (New York: Columbia Univ. Press, 1969).

Gordon, Myron J., *The Investment, Financing and Valuation of the Corporation* (Homewood, Ill.: Irwin, 1962).

Questions for discussion and problems

Phillips, Charles F., Jr., *The Economics of Regulation* (Homewood, Ill.: Irwin, 1969).

Ulmer, Melville J., *Capital in Transportation, Communications and Public Utilities: Its Formation and Financing* Princeton: Princeton Univ. Press for National Bureau of Economic Research, 1960).

Walter, James E., *Dividend Policy and Enterprise Valuation* (Belmont, Calif.: Wadsworth, 1967).

ANSWERS TO PROBLEMS 7–11

7. $P = \dfrac{\pi}{k} = \dfrac{4.72}{.0775} = \$60.90$

8. $P = \dfrac{D}{k - g} = \dfrac{3.28}{(.07 - .03)} = \dfrac{3.28}{.04} = \$82.00$ per share

9. $k_A = .05 + .04\ \ = .09$
    $k_B = .03 + .03\ \ = .06$
    $k_C = .04 + .035 = .075$
    $k_D = .04 + .05\ \ = .09$
    $k_E = .06 + .04\ \ = .10$
    A, D, and E are not eliminated.

10. (a) Earnings per share $= \$26.25/15 = \$1.75$
    Payout rate $= \$1.05/\$1.75 = .60$

    $.0825 = \dfrac{.60}{15} + g$

    $.0825 = .04 + g$
    $.0425 = g$

    (b) $.0425 + .0075 = .05$

    $P = \dfrac{D}{k - g} = \dfrac{1.05}{(.0825 - .05)} = \dfrac{1.05}{.0325} = \$32.30$

    The price of the stock will rise by $6.05.

11. $r(V - D) = iL + kE$
    $ = .095(6,800,000) + .085(8,200,000)$
    $ = \$646,000 + \$697,000$
    $ = \$1,343,000$
    $R = \$425,000 + 1,343,000$
    $ = \$1,768,000$

Capital budgeting
under constraints

13

In the last chapter, we sketched a model designed to help a utility structure its planning with respect to both the dollar outlays it should commit to new investment projects and the price it should charge the public for its services. The model was operational because both the goals of the firm and the constraints binding it were specified. The assumed goal of the utility was to minimize the cost of its services to the public. Four constraints limited its actions:

(1) a requirement that it produce a level of output adequate to meet the community's needs,

(2) a production function that linked the change in the quantity of services produced by the utility to the amount of capital it invested,

(3) a unique relationship between the prices it charged for its services and the funds it generated, and

(4) a set of prices for the capital goods it purchased.

The analysis of the public-utility model demonstrated an approach that these firms could take to solve the problem we have been grappling with since Chapter 10: how a firm can determine how much money to spend on investment projects and which projects to adopt.

Can an approach similar to that proposed for utilities be used by a firm in the competitive sector of the economy? Some will argue that a public utility differs from a profit-maximizing firm in several important respects, and that an analytical framework usable by firms in one sector of the economy will not work for those in another. Is it reasonable to assume that competitive firms, too, wish to minimize the prices they charge for their products or that they must produce an output greater than some specified target level?

Arguments about the differences between a regulated public utility and a firm that operates in the competitive sector of the economy ignore the most important property of the framework of analysis presented in Chapter 12. The reason this framework represents an advance in thinking is that it structures the capital-budgeting problem in a particular way: It requires the financial manager to recognize both an objective function and a set of constraints. A competitive corporation's objective function may differ from that of a public utility, as may the constraints binding it. However, the point to emphasize is not the differences in these functions from firm to firm, but simply that all companies planning investment expenditures must specify an objective function and a set of constraints.

This, then, is the framework we shall adopt in this chapter and the next. We shall discuss four capital-budgeting models. The two covered in this chapter have a common objective function—to maximize the present value of the cash flows of different projects. They differ, however, in the set of constraints they recognize. The two models in Chapter 14 have a different objective function, involving dividend payments. Again, the constraints specified for each of these models are different.

The four models vary in sophistication. All four, however, illustrate a systems approach to capital budgeting, and all four use the technology of linear programming. Before these models are actually discussed, however, it will be helpful to first point out some of the common assumptions that lie behind them and to illustrate the effect that different constraints can have on the decisions that a corporation will make.

A fixed-capital constraint

Suppose a firm has only a limited amount of funds—say $10,000—to spend on various projects. The returns and costs of four pieces of equipment are presented in Table 13.1. If only one of each machine can be

TABLE 13.1
Potential Investment Opportunities

Machine	Cost	Internal Rate of Return
1	$6,000	30%
2	5,000	26
3	5,000	24
4	4,000	10

purchased, which should the firm buy? How should it allocate its $10,000 among these potential investments to earn as high a rate of return as possible?

Suppose that the company first purchases machine 1 because it has the highest internal rate of return. With only $4,000 left, the firm will have to forgo machines 2 and 3, each of which cost $5,000, and can purchase only machine 4. The firm's average return on its total investment in machines 1 and 4 will be 22 percent:

$$\text{Average rate of return} = (.6)(.30) + (.4)(.1)$$
$$= .22$$

The firm could follow another strategy, however, and bypass machine 1. It would then have enough funds to purchase 2 and 3. Its return on investment, under this strategy, would be 25 percent, 3 percent more than under the first strategy.

Determining which investments to make and which to reject to earn the highest rate of return was easy in this example. Not all finance problems, however, are so trivial. It is therefore worthwhile to spend some time analyzing the structure and solution of this simple problem.

First, note that the capital-investment question was cast in a technical format. It was stated as a problem of maximizing returns subject to the constraint of limited resources. The scarce resources (dollars) were to be distributed among alternative investments to achieve a particular goal— a maximum rate of return on the entire $10,000. The problem was not one of choosing goals. We did not ask whether it was desirable for the firm to try to maximize its average rate of return or whether it should set some other goal, such as a large market share. Nor was the problem one of discovering whether all the firm's alternatives were included in the model. We took the four purchase options as given and did not search for another investment that might yield 30 percent and cost $10,000. Both these problems, setting goals for the firm and establishing the range of options, are important problems of corporate management. They are not, however, part of the technical problem posed here.

Second, the problem that was posed can be divided into a statement of the objective and a statement of the constraints. This is the classical format for decision problems; readily available mathematical procedures, or algorithms, can be used to find the solution to problems set up this way.

Not all business problems will fit this technical economic format. Policy questions, for example, can seldom be decided in this way. A different methodology is also needed to solve social, political, and legal problems. For example, how to handle employee grievances concerning work rules is a recurring business problem whose resolution depends on principles that are more legal than economic. Still other business problems, such

A fixed-capital constraint

as motivating employees and improving job performance, may be solved by applying sociological or psychological principles.

Third, it is important to stress that the rational solution to the technical economic problem of maximizing some function subject to constraints frequently conflicts with the intuitive solution. In the example, the highest rate of return on the firm's total investment was achieved by rejecting the investment with the highest return and selecting the next two options. (This result arose because of the integer and budget constraints. The firm could not purchase part of a machine, nor could it buy more than one of each. If it purchased machines 1 and 2, it would exceed its budget. Whether the constraints are considered really binding or merely guidelines for management is a matter of company policy and is not at issue here.)

These three remarks can be made more specific by considering a somewhat more complex capital-budgeting problem.

Model 1—the Lorie-Savage problem

Imagine a company with a number of divisions, whose policy concerning investment decisions is to place a fixed amount of funds at the disposal of each divisional manager. Each manager can allocate the funds he is given among the various investment alternatives he has as he sees fit.

Suppose that a manager can develop several projects that require cash outlays in more than one period. For example, one project may be a new building, which would be under construction for two years. Under these conditions, which of the acceptable projects should the divisional manager undertake, and which should he reject?

This two-period capital-budgeting problem was first posed by Lorie and Savage.[1] To make their analysis more concrete, they assumed that a manager had nine potential projects which he could undertake and that his budget was $50 in the first year and $20 in the second. The present value of the nine projects and the outlays required for each are given in Table 13.2. The question Lorie and Savage wanted to answer was, Which of the nine projects should the firm adopt to maximize the present value of all the cash flows generated by the various projects?

In Table 13.2, the present value of an investment is b_j; thus, the present value of the first project, b_1, is $14. The present value of the outlay for project 1 in year 1, $c_{1,1}$, is $12. The present value of the outlay for project 9 in year 2, $c_{9,2}$, is $3, and so forth.

One way to select the set of projects whose present value is a maximum but whose total outlays in each period satisfy the budget constraint is to proceed by trial and error. Suppose we do so. Project 5 has the highest

[1] J. Lorie and L. J. Savage, "Three Problems in Capital Rationing," *Journal of Business,* vol. XXVIII, no. 4 (October 1955) pp. 229–39.

Capital budgeting under constraints

present value, $40. If the firm adopted this project, it would have to spend $30 in period 1 and $35 in period 2. This is not a feasible option, since the firm has only $20 to spend in the second period. Suppose, then, that the firm turns to the project with the next highest present value. This would be either project 2 or 3. Project 2, however, is also not feasible; it requires a $54 outlay in the first period, when the firm has only $50 to spend. Project 3 is feasible, and if it is adopted, the firm will have $44 left over in the first period and $14 in the second. The next most attractive project can now be considered, and so on until the available funds are exhausted.

TABLE 13.2
Nine Hypothetical Investment Projects

Investment	Present Value of Investment (b_j)	Present Value of Outlay in Period 1 $(c_{1,j})$	Present Value of Outlay in Period 2 $(c_{2,j})$
1	$14	$12	$ 3
2	17	54	7
3	17	6	6
4	15	6	2
5	40	30	35
6	12	6	3
7	14	48	4
8	10	36	3
9	12	18	3

Present value of budget ceilings: $C_1 = 50, $C_2 = 20

Such a trial-and-error method is clearly inefficient. The calculations involved in allocating a fixed amount of dollars in two time periods among a large number of projects by this method are so intractable that it is more efficient to use a formal mathematical technique, that of linear programming, to find a solution.

Linear programming is a mathematical technique for finding the optimum solution to problems structured in a specific way. It is beyond the scope of this text to describe the computational procedures involved in linear programming.[2] Financial managers are, however, concerned with structuring capital-budgeting problems in such a way that this technique can be used. The problem of selecting the set of projects whose present value is a maximum but whose total outlays in each period satisfy the

---

[2] Clear statements of these procedures can be found in W. Alan Spivey, *Linear Programming: An Introduction* (New York: Macmillan, 1963) and Saul Gass, *Linear Programming* (New York: McGraw-Hill, 1964).

budget constraint could be structured as follows:

$$\text{Maximize: } \sum_{j=1}^{9} b_j x_j$$

$$\text{Subject to: } \sum_{j=1}^{9} c_{tj} x_j \leq C_t$$

$$0 \leq x_j \leq 1$$

where x_j is the fraction of the jth project undertaken.

This particular formulation of the Lorie-Savage problem was first presented by Weingartner.[3] The first equation is a statement of the *objective function*. In this problem, the objective is to find the nine x_j values that make the sum of the known present-value figures for each project, b_j, a maximum. The second and third equations are the constraints that bind the divisional manager. The first constraint is that the outlays on the projects that are adopted in each of the two years cannot exceed the amount of money the division has to spend in that period, C_t. The second constraint states that no more than one of each project can be purchased ($x_j \leq 1$) and that the percent of each project that is purchased cannot be negative ($0 \leq x_j$).

The complete mathematical formulation of this problem and its solution are presented below. The maximum present value of the nine projects is $70.27. This result is achieved by adopting projects 1, 3, 4, and 9 in full and portions of projects 6 and 7.

Linear-programming model and solution to the Lorie-Savage problem:

Maximize:

$14x_1 + 17x_2 + 17x_3 + 15x_4 + 40x_5 + 12x_6 + 14x_7 + 10x_8 + 12x_9$

Subject to:

$12x_1 + 54x_2 + 6x_3 + 6x_4 + 30x_5 + 6x_6 + 48x_7 + 36x_8 + 18x_9 + S_1 = 50$

$3x_1 + 7x_2 + 6x_3 + 2x_4 + 35x_5 + 6x_6 + 4x_7 + 3x_8 + 3x_9 + S_2 = 20$

$x_1 + q_1 = 1$	$x_4 + q_4 = 1$	$x_7 + q_7 = 1$
$x_2 + q_2 = 1$	$x_5 + q_5 = 1$	$x_8 + q_8 = 1$
$x_3 + q_3 = 1$	$x_6 + q_6 = 1$	$x_9 + q_9 = 1$

Solution:

$x_1 = 1.0$	$x_4 = 1.0$	$x_7 = .045$
$x_2 = 0$	$x_5 = 0$	$x_8 = 0$
$x_3 = 1.0$	$x_6 = .970$	$x_9 = 1.0$

Total present value: $70.27

Shadow prices: $P_1 = .136$ \quad $P_2 = 1.864$

[3] H. Martin Weingartner, *Mathematical Programming and the Analysis of Capital Budgeting Problems* (Englewood Cliffs, N. J.: Prentice-Hall, 1962).

Several comments on this solution are in order. First, in practice, a firm cannot invest in a fraction of project. It cannot buy 97 percent of one machine or 4.5 percent of another. The technical problem of adopting fractional projects can be overcome by using integer programming, which does not assume that projects are divisible and therefore does not permit the adoption of fractional projects.

Second managers are often less interested in the specific answer to linear-programming problems than they are in the general character of the results. Thus, a manager looking at the solution above might think it prudent to purchase projects 1, 3, 4, 6, and 9 and ignore project 7. To do this he would have to spend only $48 in the first year and $17 in the second. Not only would he be able to stay within his budget, he would have a margin of protection should any of the estimates with respect to the cost of specific projects turn out to be too low.

Finally, the linear-programming solution yields other data of interest to the firm. It also tells how much the firm would be prepared to pay for another dollar of cash in each period. For example, if it had $51 in period 1 rather than $50, the present value of all the projects adopted would rise by $.136; obviously, the firm would be willing to pay up to this amount in interest for another dollar. If another dollar were available in period 2, that is, if the firm had $21 instead of $20, the present value of the portfolio would increase by $1.86. These values, which are called the *shadow prices* of the constraints in each period, are obviously important. They not only suggest how much interest management would be prepared to pay in order to have another dollar to spend in each period, but they force management to reconsider how binding the constraints under which they operate really are. In this example, the firm's financial manager is likely to begin to ask himself, Can I shift some funds from period 1 to period 2? or Can I raise additional funds, particularly in period 2, so I can invest in additional projects?

To summarize, Lorie and Savage posed a practical capital-budgeting problem: A divisional manager is given a fixed sum of money each year and must allocate these funds among a large number of projects, all of which require cash outlays in more than one period. The choice of projects to be adopted in the first year thus depends on the amount of funds that will be available both in the current year and in the future. The solution to this problem (almost unsolvable by trial and error) is relatively straightforward, once it is recognized as a two-period linear-programming situation.

The Lorie and Savage problem raises a number of important issues. First, the example assumed that the present value of the nine projects under consideration was known. This implies that the divisional manager knew what cost-of-capital figure to use to discount the cash flows generated by each project. Where did he get this figure? Some clue is given by the linear-programming solution to the problem itself. Note that the shadow price indicates the contribution to the objective function (maximization of the projects' total present value) that another dollar would make if it were available. This is very close to the concept of the opportunity cost of capital. This value, in turn, is the discount rate firms should use in evaluating the cash flows of different projects. In the example, the shadow prices were $0.136 in the first period and $1.86 in the second period. Are these values then the firm's cost of capital?

Weingartner[4] has shown that these were in fact the values used in the example to calculate b_j and c_{tj}. However, there is one difficulty with considering these values as the firm's cost of capital. If more dollars were available in either period, the shadow prices (or the opportunity cost of funds) would change. But if the cost of capital changes as the amount of funds available changes, the discount rate that is applied to both the cash inflows and cash outflows must change. The c_{tj} values of the constraint set and the b_j values of the objective function then change also. This means that the values the linear-programming model takes as given are no longer constant, but vary with the amount of money available to the firm.

This criticism, that the values in both the objective function and the constraint set depend on the amount of funds the firm happens to have available, is so serious that it calls into question the validity of structuring this particular capital-budgeting problem in this way. Indeed, it is apparent that under capital rationing the concept of present value itself has no meaning. How, then, are we to proceed? Before facing this question directly, it will be useful to experiment with a different constraint than the availability of funds.

Model 2—a profit-planning model

The investment projects firms adopt will, of course, have an impact on the financial statements they give their stockholders. In determining which projects to adopt and which to reject, it is not unreasonable for a financial manager to consider the explicit impact of each project on the profit figures the firm will report in the years ahead.[5]

Assume that the firm has prepared estimates of the cash flow of various projects and that it has determined a cost-of-capital figure which it uses to discount these flows. The problem the financial manager then faces is to select from the firm's set of investment opportunities the projects

[4] *Op. cit.*, p. 27.
[5] This model was discussed by Eugene M. Lerner and Alfred Rappaport in "Limit DCF in Cash Budgeting," *Harvard Business Review* (September–October 1968), pp. 133–40.

that will both maximize the firm's net present value and generate profits subject to the constraint that profits follow a specified growth pattern through time.

The objective function in this capital-budgeting problem, then, is to select the projects that yield a maximum total return over the cost of the funds that the firm has committed to them. When the excess present value of all the projects is maximized, the return to the firm's shareholders will be at a peak. The logic of the profit constraint is equally apparent. If the firm reports rising earnings through time and the firm's shareholders attribute this to careful planning by management, the price of the firm's stock is likely to appreciate.

As an example, we shall first select a set of projects without paying any attention to the profit constraint. We shall then bring the constraint into the analysis and contrast the results in each case.

Suppose a firm has the opportunity to invest in fifteen different projects. These projects will require cash outlays of varying amounts over the next several years, and they have varying economic, or useful, lifetimes. The estimated cash flows associated with each of the fifteen capital projects are presented in Table 13.3.

Suppose, further, that the company releases a formal profit projection for the next five years. The estimated contributions to profit associated with each of the investment projects over the planning period are given in Table 13.4. The firm's present level of profits is $70, and if it makes no additional investments, the financial manager has estimated that its profits for the next five years will be $100, $95, $90, $90, and $80, respectively.

The estimated annual income (Table 13.4) and cash flows (Table 13.3) of the projects are not identical. Project 1, for example, had a cash outflow of $239 in year 1, but its contribution to profits (negative) was a loss of $20. The divergence between the two series is due to the use of the accrual accounting techniques in measuring profits and losses. To show how these differences in income and cash flows arise, detailed financial statements for the first project are presented in Table 13.5.

HE PROJECTS ADOPTED

If the firm discounts the cash flows generated by the fifteen projects at 20 percent, the present value of each project's net cash flows, PV_i, over the next n years will be given by:

$$PV_i = \sum_{t=1}^{n} \frac{CF_t}{(1 + .20)^t}$$

TABLE 13.3

Estimated Cash Flows for Projects That Can Be Initiated Within the Next Five Years

Project	1	2	3	4	5	6	7	Year 8	9	10	11	12	13	14	15	16
1	−$239	$45	$59	$64	$71	$70	$59	$150	$150	$150	$100	$60				
2	−25	−40	−30	−10	20	70	100	20	20	15	10	5				
3	−10	−10	−10	20	30	50	40	25	44	30	14					
4		−120	25	25	30	35	30	56	400	200	50					
5		−100	60	60	80	74	66	50	200	50	10					
6		20	80	100	10	50	−100	300	300	10	100					
7			−200	−100	—	−200	200	100	15	0	150	100				
8			50	100	−200	100	150	15	200	200	200	100				
9			10	50	100	−200	—	400	100	200	300					
10				80	20	20	15	—	200	500	200	10				
11				−300	50	200	300	100	300	200	300	100	$100	$100	$100	$100
12				50	200	150	100	100	70	100	200	200				
13					−300	—	—	100	200	200		200	100	200	100	50
14					−200	50	100	100	100	100		50	50			
15					−100	10	80	80	70				100			

Capital budgeting under constraints

TABLE 13.4
Estimated Income Flows Over the Next Five Years for Projects That Can Be Initiated During This Time Period

Project	Year 1	2	3	4	5
1	−$20	$ 5	$15	$ 30	$ 50
2	− 25	− 40	− 30	10	20
3	− 40	− 30	− 20	100	120
4		− 50	5	20	25
5		− 100	− 60	− 60	80
6		− 20	80	100	− 10
7			− 50	− 30	− 20
8			− 80	100	200
9			− 10	50	100
10				− 80	50
11				− 100	− 200
12				− 50	200
13					− 10
14					− 200
15					− 100

TABLE 13.5
Calculation of Cash Flows and Income Flows for Project 1

Project description—Expansion of machine capacity
Estimated investment cost—$280
Estimated economic life—Seven years
Depreciation method—Sum of the year's digits

	Year 1	2	3	4	5	6	7
Cash receipts[1]	$ 21	$70	$104	$124	$151	$160	$139
Cash disbursements	280	20	30	30	30	40	40
	($259)	$50	$ 74	$ 94	$121	$120	$ 99
Federal income tax (50% of income)	(20)	5	15	30	50	50	40
Net Cash Flow	($239)	$45	$ 59	$ 64	$ 71	$ 70	$ 59
Revenue	$ 30	$90	$110	$130	$160	$160	$130
Depreciation	70	60	50	40	30	20	10
Other operating expenses	—	20	30	30	30	40	40
	$ 70	$80	$ 80	$ 70	$ 60	$ 60	$ 50
Net income before tax	($ 40)	$10	$ 30	$ 60	$100	$100	$ 80
Federal income tax (50% of income)	(20)	5	15	30	50	50	40
Net Income	($ 20)	$ 5	$ 15	$ 30	$ 50	$ 50	$ 40

[1] Seventy percent of revenue collected in year of sales; 30 percent during next year.

Model 2—a profit-planning model

Table 13.6 gives the present value of each of the fifteen projects, using this formula.

TABLE 13.6
Net Present Values of Fifteen Projects

Project	Net Present Value	Project	Net Present Value
1	—$ 35.75	9	$ 45.07
2	96.89	10	— 9.21
3	33.20	11	151.76
4	— 10.67	12	138.42
5	— 29.82	13	— 12.19
6	187.41	14	185.45
7	31.95	15	32.84
8	72.14		

If all the projects with positive present values are purchased and no constraint is placed on earnings, the company will invest in ten projects and reject five. The present value of all the projects purchased will be $975.13, and the earnings that the company will report to its shareholders over the next five years will be as follows:

> year 1, $35;
> year 2, $5;
> year 3, —$20;
> year 4, $270;
> year 5, $190.

(Recall that if no projects are adopted, the firm will earn $100, $95, $90, $90, and $80 in each of the next five years.) Total earnings for the firm over this period will thus be $480.

This pattern of earnings, however, leaves something to be desired. Surely the decline in earnings in year 2 and the deficit reported in year 3 will be viewed by the investment community at large as a failure by the firm to use modern management tools to plan for contingencies. The dramatic rise in earnings in year 4, followed by a decline in year 5, will give rise to speculation that earnings are subject to severe cyclical swings.

Shareholders tend to know less about the investment opportunities facing a corporation than management. Thus the only objective standard they have for measuring management performance is the data reported to them. Presented with an earnings record such as the one above, shareholders will care little whether management failed to plan ahead or whether earnings are subject to cyclical swings. In either case, they will respond by placing a low multiple on reported earnings, and share prices will be lower than they would be if the earnings pattern were more stable.

What happens if we now incorporate the constraint of steadily growing earnings into our model? For example, suppose we assume that the target growth rate, g, is 5 percent per annum. The capital-budgeting problem can then be recast as the following mathematical-programming problem:

$$\text{Maximize:} \quad \sum_{j=1}^{15} \sum_{t=1}^{16} \frac{a_{jt}}{(1+k)^t} x_j$$

$$\text{Subject to:} \quad \sum_{j=1}^{15} E_{jt}x_j - (1+g) \sum_{j=1}^{15} E_{j,t-1}x_j \geqslant 0 \qquad \text{for } t = 1, 2, \ldots, 5$$

$$0 \leq x \leq 1$$

where a_{jt} represents the net cash flow of the jth project in period t. Table 13.3 tells us that $a_{1,2}$, for example, is $45 and $a_{15,16}$ is $50. x_j represents the proportion of the jth project that is adopted. E_{jt} represents the earnings of the jth project in period t. Table 13.4 tells us that $E_{1,2}$ is $5 and $E_{15,5}$ is −$100. The double sum in the objective function means

TABLE 13.7
Proportion of Each Project Adopted to Achieve a Stipulated Growth Rate in Earnings of 5 Percent

Project	Proportion Adopted	Project	Proportion Adopted
1	100.00%	9	100.00
2	—	10	71.79
3	16.25	11	100.00
4	—	12	100.00
5	—	13	—
6	89.75	14	100.00
7	5.03	15	100.00
8	100.00		

that in each of the sixteen time periods each of the fifteen cash flows is discounted. The projects that will be adopted when the capital-budgeting problem is structured this way are given in Table 13.7. The maximum net present value of the set of projects adopted is approximately $758, substantially less than the $975 found earlier, and the earnings reported to shareholders are:

year 1, $ 73.50,
year 2, $ 77.18,
year 3, $ 81.04,
year 4, $167.06,
year 5, $179.92

Thus the total earnings are $578.70. (Some hints on how to structure this linear-programming model are given in the Appendix to this chapter.)

If the projects are adopted as specified in Table 13.7, the earnings of the company will increase each year at a rate equal to or greater than 5 percent. Thus, the investment community may view the company as capable of orderly and sustained growth and place a high multiple on its earnings.

The projects adopted reported in Table 13.7, however, differ in several important respects from those adopted when no profit constraint was specified. Project 1 is adopted in full and 71.79 percent of project 10 is adopted, yet both have negative present values. They are included in this set of adopted projects because they enable the firm to report relatively large earnings during the five-year planning period. Project 2, which has the highest net present value, is not adopted in full. Moreover, projects 11, 14, and 15, which have negative earnings during the five-year planning period, are adopted because their cash flows in later years are large enough to increase the present value of the portfolio of accepted projects.

What can be said of structuring the capital-budgeting problem this way? The adoption of projects with a negative present value is surely cause for concern. After all, a negative present value means that the value of the flows generated by the project is less than the cost of the capital committed to it. Similarly, rejecting projects with high net present values just because their earnings come "on stream" late means that attractive projects are bypassed. Yet both these actions are necessary to meet the constraints and maximize the objective function when the capital-budgeting problem is structured in this way. Clearly, this solution is not a wholly satisfactory one.

The underlying problem with this model is that two different stock-valuation models are implied. The net-present-value approach rests on the assumption that shareholders will be better off (i.e., the value of their stock will be higher) if the company adopts projects whose total returns exceed their total cost. The incorporation of a five-year growth-in-earnings constraint, however, implies that shareholders are better off if the fluctuations in reported earnings are held to a minimum and if the trend in reported earnings is positive. These two valuation models may not, and in the example cited above, do not, lead to consistent results. How, then, do we proceed?

One solution might be to add another constraint, such as "no project can be adopted unless it has a positive present value." This would eliminate projects 1 and 10 from our set of potential projects.

A second option is simply to recognize that the management of a firm faces many constraints in capital budgeting and that some of these constraints are conflicting. For example, management may want to maximize profits in the short run; yet to build and hold a labor force over the long run, it may consciously decide to pay wages above the market rate. To cite another example, the firm may want to sell its products at the lowest possible price; yet to enhance its general reputation, it may engage in institutional advertising, the cost of which is passed on to customers via a higher price. Such behavioral contradictions are a fact of life and the firm may simply acknowledge this and decide to live with them.

A third, and somewhat more constructive, option might be to alter some of the parameters of the model to simulate alternative environments. For example, the financial manager could change the discount rate applied to the cash flows of various projects from 20 percent to, say, 15 percent. The growth-in-earnings constraint could be changed from 5 to 10 percent, and so on. The financial manager could then ask, If these changes are made, how will the list of approved projects compare with Table 13.7? By comparing the results of various simulations, management can assess which course of action will be most beneficial.

The thrust of these remarks is that once constraints are recognized, the capital-budgeting problem becomes more complex. The relatively simple rule "adopt the projects with a positive present value" may have to be abandoned and instead, full consideration given to the goals of the firm and the interdependencies that exist among its activities.

Summary

In this chapter we began to consider the investment decision, or the capital-budgeting decision, in a systems context. We saw that once constraints were recognized, the easy rules for adopting and rejecting projects no longer worked. We also saw how a particular algorithm, linear programming, could be used to find a solution to the capital-budgeting problem when it is recast as a technical economic problem of maximizing an objective subject to specified constraints.

Two specific models were studied with some care. The first recognized the constraint of a fixed budget; the second, the constraint of stability in earnings growth. In both cases, the firm's objective function was to maximize the investments' net present values.

Both models gave rise to difficulties. The budget constraint gave rise to questions about the meaning of the concept of present value; the growth-in-earnings constraint implied a valuation framework different from that stated in the objective function.

These difficulties are severe, but they are not the only criticisms that can be leveled against the models presented above. Two other comments are also appropriate. First, many physical constraints that bind a firm were ignored. For example, nothing was said about the production function by which the firm transformed inputs into outputs, the terms on which the firm secured its inputs, or the terms on which it sold its outputs. All these factors must be considered for the formulation of the capital-budgeting problem to be complete.

The second limitation of these models was that no progress was made toward determining the discount rate the firm should use to evaluate capital projects. The only comment made on this subject was that the management might wish to simulate a number of environments, using different cost-of-capital estimates, to determine the most preferable state of affairs. Whether these limitations can be overcome by a more complete model will be considered in Chapter 14.

APPENDIX

The earnings constraint in the profit-planning model on page 281 must be adjusted to incorporate the earnings, E_t' that would arise even if the firm made no new investments. The constraint on the firm in the example would then be:

$$E_t' + \sum_{j=1}^{15} E_{j,t}x_j - (1 + g)[E_{t-1}' + \sum_{j=1}^{15} E_{j,t-1}x_j] \geq 0$$

or

$$\sum_{j=1}^{15} E_{j,t}x_j - (1 + g) \sum_{j=1}^{15} E_{j,t-1}x_j \geq -E_t' + (1 + g)E_{t-1}'$$

Since the earnings of the company are now $70 and are planned to be $100, $95, $90, $90, and $80 in the years to come, the following table can be constructed:

Period	E_t'	E_{t-1}'	$(1 + g)E_{t-1}'$	$-E_t' + (1 + g)E_{t-1}'$
$t = 0$	$ 70	—	—	−$70.00
$t = 1$	100	$ 70	$ 73.50	− 26.50
$t = 2$	95	100	105.00	10.00
$t = 3$	90	95	99.75	9.75
$t = 4$	90	90	94.50	4.50
$t = 5$	80	90	94.50	14.50

The values in the last column are the constants of the right-hand side of the earnings constraint.

Questions for discussion and problems

1. What advantages are there in casting the capital-budgeting problem in a framework that calls for both an objective function and a set of constraints?

2. Is it reasonable to assume that a capital-budgeting decision will be affected by the volume of funds the firm has available to spend? Is it reasonable to think that if one company has abundant funds while a second company has a limited amount, additional funds will be worth less to the first company than to the second? Will the cost of capital of the two companies be different? Will they value comparable investment projects differently?

3. Can the shadow price of a fixed-budget constraint be used as an estimate of the firm's cost of capital?

4. Why does a fixed-budget constraint in the Lorie-Savage problem give rise to questions about the present value of projects?

5. What is the logic behind an objective function that calls for the maximization of the present values of a firm's projects?

6. Why might a constraint that calls for rising earnings be imposed in a capital budgeting problem?

7. What can a financial manager do if the solution that a policy constraint imposes leads to an undesirable result?

[*Answers to problems 8–10 follow references and suggested readings.*]

8. The Forward Looking Manufacturing Co. has decided to structure its capital-budgeting procedures so that linear-programming techniques can be applied. The company is considering the purchase of three machines, each of which will require some outlays in the next two periods. According to the management's best estimates, the firm will have $20 available to spend in each of these periods. Data about each of the three projects are presented below. Forward Looking wants to maximize the present value of the projects it has under review. Structure the capital budgeting problem for them.

Machine	Present Value of Investment	Present Value of Outlay in Period 1	Present Value of Outlay in Period 2
A	10	8	8
B	12	2	12
C	15	14	6

9. The Jones Company is considering the purchase of two machines. It estimates that it will receive the cash flows from each of these projects indicated below:

	Cash Flows Received	
	Year 1	Year 2
Machine A	10	15
Machine B	12	11

(a) Jones has $42 to spend, and its cost of capital is 15 percent. What is the maximum price it will pay for each of the projects?

(b) A banker tells the treasurer of Jones that he likes the way the company runs its business and that he is prepared to lend him up to $42 at 10 percent interest. What is the maximum price that the Jones Company will now pay for each of the two projects?

(c) The market price of each machine is $21. Which machines will the Jones Company buy if it does not use the bank loan and if it does?

10. The Rapid Growth Company has two goals: It wants to maximize the present value of the cash flows of the projects it adopts and it wants to report a 10-percent rise in earnings every year. To help it meet its goals, it has decided to use linear programming. The relevant facts about the projects it has under consideration are presented below. No earnings will result if no new investments are made. Structure the capital-budgeting problem of Rapid Growth.

		Planned Earnings		
Projects	Present Value	Period 1	Period 2	Period 3
A	$20	$ 5	$7	$8
B	15	10	9	8
C	30	3	6	9

REFERENCES AND SUGGESTED READINGS

Articles

Carleton, Willard, "Linear Programming and Capital Budgeting Models: A New Interpretation," *Journal of Finance,* vol. XXIV, no. 5 (December 1969), pp. 825–35.

Charnes, A., Cooper, W. W., and Miller, M. H., "Application of Linear Programming to Financial Budgeting and the Costing of Funds," *Journal of Business,* vol. XXII, no. 1 (January 1959), pp. 20–46.

Elton, Edwin J., "Capital Rationing and External Discount Rates," *Journal of Finance,* vol. XXV, no. 3 (June 1970), pp. 573–85.

Ijiri, Y., Levy, F. K., and Lyon, R. C., "A Linear Programming Model for Budgeting and Financial Planning," *Journal of Accounting Research,* vol. I (Autumn 1963), pp. 198–212.

Lerner, Eugene M., and Rappaport, Alfred, "Limit DCF in Capital Budgeting," *Harvard Business Review* (September–October 1968), pp. 133–140.

Lorie, James, and Savage, L. J., "Three Problems in Capital Rationing," *Journal of Business,* vol. XXVIII, no. 4 (October 1955), pp. 229–39.

Mao, James C. T., "Survey of Capital Budgeting: Theory and Practice," *Journal of Finance,* vol. XXV, no. 2 (May 1970), pp. 349–60.

Weingartner, H. Martin, "Capital Budgeting of Interrelated Projects: Survey and Synthesis," *Management Science,* vol. XII (March 1966), pp. 485–516.

Books

Barrin, Walter, *Introduction to Linear Programming* (New York: McGraw-Hill, 1960).

Baumol, William J., *Economic Theory and Operational Analysis* (Englewood Cliffs, N. J.: Prentice-Hall, 1965).

Beranek, William, *Analysis for Financial Decisions* (Homewood, Ill.: Irwin, 1963).

Ijiri, Y., *Management Goals and Accounting for Control* (Amsterdam: North-Holland Publishing Co.; Chicago: Rand McNally, 1965).

Mao, James C. T., *Quantitative Analysis of Financial Decisions* (London: Macmillan, 1969).

Spivey, W. Alan, *Linear Programming: An Introduction* (New York: Macmillan 1963).

Weingartner, H. Martin, *Mathematical Programming and the Analysis of Capital Budgeting Problems* (Englewood Cliffs, N. J.: Prentice-Hall, 1962).

ANSWERS TO PROBLEMS 8–10

8. Maximize: $10x_1 + 12x_2 + 15x_3$
   Subject to: $8x_1 + 2x_2 + 14x_3 \leq 20$
   $$8x_1 + 12x_2 + 6x_3 \leq 20$$
   $$x_1, x_2, x_3 \leq 1$$
   $$x_1, x_2, x_3 \geq 0$$

9. (a) The present value of the cash flows of Machines A and B is $20.04 and $18.76, respectively, when a 15 percent discount rate is used. This is the most the firm will pay for the machines.
   (b) The present value of the cash flows of Machines A and B is $21.48 and $20.00, respectively, when a 10 percent discount rate is used. Thus the firm will now pay this much for them.
   (c) The company will not buy any machines if it uses its own funds; it will purchase Machine A if it uses the bank loan.

10. Maximize: $20x_1 + 15x_2 + 30x_3$
    Subject to: $(7x_1 + 9x_2 + 6x_3) - (1.10)(5x_1 + 10x_2 + 3x_3) \geq 0$
    $$(8x_1 + 8x_2 + 9x_3) - (1.10)(7x_1 + 9x_2 + 6x_3) \geq 0$$
    These constraints can be rewritten as:
    $$1.5x_1 - 2x_2 + 2.7x_3 \geq 0$$
    $$.3x_1 - 1.9x_2 + 2.4x_3 \geq 0$$

Capital budgeting in a
systems framework

14

What did the two models that were presented in the last chapter contribute to our understanding of capital budgeting? The first problem was to select, from a larger set of investment opportunities a set of projects whose total present value would be a maximum and at the same time to satisfy certain constraints. Each project required cash outlays in more than one period, and the budget in every period was fixed. A discount rate, or a cost of capital, was assumed in order to calculate the present value of the investment projects. How was the value of the discount rate determined? This question is important because it can be shown that the discount rate depends on the amount of funds that the firm has available when the capital-budgeting problem is structured this way.

Suppose that the firm in the example studied in the last chapter had $75 and $50 to spend in the first and second periods, respectively, instead of only $50 and $20. The shadow price of the budget constraint for each period would then have been different. The shadow price measures the additional yield the firm can earn in a given period if it has an additional dollar; it is a measure of the opportunity cost of funds, or the cost of capital. When a firm's cost of capital changes, however, the present value of the projects it has under consideration will change, since the discount rate used to evaluate the cash flows of these projects will change. As a result, a set of projects different from those previously selected may now yield the maximum present value. In short, the first model taught us that when a firm has a fixed dollar budget, the concept of a cost of capital is no longer valid. The model used in the second illustration did not depend on the funds available to the firm. Instead the problem was to select a set of projects whose total present value is a maximum subject to the constraint that reported earnings grow at a specified rate.

When the projects the firm selected were examined, it was discovered that some had a negative present value; i.e., the cash flows expected were less than the cost of funds that would have to be committed to them. This anomaly occurred because the objective function and the constraints were based upon different and contradictory valuation philosophies. One valuation model considered the cash flows, the other, reported earnings. One ignored fluctuations in cash flows; the other specified an increase in earnings over time. The second example, then, underscores the fact that unless a consistent valuation philosophy is used, there may be glaring inconsistencies in the results.

These remarks suggest that we must go back to the drawing boards and restructure our capital-budgeting problem once again, exercising great care to specify accurately both the objective function of the firm and the constraints that bind its actions.

A visual approach

To focus on the problems central to capital budgeting and to understand the decisions a manager must make, it is helpful, at first, to ignore some of the empirical problems. Once the central issues are understood, these considerations can be brought back into the analysis.

Assume that an investor is endowed, in an initial period, with a fixed income of C_0.[1] These funds can be applied to either current consumption or investment outlays. If investments are made, they will yield an income stream, and, hence, consumption outlays can be made in the next period.

How will the investor allocate his current endowment between consumption now and consumption in the future? The answer to this question depends on both the investor's preferences for present consumption and the investment opportunities open to him, that is, the terms on which his current savings can be converted into future consumption outlays.

Figure 14.1 represents the investor's preferences in regard to present and future consumption. Each schedule is constructed so that the investor is equally well off at any point along the function; i.e., he is indifferent to where he is on a particular schedule since all points are equally satisfying. Each investor would, however, prefer to be on U_2 rather than U_1 and to be on U_1 rather than U_0. This is because the investor can have more of both present and future consumption as he moves in a general northeast direction on the graph.

[1] This analysis is developed most forcefully by Jack Hirshleifer in "On the Theory of Optimal Investment Decision," *Journal of Political Economy,* vol. LXVI, no. 4 (August 1958), pp. 329–52.

If he spent all his initial funds on current consumption, the investor could attain point C_0 in Figure 14.1. If he spent none of his money on current consumption and invested it all, he could consume C_1 in the next period. The schedule C_0C_1 indicates the combinations of present and future consumption streams that are potentially attainable by investing different amounts of money in the available projects.

The expenditure problem for the investor is to allocate his funds between present consumption and saving, or investment, in a way that will enable him to reach the highest schedule. In Figure 14.1, this is U_1, and it can be reached if the investor will consume $0C_0'$ of his funds and invest $C_0'C_0$. This investment outlay will enable him to consume $0C_1'$ in the next period.

This visual analysis of the capital-budgeting problem brings into focus factors that have not been explicitly incorporated in the analysis heretofore. If we think in terms of a firm rather than an individual, the analysis focuses on the firm's allocation of funds between investments and dividends. If the firm raises its dividend payments, shareholders can raise their consumption outlays immediately, or they can elect to reinvest the dividends in another investment project. On the other hand, if the firm retains and plows back the funds it generates, it will be in a position to pay higher dividends in the future. The "solution" to the problem of what percentage of available funds firms should distribute in dividends

FIGURE 14.1

An Analysis of Production and Consumption Decisions.

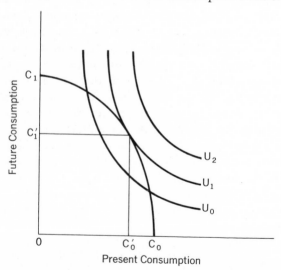

Capital budgeting in a systems framework

and what percentage they should retain therefore depends on the preferences of their shareholders for consumption today as opposed to consumption in the future.

The visual framework, however, also raises a number of questions. One concerns the construction of the production-opportunity schedule. This schedule shows the amount of consumption that can be realized in the next period if consumption is forgone today. Hence it shows the productivity of projects as successive amounts of savings are invested. Because future returns decline as the volume of savings, or current investment, rises, the production opportunity schedule C_0C_1 is concave to the origin.

The schedule C_0C_1 can be thought of as consisting of successive investment projects, ranked from high to low according to productivity. How was this ranking performed? Either the internal rate of return or the index of profitability could have been used. If we discard the internal rate of return because of the multiple-root problem associated with it, we are again left with the problem of finding a cost-of-capital figure that can be used to discount the cash flows of the investment projects.

To find this illusive cost of capital, suppose that we look, not to the corporation, but to the consumption requirements of its shareholders. Can we not use the rate at which shareholders are willing to trade current for future consumption as the firm's cost of capital? Suppose, for example, that shareholders' preferences for current and future consumption are such that $1 today is worth only $.95 to them next year. If a firm has the option of investing in a project that will enable each dollar invested to grow to $1.10 by the end of next year, it should adopt the project, because the shareholders will be better off. However, a project that will grow at only 3 percent should be rejected, because $1.03 received a year from now is worth less to the firm's shareholders than $1 received today. If this reasoning is followed, it is clear that the discount rate which should be used to rank the firm's investment projects in this example is 5 percent.

This approach to the cost of capital, however, implies that a corporation knows the value of consumption outlays to its shareholders in various future periods. Can a corporation ever know this? Surely it is difficult enough to understand the utility schedule of a single investor, let alone that of a large number of shareholders, all of whose circumstances are different.

Rather than answering this question directly, let us first ask another: If a firm knew the utility schedules of its shareholders, how would this knowledge affect its decisions? Or, what insight does a consideration of utility schedules bring to the capital-budgeting problem? Questions such as these were raised and answered by Baumol and Quandt in a widely celebrated article published in the June 1965 issue of the *Economic Journal*.[2]

Model 1—the Baumol-Quandt formulation of the capital-budgeting problem

Baumol and Quandt assumed that the objective of the corporation is to maximize the utility of consumption to the shareholders through its periodic payments (dividends) to them. The two economists postulated that if a corporation invests the funds it generates, its current dividend payments will be lower than they otherwise could be, but that in the future earnings will rise and the company will then be able to pay out a larger total number of dollars in dividends. A dollar of dividends received in the future, however, has a lower utility, or is worth less, than a dollar of dividends received immediately. The corporation must, therefore, determine whether its shareholders are better off if it pays dividends today or, by investing, enables itself to pay larger dividends in the future.

The capital-budgeting problem can now be restated as follows: If the objective of a firm is to maximize the utility of dividend payments, how should it allocate its funds between current withdrawals (dividends) and investments, given that it has only a limited amount of funds?

An important advantage of the Baumol-Quandt formulation of the capital-budgeting problem over the formulations described in the last chapter is that the firm does not have to discount the cash flows of the projects it has under consideration; it can work with the cash flows as generated. A second advantage, of course, is that it formally incorporates the preferences of shareholders in the firm's decision-making process.

To answer the capital-budgeting problem as they formulated it, Baumol and Quandt proposed the following linear-programming model:

$$\text{Maximize: } \sum_{t=1}^{n} U_t W_t$$

$$\text{Subject to: } -\sum_{j=1}^{m} a_{jt} x_j + W_t \leq M_t$$

$$0 \leq x_j \leq 1$$
$$W_t \geq 0$$

where U_t is the marginal utility of a dollar of withdrawals, W, or dividends that the shareholders receive in period t. a_{jt} is the actual cash

[2] William J. Baumol and Richard E. Quandt, "Investment and Discount Rates Under Capital Rationing: A Programming Approach" *Economic Journal*, vol. LXXV, no. 298 (June 1965) pp. 317–29.

flow of the project, j, in period t, and x_j is the proportion of project that is adopted. While no more than one of any project can be purchased, the entire project need not be adopted. M_t is the fixed-budget constraint in period t.[3]

The objective function in the capital-budgeting problem in this formulation is maximization of the utility of withdrawals. By explicitly solving for the optimal dividend payments, or cash withdrawals, the firm will learn not only the correct amount of funds to retain for investment purposes but which projects to adopt. The value of the funds that will be generated by each investment project will be contrasted with the cost of the funds in terms of their alternative use, the payment of current dividends. If the productivity of an investment is such that the shareholders will get a higher level of satisfaction over the entire period from its adoption than they would if the funds were distributed immediately, the project will be adopted. If not, it will be rejected.

AN EXAMPLE

Suppose a corporation has an opportunity to invest in four projects that have the cash flows over time indicated in Table 14.1. The funds

TABLE 14.1
Cash Flows of Four Projects

Project	Periods			
	1	2	3	4
1	−$1,200	+$ 400	+$450	+$1,500
2	− 1,500	+ 1,000	+ 900	+ 800
3	− 500	+ 1,000	+ 500	+ 500
4	− 500	+ 200	+ 200	+ 500

available to the firm from various sources are $3,000 in period 1 and $700 in each subsequent period. The coefficients of the withdrawals in each of the four periods are 1.0, .9, .8, and .7, respectively. Thus, a dollar received by a shareholder in period 1 has a utility of 1.00, a dollar

---

[3] A project's cash flows are defined as revenues less outlays. The largest withdrawal from the system that can be made in any time period, then, is $M_t + \Sigma a_{jt} x_j$. Transposing the second term from the right- to the left-hand side of the constraint equation gives rise to the negative sign.

Baumol and Quandt also discussed the possibility of allowing the firm to carry funds over from one period to the next, rather than distributing them immediately as dividends. The constraint then becomes $- \Sigma a_{jt} x_j + W_t + C_t - C_{t-1} \leq M_t$ where C is the amount carried over.

received in period 2 has the utility of .90 and so forth. For the share-holders to be as well off when the company invests funds as they would be if they received a dividend payment today, dividends must rise to $1.11 in period 2, to $1.25 in period 3, and to $1.43 in period 4. The formal structure of the problem then is:

Maximize: $1W_1 + .9W_2 + .8W_3 + .7W_4$

Subject to:

$$+1,200x_1 + 1,500x_2 + 500x_3 + 500x_4 + W_1 + S_1 = 3,000$$
$$- 400x_1 - 1,000x_2 - 1,000x_3 - 200x_4 + W_2 + S_2 = 700$$
$$- 450x_1 - 900x_2 - 500x_3 - 200x_4 + W_3 + S_3 = 700$$
$$-1,500x_1 - 800x_2 - 500x_3 - 500x_4 + W_4 + S_4 = 700$$
$$x_1 + q_1 = 1$$
$$x_2 + q_2 = 1$$
$$x_3 + q_3 = 1$$
$$x_4 + q_4 = 1$$

The solution to this problem is a maximum utility of withdrawals of $6,989.33. The firm can achieve this by paying no dividends in the first year and $2,966.67, $2,430.00, and $3,393.33, respectively, in periods 2, 3, and 4. The firm should purchase all of projects 1 and 3 and 86 percent of project 2. If project 4 were adopted, dividends would decline by $36.60.

The shadow prices of the constraints show the marginal productivity of another dollar of resources, that is, the contribution another dollar would make toward increasing the value of the objective function. In years 2, 3, and 4, when dividends are paid, the marginal productivity of funds equals the marginal utility of withdrawals. In period 1, when no dividends are paid, the marginal productivity of investment is $1.45. Since the utility of a dollar of withdrawals is 1, the shareholder is better off if the firm retains all the funds than if it disburses them.

To summarize, we have found the answer to the capital-budgeting problem of determining which of four projects to adopt as a byproduct of solving another problem—how much money the corporation should pay in dividends to maximize the utility of withdrawals to the shareholder. More accurately, we have solved both the capital-budgeting and dividend problems simultaneously. This is an appropriate procedure because the actions the corporation takes in one area influence its ability to act in another area.

Extending the capital-budgeting problem

The Baumol-Quandt treatment of capital budgeting assumed that the investor began with a fixed amount of funds. How does the capital-expenditure problem change when the opportunities open to firms change and they are permitted to borrow money? To develop an insight into this problem, it will be useful to return to a visual analysis.

In Figure 14.2, as in Figure 14.1, the C_0C_1 schedule reflects the production opportunities open to the firm, and the curves, U_1 and U_2, represent the shareholders' preferences in regard to present and future consumption. If no other opportunities were available to the firm it would retain AC_0 and pay out $0A$ as dividends. In the next period, then, it would be able to pay $0B$ in dividends. The highest schedule the firm can reach is U_1.

Suppose, however, that the firm is able to borrow money. The terms on which loans are available is represented by the line P_0P_1. Thus, if the firm borrows $0P_0$ today, it will have to pay back $0P_1$ in the future. The slope of P_0P_1 reflects the interest rate the firm must pay for the funds it borrows.

If the firm has the option of borrowing funds, it can reach U_2, which is higher than U_1. It can do this by first investing DC_0 and distributing

FIGURE 14.2

An Analysis of Production, Consumption, and Borrowing Decisions.

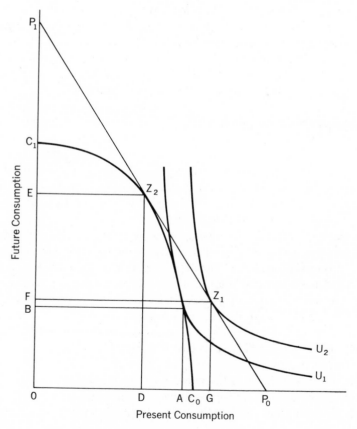

only $0D$ in dividends. The firm will then be at point Z_2 in Figure 14.2. It will generate $0E$ of funds in the next period, which can be used to pay interest on the borrowed funds and dividends. To finance an investment of DC_0, the firm can borrow money. It will move down along the curve P_0P_1, borrowing funds until it reaches the point of tangency with U_2, that is, when it has borrowed DG. It will then be at point Z_1 in Figure 14.2. At this point, it will be able to distribute $0G$ in dividends to its shareholders in the current period and $0F$ in dividends in the next period. The interest payments it will have to make on the borrowed funds, DG, is EF.

An evaluation of this analysis of capital expenditures

The visual analysis presented above links an individual's investment and borrowing decisions to the utility of consumption now and in the future. When the firm is in equilibrium, the schedule indicating the terms upon which it can borrow funds is tangent to both the schedule of consumer preferences (at Z_1) and the schedule of available production opportunities (at Z_2). The interest rate the firm pays for borrowed funds is therefore equal to both the marginal rate of substitution between consumption today and consumption tomorrow (at Z_1) and the marginal productivity of capital, that is, the rate at which savings today can be converted into consumption tomorrow (at Z_2). Hence in equilibrium, all three rates are equal.

This equality of the interest rate, the productivity of capital, and the marginal rate of substitution between present and future consumption—suggests one answer to the question of what rate of discount the corporation should use to evaluate the cash flows of different projects: the market rate at which it can secure additional funds. This rate of interest is a market value, and if the capital market were perfect, it would be determined by forces outside the firm.

A "perfect" capital market implies that firms can borrow and lend funds without influencing the price, or the interest rate, of such transactions. If the firm does not operate in a perfect capital market, however, the rate it must pay for additional funds, or the rate it receives when it lends funds, depends in part on the volume of its own activity. Generally, the more heavily a firm borrows, the higher the interest rate it will have to pay. Thus its cost of borrowed funds will not be, entirely, imposed on it from outside. This cost will depend, in part, on the corporation's own activities.

How much should a firm borrow? Can the Baumol-Quandt framework be used to determine the optimal size of corporate borrowings, just as it was to determine how much money the firm should invest and how large dividend payments should be? It can indeed. However, once imperfect factor markets are explicitly recognized, the problems of determining how much to spend on investment projects, to borrow, and to pay in dividends become more complex. To see the reason for this added complexity, suppose a firm produces two products that use a common input, such as borrowed funds or a certain type of skilled labor. The more of this common input the firm uses, the higher will be its cost to the firm. But this implies that if the demand for one of the two products increases so that the use of common input expands, the cost of the input to both products will rise. As costs change, the cash flows associated with each product will be altered. In short, the cash flow that each project will generate cannot be determined until the final output mix of the firm is known, that is, until the financial manager knows the amount of output of both products that will be produced.

Once we recognize that firms purchase their factor inputs in imperfect markets, i.e., that the firms' own actions influence the price they pay for the products they buy, we can no longer assume, as did Baumol and Quandt, that the cash flows of each investment project is independent of the other projects the firm adopts. Rather, if a firm produces more than one product and uses inputs common to all, and it purchases these inputs in an imperfect market, the firm itself, by its own actions, will affect the cash flows associated with each activity.

To put this another way, it may appear to be reasonable to assume that the capital-budgeting problem can be divided into two parts: first, determine the cash flows of various projects and, second, with this knowledge in hand, select the projects whose cash flows lead to an optimal solution. Unfortunately, such a two-step procedure introduces the possibility that a suboptimum solution will be found because of the bias inherent in the way projects are selected.

How can a financial manager proceed? If projects use common inputs, so that the cash flows of different projects are related, is the capital-budgeting problem intractable? The answer, fortunately, is No. In fact, the capital-budgeting problem can still be formulated as a straightforward linear-programming problem. However, care must be taken to structure both the objective function and the constraints in a way that takes account of the systematic interaction of the different decisions a firm must make.

The ultimate criterion, in capital budgeting, for accepting or rejecting projects is not the total profit a project generates or its total cash flow. Rather, the visual analysis presented in this chapter suggests that this criterion is the contribution the project makes to satisfying the shareholder's consumption requirements. Thus a formulation of the capital-budgeting problem is called for that does not require the specification in advance of precise output levels, or production methods, or input requirements for each product. All these decisions should be made with a view toward their contribution to the utility of withdrawals (dividends) to the shareholder.

If we do not know the cash flows of various projects before they are adopted, what constraints do bind a firm's actions, and what options are even open to the firm? *The constraints binding a firm when it makes investment decisions are the economic functions that lie behind the cash-flow estimates prepared for various projects.* These economic functions are the firm's demand schedule, its production function, and the supply schedule of its inputs. A precise and accurate formulation of the firm's capital-budgeting problem, then, is that financial managers must maximize the utility of shareholder withdrawals subject to these three constraints.

When the capital-budgeting problem is formulated in this way, the solution to the problem of which projects to adopt and which to reject will simultaneously resolve such difficult managerial problems as:

(1) how many physical units of each product to produce,

(2) how many units of capital to purchase,

(3) how many units of labor to employ,

(4) which production method to adopt for each product,

(5) what volume of funds to borrow from outside sources,

(6) when to pay dividends, and

(7) how large dividend payments should be.

Let us now see how this systems approach works in practice by taking an example.

Reformulating the capital-budgeting problem

To illustrate how capital budgeting is done when a systems approach is adopted, consider a hypothetical firm with the characteristics described below.

THE INPUTS

To make the various products the firm manufactures, it uses only two inputs, labor and machinery. Estimates of the total labor cost associated with different levels of employment is given in Table 14.2.

Because the market for labor is imperfect, the first four man-years of labor cost $2,000 each. If more than four man-years of labor are used, the rate rises to $2,400 per annum. If more than eight man-years are used, the rate increases to $2,800 per annum, and so on. Because the workers can be used to produce any product the firm makes, the labor costs are independent of the specific products produced.

TABLE 14.2
Total Labor Costs

Man-Years	Total Wage Bill
4	$ 8,000
8	17,600
12	28,800
16	44,000
20	60,000

Estimates of the total annual interest that the firm will pay for different amounts of borrowed funds are given in Table 14.3.

TABLE 14.3
Total Entered Payments

Funds Borrowed	Total Interest Payments
$10,000	$ 800
25,000	2,300

The cost of borrowed funds, like the cost of labor, is assumed to be a rising function of the amount used. Small amounts can be borrowed at 8 percent; once $10,000 is borrowed, however, the marginal rate increases to 10 percent.

In this example, we shall assume that all borrowings that take place occur in the first period and that the funds that are borrowed will be repaid in the second and third periods in equal installments. The interest payments that the firm makes in each year, however, will be based on the original size of the loan, not on the unpaid balance. Thus, if the firm were to borrow $5,000, it would have to pay $400 in interest in both years 2 and 3, even though it repaid half the loan in year 2. Different assumptions about repayment patterns and interest payments could be made without affecting the structure of the problem.

The firm is assumed to have $2,000 initially, which it can use to pay dividends, to purchase machinery, or to pay wages.

THE PRODUCTION PROCESS

The firm produces two products, A and B. To produce them, it uses both labor and machinery. Each machine it uses costs $5,000. The specific quantities of each input that it will use, however, depends on two things:

the output of each product and the technology, or production configuration, it will use to produce that output. Thus any specific output level, say 50 units of product A, can be produced by using different combinations of labor and machinery. For example, 50 units of product A could be produced by using 2 man-years of labor and 2 machines or 1 man-year of labor and 4 machines. The range of production options open to the firm are given in Table 14.4.

TABLE 14.4
Alternative Production Functions

	Output	Machines Required	Man-Years of Labor Required
Product A	50	2	2
	50	1	4
	100	3	4
	100	1.5	9
	150	3	15
	150	4	8
Product B	25	2	0.5
	25	1	1
	50	1.25	1.5
	50	2	1.1
	100	2	3
	100	3	1.5

The choice of a production method, as well as a particular output level, will depend on how the decision affects the ability of the firm to make dividend payments to its shareholders.

THE OUTPUTS

The total revenue the firm will receive from selling its output is given in Table 14.5. These revenue figures imply that the firm's demand curve slopes downward. Each of the first 50 units of product A it sells allows the firm to realize $220; each of the second 50 brings in only $180; and so on.

THE UTILITY OF WITHDRAWALS

In addition to these data on the costs of inputs, the possible production-function configurations, and the firm's demand schedule, we assume that the financial manager also knows the utility of a dollar of withdrawals to its shareholders over the next three years. These values are 1.00, .91, and .82, respectively.

TABLE 14.5
Total Revenue

	Output	Total Revenue
Product A	50	$11,000
	100	20,000
	150	26,000
Product B	25	5,000
	50	6,500
	100	10,000

In this example, then, we assume that the financial manager has information only about the economic schedules that limit his actions. Thus, he knows what will happen to wage costs if he hires an additional man-year of labor, what will happen to total revenue if he produces more units of product B, and so on. What he does not know, however, is how many units of capital he should purchase, how many units of each product to produce, how to produce each product, how much money to borrow, how large dividend payments should be, or when dividends should be paid.

The answer to all these questions can be found by formulating the capital-budgeting problem as follows:

Maximize: the sum of the utility of withdrawals over the three-year planning horizon

Subject to: (period-1 constraint) total revenues — capital outlays — labor outlays — withdrawals + borrowings + initial endowment ≥ 0,

(period-2 constraint) total revenues — repayment of borrowings — interest payments — labor costs — withdrawals ≥ 0,

(period-3 constraint) total revenues — repayment of borrowings — interest payments — labor costs — withdrawals ≥ 0.

Some hints on how to structure this problem are presented in the appendix to this chapter. We shall pass over this technical material here, however, and present only the solution to the problem.

The maximum utility of withdrawals is $22,199.36. This will result if the firm (1) pays no dividends in the first year but pays dividends of $12,832 in both year 2 and year 3; (2) produces 100 units of product A and 100 units of product B (thus generating the revenues to pay these dividends); (3) produces product A with 3 machines and 4 man-years of labor and product B with 3 machines and 1.5 man-years of labor; (4) hires 5.5 man-years of labor and purchases 6 machines; and (5) borrows $9,600 in the first year to finance these purchases, and repays $4,800 in years 2 and 3.

The solution to this particular capital-budgeting problem is not important. The reason this example was pursued in such depth is that *it illustrates the power of the systems approach to capital budgeting*. The decision as to what machines to buy cannot be made without taking into account the labor- and capital-market conditions. The amount of output to produce cannot be decided without considering the effect of the decision on dividends, and so on. A number of decisions must be made *simultaneously*, because the actions taken in one part of the firm will affect the options that are available in another. Moreover, all the decisions that are made, to be internally consistent, must be made with the objective function of the firm in mind. When such a systems approach is adopted, the course a firm should take to maximize its objectives can be readily calculated.

Summary

The capital-budgeting problem—selecting which investment projects to adopt—touches all aspects of the corporation's affairs. We saw that if a firm knows in advance the cash flow a project will generate and the utility of its dividend payments to its shareholders, then the Baumol-Quandt framework will enable the firm to simultaneously determine both its optimum dividend and investment policy.

When corporate borrowings are introduced, the capital budgeting problem changes. If the firm operates in a perfect capital market and knows the cash flow of each project, it can use the market interest rate as a criterion for discounting each project's cash flow and for selecting those with a positive present value. If it does not operate in a perfect capital market, however, then the interest rate it will pay for borrowed funds depends in part on the volume of funds it uses. Since the interest rate is determined, in part, by the corporation's own actions, it cannot be known in advance.

Other markets than that for borrowed funds are also likely to be imperfect. Specifically, the rate that the corporation must pay for labor is likely to depend on the number of workers it hires, and the prices it can charge for its products is likely to depend on its volume of output. Moreover, more than one production technology is likely to be available.

Once these facts are recognized, once it is understood that a systems problem must be solved, the capital-budgeting problem can be properly

Capital budgeting in a systems framework

stated: Maximize the utility of withdrawals subject to the demand curve, the production function, and the supply schedule of inputs of the firm.

To satisfy the information requirements of this systems approach to capital budgeting, we must know the parameters of its demand schedule, its supply schedule, and its physical production function. These requirements, however, are no more severe than those of other capital-budgeting models. In the Baumol-Quandt model, the firm had to know these values to arrive at estimates of each project's cash flow.

The advantages of formulating the capital-budgeting problem in a way that reflects the systematic interaction of the parts of the firm with one another and of the firm with its environment are many.

First, a large number of relevant operating problems can be solved simultaneously with the determination of capital expenditures—the amount of dividends to pay, the amount of funds to borrow, the product mix, the number of workers to employ, and the number of machines to buy.

Second, the correct volume of capital expenditures can be determined without first having to calculate the cash flow associated with specific pieces of capital.

Third, the severe problems caused by the interdependencies that arise when inputs are purchased in imperfect markets and used to produce different products can be overcome.

And fourth, the utility of withdrawals can be used as a common standard for making a number of corporate decisions, thus ensuring their internal consistency.

APPENDIX

The total labor cost and interest payments are nonlinear functions. To estimate these functions with a series of linear approximations, the following strategy, attributable to Charnes, Cooper and Ijiri,[1] can be employed:

Let L_0 represent the total number of workers that can be employed in the example given earlier. The first four workers can be hired at the marginal rate of $2,000. Once four workers are hired at this rate, the marginal wage rate increases by $400, to $2,400; once eight workers are hired, the marginal wage rate increases by another $400, to $2,800. The total wage bill can thus be found by the expression:

$$2,000L_0 + 400L_1 + 400L_2$$

[1] Yuji Ijiri, *Management Goals and Accounting for Control* (Amsterdam: North Holland Publishing Co., 1965).

where

$$L_0 - L_1 \leq 4$$
$$L_0 - L_2 \leq 8$$

Six different methods can be used to produce each commodity; that is, three different output levels can be selected for each product and each output level can be produced two ways. It is convenient to subtract the total machinery costs from the revenue associated with the level of output in the first year. Thus, if 50 units of product A are sold, $11,000 in revenues will be realized. One method of producing this output requires the use of two machines, at a cost of $5,000 for each machine. If this method is used, the net revenues in the first period are $1,000. The second method requires the use of only one machine. If this method is used, the net revenues are $6,000. In later years, the revenues associated with both methods will, of course, be $11,000.

The variables and the system equations for the example in the chapter are:

Table of Variables

x_1	Withdrawal in period 1	x_{13}	Fourth Method of producing B
x_2	Withdrawal in period 2	x_{14}	Fifth Method of producing B
x_3	Withdrawal in period 3	x_{15}	Sixth Method of producing B
x_4	First Method of producing A	x_{16}	Total wage bill
x_5	Second Method of producing A	x_{17}	Total amount borrowed
x_6	Third Method of producing A	x_{18}	Yearly interest bill
x_7	Fourth Method of producing A	x_{19}	Amount of loan over $10,000
x_8	Fifth Method of producing A	x_{20}	Total labor requirement
x_9	Sixth Method of producing A	x_{21}	Amount of labor over 4
x_{10}	First Method of producing B	x_{22}	Amount of labor over 8
x_{11}	Second Method of producing B	x_{23}	Amount of labor over 12
x_{12}	Third Method of producing B	x_{24}	Amount of labor over 16

Objective function

$$z = x_1 + .91x_2 + .82x_3$$

First-period constraint

$$-x_1 + 1{,}000x_4 + 6{,}000x_5 + 5{,}000x_6 + 12{,}500x_7 + 11{,}000x_8 + 6{,}000x_9$$
$$-5{,}000x_{10} + 0x_{11} + 250x_{12} - 3{,}500x_{13} + 0x_{14} - 5{,}000x_{15} - x_{16}$$
$$+ x_{17} + 2{,}000 \geq 0$$

Second-period constraint

$$-x_2 + 11{,}000x_4 + 11{,}000x_5 + 20{,}000x_6 + 20{,}000x_7 + 26{,}000x_8$$
$$+26{,}000x_9 + 5{,}000x_{10} + 5{,}000x_{11} + 6{,}500x_{12} + 6{,}500x_{13} + 10{,}000x_{14}$$
$$+ 10{,}000x_{15} - x_{16} - 0.5x_{17} - x_{18} \geq 0$$

Third-period constraint

$-x_3 + 11,000x_4 + 11,000x_5 + 20,000x_6 + 20,000x_7 + 26,000x_8$
$+26,000x_9 + 5,000x_{10} + 5,000x_{11} + 6,500x_{12} + 6,500x_{13} + 10,000x_{14}$
$+10,000x_{15} - x_{16} - 0.5x_{17} - x_{18} \geq 0$

Production-of-A constraint

$x_4 + x_5 + x_6 + x_7 + x_8 + x_9 = 1$

Production-of-B constraint

$x_{10} + x_{11} + x_{12} + x_{13} + x_{14} + x_{15} = 1$

Total labor

$x_{20} - 2x_4 - 4x_5 - 4x_6 - 9x_7 - 15x_8 - 8x_9 - 0.5x_{10} - x_{11} - 1.5x_{12}$
$- 1.1x_{13} - 3x_{14} - 1.5x_{15} = 0$

Wage bill

$x_{16} - 2,000x_{20} - 400x_{21} - 400x_{22} - 1,000x_{23} - 200x_{24} = 0$

Amounts of labor above points of wage-scale changes

$x_{20} - x_{21} \leq 4$
$x_{20} - x_{22} \leq 8$
$x_{20} - x_{23} \leq 12$
$x_{20} - x_{24} \leq 16$

Yearly interest bill

$x_{18} - .08x_{17} - .02x_{19} = 0$

Amount of loan under $10,000

$x_{17} - x_{19} \leq 10,000$

Questions for discussion and problems

1. Why must a firm consider the dividend problem at the same time it considers its investment problem?

2. What contribution did Baumol and Quandt make to understanding of capital budgeting?

3. If a firm can borrow and lend in a perfect capital market, why is the capital-budgeting problem trivial?

4. If a firm buys its inputs in an imperfect market and the same inputs are used to produce more than one product, how does this make the capital-budgeting problem more difficult?

5. How do the assumptions in question 4 complicate the task of estimating the present value of the cash flows of different projects?

6. Why must a firm know its demand curve, its production function, and its supply schedule of inputs to solve its capital-budgeting problem?

7. Why does a systems approach to capital budgeting provide a simultaneous solution of a large number of corporate problems?

[Answers to problems 8–11 follow references and suggested readings.]

8. Consider Figure 14.1.
   (a) If the C_0C_1 production-opportunity schedule shifted outward, would the utility of the firm's shareholders increase?
   (b) How could such a shift occur?
   (c) If the utility schedules change their shape and become tangent to C_0C_1 at a point to the right of C_0' and below C_1' in Figure 14.1, will the firm invest more or less funds in the current period?

9. The Happy Shareholder Company estimated that the utility schedule of its shareholders was as follows: $U_1 = 1$, $U_2 = .87$, $U_3 = .75$, and $U_4 = .66$ (where the subscript stands for the year). It has allocated $100 for new projects and it does not plan to spend any more funds in later periods for investment projects. It is considering the purchase of projects with the following cash flows:

Cash Flow in Various Years

Project	1	2	3	4
A	−$50	+$ 6	+$ 20	+$100
B	− 50	+ 50	+ 50	+ 50
C	− 40	− 40	+ 100	+ 200

Construct a linear-programming problem for the firm that will help decide which projects to adopt.

10. (a) Suppose that a dollar of consumption next year is worth $.90 today. Should a firm invest in a project that costs $1 today and will yield $1.20 next year?
    (b) If the firm can borrow money at 5 percent, should it finance this investment with borrowed funds?
    (c) If it can either lend or borrow money at 12 percent and a dollar of consumption in the future is worth $.90 today, which course of action should the firm follow?
    (d) In equilibrium, what is the relationship between the interest rate, the marginal rate of substitution, and the productivity of capital?

11. The Simple Machine Company produces two products, A and B. It can manufacture each of these products in two ways. Both ways of producing A, methods 1 and 2, generate $10 in revenue; both

ways of producing B, methods 3 and 4, generate $15 in revenue. The four production functions are described below:

		Units of Labor	Units of Capital
Product A	Method 1	1	2
	Method 2	2	1
Product B	Method 3	3	1
	Method 4	1	3

The total cost of using different amounts of labor and capital is as follows:

Units of Labor	Total Cost	Units of Capital	Total Cost
1	$ 1.00	1	$ 2.00
2	2.50	2	4.25
3	4.75	3	6.25
4	8.00	4	8.25
5	11.00	5	10.25

(a) If only product A is produced, which is the cheaper production method, 1 or 2?

(b) If only product B is produced, which is the cheaper production method, 3 or 4?

(c) When both products are produced together, how much will it cost the firm if it uses methods:

(1) 1 and 3?
(2) 1 and 4?
(3) 2 and 3?
(4) 2 and 4?

REFERENCES AND SUGGESTED READINGS

Articles

Baumol, W., and Quandt, R., "Investment and Discount Rates Under Capital Rationing—A Programming Approach," *Economic Journal,* vol. LXXV (June 1965), pp. 317–29.

Gale, D., "Optimal Programs for Sequential Investments," in M. J. Brennan, ed., *Patterns of Market Behavior* (Providence, R. I.: Brown Univ. Press, 1965), pp. 17–26.

Hirshleifer, J., "Investment Decision Under Uncertainty: Choice Theoretic Approaches," *Quarterly Journal of Economics,* vol. LXXIX, no. 4 (November 1965), pp. 506–36.

———, "On the Theory of Optimal Investment Decision," *Journal of Political Economy,* vol. LXVI, no. 4 (August 1958), pp. 329–56.

Ijiri, Y., Levy, F. K., and Lyon, R. C., "A Linear Programming Model for Budgeting and Financial Planning," *Journal of Accounting Research,* vol. I (Autumn 1963), pp. 198–212.

Mao, James C. T., "Survey of Capital Budgeting: Theory and Practice," *Journal of Finance,* vol. XXV, no. 2 (May 1970), pp. 349–61.

Moag, Joseph S., and Lerner, Eugene M., "Capital Budgeting Decisions Under Imperfect Market Conditions," *Journal of Finance,* vol. XXIV, no. 4 (September 1969), pp. 613–23.

Reiter, Stanley, "Choosing an Investment Program Among Interdependent Projects," *Review of Economic Studies,* vol. XXX, no. 1 (January 1963), pp. 32–36.

Books

Baumol, William J., *Economic Theory and Operations Analysis* (Englewood Cliffs, N. J.: Prentice-Hall, 1965).

Fisher, I., *The Theory of Interest* (New York: Macmillan, 1930).

Hirshleifer, J., *Investment, Interest and Capital* (Englewood Cliffs, N. J.: Prentice-Hall, 1970).

Ijiri, Y., *Management Goal and Accounting for Control* (Amsterdam: North-Holland Publishing Co.; Chicago: Rand McNally, 1965).

Lerner, Eugene M., and Carleton, Willard T., *A Theory of Financial Analysis* (New York: Harcourt Brace Jovanovich, 1966).

Mao, James C. T., *Quantitative Analysis of Financial Decisions* (London: Macmillan, 1969).

Masse, Pierre, *Optimal Investment Decisions* (Englewood Cliffs, N. J.: Prentice-Hall, 1962).

Vickers, Douglas, *The Theory of the Firm: Production, Capital and Finance* (New York: McGraw-Hill, 1968).

ANSWERS TO PROBLEMS 8–11

8. (a) Yes.
   (b) It could occur if a change in technology or some similar development took place.
   (c) It will invest less.

9. Maximize: $1W_1 + .87W_2 + .75W_3 + .66W_4$
   Subject to: $50x_1 + 50x_2 + 40x_3 + W_1 \leq 100$
   $-6x_1 - 50x_2 + 40x_3 + W_2 \leq 0$
   $-20x_1 - 50x_2 - 50x_3 + W_3 \leq 0$
   $-100x_1 - 50x_2 - 200x_3 + W_4 \leq 0$
   $x_1, x_2, x_3 \geq 0$
   $x_1, x_2, x_3 \leq 1$

10. (a) Yes.
    (b) Yes.
    (c) It should lend money.
    (d) All rates are equal.

11. (a) Method 1 costs \$5.25 and method 2 costs \$4.50; therefore 2 is cheaper.
    (b) Method 3 costs \$6.75 and method 4 costs \$7.25; therefore 3 is cheaper.
    (c) (1) 1 and 3 together cost \$14.25.
        (2) 1 and 4 together cost \$12.75.
        (3) 2 and 3 together cost \$15.25.
        (4) 2 and 4 together cost \$13.00.

Note that while methods 2 and 3 are cheaper than 1 and 4 if they are considered individually, methods 1 and 4 are the cheapest when they are considered together.

Variations in return, capital budgeting, and risk

15

A firm's investment decisions have a wide impact on other corporate activities. To study their systemic effects, models have been designed in preceding chapters that viewed the firm as maximizing an objective function subject to certain constraints. In Chapter 14, the assumption was made that the corporation's objective function was to maximize the utility of dividend payments made to shareholders. The constraints limiting the firm's ability to make these payments were the demand for its output, its production function, and the supply schedule of its inputs. The principal conclusion the model led to was that, in determining the amount of dividends to pay, the firm simultaneously determines the price to charge for each product, the quantity of each product to produce, the number of machines to purchase, the amount of labor to hire, and the amount of funds to borrow.

The precision of the analysis presented in Chapter 14, however, rests on a number of assumptions that are not entirely realistic. Perhaps the most tenuous of these assumptions is that the manager of the firm can specify, positively, the constraints binding him. It is unlikely that many chief financial officers can do this. Few firms have developed a formal information system that keeps track really effectively of either their internal operations or their interactions with the environment. In fact, many large firms decentralize much of their decision making to ensure that decisions are made by persons "close to the facts."

However, although decentralization may lower the firm's information costs, it gives rise to another problem: as decentralization increases, the costs of coordination rise. While, a decentralized unit may have a good grasp of the important factors at work in its own area, it is unlikely to be aware of the consequences of its actions for other parts of the firm. This is precisely the problem we encountered in the capital-budgeting problem in the last chapter. When one part of the firm expanded its output, the wage rates and borrowing costs in another part increased. To coordinate one unit's activities with those of the rest of the firm, an effective, centralized information system is needed. However, once again we have come full circle, for the lack of such a system was the reason for decentralization in the first place.

The practical consequence of the current status of information systems and organizational structure is that a firm cannot ascertain precisely what the effects of its actions will be. A firm cannot know, for example, the number of units of its various products that will be sold as a result of a specific action. Rather, the most any manager can be expected to know is that sales are likely to be within a certain range. The actual number of sales within this range may depend on such varied factors as the weather, the number of calls the salesmen make, the intensity of competition, and the level of economic activity.

One way to include this economic truth in our model is to specify as the demand curve for the firm $Q = a_0 - a_1 P + u$ where $Q =$ quantity, P equals price, u is a random term that can be either positive or negative, and a_0 and a_1 are parameters. Similar statements can be made about the other constraints a firm faces. The amount of output produced by a man or a machine will depend on such unpredictable factors as the number of times the machine breaks down or the enthusiasm of the employee on any particular day.

The problem that must be faced, then, as models of the firm approach reality is, How can the fact of variability be incorporated in a framework for financial decision making? Furthermore, once an allowance is made for the variability of an activity's returns, must the results reached in earlier chapters be amended? We shall find answers to these problems as the chapter progresses.

Break-even charts

One technique widely used by financial officers to evaluate whether a new product should be introduced or a new activity begun is the break-even chart. This chart shows the number of units that must be sold at a stipulated price to break even, i.e., to generate enough revenue to cover both the fixed and variable costs of production. Such a chart is presented in Figure 15.1.

The fixed costs of producing a new product include such factors as the rent, light, and heating expenses associated with the production process. Because these factors are invariant under changes in output, they

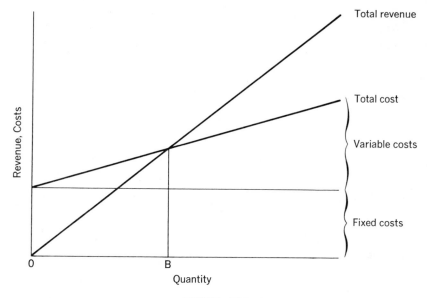

FIGURE 15.1
Break-even Chart.

are represented by a horizontal line in Figure 15.1. The variable costs are outlays that vary directly with output, such as the expenditures for materials, wages, and sales commissions. The firm's total cost is the sum of its fixed and variable costs.

The variable-cost schedule is drawn as a straight line in Figure 15.1, reflecting an implicit assumption that costs are proportionate to output. If the firm's variable costs rise more than proportionately as output rises (which would occur if the firm experienced diminishing returns to scale), the variable-cost curve would be concave upward. Conversely, if the firm experienced increasing returns to scale, variable costs would rise less than proportionately as output rose, and the variable-cost curve would be concave downward.

The total revenues of the firm are the product of the price charged for each unit and the number of units sold. If the price per unit does not change over wide ranges of output, then a graph of the firm's total revenues will be a straight line through the origin, as in Figure 15.1. *The slope of the total revenue line is the price per unit of the product.* If the price per unit falls as the quantity of goods sold increases, the firm's total revenue function will be concave downward.

The gross profits that will result from difference levels of output are equal to the vertical distance between total revenues and total costs. If output is to the right of the break-even point, *B*, a profit results; if it is to the left of the break-even point, a loss occurs.

Suppose that the fixed costs of producing a product are $500, the variable cost per unit is $.50, and the selling price of the product is $1.00. The break-even level of output will be that level where total costs equal total revenues—in this illustration, 1,000 units. The break-even point is calculated arithmetically as follows:

$$500 + .50Q = 1.00Q$$
$$500 = .50Q$$
$$1,000 = Q$$

Let us assume that the financial manager of the firm has received estimates from the marketing department of the volume of sales that will occur when different prices are charged. These reports indicate that at a price of $1.00 the most likely volume of sales is 1,100 units. However, more or less than this amount could be sold, depending on a number of random events. If the weather is good and competitors are slow to introduce rival products, there is some probability that sales will exceed the 1,100 mark; on the other hand, adverse developments could cause sales to be below the expected level.

Let the distribution of expected sales be represented by a normal curve, with a mean of 1,100 and a standard deviation of 100 units. The estimates of the sales volume can now be combined with analysis of the break-even point. To do this, we simply graph the profit contribution of each additional unit of sales so that total profits change from negative to positive at the break-even point of 1,000 units of output. The probability distribution of sales is then superimposed on the profit line, as in Figure 15.2.

The break-even point, 1,000 units, is one standard deviation below the expected level of sales. Since 16 percent of the area of a normal curve is more than one standard deviation below the mean, the sales of the product should be profitable 84 percent of the time. When sales

FIGURE 15.2

The Profits That Result at Different Levels of Sales When Price of $1 per Unit Is Charged.

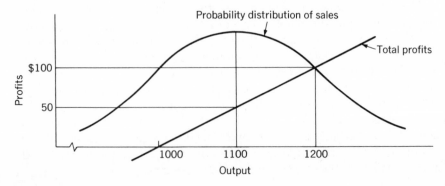

        Variations in return, capital budgeting, and risk

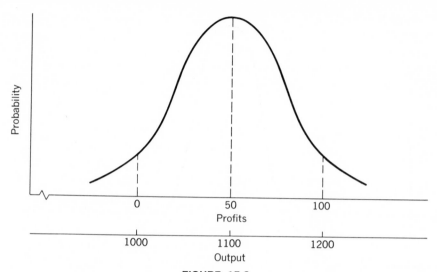

FIGURE 15.3
Profit Profile at $1 per Unit.

reach 1,100 profits will be $50 (since each unit of sales above the break-even point contributes $.50 in profits). Sixteen percent of the time profits will be greater than $100 (sales will be greater than 1,200 units); and 2.3 percent of the time profits will be greater than $150 (sales will be greater than 1,300 units).

These data indicate that when a price of $1 per unit is charged, the expected distribution of profits is a normal curve with a mean of $50 and a standard deviation of $50. Such a distribution is presented in Figure 15.3.

Let us now contrast this profit profile with the one that would result if a different pricing policy were followed. Suppose that the firm's marketing department expects that if a price of $2.50 were charged only 270 items would be sold. However, the probable deviation from this number is quite small—only 5 units—because the buyers that want the product will pay the high price and not search for less expensive substitutes. We assume that the fixed costs remain $500 and that the variable costs continue to be $.50 per unit.

The break-even point under this pricing policy is 250 units, and each additional unit sold contributes $2 to total profits. The profit profile now is as in Figure 15.4. At 270 units of output, the firm will earn $40 in profits. There is virtually no chance of loss because the break-even point lies 4 standard deviations below the expected sales level. On the other hand, profits will be above $50 (sales will be above 275 units) only 16 percent of the time.

The profit profiles of both pricing strategies are shown in Figure 15.5.

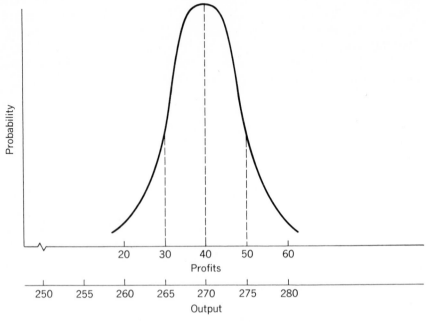

FIGURE 15.4
Profit Profile at $2.50 per Unit.

FIGURE 15.5
Profit Profiles at $1 and $2.50 per Unit.

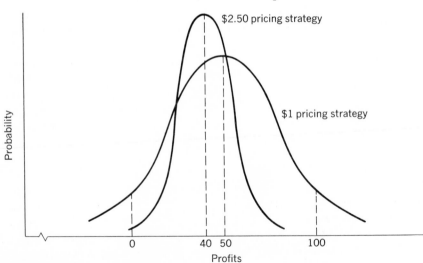

$2.50 pricing strategy

$1 pricing strategy

Variations in return, capital budgeting, and risk

Obviously, the expected return of the $1 pricing strategy is greater than the expected return of the $2.50 strategy. On the other hand, the standard deviation of the $1 strategy is also higher. Profits under the $1 strategy could be greater than $100 or less than $0; profits under the $2.50 strategy are unlikely to be greater than $60 or less than $30. Which of these pricing strategies should the firm adopt?

Coping with variability

The question of which pricing strategy to adopt is a specific example of a broader class of problems that a financial manager faces—how to cope with the expected variations of an economic variable in which he has an interest. This same problem also arose in Chapter 10. We saw there that one method a financial manager can use to determine the present value of a variable stream of cash is to adjust either the numerator or the denominator in the present-value calculation. It makes a difference, however, which we do—lower the numerator or raise the denominator. If the numerator is lowered, the adjustment for uncertainty is constant through time. If the denominator is raised, however, the adjustment for uncertainty is compounded through time.

LOWERING THE NUMERATOR IN THE PRESENT-VALUE CALCULATION

Suppose project A costs $1,000; its expected cash flow is $300 per annum and the standard deviation of these flows is $60 per annum. Project B costs $2,000 and has both a larger expected annual cash flow and a higher standard deviation than project A. The mean and standard deviation of B's annual cash flows are $700 and $200, respectively. Both projects have a 5-year life, and at the end of this period will have only a nominal salvage value.

To adjust the numerator in the present value calculation for uncertainty, we must know the project's *certainty equivalent cash flow*—how much the financial manager would be willing to pay to convert the uncertain stream of cash into a certain one. Project A, for example, has an expected value of $300, but the standard deviation from this value is $60. There is a 50 percent chance that the firm will receive less than $300 and a 16 percent chance that it will receive less than $240. If the financial manager wants to avoid these risks, he will be willing to pay some price to eliminate the variability in the return. Suppose that this price is $30, that he is indifferent whether project A generates the uncertain revenues described above or a certain revenue stream of $270. This value, $270, is the financial manager's certainty equivalent of the distribution whose mean is $300 and whose standard deviation is $60. Other financial managers could, of course, have different certainty equivalents for this distribution of returns.

To obtain a more precise statement of the certainty equivalent, we let the cash flows generated each year by a project be a random variable with an expected value, $E(x)$, and a standard deviation, σ. The certainty equivalent of the random variable is then:

$$CE = E(x) - b\sigma$$

where b is a measure of the unwillingness of the manager to accept uncertainty.

In our example,

$$270 = 300 - b(60)$$
$$b = \tfrac{1}{2}$$

If the financial manager is consistent, the certainty equivalent cash stream for project B each year is $600. For

$$CE = 700 - \tfrac{1}{2}(200)$$
$$CE = 600$$

To determine their relative attractiveness, the financial manager could calculate the profitability index of projects A and B using the certainty equivalent cash flow instead of the expected annual cash flow. The data in Table 15.1 show that if the firm uses a 10 percent rate of discount, the profitability index of project A is 112.6, whereas that of project B is 125.1 percent. Project B is therefore more attractive.

TABLE 15.1
A Comparison of Two Investment Projects

Year	Present Value of $1 at 10%	Certainty Equivalent of A's Cash Flow	Present Value of A's Cash Flows	Certainty Equivalent of B's Cash Flow	Present Value of B's Cash Flows
1	$1.00	$270	$ 270	$600	$ 600
2	.91	270	246	600	546
3	.83	270	224	600	498
4	.75	270	202	600	450
5	.68	270	184	600	408
		Total	$1,126		$2,502

Profitability index of project A = 1,126/1,000 = 112.6
Profitability index of project B = 2,502/2,000 = 125.1

RAISING THE DENOMINATOR IN THE PRESENT-VALUE CALCULATION

If the financial manager decides to raise the discount rate to cope with the variation of returns, he might proceed as follows: Let the discount rate, k, be the sum of two components. The first is the rate of return the firm can earn by purchasing an asset that yields a certain return over the same period as the project in question. A five-year government bond would be such an investment. The second term in the discount rate is a measure of the variability of the project's cash flows—the coefficient of variation, which is the standard deviation divided by the mean. Then:

$$k = i + \alpha \frac{\sigma}{\bar{X}}$$

where i is the rate on government bonds, $\bar{X}$ is the expected value of the cash flows, σ is the standard deviation of the flows, and α is an arbitrary scaler that indicates the amount by which k rises as the coefficient of variation increases. Suppose that i is .05 and α is $\frac{1}{4}$. The discount rate that will be applied to the expected value of project A's cash flow is then

$$k_a = .05 + \tfrac{1}{4}(60/300) = .10$$

The discount rate that will be applied to the expected value of B's cash flows is

$$k_b = .05 + \tfrac{1}{4}(200/700) = .12$$

Using these discount rates, the profitability indexes of projects A and B can be readily calculated. Table 15.2 shows that the profitability index of A is 131 percent, while that of B is 141 percent.

TABLE 15.2
A Comparison of Two Investment Projects

Years	Present Value of $1 at 10%	Expected Cash Flow from Project A	Present Value of A's Cash Flow	Present Value of $1 at 12%	Expected Cash Flow from Project B	Present Value of B's Cash Flow
1	$1.00	$300	$ 300	$1.00	$700	$ 700
2	.91	300	273	.89	700	623
3	.83	300	249	.80	700	560
4	.75	300	225	.71	700	497
5	.68	300	264	.64	700	448
		Total	$1,311			$2,828

Profitablity index of project A = 1,311/1,000 = 131.1
Profitability index of project B = 2,828/2,000 = 141.0

Coping with variability

An evaluation of coping with variation by adjusting variables

Variations in return can be incorporated in the analysis of specific investment projects by modifying either the cash flows that are to be discounted or the discount rate itself. The cash-flow figure can be lowered by substituting the certainty equivalent cash flow for the expected cash flow, and the discount rate can be raised by adding to it a term such as the adjusted coefficient of variation $\alpha(\sigma/X)$.

Both methods, however, can be criticised on several counts. First, both treat each project as self-contained, whereas we have seen that all the firm's activities are related to one another in rather complicated ways. To ignore the linkages that exist between projects and between the various parts of a firm is to miss the very essence of the managerial task—the coordination of all the company's resources to achieve a desired state of affairs.

Second, both methods merge two attributes of the distribution of return of an activity—its expected value and its variation—into a single value. As a result, a good deal of information about the cash flows is lost. A more appropriate way to handle the problem of variations in the returns of activities is to recognize that both dimensions exist. But how can a one-dimensional framework be extended to incorporate both the return of a project and the variation of its returns? We shall see in the following section.

A simulation

In the examples presented above, multiple profit figures arose because the company was not certain of the number of units of the product it could sell. In practice, of course, demand is not the only random variable in the investment decision problem. For example, a firm considering an investment project might have developed the data on nine important variables given in Table 15.3.

Note that each of the nine variables which affect the investment decision have a range of possible values. Moreover, the distribution of many of the variables is not normal; i.e., the best estimate (the one most likely to occur) does not lie at the midpoint of the range of values. Most of the distributions are skewed to the left. Figure 15.6, for example, shows the distribution of expected market size.

The internal rate of return of the project can be readily calculated from the data in Table 15.3. Using only the best estimate, the internal rate of return is 25.2 percent. However, if all the facts that are known about the project are included in the analysis, it becomes apparent that this estimate is very high.

TABLE 15.3
Estimates of Relevant Variables in Investment Analysis

	Best Estimate	Range of Values
1. Market size		
Expected value (tons)	250,000	100,000–340,000
2. Selling price		
Expected value ($/ton)	$510	$385–$575
3. Market growth rate		
Expected value	3%	0–6%
4. Eventual share of market		
Expected value	12%	3%–17%
5. Total investment required		
Expected value ($ millions)	$9.5	$7.0–$10.5
6. Useful life of facilities		
Expected value (years)	10	5–15
7. Residual value (at 10 years)		
Expected value ($ millions)	$4.5	$3.50–$5.00
8. Operating costs		
Expected value ($/ton)	$435	$370–$545
9. Fixed costs		
Expected value	$300	$250–$375

SOURCE: David Hertz, "Risk Analysis in Capital Investment," *Harvard Business Review*, vol. 42, no. 1 (January–February, 1964) pp. 95–106.

One way to include all the data is to draw sample observations from each of the nine distributions indicated in Table 15.3. Thus, a single figure for market size could be picked at random, a single selling price could be selected, and so forth.[1] These data can then be combined to

[1] The distribution of each of the nine series, of course, must be known, so that the probability of any one value can be determined. If the range and modal values are known, as in this example, it is convenient, for mathematical reasons, to assume that the data take on a triangular distribution. Computer programs that can select random samples from such distributions are widely available.

FIGURE 15.6
Distribution of Expected Market Size.

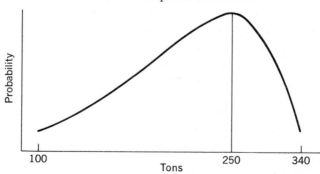

determine the internal rate of return. If this procedure is repeated a large number of times, an entire distribution of internal rates of return can be calculated. The results of just such a simulation are given in Table 15.4. These new data show that there is less than a 50-percent chance that the project will earn as much as 20 percent. This additional knowledge about the distribution of expected returns, therefore, places the best estimates in a new perspective; it now appears that 57 percent of the time the return will be less than 20 percent.

TABLE 15.4
The Probability of Achieving a Particular Return

Expected Return	Probability of Achieving at Least This Return
0%	96.5%
5	80.6
10	75.2
15	53.8
20	43.0
25	12.6
30	0

Suppose that the firm now simulates the possible results of a second project and, once again, finds the entire range of values that can result. If the profit profiles of the two projects are similar to those in Figure 15.5, the firm will again have to decide between a project with a lower, but less variable, return and one with a higher, but more variable, return.

The uncertainty problem in general

The choice among pricing strategies described earlier, as well as the choice between projects, is typical of many problems in finance. Situations frequently occur in which the expected mean and standard deviation of one activity are greater than the expected mean and standard deviation of another. For example, individuals often have a problem determining which securities to buy. The choice may be between government bonds that yield a small, but certain, return and the common stock of a small, but rapidly growing, company. The expected return of the common stock may be greater, but there is some chance that the company will fail and the investment will become worthless.

The nature of the problem in each of the situations described above—what price to charge for a product, which investment to make, and which securities to buy—is identical. Two alternatives are available, and the outcome of one has both a higher expected value and a higher standard deviation than the outcome of the other. If the expected value of the outcome were the sole criterion for ordering activities, no difficulty would be encountered. The firm would price the product at $1, and the individual investor would purchase the common stock of the small company. But the expected value of an activity is not the only criterion used to make decisions. The variation of the return must also be considered.

The utility function again

One way to link the expected return and the variation in the return of a project is to assume that an investor's utility curve depends on both of these factors rather than on the project's expected return alone. Several utility curves constructed on this basis are presented in Figure 15.7. The expected return of a project is measured along the horizontal axis, and an index of the variation in the return, its standard deviation, is measured along the vertical axis. The utility schedules rise monotonically and are concave downward, implying that, as a project's return rises, the utility afforded by it increases if the standard deviation remains constant. However, an increase in the project's standard deviation, for a given level of return, will lead to a lower level of utility.

The slope of any one utility function indicates the trade-off between the project's level of return and its variation. The schedules, as drawn,

FIGURE 15.7

An Investor's Utility Map.

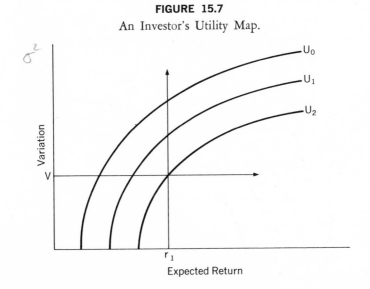

assume that at low levels of return, an investor is willing to accept a great deal of additional variation to increase his return by a modest amount. As the return increases, however, the investor's willingness to sustain additional variation for a modest increase in return falls.

In Figure 15.7, U_2 represents a higher level of utility than U_1, and U_1 is preferable to U_0. For a given level of variation, v_1, utility rises as return increases; on the other hand, for a given return, r_1, utility falls as variation rises. This is because as an investor moves in a general southeast direction, he receives both a higher level of return and a lesser amount of variation.

Let us now consider three projects, A, B, and C, in light of the utility schedules in Figure 15.7. Project B has both a higher standard deviation and a higher return than project A. Project C has both a higher return and a higher standard deviation than B.

When the variation and expected return of these three projects are plotted, as in Figure 15.8, it is apparent that projects C and A are equivalent, since both lie on the same utility function. The increase in project C's return is just sufficient to offset the greater variation in its expected return. Both projects A and C, however, are inferior to project B.

The problems that were posed earlier in this chapter can now be structured in a more formal way. Consider the two pricing alternatives: Should the firm adopt the policy that results in an expected profit level of $50 and a standard deviation of $50 or the one that results in a $40 profit level and a standard deviation of $10? If the manager's utility schedule depends on both the firm's level of profits and the variation of these profits, and if the trade-off between these variables is known, the answer

FIGURE 15.8

A Comparison of Three Investment Projects.

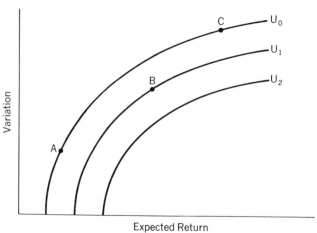

Variations in return, capital budgeting, and risk

to the question of which policy to adopt can be found. The results of the two policies can be plotted on a graph such as Figure 15.8; the one that lies along the highest utility schedule is the preferred policy. To summarize, the returns of a project or an activity will usually vary over some range. The firm's decision as to which of several projects to adopt and which to reject, therefore, cannot be made solely on the basis of the mean or expected value of the distribution of returns. Other properties of the distribution, such as its standard deviation, must also be considered. This is not a difficult task, however, if the utility function of the decision-maker is recognized as having two components. For example, if a decision-maker likes large returns and is not bothered by variability, the relative attractiveness of different projects can be readily determined. We have only to identify the utility curve on which the project lies.

The portfolio problem

The fact that activities generate a distribution of possible values, rather than a single value, has been widely recognized in recent years. Perhaps the most important reason for this is that this framework helps to explain one frequently observed aspect of investor behavior: Most people hold a diversified portfolio and do not concentrate their assets in a single venture.

Suppose an investor places half his funds in a project that has an expected return of 10 percent and a standard deviation of 15 percent. The other half he places in a project with an expected return of 10 percent and a standard deviation of 20 percent. It follows that the expected return on his total portfolio will also be 10 percent, but how large will the standard deviation of the portfolio be?

To answer this question, we need some information about the *covariance* of the two projects. Covariance is a statistical measure that indicates whether the returns of two or more projects vary together. The covariance of two projects will be negative if the returns on one project are high when the returns on the other are low; the covariance will be zero if the returns are independent; and it will be positive if the two returns fluctuate in the same direction. Let us suppose that the covariance of the returns of the two projects in question is —.03; i.e., their covariance is moderately negative. We can now calculate the standard deviation of the portfolio as a whole.

The square of the standard deviation is the *variance*. It is a well-known mathematical theorem that the variance of a weighted sum of two variables is given by the formula:

(15–1) $$\text{Var}(w_1A + w_2B) = w_1{}^2\text{Var}A + w_2{}^2\text{Var}B + 2w_1w_2\text{Cov}(AB)$$

where w_1 and w_2 are the weights applied to the variances of the two variables, A and B.

In our example, $w_1 = w_2 = \frac{1}{2}$. $\text{Var}A = (.15)^2 = .0225$, $\text{Var}B = (.2)^2 = .04$, and $\text{Cov}(AB) = -.03$. By substituting these values in the equation 15–1, we can find the variance of the portfolio. Thus:

$$\text{Var}(\tfrac{1}{2}A + \tfrac{1}{2}B) = \tfrac{1}{4}(.0225) + \tfrac{1}{4}(.040) + 2(\tfrac{1}{4})(-.03)$$
$$= \tfrac{1}{4}(.0225 + .04 - .06)$$
$$= .0006$$

The standard deviation of a portfolio with half the funds invested in A and half in B is the square root of .0006, or .0245. Buying both projects, then, reduces the variability of the portfolio's return substantially.

Figure 15.9 shows this argument visually. Projects A and B both yield a return of 10 percent. If half the investor's funds are put in each project, the rate of return will, of course, be 10 percent. However, because the covariance of the two projects is negative, the standard deviation of the return on both projects combined (C) will be lower than the standard deviation of either project by itself. The utility of the investor will therefore be higher (U_2) than it would be (U_1 or U_0) if he purchased only one project.

More frequently, both the return and the standard deviation of two projects are different. Suppose the mean and standard deviation of one project were 15 and 10 percent respectively, the corresponding values of another project were 25 and 35 percent, and the covariance of the two projects was −2 percent. Then, the portfolio mean and standard deviation would change as the proportion of the two securities purchased changed. For example, if the investor allocated his funds so that 80 per-

FIGURE 15.9
The Utility of Two Projects Alone and in Combination.

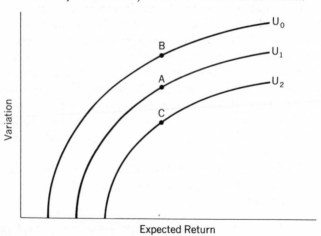

cent of his resources were committed to project A and 20 percent to project B, the expected return of his portfolio would be:

$$\text{Portfolio return} = (.8)(.15) + (.2)(.25)$$
$$= .17$$

The expected standard deviation of the portfolio (the square root of the variance), would be approximately 7 percent:

$$\text{Portfolio variance} = w_1{}^2\text{Var}A + w_2{}^2\text{Var}B + 2w_1w_2\text{Cov}(AB)$$
$$= (.8)^2(.10)^2 + (.2)^2(.35)^2 + 2(.8)(.2)(-.02)$$
$$= .0064 + .0049 - .0064$$
$$= .0049$$

This alternative, a return of 17 percent and a standard deviation of 7 percent, may be more attractive to the investor than purchasing either project A or project B alone.

To illustrate further the use of this framework, let us assume that the firm can purchase a number of potential projects. The returns and standard deviations of these projects are represented by the scatter of dots in Figure 15.10. By combining the projects in various proportions, the firm can, theoretically, construct a line, such as *AB*, which represents an *efficient frontier*. Each point along the frontier represents that combination of projects which, for any given value of σ, offers the highest return, or, alternatively, for any given return, the minimum σ that can be obtained. The exact combination of investments adopted depends on where the efficient frontier is tangent to the investor's utility curve. In Figure 15.10, one combination of projects is tangent to *U*, and this is the combination the investor will adopt.

FIGURE 15.10
An Efficiency Frontier and Utility Schedule.

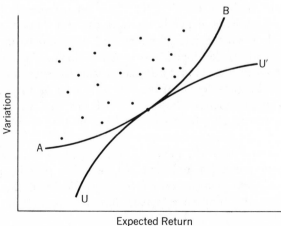

The portfolio problem

Advantages and disadvantages of this approach

Incorporating both the mean and the standard deviation of the return of an activity in the decision-making process has two principal advantages. First, it enables the financial manager to focus directly on important properties of the entire distribution of possible returns, rather than on some single measure that then must be adjusted, or modified, to reflect other values. Second, this framework can be used to develop models that explain why investors diversify their holdings rather than concentrate their funds in a single activity or project. It can easily be shown that the variation of the return of a portfolio of projects may be less than the variation of the return of any single project in the portfolio. This emphasizes the fact that the value to a firm of any specific investment cannot be measured solely in terms of its own return and the interaction of any new investment with ongoing projects must be considered.

However, several criticisms can be leveled at this framework. One is pragmatic. It is extremely difficult, if not impossible, for a firm to know what the covariance among projects actually is, since the returns of two projects may vary in the same direction under one set of circumstances and in the opposite direction under a second set of circumstances. For example, a paint manufacturer may produce some products that are used by homeowners and some that are used by professional painters. During a slowdown in economic activity, sales of one line may be high and those of the other low; during prosperity, the sales of both lines may move in the same direction. Unless the financial manager knows which state of affairs will prevail in the future, he cannot effectively determine what the covariance of different projects will be.

A second criticism is more fundamental. The underlying assumption of this framework is that only the mean and the standard deviation of the distribution of returns are important components of the investor's utility schedule. If the investor's utility function is more complicated than this, if, for example, it depends on how the distribution of returns is skewed as well as on the rate of return and the standard deviation, then the portfolio analysis developed above breaks down. To find an optimal portfolio, the mean, the standard deviation, and the skewness of the portfolio must all be considered. When the skewness of the distribution is incorporated in the analysis, however, portfolios that are inside the efficient frontier may touch a higher utility schedule than those that lie along the frontier.

One way to cope with the fact that other properties of the distribution of returns than the mean and standard deviation may be important to investors is to investigate the *cumulative distribution* of the project's returns. For example, suppose a person has the opportunity to purchase either of the two portfolios in Table 15.5. Neither distribution is normal, so the mean and standard deviation do not reflect all that is of interest here.

TABLE 15.5
Cumulative Distribution of Returns

	Portfolio A	Portfolio B
Percentage of returns that are less than 5%	5%	10%
Percentage of returns that are less than 10%	20	25
Percentage of returns that are less than 15%	25	35
Percentage of returns that are less than 20%	50	55
Percentage of returns that are less than 25%	60	80
Percentage of returns that are less than 30%	100	100

There is a 5 percent chance that the return on portfolio A will be less than 5 percent; the corresponding probability for portfolio B is 10 percent. There is only a 50 percent chance that the return on portfolio A will be less than 20 percent; for B, the probability is 55 percent; and so forth. Since portfolio A dominates portfolio B at every level of return, it is the preferred combination of projects.

In Figure 15.11, portfolio C lies to the right and therefore dominates portfolio D for some range of values and then the order changes, i.e., D lies to the right of C and dominates it. To determine which of these portfolios is superior, the utility of the slashed C's area of dominance must ultimately be compared to the utility of the D's area of dominance.

To summarize, the distribution of returns of different projects or different combinations of projects may not be normal. When this occurs, the

FIGURE 15.11
Cumulative Distribution of Returns of Two Projects.

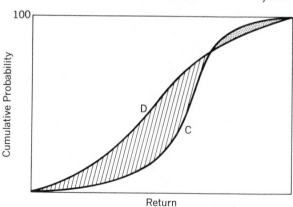

Advantages and disadvantages of this approach

mean and the standard deviation do not reflect all the data that is of interest, for they ignore the skewness of the distribution. To take this third factor into consideration, the investor must compare the entire cumulative distribution of the returns of the two projects by plotting the cumulative distribution of the expected results of different portfolios and ascertaining which one dominates the other. If one distribution dominates the other at all points, there is little difficulty in choosing between the two. However when the distributions cross, so that each dominates the other for some range of values, the problem is more difficult. The investor must then assign subjective values to various possible returns and determine which distribution gives him the most utility.

The role of risk in investment analysis

In the last section, stress was placed on the need to consider the entire distribution of expected returns rather than just one or two properties of the distribution such as the mean or the standard deviation. Some financial writers, unfortunately, have come to look upon the standard deviation of the distribution of returns as a measure not only of variability (which it is) but of the risk inherent in a project (which it is not).

In everyday usage, risk means the probability of a loss or the probability that a return will be lower than some target level. In Figure 15.12, this target level is T. Although the investor obviously would like to earn as high a return as possible he will not consider that he has sustained a loss unless the return falls below this level. *Risk can be measured by the area under the distribution of returns that lies below the target level.*

FIGURE 15.12
The Risk Associated with Three Distributions of Returns.

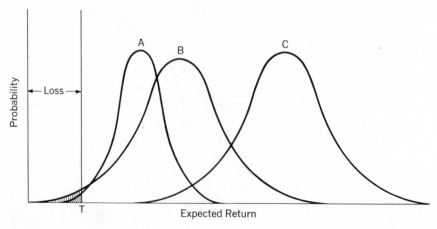

Variations in return, capital budgeting, and risk

Figure 15.12 shows the distribution of returns offered by three different investments. Distribution A has a smaller standard deviation than distribution B. The probability that the return earned on project A will fall below the target level is the dotted area in Figure 15.12. This area is less than the hatched area, the probability that the return on B will fall below the target level. Project A is therefore less risky than B. Project C has the highest standard deviation of the three. However, since the chance that its return will fall below the target level is negligible, it is the least risky project.

The relationship between risk and the standard deviation of a distribution of returns is now clear. If the two distributions have the same expected return, the project with the larger standard deviation is the riskier. However, if the returns are not equal, the risk associated with a project cannot be determined until a minimum target level of return has been established. At times, a distribution with a high standard deviation is less risky than one with a low standard distribution. (C in Figure 15.12 is less risky than B.) At other times, a distribution with a high standard deviation is more risky than one with a small standard deviation. (B is more risky than A.)

One question uppermost in the minds of investors is, How can the risk associated with an activity be lowered? The first and most obvious strategy is to select projects with a high expected rate of return. The higher the expected return is, the smaller is the probability that the actual return will be below the minimum target level. A second strategy is to distribute investment resources among several different securities. If the covariance of the distribution of the returns of the investments in a portfolio is negative, the standard deviation of the portfolio as a whole will be lower than the standard deviation of the specific investments.

A third strategy is to hold the investments for a relatively long period. If a portfolio with a positive expected return is held over successive time periods, the probability that a loss will occur eventually becomes negligible. For example, an investment may have an expected rate of return of 10 percent per annum and a standard deviation of 5 percent. Let the target loss level be 5 percent. This is a moderately risky situation in the first year, since a loss will occur (i.e., a return below 5 percent will be realized) 16 percent of the time. The expected value of the investment at the end of two years, however, is 21 percent. More important, the distribution of the expected return in each subsequent year becomes more sharply skewed to the right, and the probability that the realized rate of return will fall below 5 percent becomes negligible in only a few years.

All three of these strategies—purchasing investments with high expected returns, diversifying, and holding investments for long periods—are followed by financial managers. As a result, random fluctuations in return are seldom an important managerial problem. What is important, however, is the information system the manager has developed. If the information system is a poor one, he may overlook, through ignorance, some major consideration that will alter the entire character of a project. The probability of loss, or risk, is therefore more intimately connected to the information system of the firm than it is to possible variations in return.

Summary

All corporations are challenged to create an effective information system. A good cost-accounting system can provide some data about the internal operations of the firm, but a financial manager needs to know more than what his production costs will be for a specified mix of outputs. He must know about developments outside the firm that influence the demand for his product, his production function, and the supply of his inputs. He must also know the effects of a change in one activity on the costs and profits of another. Without this information, he must operate under conditions of uncertainty, and the returns the firm earns on its investments may be highly variable.

Financial analysts have attempted to come to grips with the economic reality that managers frequently do not know all the consequences of their actions in several ways. One method is to adjust the expected cash flow from an activity for possible variations. Another is to raise the discount rate used to determine the cash flows' present values. Both these methods reduce the entire distribution of possible returns to a point estimate.

A third and more promising method is to work directly with the entire distribution of returns, recognizing that if the distribution of returns is normally distributed, the mean and standard deviation will effectively reflect all the relevant factors. Moreover, if investors have a utility schedule that values returns and disvalues variations, the distributions of returns associated with the different projects can themselves be ordered.

This *mean-variance approach* to investment projects has gained favor in recent years for several reasons. It permits a more realistic assessment of projects because it recognizes another dimension than return. More important, it effectively explains the widely observed phenomenon that most financial managers prefer to maintain a portfolio of projects rather than concentrating all their wealth and energy in a single activity. As long as the covariance between projects is negative, the variance of the entire portfolio may be less than the variance of any single activity.

This approach, however, depends on an investor utility function that has only two components. If investors are interested in other properties of the distribution of possible returns than the mean and the standard deviation, and they will be if the returns generated by a project are not normally distributed, a broader formulation of the investment problem is needed. One solution is to compare the entire distribution of returns of projects and to see which one is dominant. If one project always dominates another, it is obviously superior and should be selected. If one distribution dominates another only for some values, the utility of the returns over the various ranges of values must be studied.

The riskiness of a project is related to the variability of its returns, but the link between risk and variability is subtle. If two projects have the same expected value, then the project whose returns are more variable is riskier. But risk means the probability of loss. Thus a project with a high expected return may be less risky than one with a lower expected return, even though the standard deviation of the first project is greater. In the final analysis, risk depends on the adequacy of the information system of the firm.

Questions for discussion and problems

1. What is the nature of the trade-off between the costs of organizational design and the costs of information?

2. What factors are likely to give rise to a distribution of expected sales as a result of a specific corporate action rather than to a single expected value?

3. If a firm experiences diminishing returns to scale, what will happen to the profit per unit as sales increase?

4. What are the important differences between adjusting the expected cash flows of a project by lowering the numerator of the present-value calculation and raising the denominator of the calculation?

5. How can two projects with normally distributed expected returns be ordered in a way that takes account of both the returns and the variability of the returns?

6. Under what conditions will a portfolio of several projects have a lower standard deviation than each of the projects alone?

7. Why does diversification lead to a lower level of variability?

8. What are some limitations of the mean-variance framework of analysis?

9. Why is the determination of the dominance of one distribution over another a more satisfactory way to compare projects than an analysis of only the mean and variance of each project?

10. Why are the terms "risk" and "variability" not equivalent in financial matters? Is variability always considered bad?

[*Answers to problems 11–14 follow references and suggested readings.*]

11. (a) The Happy Medium Entertainment Center has fixed costs of $3,300 a month. These costs include the outlays for rent, go-go girls, etc. If its variable costs are $.40 per drink and the average price per drink is $1.50, how many drinks a month must the Happy Medium sell to break even?

    (b) A typical customer at the Happy Medium buys three drinks. The owner of the Happy Medium estimates that he has 1,200 customers a month. However there is some variation in this figure: In about two-thirds of the months, he has from 800 to 1,600 customers. The Happy Medium is up for sale, and the prospective buyer wants to know the expected monthly profit. In addition, he wants to know (c) what percent of the time he can expect to lose money and (d) what percent of the time he can expect to make roughly $2,000 a month profit.

12. An investor is considering the purchase of two businesses. One, a racing stable, has an expected annual return of $5,000 and a standard deviation about this value of $1,000. The second, a nursing home, has an expected return of $4,000 and a standard deviation about this value of $400. The investor is moderately averse to risk in the sense that his b coefficient in the certainty-equivalent formula is .5. He has a four-year horizon and expects that the salvage value of both investments at the end of this period will be zero. If he wants to earn 15 percent on his money, how much should he offer the sellers of each investment?

13. The interest rate on government bonds was 8 percent at the time the investor in problem 12 was considering making his investments. If his α coefficient is $\frac{1}{2}$, what discount rate would he use to evaluate the two investments?

14. Calculate the returns and standard deviation of a portfolio if half the funds are invested in a project that has a 10 percent return and a standard deviation of .10 while the other half is invested in a project that has a 20 percent return and a standard deviation of .2. The covariance of the two projects is −.005.

REFERENCES AND SUGGESTED READINGS

Articles

Agnew, N. H., *et al.,* "An Application of Chance Constrained Programming to Portfolio Selection in a Casualty Insurance Firm," *Management Science,* vol. XV, no. 10 (June 1969), pp. B512–21.

Alderfer, Clayton, and Bierman, Harold, Jr., "Choices with Risk: Beyond the Mean Variance," *Journal of Business,* vol. XLIII, no. 3 (July 1970), pp. 341–54.

Arditti, F. O., "Risk and Required Return on Equity," *Journal of Finance*, vol. XII, no. 3 (March 1967), pp. 19–36.

Bauman, W. Scott, "Evaluation of Prospective Investment Performance," *Journal of Finance*, vol. XXIII, no. 2 (May 1968), pp. 276–95.

Briscoe, G., Samuels, J. M., and Smyth, D. J., "The Treatment of Risk in the Stock Market," *Journal of Finance*, vol. XXIV, no. 4 (September 1969), pp. 707–13.

Byrne, R., Charnes, A., Cooper, W. W., and Kortanek, K., "A Chance Constrained Approach to Capital Budgeting with Portfolio Type Payback and Liquidity Constraints and Horizon Posture Controls," *Journal of Financial and Quantitative Analysis*, vol. II. no. 4 (December 1967), pp. 339–64.

Cohen, Kalman J. and Elton, Edwin J., "Inter-temporal Portfolio Analysis Based on Simulation of Joint Returns," *Management Science*, vol. XIV, no. 1 (September 1967), pp. 5–18.

Fisher, I. N., and Hall, G. R., "Risk and Corporate Rates of Return," *Quarterly Journal of Economics*, vol. LXXXIII, no. 1 (February 1969), pp. 79–93.

Friedman, M., and Savage, L. J., "The Utility Analysis of Choices Involving Risk," *Journal of Political Economy*, vol. LVI (August 1958), pp. 279–306.

Hadar, Josef, and Russell, William P., "Rules for Ordering Uncertain Prospects," *American Economic Review*, vol. LIX, no. 1 (March 1969), pp. 25–34.

Hakanson, Nils, "On the Dividend Capitalization Model Under Uncertainty," *Journal of Financial and Quantitative Analysis*, vol. IV, no. 1 (March 1969), pp. 65–89.

Hertz, David B., "Risk Analysis in Capital Investment," *Harvard Business Review*, vol. 42, no. 1 (January–February 1964), pp. 95–106.

Hespos, Richard F., and Strassmann, Paul A., "Stochastic Decision Trees for the Analysis of Investment Decisions," *Management Science*, vol. XI (August 1965) pp. 244–59.

Hillier, Frederich S., "The Evaluation of Risky Interrelated Investments," Technical Report No. 73, Department of Statistics, Stanford University, Stanford, Calif. (July 1964).

Hirshleifer, J., "Investment Decision Under Uncertainty: Choice—Theoretic Approaches," *Quarterly Journal of Economics*, vol. LXXXIX, no. 4 (November 1965), pp. 509–36.

———, "Investment Decision Under Uncertainty: Application of the State-Preference Approach," *Quarterly Journal of Economics*, vol. LXXX, no. 2 (May 1966), pp. 252–77.

Jaedicke, Robert K., and Robichek, Alexander A., "Cost-Volume Profit Analysis Under Conditions of Uncertainty," *Accounting Review* (October 1964), pp. 917–26.

Joyce, Jon M., and Vogel, Robert C., "The Uncertainty in Risk: Is Variance Unambiguous?" *Journal of Finance*, vol. XXV, no. 1 (March 1970), pp. 127–35.

Latane, H. A., "Criteria for Choice Among Risky Ventures," *Journal of Political Economy*, vol. LXVII, no. 2 (April 1959), pp. 144–55.

Levy, Haim, "A Utility Function Depending on the First Three Moments," *Journal of Finance*, vol. XXIV, no. 4 (September 1969), pp. 715–19.

Machol, Robert E., and Lerner, Eugene, "Risk, Ruin, and Investment Analysis." *Journal of Financial and Quantitative Analysis*, vol. IV, no. 4 (December 1969), pp. 473–93.

Magee, John F., "Decision Trees for Decision Making," *Harvard Business Review*, vol. 42 (July–August 1964), pp. 126–38.

Questions for discussion and problems   **333**

Magee. John F., "How to Use Decision Trees in Capital Investment," *Harvard Business Review* vol. 42 (September–October 1964), pp. 79–96.

Mao, James C. T., and Helliwell, John F., "Investment Decisions Under Uncertainty: Theory and Practice," *Journal of Finance,* vol. XXIV, no. 2 (May 1969), pp. 323–39.

Markowitz, Harry, "Portfolio Selection," *Journal of Finance,* vol. VII, no. 1 (March 1952), pp. 77–91.

Naslund, Bertil, "A Model of Capital Budgeting Under Risk," *Journal of Business,* vol. XXXIX, no. 2 (April 1966), pp. 257–71.

Resik, Robert, "Multidimensional Risk and the Modigliani-Miller Hypothesis," *Journal of Finance,* vol. XXV, no. 1 (March 1970), pp. 42–53.

Robichek, Alexander, and Myers, S. C., "Conceptual Problems in the Use of Risk-Adjusted Discount Rates," *Journal of Finance,* vol. XXI, no. 4 (December 1966), pp. 727–30.

Roy, A. D., "Safety First and the Holding of Assets," *Econometrica* (July 1952), pp. 431–49.

Sharpe, W. F., "Risk Aversion in the Stock Market: Some Empirical Evidence," *Journal of Finance,* vol. XX, no. 3 (September 1965), pp. 416–23.

————, "Capital Asset Prices: A Theory of Market Equilibrium Under Conditions of Risk," *Journal of Finance,* vol. XIX, no. 3, (September 1964), pp. 425–42.

Shinju, Kataoka, "A Stochastic Programming Model," *Econometrica,* vol. XXXI. no. 1–2 (January–April 1963), pp. 181–96.

Soldofsky, Robert M., and Miller, Roger L., "Risk-Premium Curves for Different Classes of Long-Term Securities, 1950–1966" vol. XXIV, no. 3, *Journal of Finance* (June 1969) pp. 429–45.

Swalm, Ralph D., "Utility Theory—Insights into Risk Taking," *Harvard Business Review,* vol. 44, no. 6 (November–December 1966), pp. 123–36.

Tuttle, Donald L., and Litzenberger, Robert H., "Leverage, Diversification and Capital Market Effects on a Risk Adjusted Capital Budgeting Framework," *Journal of Finance,* vol. XXIII, no. 3 (June 1968) pp. 427–45.

Van Horne, James, "Capital Budgeting Decisions Involving Combinations of Risky Investments," *Management Science,* vol. XIII, no. 2 (October 1966), pp. 84–92.

Woods, Donald H., "Improving Estimates That Involve Uncertainty," *Harvard Business Review,* vol. 45, no. 4 (July–August 1966), pp. 91–98.

Books

Borch, Karl, and Jan Mossin, ed., *Risk and Uncertainty: Proceedings of a Conference Held by the International Economic Association* (London and New York: Macmillan, 1969).

Brealey, Richard A., *An Introduction to Risk and Return from Common Stocks* (Cambridge, Mass.: MIT Press, 1969).

Grayson, C. Jackson, Jr., *Decisions Under Uncertainty: Drilling Decisions by Oil and Gas Operators* (Boston, Mass.: Harvard Business School Division of Research, 1960).

Hillier, Frederich, and Lieberman, Gerald, *Introduction to Operation Research* (San Francisco: Holden-Day, 1967).

Kogan, Nathan, and Wallach, Michael, *Risk Taking* (New York: Holt, Rinehart and Winston, 1964).

Markowitz, Harry, *Portfolio Selection—Efficient Diversification of Investments* (New York: Wiley, 1959).

McMillan, Claude, and Gonzalez, Richard F., *Systems Analysis—A Computer Approach to Decision Models* (Homewood, Ill.: Irwin, 1965).

Naylor, Thomas, *et al., Computer Simulation Techniques* (New York: Wiley, 1966).

Rappaport, Alfred, ed., *Information for Decision Making: Quantitative and Behavioral Dimensions* (Englewood Cliffs, N. J.: Prentice-Hall, 1970).

Robichek, Alexander, and Myers, S. C., *Optimal Financing Decisions* (Englewood Cliffs, N. J.: Prentice-Hall, 1965).

Von Neuman, J., and Morgenstern, O., *Theory of Games and Economic Behavior*, 3rd ed. (Princeton, N.J.: Princeton Univ. Press, 1953).

ANSWERS TO PROBLEMS 11–14

11.
(a) It must sell 3,000 drinks a month.
(b) The company will sell, on the average, 3,600 drinks a month. This is 600 over the break-even amount and will yield a profit of $660.
(c) One standard deviation is 1,200 drinks (400 customers). The probability that sales will fall below the break-even amount of 3,000 drinks is .31. Therefore, in 31 percent of the months the company will lose money.
(d) If the company sells 4,800 drinks, it will earn approximately $2,000 per month ($1,980). Since this value is two standard deviations greater than the mean, profits will be about $2,000 in 2.3 percent of the months.

12.

Year	Present Value of $1 at 15 Percent	Certainty Equivalent of Stable's Cash Flows	Present Value of Stable's Cash Flows
1	.87	$4,500	$ 3,915
2	.75	4,500	3,375
3	.66	4,500	2,970
4	.57	4,500	2,565
			$12,825

Year	Present Value of $1 at 15 Percent	Certainty Equivalent of Nursing-Home Cash Flows	Present Value of Nursing Home's Cash Flows
1	.87	$3,800	$ 3,306
2	.75	3,800	2,850
3	.66	3,800	2,508
4	.57	3,800	2,166
			$10,830

Thus he should offer $12,825 for the racing stable and $10,830 for the nursing home.

13. He should use a discount rate of 18 percent for the race track and 13 percent for the nursing home.

14. Expected return $= \frac{1}{2}(.10) + \frac{1}{2}(.20) = .15$
$\mathrm{Var}(\frac{1}{2}A + \frac{1}{2}B) = (\frac{1}{4})(.1)^2 + (\frac{1}{4})(.2)^2 + 2(\frac{1}{2})(\frac{1}{2})(-.005) = .01$
Therefore the standard deviation is .1

Influencing the market value of the system: investment analysis and portfolio management

FIVE

The decisions financial managers make with respect to dividend payments, capital structure, and the rate of return have effects beyond the narrow confines of the corporation itself. They touch, to a greater or lesser degree all the markets in which the firm operates. In particular, they affect the financial market in which the company's stock is traded and the price of the company's shares.

Part Five focuses on several aspects of the security market. Chapter 16 discusses why many firms have adopted the maximization of shareholder wealth as a corporate goal, even though financial managers must contend with economic and market forces outside their direct control to achieve this end. Chapter 17 describes the relationship between the actions of a corporate manager and the change in the price of the company's shares.

The investment community, of course, follows corporate activities closely, in order to be able to make informed judgments about the future price of the company's stock. Chapter 18 describes some of the models working investment analysts use to determine whether the price of a company's stock is at a level that indicates an extraordinary opportunity for gain.

The behavior of the price of a company's securities affects its ability to grow through mergers and acquisitions. If the price of the stock is relatively low, merging is a high-cost strategy; if the price of the stock is relatively high, merging becomes a viable strategy for corporate growth. The reasoning behind these claims is discussed in Chapter 19.

Finally, Chapter 20 is concerned with the management of security portfolios. This material is important to many financial managers, who are deeply involved with the management of their company's pension fund or profit-sharing plan.

Corporate goals and the equity market

16

The models of the firm discussed in Part Four rested on an implicit assumption that it is important for a firm to strive to maximize the welfare of its shareholders. Almost nothing was said of the corporation's responsibility to help eliminate national social problems, to work for the goals of the community in which it operates, or to further the hopes and aspirations of its employees.

These models indicated what decisions management should make to realize its objectives. Thus they also assumed that the forces beyond the control of management were not so powerful that they could frustrate the realization of well-conceived corporate goals.

Both these assumptions must now be questioned. Why should a financial manager urge his firm to pursue the goal of shareholder wealth? If he does, can the manager achieve the ends he wishes with the means he has at his command?

These are far-reaching questions. Perhaps the most that can be done in this chapter is to sketch some of the considerations that must be kept in mind before a judgment can be reached. The first section of the chapter discusses whether the maximization of shareholder wealth is a reasonable goal for a firm to set for itself. To reach an answer, we shall analyze how the competitive economy operates and what its strengths and weaknesses are. Even if maximization of shareholder wealth is an appropriate corporate goal, the extent to which the actions of the financial manager determine the price of his company's shares is questionable. No financial manager can control macroeconomic variables such as the general level of interest rates or the rate of growth of the economy. Yet these factors have a great effect on stock prices. Moreover, technical properties of the market for securities condition the volatility of the price movements that take place. These market properties also are outside the control of individual managers. Some knowledge of the economic and technical market factors that influence the thinking and perspective of financial managers is essential to any real understanding of capital budgeting, security-valuation strategies, merger policies, and portfolio problems.

The logic of wealth maximization

There is widespread agreement that if a society is to meet its economic commitments to its citizens, and these include the obliteration of hunger and poverty, two conditions must be met. First, all the resources in the economy that seek work must be able to find it. Second, the amount of waste in the system must be a minimum. The resources that are employed should produce the goods and services society wants and needs in as socially efficient a manner as possible.

Chapter 21 presents a framework for analyzing the capacity of the economy to provide full employment. Here we shall see how a society can structure itself so that it uses its resources in a socially efficient way.

An economy can organize its resources to produce goods and services in several ways. In a dictatorship, a central bureaucracy can control strategic factor inputs and arbitrarily direct the production of the goods and services it deems desirable. Such centrally controlled economies have existed in different parts of the world in the past, and they continue to exist in the present.

Another way to determine what goods and services the economy will produce is to allow consumers to purchase the products they want. If there are a large number of firms operating in each industry and if each strives to maximize the wealth of its shareholders, they will compete with one another for the consumers' dollars. They will produce the products consumers want and they will produce them as efficiently as they know how.

To illustrate how a competitive economy works, suppose that the demand for a firm's products rises. To expand its output to meet this demand, the profit-maximizing firm will bid resources away from other firms in the economy. It will be able to hire the resources by offering them a higher price than they now earn. But the firm can continue to pay this price only as long as it can generate enough revenue from the products it sells. If consumers are unwilling to pay the prices for goods that the firm charges, it will be unable to continue paying for the production inputs it needs. Its resources will then be bid away from it by firms that are producing the goods and services that consumers want to buy and are willing to pay for. If the cost of producing a unit of output exactly equals the price the consumer is willing to pay for that unit, i.e., if the marginal cost of the unit equals the marginal revenue it produces, and if this is true for all firms in the economy resources are being allocated in a socially optimum way.

A number of assumptions lay behind the sweeping statements made above about the operation of the competitive economy. We assumed that resources were mobile and that they could shift from one firm to another at no social cost; that products were sold in competitive markets, so that the marginal revenue earned by the firm equaled the price that the consumer paid for the product; that consumers knew the prices of comparable goods; and that producers had the knowledge and ability to change their production function in response to changes in either factor prices or market demands. All these assumptions are more or less untenable in the short run. In the short run, resources are not highly mobile, markets are not perfect, and the consumers' knowledge about the relative prices and quality of goods varies. Moreover, we have ignored certain situations in which the competitive market will not produce an optimum allocation of resources for society as a whole.

One such case where the competitive system fails to perform well arises when a firm has continuous economies of scale, that is, when the more output it produces, the lower the cost of each unit becomes. Whenever such a situation prevails, the economy will be able to obtain these goods at the lowest price only if a single firm, a monopoly, operates in the industry.

A second situation that will not result in an optimum allocation of resources occurs when the utility curves of consumers are interdependent. Thus, if the consumption of drugs is offensive to a large segment of the population a law may be passed making it a crime for some people to spend their income as they see fit, i.e., to purchase drugs. Or, if the community believes that it is desirable for the aged to have a guaranteed income, a law may be passed making it mandatory for every working person to contribute a portion of his salary to social security. Both these laws arise because the consumption expenditures of one person influence not only his own utility curves but those of others as well. The welfare of society as a whole may therefore be improved by their passage. But there is no way that a competitive economy, left to itself, could have produced the particular allocation of resources achieved by these laws.

The third case in which the market system will fail to provide an optimum allocation of resources arises when the production function has *indivisibilities*. By this we mean that a whole dam must be built to stop a river, or a whole bridge must be built to cross a gully; half a dam or a quarter of a bridge will not suffice. The market economy provides an optimum allocation of resources when small-scale adjustments must be made; it works well if a little more or a little less of a product is to be produced. But there is no assurance that it will provide the best allocation of the economy's resources when major indivisibilities characterize the production process.

There are limitations, then, to the ability of the competitive economy to solve certain problems in a socially optimum way. Nevertheless, the market economy continues to enjoy widespread support because of the deep ethical beliefs of many people about the kind of society in which they want to live.

The economy described so briefly above was that which exists in a free society under ideal conditions and is approximated to some extent in western society today. People have the right to buy whatever goods they want, sell the resources they own to any bidder, and change their jobs when they perceive better opportunities elsewhere. People vote not only with their dollars for the goods they want to buy but with their feet, because in a free society people are mobile. Any person who has had first-hand experience with a dictatorial society will testify that these are not liberties to be valued lightly.

A second reason a competitive economy enjoys support is that a real profit-maximizing firm in a free society is color-blind. It is indifferent to whether its customers are black or white, college graduates or unlettered. Its sole concern is with which buyer will pay the highest price. In an ideal competitive society, the firm is equally indifferent as to the inputs it buys: It will purchase the resources that can produce a given level of output at the least cost. It does not matter whether the seller is handsome, has the proper ethnic background, or wears the right clothes. The alternative to the color-blindness of the profit-maximizing firm operating in a competitive environment is a social system of favoritism, segregation, and quotas.

Finally, a free-enterprise society enables each person to develop to the full extent of his ability. Any person is free to produce the goods he thinks society needs in any way that he wishes as long as he does not break the law. This is true whether the product is an underground newspaper, a novel on the ills of society, a painting, or a detergent. Moreover, the entrepreneur can continue to do his thing as long as his resources hold out.

An outsider will never be able to tell what impelled him to produce the product, and, in fact, it makes no difference whether his motive was to benefit society, or only himself. If he anticipated the needs of society correctly, people will not only buy his product but will make him rich. If people do not want the product (even if it is "good" for them), he will lose whatever resources he has invested.

The competitive economy, then, has important strong points: It is a necessary part of a free society; it operates without prejudice; and it lets any man venture into any activity that he thinks will let him fulfill himself. Profit-maximizing firms within the system will produce the goods society wants as efficiently as they know how. As we have seen, however, the market system also has limitations that must be corrected: It cannot remain competitive when there are massive economies of scale in an industry, and it may not lead to an optimum allocation of resources when consumers' utility curves are interdependent or when the production process is characterized by indivisibilities. Moreover, there is no automatic mechanism that helps people who can contribute no useful inputs to survive.

These limitations of the free, competitive economy can be overcome by legal and political action. Monopolies can be regulated or operated by the government. Laws can be passed and agencies established to ensure that the aged, the infirm, or the indigent and others who do not directly contribute to the economic system can have an adequate living standard. Government plays an important and vital role in a free society, for it both defines the rules of the game and enforces them.

Within the ground rules set by law, the profit-maximizing firm is, in a free society, the instrument through which decisions are made as to which goods the economy will produce and how it will produce them. There is, however, a certain ambiguity about the term "profit-maximizing firm." It does not mean that a firm will charge what the traffic will bear at every moment or that it will dismiss its employees the instant a cheaper production process becomes available. It is easy to show that a pricing policy or an employment policy that does not consider the effects of an action on the future position of the firm is suboptimum. Because of the misunderstanding that surrounds the term "profit maximizing," a more appropriate phrase has now gained acceptance: Corporations seek to maximize "the wealth of their shareholders."

A wealth-maximizing framework looks beyond the short run and explicitly seeks to incorporate into its thinking and planning the entire future stream of earnings that the firm will generate. In addition, since the future earnings generated by the firm are evaluated in present dollars, this framework adds a new dimension to the classical theory of the firm; it requires information about the discount rate that shareholders use to convert a firm's future earnings into present value.

The most widely used measure of wealth is the market price of the corporation's shares. Another, more concrete way of stating that firms seek to maximize the wealth of their shareholders is therefore to say that firms seek to maximize the market value of their shares.

To summarize, a corporation should strive to maximize the wealth of its shareholders because, under a specified set of conditions, such action by all firms will lead to an efficient allocation of resources throughout the economy. Goods will be produced that consumers want to buy; firms will operate without regard to race, color, or creed; and each individual will be free to develop his talents to fullest.

The concept of "maximizing the wealth of shareholders" is a broader concept than "maximizing long-run profits." It implies that firms are interested in more than just the efficient production and marketing of goods and services in a single period—that they are also interested in how the marketplace evaluates their performance. It is for this reason that financial managers weigh so carefully the effect on the corporate image of a change in the firm's debt structure, a merger with a firm in an unrelated business, or the establishment of a research and development department.

Fluctuations in market averages

A corporation, however, is not the complete master of its fate in regard to share prices. Even though it may strive to maximize shareholder wealth, certain macroeconomic events will influence the price of all the shares that are traded, and their influence may be powerful enough to outweigh the specific actions of corporate management. Moreover, certain structural characteristics of the market in which the firm's securities are traded can also influence the price of the shares. These macroeconomic market forces, are largely outside the control of the firm.

Imagine a composite company, one made up of all the companies listed on the New York Stock Exchange. The price of this composite's stock would then behave in a manner similar to the way an index of all securities (such as the Dow Jones average or the Standard and Poor's average of security prices) now behaves.

To analyze this behavior, we can imagine that the price of the company's stock, like that of any single company, would be given by the equation:

$$P = \frac{D}{k - g}$$

where D is the dividend payment, k is the discount rate, g is the growth rate, and P is the price. If k rises abruptly, the price of the security will fall dramatically; if g rises, the price of the security will rise sharply; and as D rises and falls, corresponding fluctuations will occur in the price of the composite's stock.

The values of k, g, and D in this valuation equation, are affected by macroeconomic forces, rather than by specific corporate developments, since the company in question is a composite of all companies. For example, the discount rate, k, applied to the composite company's expected stream of dividends is likely to be a function of the prevailing interest rate on government bonds, since these bonds are an alternative outlet for funds available to all investors. The value of k used to discount the composite company's dividend stream is likely to be greater than the interest rate on government bonds, since the interest payments that bondholders receive are more certain than the growth rate of the composite company's dividend stream. As the interest rate on government bonds rises from, say, 5 to 7 percent, investors might want the return of the securities they buy to increase from, say, 7 to 10 percent.

The growth rate of the composite company's dividend payments will be functionally related to the growth rate of the economy. If the economy expands rapidly, corporate profits are likely to rise, and the financial manager is likely to urge that dividends be raised to maintain and enhance the value of its shares. Investors will thus come to recognize that the same factors which indicate a change in the growth rate of the economy are effective indicators of the growth rate of the company's dividend payments.

Economists, who are very interested in methods of forecasting changes in economic events, have found that gross national product tends to expand when the money supply rises and level off or decline when it falls. Investors in the composite company's securities are likely to come to the same conclusion.

Using the interest rate on bonds as a proxy for k in the valuation equation of the composite security and changes in the money supply as a proxy for g, we can predict how the price of the stock, or the value of any index of security prices, is likely to behave over a business cycle.

The interest rate on government bonds is a *lagging series*. By this we mean that interest rates continue to rise for some time after the economy as a whole has reached a peak. Similarly, interest rates continue to fall for some time after the economy as a whole has reached the bottom of a recession. The graph of typical lagging function is presented in Figure 16.1. The occurrence of a peak or a trough in the business cycle is indicated on the time axis by P and T, respectively.

FIGURE 16.1

A Typical Lagging Series.

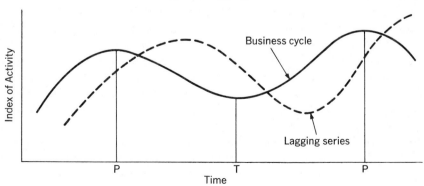

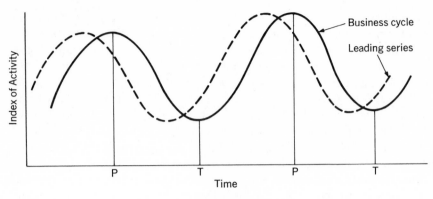

FIGURE 16.2

A Typical Leading Function.

The rate of change of the money supply, on the other hand, is a *leading series.* The rate of change of the money supply tends to turn down before the economy as a whole reaches the peak of a business cycle and to turn up before the economy as a whole begins to recover from the trough of a recession. The graph of a typical leading function is presented in Figure 16.2.

The length of the lag of interest rates and the length of the lead of changes in the money supply during business cycle peaks and troughs varies from period to period. For example, the change in the money supply might turn up anywhere from a year to six weeks before business conditions improve. Similarly, the interest-rate peak can occur from one to nine months after economic activity reaches a peak.

Let us now combine these proxies for k and g in a single graph, Figure 16.3, to determine how an average of all security prices may be expected to behave over a business cycle.

How will security prices behave between periods 1 and 2, just before and after the peak of a business cycle? During this period, the leading series has turned down and is declining. The drop in the rate of change of the money supply will lead investors to expect a fall in the growth rate of national income, aggregate profits, and aggregate dividends. The lagging series, however, is still rising during this period. Since the interest rate is continuing to rise, the discount rate that shareholders apply to the stream of revenues they will receive from their securities will also keep on rising. The combination of a fall in g and a rise in k will tend to drive security prices down.

The behavior of security prices between periods 2 and 3 is more difficult to predict. This period corresponds to a downturn in economic activity. The leading series is still declining, indicating that an upturn in the growth rate of national income is not yet in sight. However, the rate

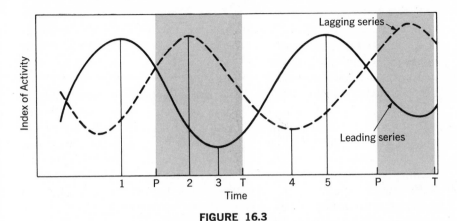

FIGURE 16.3

The Behavior of Leading and Lagging Series over the Business Cycle.

of interest is also falling. This will lower k, the discount rate that shareholders apply to the composite company's dividends. Whether security prices will continue to fall, hold steady, or rise moderately will depend on whether the change in g is greater than, equal to, or less than the change in k.

The period between 3 and 4 spans the bottom of a recession. During this period, the rate of change in the money supply begins to increase, indicating that the rate of growth of the economy will soon pick up, and hence that earnings and dividends will begin to rise. Moreover, interest rates (the lagging series) are still falling, causing ever-lower values of k to be adopted. The combination of a rise in g and a fall in k will lead to a rapid increase in security prices.

From period 4 to 5, security prices will behave much as they did between periods 2 and 3, since k and g again move in opposite directions.

The fact that stock-price indexes fall while the economy is prospering and rise when it is not is so puzzling to some observers that they ascribe the behavior of security prices to "market psychology" or the "madness of crowds" or simply to chance. In fact, there is an explanation of the movements.

To summarize, security prices will rise most rapidly near the trough of a business cycle, and they will fall most rapidly near the peak of a business cycle. In between the peaks and troughs, prices will tend to be stable. However, because the length of the lead and the lag of the rate of growth of the money supply and interest rates vary, the movement of security prices is difficult to predict.

The fact that security prices rise most rapidly near the trough of a business cycle and fall most rapidly near the peak is well documented. For example, the Dow Jones average of security prices fell by more than

25 percent during 1969 and early 1970. During this period, also, the economy reached a peak and began to decline. Not until the rate of change of the money supply began to rise and interest rates leveled off did security prices in general start to rise.

To a shareholder, all securities are substitutes for one another, and the expected return on any one, with due allowance for uncertainty, is related to the expected return on any other. As a consequence, even though the dividends of a company may rise, the price of its stock may fall if stock prices generally decline. The price of the company's stock may not fall as much or as rapidly as prices in general, but it will probably decline. Similarly, when the market average rises, the price of a company's stock can be expected to rise to some extent even if the company does not raise its dividends.

Many students of financial matters have attempted to measure the relationship between the return earned by a single security and the return earned by an average of all securities. They have postulated the relationship to be of the form:

$$r_i = a + bI$$

where r_i is the return that can be earned by investing in company i and I is the return that can be earned by investing in a composite of all securities. The values of a and b are the parameters that must be found. The parameter b indicates how much r_i will rise when I increases by one unit; the parameter a indicates the value of r_i when the composite index I is equal to zero. These studies consistently show that the value of b is positive.

Changes in macroeconomic variables can change the value of the index I. Since changes in I, in turn, affect the return that a single security offers, macroeconomic factors are of extreme importance to financial managers. Indeed, the manager may not be the most important agency behind the changes in the price of his company's securities.

However, macroeconomic events such as a change in interest rates or in the rate of growth of the money supply are not the only factors outside the direct control of the firm which influence the price of a company's stock. The liquidity of the market in which the security is traded can affect the volatility of price movements that result from buy and sell orders. It is important, therefore, to know how the security market itself operates, in order to understand the problems financial managers face in trying to achieve corporate goals with the limited tools at their command.

The structure of the securities market

The securities of most American corporations are bought and sold in a market that is organized in a slightly different way than the market for most products consumers buy. First, the negotiations concerning the price at which the purchase or sale will take place are carried on by brokers, who are agents for the ultimate buyers or sellers. These brokers charge a fee, or commission, for their services. Merrill, Lynch, and Co.; Bache and Co.; and Dean Witter and Co. are three well-known security brokerage firms.

Second, if the customer's buy or sell order is relatively small say 100 or 200 shares, the brokers will often fill the order by trading with a person who is a dealer in the stock, rather than with a broker representing another customer. A dealer maintains inventories of stocks and buys for or sells from these inventories.

In security markets, such as the New York Stock Exchange, the American Stock Exchange, or the Midwest Stock Exchange, dealers that stand ready to buy and sell are called specialists. These organized exchanges have allocated all the securities that are listed with them for trading among these specialists. There are approximately 360 specialists on the New York Stock Exchange and some 1,700 securities listed there. Each specialist on the exchange therefore handles approximately five securities. Usually, only one specialist handles an issue; however, when the public interest in a particular security is large, as in the case of, say, American Telephone and Telegraph, more than one specialist may "make a market" in the security. The American Stock Exchange has approximately 159 specialists and roughly 1,000 securities listed for trading. The average specialist in that market stands ready to buy and sell roughly six different securities.

The specialist on the floor of an exchange also performs another function. At times, he may act as a broker. For example, suppose that the price of a security is $50 a share and a customer wants to sell 100 shares when the price reaches $53. If he gives an order to sell at $53 to his broker, the broker, in turn, will give the order to the specialist handling the stock to fill. When the price of the security reaches $53, the specialist will fill the order and notify the broker that his customer sold his stock.

Not all securities, however, are traded on organized exchanges. Government bonds, as well as the common stocks of most smaller companies, banks, and insurance companies are traded in the *over-the-counter* market. This market is made up of a large number of firms who keep in contact with one another by telephone instead of speaking directly to each other as brokers do when they complete a trade on the floor of an exchange. A brokerage firm operating in this market can become a dealer in any security.

In recent years, a so-called "third market" has developed, consisting of firms that are not members of the New York Stock Exchange, but deal in securities listed on the exchange. Weeden and Co., for example, is a large brokerage firm that operates in this third market. It maintains inventories of approximately 250 securities and competes with the specialists on the floor of the exchange who deal in these issues.

A dealer in securities makes money by buying securities at one price and selling them at a higher price. The difference between the price the dealer will pay for a security (the *bid*) and the price at which he will sell (the *ask*) is called the *spread*. Any dealer in securities whether he is a specialist operating on the floor of an exchange or a firm like Weeden operating in the third market, exposes himself to a great deal of risk. For example, during the first quarter of 1969, the range of Weeden's weekly inventories were as follows: tax-exempt bonds, $30,400,000 to $51,500,000; common stocks and convertible bonds, $27,900,000 to $39,900,000; corporate and government-agency bonds, $300,000 to $3,000,000; and tax-exempt notes, $850,000 to $40,000,000. Since the company finances its inventories with loans payable on demand from commercial banks and since its inventories average four to five times its capital, an unexpected change in the market price of the securities it holds could cause a decline in the value of its inventory that would substantially lower or even destroy, the value of its stockholders' equity.

One way for a dealer to reduce his exposure to risk is to decline to carry a large inventory of highly volatile securities. A specialist on the New York Stock Exchange, for example, need buy only 100 shares of the stock that is offered for sale at a specified price; and an over-the-counter firm can "walk away" from a customer that wants to sell it a large block of stock. Of course, if a dealer turns down sell offers too often, brokers will not continue to offer him their business.

A second way for a dealer to reduce his exposure to risk is to change the ask price, or the spread, of the securities he handles. For example, suppose a buyer wants to purchase a substantial number of shares and the dealer does not have them in inventory. The dealer may offer to sell the shares to the buyer at a price substantially higher than the price at which the last transaction occurred. When other holders of the stock become aware of the high price quoted by the dealer, they may offer their shares for sale, and the dealer can then "cover" his short position by buying from them.

The smaller the spread between the bid and ask price and the more willing the dealer is to buy securities for, and sell them from, his own inventory, the better the quality of the market, or the more liquid the security. The ability of the dealer to make a good market by exposing himself to the risk of price fluctuations in his inventory ultimately depends on the amount of capital that he is prepared to commit to an issue.

To summarize, the dealer function in the securities market arises because buyers and sellers interested in the same number of shares of the same issue rarely arrive on the scene at the same time. When this happens, their brokers can, of course, negotiate the trade. However, since a dealer in a security is always willing to take a position in it and carry it in his inventory for later resale, both buyers and sellers can trade with him at any time.

Corporate goals and the equity market

As long as a firm acts only as a broker, its need for capital is limited to the normal demands of the business; when a firm becomes a dealer, however, its need for capital increases sharply, since it must now carry a large inventory of securities and expose itself to possible losses from sharp price changes. A dealer can limit the degree of risk to which he exposes himself by widening the spread between bid and ask prices or simply by turning down some trading opportunities. When this happens, however, the liquidity of the securities in which the dealer makes a market is substantially reduced.

The quality of the securities market

The structure of the security market was described in detail in the preceding section to provide a background for understanding some of the factors outside the immediate control of the corporation that influence the price of a company's shares.

The organized exchanges have been structured to meet the trading needs of a large number of relatively small investors. They perform this task well. The normal trading unit is 100 shares, a reasonable size for most individual investors. Moreover, a specialist on the New York Stock Exchange is required to have enough capital to be able to carry in inventory 1,200 shares of each security in which he makes a market. This is probably an adequate amount of capital to provide liquidity as long as the individual transactions are small and a large number of buy and sell orders cross the floor during a day.

Over the past decade, however, a marked change has taken place in the distribution of holdings of securities. The holdings of trust departments of banks, mutual funds, pension and profit-sharing plans, insurance companies, and other institutional holders of securities have increased in both size and importance. This change has occurred because more and more of the savings of the community have become institutionalized.

These institutions have placed new demands on the securities market. For example, they tend to buy and sell large blocks of stock, rather than 100 or 200 shares, simply because their holdings are so extensive. Also, they do not require, by and large, the same type of services that a typical brokerage firm gives its small investors. They do not, as a rule, require the customary brief reports on new developments in specific corporations, for they are capable of doing their own analyses of companies. Nor do they need analyses of market trends, economic indicators, or world events, since they tend to have their own research staff. What these institutional holders demand is to be able to buy and sell large blocks of stock quickly and without affecting the price of the security adversely; that is, without driving it up against themselves as they buy, and without driving it down against themselves as they sell. In short, they want a liquid market.

Institutions, therefore, generally prefer to do business with brokerage firms from whom they can buy or to whom they can sell the securities in which they have an interest quickly and efficiently. To do this, the brokers themselves may have to become dealers and buy or sell the securities directly. At the very least, the brokerage firms must be able to find other large buyers and sellers of the same securities quickly so that the trade can be accomplished with a minimum of delay. Behind the preference to do business with such firms is the assumption that the specialist on the floor of the exchange, to whom the broker would ordinarily take the trade, may be unable to handle the business because of his inadequate capital or unwillingness to expose himself to the risk of a price fluctuation.

It was to meet this demand for increased liquidity that the third market developed, for dealers like Weeden do take substantial positions in securities. Moreover, to meet the demands of institutional shareholders, major member firms of the New York Stock Exchange such as Solomon Bros. and Hutzler, Bear, Stearns and Co., and others have become dealers, rather than remaining exclusively brokers to small investors.

With specialists, third-market firms, and a growing number of brokerage houses willing to trade for their own account, how liquid is the market for the type of securities an institution might purchase? The answer to this question is important to the financial manager of the firm. If the market for the company's shares is not liquid, their price can be affected by events that are unrelated to the profit and dividend prospects of the firm or to other factors under the control of management. For example, a pension-fund manager may have to make an unexpected payment to a group of retired workers. To raise the funds he may be forced to liquidate his holdings of a company's shares. If the sale drives down the price of the company's stock, it may lead other holders to change their minds about the future prospects of the company and create further instability in the price. A corresponding situation would arise if a substantial buy order should suddenly take place. If the market is not liquid, the buy order will drive the price of the stock up, and this movement in turn may cause a speculative flurry.

In spite of its obvious potential importance, little empirical work has been done to measure just how liquid the market for corporate securities is. To obtain a partial answer to the question, however, let us examine the transactions of one investment fund during a nine-month period from September 1968 to June 1969.

During the period, the fund made 46 purchases and 29 sales. A sample list of the securities it dealt with is given in Table 16.1. All these companies are well known, and most are listed on the New York Stock Exchange.

The 46 orders that were placed ranged in size from 600 to 6,800 shares. The data in Table 16.2 show that the order size of both purchases

Corporate goals and the equity market

TABLE 16.1
Companies Whose Shares the Fund Purchased or Sold from September 1968 to June 1969

Goodyear Tire and Rubber Company	Motorola, Inc.
Smith Kline & French Laboratories	American Cyanamid Company
Litton Industries, Inc.	Aluminum Co. of America
National Lead Company	Bethlehem Steel Corporation
Zenith Radio Corporation	Mortgage Guarantee Insurance Corp.
Weyerhaeuser Company	J. C. Penney
Westinghouse Electric Corporation	Scott Foresman
Reynolds Metals Company	Becton Dickinson & Company
Hewlett-Packard Company	Honeywell, Inc.
Armstrong Cork Company	Parker-Hannefin Corporation
R. R. Donnelley & Sons	Trane Company
Dun & Bradstreet, Inc.	Ford Motor Company
Eastman Kodak Company	General Electric Company
International Business Machines	G. D. Searle & Company
Monsanto Company	Western Publishing Company
Pfizer (Chas.) & Company, Inc.	Max Factor & Company
Scott Paper Company	U. S. Steel Corporation
American Metal Climax	O. M. Scott & Sons
Caterpillar Tractor Company	American Tel. & Tel.
Sunbeam Corporation	Merck & Company
U. S. Gypsum Company	Sterling Drug, Inc.

and sales clustered between 1,500 and 4,500 shares. These are not large blocks, which are usually defined as orders of 10,000 or more shares. They are, rather, the medium-sized orders that a typical institution tends to purchase.

One measure of the quality of a market is the number of transactions that are needed to fill an order. The data in Table 16.3 indicate that

TABLE 16.2
A Distribution of Order Sizes Placed by the Fund

Order Size	Buy Orders	Sell Orders
Less than 1,500 shares	2	1
1,600–2,500 shares	12	7
2,600–3,500 shares	11	7
3,600–4,500 shares	13	8
4,600–5,500 shares	3	3
5,600–6,500 shares	2	2
6,600–7,500 shares	3	1
Total	46	29

10 of the 46 purchase orders were handled in a single trade; 13 required two trades, and one order required 10 separate transactions to fill it. Some of these transactions took several days, though most were completed within a single day. Since less than a third of the purchase orders were filled in a single trade, it was apparently relatively difficult for the fund to accumulate even modest holdings of the securities it wanted to buy.

TABLE 16.3
Number of Orders Filled at
Varying Transaction Levels

Transactions Required to Fill Order	Buy Orders	Sell Orders
1	10	16
2	13	4
3	10	5
4	8	1
5	3	1
6	1	0
7	0	1
8	0	0
9	0	1
10	1	0
Total	46	29

When more than one transaction is required to fill an order, different prices may be paid for the security. The data in Table 16.4 show the range of prices that resulted from filling a single order. For example, the figures in the top row show that 13 purchase orders were filled in two separate transactions. Eight times both transactions took place at the same price; twice $\frac{1}{8}$ of a point separated the two trades; once $1\frac{1}{4}$ points separated the two transactions. The bottom line of Table 16.4 provides a summary of the price differences between transactions of the same order. Sixteen of the 36 buy orders that involved more than one transaction were filled at the same price or at a price only $\frac{1}{8}$ of a point different; only two of the 12 sell orders, however were filled at the same price or at a price only $\frac{1}{8}$ of a point different. A spread of a point or more characterized seven of the 36 buy orders and two of the 13 sell orders. Thus not only were several transactions required to fill most of the orders placed by the fund, but the transactions themselves took place at widely varying prices.

Each decision to buy or sell that the fund made was reached at the close of a business day, and the order placed the following morning. The price at which the security closed on the day the decision to buy

Corporate goals and the equity market

or to sell was noted, and an estimate prepared of the cost of the transaction. For example, if 4,000 shares of a stock selling at $50 were to be purchased, the estimated cost would be $200,000. This figure ignores commissions, which in this example would be $440 for the first 1,000 shares and $840 for the next 3,000 shares (if the trade is completed on the same day), or a little less than 1 percent of the value of the trade.

TABLE 16.4
Price Spread in Multiple-Transaction Orders

Buy Orders

Orders	Transactions	Price Spread Between Highest and Lowest Transaction										
		0	$\frac{1}{8}$	$\frac{1}{4}$	$\frac{3}{8}$	$\frac{1}{2}$	$\frac{5}{8}$	$\frac{3}{4}$	$\frac{7}{8}$	1	$1\frac{1}{8}$	$1\frac{1}{4}$
13	2	8	2	1						1		1
10	3	3		4		1		1		1		
8	4	1	1			1	1		2	1		1
3	5			2								1
1	6	1										
0	7											
0	8											
0	9											
1	10											1
36		13	3	7		2	1	1	2	3		4

Sell Orders

Orders	Transactions	Price Spread Between Highest and Lowest Transaction												
		0	$\frac{1}{8}$	$\frac{1}{4}$	$\frac{3}{8}$	$\frac{1}{2}$	$\frac{5}{8}$	$\frac{3}{4}$	$\frac{7}{8}$	1	$1\frac{1}{8}$	$1\frac{1}{4}$	$1\frac{1}{2}$	$3\frac{1}{2}$
4	2	2			1	1								
5	3			2		1	1							1
1	4							1						
1	5			1										
1	6					1								
0	7													
0	8													
1	9												1	
13		2		3	1	3	1	1					1	1

The data in Table 16.5 show the actual dollars spent by the fund for the securities it purchased as a percentage of the expected outlays during the months in which the transactions occurred. The average buy order cost 1.46 percent more than estimated, and the average sell order realized only 98.44 percent of the expected return. In short, on the buy side the company paid about one-half of one percent more than it expected to pay, and on the sell side it realized about one-half of one percent less than it expected to.

TABLE 16.5
Percentage Difference Between
Realized and Expected Outlays

	Buy Orders	Sell Orders
September 1968	101.41%	
November 1968	100.71	99.35%
December 1968	100.39	97.75
February 1969	101.52	97.82
March 1969	102.55	96.29
April 1969	97.81	99.51
May 1969	101.02	98.48
June 1969	106.32	99.86
Average	1.46%	98.44%

The one-half of one percent variation in payments and returns is, of course, because of price changes. Securities can not always be purchased on one day at the closing price of the day before. The fact that the fund's buy orders tended to take place at higher prices than expected and its sell orders at lower prices indicates that the market was so thin and there was so little liquidity that even these relatively modest transactions could alter the price of the stocks traded. Although further research is needed before any definitive statements can be made, the problems associated with block trading and a lack of liquidity in the securities market are likely to increase rather than diminish in the years to come since more and more shares are being managed by institutions. The lack of liquidity in the securities market means that the price of a company's shares can change sharply as a result of events over which its management has no control. Financial managers may find it even more difficult in the future to control the price of their company's shares.

Summary

In the first section of this chapter we asked whether it was desirable for a firm to try to maximize shareholder wealth. A review of the strengths and weaknesses of a competitive economy showed that if firms do pursue this goal, a competitive economy will produce many highly desirable results. Goods will be produced that consumers want, and in a socially efficient way. Economic prejudice will be absent, and each participant in the economy will be able to develop to the limit of his capabilities.

Many events can occur in the economy at large, however, that frustrate the financial manager's efforts to ensure a high and rising price for his company's shares. For example, a rise in interest rates or a slowdown in the growth rate of the economy can drive down the average price of all shares. Even if these macroeconomic forces do not influence the business prospects of the corporation, they are likely to induce a fall in the price of its shares. Conversely, if the market average is rising, the price of the corporation's shares is likely to rise even if the firm's prospects are unchanged.

A second factor that influences security price movements is the liquidity of the market itself. If the market for a corporation's shares is thin, the sale of a substantial number of shares can cause the price to spiral either upward or downward. Thus the financial manager's actions may be offset by macroeconomic and market forces.

Questions for discussion and problems

1. Prepare a list of economic goals for the nation. Which of these goals are primarily the responsibility of government, and which are primarily the responsibility of companies? Can the goals that are the companies' responsibility be better satisfied by competitive firms or by monopolies?

2. Three shortcomings of the competitive system were described in the first section of this chapter. Why is government action necessary to overcome these shortcomings?

3. Why will a wealth-maximizing firm in a competitive environment allocate goods in a socially optimal way? Why will it be color-blind and welcome individual incentive?

4. Suppose that the interest rate lenders will charge for funds is the sum of an expected real return and an estimate of how much prices will change. Suppose, further, that the expected growth rate depends on the expected price change. Will securities be a good hedge against inflation?

5. Why are stock prices a leading series in relation to the business cycle?

6. What is the function of a dealer, or specialist, in the securities market?

7. What risk does a dealer in securities face? If dealer firms had more equity, would they be able to make better markets? If they had less equity, would they make better markets? What is the function of equity for firms operating in the securities market?

8. From your own experience, what factors might account for the growing amount of individual savings held by institutions?

9. What demands do institutional buyers make on the security market that individuals do not?

10. Why is the problem of liquidity in the securities market important to financial managers?

[*Answers to problems 11 and 12 follow references and suggested readings.*]

11. Suppose that the index values of all securities could be captured by the expression $P = D/(k - g)$. Suppose, further, that k is a function of the interest rate.
   (a) If the price level is expected to rise by 5 percent, what will happen to the value of k?
   (b) If prices are expected to rise, what will happen to the nominal growth rate of dividends?
   (c) If both k and g increase by 5 percent and the dividends remain constant, what will happen to the value of the index of stock prices?
   (d) If the assumption in (c) is true, are stocks a good hedge against inflation?
   (e) For stocks to be a hedge against inflation, what must be the relationship between k and g?

12. (a) At the trough of a depression, the dividends of a composite company are $5 per share. What is the per-share price of its stock company if the expected growth rate is 2 percent and the discount rate is 8 percent?
   (b) As the economy begins to expand, the growth rate rises to .04, while the discount rate falls to .07. What is the price per share if dividends remain constant?
   (c) As the economy approaches a peak, the growth rate falls to .03 and the discount rate rises to .08. What is the price per share if dividends increase to $6?
   (d) As the economy passes a peak, the growth rate falls to .02 and the discount rate falls to .07. What is the price per share if dividends are reduced to $5.50?

REFERENCES AND SUGGESTED READINGS

Articles

Eiteman, David K., "The S.E.C. Study and the Exchange Markets," *Journal of Finance,* vol. XXI, no. 2 (May 1966), pp. 311–23.

Fama, Eugene F., "Efficient Capital Markets: A Review of Theory and Empirical Work," *Journal of Finance,* vol. XXV, no. 2 (May 1970), pp. 383–418.

Fand, David I., "A Monetarist Model of the Monetary Process," *Journal of Finance*, vol. XXV, no. 2 (May 1970), pp. 275–91.

Friend, Irwin, "Broad Implications of the S.E.C. Special Study," *Journal of Finance*, vol. XXI, no. 2 (May 1966), pp. 324–32.

"Research in the Capital Markets," An Exploratory Report by the National Bureau of Economic Research, *Journal of Finance*, vol. XIX, no. 2, part 2 (May 1964), Supplement, pp. 1–43.

Upson, Roger B., and Jessup, Paul, "Risk Return Relationships in Regional Securities," *Journal of Financial and Quantitative Analysis*, vol. IV, no. 5 (January 1970), pp. 677–97.

Whitmore, G. A., "Market Demand Curve for Common Stock and the Maximization of Market Value," *Journal of Financial and Quantitative Analysis*, vol. V, no. 1 (March 1970), pp. 105–15.

Books

Baumol, William J., *The Stock Market and Economic Efficiency* (New York: Fordham Univ. Press, 1965).

Cohen, Jerome B., and Zinbarg, Edward, *Investment Analysis and Portfolio Management* (Homewood, Ill.: Irwin, 1967).

Cootner, P. H., ed., *The Random Character of Stock Market Prices* (Cambridge, Mass.: MIT Press, 1964).

Dougall, Herbert E., *Capital Markets and Institutions* (Englewood Cliffs, N. J.: Prentice-Hall, 1965).

Facts Affecting the Stock Market, U. S. Government, 84th Congress, 1st Sess., Senate Comm. on Banking and Currency.

Friedman, Milton, *Capitalism and Freedom* (Chicago, Ill.: Univ. of Chicago Press, 1962).

Friend, Irwin, *et al.*, *Investment Banking and the New Issue Market* (Cleveland: World, 1967).

Friend, Irwin, *et al.*, *The Over the Counter Securities Market* (New York: McGraw-Hill, 1958).

Galbraith, John Kenneth, *The New Industrial State* (New York: New American Library, 1967).

Heilbroner, Robert L., *The Wordly Philosophers* (New York: Simon and Schuster, 1967).

Leffler, G. L. and Farwell, L. G., *The Stock Market*, 3rd ed. (New York: Ronald Press, 1963).

Lerner, Eugene M. and Carleton, Willard T., *A Theory of Financial Analysis* (New York: Harcourt Brace Jovanovich, 1966).

Robinson, Roland, *Money and Capital Markets* (New York: McGraw-Hill, 1964).

Sauvain, Harry, *Investment Management*, 3rd ed. (Englewood Cliffs, N. J.: Prentice-Hall, 1967).

Securities and Exchange Commission, *Special Study of Securities Markets* (Washington, D. C.: Government Printing Office, 1963).

Sobel, Robert, *The Big Board* (New York: Macmillan, 1965).

Sprinkel, B. Y., *Money and Stock Prices* (Homewood, Ill.: Irwin, 1964).

A Study of Mutual Funds, U. S. Government, 87th Congress, 2nd Sess., Comm. on Interstate and Foreign Commerce.

Van Horne, James C., *Functions and Analysis of Capital Market Rates* (Englewood Cliffs, N. J.: Prentice-Hall, 1970).

Questions for discussion and problems 359

ANSWERS TO PROBLEMS 11 AND 12.

11.

   (a) k can be expected to rise by 5 percent.
   (b) The growth rate can be expected to rise by approximately 5 percent.
   (c) The value of the index will remain constant.
   (d) No.
   (e) g must rise faster than k.

12.

   (a) $83.30
   (b) $166.65
   (c) $120.00
   (d) $110.00

The effect of corporate actions
on share prices

17

Financial managers do not, we have seen, have complete control over the price of their company's shares; they cannot regulate either macroeconomic variables or the liquidity of the market in which their stock is traded, even though these factors affect both the level and volatility of prices. Even so, the decisions corporate managers make and the financial policies they follow are the single most important determinant of the price of a company's shares in the long run.

In this chapter, we shall temporarily ignore the economic and market factors that managers cannot influence and concentrate instead on the factors they can control. We shall outline a framework that financial managers and security analysts alike can and do use to answer such questions as, How are the firm's financial policies related to one another? and, How will a change in a specific policy affect the price of the stock?

Dividends and share prices

The dominant valuation equation used in preceding chapters set the price of a share of stock equal to the present value of its future stream of dividends where the dividends are expected to grow at a rate g and are discounted at a rate k. It is common knowledge, however, that many securities which pay no dividends at all command high prices. Yet the model $P = D/(k - g)$ seems to imply that if $D = 0$, then $P = 0$, not a high value. How can this conclusion be reconciled with the empirical evidence?

The paradox suggested by the dividend model can be matched by still another. It is common knowledge, also, that many companies sustain operating losses in some years. Consider the valuation equation $P = m\pi$, where π is the earnings per share of the company. If π is negative, and it will be if a loss is sustained, how can any positive price of the security be rationalized?

The answer to both the zero-dividend and the negative-earnings problem is straightforward. In both cases, incorrect measurements of the relevant variables were used. No one would pay anything for shares of a company that lost money year after year and was expected to continue losing it in the foreseeable future. Indeed, the company would be liquidated immediately. The fact that a company sustains losses in some years and still commands a price greater than zero for its shares means that both actual and potential shareholders expect the negative earnings' trend to reverse. What a shareholder really buys is some "permanent" earnings stream. The actual earnings, measured at any moment (π_m), have both a permanent (π_p) and a transitory (π_t) component. Thus, $\pi_m = \pi_p + \pi_t$. If a company's shares command a positive (greater than zero) price and if measured earnings, π_m, are negative, transitory earnings, π_t, must be negative and greater than π_p. By definition, the transitory loss must vanish and may be replaced by a transitory gain the following year. In any event, the transitory component of earnings is not what the shareholder purchases; he purchases the permanent component. Thus the earnings paradox is resolved.

A similar logic applies to the case where current dividends are zero. If a security were guaranteed never to pay a dividend, so that no shareholder would ever receive a return from owning it, the price of the stock would be zero. Some securities that do not pay dividends now command a positive price because purchasers expect dividends at some future date. To influence the price of its shares, a company must influence its "permanent" dividends, its "permanent" growth rate, and the discount rate shareholders apply to the growing earnings stream.

The valuation equation with no debt

If a company has no debt in its capital structure, both the dividends and the rate of growth of dividends can be expressed in terms of two other variables, r, the rate of return on assets and b, the retention rate. To see the relationship between dividends, the rate of growth, the rate of return, and the dividend-payout ratio, consider a firm whose balance sheet shows $100 in both assets and equity. If the firm has 10 shares of stock outstanding, the asset value per share will be $10.

Suppose the firm earns $20 in profits before interest and taxes and is in a 50-percent tax bracket. The rate of return on assets is then 20

The effect of corporate actions on share prices

percent:

$$r = \frac{\text{Profits before interest and taxes}}{\text{Total assets}}$$

$$20\% = \tfrac{20}{100}$$

The company has no debt, so interest payments are zero. Profits after taxes are found as follows:

$$\begin{aligned}
\text{Profits after taxes} &= (1 - T)rA \\
&= (.50)(.20)100 \\
&= 10
\end{aligned}$$

where T is the tax rate and A is total assets. Since the company has 10 shares of stock outstanding, profits per share are $1.

Dividends are paid from profits after taxes. If b is the retention rate, then $1 - b$ is the dividend-payout rate. The actual dollars in dividends paid to shareholders are:

(17–1)
$$\text{Dividends} = (1 - T)(1 - b)rA$$

Thus, if the retention rate is .75, the total dividends are:

$$\begin{aligned}
\text{Dividends} &= (.5)(.25)(.20)100 \\
&= 2.50
\end{aligned}$$

With 10 shares of stock outstanding, dividends per share are 25 cents.

The amount of profits that the firm will retain and the increment to both assets and equity are given by:

$$\begin{aligned}
\Delta A &= (1 - T)brA \\
&= (.5)(.75)(.20)(100) \\
&= 7.50
\end{aligned}$$

The rate of growth of assets is, of course, the change in $A(\Delta A)$ divided by A, or

(17–2)
$$\begin{aligned}
g = \frac{\Delta A}{A} &= (1 - T)br \\
&= (.5)(.75)(.20) \\
&= 7.5\%
\end{aligned}$$

When equations 17–1 and 17–2 are substituted into the valuation equation,

(17–3)
$$\begin{aligned}
P &= \frac{D}{k - g} \\
&= \frac{(1 - T)(1 - b)rA}{k - (1 - T)br}
\end{aligned}$$

The valuation equation with no debt

363

The price of a company's shares, therefore, depends on two corporate decision variables, r and b, and three parameters, k, T, and A. Suppose we let k be .09. Then, since the per-share value of A is \$10, $T = .5$, $b = .75$, and $r = .20$, the price of a share of stock is:

$$P = \frac{(.5)(1 - .75)(.20)10}{.09 - (.5)(.75)(.20)}$$

$$= \frac{.25}{.09 - .075}$$

$$= \$16.66$$

Equation 17-3 implies that any particular price for a share of stock can be achieved by an infinite number of r,b combinations. For example, using the data in the example above, a price of \$20 can be achieved if the company selects any of the r,b combinations in Table 17.1.

TABLE 17.1
r,b Combinations That Satisfy the
Valuation Equation When $P = \$20$,
$A = \$10$, $T = .5$, and $K = .09$

r	b
.30	.2
.24	.5
.20	.8

The r,b values that satisfy the valuation equation when the price of a share is \$20 are found as follows. Since $A = 10$, $T = .5$, and $P = 20$, the equation

$$P = \frac{(1 - T)(1 - b)(r)A}{k - (1 - T)rb}$$

can be written

$$20 = \frac{(.5)(1 - b)(r)(10)}{.09 - (.5)(r)(b)}$$

The values of r and b that satisfy this equation can be found by multiplying both sides of the equation by $(.09 - .5rb)$. Thus:

$$1.8 - 10rb = 5r - 5rb$$
$$-5rb = 5r - 1.8$$
$$r = \frac{+1.8}{5(b + 1)}$$

If b is arbitrarily set at .2,

$$r = \frac{1.8}{5(1.2)} = 30\%$$

the value indicated in Table 17.1.

The three values of r and b given in Table 17.1 are consistent with a price of $20, a book value of $10 per share, a tax rate of 50 percent, and a value of k of 9 percent. There are, however, an infinite number of r,b combinations that are consistent with a price of $20. The locus of these points, plotted in Figure 17.1, is called an *isoprice line,* since the price is the same ($20) at all points on the line.

Figure 17.2 indicates the r,b combinations that give rise to isoprice lines of $15, $20, and $25. Note that, for any given r, the price of a security will rise as b increases; and for any given b, the price of a security will rise as r increases. The logic behind these results is simple. If a firm's shareholders demand a return of k and if the corporation can earn a rate of return on their investments such that r is greater than k, shareholders are better off if the firm retains its earnings than if it distributes them. Similarly, for any given retention-rate policy, i.e., for any given value of b, shareholders are prepared to pay more for the shares of companies that can earn a higher rate of return.

What if r is less than k? Figure 17.3 shows three isoprice lines along which share prices are less than the book value of the shares. When r is less than k, the price of the company's stock falls as the retention rate increases because shareholders have better alternatives for their funds than continuing to invest them in the company. Of course, for a given

FIGURE 17.1

An Isoprice Line.

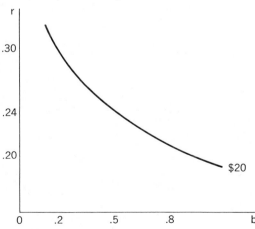

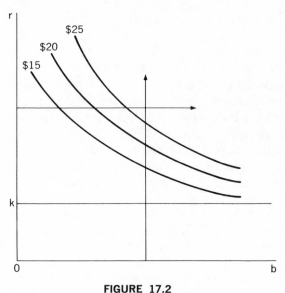

FIGURE 17.2

Three Isoprice Lines, $r > k$.

value of b, the price of the company's securities will appreciate as r increases and approaches k.

Given T, and the book value per share, Figures 17.1, 17.2, and 17.3 indicate what the market will pay for securities that offer different r,b combinations. Since a price of, say, \$20, can be achieved by an infinite number of r,b combinations, which r and which b should the company choose?

FIGURE 17.3

Three Isoprice Lines, $r < k$.

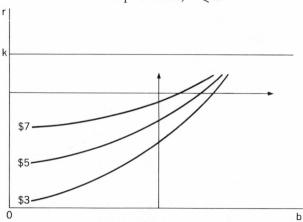

The effect of corporate actions on share prices

Corporate opportunities

The problem of selecting an r,b combination is less difficult than it appears since, in practice, corporate-investment opportunities at any point in time are limited. The more the corporation exploits its opportunities, i.e., the more projects it adopts, the lower the average rate of return it will earn on its assets will be.

Suppose that the relationship between the after-tax rate of return on assets and the corporate retention rate is described by the equation:

(17–4)
$$(1 - T)r = a_0 + a_1b$$

where $a_1 \leq 0$.

Equation 17–4, plotted in Figure 17.4, states that, as the retention rate rises, other things being equal, the rate of return the corporation can earn on its assets will fall. There are several reasons why this result may be expected. As the company retains more of its earnings and expands its assets, its output will increase. If it operates in an imperfect market (i.e., if its demand curve is downward sloping), the price it can charge for its products will tend to fall as output rises. If the lower prices are not offset by operating economies, the rate of return it earns on its assets will decline. Moreover, even if the firm can sell its increased output at the same price as before, it may incur higher operating costs as it expands. Whether the cause is a decrease in demand or a rise in costs, the result is the same: As the firm expands its assets, the average rate of return earned on the assets will decline.

Corporate financial officers would obviously prefer to always have the opportunity of investing in projects that will lead to an increase in the rate of return on their assets or, at least, will not lower the current rate of return. Thus they would like a *profit-opportunity schedule* that slopes

FIGURE 17.4
The Relationship Between the Retention Rate and the Rate of Return.

upward and to the right. Unfortunately, they are not given this option by the market. If they were, however, the more funds a company retained, the higher its rate of return would be. Furthermore, since the largest companies would profit most from this situation, ultimately each industry would have only one firm.

Corporations can, however, shift their profit-opportunity schedule to the right through time. For example, a firm might develop a new technological process that lowers its production costs, so that for any given level of sales and assets, its profits increase. Or, through advertising, a firm may increase the demand for its products and be able to charge higher prices for the goods it sells. If the advertising campaign is successful, i.e., if revenues rise faster than costs, the profit-opportunity schedule will shift to the right.

Most of a firm's activities, to a greater or lesser degree, are undertaken with a view toward shifting the investment-opportunity schedule (which is also the profit-opportunity schedule) to the right. Research departments, for example, are usually concerned with discovering new processes or new products; development staffs are concerned with tailoring current products to fit changing markets; advertising outlays are geared to shifting the demand for the company's products. Some companies also have tried to shift their profit-opportunity schedules by merging with companies in different fields. These mergers provide new outlets for both the firm's management skills and its financial resources. Instead of making new commitments that would only carry the firm down along a particular investment schedule, the management may now be able to select investment projects from a broader set of potential opportunities and thereby shift the entire schedule to the right.

These considerations can affect both the position and the slope of the firm's profit-opportunity schedule through time. At any given moment, however, the profit-opportunity schedule will be downward sloping. In view of this fact, what rate of return and retention rate should the firm strive to achieve? How far down along its profit-opportunity schedule should it go before stopping?

Combining the valuation model and the profit-opportunity schedule

The solution to the problem of what rate of return and retention rate a firm should adopt if it wishes to maximize shareholder wealth becomes clear if the isoprice lines are combined with the investment-opportunity schedule. In Figure 17.5, a firm's investment-opportunity schedule and a series of isoprice lines are brought together. The highest price of the stock that is obtainable is P_1, the price that results if the firm adopts a rate of return of r' and a retention rate of b'.

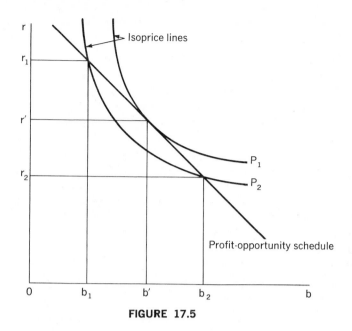

FIGURE 17.5

Suppose a firm arbitrarily selects r_1 as its target rate of return. Then, if it adopts no projects that bring its average return below r_1, it will retain only b_1 percent of its earnings and have a payout rate of $(1 - b_1)$. At this point, the price of the corporation's shares will be P_0.

P_0, however, is not the maximum price that the firm could achieve. Rather, if it were to cut back its dividends and expand its assets at a more rapid rate by retaining a larger percentage of its earnings, the price of its shares would rise. This is because the firm's shareholders value the larger stream of dividends that they will receive in the future more highly than the last increment of their current dividend payments.

To cite another example, suppose the company arbitrarily elects to retain b_2 percent of its current earnings and distribute only $1 - b_2$ percent of its income in dividends. Under these conditions, the price of its shares will again be a suboptimum one. By retaining so large a percentage of its earnings, the firm is compelled to adopt projects that force the rate of return below the level shareholders prefer. If it lowered its retention rate, raised its payout rate, and raised its rate of return, the price of the stock would appreciate to P_1.

Figure 17.5 shows how a firm can make an optimum decision at a moment of time with respect to both its rate of return and its payout rate. What happens to the price of the stock, however, if the firm suddenly encounters new and more profitable investment opportunities?

Figure 17.6 shows that if the profit-opportunity schedule shifts to the right, from I_1 to I_2, and becomes a bit steeper, the price of the company's

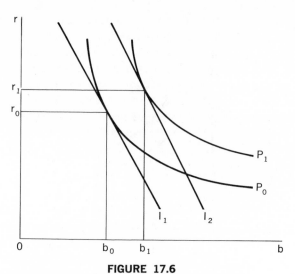

FIGURE 17.6
A Shift in the Profit Opportunity Schedule.

securities will rise from P_0 to P_1; the rate of return that it will earn on its assets will rise to r_1, and its retention rate will rise to b_1. Current dividends will fall, but the lower payout rate will lead to a higher growth rate.

This graph explains why a relatively high-priced stock may have a low dividend-payout rate. If the firm's investment opportunities are high, retained earnings can be reinvested to yield a high rate of return. A firm does not become a high-growth company because it has a low payout rate, but because it has good investment opportunities it may pay out little in dividends.

A change in k

The valuation equation specifies three factors that influence the behavior of stock prices: current dividends, growth rates, and the discount rates applied to the growing streams of dividends. How do changes in k influence the price of a company's shares, the rate of return it will seek to earn, and the retention rate it will adopt?

It is apparent from the equation that a fall in k will lead to a rise in P, and a rise in k to a fall in P. However, this is not all that happens when the discount rate changes. A fall in k shifts all the isoprice lines to the left. It also changes their slope, and, as a consequence, the wealth-maximizing firm will choose a different r,b combination when k is at one level than when it is at another.

A fall in k means that future dividends are accorded a higher present

The effect of corporate actions on share prices

value than formerly. A wealth-maximizing firm will therefore be inclined to retain and invest a larger percentage of its current earnings when k is low than when it is high. On the other hand, when k is relatively high, current dividends are valued more highly than future dividends, and a low retention rate will maximize stock prices. Table 17.2 shows some of the r,b combinations that will enable the company described in the earlier example to maintain the price of $20 when k is .08. A comparison of Tables 17.1 and 17.2 indicates that, for any level of b, a price of $20 can be achieved with a lower r when k is .08 than when it was .09.

TABLE 17.2
r,b Combinations That Satisfy the
Valuation Equation When $P = \$20$,
$A = \$10$, $T = .5$, and $k = .08$

b	r
.2	.278
.5	.212
.8	.178

Figure 17.7 contains two $20 isoprice lines. In one case k is .09, and in the other k is .08. The profit-opportunity line that led to a maximum

FIGURE 17.7
A Change in Isoprice Lines When k Changes.

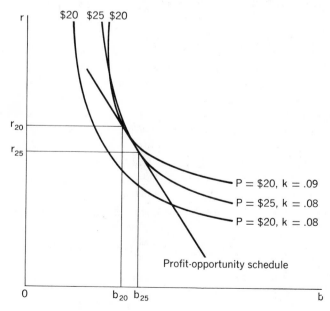

price when k was .09 required the firm to earn r_{20} and retain b_{20} percent of its earnings. When k falls to .08, however, the same profit-opportunity line is tangent to a higher isoprice line, a $25 line. Thus the value of b will be higher, b_{25}, and the value of r will be lower, r_{25}.

Implications for security analysis

The analysis developed in the first part of the chapter clearly indicates that for the price of a firm's stock to appreciate through time, either its profit-opportunity schedule must constantly shift to the right or the discount rate shareholders apply to its dividend stream must constantly fall.

For the profit-opportunity schedule to keep shifting to the right the management of the company must be continually alert, not only to new and better ways of producing the same product but to the constantly changing demands of its customers. If the firm concentrates on maintaining old markets, protecting entrenched business practices, and resisting change, the price of its stock will rapidly settle around a level and will change little over time.

The task of a professional security analyst is to appraise the present set of investment opportunities facing corporate management and to ask two fundamental questions: First, given the set of opportunities available, is the firm operating as effectively as it can? Second, is the set of opportunities in the future likely to be superior to the current set to opportunities?

To answer the first question, most analysts are content to compare the financial statements of the firm with those of others in the same industry. Using methods such as those in Chapter 3, the analyst may ask whether the firm's profit margins are higher or lower than the industry average, whether its turnover rates are adequate, whether its average return is relatively high or low, and so forth. This type of comparative analysis is relatively straightforward and can probably be performed better by a computer than by an individual.

The second question—whether the firm's investment opportunities will improve—is more difficult to answer. The analyst must know as much about the developments that are unfolding in an industry as any corporate manager. More important, he must be able to recognize which firm in the industry is best equipped to take advantage of the opportunities that are unfolding. To complicate the task of the analyst still further, most large firms today have divisions in many different industries. Thus an analyst specializing in petroleum firms must know not only about the oil industry, but about other industries such as chemicals, coal, and transportation as well.

The second way that stock prices can rise is if the discount rate continues to fall. The discount rate shareholders apply to a firm's stream of dividends does change from time to time, but the changes are not always in the same direction. When interest rates on government bonds are high, the discount rate is high; and when interest rates fall, the discount rate falls as well. Thus an analyst, like a financial manager, must be concerned with the changes that are constantly occurring in the economy as a whole.

Incorporating capital structure into the valuation equation

The valuation equations presented above were predicated on the assumption that the only source of funds for the firm is equity capital. This assumption is clearly untenable, since most firms use some debt to finance their assets. Clearly, to make the valuation models more useful, we must incorporate the phenomenon of debt in the analysis.

Suppose a company has the following income statement and balance sheet:

Balance Sheet				Income Statement	
Assets	$100	Debt	$50	Profits before interest	
		Equity	50	and taxes	$10.00
				Interest	2.50
				Profits before taxes	$ 7.50
				Taxes	3.00
				Profits after taxes	$ 4.50

Then:

$$r = \frac{PBIT}{A} = \frac{10}{100} = .10$$

$$i = \frac{Interest\ payments}{Liabilities} = \frac{2.50}{50} = .05$$

$$T = \frac{Taxes\ paid}{PBT} = \frac{3}{7.50} = .4$$

Substituting these values in the valuation equation gives us the profits after taxes of $4.50:

$$
\begin{aligned}
\text{Profits after taxes} &= (1 - T)(rA - iL) \\
&= (1 - .4)[.10(100) - .05(50)] \\
&= .6(10 - 2.50) \\
&= 4.50
\end{aligned}
$$

Expressing profits after taxes as the difference between rA and iL is useful for focusing on the factors that determine a corporation's growth rate. Since assets are equal to liabilities plus equity $(L + E)$,

(17–5)
$$
\begin{aligned}
\text{Profits after taxes} &= (1 - T)[r(L + E) - iL] \\
&= (1 - T)[rE + L(r - i)] \\
&= (1 - T)[r + (r - i)L/E]E^1
\end{aligned}
$$

Substituting the values of T, r, i, L, and E in this expression, we have:

$$
\begin{aligned}
\text{Profits after taxes} &= (1 - .4)[.10 + (.10 - .05)50/50]50 \\
&= (.6)(.10 + .05)(50) \\
&= 4.50
\end{aligned}
$$

Some proportion of the profits of the company will be retained and some will be distributed in the form of dividends. If b is the retention rate of the corporation, then its dividends will be as follows:

$$
\text{Dividends} = (1 - T)(1 - b)[r + (r - i)L/E]E
$$

The change in equity for the firm is given by the following expression:

$$
\Delta E = b(PAT) = b(1 - T)[r + (r - i)L/E]E
$$

The rate of growth of equity can be found by dividing both sides of this equation by E.

(17–6)
$$
g = \frac{\Delta E}{E} = b(1 - T)[r + (r - i)L/E]
$$

For example, assume that the firm paid out as dividends one-third of its $4.50 in profits. The retention rate, b, would then be two-thirds, and the growth rate of equity would be 6 percent.

$$
\begin{aligned}
\frac{\Delta E}{E} &= \tfrac{2}{3}(.6)[.10 + (.10 - .05)1] \\
&= \tfrac{2}{3}(.6)(.15) \\
&= \tfrac{2}{3}(.09) \\
&= .06
\end{aligned}
$$

Since the actual retained earnings were $3 and the original equity was $50, the new level of equity is $53. This is, of course, consistent with the 6-percent growth rate given by the equation.

Suppose, now, that the company wants to maintain the same ratio of debt to equity as it had in the past. Since equity is now $53, it must

---

[1] If both sides of this equation are divided by equity, the following expression results:

$$
\frac{\text{Profits after taxes}}{\text{Equity}} = (1 - T)(r + (r - i)L/E)
$$

This expression is formally equivalent to one of the propositions put forth by Modigliani and Miller in a widely celebrated 1958 paper. While the proposition is trivially true from an accounting point of view, Modigliani and Miller have developed an impressive superstructure of economic logic to demonstrate its validity under conditions of perfect knowledge, perfect competition and no transaction costs.

raise $3 in debt to maintain a one-to-one ratio of debt to equity. Suppose, further, that r, b, and i also remain at the same levels as formerly. Then we can say that

(1) debt will be $53, or grow at a rate of 6 percent;

(2) assets will be $106, or grow at a rate of 6 percent;

(3) profits before interest will be 10 percent of $106, or $10.60, consistent with a growth rate of 6 percent;

(4) profits after taxes will be $4.76, or 6-percent higher than $4.50;

(5) the dividend will be $1.59 ($\frac{1}{3}$ of $4.77), or 6 percent greater than $1.50.

In short, if the debt ratio and the values of r, i, and b remain constant, the growth rate of the entire enterprise will be 6 percent. The valuation equation $P = D/(k - g)$ now becomes

(17-7)
$$P = \frac{(1 - T)(1 - b)[r + (r - i)L/E]E}{k - (1 - T)(b)[r + (r - i)L/E]}$$

These results are, however, largely a matter of accounting identities. The task of the financial analyst, or anyone interested in security prices, is to probe behind these numbers to discover the developments that are unfolding within the corporation with respect to the rate of return, the retention rate, the ratio of debt to equity, the tax rate, and so forth.

For example, consider the growth-rate equation

$$g = b(1 - T)[r + (r - i)L/E]$$

As long as r is greater than i, g will rise as L/E increases. However, as L/E rises, i is likely to rise as well. Moreover, as the value of L/E rises, the firm may undertake new investment projects that drive its average rate of return down. To be able to estimate the future growth rate of a company, we must analyze the economic relationships that link the variables in our equations.

Some behavioral equations that determine stock prices

When the firm had no debt, the valuation equation $P = D/(k - g)$ gave rise to the question, What r,b combination should the company adopt? The answer was found by examining the company's investment-opportunity schedule and integrating that function with the valuation equation. However, the firm must choose not only the rate of return and retention rate that it wants to achieve, but the capital structure and interest rate as well. Four variables, not just two, must be selected. Furthermore, once the relationships that link these variables are specified, the freedom of the firm is sharply curtailed.

THE AVAILABLE-FUNDS SCHEDULE

Consider, first, the relationship between the interest rate a company must pay on its debt and the firm's ratio of debt to equity. It is reasonable to expect that, as a firm increases its ratio of debt to equity, the interest rate it will have to pay for borrowed funds will increase. Thus:

$$(17\text{--}8) \qquad i = b_0 + b_1 L/E$$
$$b_1 \geq 0$$

The reason the interest rate rises as the ratio of debt to equity increases is that the probability of loss to the lender rises as the firm increases its debt ratio. A reduction in the earning power of the firm will jeopardize its ability to pay interest. Moreover, any shrinkage in the value of the firm's assets will jeopardize the ability of the lending institution to recover its loans in the event of bankruptcy. For both these reasons, then, one would expect to find that the interest rates paid by firms with a high ratio of debt to equity are higher, other things being equal, than those paid by firms with a low ratio.

When the actual experience of corporations is examined, however, it is difficult to prove that this is indeed the case. There are several reasons that could account for this lack of empirical confirmation of the logic described above. First, lenders may be reluctant to make a loan that increases a firm's debt-to-equity ratio above what the lenders themselves consider prudent and therefore high enough to warrant a higher interest rate. Second, lenders tend to place other restrictions on the firm, so that the interest rate does not reflect the full cost of borrowed funds. Among these restrictions are limitations on the use of borrowed funds, limitations on dividend payments, and an enforced level of compensating balances.

Even though it is difficult to measure the parameters of the equation

$$i = b_0 + b_1 L/E$$

this expression of the relationship between interest rates and capital structure serves an important analytical function. For if such a relationship exists—as it surely does—the firm does not make two independent decisions, one about the interest rates that it will pay and one about the ratio of debt to equity. Rather, it makes only one decision. Earlier, we saw how, once a firm selects a retention rate, it can earn only one rate of return. So too, once it selects a ratio of debt to equity, it necessarily selects the interest rate consistent with that ratio. In short, these constraints simplify the analysis by reducing the number of variables for which the firm must select values and hence the number of decisions it must make.

THE INVESTMENT-OPPORTUNITY SCHEDULE

A corporation can finance its assets with two sources of funds, retained earnings and borrowings. Whichever source is used, as the assets grow the firm will move down along its profit-opportunity schedule and the rate of return it earns will fall. Companies, of course, would prefer to have both a high growth rate and a rising rate of return. However, as we saw earlier, the investment-opportunity schedule of a firm slopes downward at any moment of time.

Suppose that the investment-opportunity schedule is a falling function of the growth of the firm, as indicated by the following equations:

(17–9)
$$r = a_0 + a_1(1 - T)(b)[r + (r - i)L/E]$$

or

$$b = \frac{r - a_0}{a_1(1 - T)[r + (r - i)L/E]}$$

When the investment-opportunity schedule is written this way, it is clear that once r, i, and L/E are known, b is also known.

The valuation equation once again

If a firm faced no constraints, it would have to make four financial decisions to maximize the price of its shares. It would have to select values for r, b, i, and L/E. In reality, however, firms do face a number of constraints. One is the available-funds schedule that links L/E and i. Another is the investment-opportunity schedule that reveals b as a function of r, i, and L/E. Each constraint eliminates one variable. When the two constraints are combined with the valuation equation itself, the financial manager striving to maximize the price of his company's shares must make two independent decisions. He must choose a target level of r or b, and a target value of i or L/E. His choice of, say, a particular r and a particular L/E, will mean that b and i are automatically determined, and the price of the corporation's shares can be readily calculated.

A financial manager operating within this framework would proceed by substituting its available-funds schedule and its investment-opportunities schedule in the valuation model, which will then have only two independent variables. By experimenting with different values of each variable, the manager can determine which combination will yield an optimum price for the company's shares. The power of these simulations depends, of course, on how accurately the constraints (the relationships that link the decision variables) are specified. If the constraints specified are different from those in the analysis above, different answers will result. For example, if the claim is made that

$$r = a_0 + a_1 b^2$$

instead of

$$r = a_0 + a_1 b$$

a different r,b combination will appear optimum.

The question that must always be uppermost in the mind of the financial manager is, What are the facts about the relationship under discussion? Frequently, he will not have enough data at his command to make a conclusive statement about the relationship that concerns him, and he will be forced to use his judgment about what the facts are in the case. To this extent, financial management remains an art. Once the constraints are specified, only mechanical calculations are needed to obtain optimum values.

Summary

While a financial manager cannot control all the factors that affect the price of his company's shares, he can influence the firm's financial policies.

The valuation equation $P = D/(k - g)$ can be recast several ways. If a firm has no debt and pays no taxes, the valuation equation can be written

$$P = \frac{(1 - b)rA}{k - rb}$$

to highlight the importance of the rate of return, r, and the retention rate, b, as variables that affect the price of the company's shares.

If the firm has some debt in its capital structure and pays taxes, the valuation equation becomes

$$P = \frac{(1 - T)(1 - b)[r + (r - i)L/E]E}{k - (1 - T)(b)[r + (r - i)L/E]}$$

where r and b are as defined above; T is the tax rate; i, the interest rate; and L/E, the ratio of debt equity.

Valuation equations bring together in a single statement the variables that are of interest. They do not specify the other economic relationships that exist between the variables. To make a model operational, these relationships must be specified and incorporated in the valuation equation. When this is done, it becomes apparent that the profit-opportunity schedule and the available-funds schedule are the dominant functions linking the variables that a financial manager must consider. Once these two functions are specified, the financial manager can select the points along the functions that maximize the price of the company's shares by simulation. The difficult task is not selecting the points, but, rather, determining the location and form of the functions themselves.

Questions for discussion and problems

1. Why do the shares of some firms that pay no dividends command high prices? If you were a financial consultant to a firm, would you

recommend to its management that, to raise the price of the stock, they increase or decrease the dividend payment?

2. In the models developed in this chapter, the growth rate of assets, earnings, dividends, and stock prices was identical. What assumptions were required for this to occur? Are these assumptions reasonable?

3. How many different r,b combinations can satisfy the valuation equation for any particular stock price? When the profit-opportunity constraint is introduced, how many r,b combinations will lead to the maximum possible price?

4. Why does a firm's profit-opportunity schedule slope downward? What evidence is there that the function slopes downward? What kind of evidence would you require to satisfy yourself that this is the slope of the function? How would you develop this evidence?

5. Why should a firm try to shift its profit-opportunity schedule to the right over time?

6. What is the effect of a change in k on stock prices and on the r,b values that a firm will select?

7. How does the presence of corporate debt complicate the valuation model?

8. Is either function, the profit-opportunity schedule or the available-funds schedule, more important than the other in determining the price of a company's shares?

9. If different constraints than those specified in the text are assumed, how will this affect the security-valuation procedures outlined in the chapter?

[Answers to problems 10–14 follow references and suggested readings.]

10. The income statement of company A is reproduced below:

Sales	$200
Cost of goods sold	150
Gross profits	$ 50
Administrative expenses	10
Profits before taxes	40
Taxes	10
Profits after taxes	$ 30

Company A has $160 in assets, financed entirely through equity. The company has adopted the policy of retaining one-half its earnings and distributing the other half to shareholders. There are 40 shares of stock outstanding.

(a) What rate of return does the firm earn on its assets?

(b) How large are its per-share dividends?

(c) If the firm continues to earn the same rate of return, maintain the same dividend policy, and pay taxes at the same rate, how fast will its assets grow?

(d) If shareholders apply a discount rate of .11375 to the firm's dividend stream, what is the price of company A's shares?

11. If $A = 20$, $T = .5$, $k = .10$, and $P = 25$, what values of r satisfy the equation $P = D/(k - g)$ when b equals (a) .2, (b) .5, (c) .75?

12. Suppose that the investment opportunities open to a firm can be captured by the expression $(1 - T)r = a_0 - a_1 b$. If $T = .5$, $a_0 = .3$, and $a_1 = .5$, what rate of return can the firm earn if (a) $b = .25$, (b) $b = .40$, (c) $b = .50$?

13. How would you explain the following events?

(a) The price of a firm's shares increases when it announces a new breakthrough in its R and D program.

(b) The price of a firm's stock rises when it raises its retention rate.

(c) Interest rates fall and stock prices rise.

(d) The price of a company's stock falls when a new competitor appears.

(e) The price of a firm's stock falls when it raises its retention rate.

14. A company has the following balance sheet and income statement:

Balance Sheet				Income Statement	
Assets	$200	Debt	$100	Profits before interest and taxes	$40
		Equity	100	Interest	8
				Profits before taxes	32
				Taxes	16
				Profits after taxes	$16

The firm distributes three-fourths of earnings in dividends; it has 10 shares of stock outstanding; and investors discount its future dividend stream at a 9 percent. Calculate:

(a) the rate of return on assets.

(b) the interest rate.

(c) the rate of return on equity.

(d) the growth rate.

(e) the dividends per share.

(f) the price per share.

REFERENCES AND SUGGESTED READINGS

Articles

Baumol, William, "On Dividend Policy and Market Imperfection," *Journal of Business,* vol. XXXVI (January 1963), pp. 112–15.

Baumol, W., and Malkiel, B., "The Firm's Optimum Debt-Equity Combination and the Cost of Capital," *Quarterly Journal of Economics,* vol. LXXXI, no. 4 (November 1967), pp. 548–78.

Baxter, N., "Leverage, Risk of Ruin, and the Cost of Capital," *Journal of Finance,* vol. XXII, no. 3 (September 1967), pp. 395–403.

Benishay, Haskel, "Variability in Earnings Price Ratios of Corporate Equities," *American Economic Review,* vol. LI, no. 1 (March 1961), pp. 81–94.

Bierman, H., "Risk and Addition of Debt to the Capital Structure," *Journal of Financial and Quantitative Analysis,* vol. III, no. 4 (December 1968), pp. 415–26.

Carleton, W. T., and Lerner, Eugene M., "Measuring Corporate Profit Opportunities," *Journal of Financial and Quantitative Analysis,* vol. II, no. 3 (September 1967), pp. 225–41.

Chen, Houng-Yhi, "Valuation Under Uncertainty," *Journal of Financial and Quantitative Analysis,* vol. II, no. 3 (September 1967), pp. 313–26.

Darling, Paul G., "The Influence of Expectations and Liquidity on Dividend Policy," *Journal of Political Economy,* vol. LXV (June 1957), pp. 209–24.

Durand, David, "The Cost of Capital, Corporation Finance, and the Theory of Investment: Comment," *American Economic Review,* vol. XLIX, no. 4 (September 1959), pp. 639–55.

Friend, Irwin, and Puckett, Marshall, "Dividends and Stock Prices," *American Economic Review,* vol. LIV, no. 5 (September 1964), pp. 656–82.

———, "Optimal Investment and Financing Policy," *Journal of Finance,* vol. XVIII, no. 2 (May 1963), pp. 264–72.

Gordon, M. J., "Dividends, Earnings and Stock Prices," *Review of Economics and Statistics,* vol. XLI (May 1959), pp. 99–105.

Gordon, M. J., and Shapiro, E., "Capital Equipment Analysis: The Required Rate of Profit," *Management Science,* vol. III (October 1956), pp. 102–10.

Harkavy, Oscar, "The Relationship Between Retained Earnings and Common Stock Prices for Large Listed Corporations," *Journal of Finance,* vol. VIII (September 1953), pp. 283–97.

Krainer, Robert E., "Liquidity Preference and Stock Market Speculation," *Journal of Financial and Quantitative Analysis,* vol. IV, no. 1 (March 1969), pp. 89–98.

Lerner, Eugene M., and Carleton, Willard T., "The Integration of Capital Budgeting and Stock Valuation," *American Economic Review,* vol. LIV, no. 5 (September 1964), pp. 683–703.

Lintner, John, "Dividends, Earnings, Leverage, Stock Prices and the Supply of Capital to Corporations," *Review of Economics and Statistics,* vol. XLIV (August 1962), pp. 243–69.

————, "The Cost of Capital and Optimal Financing of Corporate Growth," *Journal of Finance,* vol. XVII, no. 2 (May 1963), pp. 293–310.

————, "Distribution of Incomes of Corporations Among Dividends, Retained Earnings and Taxes," *American Economic Review,* vol. XLVI, no. 2 (May 1956), pp. 97–113.

Miller, Merton, and Modigliani, Franco, "Dividend Policy, Growth, and the Valuation of Shares," *Journal of Business,* vol. XXXIV (October 1961), pp. 411–33.

Modigliani, Franco, and Miller, Merton, "The Cost of Capital, Corporation Finance, and the Theory of Investment," *American Economic Review,* vol. XLVIII, no. 3 (June 1958), pp. 261–97.

Myers, Stewart, "A Time-State-Preference Model of Security Valuation," *Journal of Financial and Quantitative Analysis,* vol. III, no. 1 (March 1968), pp. 1–34.

Reisman, Arnold, and Buffa, E. S., "A General Model for Investment Policy," *Management Science,* vol. 8 (April 1962), pp. 204–310.

Robichek, Alexander, and Myers, Stewart C., "Problems in the Theory of Optimal Capital Structure," *Journal of Financial and Quantitative Analysis,* vol. I, no. 2 (June 1966), pp. 1–35.

Schwartz, Eli, "Theory of the Capital Structure of the Firm," *Journal of Finance,* vol. XIV, no. 1 (March 1959), pp. 18–39.

Sloane, William, and Reisman, Arnold, "Stock Evaluation Theory: Classification, Reconciliation, and General Model," *Journal of Financial and Quantitative Analysis,* vol. III, no. 2 (June 1968), pp. 171–205.

Solomon, Ezra, "Leverage and the Cost of Capital," *Journal of Finance,* vol. XVIII, no. 2 (May 1963), pp. 273–80.

Tinsley, P. A., "Capital Structure, Precautionary Balances and Valuation of the Firm: The Problem of Financial Risk," *Journal of Financial and Quantitative Analysis,* vol. V, no. 1 (March 1970), pp. 33–62.

Vickers, Douglas, "Profitability and Reinvestment Rates: A Note on the Gordon Paradox," *Journal of Business,* vol. XXXIX (July 1966), pp. 366–70.

Walter, James E., "Dividend Policies and Common Stock Prices," *Journal of Finance,* vol. XI, no. 1 (March 1956), pp. 29–41.

————, "Dividend Policy: Its Influence on the Value of the Enterprise," *Journal of Finance,* vol. XVIII, no. 2 (May 1963), pp. 280–92.

Books

Brittain, J. A., *Corporate Dividend Policy* (Washington, D. C.: Brookings Institute, 1966).

Donaldson, G., *Corporate Debt Capacity* (Boston: Harvard Univ. Press, 1961).

Gordon, Myron, *The Investment, Financing and Valuation of the Corporation* (Homewood, Ill.: Irwin, 1962).

Robichek, Alexander, and Meyers, Stewart, *Optimal Financing Decisions* (Englewood Cliffs, N. J.: Prentice-Hall, 1965).

Vickers, Douglas, *The Theory of the Firm: Production, Capital and Finance* (New York: McGraw-Hill, 1968).

Walter, James E., *Dividend Policy and Enterprise Valuation* (Belmont, Calif.: Wadsworth, 1967).

10. (a) $r = \frac{40}{160} = .25$
    (b) Dividends per share $= (1 - T)(1 - b)rA$
    $\quad\quad = (.75)(.5)(.25)4$
    $\quad\quad = .375$
    (c) $g = (1 - T)br$
    $\quad\quad = (.75)(.5)(.25)$
    $\quad\quad = .09375$
    (d) $P = \dfrac{D}{k - g}$
    $\quad\quad = \$18.75$

11. (a) .238
    (b) .222
    (c) .210

12. (a) .35
    (b) .20
    (c) .10

13. (a) The profit-opportunity schedule shifts to the right.
    (b) The company moves down along its profit-opportunity schedule.
    (c) The entire family of isoprice lines shifts downward.
    (d) The profit-opportunity schedule shifts to the left.
    (e) The company has moved down along its profit opportunity schedule past the point of maximum price.

14. (a) 20 percent
    (b) 8 percent
    (c) 16 percent
    (d) 4 percent
    (e) $1.20
    (f) $24

Implementing valuation models

18

If a firm's profit-opportunity schedule shifts to the right, the price of its stock will increase. If this schedule shifts to the left, the price of its stock will fall. These shifts can result from either managerial decisions or economic developments outside the control of the firm. Research and development outlays can lead to the creation of new products and to cost reductions in the manufacture of old products. More effective marketing programs can raise the firm's demand curve. New manpower policies can lower labor costs. All these developments will lead to upward shifts in the profit-opportunity schedule attributable to managerial actions. A change in the nation's monetary policy or in the government's tax and expenditure policy can lead to a faster or slower rate of growth of national income. When the growth rate of the economy changes, the demand for the output of many firms also changes, resulting in shifts in their profit-opportunity schedules attributable to forces outside the firm's control.

The price of a company's shares will also be affected when the discount rate that shareholders apply to its expected dividend stream rises or falls. Here, too, both specific corporate actions and changes in macroeconomic variables can have an effect. Managerial decisions with respect to the amount of debt in the firm's capital structure influence the variability and potential growth of the dividend stream and hence the discount rate. When interest rates rise as a result of government actions, shareholders will apply a higher discount rate to a company's expected dividend stream than when interest rates fall.

Because changes in the government's monetary and fiscal policies affect both the profit-opportunity schedules of firms and the rate at which future streams of dividends are discounted, prices of many companies' stock tend to move together. During some periods, almost all the securities listed on an exchange will rise in price; while during other periods, almost all will fall in price. Economic forecasting and studies of when changes in government policy are likely to occur therefore play a major role in the timing of the investment decisions of major trust companies, pension funds, mutual funds, and similar organizations.

Not all securities, however, will rise or fall by the same amount during a particular period. When the market as a whole is rising, the price of some securities may fall while the price of others rises dramatically. Similarly, when the market as a whole is declining, the price of some issues may rise while that of others may drop sharply. These differences arise because of managerial decisions unique to each firm.

From an investor's point of view, the crucial question is, How can the securities that are likely to outperform the average be detected? How can the analysis developed in Chapter 17 help an investor decide which securities to buy? How does it help professional analysts structure the information they collect about a company?

Industry and company analysis

Perhaps the greater part of the research effort of all security analysts is directed toward estimating the likelihood of a change in a company's profit-opportunity schedule. To prepare this estimate, an analyst will gather information from a wide variety of sources: articles in trade and financial magazines, industry conventions at which new products are exhibited, interviews with corporate managers, discussions with other security analysts, and so forth.

In their work, many analysts make the implicit assumption that for a firm's profit-opportunity schedule to shift further to the right than the schedules of other firms in the industry, the quality of its management must be superior. Since many different management styles can prove effective, they generally use several yardsticks to measure corporate management. Many of the better analysts, for example, look for at least the following four behavioral qualities when they evaluate management[1]:

(1) A RESULTS-ORIENTED ATTITUDE.

This implies that the firm has established a performance standard for itself and that current operations are measured against this yardstick. When discrepancies between the actual and planned results occur, corrective actions are taken promptly.

(2) A CONCERN FOR PEOPLE.

Everyone recognizes that managers do not have to be gregarious, outgoing, or solicitous toward their employees. Effective managers are, how-

[1] For a fuller discussion of problems in measuring corporate management, see Phil Dutter, "The Quality of Management," *Financial Analysts Journal,* vol. XXV, no. 2 (March–April 1969), pp. 105–13.

ever, concerned about the quality of the people whom they hire, the progress they make once they are on the job, and the atmosphere of the organization in which they work.

(3) A STRATEGY ORIENTATION.

A forward-looking manager will be concerned with any developments that are unfolding in the environment which will affect the company. He will allocate some portion of his time to creating programs not only to meet these impending changes, but to guide and direct them.

(4) AN IMPROVEMENT ORIENTATION.

An organization can be structured so that it constantly strives for improvement; past results are expected to be exceeded and new challenges are expected to be met and overcome. Such an organization will tend both to produce capable future managers and to generate superior short-term results.

Determining whether the management of a firm has these four qualities is not easy. A series of carefully structured interviews must be carried on, not only with the chief executive officer of the firm but with several other key employees, its competitors, and its customers. Moreover, conditions change rapidly within a corporation. A chief executive officer can leave or retire, and his replacement may not be as capable or effective. A firm that was once a leader in its field can in a few short years become a laggard; and a relatively unimaginative corporation, under new leadership, can in the same space of time become dynamic and creative. Thus analysts must constantly audit the management of companies, as well as the productivity of their financial and physical assets.

Even after an analyst preparing an evaluation of a company has audited the firm's management and reached the conclusion from his study that it has the capacity to continually shift its profit-opportunity schedule, his job is only half done. The price of the company's stock may already reflect widespread expectations of future growth. The price may already be so high that, unless all the favorable predictions of the analyst come true, it will fall substantially. On the other hand, if the expected growth does occur, the price of the stock, since it is already high, may appreciate only slightly. An analyst must therefore determine whether *the combination of the present price and future prospects* of one security make it more or less attractive than the combination of the present price and future prospects of another security.

Comparative analysis

The relative attractiveness of various companies can be readily graphed. Suppose an analyst concludes that six companies have approximately the

Implementing valuation models

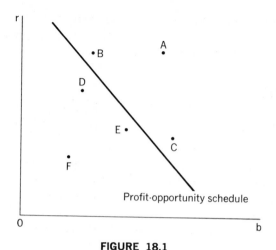

FIGURE 18.1
Several Companies with an Identical Profit-Opportunity Schedule.

same long-run profit-opportunity schedule. For one reason or another, however, the price of each company's stock, its rate of return on assets, r, and its retention rate, b, are different and are as shown in Figure 18.1. (The isoprice lines are not shown on this graph.) Company F is the most attractive, from an investment standpoint, and company A is the least attractive. The price of company F's shares is likely to rise as the market comes to recognize its potential for growth, while company A's shares are likely to fall in price. The prices of B, C, D, and E's shares are unlikely to change substantially.

Two methods are commonly used by analysts to ascertain the relative attractiveness of different companies (i.e. to find those that most nearly resemble F and those that most nearly resemble A). Under the first method, an analyst begins by examining a series of financial ratios such as those developed in Chapter 3. For example, he might examine the price-earnings ratio, debt-equity ratio, dividend-payout rate, sales-growth rate, profit margins, and return on assets of several companies with comparable profit-opportunity schedules. He then makes a subjective evaluation of each company's position. For example, if a firm has a relatively low debt-equity ratio, a high profit margin, a high growth rate of sales, and a low price-earnings ratio, it may correspond closely to company F in Figure 18.1; that is, it may be a company whose shares are likely to rise rapidly in value in the months ahead. If these ratios are different, if the debt-equity ratio and the price-earnings ratio are high and the profit margin and growth rate of sales low, the company may correspond closely to company A.

The second method of determining the relative attractiveness of different securities is more formal. The analyst establishes the statistical relationship between a measure such as the price-earnings ratio and several independent variables. The procedure for calculating this statistical relationship is called *regression analysis*. Regression analysis refers (1) to the methods by which estimates are made of the values of one variable from a knowledge of the values of one or more other variables and (2) to the measurement of the errors involved in this estimation process. For example, based on his knowledge of a company's past growth rate, debt-equity ratio, and dividend payout rate, an analyst could try to forecast its P/E ratio. Firms whose actual P/E ratios are less than the value forecast by such a regression equation are considered attractive investments, and those whose current P/E ratios are above the level forecast are considered unattractive.[2]

Bower and Bower[3] recently prepared such a regression, using the data for 100 companies for the years 1960–1964. The variables they used to estimate the P/E ratio were: (1) growth rate, (2) payout ratio, (3) marketability, (4) market conformity, (5) price variability, and (6) firm effects. How each of these variables were defined and measured will be described later. The coefficients that indicate how much a change of one unit in each of these variables will induce in the dependent variable (P/E) are given in the second column of Table 18.1. The *t* values in the third column are a measure of the significance of each of the variables. The larger the *t* value, the more confident the researcher can be that the coefficient of each variable is not zero.

TABLE 18.1
Coefficients Found in the Bowers' Study

Variable	Value of Coefficient	*t* Value
growth rate	.847	4.76
payout ratio	.095	4.04
marketability	.080	12.20
market conformity	−.077	5.76
price variability	.534	12.42
firm effects	.976	29.00

SOURCE: Richard S. and Dorothy H. Bower, "Risk and the Valuation of Common Stock," *Journal of Political Economy*, vol. LXXVII, no. 3 (May–June 1969), University of Chicago Press.

Although the Bowers did not use the results of the regression to recommend different securities for an investment portfolio, they could have proceeded to do so as follows: Tabulate the growth rate, payout rate,

[2] There are several excellent texts that describe this technique in detail. Among them are Morris Hamburg, *Statistical Analysis for Decision Making* (Harcourt Brace Jovanovich, 1970) and Taro Yamane, *Statistics* (Harper and Row, 1964).

[3] Richard S. and Dorothy H. Bower, "Risk and the Valuation of Common Stock," *Journal of Political Economy*, vol. LXXVII, no. 3 (May–June 1969), pp. 349–63.

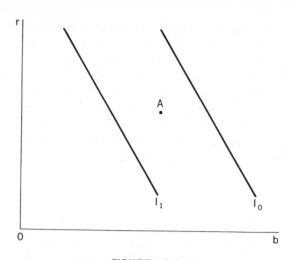

FIGURE 18.2
Two Possible Profit-Opportunity Schedules for Company A.

and the values of the other variables for the security under consideration. Multiply each value by the estimated coefficient indicated in Table 18.1 to obtain an expected normal P/E ratio, that is, the P/E ratio the security can be expected to maintain. Then compare the actual prevailing P/E ratio to the estimated ratio. If the actual ratio exceeds the estimate, the security may be considered relatively unattractive; if it is less than the estimate, it is relatively attractive.

Although popular, this technique is not an infallible guide because it makes the implicit assumption that the P/E ratio will move toward its calculated value faster than the independent variables themselves will change. This assumption, however, may not always be true; as a result, securities that appear relatively attractive may fall in price. For example, consider company A in Figure 18.2. If I_0 represents its opportunity schedule, the price of its shares is relatively low. However, if the investment schedule changes to I_1 the price of the shares will be relatively high.

Let us now return to the specific procedures followed by the Bowers and evaluate their results. The coefficients the Bowers report indicate that high P/E ratios arise because of high payout rates and high growth rates. The P/E ratio declines as the marketability of the security falls, as the conformity to the general market index rises, and as the variability of the security itself falls. Before we can use their results, however, we must examine how the variables in the regression were defined and measured.

THE P/E RATIO

The P/E ratio is the dependent variable in the Bowers' study. It is the value that they are trying to explain. For all its apparent simplicity, the price-earnings ratio is difficult to define operationally. Which price should be used as the numerator? The high price for the year? the low price? the median price? And which earnings should be chosen for the denominator? The annual figure? the figure for the last twelve months? the seasonally adjusted quarterly rate? The Bowers selected none of these, using instead the year-end price of the security as the numerator and an average of past annual earnings (adjusted to give more weight to the current year's earnings) as the denominator. They called this measure of earnings the *normal earnings for the year*.

THE GROWTH RATE

A similar set of questions arise with respect to the growth rate. Which growth rate should be used? The growth in earnings, dividends, sales, assets, or still another variable? Over what period should growth be measured? One year? three years? or five? The Bowers calculated the annual growth rate by dividing the annual increment in the trend of normal earnings by normal earnings for the year.

THE DIVIDEND-PAYOUT RATIO

Two estimates of the payout rate were tested. The first was the ratio of annual dividends to normal earnings, defined as above. The second was a statistical estimate of the payout rate based on a regression of actual dividends paid and actual earnings reported each year.

MARKETABILITY

The marketability of a security was calculated by multiplying the number of shares traded during a year by the average of the high and the low price for the year. Thus, the higher the aggregate market value of securities that are traded, the greater they assume the marketability of the issue to be.

CONFORMITY WITH MARKET MOVEMENTS

To estimate this value, the Bowers first calculated the annual return on security, defined as the change in its closing price from year-end to year-end, plus the dividends paid during the year, divided by the price at the beginning of the year. They then performed a similar computation to calculate the return an investor would have earned had he bought the Dow Jones Index. Finally, they ran a regression between the two series, using the Dow Jones return as the independent variable and the company's return as the dependent variable. Thus, $r_s = a_0 + a_1 r_{DJ}$ where r_s is the return of the security under study and r_{DJ} is the return of the Dow Jones Index. The value of the coefficient a_1 is the measure of conformity with market movements that the Bowers use in their work.

PRICE VARIABILITY

The spread between the security's highest and lowest price each year was expressed as a percentage of the average price during the year. The average percentage for all the years studied was then calculated and used as the measure of price variability.

THE "FIRM EFFECT"

To capture the systemic effect of other variables that are associated with the firm but are not explicitly taken into account by the five independent variables described above, the Bowers proceeded as follows. For each year of the study, they ran a regression between the price-earnings ratio and the five independent variables described. The difference between the predicted and actual P/E ratios was divided by its standard error, and the resulting ratio used as an estimate of the persistently influential variables that were not part of those explicitly considered. The Bowers called this ratio the *firm effect*, and, in their subsequent tests, used it as a sixth independent variable.

We have described the variables the Bowers used to estimate P/E ratios in such detail to indicate the care with which their study was performed. Let us now see what questions are raised by the statistical results.

One problem was noted by the Bowers themselves. In commenting on the firm effect, they said, "The firm effect, as might be inferred from the *t*-ratio makes more of a contribution to the explanation of price-earnings ratios than any other variable. Its addition to the group of explanatory variables results in the approximate doubling of explained variance." In other words, the various financial variables that were so laboriously selected and calculated were of limited value in explaining the variations observed in the actual P/E ratios. Not until the firm effect was added to the final estimating equation did statistically powerful results emerge.

Unfortunately, the firm effect has no economic meaning. It is not a set of decisions that management can take to improve performance, it is not even a value that can be known in advance of the particular sample of companies studied. It is purely a statistical artifact, yet it contributes more than any of the other variables used to the explanation of the behavior of the price-earnings ratios of different companies provided by the study.

The second problem raised by the Bowers' analysis centers on the differences in the signs of the coefficients for market conformity and price variability. The market-conformity coefficient can be considered a measure of volatility: When the coefficient of a security is greater than 1, the return on the security is more volatile than the return on the market index; when the coefficient is less than 1, the security fluctuates less than the market as a whole. A negative coefficient for this variable indicates that the market penalizes highly volatile securities. If this is the case, how can a positive value for price variability be explained?

The argument over the signs of these variables can be viewed in another way. The positive value of the price-variability factor can be rationalized as follows: Investors look to bonds or other fixed-return investments when they want a stable return but when they purchase stocks, they want "action" and will pay to get it. But if this reasoning is correct, how can the negative market-conformity value be explained? In some sense, then, the statistical results are not internally consistent.

Monitoring changes in the profit-opportunity schedule

The analytical model presented in the last chapter indicated that security prices will change when the firm's profit-opportunity schedule changes. One way for an analyst to determine whether this is likely to occur is to interview the management of different companies. Once he has obtained information about several companies he can perform a comparative analysis, either subjective or statistical to ascertain which company is likely to enjoy the greatest increase in the price of its shares.

A second strategy is simpler. Rather than interviewing the management of several companies and making various tests to measure the relative attractiveness of their securities, the analyst can wait until a shift actually occurs in the firm's profit-opportunity schedule to recommend the purchase of the stock. If there is a lag between the time the schedule shifts and the price of the security changed, there is still an opportunity for gain.

But how can companies whose profit opportunities are improving be detected? Analysts use various "filter rules" to determine when the profit-opportunity schedule of a firm shifts.[4] Several analysts have suggested that the percentage change in a company's earnings from quarter to quarter be used as a proxy for a shift in its profit-opportunity schedule. For example, suppose that earnings for the first two quarters of two years

---

[4] See Manoun Kisor and Van A. Messner, "The Filter Approach and Earnings Forecasts," *Financial Analysts Journal* (January 1969), pp. 109–15; H. A. Latane, D. L. Tuttle, and C. P. Jones, "E/P Ratios v. Changes in Earnings in Forecasting Future Price Changes," *Financial Analysts Journal* (January 1969), pp. 117–20; Robert Levy, "Random Walks: Reality of Myth," *Financial Analysts Journal* (November 1967), pp. 69–77.

are as follows:

Year	Earnings in Quarter 1	Earnings in Quarter 2
1	$ .80	$ .90
2	.90	1.10

Since the percentage change in earnings in year 2 was greater than the percentage change in earnings in year 1 (i.e., since 1.10/.90 > .90/.80), a shift to the right of the firm's profit-opportunity schedule can be assumed to have occurred during the second year. If the price of the company's shares has not risen before the figures for the second quarter of year 2 become available, in anticipation of the change, and if the firm's profit-opportunity schedule actually did change, the price of the security can be expected to rise in the near future.

Another way of understanding this strategy is to consider the valuation equation $P = D/(k - g)$. If the growth in dividends follows the growth in earnings, then a rise in earnings means that the value of g in the valuation equation will also rise. As g rises, other things being equal, P, of course, rises as well.

This approach to security analysis rests on a series of conditions: If earnings rise, it is likely that a firm's profit-opportunity schedule has shifted; if the profit-opportunity schedule shifts and if the price of the security has not already gone up, the price is likely to rise in the near future. An investor purchasing securities on this basis does not expect that the price of every stock he buys will rise. Those who practice this style of security analysis contend only that a greater percentage of the securities selected according to these rules are likely to increase in value than securities selected, say, at random. If a higher percentage of the securities chosen do rise in price, the value of the portfolio as a whole is, of course, increased.

Different writers in this tradition have used different proxy variables for detecting a change in the profit-opportunity schedule. For example, instead of quarterly changes in earnings from the preceding year, changes in the rate of return on assets can be monitored. Instead of investing on the basis of data from only two quarters, data from three, four, or five quarters can be used. In short, just as the Bowers could have used different constructs to measure parameters, so different analysts operating in this tradition have found different series convenient.

An important test of this approach to security analysis and portfolio management was performed by Breen and Savage,[5] who compared the return that an investor would have earned had he consistently followed three different strategies:

[5] William Breen and James Savage, "Portfolio Distribution and Tests of Security Selection Models," *Journal of Finance,* vol. XXIII (December 1968), pp. 805–21.

STRATEGY 1: Compute the five-year average growth rate of earnings per share for each company under consideration. Calculate the price earnings ratio for each security whose growth rate exceeds 10 percent per annum. Purchase equal dollar amounts of the ten securities with the lowest price-earnings ratio each year.

STRATEGY 2: Purchase the securities of the ten companies with the highest dividend-price ratio in the preceding year.

STRATEGY 3: Purchase the securities of the ten companies with the highest rate of return on total assets in the preceding year, where return is measured by earnings available to the common shareholder divided by total assets.

To evaluate these strategies, Breen and Savage constructed 1,000 portfolios, each consisting of ten randomly selected securities, for the years 1951–1966. They then calculated the return on these portfolios, measured by dividends plus capital gains over the one-year holding period, divided by the initial outlay. Finally, they arrayed the 1,000 portfolios, listing those with the lowest return first, and calculated 20 points along the distribution. When they compared the performance of the portfolios selected by the three strategies presented above with the performance of the 1,000 randomly selected portfolios to determine where along the distribution these portfolios would lie, they obtained the results presented in Table 18.2.

TABLE 18.2
Annual Rates of Return

Year	Under Strategy 1	Percentage of Sample Portfolios That Earned Less	Under Strategy 2	Percentage of Sample Portfolios That Earned Less	Under Strategy 3	Percentage of Sample Portfolios That Earned Less
1954	.6569	.95	.4806	.90	.5196	.95
1955	.3594	.95	.3566	.95	.1693	.75
1956	.1883	.90	.3226	.95	.1427	.70
1957	− .0927	.45	− .1292	.30	− .0379	.70
1958	1.1789	.95	.5931	.90	.8261	.95
1959	.6799	.95	.2492	.80	.6385	.95
1960	.1077	.85	− .0313	.40	.3255	.95
1961	1.4409	.95	.1997	.25	.5142	.90
1962	− .0493	.95	− .1071	.80	− .3336	.00
1963	.2716	.80	.2134	.65	.1114	.30
1964	.4431	.95	.4525	.95	.2054	.60
1965	.9582	.95	.2845	.30	.2862	.30
1966	.3304	.95	− .0680	.55	− .1820	.05

SOURCE: William Breen and James Savage, "Portfolio Distribution and Tests of Security Selection Models," *Journal of Finance*, vol. XXIII (December 1968), p. 817.

Except in 1957, strategy 1, the selection of high-growth-rate companies with low price-earnings ratios, consistently produced dramatically superior results. Strategies 2 and 3 were much less successful.

The results obtained by Breen and Savage are important for a number of reasons.

First, they indicate that a lag exists in the response of security prices to changes in corporate earnings and growth. If these changes can be detected promptly, a portfolio of securities can be constructed that will increase in value faster than a portfolio of securities selected at random.

All the securities in the portfolio that pass a particular filter rule may not increase in value. Indeed, the price of some of these stocks may fall. Similarly, some stocks whose price will rise rapidly may be left out of the portfolio. The point to emphasize is that Breen and Savage were able to specify the properties of a class of securities whose members have a higher probability of appreciation than securities not included in the class.

Second, Breen and Savage's study demonstrates the feasibility of a new style of security analysis. Instead of studying a single company in depth to determine whether the price of its stock is relatively high or low, they treat the price of a security as a random variable and ask questions only about the probability of the price rising or falling. The probability that the securities which pass the established filter rules will show some degree of price appreciation is greater than the probability that those which do not pass the rules will increase in value.

Two things are required to use this type of security analysis. First, the investor must be able to scan a large number of securities to ascertain which ones pass the filter rules and which do not. In practice, this kind of scanning requires the use of a computer. Second, the data available about the company must be reasonably current, since the lag between corporate developments and the change in security prices is likely to be short.

Monitoring price change

Some financial analysts have attempted to design filter rules that, unlike those proposed by Breen and Savage, consider only the past changes in the price of the security itself. Rather than trying to determine when a firm's profit-opportunity schedule shifts by examining changes in corporate earnings, they monitor only price data. The argument here, in terms of the analysis developed above, is that when a change occurs in either the profit-opportunity schedule or the discount rate, the price of the security will begin to move toward its new equilibrium level. It may take only a short time to reach this level, but substantial gains can be realized if the security is purchased early in the adjustment process.

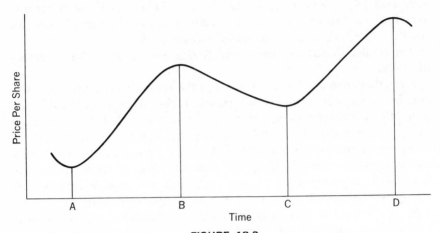

FIGURE 18.3
Time Path of Stock Prices.

A change in either the profit-opportunity schedule or the discount rate could lead to a time path of prices like that in Figure 18.3. With the benefit of hindsight, it is obvious that a purchase at points *A* and *C* and a sale at points *B* and *D* would have been rewarding. The problem is to recognize when *A*, *B*, *C*, and *D* occur in time to take advantage of the opportunity they afford by buying or selling.

One way that has been suggested for determining when purchases and sales should be made is to design a set of filter rules based on turning points in the price of the stock. For example, in Figure 18.4, purchases and sales are triggered by a 10-percent filter. Suppose a low price for shares of the company under review is $40. When the security appreciates 10 percent (to $44), it should be purchased. The stock is then held

FIGURE 18.4
Time Path of Stock Prices.

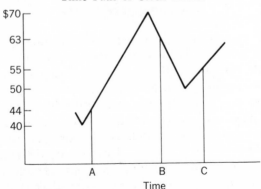

Implementing valuation models

until it reaches a peak and falls 10 percent. The security in Figure 18.4 rises to a high of $70 and is sold at $63, when it seems clear that a peak has been passed. It continues to fall, this time to $50. When it goes back up to $55, a second purchase is made.

A typical x percent filter rule would be: If the daily closing price of a particular security moves up at least x percent, buy and hold the security until its price moves down at least x percent from a subsequent high. At this time, sell the holding and go short (sell more of the stock then you actually own). Maintain the short position until the daily closing price rises at least x percent above a substantial low. At this time, cover the short position and go long (purchase shares for your own account). Moves of less than x percent in either direction are ignored. Variations of this filter rule may specify a different percentage price change to trigger a purchase than that required to trigger a sell.

Filters of various sizes, ranging from half of one percent to 50 percent, have been constructed by analysts, and the portfolios generated by them have been compared to those generated by a simple buy-and-hold rule. Similarly, the returns generated by buying and selling a specific security under different filter rules have been compared with a simple buy-and-hold rule for the same security. The results of these studies generally show that even if brokers' commissions are not included, a simple buy-and-hold strategy is superior to a price-based filter-rule. For example, when Fama and Blume studied the closing prices of the 30 securities that make up the Dow Jones Industrial Index from 1957 to 1962,[6] they found that all filters below 12 percent and above 25 percent produced negative average returns per security. The returns on filters between 12 and 25 percent were positive; however, they were less than the returns that would have been received from a buy-and-hold strategy. Moreover, when the filter rules were applied to individual securities, the results were inferior to those of the buy-and-hold strategy in 28 of the 30 cases studied. The two exceptions were Alcoa and Union Carbide.

To see why filter rules can produce either better or worse portfolios than a buy-and-hold rule, let us take a look at Figures 18.4 and 18.5. Figure 18.4 shows the conditions under which a filter will produce substantially better results than a buy-and-hold strategy. If a long and sustained period of price increases is followed by a relatively sharp break in prices, a filter rule such as "buy 10 percent above the low and sell 10 percent below the high" will ensure capital gains for investors. Figure 18.5, however, shows what can happen when the 10-percent rule is applied blindly.

Suppose that an initial purchase is made at $49.50, a price 10 percent above the low price of $45 per share. The price of the security increases

[6] Eugene F. Fama and Marshall E. Blume, "Filter Rules and Stock Market Trading," *Journal of Business,* vol. XXXIX, no. 1 (January 1966), pp. 226–41.

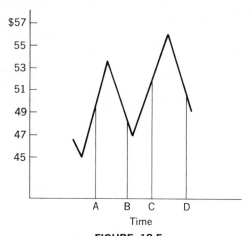

FIGURE 18.5

Time Path of Stock Prices.

to a high of $53.50 and then falls back 10 percent, triggering a sale. Since the price of the stock is now $48.20, this will mean a loss of $1.20 before commissions. A second transaction can have equally poor results. Suppose the price of the security continues to fall to $47, then reverses itself and rises to $51.70. Since this is 10 percent above the low of $47, a purchase is made. The stock continues to rise and reaches a peak of $56. From this point it declines 10 percent, triggering a sale at $50.40 and resulting in a loss of $1.30 before commissions. Thus, when the price movements are saw-toothed, a mechanical trading strategy such as a filter rule may be dramatically inferior to a buy-and-hold strategy. Furthermore, the empirical evidence cited by Fama and Blume suggests that the actual behavior of security prices resembles the pattern in Figure 18.5 more closely than the pattern in Figure 18.4.

Momentum series

A second purchasing strategy based on the behavior of security prices alone is to purchase only those securities whose prices have shown the greatest increase over a given period, such as a week. Thus, at the end of a week, all the securities under consideration are ranked according to the percentage change in their price and, say, the 20 or 25 securities that appreciated the most are then purchased. The following week a new ranking is made. Some of the securities that are held will appear again in the list of the 20 or 25 securities that appreciated the most, and some will drop down to a lower ranking. An arbitrary sell point is then deter-

Implementing valuation models

mined. For example, a security may be sold when it drops below the rank of 50. The proceeds from the sale of low-ranking securities are used to purchase securities in the top 20 or 25 group not already represented in the portfolio. By constantly selling securities that have ceased to appreciate rapidly and purchasing those that do, the investor constructs a portfolio that contains only the securities with the greatest *momentum*.

The rationale for this strategy is the assumed lag in the securities market. If the market does not adjust instantly to changes in corporate investment opportunities, the price of a security may continue to rise rapidly for two, three, four, or even five weeks at a time.

Robert Levy, a researcher who tested this strategy using portfolios of various sizes and different sell points, reported that a portfolio for the period October 1960 to October 1965 constructed according to the general procedure outlined above yielded a rate of return of 20 percent.[7] A similar portfolio for the period July 1962 to November 1966 yielded an annual rate of return of 32 percent. Both these values are greater than the return that would result from a buy-and-hold strategy.

Unfortunately, Levy did not document his findings well. He does not explain why these results occurred, i.e., whether a small percentage of the total purchases accounted for the gains or whether modest profits were realized in the great majority of transactions. Nor does he reveal the number of periods during which gains occurred and during which losses resulted. Furthermore, the number of physical transactions required to support this portfolio procedure is, of course, very high. Levy did not indicate whether, during periods of falling or even stable prices, the commission charges exceeded the returns earned on the portfolio. Finally, he did not estimate trading costs above and beyond the commissions that were paid, i.e., whether the markets for the securities selected were sufficiently liquid that substantial purchases could be made without adversely affecting their price.

In spite of these empirical defects, Levy's study is provocative. His results are consistent with the hypothesis that when a sharp change in the price of a security occurs, a new equilibrium level is not achieved immediately and the price will continue to appreciate for some time.

The random-walk hypothesis

Many of the writers in the field of security analysis maintain that the direction of the change in the price of a security is random and that past price changes are no clue to future price changes. The reason past

[7] Robert A. Levy, "Random Walks: Reality or Myth," *Financial Analysts Journal* (November 1967), pp. 69–77.

price movements are not a guide to future movements, they contend, is that the securities market is constantly in equilibrium. All the available information about both macroeconomic and corporate variables is reflected in the existing price. The movement in prices about this equilibrium will be random from trade to trade and from day to day. If developments suddenly occur that indicate a change in a firm's prospects, this information immediately becomes known to all. A new equilibrium price is immediately established, and, once again, only random changes in prices will take place about this level. This theory is known as the *random-walk hypothesis.*

If security price changes dance randomly about an equilibrium level, two conclusions follow. First, there is no point in studying past price trends, since they can reveal nothing. And second, no filter rule based on past price data alone can generate a portfolio that will consistently yield a higher return than a portfolio of randomly selected securities.

A substantial amount of empirical data is consistent with the random-walk hypothesis. One piece of evidence has already been discussed: No price-filter rule, with the possible exception of the momentum strategy, has yet been found and documented that is superior to a buy-and-hold strategy. A second fact which supports random-walk hypothesis is that the performance record of portfolios selected by professional managers of pension funds, mutual funds, and trusts is not consistently better than that of a group of randomly selected securities. Finally, a tabulation of the price changes of specific securities indicates that they do conform closely to distributions generated by a random process.

If there were no lags between the time a change takes place in a corporation and its recognition by investors, price changes would indeed be random. Alternatively, if all investors had the same information about a company, price changes would be random. What is at issue, then is a question of fact: Do these two conditions hold?

Studies such as those conducted by Breen and Savage suggest that the first condition does not hold. They have martialed evidence that they can forecast the direction of price change through reported earnings. Moreover, the intense interest on the part of investors in the conversations that analysts have with corporate officers suggests that the second condition does not hold either—that there is a group of men, the corporate officers, who know more than others about the future performance of a company.

All investors are interested in the future equilibrium price level of the company's shares. If it will be above the current level, they can expect to make a profit by purchasing the stocks. If it will be below the current level, they can make a gain by selling short. The pattern of price changes between the two equilibrium levels can indeed be random, and the investor is indifferent to the fact. Indeed, if the pattern were not random—if there were, say, ten or twenty days in which the price of a security moved in the same direction—most investors would believe that it was being manipulated.

The random-walk hypothesis, then, is recognized as a valid statement about the short-run behavior of security prices by most investors. Unfortunately, since no stock-selection strategy other than random selection can be based on random movements, it is also nonoperational.

Summary

Several strategies for selecting securities are used by security analysts. All draw heavily on the assumption that changes in security prices are caused by changes in the firm's profit-opportunity schedule or changes in the discount rate.

Many security analysts attempt to estimate when a change in the firm's profit-opportunity schedule will take place by interviewing the management of the company, studying the firm's products and its competitive position, and so on. After this research is completed, they then must evaluate whether the market price of the security already reflects the change they foresee in the profit-opportunity schedule. This evaluation can be either subjective or formal and statistical. Even statistical comparisons, however, must be considered tentative, since unspecified "firm effects" seem to explain more of the variation in price-earnings ratios among firms than such variables as their growth rates and dividend payout ratios.

A second strategy for selecting securities is to wait until the profit-opportunity schedule shifts and purchase those securities whose price has not already risen. One way to measure whether a shift has taken place is to monitor the growth rate of earnings. Some analysts look for changes on a quarter-to-quarter basis, while others use a longer time span, such as five years.

A third strategy for selecting securities is to examine the price data itself and to purchase those securities whose price shows the greatest increase over a short period. This strategy rests on the assumption that price movements to new equilibrium levels take time and that if the securities can be purchased just as their movement toward the new equilibrium level begins, substantial gains can be made.

Questions for discussion and problems

1. Why do many securities tend to move in the same direction?
2. If an analyst is satisfied that the management of a company is capable and that its products have a good reputation, should he recommend its stock to investors?

3. How can an analyst use financial ratios to measure the attractiveness of a security?

4. What are some of the difficulties practicing analysts often encounter when they use regression analysis to evaluate securities?

5. What are some other plausible measures of the variables used by Bower and Bower in their analysis of security prices?

6. How can a shift in the profit-opportunity schedule be detected? Does the schedule shift every time a firm's reported profits rise?

7. Design and defend a set of plausible filter rules.

8. Why have price filters alone been useless in portfolio analysis?

[Answers to problems 9–12 follow references and suggested readings.]

9. A security analyst has collected the following data on three companies in a particular industry. Based upon these data alone, how might he rank their securities companies in terms of their attractiveness to a prudent investor?

	A	B	C
Current price	$60	$40	$50
Price range in the preceding year	$70–$85	$33–$55	$45–$80
Current earnings per share	$6.25	$3.00	$4.00
Current price-earnings ratio	9+	13+	12+
Growth rate of earnings for the past 3 years	−.02	+.06	+.08
Growth rate of earnings for the past 5 years	+.04	+.07	+.06
Dividends per share	$4.00	$1.00	$2.00
Ratio of debt to equity	1.6/1	1.3/1	1.8/1

10. Suppose that a regression analysis indicates that the following relationship characterizes an industry.

$$P/E = 100(\text{Growth rate}) - 1(\text{debt-equity ratio}) + 4(\text{payout ratio}) - .5(\text{price variability})$$

Two companies in the industry have the following characteristics:

	A	B
Growth rate	.16	.10
Debt-equity ratio	1.1	.8
Payout ratio	.6	.3
Price variability	.3	.5

If the actual P/E ratios for companies A and B are 20 and 9, respectively, which is statistically the more attractive?

11. Given the following seasonally adjusted quarterly-earnings pattern of three companies, where E_t is the current quarter, what might an analyst conclude about the profit-opportunity schedule of each?

	A	B	C
E_{t-3}	$1.00	$1.00	$1.00
E_{t-2}	1.10	.80	1.10
E_{t-1}	1.25	.90	.80
E_t	1.50	1.00	.80

12. The weekly closing price for a company's stock has been as follows:

Week	Price	Week	Price
1	$30	6	$33
2	28	7	31
3	26	8	38
4	35	9	37
5	34	10	38

Starting in period 1 with the purchase of the stock at $30, design a 10 percent buy-and-sell rule. (All purchase and sells must take place at week-end prices).
(1) When does the first sale take place, and how large a gain or loss occurs?
(2) When does the second purchase take place?
(3) When does the second sale take place, and how large a gain or loss occurs?
(4) When does the third purchase take place?

REFERENCES AND SUGGESTED READINGS

Articles

Alexander, Sidney, "Price Movements in Speculative Markets: Trends or Random Walks, No. 2," *Industrial Management Review,* vol. V (Spring 1964), pp. 25–46.

Bower, Richard S. and Dorothy H., "Risk and the Valuation of Common Stock," *Journal of Political Economy,* vol. LXXVII, no. 3 (May–June 1969), pp. 349–63.

Breen, William, and Savage, James, "Portfolio Distribution and Tests of Security Selection Models," *Journal of Finance,* vol. XXIII (December 1968), pp. 805–21.

Carlson, Robert S., "Aggregate Performance of Mutual Funds, 1948–1967," *Journal of Financial and Quantitative Analysis,* vol. V, no. 1 (March 1970), pp. 1–33.

Cragg, John G., and Malkiel, Burton F., "The Consensus and Accuracy of Some Predictions of the Growth of Corporate Earnings," *Journal of Finance,* vol. XXIII, no. 1 (March 1968), pp. 67–84.

Crum, M. Colyer, "Performance Investing and the Breakdown of Respect for Authority," *Financial Analysts Journal*, vol. XXV, no. 3 (May–June 1969), pp. 142–46.

Dutter, Phil, "The Quality of Management," *Financial Analysts Journal*, vol. XXV, no. 2 (March–April, 1969), pp. 105–13.

Evans, John L., "The Random Walk Hypothesis, Portfolio Analysis, and the Buy-and-Hold Criterion," *Journal of Financial and Quantitative Analysis*, vol. III, no. 3 (September 1968), pp. 327–42.

Fama, Eugene F., "The Behavior of Stock Market Prices," *Journal of Business*, vol. XXVIII (January 1965), pp. 34–105.

———, "Random Walks in Stock Market Prices," *Financial Analysts Journal*, vol. XXI (September–October 1965), pp. 55–59.

———, and Blume, Marshall E., "Filter Rules and Stock Market Trading," *Journal of Business*, vol. XXXIX, no. 1 (January 1966), pp. 226–41.

Fisher, Lawrence, "Some New Stock Market Indexes," *Journal of Business*, vol. XXXIX, no. 1, part II (January 1966), pp. 191–225.

Friend, Irwin, and Vickers, Douglas, "Portfolio Selection and Investment Performance," *Journal of Finance*, vol. XX, no. 3 (September 1965), pp. 391–415.

Gould, Alex, and Buchsbaum, Maurice, "A Filter Approach Using Earnings Relatives," *Financial Analysts Journal*, vol. XXV, no. 6 (November–December 1969), pp. 62–64.

Granger, C. W. J., "What the Random Walk Model Does Not Say," *Financial Analysts Journal*, vol. XXVI, no. 3 (May–June 1970), pp. 91–94.

King, Benjamin F., "Market and Industry Factors in Stock Price Behavior," *Journal of Business*, vol. XXXIX, no. 1 (January 1966), pp. 139–90.

Kisor, Manown, and Messner, Van A., "Filter Approach to Earnings," *Financial Analysts Journal*, vol. XXV, no. 1 (January–February 1969), pp. 109–16.

Latane, Henry, Tuttle, Donald L., and Jones, Charles P., "E/P Ratios vs. Changes in Earnings in Forecasting Future Price Changes," *Financial Analysts Journal*, vol. XXV, no. 1 (January–February 1969), pp. 117–20.

Latane, Henry, and Tuttle, Donald L., "Analysis of Common Stock Price Ratios," *Southern Economic Journal*, vol. XXIII (January 1967), pp. 343–54.

Levy, Robert A., "Conceptual Foundations of Technical Analysis," *Financial Analysts Journal*, vol. XXII (July–August 1966), pp. 83–89.

———, "Measurement of Investment Performance," *Journal of Financial and Quantitative Analysis*, vol. III, no. 1 (March 1968), pp. 35–57.

———, "Random Walks: Reality or Myth," *Financial Analysts Journal*, vol. XXIII, no. 6 (November–December 1967), pp. 69–77.

Levy, Robert A., and Kripotos, Spiro L., "Earnings Growth, P/E's and Relative Price Strength," *Financial Analysts Journal*, vol. XXV, no. 6 (November–December 1969), pp. 61–67.

Myers, Thomas S., "A Leading Indicator Approach to Stock Selection," *Financial Research, Investment Analysis and the Computer*, Tuck School (Hanover, N. H.), Bulletin 31 (November 1967), pp. 3–9.

Nicholson, S. Francis, "Price-Earnings Ratios," *Financial Analysts Journal*, vol. XVI, no. 4 (July–August) 1960, pp. 43–45.

Pinches, George E., "The Random Walk and Technical Analysis," *Financial Analysts Journal*, vol. XXVI, no. 2 (March–April 1970), pp. 104–09.

Pope, Alan, "The X Factor and the High Flyers," *Fortune*, vol. LXXVII (June 1, 1968), pp. 138–39.

Books

Brearley, Richard, *An Introduction to Risk and Return from Common Stocks* (Cambridge, Mass.: MIT Press, 1969).

Cohen, Jerome B., and Zinbarg, Edward D., *Investment Analysis and Portfolio Management* (Homewood, Ill.: Irwin, 1967).

Cootner, P. H., ed., *The Random Character of Stock Market Prices* (Cambridge, Mass.: MIT Press, 1964).

Edwards, Robert D., and Magee, John, *Technical Analysis of Stock Trends,* 5th ed. (Springfield, Mass.: John Magee, 1967).

Lerner, Eugene M., ed., *Readings in Financial Analysis and Investment Management* (Homewood, Ill.: Irwin, 1963).

Little, Ian M. D., and Rayner, A. C., *Higgledy Piggledy Growth Again* (Oxford: Basil Blackwell, 1966).

Sprinkel, Beryl W., *Money and Stock Prices* (Homewood, Ill.: Irwin, 1964).

Thorpe, E. O., and Kassouf, S., *Beat the Market* (New York: Random House, 1967).

ANSWERS TO PROBLEMS 9–12

9. Company C has the highest growth rate, and in recent years the rate has accelerated. Its current price is near the bottom of the range indicated for last year, and its P/E ratio is quite low for the indicated growth. While its debt to equity ratio is slightly higher than that of the other firms, it may not be excessive. Based on this information alone, C appears to be the most attractive.

   Ranking A and B is more difficult. A's growth rate is falling, and it has more debt than B. On the other hand, its P/E ratio is lower and its price, compared to last year, is low. If further research indicates that the growth rate may pick up, it may be more attractive than B. On the hand, if the downward trend in earnings is likely to continue, it is probably a less attractive investment than B.

10. Company A has an expected P/E ratio of 17.2, and company B has an expected P/E ratio of 10.15. Since B's actual ratio is below its expected value, it is the more attractive.

11. The profit-opportunity schedule of A appears to be rising; that of B appears to be constant; and C appears to be falling.

12. (1) In week 3 at a loss of $4 per share.
    (2) In week 4 at $35.
    (3) In week 7 a loss of $4 per share.
    (4) In week 8 at $38.

Mergers and corporate growth

19

Several mechanical investment strategies were presented in the last chapter. Some of the strategies recommended building portfolios of securities whose earnings followed a specified pattern. Others were more concerned with the pattern of changes in the price of the firm's stock, and still other strategies for building a portfolio called for purchasing securities that had both a high earnings growth rate and a low price-earnings ratio.

None of the strategies described really emphasized the need to look behind the reported figures to determine whether a shift in a firm's profit-opportunity schedule did, in fact, take place. They all implicitly assumed that when reported earnings rise, the firm's stock should be revalued upward because the underlying functions that limit its opportunities have changed. This assumption, however, may not always be correct. Reported earnings can increase for reasons that have nothing to do with a change in investment opportunities. Under these conditions, there may be no reason to revalue the firm.

Nevertheless, it remains a well-known fact that investors will pay relatively high prices for the shares of companies that can report rising earnings year after year and quarter after quarter. As a consequence of this market fact, a new phenomenon has arisen on the business scene: the conglomerate. A *conglomerate* is created when two or more companies in wholly different businesses merge. Conglomerate mergers should be distinguished from vertical or horizontal ones. A *vertical merger* arises when two companies combine and the output of one is the input of the other—when, for example a steel company combines with a coal mine or an equipment manufacturer merges with a distributor of its products. A *horizontal merger* arises when two companies that produce competing products and sell them to a common market combine. The merger of two coal companies, two steel mills, or two distributors would be a horizontal merger.

Both vertical and horizontal mergers involve companies in closely related activities, and it is not difficult to find the economic motive behind them: By combining their resources the firms can increase both their operating economies and their market power. Recent court decisions, however, have sharply curtailed the ability of companies to expand this way, and for all intents and purposes, such mergers can no longer take place between large firms.

A conglomerate merger arises when unrelated firms such as a dress manufacturer and a railroad, a flour mill and a toy manufacturer, or a chemical company and a boat manufacturer combine. When a conglomerate merger occurs, no operating economies arise because the companies are in different businesses. Nor is there an increase in market power. The merged companies can neither sell their output at a higher price nor purchase their inputs at a lower price because their products are unrelated. Why, then, would a rational manager seek such a merger, and how can his firm benefit from it? The answer lies largely in financial considerations.

An example of a merger

To understand how a merger between two companies in widely separated industries can produce a rise in reported per-share earnings, consider the following example. The balance sheets and income statements of two hypothetical companies, 1 and 2, are presented below:

Balance Sheets

Company 1		Company 2	
Assets	$100	Assets	$300
Debt	50	Debt	100
Equity	50	Equity	200
Total	$100	Total	$300

Income Statements

Company 1		Company 2	
Earnings before interest and taxes	$20	Earnings before interest and taxes	$47
Less interest (at 8%)	4	Less interest (at 7%)	7
	$16		$40
Taxes	8	Taxes	20
Earnings after taxes	$8	Earnings after taxes	$20

Suppose that company 1 has five shares of stock outstanding; its earnings per share will then be $1.60. Assume that the market price of each share of this company is $16.

Company 2 is a larger firm. It has ten shares of stock outstanding, and its earnings per share are $2. Suppose that for one reason or another, company 2's shares have a market price of $40. Thus, company 1 sells at ten times its earnings, while company 2 sells at twenty times its earnings.

The total market value of company 1 is $80 ($16 per share times the five shares of stock outstanding). Since the market price of company 2 is $40 per share, a merger between the two companies could take place if company 2 exchanged two shares of its stock (worth $80 in the market) for the five shares of company 1.

If these are the terms of a merger, and the companies continue to earn as much in the future as they have in the past, the income statement of the newly merged company will be simply a combination of the two earlier statements:

Income Statement of Merged Company When Two Shares of Company 2's Stock Are Exchanged for the Five Shares of Company 1

Earnings before interest and taxes	$67
Less interest ($50 at 8% and $100 at 7%)	11
	$56
Taxes	28
Earnings after taxes	$28

Since there are now twelve shares of stock outstanding (company 2's original ten shares and the two that arose out of the merger), the earnings per share of the merged company will be $2.33. If the newly merged company also commands a market price of twenty times its earnings, the market price of its shares will promptly rise to $46, and the shareholders of both companies will realize substantial capital gains. The former shareholders of company 1 will now own securities that have a market value of $92 (instead of $80), and the old shareholders of company 2 will own securities worth $460 (instead of $400).

A merger on other terms may be still more profitable. Suppose that the shareholders of company 1 want to be paid $100 for their five shares, which is $20 per share, or 25 percent above the current market price of $16. Suppose, further, that they are willing to accept a 7 percent $100-par bond issued by company 2 in exchange for their five shares. The balance sheet and income statement of the merged company will then be:

Balance Sheet

Tangible assets	$400	Liabilities		
		Old debt	$150	
		New debt	100	
Goodwill	50	Total	$250	
Total assets	$450	Equity	200	
		Total liabilities and equity	$450	

Income Statement

Earnings before interest and taxes	$67.00
Interest payments ($50 at 8% and $200 at 7%)	18.00
	$49.00
Taxes	24.50
Earnings after taxes	$24.50

The earnings of the merged company are now $24.50, and since only ten shares of stock are outstanding, its earnings per share will be $2.45. Before the merger, earnings per share were only $2.00. This substantial increase may persuade those investors who look only at changes in reported figures and not at the factors that cause them that a change has occurred in the firm's profit-opportunity schedule. The multiple they apply to the firm's reported earnings may rise from 20 to 25 or 30. Should this happen, the price of the stock may rise to $61.25 or even $73.50. Even if the old multiple of 20 is retained, the price of the company's shares will rise to $49. Since the price per share before the merger was $40, the motive for merging is obvious.

In short, it made no difference, in our example, whether the two companies that merged were in related industries, whether the management skills of the companies complemented one another, or whether any operating benefits would arise from the merger. The major reason the merger was attractive to both companies was that the market valued the earnings of the acquiring company more than it did the earnings of the acquired company and applied a higher multiple to them. By merging, the companies may be able to raise the multiple applied to earnings of the acquired company. Moreover, if earnings per share rise as a result of the merger, and they probably will, the multiple that is applied to the earnings of the acquiring company may also rise. Under these conditions, substantial benefits will accrue to the shareholders of both companies.

Suppose, now, that the price-earnings ratios of the two companies discussed above are reversed; that is, the larger company that is acquiring the smaller one has a lower price-earnings ratio. Under these conditions, it will be more difficult for the two companies to reach an agreement, for if the merger takes place through an exchange of shares, the earnings per share of the surviving company are likely to fall immediately. In time, of course, earnings may rise; but the initial effect of the merger will be to lower reported earnings and possibly the price of the company's stock. Thus, if the two companies decide to join forces, it is more likely that they will do so through an acquisition than through a merger. Moreover, the terms of the acquisition will be either cash or some form of delayed payment.

The terms of exchange in a merger

The examples in the last section raise a number of questions. For example, what determines the price of the merger? What is the minimum price that the seller will accept, and what is the maximum price that the buyer will pay?

Different standards may be used to arrive at the terms for a merger. Several widely used yardsticks are listed below.

(1) THE BOOK VALUE PER SHARE.

In the example cited above, the book value per share of company 1 was $10, and the book value per share of company 2 was $20. Had this standard been used, each share of company 1 would have been exchanged for one-half of a share of company 2.

One difficulty with using this yardstick to determine the exchange ratio is that a company's book value depends on its accounting practices. Thus, if one company has a more rapid depreciation policy than another, their book value will be different even if they own identical assets. A second difficulty with this yardstick is that the recorded value of a firm's assets depends on when they were purchased. If the price of the assets has risen substantially since they were acquired, the market value or replacement value of the firm's physical plant and machinery may be greater than their book value. On the other hand, if new production techniques have been developed since the equipment was purchased, the market value of the assets may be less than their recorded value. Finally, the book value does not necessarily reflect the earning power of either the firm's plant and equipment or the intangible assets it has acquired over the years. A vigorous management team, a brand name, an effective distribution system, for example, are all valuable intangible assets. For all these reasons, book-value figures are seldom given much weight in arriving at the terms of an exchange.

(2) THE EARNINGS PER SHARE.

Company 1 in the example earned $1.60 per share, and Company 2 earned $2 per share. If this yardstick were used to determine the terms of exchange in a merger, each share of company 1's stock would be exchanged for four-fifths of a share of company 2's stock, since the per-share earnings of company 1 ($1.60) are four-fifths of those of company 2 ($2).

Even if both firms use a similar accounting procedure, difficulties can arise in applying this standard. Much legitimate debate may arise over which earnings figure should be used—the current figure, an average of reported earnings over the past few years, or the earnings that are likely to be reported in the future when the new projects that both firms have under development come on stream.

Nevertheless, earnings are given great consideration in setting the terms of exchange. The purchasing company, in particular, will not want its per-share earnings diluted or reduced as a result of the merger.

(3) THE MARKET PRICE PER SHARE.

The market price of a company's shares is an independent and imper-sonal appraisal of the value of the company. In the example cited above, the price of one security was $16, and the price of the other was $40. If an exchange were based on market prices, two-fifths of a share of company 1's stock would be traded for each share of company 2's stock $(\frac{16}{40} = \frac{2}{5})$.

There are, of course, difficulties with this yardstick too. One company's stock may be traded in a relatively thin market, and the purchase or sale of relatively few shares may change the market price dramatically, whereas the shares of another company may be traded in a market that is relatively broad and deep. If the market is thin, the price of the few shares that are traded in any given period may not adequately reflect the value of the company to the prospective buyer. There may also be some question as to which market price should be used—the last price, the high or low price for the year, or the average price for some past period.

Despite the obvious problems involved in using the current price as a standard, it is difficult to argue convincingly that the value of a com-pany's shares is much less than the current market price. As a practical matter, both parties must agree on the terms of a merger before it can be effected. If a shareholder can sell his shares on the open market at $16 a share, how can a potential buyer convince him to accept a lesser amount, such as $10 a share, for his holdings? In most mergers, therefore, the current market price of the company's shares is the minimum price that the shareholders of the selling company will accept. More often than not, selling shareholders will demand a premium of 20 percent or more over the current market price.

(4) THE DIVIDENDS PER SHARE.

No mention was made, in the example, of the dividends that company 1 and company 2 paid their shareholders. However, if the selling company pays a regular dividend, its shareholders may demand an equivalent return from the securities offered by the acquiring company.

Suppose, for example, that company 1 paid $5 of its $8 in earnings to shareholders as dividends and that the acquiring company did not pay any dividends. Under these conditions, the acquiring company may have to offer a package of securities that would give the selling shareholders both the price that they want for their shares and at least the $5 income that they previously enjoyed. Such a package might include some bonds or preferred stock as well as common stock.

In view of these considerations, what is the minimum dollar amount that the selling company in our example will accept, and what is the maximum price that the acquiring company will pay? The minimum price that the selling company will accept is obviously $80, the market value of the company's shares. The maximum price that the acquiring company will pay is more difficult to determine. All that can really be said is that the acquiring company will be reluctant to pay a price which is so high that it may drive the price of its shares down. In practice this means that the purchasing company will not want to pay a price that will lower its per-share earnings.

The acquired company earned $16 in profits before taxes. If the acquiring company pays the selling shareholders with debt yielding an 8 percent return, the maximum face value of the bonds that the acquiring company can issue without lowering its per-share earnings is $200. If the multiple that the market applies to the earnings of the purchasing company falls as a result of the substantial increase in debt, however, the price of the company's stock will also fall. It is up to management to decide whether this will happen. On the basis of the facts presented so far, most managers would probably consider the $200 figure too high.

If shares are used to effect the merger, the purchasing company may arrive at still another market value for the acquired company. The combined company will report $28 in earnings. If earnings per share are not to fall below the current level of $2, no more than fourteen shares can be outstanding. Since the acquiring company now has ten shares outstanding, four shares is the maximum number it will be prepared to issue in exchange for the smaller company's shares. Since each share sells at $40, the maximum price the larger company will pay for the smaller company is $160.

If shares alone are used to effect the merger, the minimum terms that the selling company will accept are two shares of stock; the maximum terms that the acquiring company will offer are four shares of stock. The final terms at which the merger will take place will therefore lie somewhere between these two extremes. If the terms are close to two shares, the buyer will benefit the most; if they are close to four shares, the seller will benefit the most. The number of shares that are issued, rather than the purchase price, is stressed in merger negotiations because of the concern over per-share earnings. For, other things being equal, the more shares that are outstanding, the lower per-share earnings will be.

Alternative financial packages

The fact that the earnings per share after a merger are frequently more important than the actual price paid for the company's assets has given rise to both innovative financial arrangements and creative accounting practices. We shall consider each in turn.

FINANCING A MERGER WITH CONVERTIBLE BONDS

One common way of financing a merger is by issuing convertible bonds. These are bonds which, at a later date, can be converted into a fixed number of shares.

Suppose that the selling company in our example wanted three things:

(1) a price for its assets that is above $80 and as close to $100 as possible,

(2) the ability to participate in any subsequent rise in the value of the acquiring company's equity, and

(3) a minimum cash return of $7 per year.

To complicate the problem further, suppose that the shares of the acquiring firm do not pay any dividends. All three of the selling company's objectives could be met by a $100 bond paying 7 percent interest and convertible into two shares of common stock. The earnings per share of the acquiring company, after the merger, would be $2.45 since it earned $24.50 and only ten shares of stock were outstanding.

As long as the shareholders of the selling company hold the bond, they will receive an annual cash return of $7. If the market continues to value the acquiring company at twenty times its reported earnings, the price of its shares will rise to $49. Thus, if the bond were converted immediately into 2 shares of stock, the bondholders would receive securities with a market value of $98. However, if they do not convert it immediately, and if the price of the security rises above $49 per share, the bond will increase in value, since it can be converted into two shares of stock at any time.

The earnings figure of $2.45 is called the *primary earnings figure.* Companies are also required by the Securities and Exchange Commission to report a second earnings figure, called the *fully diluted earnings.* These are the per-share earnings that would result if all the convertible bonds that are outstanding were converted and an adjustment were made for the interest that the firm would save. In this example, the bond conversion would save $7 in interest, raising the after-tax earnings to $28. Since twelve shares of stock will be outstanding after the conversion (instead of only ten shares), the fully diluted earnings per share that the firm will report will be $2.33.

EARN OUTS

Mergers can be financed in other ways than by issuing convertible bonds. For example, the acquiring firm may divide the total payment it makes to the selling firm into two parts. The first part is a payment for the present assets or present earning power of the selling company; a second sum is paid at a later date when the acquired company reports a rise in earnings. This arrangement is called an *earn out.*

Suppose that the small firm in our example is reluctant to sell at a price of $80, or even $100, because it has under development some products that its management believes will increase its earnings substantially in the future. At a later date, therefore, it will be able to command a market price in excess of $80. The acquiring firm may also believe that this is the case. In fact, the new products that are being developed may have been what brought the smaller company to the attention of the larger company in the first place. However, even though both companies believe that the new products will be successful, the acquiring firm may be reluctant to issue more than two shares of stock for the company at the present time.

Under these conditions, the following two-part arrangement might be made. First, two shares of stock will be issued immediately to the shareholders of the smaller company in exchange for their shares. These two shares are equal to the market value of the smaller company today. Second, over the next five years, as the earnings of the acquired company rise, the acquiring company will issue additional shares to the selling shareholders.

A possible formula for determining how many additional shares to issue in the future would be:

$$\text{New shares issued} = \frac{(\text{increase in annual earnings over base}) \cdot (\text{multiple})}{\text{current market price}}$$

It would work as follows. Suppose that in the first year after the merger, the acquired company, now an autonomous division of the conglomerate, earns $11, an increase of $3 over the base-period figure of $8. If the multiple agreed on were 15, the acquiring company would issue that number of shares which would enable the selling shareholders to realize $45 in the current securities market. Thus, if at the end of the year the market price of the acquiring company's stock was $45, it would issue one new share to the sellers; if the market price of its stock was $22.50, it would issue two new shares.

Numerous variations of this formula are possible: A price other than the current market price can be used as the denominator, a sliding scale can be used instead of a constant multiple in the numerator, and an average of the earnings in two or more years can be used instead of the annual earnings. The duration of the earn-out period can vary, and an upper limit can be set on the number of shares to be issued. No set rules exist in this area; rather, the terms of a merger depend only on the interests of the parties involved and the imagination of the financial negotiators.

An earn out, then, enables the shareholders of the selling company to participate in their company's future growth. It permits the acquiring company to buy a company that may have high earnings in the future without paying so high a price for it immediately that its own earnings per share are diluted. Moreover, it is a low-risk way for a large company to merge, since if the acquired company does not do as well as expected, no additional shares need be issued. If the selling company's earnings do rise, the shareholders of both the selling and the buying company will benefit.

Under an earn-out arrangement, the rise in total earnings offsets the dilution in per-share earnings as new shares are issued. If an earn out had been used in our example, and two shares of company 1's stock were exchanged for the five shares of company 2, total corporate earnings would have been $28 when the merger took place, and 12 shares of stock would have been outstanding. Earnings per share would have been $2.33. If the acquired company's earnings then rose to $11, and no other changes took place, the earnings of the entire company would rise to $31. If a multiple of 15 were assigned to the increase in earnings and if the market price of the acquiring company's stock rose to $45, one new share of stock would then be issued to the shareholders of the selling company. The number of shares outstanding would increase to 13. The reported earnings per share, however, would rise to $2.38 ($31/13 = $2.38). Thus, earnings per share would rise under the earn-out arrangement even though the number of shares outstanding increased.

The multiple that will be applied to the increase in the acquired firm's earnings over the base is a negotiated figure. If it is below the market multiple of the acquiring company, as in the example above, earnings per share for the entire company will rise as the acquired company raises its earnings above the base figure. However, if the multiple is above the current multiple of the acquiring company, the merged company's per-share earnings will be diluted.

For an earn out to be successful, the acquired company must be operated as a wholly independent division. The acquiring company should not interfere with the business judgments of the divisional management, for the latter has a continuing interest in the profits of the division. On the other hand, the agreement should spell out carefully the methods by which the earning power of the assets of the division is to be maintained; the level of advertising outlays, the accounting practices to be followed, and so forth. This will ensure that the acquiring company does not inherit a division that is depleted of all its tangible and intangible assets at the end of the earn-out period.

Accounting practices

The firm's accountants can handle a merger in two ways: as a pooling of interests or as a purchase. The important difference, from the financial analyst's point of view, is that when the merger is treated as a purchase, the premium which the acquiring firm pays over the tangible book value of the acquired firm is considered a payment for the "goodwill" acquired whereas if a pooling of interests occurs no goodwill is officially recognized.

Consider, once again, the example that we have been working with. If company 2 issues two shares of stock worth $80 for the shares of company 1, and the merger is treated as a pooling of interests, the balance sheets of the two companies are simply added together. Thus:

Balance Sheet of Company 1		Balance Sheet of Company 2		Balance Sheet of Merged Company (pooling of interest)	
Assets	$100	Assets	$300	Assets	$400
Debt	$ 50	Debt	$100	Debt	$150
Equity	50	Equity	200	Equity	250
Total	$100	Total	$300	Total	$400

If the merger is treated as a purchase, however, the fact that securities worth $80 in the market were paid for the $50 book value of company

1's equity is explained by treating the $30 excess as a payment for goodwill. Thus, under a purchase arrangement, the balance sheet of the merged company will be:

Balance Sheet of
Merged Company
(Purchase)

Assets	
Tangible	$400
Goodwill	30
Total	$430
Debt	$150
Equity	280
Total	$430

How the merger is treated on the balance sheet can be important to the firm. If the $30 in additional assets acquired under the purchase arrangement (the goodwill) is written off against the future earnings of the company, earnings per share in future years will be penalized. Under a pooling arrangement there is no goodwill to write off, and the entire issue is bypassed.

If the merger were treated as a purchase and if the goodwill were written off over ten years, the earnings of the combined company in our example would be $25 per year instead of $28. Since there are twelve shares of stock outstanding, earnings per share would be $2.08. If the merger were treated as a pooling of interests, the reported earnings per share would be $2.45. This difference in reported earnings ($2.45 as opposed to $2.08) could have a substantial effect on the price of the company's shares. If the firm reports $2.45 in earnings, investors may believe that its profit-opportunity schedule has shifted, whereas if it reports only $2.08 in earnings, they may assume that only normal growth has occurred.

It is difficult to overstate the effect that pooling has on reported earnings. A study of companies listed on the New York Stock Exchange in the year 1967 indicates that for six companies the effect of pooling was to "overstate" earnings by 50 percent or more. This conclusion is based on what the companies would have reported had they been required to write off the difference between the book value and the purchase price over five years. The six companies were Continental Telephone Corp., International Telephone and Telegraph, United Utilities Inc., Ashland Oil and Refining Co., Occidental Petroleum Co., and Walter Kidde and

Co.[1] Of course, many of these firms would claim, in any event, that goodwill is an intangible asset of indefinite life and, as such, should never be written off. When the goodwill that arises in a purchase should be written off and whether it should be written off at all is a question intensely debated by accountants and financial analysts.

Some managerial considerations

The entire treatment of mergers up to this point has been couched in terms of their financial rationale and the accounting practices that support their development. However, our analysis would be incomplete if it did not touch on the managerial problems that arise once a merger is consummated. Once a merger is completed, the acquiring company can no longer think of the merged company as an investment, i.e., as an asset that can be disposed of if it does not come up to expectations. If the merged company is not doing well, the management of the parent company must take corrective action.[2]

A firm that expands through mergers may find itself faced with problems that a company which expands from within is unlikely to encounter. When growth occurs through a merger, the firm acquires new product lines and new plants, often in different parts of the nation, virtually overnight. The organization immediately becomes both more complex and more dispersed. Expansion from within is likely to be gradual and to involve either products that are already being produced in the old plants or related products.

As a firm increases in complexity and dispersion, both the absolute and the relative costs of administration increase. Several factors account for this increase:

(1) THE EFFICIENCY OF THE INTERNAL COMMUNICATION SYSTEM DETERIORATES.

Not only does the number of possible channels of communication increase dramatically as organizations become more complex, but members of the organization simply "tune out" much of what is going on about them in order to perform their own perceived tasks more effectively. Thus the costs of effective communication rise sharply as the organization grows.

---

[1] *Wall Street Journal* (February 27, 1970), p. 16.
[2] Much of the analysis that follows draws heavily on Thomas Whisler's "Organization Aspects of Corporate Mergers," in Alberts and Segall, eds, *The Corporate Merger* (Chicago: Univ. of Chicago Press, 1966).

(2) THE NUMBER OF ORGANIZATIONAL LEVELS INCREASES.

As an organization becomes more complex and dispersed the number of levels of hierarchy needed to coordinate its activities increases. Thus the costs of coordination also mount.

(3) THE DEGREE OF DECENTRALIZATION RISES.

The control of complex and dispersed activities tends to be decentralized. It is somewhat paradoxical that as the levels of hierarchy increase, the degree of decentralization increases. Control in a large organization is generally shared by a large number of people, not concentrated in a single person or a single group. As decentralization increases, the costs of coordination again increase.

Although expanding through mergers can be expensive, in this sense, careful planning by management can minimize the problems involved. Many conglomerates also stress the importance of merging with companies that already have "good" managements. The implication is that the management of the conglomerate will permit the merged company to continue to operate as an autonomous division and that there will be a minimum of control exercised over its activities. In practice, of course, no division can operate independently for long. Since it must compete for funds with other divisions, many parts of the organization will come to know something of its activities. The task of the conglomerate's management is to reduce the degree of divisional autonomy when this is economically necessary, to develop new communication patterns among the various divisions and between the divisions and headquarters, and to eliminate duplicate functions wherever possible.

The increased use of debt

We have seen that the benefits of a conglomerate merger are more financial than structural. The acquiring company usually has a higher price-earnings ratio than the acquired company and is capable of transferring its market multiple to the earnings of the acquired company, especially if its reported earnings per share rise as a result of the merger.

In periods of prosperity, earnings per share will rise more rapidly if debt instruments rather than new shares are issued in exchange for the assets of the acquired company. The use of debt, however, produces problems of its own that not all financial managers fully appreciated in the mid-1960's. High interest payments and amortization charges can cause severe cash problems for the firm during a period of recession.

During the last half of 1969 and the first half of 1970, many investors became convinced that the American economy had passed a peak and was entering a recession. It became increasingly apparent that certain conglomerates were going to have trouble not only in maintaining their previous growth in earnings but in meeting their interest and amortization payments. As a result, the prices of both the bonds and stocks of conglomerates declined dramatically. For example, a bond series sold by Ling-Temco-Vought that had a face value of $1,000 fell to $260 in 1970. The price of the stock of Litton Industries fell from a high of $74 in 1969 to a low of $16 in the first half of 1970; in the same period Bangor Punta fell from $50 to $8 and Victor Comptometer fell from $63 to $12.

Of course, many factors other than the increase in the value of the outstanding debt contributed to the sharp fall in the price of many of the conglomerates' stocks. Government regulations requiring more detailed financial reports to shareholders and threatened Justice Department antitrust suits no doubt contributed to their fall from favor. Moreover, the decline in conglomerate stock prices was undoubtedly excessive, just as was the prior increase in the price of the shares of conglomerates. Even so, the financial experience of the conglomerates remains a story that will be told and retold in financial circles for many years to come.

Summary

If the earnings of two companies are valued differently by the market, i.e., if they have different price-earnings ratios, a merger may increase the market value of both firms. This result can be achieved if the acquiring company, through the merger, is able to report an increase in its earnings per share and if the multiple that is applied to its earnings rises.

Different bases can be used to set the terms of a merger. For example, the book value of the company, its earnings, the market price of its shares, and the level of dividends it pays can all enter into the final determination of the merger price. The limits within which the terms will be set, however, can be readily specified. The seller will not accept less than the current market value of its shares, and the buyer will not pay a price so high that it will force the market value of its shares down. Many companies prefer to issue convertible bonds rather than shares to effect a merger and to work out an earn-out arrangement of some kind.

A prime concern of both parties in a merger is to ensure a continued rising trend in the earnings of the acquiring company. To avoid penalizing future earnings, a merger is frequently treated by the firm's accounting department as a pooling of interests rather than as a purchase.

While there are usually definite financial benefits from a merger, the control and coordination problems that arise once a merger is consummated can be both complicated and costly to solve. Moreover, many mergers involve the use of debt instruments. A large amount of outstanding debt can cause such severe cash problems during a recession that the price of the company's shares declines dramatically.

Questions for discussion and problems

1. What is the difference between vertical, horizontal, and conglomerate mergers? What are some of the social advantages and disadvantages of each?

2. Why may earnings per share rise when a conglomerate merger occurs? Is this rise in earnings the result of a shift in the profit-opportunity schedule?

3. What difficulties can be anticipated when a large company with a low price-earnings ratio seeks to merge with a small company with a high price-earnings ratio?

4. Why may there be some difficulty in arriving at the terms of a merger? What standards can be used to determine the "price"?

5. Why are convertible bonds frequently used to effect a merger?

6. If a merger involves an earn-out arrangement, who benefits from this—the buyer or the seller? Is there any risk to the buyer under an earn-out arrangement? to the seller?

7. Why does the use of debt instruments add to the risks a conglomerate faces during a period of economic decline?

8. What are some special management problems of conglomerates?

   [*Answers to problems 9–12 follow references and suggested readings.*]

9. The following are income statements of two firms:

	A	B
Earnings before interest and taxes	$20	$40
Interest	4	8
	$16	$32
Taxes	8	16
Earnings after taxes	$ 8	$16

Company A has 4 shares of stock outstanding and company B 8 shares. The market price of A is $20 per share, and the market price of B is $40 per share.

(a) What are the earnings per share of each company?

(b) What is the price-earnings ratio for each company?

(c) If a merger occurs and two shares of A are issued in exchange for each share of B, how many shares will company B now have outstanding?

(d) If no other changes take place, what will the earnings per share of company B now be?

(e) If company B continues to have a price-earnings ratio of 20, what will be the price of its shares?

10. Suppose that the stockholders of company A in problem 1 wanted $30 in cash for each of their shares and that company B could borrow the money at 7 percent interest. Assume that company B is in a 50-percent tax bracket.

(a) What will happen to earnings per share?

(b) Is the purchase of A still attractive to B?

11. Consider the following data about two companies:

	A	B
Book value	$10	$20
Earnings per share	3	4
Dividends	1	2
Market price per share	48	48

(a) What difficulties will arise if B tries to acquire A?

(b) What would the exchange rate be if a merger took place on the basis of (1) book value, (2) earnings, (3) dividends, and (4) market price?

12. Two companies decide to merge on the following terms.

1. Company A is to buy company B for an immediate payment of $1,000,000. The form of payment is to be shares of company A's securities, which have a market price of $50.

2. Company B is also to receive a deferred payment based on its earnings for the next three years. At present, company B earns $100,000 a year. When earnings rise above this figure, company A is to pay 8 times the amount of the increment. This payment also will be in the form of shares of company A's stock, valued at their market price.

Assume that company B reports earnings of $110,000, $145,000, and $126,000 over the next three years and that the market price of A's shares rises to $60 in the first year, rises to $80 in the second year, and falls to $65 in the third year. How many shares of company A's stock does B receive, and what is the total value of the transaction in terms of the market price of the shares in the third year?

REFERENCES AND SUGGESTED READINGS

Articles

Adelman, Morris A., "The Antimerger Act, 1950–1960," *American Economic Review,* vol. LI, no. 2 (May 1961), pp. 236–44.

Ansoff, H. Igor, and Weston, J. Fred, "Merger Objectives and Organizational

Structure," *Quarterly Review of Economics and Business,* vol. II (August 1968), pp. 49–58.

Barr, Andrew, "Accounting Aspects of Business Combinations," *Accounting Review,* vol. XXXIV (April 1959), pp. 175–81.

Carroll, Daniel T., "What Future for the Conglomerate?" *Harvard Business Review* (May–June 1969), pp. 4–12, 167–68.

Dewing, Arthur S., "A Statistical Test of the Success of Consolidations," *Quarterly Journal of Economics,* vol. XXXVI (November 1921), pp. 231–58.

Gort, Michael, "An Economic Disturbance Theory of Mergers," *Quarterly Journal of Economics,* vol. LXXXIII (November 1969), pp. 624–42.

Hayes, Samuel L., III, and Taussig, Russell A., "Tactics of Cash Takeover Bids," *Harvard Business Review* (March–April 1967), pp. 135–48.

Hogarty, Thomas F., "The Profitability of Corporate Mergers," *Journal of Business,* vol. XLIII (July 1970), pp. 317–27.

Jacoby, Neil H., "The Conglomerate Corporation," *Financial Analysts Journal,* vol. XXVI (May–June 1970), pp. 35–50.

Jaedicke, H. R., "Management's Choice to Purchase or Pool," *Accounting Review,* vol. XXXVII (October 1962), pp. 758–65.

Leighton, Charles M., and Todd, G. Robert, "After the Acquisition: Continuing Challenge," *Harvard Business Review* (March–April 1969), pp. 90–99.

Levinson, Harry, "A Psychologist Diagnoses Merger Failures," *Harvard Business Review* (March–April 1970), pp. 139–47.

MacDougal, Gary E., and Malek, Fred V., "Master Plans for Merger Negotiations," *Harvard Business Review* (January–February 1970), pp. 71–82.

Markham, Jesse W., "Survey of the Evidence and Findings on Mergers," in *Business Concentration and Price Policy* (Princeton: National Bureau of Economic Research, 1955), pp. 141–212.

Mossin, Jan, "Merger Agreements: Some Game Theoretic Considerations," *Journal of Business,* vol. XLI (October 1968), pp. 460–72.

Mueller, Dennis C., "A Theory of Conglomerate Mergers," *Quarterly Journal of Economics,* vol. LXXXIII (November 1969), pp. 643–59.

Reilly, Frank K., "What Determines the Ratio of Exchange in Corporate Mergers?" *Financial Analysts Journal,* vol. XVIII (November–December 1962), pp. 47–50.

Reum, W. Robert, and Steele, Thomas A., III, "Contingent Payouts Cut Acquisition Risks," *Harvard Business Review* (March–April 1970), pp. 83–91.

Silberman, Irwin H., "A Note on Merger Valuation," *Journal of Finance,* vol. XXII (June 1968) pp. 528–34.

Vance, Jack O., "Is Your Company a Takeover Target?" *Harvard Business Review* (May–June 1969), pp. 4–12. 167–68.

Books

Alberts, William W., and Segall, Joel E., eds., *The Corporate Merger* (Chicago: Univ. of Chicago Press, 1966).

Boch, Betty, *Mergers and Markets: 7* (New York: National Industrial Conference Board Studies in Business Economics, no. 105, 1969).

Butters, J. Keith, Lintner, John. and Cary, William S. *Effects of Taxation: Corporate Mergers* (Boston: Harvard University Graduate School of Business Administration Division of Research, 1951).

Gort, Michael, *Diversification and Integration in American Industry* (Princeton, N. J.: Princeton Univ. Press, 1962).

Questions for discussion and problems

Kelly, Eamon M., *The Profitability of Growth Through Mergers* (University Park, Pa.: Pennsylvania State Univ. Press, 1967).

McCarthy, George D., *Acquisitions and Mergers* (New York: Ronald Press, 1963).

Nelson, Ralph, *Merger Movement in American Industry* (Princeton, N. J.: Princeton Univ. Press, 1959).

Rappaport, Alfred, Firmin, Peter A., and Zeff, Stephen A., eds., *Public Reporting by Conglomerates* (Englewood Cliffs, N. J.: Prentice-Hall, 1968).

Reid, Samuel R., *Mergers, Managers and the Economy* (New York: McGraw-Hill, 1968).

Scharb, C. A., *Techniques for Buying, Selling and Merging Business* (Englewood Cliffs, N. J.: Prentice-Hall, 1964).

U. S. Bureau of the Census, *Acquisitions and Disposals of Manufacturing Facilities, 1959 and 1960,* based on 1959 and 1960 *Annual Survey of Manufacturers* (Washington, D. C.: Government Printing Office, June 1963).

Weston, J. Fred, *The Role of Mergers in the Growth of Large Firms* (Berkeley, Calif.: Univ. of California Press, 1953).

ANSWERS TO PROBLEMS 9–12

9. (a) Both companies earn $2 per share.
   (b) The price-earnings ratio for A is 10 and for B, 20.
   (c) 10 shares.
   (d) $2.40.
   (e) $48.

10. (a)

Earnings before interest and taxes	$60.00
Less interest payments	20.40
Profits before taxes	$39.60
Taxes	19.80
Profits after taxes	$19.80

   Since 8 shares of stock are outstanding, earnings per share will be $2.47.
   (b) Yes.

11. (a) Since the price-earnings ratio of A is higher than that of B, a dilution of earnings will take place if a merger takes place at market value.
    (b) (1) 2 shares of A for 1 share of B.
        (2) $1\frac{1}{3}$ shares of A for 1 share of B.
        (3) 2 shares of A for 1 share of B.
        (4) 1 share of A for 1 share of B.

12. B will receive 20,000 shares immediately, 1,333 in year 1, 4,500 in year 2 and 3,200 in year 3, for a total of 29,033 shares. At $65 per share, the value of the transaction is $1,887,145.

Portfolio analysis

20

A shift in the rate of growth of national income affects the profit opportunities of firms in many different industries, and a change in the level of interest rates affects the rate that investors use to discount a company's future earnings. When macroeconomic variables such as these fluctuate, the prices of a large number of securities rise and fall together.

Not all securities, however, will rise or fall by the same amount. A merger, the development of a new product, the installation of an effective cost-control program, or a change in the firm's marketing apparatus—all these are factors under the control of management. When firms initiate programs of this kind, their earnings may rise, and as a result, the price of their stock may increase more rapidly than the price of other securities. These diverse movements in the behavior of stock prices create problems for investors trying to develop a security portfolio that meets their needs. We shall explore several aspects of the portfolio problem in this chapter. We shall see, first, how some financial theorists approach the problem of building a portfolio and then go on to review some empirical studies of portfolio performance.

Return and variability

It is obvious, other things being equal, that investors will always prefer a high return to a low one and that most investors probably prefer to have less variability in their expected returns rather than more. The relevant operating problem is, How, for a given level of variability, can the expected return of the portfolio be maximized? Or how, for a given expected return, can the variability be minimized? Some of the issues surrounding this question were briefly discussed in Chapter 15, and it may be helpful to restate the high points of that analysis before extending it here.

One way to explore the problem of risk and return, the basic problem in portfolio analysis, is to ask: Why do investors generally hold a portfolio of securities instead of concentrating their holdings in a single issue, the one that is expected to increase in value the most? Suppose that the price of one security, A, is guaranteed to increase exactly 20 percent in a year and that the price of another security, B, is guaranteed to increase by exactly 12 percent. If their current market value was the same, every rational investor would purchase as many shares as possible of the 20-percent security and none at all of the other security.

Now, suppose that the return on both securities is uncertain. There is some chance that the prices of these securities will rise more than the amount predicted and some chance that they will rise less. Suppose that the expected returns for security A are normally distributed and the predicted standard deviation of the return is 10 percent. There is then a 2.3 percent chance that the security will have a negative return (or, lie more than two standard deviations from the mean). Conversely, there is a 16 percent chance that the return will be greater than 30 percent and a 2.3 percent chance that it will be above 40 percent. Suppose, further, that the expected return of security B is 12 percent and that its predicted standard deviation is 2 percent.

The decision facing the investor is now considerably more complex. He can purchase a security that has a high but greatly variable expected return, or he can purchase one that offers a lower but more stable return. Furthermore, he may be better off if he divides his funds between the two securities rather than investing all of them in either one. If the two securities have a negative covariance, the return on one can be expected to rise when the return of the other falls, and vice versa. The variance of a portfolio may therefore be less than the variance of the securities in it. In Chapter 15, the variance of the sum of two random variables was given by the expression:

$$\text{Var}(w_1A + w_2B) = w_1{}^2\text{Var}(A) + w_2{}^2\text{Var}(B) + 2w_1w_2\text{Cov}(AB)$$

where w_1 and w_2 are the weights assigned to securities A and B (or the proportion of the portfolio comprising A and B).

The variance, or the square of the standard deviation, of security A is $(.1)^2$, or .01; the variance of security B is $(.02)^2$, or .0004. Let the covariance between the two securities be $-.002$. Then, if half the investor's funds are invested in A and half in B ($w_1 = w_2 = \frac{1}{2}$), the variance of the portfolio is:

$$
\begin{aligned}
\text{Var}(w_1A + w_2B) &= (\tfrac{1}{2})^2(.01) + (\tfrac{1}{2})^2(.0004) + 2(\tfrac{1}{2})(\tfrac{1}{2})(-.002) \\
&= \frac{.01 + .0004 - .004}{4} \\
&= .0016
\end{aligned}
$$

The standard deviation of the portfolio if half the funds are invested in security A and half in security B will therefore be .04. The expected return of the portfolio if half of the funds are invested in a security that is expected to earn 20 percent and half are invested in one that is expected to yield 12 percent is:

$$\text{Expected return} = \tfrac{1}{2}(.20) + \tfrac{1}{2}(.12)$$
$$= .10 + .06$$
$$= .16$$

Different proportions of securities A and B in a portfolio will produce other expected returns and standard deviations. A comparison of the returns and standard deviations of three possible portfolios made up of securities A and B is presented in Table 20.1. Which of the three will the investor choose?

TABLE 20.1
The Expected Mean and Standard
Deviation of Three Portfolios

Contents of Portfolio	Expected Return (%)	Standard Deviation (%)
Security A alone	20	10
Security B alone	12	2
Half A and half B	16	4

If an investor is interested only in obtaining the greatest expected return, he will ignore the variability indicated by the standard deviation and purchase security A alone. It is unlikely, however, that many investors would act this way. Carried to its logical extreme, such conduct would imply that a person would be willing to wager all his capital in a venture even if there was only a small probability of gaining an enormous sum and a high probability of losing all, as long as the expected return of the investment was greater than that of any alternative.

If an investor were interested only in minimizing the fluctuations in his return, he would purchase security B alone. Though many investors are in a position where they cannot afford fluctuations in the expected return of their investments, it is difficult to imagine that this is an appropriate description of most of the individuals who commit a large percentage of their resources to securities that are traded on exchanges.

If an investor is interested in both the return on an investment and the variability of this return, he will invest some of his funds in A and some of his funds in B.

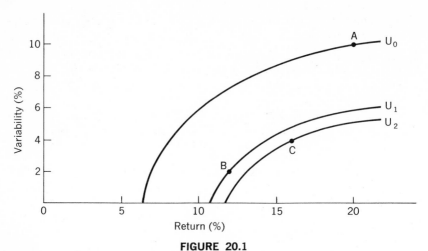

FIGURE 20.1

Utility Curves That Make Portfolio C the Most Attractive.

Which of the three portfolios described in Table 20.1 is preferable will depend on the shape of the investor's utility curves. Suppose we call the portfolios A, B, and C. Three utility functions that make portfolio C the most attractive are shown in Figure 20.1.

If the investor's utility curves resemble those in Figure 20.2, portfolio B will be the most attractive; and if they resemble those in Figure 20.3, portfolio A will be chosen. A person whose utility curves resemble those in Figure 20.2 requires a substantial increase in returns before he will expose himself to more variability in return. Conversely, a person whose

FIGURE 20.2

Utility Curves That Make Portfolio B the Most Attractive.

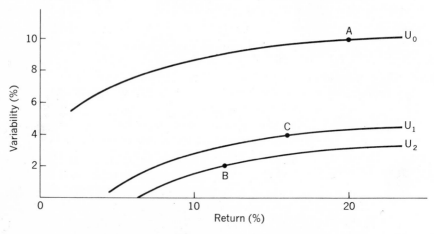

Portfolio analysis

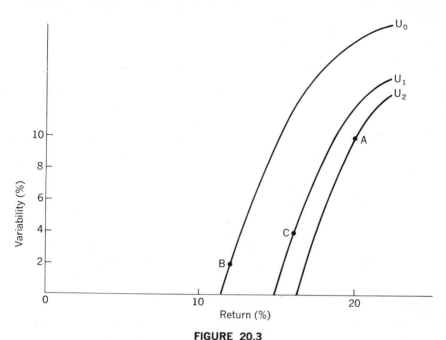

FIGURE 20.3
Utility Curves That Make Portfolio A the Most Attractive.

utility curves resemble those in Figure 20.3 will expose himself to substantially more variability for a modest increment in return.

To summarize, if the expected returns of different securities fluctuate at different times, i.e., if some returns rise while others fall, a portfolio constructed of a combination of these securities will have a more stable return through time than the securities themselves. The stability of the portfolio and the return it provides will depend on how the securities are combined. The trade-off that an investor is willing to make between the expected return and the variability of the return must therefore be known before a choice among different portfolios can be made.

Constructing a portfolio when risk is measured by variance

When two securities are combined to form a portfolio, the variance of the distribution of returns that the investor will receive may be reduced because the adverse fluctuations in the return of one security may be offset by favorable fluctuations in the other. Portfolio managers have always been aware of this fact, and, consequently, have always held that diversification is the first principle of good management. Although many rely primarily on intuition in assembling a good, diversified portfolio,

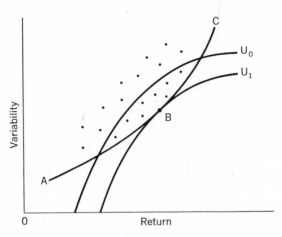

FIGURE 20.4

The Set of Feasible Points of a Portfolio and a Set of Investor's Utility Curves.

a more formal approach to this problem has been developed in recent years.

Suppose, for example, that each point in the scatter in Figure 20.4 represents a security. Obviously, the "best" portfolio made up of these securities will lie somewhere along the frontier of the set of feasible points. Portfolios lying along the frontier *ABC* are called *efficient*.

In Figure 20.4, the single best portfolio is represented by point B. If an investor had a different set of utility curves, another combination of securities would, of course, be more appropriate.

Some portfolio theorists have approached the problem of combining securities as follows: Consider the function $Z = E(R) - V(R)$ where $E(R)$ is the expected return of the portfolio and $V(R)$ is the variance of the portfolio. Then, by maximizing Z subject to the constraint that at least one point on the line Z can in fact be achieved, this solution point will be an efficient portfolio (i.e., it will lie along the boundary ABC in Figure 20.4).

The function $Z = E(R) - V(R)$ implies that a unit of variance lowers the objective function by the same amount that a unit of return raises it. Suppose, however, that an investor wants to penalize the variations in the return of his portfolio more heavily. Then, he may choose to maximize a function such as $Z = 2E(R) - V(R)$, in which a unit of variance is equivalent to two units of return (a unit of variance changes the objective function by as much as two units of earnings). Similarly, if the investor is willing to bear more fluctuation, he may maximize the function $Z = \tfrac{1}{2}E(R) - V(R)$. These three Z functions are graphed in Figure 20.5. In general, the function $Z = \lambda E(R) - V(R)$ where λ ranges from 0 to ∞ will trace out the entire set of efficient portfolios.

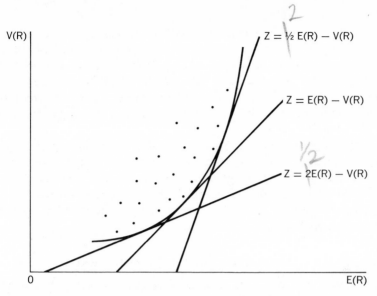

V(R)

$Z = \frac{1}{2} E(R) - V(R)$

$Z = E(R) - V(R)$

$Z = 2E(R) - V(R)$

0

E(R)

Three Maximum Z Functions.

The problem of combining securities to achieve an optimum portfolio can now be set up as follows:

$$\text{Maximize } Z = \lambda E(R) - V(R)$$

$$\text{Subject to } \sum_{i=1}^{n} x_i = 1$$

$$x_i \geqslant 0$$

where

$x_i =$ the proportion of each security held in the portfolio;

$$E(R) = \sum_{i=1}^{n} x_i r_i,$$

$r_i =$ the return of the ith security,

$$V(R) = \sum_{i=1}^{n} x_i^2 v_i + \sum_{i=1}^{n} x_i x_j c_{ij}, \text{ where } i \neq j,$$

$v_i =$ the variance of the ith security, and

$c_{ij} =$ the covariance of the ith and jth securities.

The investor specifies the value of λ that he wants to achieve, and once the variance and covariance terms are known, an optimum portfolio can be calculated.[1]

[1] This framework of analysis was pioneered by Harry Markowitz in *Portfolio Selection: Efficient Diversification of Investments* (New York: Wiley, 1959).

The solution to this programming problem, however, is quite difficult. First, because the objective function is nonlinear, highly sophisticated quadratic programming techniques must be used. Second, it is virtually impossible to know the covariance between every security that could enter the portfolio. A portfolio manager trying to build a portfolio from 100 securities would have to estimate 100 variances, 100 expected returns, and 4,950 covariance terms.

To simplify the calculation, Sharpe proposed the following strategem. Instead of calculating all the covariance terms, an analyst could relate the return of each security to a general market index such as the Dow Jones average.[2] Once he found the relationship between the return that a security offered and changes in the index, he could relate the returns of each security to one another.[3]

---

[2] William A. Sharpe, "A Simplified Model for Portfolio Selection," *Management Science* (January 1963), pp. 277–93.

[3] Let $r_i = A_i + b_iI + e_i$, where I is the market index, b_i is the coefficient indicating the change in r_i that will result if the market index changes by a unit, A_i is the return that the security will earn if the market does not change at all, and e_i is a random term with an expected value of zero and a variance of Q_i. The variance of any security will now depend on two variables, the variance in the market index, Q_{n+1}, and the variance of the security itself, Q_i. Thus:

$$v_i = E[A_i + b_iI + e_i - (A_i + b_i\bar{I} + 0)]^2$$
$$= [b_i(I - \bar{I}) + e_i]^2$$
$$= b_i^2 Q_{n+1} + Q_i$$

The variance of a security due to fluctuations in the market index, $b_i^2 Q_{n+1}$, cannot be eliminated or reduced as long as stocks are the only securities held in the portfolio. Thus this component of variance is called *nondiversifiable risk;* the variance due to movements in the price of the security itself, which can be reduced through diversification, is called *diversifiable risk.*

The covariance between securities is simply:

$$C_{ij} = b_ib_jQ_{n+1}$$

Now, if

$$x_{n+1} = \sum_{i=1}^{n} x_ib_i$$

and

$$A_{n+1} = I$$

the expected value of a portfolio becomes:

$$E(R) = \sum_{i=1}^{n} x_ir_i = E\left[\sum_{i=1}^{n} (x_iA_i + x_ib_iI) \right]$$
$$= \sum_{i=1}^{n} x_iA_i + x_{n+1}I$$
$$= \sum_{i=1}^{n+1} x_iA_i$$

Similarly, by substitution, the variance of the portfolio can be shown to become:

Although fewer calculations are needed to find an optimum portfolio, using this formulation, the computations that remain, such as those needed to forecast the precise mean and variance of the market index, are still very difficult.

Introducing riskless assets

The formal work on portfolio theory within this mean-variance tradition has been extended in still another direction in an effort to incorporate another security, such as a deposit in a savings and loan association or a savings account in a commercial bank, into the analysis. The reason this extension is so important is that these securities yield a return and involve no risk of price fluctuation. An investor can withdraw the principal he invested at any time.

Let point A in Figure 20.6 represent the return and variance associated with a risk-free asset, and let Point B represent the return and variance associated with the market average of all securities other than the risk-free one. By dividing his funds between the risk-free asset and a portfolio of the other securities, an investor can operate anywhere along the line AB.

$$V(R) = \sum_{i=1}^{n+1} x_i^2 Q_i$$

The portfolio programming problem now becomes:

Maximize:
$$Z = \lambda \sum_{i=1}^{n+1} x_i A_i - \sum_{i=1}^{n+1} x_i^2 Q_i$$

Subject to:
$$x_{n+1} = \sum_{i=1}^{n} x_i b_i$$

$$\sum_{i=1}^{n} x_i = 1$$
$$x_i \geq 0$$

Thus the portfolio manager need calculate only the values of A_i, b_i, and Q_i for each security and the values of A and Q for the index itself, not the covariance between securities. It is not an easy task, however, to estimate even these values, for there is no assurance that the parameters A_i, b_i, and Q_i remain stable through time. Moreover, the value of A and Q, the market average and its variance, are extremely difficult to forecast with any degree of precision.

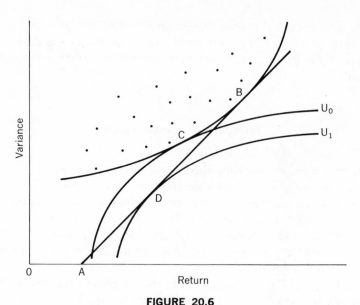

FIGURE 20.6
Maximization of an Investor's Utility Given a Risk-Free Asset.

Suppose an investor ignores the opportunity to invest in the risk-free asset. The best portfolio he can select, then, is C, for this will place him on utility curve U_0. However, by investing in both the risk-free asset and the other securities, he can reach a higher level of utility, U_1. Note that any portfolio lying above the line AB, such as C, is clearly inferior to a portfolio, such as D, that lies along the line itself. We shall return to these observations after we have considered the methods that have been proposed for measuring portfolio performance.

To summarize, suppose that return on an investment is positively valued and that variability in the return is negatively valued. Then, if variability is measured by the variance of the portfolio's return, an entire frontier of efficient portfolios can be constructed using the objective function $Z = \lambda E(R) - V(R)$ and selecting values for λ.

This framework of analysis is quite difficult to use effectively because the investor must know the covariance of all the securities under consideration. Hence a modification of this approach has been developed which eliminates the need to determine the covariances of returns by relating the returns of any one security to the market average of all securities.

The analytical work in portfolio analysis has also been extended to include risk-free securities. It can be shown that by dividing his funds between a risk-free asset, such as a deposit in a savings and loan association, and a portfolio of stocks, an investor can reach a higher utility curve than by investing only in variable securities.

An evaluation of the portfolio framework

The outlined framework for analyzing portfolios can be criticized on several grounds. It does not adequately capture the basic characteristics of the investment problem faced by a portfolio manager because it considers only the total rate of return on a security. The dividends and capital gains are added together and treated as equivalent; whereas, in practice, a distinction is often made between these two components of a stock's total return.

For example, a will may specify that the income earned by the securities in an estate be paid to the widow, while the securities themselves are given to the children. Upon the widow's death her income passes to the children, who also benefit from any capital gains that have occurred. If the portfolio manager of the estate purchases securities that pay no dividends but enjoy substantial capital gains, the children are favored at the expense of the mother. On the other hand, if the portfolio manager purchases only securities that pay high dividends, but enjoy no appreciation, the mother is favored and the children will receive a smaller terminal estate than they might have.

The distribution of each of the two components of a security's total return, the dividends and the capital gain, is also likely to be different. The capital-gains portion of a security's total cash return is likely to have both a higher expected value and a higher standard deviation than the dividend portion. By suppressing this fact and considering only a single rate of return in the equation, valuable information about the performance of the portfolio may be lost.

A second situation in which a distinction must be drawn between current income and capital gains occurs in the case of hospitals and universities which have restrictions placed on their endowment. Frequently the income from the endowment is to be used to help finance the current operations of the institution but the endowment funds themselves cannot be invaded, or used to support current activities. The problem institutions face is how to allocate their endowment between "growth" and "income" securities so as to maximize the funds that can be applied to current operations over the life of the institution.

Suppose that a university has a $1-million endowment and it can purchase bonds that yield 5 percent or stocks that pay no current dividends but are expected to appreciate at a rate of 10 percent per annum. If all the funds are invested in growth stocks, the university will forgo $50,000 in current income, but its endowment will rise to $1,100,000 by the end of the year. In year 2, it can then switch its portfolio and buy the bonds. If it does this, its current income in year 2 and in all succeeding years will rise to $55,000. If it forgoes current income for 10 years, its endowment will grow to $2,593,740 and, starting in year 11, its current income will be $129,687.

A hospital or a university, then, is not so much concerned with maximizing the return for a given level of risk at a moment of time as with choosing between using their resources to support operations now and using them to increase the resources that will be available in a later period.

These criticisms arise because in real situations most portfolio problems are multiperiod problems, not single period ones.

Risk as the probability of loss

Another criticism that can be leveled against the single-period portfolio framework has to do with the definition of risk. The analysis that was presented defined risk as variability in return and measured it by either the standard deviation or the variance of an expected return. It is intuitively obvious that risk increases with variability. Whether variability is an appropriate definition of risk, however, is debatable, and this position has been challenged by several financial writers.[4] These writers have suggested that risk is simply *the probability of earning less than some specified target return.* Suppose, for example, that a person sets a zero return as his target. If risk is defined in this way, then, if a security has an expected return of 20 percent and a standard deviation of 10 percent, the probability of loss would be 2.3 percent, since this is the probability that the return will be zero or negative. This security is more risky than one that has an expected return of 30 percent and a standard deviation of 12 percent, which would have a probability of loss of only 1 percent. On the other hand, the first security is less risky than one with an expected return of 5 percent and a standard deviation of 3 percent because the probability of loss of the latter is 5 percent.

The minimum level of return that an investor must receive is called his *ruin level*, or *target level.* If a person must earn at least a 5-percent return to, say, pay the rent or buy food, his ruin level would be 5 percent. Any investment that is likely to earn less than 5 percent is risky for him, regardless of the size of the standard deviation of the distribution of returns. Some investors, widows and orphans, for example, may have a target level of return which is marginally lower than the rate on government bonds; hence they will prefer bonds, preferred stock, and savings accounts, all instruments whose return fluctuates very little, to other investments with a higher but more variable return. The manager of a pension fund might have a slightly lower target level of ruin, say zero gain or, at most, a very slight loss; the manager of a "go-go" fund, whose customers have explicitly accepted risk might have a still lower target ruin level; and an individual investor who has some extra money to "play with" might be willing to lose all this extra money. It must be stressed, of course, that the investor does not *desire* to reach this target level of

---

[4] See for example, A. D. Roy, "Safety First and the Holding of Assets," *Econometrica* (July 1952), pp. 431–49.

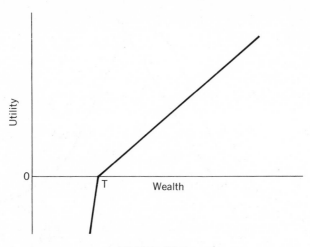

FIGURE 20.7

An Investor's Utility Function When Risk Is Defined as the Probability of Loss.

ruin; he prefers to be above it, and the farther above the better.

Those who hold that risk is the probability of loss typically assume that the investor's utility function breaks sharply at the target loss point, as in Figure 20.7. Utility rises linearly with wealth as long as the level of wealth is greater than the target level; i.e., $U = a + bW$ (for $T < W < \infty$). If the actual level of wealth is below T, however, the utility level is below the line $a + bW$.

The attractiveness of an investment can be calculated by multiplying the utility of a return times its probability and summing over the products. Figure 20.8 combines both the distribution of returns for a $100 portfolio, portfolio A, and a utility function whose slope is 2 when $W > T$ and -8 when $W < T$. Let T be the target ruin level of $10. We can now approximate the attractiveness of this investment.

Roughly 16 percent of the time, the expected return of the portfolio will be between 0 and $10. As an approximation, assume that a return of $5 will occur 16 percent of the time. Similarly, we can assume that a return of $15 will occur 34 percent of the time. The total utility of the investment, 15.2 units, is shown in Table 20.2.

A similar calculation can be performed to determine the utility of a portfolio with an expected return of 16 percent and a standard deviation of 4 percent, as in Table 20.3. The total utility of this portfolio, call it portfolio B, is 11.62. By this criterion, then, portfolio A is more attractive. Clearly, however, if a different utility value were assigned to returns that were below the target level or if the utility of returns greater than the target value were prized more highly, a different choice could have been made.

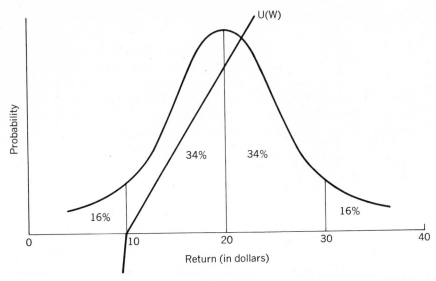

FIGURE 20.8

The Distribution of Returns of Portfolio A and an Investor's Utility Function.

TABLE 20.2

The Probability and Utility of Different Returns
for Portfolio A

Return	Target	Return Less Target	Utility	Probability	(Utility) · (Probability)
$ 5	$10	−$ 5	−40	.16	− 6.40
15	10	+ 5	+10	.34	+ 3.40
25	10	+ 15	+30	.34	+10.20
35	10	+ 25	+50	.16	+ 8.00
					15.20

TABLE 20.3

The Probability and Utility of Different Returns
for Portfolio B

Return	Target	Return Less Target	Utility	Probability	(Utility) · (Probability)
$ 9	$10	−$ 1	− 8	.07	− .56
11	10	+ 1	+ 2	.09	+ .18
14	10	+ 4	+ 8	.34	+ 2.72
18	10	+ 8	+16	.34	+ 5.44
22	10	+ 12	+24	.16	+ 3.84
					11.62

Portfolio analysis

To summarize, when risk is defined as the probability of loss, a target level of return is used to evaluate investments. This target level varies with each investor, depending on his needs. Returns below this level will be negatively valued; returns above it will be positively valued. This definition of risk and the specification of the parameters a and b in the equation $U = a + bW$ have several implications for portfolio analysis.

First, if two portfolios have the same mean, the one with the smaller standard deviation will have a lower probability of loss and will be valued more highly. Second, if a portfolio has both a higher mean and a higher standard deviation than another, it may or may not be preferred. Clearly, if the returns and standard deviations of both are such that neither results in a loss, neither involves any risk. The portfolio with the higher expected return will then be most valued. In general, however, the ordering of the portfolios will depend on the slope of the investor's utility function both above and below the target level of return.[5]

Measuring portfolio performance

Up to now, we have dealt primarily with the considerations that enter into the construction of a portfolio. But once a portfolio is selected, how should its performance be measured? An obvious answer is to say that the portfolio which rises the most in value is best. But not everyone would agree with this answer. Some theorists would argue that a measure of risk should be included in the performance measure.

Did a portfolio that produced an average return of 20 percent over several years, but whose returns fluctuated wildly within this period, perform better than a portfolio that earned an average return of 10 percent over the same period but whose returns fluctuated less? Suppose that the fluctuation in realized returns, as well as their level, is a valid criterion for judging investment performance. How can the two measures be combined to produce a single measure for ranking portfolio performance?

To answer this question, we might argue as follows: Suppose that a regression is run between the portfolio's annual return and a market index such as the Dow Jones or the Standard and Poor's Average of 425 Securities over a period of several years. Thus: $Y = a + bI$ where Y is the portfolio's annual return and I is the index. The coefficient b can then be taken as a measure of the volatility of the portfolio. If b is greater than 1, the returns of the portfolio will fluctuate more than the market average, whereas if b is less than 1, they will fluctuate less.

[5] For a statement of the formal programming model that can be used to solve the portfolio problem when risk is defined as the probability of loss, see Robert Machol and Eugene M. Lerner, "Risk, Ruin and Investment Analysis," *Journal of Financial and Quantitative Analysis* (December 1969), pp. 473–93.

The value of b for each portfolio can then be used to "normalize" its average return over a long period for its instability. Thus, if one portfolio has a higher annual return (a high Y) but a large b, its normalized return, that is, its risk-adjusted annual return, may be less than the normalized return of a portfolio with a smaller return and a lower b value. One way to rank the performance of portfolios in terms of both their return and their volatility is, therefore, by the size of the ratio Y/b.

This measure, however, ignores another important dimension of the portfolio-selection problem: An investor could place his funds in, say, a savings and loan company and earn a risk-free return of, say, r'. We can take into consideration the alternative risk-free rate of return the investor forgoes by adjusting the numerator of the performance measure. The Y/b ratio now becomes $(Y - r')/b$. If r' is greater than Y, the performance measure is negative, since the portfolio earned less than the riskless rate. The higher the positive value of this measure, the more satisfactory is the performance of the portfolio.

If we substitute the right-hand side of the equation $Y = a + bI$ for Y, the performance measure can be rewritten as

$$\text{Performance measure} = \frac{a + bI - r'}{b}$$

or

$$\text{Performance measure} = \frac{a - r'}{b} + I$$

If we state the measure this way, we can see that it takes two things into consideration: $(a - r')/b$ measures how the portfolio itself performs, and I measures how the market as a whole acted. The performance of the portfolio thus depends on (1) which securities are selected and (2) conditions in the securities market as a whole.

Variations of this performance measure have been proposed by Treynor, Sharpe, and Jensen.[6] All three of these writers have studied the performance of mutual funds in depth, and all three have attempted to measure the contribution of the portfolio manager (the selection of securities) to the fund's return. All three men found that their particular variation of the term $(a - r')/b$ had a value close to zero; that is, they found that the managers of most mutual funds do not make a positive contribution to the performance of the fund. Rather, the performance of any portfolio is largely attributable to market conditions.

[6] See J. L. Treynor, "How to Rate Management of Investment Funds," *Harvard Business Review*, vol. 43 (January–February 1965), pp. 63–75; W. F. Sharpe, "Mutual Fund Performance," *Journal of Business*, vol. 39, pt. 2 (January 1966), pp. 119–38; and M. C. Jensen, "The Performance of Mutual Funds in the Period of 1945–1964," *Journal of Finance*, vol. 27 (May 1968), pp. 389–419.

This approach to measuring portfolio performance has several weaknesses. First, a performance is usually measured over a period of several years. If the return on the risk-free assets changed over this period, the return represented by r' cannot have been entirely riskless. Moreover, the value assigned to r' may vary since not all risk-free assets yield the same return. Whether the manager's contribution is found to be positive or negative may depend on which value of r' is used.

A second criticism is more serious. Portfolio performance is penalized, in the measures presented above, if the value of b is high. But if the prices of securities in general rise over the period, then the owners of the portfolio are likely to be quite pleased if it has a high b value, since this means that their return increased more than the market index. Rather than penalizing portfolios for a high b value, investors may applaud them.

Investors tend to behave this way, of course, because after the fact, there is no risk. In the end, a result is either above or below a certain target. If the investment alternative is the riskless security, the only question is whether the return exceeds the target. In Figure 20.9, all portfolios to the right of the first perpendicular line did well if the target was to earn more than a risk-free asset. If the target was to beat the market index, only the securities to the right of the second perpendicular line performed well, and all the securities to the left performed badly.

Most of the portfolios whose performance has been reported in empirical studies have been mutual-fund portfolios, and most of them have earned returns higher than the returns on government bonds but not better than the market index. It is not surprising that mutual funds should earn more than the rate on riskless assets; one reason many of them have not earned more than the market average is that they have bonds, as well as stocks, in their portfolio. Why bonds were held in these port-

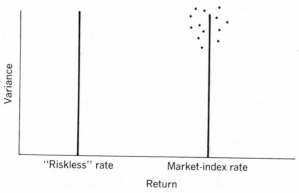

FIGURE 20.9

Portfolio Performance Given Two Target Ruin Levels of Return.

folios at all during a period when stocks appreciated more than bonds is not clear. Obviously they were held for a purpose, but with the benefit of hindsight, it seems clear that the reasoning behind their inclusion was probably falacious.

Another reason the portfolios of some mutual funds may not do as well as the market index is that their trading costs are high. A large mutual fund's purchase or sale may cause adverse price movements as much as 3 or 4 percent. This is seldom taken into consideration in comparing the returns from the fund and the return that could have been earned by buying and holding a market average. Finally, the net return of a fund may not have exceeded the market average because of the management fees, which are paid out of the fund's gross returns.

Summary

Portfolio management is a serious problem for all investors, and in recent years it has been the subject of intense formal analysis. Many consider it the task of a portfolio manager to select securities that can achieve a maximum return for a given level of risk. When risk is defined as the standard deviation of the expected return and the shape of the investor's utility function is known, formal programming models can be developed that can be used to calculate optimum single-period portfolios. These models show why investors typically hold a diversified portfolio rather than concentrating all their funds in a single asset. They also demonstrate why an investor will frequently hold both a riskless asset, such as a time deposit in a bank, and a portfolio of risky securities.

Many portfolio problems, however, do not readily lend themselves to this kind of formal analysis. All the programming models developed treat the dividends and the capital gains that a security offers as equivalent returns. Frequently, however, one person may receive the dividend income and another the capital gain. These parties are certainly not indifferent to the relative importance of each component of total return. Another important portfolio problem concerns the timing of the returns. Should a hospital or a university, for example, design a portfolio that will yield as high a current income as possible, or should it forgo some current income to obtain larger returns at a later date? Again, the single-period models provide no answer.

A technical criticism, involving the definition of risk, can also be leveled against the formal portfolio models that were presented. Most investors think of risk as the probability of loss, not as a variance or a standard deviation of expected returns, as indicated in the models. How risk is defined will affect the investor's evaluation of a portfolio's performance. Those who think of risk as variation will penalize a fund that is more volatile than a market index; those who think of risk as the probability of loss would not consider this relevant; they would be interested only in whether the fund surpassed a target rate of return.

Questions for discussion and problems

1. Why are the indifference curves of an investor positive with respect to return and negative with respect to variability? What would another shape imply about an investor's preferences?

2. Why does diversification reduce the variance of the returns of a portfolio?

3. How can an efficient frontier be calculated?

4. Can a riskless yield ever be greater than the realized return on a portfolio of securities?

5. Is the total return offered by a portfolio always an appropriate measure of its return? If not, what new problems are introduced into the analysis?

6. When the utility of the entire distribution of the expected returns of a portfolio is incorporated into the analysis, what problem can be easily handled that was difficult to cope with in another framework?

7. Suppose that the Dow Jones Index falls by 20 percent and that a particular portfolio falls by 10 percent during the same period. The interest rate on Treasury Bills during this period was 6 percent. Did the portfolio manager do a good job of managing the fund?

8. Should the annual variations in realized returns be used as a measure of a portfolio's performance?

   [Answers to problems 9–13 follow references and suggested readings.]

9. Compute the mean and variance of a portfolio that consists of 60 percent security A and 40 percent security B, where A has an expected return of 10 percent and a variance of .10 and B has an expected return of 20 percent and a variance of .30. The covariance between the two securities is —.05.

10. Assume that the general shape of an investor's utility curves depend on the expected level and variability of return. Sketch the utility curve of (a) a widow who cannot afford to take much of a risk, (b) a speculator, and (c) a prudent businessman.

11. Using the mean-variance framework, construct an efficient frontier and a set of utility curves. Introduce a risk-free rate and let it increase in value by 5 percent. What happens to (a) the utility that will

be realized, and (b) the percentage of securities held in the portfolio and the percentage of risk-free asset held?

12. Assume that an investor invests $100 and has a target rate of return of 10 percent. If the utility associated with a return of less than $10 is −50; the expected return is normally distributed around a mean of $20; the standard deviation is $10, and the utility of each dollar earned above $10 is +1, what is the utility of the investment?

13. Suppose that the annual return of a portfolio is captured by the equation $Y = a + bI$ where Y is the annual return and I is a market index. For a particular fund, the values of a and b are .06 and 1.1, respectively. During a year, the market index rose 12 percent; during the same period, the rate of return on government bonds was 5 percent.
   (a) What was the expected return on the portfolio?
   (b) How much of this total return can be attributed to market conditions and how much to the management of the fund?
   (c) What is the value of the portfolio-performance measure when an adjustment is made for variability?
   (d) How much of the return in (c) is due to management and how much is due to the market?

REFERENCES AND SUGGESTED READINGS

Articles

Agnew, N. H., *et al.,* "An Application of Chance-Constrained Programming to Portfolio Selection in a Casualty Insurance Firm," *Management Science,* vol. XV, no. 10 (June 1969), pp. 512–21.

Baumol, William, "An Expected Gain-Confidence Limiting Criterion for Portfolio Selection," *Management Science,* vol. X, no. 1 (October 1963), pp. 174–83.

Bower, Richard S., and Wippern, Ronald F., "Risk Return Measurement in Portfolio Selection and Performance Appraisal Models: Progress Report," *Journal of Financial and Quantitative Analysis,* vol. IV (December 1969), pp. 417–48.

Breen, William, and Savage, James, "Portfolio Distribution and Tests of Security Selection Models," *Journal of Finance,* vol. XXIII (December 1968), pp. 805–21.

Carlson, Robert S., "Aggregate Performance of Mutual Funds, 1948–1967," *Journal of Financial and Quantitative Analysis,* vol. V (March 1970), pp. 1–32.

Cohen, Kalman J., and Pogue, Jerry A., "An Empirical Evaluation of Alternative Portfolio Selection Models," *Journal of Business,* vol. XL (April 1967), pp. 167–93.

Evans, John L., "The Random Walk Hypothesis, Portfolio Analysis and the Buy-and-Hold Criterion," *Journal of Financial and Quantitative Analysis,* vol. III (September 1968), pp. 327–42.

Fama, Eugene F., "Portfolio Analysis in a Stable Paretian Market," *Management Science,* vol. XI (January 1965), pp. 404–19.

———, "Risk and the Evaluation of Pension Fund Profit Performance" (Park Ridge, Ill.: Bank Administration Institute, 1968).

Fisher, Laurence, "Some New Stock Market Indexes," *Journal of Business,* vol. XXXIX, no. 1, part II (January 1966), pp. 171–226.

Fisher, Lawrence, and Lorie, J. H., "Rates of Return on Investments in Common Stocks," *Journal of Business,* vol. XXXVII, no. 1 (January 1965), pp. 1–22.

Friedman, Multon, and Savage, L. J., "The Utility Analysis of Choices Involving Risk," *Journal of Political Economy,* vol. LVI (August 1948), pp. 279–304.

Friend, Irwin, and Vickers, Douglas, "Portfolio Selection and Investment Performance," *Journal of Finance,* vol. XX (September 1965), pp. 391–415.

Hadar, Josef, and Russel, William P., "Rules for Ordering Uncertain Prospects" *American Economic Review,* vol. LIX, no. 1 (March 1969), pp. 25–34.

Homer, Sidney, "Stocks Versus Bonds: A Comparison of Supply and Demand Factors," *Institutional Investor,* vol. II (August 1968), pp. 45–47, 87–93.

Horowitz, Ira, "A Model for Mutual Fund Evaluation," *Industrial Management Review,* vol. VI, (Spring 1965), pp. 81–92.

———, "The 'Reward-to-Variability' Ratio and Mutual Fund Performance," *Journal of Business,* vol. XXXIX (October 1966), pp. 485–88.

Horowitz, Ira, and Higgins, Harold B., "Some Factors Affecting Investment Fund Performance," *Quarterly Review of Economics and Business,* vol. III (Spring 1963), pp. 41–49.

Jensen, Michael, "The Performance of Mutual Funds in the Period 1945–1964," *Journal of Finance,* vol. XXIII (May 1968), pp. 389–419.
———, "Risk, the Pricing of Capital Assets, and the Evaluation of Investment Portfolios," *Journal of Business,* vol. XLII, no. 2 (April 1969), pp. 167–248.

King, Benjamin F., "Market and Industry Factors in Stock Price Behavior," *Journal of Business,* vol. XXXIX, no. 1, part II (January 1966), pp. 139–90.

Levy, Robert A., "Measurement of Investment Performance," *Journal of Financial and Quantitative Analysis,* vol. III (March 1968), pp. 35–57.

Lintner, John, "The Aggregation of Investors' Diverse Judgments and Preferences in Purely Competitive Security Markets," *Journal of Financial and Quantitative Analysis,* vol. IV (December 1969), pp. 347–400.

———, "The Valuation of Risk Assets and the Selection of Risky Investments in Stock Portfolios and Capital Budgets," *Review of Economics and Statistics,* vol. LXVII (February 1965), pp. 13–37.

———, "Security Prices, Risk, and Maximal Gains from Diversification," *Journal of Finance,* vol. XX (December 1965), pp. 587–615.

Machol, Robert, and Lerner, Eugene M., "Risk, Ruin, and Investment Analysis," *Journal of Financial and Quantitative Analysis,* vol. IV (December 1969), pp. 473–92.

Pope, Alan, "The X Factor and the High Flyers," *Fortune,* vol. LXXVII (June 1, 1968), pp. 138–39.

Pratt, John W., "Risk Aversion in the Small and in the Large," *Econometrica,* vol. XXXII (January–April 1964), pp. 122–37.

Roy, A. D., "Safety First and the Holding of Assets," *Econometrica* (July 1952), pp. 431–49.

Sharpe, William F., "Capital Asset Price: A Theory of Market Equilibrium Under Conditions of Risk," *Journal of Finance,* vol. XIX (September 1964), pp. 425–42.

———, "Mutual Fund Performancs," *Journal of Business,* vol. XXXIX, no. 1, part 2 (January 1966), pp. 119–39.

———, "Risk-Aversion in the Stock Market: Some Empirical Evidence," *Journal of Finance,* vol. XX (September 1965), pp. 416–22.

Shinji, Kataoka, "A Stochastic Programming Model," *Econometrica,* vol. XXXI, no. 1–2 (January–April 1963), pp. 181–96.

Smith, Keith and Tito, Dennis A., "Risk-Return Measures of Expost Portfolio Performance," *Journal of Financial and Quantitative Analysis,* vol. IV (December 1969), pp. 449–72.

Tobin, James, "Liquidity Preference as Behavior Towards Risk," *Review of Economic Studies,* vol. XXV, no. 67 (February 1958), pp. 65–86.

Treynor, Jack, "How to Rate Management of Investment Funds," *Harvard Business Review,* vol. 43 (January–February 1965), pp. 63–75.

Treynor, Jack and Mazuy, Kay K., "Can Mutual Funds Outguess the Market?" *Harvard Business Review,* vol. 44 (July–August 1966), pp. 131–136.

Treynor, Jack, *et al.,* "Using Portfolio Composition to Estimate Risk," *Financial Analysts Journal,* vol. XXIV (September–October 1968), pp. 93–100.

Books

Farrar, Donald E., *The Investment Decision Under Uncertainty* (Englewood Cliffs, N. J.: Prentice-Hall, 1962).

Friend, Irwin, *et al., A Study of Mutual Funds* (Washington, D. C.: Government Printing Office, 1962).

Knight, Frank H., *Risk, Uncertainty and Profit* (Boston: Houghton-Mifflin, 1921).

Markowitz, Harry, *Portfolio Selection* (New York: Wiley, 1959).

Mood, A. M., and Graybill, F. A., *Introduction to the Theory of Statistics* (New York: McGraw-Hill, 1963) ch. 8.

Standard & Poor's Corporation, *Standard & Poor's Trade and Securities Statistics: Security Price Index Record* (Orange, Conn.: Standard & Poor's Corporation, 1968).

U. S. Securities and Exchange Commission, *Report of the Securities and Exchange Commission on the Public Policy Implications of Investment Company Growth,* 89th Congress, 2nd Sess., House Report No. 2337 (Washington, D. C.: Government Printing Office, 1963–1965) 6 vols.

———, *Report of Special Study of Securities Markets of the Securities and Exchange Commission,* 88th Congress, 1st Sess., House Document No. 95, pts. 1–6 (Washington, D. C.: Government Printing Office, 1963–1965) 6 vols.

Wiesenberger, Arthur, *Investment Companies* (New York: Arthur Wiesenberger & Co., 1948–1967, including supplement to 1967 ed.).

ANSWERS TO PROBLEMS 9–13

9. Expected return $= (.60)(.10) + (.40)(.20)$
    $$= .14$$
    Variance $= (.60)^2(.1) + (.4)^2(.3) + 2(.6)(.4)(-.05)$
    $$= .060$$

10.

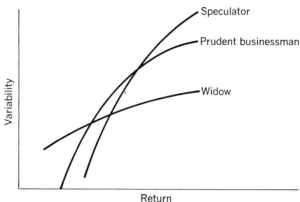

11. (a) A higher utility curve can be reached.
(b) The proportion of the risk-free instrument held increases.

12.

Return	Target	Return Less Target	Utility	Probability	(Utility) · (Probability)
$ 5	$10	−$ 5	−50	.16	−8.00
15	10	+ 5	+ 5	.34	+1.70
25	10	+ 15	+15	.34	+5.10
35	10	+ 25	+25	.16	+4.00
					+2.80

13. (a) $Y = .06 + 1.1\,(.12)$
    $= .192$
(b) Since the market rose 12 percent and the portfolio increased in value by 19.2 percent, 7.2 percent of the return is attributable to management.
(c) $\dfrac{a - r'}{b} + I = \dfrac{.06 - .05}{1.1} + .12$
    $= .129$
(d) Thus, according to this measure the market contributed .12 and the management .009.

Macroeconomic factors affecting the system: money and capital market forces

Changes in macroeconomic variables affect financial planning, capital budgeting, and security valuation. The chapters in this part present some of the analytical tools financial managers use to structure their thinking about these variables.

Chapter 21 presents the two analytical approaches that dominate discussions of macroeconomic events today: the monetarist and the income-expenditure approach. Both these frameworks emphasize the importance of changes in the money supply. Chapter 22, therefore, presents an analysis of how changes in the money supply come about and the critical role of the Federal Reserve, the nation's central bank, plays in this process.

Since the Federal Reserve works through the commercial-bank system in controlling the money supply, Chapter 23 studies some of the operating problems of banks and the constraints that bind their actions.

The monetarist and the income-expenditure approaches to economic activity

21

Earlier chapters repeatedly emphasized the importance of changes in the level of economic activity to financial managers. In the capital-budgeting section, we saw how the demand schedule for a firm's output and the supply schedule of its inputs constrained its outlays for new plant and equipment. Since these functions can shift if a change occurs in the price level, the rate of unemployment, or the net amount of government expenditures, management has good reason for concern when these macroeconomic variables fluctuate.

The chapters on security valuation were built around the equation $P = D/(k - g)$. There we saw how the discount rate shareholders apply to a firm's future stream of dividends, k, depends in part on an assessment of the risks that are inherent in the business and in part on the level of interest rates. The higher interest rates are, other things being equal, the greater the value of k will be, and the lower the price of stock. Similarly, the growth rate, g, that shareholders expect a corporation to achieve depends on both managerial actions and macroeconomic factors such as the growth of national income. Since the price of the company's stock will rise as the expected growth rate increases, the interest of the financial manager in the performance of the economy is understandable.

The level of the macroeconomic variables influencing corporate activities has been taken as given up to now. The models developed in earlier chapters did not question why an economic series followed a certain path over time or why it might be expected to rise or fall in the future. These questions cannot, however, be ignored, for they are crucial to understanding the environment of the firm. We must investigate what factors lead to changes in the level and the rate of growth of overall economic activity; how financial analysts come to grips with such problems as inflation, recession, unemployment, and rising interest rates; and what frameworks economists and financial analysts use to study the behavior of macroeconomic variables.

Although many approaches can be used in assessing the period-to-period changes in economic activity, two analytical frameworks dominate the thinking of economists and financial analysts today. The first is the *monetarist approach;* the second is the *income-expenditure approach.* The former has been carefully developed by, and is associated with, the economist Milton Friedman;[1] the latter is associated primarily with its chief architect, John Maynard Keynes.[2]

To contrast these two frameworks, it is necessary to distinguish between two kinds of variables that are encountered in building models of an economic process: *exogenous variables* and *endogenous variables.*

The values of exogenous variables are determined outside the system under study. They are the forces that both drive and constrain the economic process being studied. Some exogenous variables are controlled by the government; they can be changed by political action. Others, such as the work habits of the nation, are elements of the culture of society and change only slowly. Still others, such as last year's rate of change in prices, are the result of past actions of the economy, and are history. In model building, the direction of influence is *from* the exogenous variables *to* the economic system. Exogenous factors cannot be changed by the system at any moment of time; the system can only react to them.

The values of endogenous variables, on the other hand, are determined by the operations of the system itself. The level of an endogenous variable and its rate of change will depend on the level and rate of change of the exogenous variables and the relationships that link the exogenous and endogenous variables. The difference between the monetarist and the income-expenditure approaches lies in both the specification of the variables that are considered exogenous to the economic system and the relationships that link them.

The monetarist approach

The Federal Reserve Bank of St. Louis is a leading champion of the monetarist approach, and the pages that follow draw heavily on its work.[3]

[1] Milton Friedman, *The Optimum Quantity of Money and Other Essays* (Chicago: Aldine Press, 1969).
[2] John Maynard Keynes, *The General Theory of Employment, Interest and Money* (New York: Harcourt Brace Jovanovich, 1936).
[3] See, in particular, "A Monetarist Model for Economic Stabilization," Federal Reserve Bank of St. Louis *Review* (April 1970).

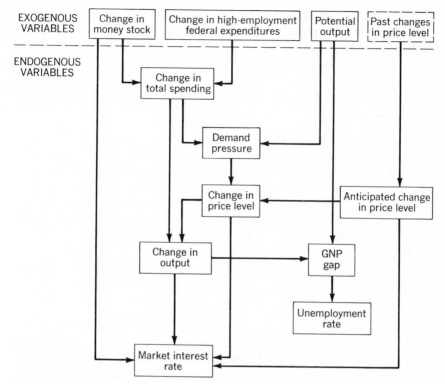

SOURCE: "A Monetarist Model for Economic Stabilization," Federal Reserve Bank of St. Louis *Review* (April 1970), p. 10.

FIGURE 21.1

A Flow Diagram of the Monetarist Approach.

The elements of the monetarist framework and the relationships between them are shown in Figure 21.1.

Exogenous variables

Monetarists consider four exogenous variables of strategic importance:

(1) CHANGES IN THE SUPPLY OF MONEY.

Changes in the money supply are caused by the actions of a government agency, the country's central bank. Through a process we shall describe in Chapter 22, the central bank can increase or decrease the amount of reserves available to commercial banks. As the level of their reserves changes, the ability of banks to extend credit to borrowers increases or decreases. Since the amount of funds that the central bank makes available depends entirely on the decisions of its board of governors, monetarists assume that changes in the money supply are exogenous to the economic system.

(2) CHANGES IN FEDERAL SPENDING.

Changes in government expenditures, which are financed by taxing and borrowing, are a second exogenous variable. These outlays can be altered by the actions of Congress or the President, who have discretionary control over them, although in practice a substantial amount of time may pass before the government decides whether a particular increase or decrease is appropriate.

(3) POTENTIAL OUTPUT.

The amount of goods and services that an economy has the potential to produce depends on such factors as its stock of physical capital, the size and skill of its labor force, and the cultural characteristics of the community as a whole. If an economy has a relatively large stock of capital, it will have the potential to produce a large quantity of goods. Similarly, if the labor force is large and technologically sophisticated, the potential output of the nation will be higher than if this were not the case. Finally, if the people as a whole value hard work and high productivity, output will also tend toward a higher level.

(4) PAST CHANGES IN PRICE LEVELS.

While monetarists consider the changes in the country's price level to be an endogenous variable at any moment of time, the past changes in prices are exogenous to the current state. Past changes in prices are important because they influence the expectations of consumers and businessmen about what will happen to prices in the current period.

Endogenous variables

Once the value of each of these four exogenous variables is known, the monetarist can determine the level of many of the endogenous macroeconomic variables that were referred to in earlier chapters. Among the endogenous variables are:

ΔY_t = the change in total spending (the change in the money value of gross national product),

D_t = demand pressure,

ΔP^{A_t} = the anticipated change in the price level,

ΔP_t = the change in the price level,

ΔX_t = the change in output (the change in the real value of gross national product),

G_t = the GNP gap (the difference between potential and realized gross national product),

U_t = the unemployment rate, and

R_t = the market rate of interest.

To understand how these endogenous values are determined, within the monetarist framework, we need to examine the equations monetarists use to describe the economic system.

CHANGES IN TOTAL SPENDING

The changes in the total expenditures that a community makes to purchase the goods and services it produces is a function of the change in the money supply, ΔM, and a change in amount of federal spending, ΔE. Thus:

$$(21\text{--}1) \qquad \Delta Y_t = f(\Delta M_t, \ldots \Delta M_{t-n}, \Delta E_t \ldots \Delta E_{t-n})$$

where ΔY is the change in spending, ΔM is the change in the money supply, and ΔE is the change in federal expenditures. The subscripts indicate the dates when these changes occur.

The Federal Reserve Bank of St. Louis, which estimated the parameters of equation 21–1, found that the best statistical results were obtained when the values of the independent variables for the past four years were incorporated in the analysis. The bank also found that the changes in the money supply were more important in explaining fluctuations in the dollar value of national income than the changes in government expenditures.

The change in total spending, or the dollar value of the gross national product, has two components, the change in the real output of the economy and the change in the price level. To estimate these two components, a monetarist must first estimate the *demand pressure* in the economy, for this is a principal determinant of changes in prices.

DEMAND PRESSURE

Demand pressure is a construct that relates the change in total spending (calculated in equation 21–1) and the potential output of the system (an exogenous variable). Thus:

$$(21\text{--}2) \qquad D_t = \Delta Y_t - (X_t^F - X_{t-1})$$

where D_t is demand pressure, X_t^F is the potential level of output at full employment, and X_{t-1} is the nation's real level of output in the past year.

If the economy is operating at full employment, $X_t^F = X_{t-1}$ and any increase in spending, ΔY_t, since it raises the demand pressure at a time when the economy is already producing all the output it has the potential to produce, will ultimately lead to an increase in prices. However, if there is a gap between potential and realized output, the demand pressure on prices will not be so great. Under these conditions, an increase in ΔY_t can lead to an increase in real output.

A number of methods are available for measuring potential GNP.

The estimates of the Council of Economic Advisors to the President indicate that potential GNP is increasing at an annual rate of 4.3 percent.

ANTICIPATED CHANGES IN PRICES

Most people have some idea of how they expect prices to behave in the current period. These expectations will affect both the actual prices that will prevail and the interest rates that lenders demand when they advance credit. The amount of change in prices that the community as a whole anticipates usually depends on how prices behaved under similar economic conditions in the past. For example, if prices have risen rapidly during the last few years, people may expect this trend to continue. However, if the level of unemployment begins to increase, consumers and businessmen alike may moderate their expectations, for a high level of unemployment has historically been associated with periods of declining prices.

Anticipated changes in prices, of course, cannot be observed directly and therefore must be constructed. The weights that are assigned to past price changes and to past levels of unemployment are, in the final analysis, arbitrary. Even so, a reasonable estimate of the anticipated price change can be found by using an equation such as 21–3.

(21–3)
$$\Delta P^{A_t} = f(\Delta P_{t-1} \ldots \Delta P_{t-n})$$

THE PRICE EQUATION

The change in prices that will actually occur during any period will depend on the demand pressure (equation 21–2) and the anticipated change in prices (equation 21–3). Thus:

(21–4)
$$\Delta P_t = f(D_t \ldots D_{t-n}, \Delta P^{A_t})$$

Equation 21–4 says that if the demand pressure has been at a high level during the recent past and if the anticipated change in prices is high, the actual change in prices will be high.

Empirical estimates of the parameters of this equation prepared by the Federal Reserve Bank of St. Louis indicate that the anticipated change in prices is a significant determinant of the actual price change that occurs. However, it is difficult to evaluate this conclusion since anticipated price changes cannot really be considered independent of the demand-pressure variable. The two variables in equation 21–4 should, properly, be considered in combination rather than separately.

CHANGES IN REAL OUTPUT

The change in the money value of gross national product is defined as:

$$\Delta Y_t = \Delta P_t + \Delta X_t + (P_t - P_{t-1})(X_t - X_{t-1})$$

The product of the change in prices times the change in output, however, is small enough to be dropped without influencing the value of the change in real output noticeably.

Equation 21–1 gave us the value of ΔY_t, the change in the money value of the gross national product, and equation 21–4 gave us ΔP_t, the change in prices. Once these values are known, the change in real output, ΔX_t, can be readily computed by subtracting one variable from the other. Thus:

$$(21\text{–}5) \qquad \Delta X_t = \Delta Y_t - \Delta P_t$$

THE GROSS NATIONAL PRODUCT GAP

The real value of the gross national product, or the actual amount of physical goods and services produced, was calculated in equation 21–5. By combining this value and the exogenous variable potential output, the GNP gap, G_t, can be computed. This gap is the difference between the real and the potential output, expressed as a percentage of the real level of output. Thus:

$$(21\text{–}6) \qquad G_t = \frac{X_t^F - X_t}{X_t}$$

The GNP gap is a measure of how effectively the resources of the community are being utilized. If the gap is large, the community as a whole is forgoing a substantial amount of goods and services that are potentially available to it. If the gap is small, the economy is operating close to capacity.

THE LEVEL OF EMPLOYMENT

The level of employment of one resource in particular, labor, has always been of concern to economists. The amount of unemployment, U_t, likely to exist at any time can be forecast from estimates of the GNP gap as follows:

$$(21\text{–}7) \qquad U_t = f(G_t, G_{t-1})$$

Equation 21–7 indicates that as the GNP gap increases, the amount of unemployment rises.

INTEREST RATES

In the monetarist framework, the interest rate that will prevail in the economy is a function of a number of variables, including current and past rates of change of output, the current rate of change of the money supply, and current and past rates of change of prices. Thus:

$$(21\text{–}8) \qquad R_t = f(\Delta M_t, \Delta X_t \ldots \Delta X_{t-n}, \Delta P_t, \Delta P^A_t)$$

Empirical estimates of long- and short-term interest rates reached by using equation 21–8 show that the full impact of changes in the money supply does not occur immediately. The first effect of an increase in the supply of money is to lower interest rates because more funds are available to meet current demands. However, as real output increases and as prices begin to rise (because of the increase in demand pressure), interest rates will also rise. A sudden increase in the money supply will therefore lead to a cyclical pattern of interest rates; i.e., rates will first fall and then rise as the effects of the increase in the stock of money spread throughout the economy.

A summary of the monetarist approach

An effective summary of the monetarist framework, which appeared in the April 1970 issue of the Federal Reserve Bank of St. Louis *Review*, is quoted below:

> The workings of the model can be demonstrated with graphical techniques. Figure 21.2 is a representation of the core of the model, showing the determination of changes in spending, output, and prices.
>
> Panel A of Figure 21.2 is a graphical representation of the total spending equation with ΔM on the horizontal axis and ΔY on the vertical axis. Changes in ΔE shift the total spending line.
>
> Panel B shows prices (ΔP) as a function of ΔY. A short-run price line (ΔP_1) is drawn consistent with empirical results showing that ΔP is not very sensitive to ΔY in the short run. Important determinants of the position of the short-run price line are the size of the GNP gap and anticipated price changes. The long-run price line ($\Delta P(LR)$) is drawn to show the relationship between ΔP and ΔY when the GNP gap is zero and anticipated prices are equal to actual prices. Its slope (45 degrees from its origin in the ΔY axis) is based on the monetarist view that in the long run, ΔM influences only ΔP.
>
> Panel C expresses the total spending identity in graphical terms. Total spending is divided between output and prices; to reflect this, the line in panel C is drawn as a 45-degree line with its position determined by the magnitude of total spending (ΔY). There is a family of 45-degree lines, one for each possible ΔY. Also included in panel C is a horizontal line representing the long-run growth rate of output. It is shown as a horizontal line to indicate that long-run output growth is exogenously determined by resource growth and technology.
>
> In panel D, the ΔX_1 line shows the relationship between money (ΔM) and output (ΔX) as derived from the other three panels. . . .
>
> Figure 21.2 is drawn to represent an initial equilibrium for a given ΔM, which has associated with it the short-run price and output lines, ΔP_1 and ΔX_1. The effect of a change in ΔM, given ΔE, is shown as a movement along the spending line in panel A from ① to ②. Given the

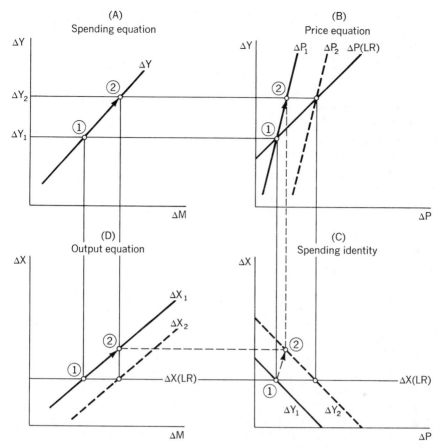

SOURCE: "A Monetarist Model for Economic Stabilization," Federal Reserve Bank of St. Louis *Review* (April 1970), p. 23.

FIGURE 21.2

Model in Graphical Form.

initial price line, ΔP_1, and the changed ΔY, the effect on prices and output is shown in panels B, C, and D as a movement from ① to ②.

This case illustrates the impact of a change in ΔM in the short run. For longer periods, anticipated price changes and the GNP gap will also change; they become endogenous variables in a long-run model. To illustrate the effects for the long run, the long-run price line, $\Delta P(LR)$, in panel B, is relevant. The interpretation of the long-run price line is that changes in ΔM are reflected only in ΔP, with ΔX determined by considerations of resource growth and technology. The horizontal line in panels C and D is the long-run relation between prices and output.

In the short run, the solution of the model need not lie on the long-run price line in panel B (or the long-run output line in panels C and D). However, a succession of short runs (shown as a shift of the ΔP and

A summary of the monetarist approach

ΔX lines to ΔP_2 and ΔX_2) will tend to move equilibrium toward the long-run price and output lines, as anticipated prices adjust to actual prices and the GNP gap goes to zero.[4]

The income expenditure approach

The Keynesian income-expenditure framework attempts to explain fluctuations in economic activity by focusing on the behavior of spending units. To see whether this approach leads to a useful understanding of the economic process, i.e., whether it enables policymakers to achieve the economic goals of the nation, let us begin, as in the preceding section, by asking which variables in the framework are exogenous and which are endogenous.

Exogenous variables

THE PRICE LEVEL

The monetarist approach considers the current price level an endogenous variable; the income-expenditure approach considers it an exogenous variable. The prevailing price level in the income-expenditure framework is assumed to be determined in part by the historical pattern of prices and in part by the institutional structure which keeps prices rigid in the short run. Changes in prices over time are caused by changes in the relative bargaining power of business, labor, government, and powerful consumer groups.

The assumption that the current price level is exogenous forces the income-expenditure framework to concentrate on those factors that contribute to changes in the real output of the nation. It is thus of little use in periods when the economy is operating close to capacity and the GNP gap is close to zero.

EXPENDITURES BY GOVERNMENTS AND FOREIGNERS

Both monetarists and Keynesians assume that government outlays are exogenous, not because they are unimportant to the level of economic activity, but simply because their level is not determined by the forces described in the model.

The expenditures of foreigners are considered an exogenous variable by Keynesians. Since they constitute only a small percentage of the total outlays for goods and services that occur in an economy as large as that of the United States, they can be ignored without doing violence to the model of

[4] *Ibid.*, p. 23.

the economic process. However, the model will be strictly valid only for a closed economy.

THE NOMINAL STOCK OF MONEY

The nominal supply of money is a third exogenous variable in the income-expenditure approach. How the actions of the central banks lead to changes in the money supply is described in Chapter 22.

Endogenous variables

The endogenous variables in the income-expenditure framework are

Y = the level of real income,
C = the level of real consumption outlays,
I = the level of real investment outlays,
R = the interest rate, and
M_d = the demand for nominal money balances.

THE NATIONAL INCOME DEFINITION

The total real outlays by consumers and investors are, by definition, equal to the real value of national income. Thus:

$$(21\text{–}9) \qquad Y = C + I$$

Although this equation yields no insights into the workings of economy, it does serve to raise the question of what determines the size of each component of national income.

THE CONSUMPTION FUNCTION

The belief that consumption outlays are a function of income is an important cornerstone of the income-expenditure framework. This relationship between these two variables is postulated to be

$$(21\text{–}10) \qquad C = a_0 + a_1 Y$$

where $a_1 \leq 1$. For example, suppose that a_0 is $10 and a_1 is .8. Then, if Y is $100, C will be $90, and every $1 change in Y will cause an $.80 increase in consumption outlays. The consumption function will then resemble line C in Figure 21.3.

If every dollar that the community earned were spent on consumption, the value of a_1 in equation 21–10 would be +1. Moreover, if consumption fell to zero when income fell to zero, the value of a_0 would be zero.

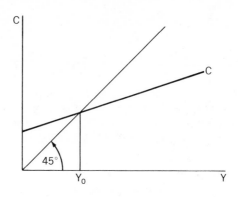

FIGURE 21.3

The Consumption Function.

The consumption function would then be the 45-degree line in Figure 20.3.

If income is to the right of Y_0 and C is the consumption function of the community, consumers will not spend all the income that they have, but will save some. For national income to remain to the right of Y_0, spending from some other source, such as private investment or government outlays, must offset the volume of consumers' savings.

Equation 21–10, however, is not a complete statement of the consumption function. Studies of consumer outlays indicate that consumption expenditures are also sensitive to changes in wealth: As wealth rises, tastes change and the standard of living of the community rises and the entire consumption function shifts upward. The interest rate is a good proxy for wealth, since it moves inversely with the wealth position of the community. A more complete statement of the consumption function, then, is

(21–10a)
$$C = f(Y, R)$$

THE INVESTMENT FUNCTION

Few economic series have been as carefully and intensively studied as the level of the nation's investment outlays. This is because in the income-expenditure framework, changes in the level of investment outlays affect national income. For example, a change in investment outlays from, say, $10 to $12 will affect national income as follows:

If $a_0 = \$10$ and $a_1 = .8$ in equation 21–10,

$$C = 10 + .8Y$$

Since

$$Y = C + I$$

by substitution,

$$Y = 10 + .8Y + I$$
$$Y(1 - .8) = 10 + I$$
$$Y = \frac{10 + I}{(1 - .8)}$$

When $I = \$10$, $Y = \$100$:

$$Y = \frac{\$20}{.2} = \$100$$

If I now increases by $2 to $12, Y will increase by $10 to $110:

$$Y = \frac{\$22}{.2} = \$110$$

A $2 increase in investment outlays thus led to a fivefold increase in national income. This multiple expansion in income occurred because consumption outlays, as well as investment outlays, rose. The $2 rise in investment raised income by $2, initially. This rise, however, led to an increase in consumption outlays that led to a still further increase in income, and so on. Ultimately, the $2 rise in investment outlays induced an increase of $8 in consumption outlays, raising national income a total of $10.

Economists believe that aggregate investment outlays are a function of two principal variables: the interest rate and the change in the income. Consider the first relationship of investment to interest rates:

(21–11) $I = f(R)$

If interest rates fall, other things being equal, the level of investment will rise. Funds will not only be less expensive to borrow, which will facilitate expansion, but more investment will take place because business-men will not discount the future cash flows from investment outlays at as high a rate as previously.

When equations 21–9, 21–10, and 21–11 are combined, as they are in Figure 21.4, a schedule called the *IS* (*investment-saving*) *function* can be constructed that shows the equilibrium relationship between the level of income and the rate of interest.

The *IS* schedule is downward sloping because as interest rates fall, investment outlays rise and lead to a higher level of income. The exact shape and position of the *IS* function (i.e., whether it will be to the right or left of the line in Figure 21.4 and whether it will be steeper or flatter) depends on the value of the parameters of equations 21–10 and 21–11.

Figure 21.4, then, shows the level of income interest consistent with various rates. We shall see what factors determine the interest rate when we study the money market later in the chapter.

Endogenous variables

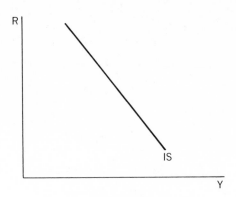

FIGURE 21.4

The *IS* Function.

Let us now examine the second assumption made by the income-expenditure approach about aggregate investment: that it is a function of changes in income. What are the consequences of assuming that investment changes in response to a change in income?

If income rises and markets expand, investment outlays may rise, as entrepreneurs see new profit opportunities. Let α be the relationship between investment and the change in income. Then,

(21–12) $$I = \alpha \Delta Y$$

If consumption is now expressed as a linear function of income,

$$C = \beta Y$$

then the national income identity, $Y = C + I$, becomes

$$Y = \beta Y + \alpha \Delta Y$$

Rearranging the terms in this equation gives us

$$\frac{\Delta Y}{Y} = \frac{1 - \beta}{\alpha}$$

The solution to this equation shows that the growth rate of national income will be $(1 - \beta)/\alpha$. Note that if β falls, i.e., if people save more of their income, national income can grow at a faster rate. Similarly, if α falls, i.e., if investments become more productive so that a given dollar outlay of investment can support a larger change in income, the growth rate of national income will rise. The term $(1 - \beta)/\alpha$ is sometimes called the *warranted rate of growth*.

To summarize, the aggregate investment function is crucial in the income-expenditure framework because changes in investment greatly affect the level of national income. When aggregate investment is expressed as a function of the interest rate, an *IS* schedule can be constructed to show the relationship between the change in income and the change in interest rates. When aggregate investment is expressed as a function of the rate of growth of income, it provides an insight into factors that promote economic growth.

THE DEMAND FOR MONEY

In the income-expenditure framework, the interest rate is set by the supply of, and demand for, money. The demand for real money balances (the stock of money deflated by the price level) is assumed to be a function of two variables, national income and the interest rate. Thus,

(21–13) $$M_d = f(Y, R)$$

A graph of this equation is presented in Figure 21.5.

The demand for money balances is a falling function of the interest rate: As rates rise, the opportunity to earn a return on money increases; and the community as a whole will want to hold a lower level of real money balances. On the other hand, as national income increases, the demand for money balances will increase, not only because more funds are needed for transactions but because money is a superior good; i.e., as national income increases, the demand for money increases more than proportionally. In Figure 21.5, Y_1 is a higher level of income than Y_0, and at every level of interest rates, the demand for money is greater than along Y_0.

FIGURE 21.5
The Demand for Money.

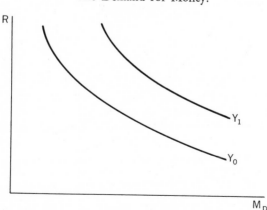

The equilibrium conditions in the money market

In the income-expenditure framework, the supply of money is determined exogenously. Thus,

$$(21\text{--}14) \qquad\qquad M_s = \overline{M}$$

where $\overline{M}$ is a given value. (Some economists hold that the supply of money is a rising function of the interest rate. This modification could be made, but it would not alter the analysis significantly.)

The money market is in equilibrium when the demand for money equals the supply—when

$$(21\text{--}15) \qquad\qquad M_D = M_S$$

For example, Figure 21.6 shows that when the money supply increases from M_0 to M_1, the interest rate falls from R_0 to R_1, as long as national income remains Y_0. If national income rises to Y_1 as the money supply increases, the equilibrium interest rate in Figure 20.6 will rise to R_2.

The relationship in Figure 20.6 is described in another way in Figure 21.7. Figure 21.7 shows the equilibrium relationships between the interest rate and national income for a given stock of money. This function, called the *LM* (*liquidity-money*) *function,* slopes upward because a higher interest rate is needed to support a higher level of income if the stock of money remains constant. The exact location of the *LM* schedule depends on the money supply; if M_s increases, the entire *LM* schedule shifts to the right; if it falls, the schedule shifts to the left. The exact slope of the *LM* schedule depends on the demand for money balances.

FIGURE 21.6

Equilibrium Conditions in the Money Market.

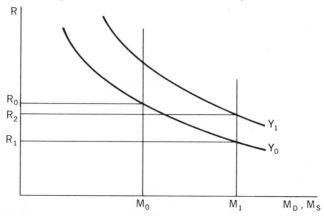

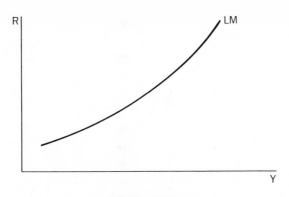

FIGURE 21.7
The *LM* Function.

The simultaneous determination of interest rates and national income

The *IS* schedule was constructed from three equations:

(21–9) $\qquad\qquad\qquad Y = C + I$
(21–10a) $\qquad\qquad\quad\; C = f(Y, R)$
(21–11) $\qquad\qquad\qquad I = f(R)$

The *LM* schedule was also constructed from three equations:

(21–13) $\qquad\qquad\qquad M_d = f(Y, R)$
(21–14) $\qquad\qquad\qquad M_s = \overline{M}$
(21–15) $\qquad\qquad\qquad M_D = M_S$

These six equations can be combined to determine, simultaneously, the interest rate and the level of national income.

Figures 21.4 and 21.7 can be combined to show the level of national income and the interest rate determined by the economic system. In Figure 21.8, for example, the equilibrium interest rate is R_0 and the equilibrium level of income is Y_0.

This visual analysis can be extended to trace the effect of changes in exogenous variables. If investment outlays increase because of additional government spending, the *IS* schedule will shift to the right (to IS_1 in Figure 21.9). Both interest rates and national income will rise. Since there is no change in the money supply, the rise in income will be accompanied by an increase in the velocity of money (the rate at which it is being used).

An increase in the money supply can also lead to an increase in the national income. In Figure 21.10, for example, the shift in the *LM* schedule to LM_1 causes national income to rise and interest rates to fall.

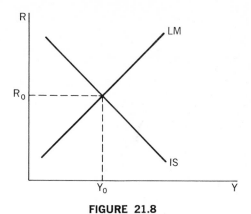

FIGURE 21.8

National Income and the Interest Rate as a Function of *IS* and *LM*.

The effect of a change in investment outlays or the money supply on national income and interest rates depends on the slope and position of the *IS* and *LM* schedules. Clearly, if the slope of the *IS* schedule is steep, a shift in the *LM* schedule will affect interest rates more than national income. Similarly if the *LM* schedule is steep, a shift in *IS* will lead to a greater rise in rates. If either schedule is nearly horizontal, changes in one or the other will affect national income more than interest rates.

Note that a rise in national income can be accompanied by either a rise or a fall in interest rates. If the rise in income reflects an upward shift in the *IS* schedule, interest rates will rise; if it reflects an upward shift in the *LM* schedule, interest rates will fall.

FIGURE 21.9

A Shift in the *IS* Schedule.

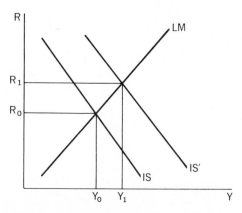

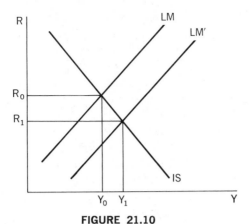

FIGURE 21.10

A Shift in the *LM* Schedule.

Summary

The two dominant approaches to macroeconomic analysis are the monetarist approach and the income-expenditure approach. There are several important differences between the two analytical frameworks:

First, the monetarist framework attempts to come to grips directly with the forces that lead to changes in prices. Monetarists consider the price level to be endogenous to the economic system. Thus they tend to believe that changes in the price level can be controlled by changes in the exogenous variables that lie behind total spending. The income-expenditure framework does not take this position. The price level is considered an exogenous variable and is excluded from the system of equations used to describe the economy. Those who hold to the income-expenditure framework are inclined to feel that price controls or wage and price guidelines are the answer to controlling rapidly rising prices.

Second, monetarists attempt to determine the endogenous variables of the economic system sequentially. They believe that changes in the money supply lead to changes in total spending, that the potential output of the economy and the change in total spending give rise to the demand pressure, that the demand pressure in the economy and the anticipated change in prices cause the changes in the price level, and so on. Under the income-expenditure approach, all the relevant endogenous variables—consumption, investment, income, the interest rate, and the demand for money balances—are found simultaneously. Users of this framework are thus deeply concerned with the effect of a change in one part of the economic system on every other part. From a policy point of view, they are interested in "fine tuning" the various relationships to keep the economy running smoothly. Monetarists, on the other hand, are not greatly concerned when a slight change occurs in one subsector of the economy since they believe that controlling monetary aggregates will resolve problems of the overall performance of the system as a whole.

Third, the interest rate plays a crucial role in the determination of national income in the income-expenditure framework. The level of interest rates is a determinant of investment outlays, which in turn lead to changes in income. Users of this framework are thus deeply concerned about the level and stability of interest rates. High and rising interest rates are taken as an indication that investment outlays and thus national income will fall. In the monetarist framework, the dollar value of national income is a direct function of the change in the money supply. Interest rates are determined by the level of real output, not output by the interest rate. The monetarist is therefore less concerned about the behavior of interest rates. While changes in rates may have an effect on financial institutions, they need not directly affect the aggregate level of income.

The monetarist and income-expenditure approaches also have elements in common. Both analyze short-term adjustments in terms of shifts from one static equilibrium position to another, both implicitly consider the equilibrium position of the economy to be characterized by stable prices and output, and both consider changes in government spending and in the money supply as exogenous forces that will lead to a change in national income. Monetarists, however, believe that changes in the money supply are more important, while followers of the income-expenditure approach tend to believe that changes in government spending are more important.

The slope and position of the functions that characterize the relationships between the exogenous and endogenous variables are also important to both frameworks. For example, if the IS schedule is steep, the Keynesians believe that an increase in the money supply will affect interest rates more than national income; if it is flat, they believe the reverse to be true. The monetarists believe that if the economy is operating close to capacity, demand pressure will be high; and an increase in the money supply will lead to a rise in prices. If it is not, they will expect the increase in the money supply to lead to an increase in real output.

Both these positions have been carefully developed, and both are useful guides for financial managers who need to assess the impact of a change in government policy on the parameters that affect the firm.

Questions for discussion and problems

1. Why are the financial decisions of the firm affected by changes in macroeconomic variables?
2. Why is the distinction between endogenous and exogenous variables an important one for students of the economic system?
3. What are the most important exogenous variables to a monetarist?

4. What endogenous variables are explained by the monetarist economic model?

5. What role does demand pressure play in the monetarist framework?

6. How does an increase in the money supply lead to a rise in interest rates in the monetarist framework?

7. What factors determine the growth of real output in the long run in the monetarist framework?

8. Why are the consumption function and the investment function important in the income-expenditure framework?

9. What effect do changes in the level of investment outlays have on total spending in the income-expenditure framework?

10. What relationships are described by an *IS* schedule? by an *LM* schedule? by both schedules together?

11. What is the effect of an increase in the stock of money on interest rates in the monetarist framework? in the income-expenditure framework?

[*Answers to problems 12–15 follow references and suggested readings.*]

12. In the monetarist framework, what is the effect of:
   (a) an increase in the money supply on the dollar value of national income?
   (b) an increase in potential output on demand pressure?
   (c) a steady decline in prices on anticipated prices?
   (d) an increase in demand pressure on prices?
   (e) an increase in prices on real output when no change occurs in the dollar value of national income?
   (f) an increase in real income on the GNP gap?
   (g) a rise in the GNP gap on employment?
   (h) an increase in the money supply on interest rates?

13. Take another look at Figure 21.2.
   (a) If the economy is operating close to full employment, what is the shape of the function linking changes in the money supply to changes in real output?
   (b) If the economy is operating at close to full employment, what is the shape of the function linking changes in the money supply to changes in the price level?
   (c) Under what conditions will the function linking changes in prices to the change in income be a 45-degree line?
   (d) Under what conditions will the function linking changes in prices to changes in income be nearly vertical?

14. Consider the model $Y = C + I$, $C = 50 + .6Y$.
   (a) What is the value of C and Y when $I = 10$?
   (b) What is the value of C and Y when $I = 12$?

15. In the income-expenditure model, what is the effect on both national income and the interest rates of:
    (a) an increase in the money supply?
    (b) an upward shift in the consumption function?
    (c) an upward shift in the investment function?

REFERENCES AND SUGGESTED READINGS

Articles

Anderson, L. C., and Jordan, J. L., "Monetary and Fiscal Actions: A Test of Their Relative Importance in Economic Stabilization," *Federal Reserve Bank of St. Louis Review*, vol. L (November 1968), pp. 11–24.

Brainard, W. C., and Tobin, James, "Pitfalls in Financial Model Building," *American Economic Review*, vol. LVIII (May 1968), pp. 99–122.

Breen, William, "An Exploratory Econometric Model of Financial Markets," *Journal of Financial and Quantitative Analysis*, vol. IV (September 1969), pp. 233–70.

Brunner, Karl, "A Schema for the Supply of Money," *International Economic Review*, vol. II (1962), pp. 79–109.

Brunner, Karl, and Meltzer, Allan H., "Predicting Velocity," *Journal of Finance*, vol. XVIII (May 1963), pp. 319–34.

de Leeuw, F., and Gramlich, E., "The Federal Reserve-M.I.T. Econometric Model," *Federal Reserve Bulletin*, vol. LIV (January 1968), pp. 11–40.

Duesenbury, James S., "Tactics and Targets of Monetary Policy," in *Controlling Monetary Aggregates* (Boston, Mass.: Federal Reserve Bank of Boston, 1969), pp. 105–26.

Fand, David I., "A Monetarist Model of the Monetary Process," *Journal of Finance*, vol. XXV (May 1970), pp. 275–89.

Friedman, Milton, "A Theoretical Framework for Monetary Analysis," *Journal of Political Economy*, vol. LXXVIII (March–April 1970), pp. 193–238.

Guttentag, J. M., "The Strategy of Open Market Operations," *Quarterly Journal of Economics*, vol. LXXX (February 1966), pp. 5–38.

Hicks, J. R., "Mr. Keynes and the Classics: A Suggested Interpretation," *Econometrica*, vol. V (April 1937), pp. 147–159.

Levhari, D., and Patinkin, D., "The Role of Money in a Simple Growth Model," *American Economic Review*, vol. LVIII (September 1968), pp. 713–53.

Mundell, Robert A., "A Fallacy in the Interpretation of Macroeconomic Equilibrium," *Journal of Political Economy*, vol. LXXIII (February 1965), pp. 61–66.

Phillips, A. W., "The Relation Between Unemployment and the Rate of Change of Money Wage Rates in the United Kingdom, 1861–1957," *Economica* (November 1958), pp. 283–99.

Raasche, R., and Shapiro, H., "The FRB-MIT Model: Its Special Features," *American Economic Review*, vol. LVIII (May 1968), pp. 123–49.

Samuelson, Paul A., "The Role of Money in National Economic Policy," in *Controlling Monetary Aggregates* (Boston, Mass.: Federal Reserve Bank of Boston, 1969), pp. 7–15.

Smith, Warren L., "A Neo-Keynesian View of Monetary Policy," in *Controlling*

Monetary Aggregates (Boston, Mass.: Federal Reserve Bank of Boston, 1969), pp. 105–26.

Solow, R. M., "A Contribution to the Theory of Economic Growth," *Quarterly Journal of Economics,* vol. LXX (February 1956), pp. 65–94.

Teigen, Ronald, "Demand-Supply Functions for Money in the United States: Some Structural Estimates," *Econometrica,* vol. XXXII (1964), pp. 476–509.

Books

Bailey, Martin J., *National Income and the Price Level* (New York: McGraw-Hill, 1962).

Council of Economic Advisors, *The American Economy in 1961: Problems and Policies* (Washington, D. C.: Government Printing Office, 1961).

Fisher, Irving, *The Purchasing Power of Money* (New York: Macmillan, 1911).

Friedman, Milton, *The Optimum Quantity of Money and Other Essays* (Chicago: Aldine Press, 1969).

Friedman, Milton, ed., *Studies in the Quantity Theory of Money* (Chicago, Ill.: Univ. of Chicago Press, 1958).

Friedman, Milton, and Schwartz, Anna, *A Monetary History of the United States, 1867–1960* (Princeton, N. J.: Princeton Univ. Press, 1963).

Heller, W. W., *New Dimensions of Political Economy* (New York: Norton, 1966).

Heller, W. W., ed., *Perspectives on Economic Growth* (New York: Random House, 1968).

Keynes, John Maynard, *The General Theory of Employment, Interest, and Money* (New York: Harcourt Brace Jovanovich, 1936).

Mints, L. W., *History of Banking Theory* (Chicago: Univ. of Chicago Press, 1945).

Weintraub, Robert E., *Introduction to Monetary Economics* (New York: Ronald Press, 1970).

ANSWERS TO PROBLEMS 12–15

12. (a) A rise in national income.
    (b) A fall in demand pressure.
    (c) A fall in anticipated prices.
    (d) A rise in prices.
    (e) A fall in real output.
    (f) A fall in the GNP gap.
    (g) A fall in employment.
    (h) An initial drop in rates, followed by a rise in rates.

13. (a) It is more vertical.
    (b) It more nearly approaches the 45-degree line.
    (c) When a change in the money supply does not lead to a rise in output.
    (d) When there is substantial unemployment and changes in national income are almost fully matched by changes in real output.

14. (a) $Y = 150$; $C = 140$.
    (b) $Y = 155$; $C = 143$.

15. (a) The *LM* schedule shifts to the right, leading to a rise in national income and a fall in interest rates.
    (b) The *IS* schedule shifts to the right, leading to a rise in national income and a rise in interest rates.
    (c) The *IS* schedule again shifts to the right.

Money mechanics

22

The process linking a change in the money supply to national income, prices, and interest rates was described in the last chapter; however, the relationships that bring about a change in the money supply itself were not discussed. In this chapter, we shall see how the Federal Reserve Banks, which are an arm of the government, play a strategic role in the expansion and contraction of the money supply. Indeed, most monetarists would contend that the Federal Reserve has enormous power and that the actions it takes or fails to take significantly influence the dollar value of national income.

The dollar value of national income, as we saw in Chapter 21, is equal to the product of the country's real output (Y) multiplied by the price level (P). Thus,

$$\text{National income} = PY$$

If real output grows at 4 percent per annum and the price level also rises 4 percent, the money value of national income will increase by slightly more than 8 percent per annum.

The dollar value of national income is also equal to the product of the total dollars available (M) multiplied by the number of times each dollar is spent (V). Thus,

$$\text{National income} = MV$$

If the Federal Reserve allows the money supply to grow at a rate of 8 percent per annum and the rate at which the community spends money remains constant, national income will rise 8 percent per annum.

The dollar value of national income can therefore be defined in two ways: (1) as the product of real income times the price level and (2) as the product of the money supply times the rate at which dollars are spent. Thus,

$$\text{National income} = MV = PY$$

This view of the economic process implies that if the Federal Reserve can keep the rate of growth of the money supply equal to the rate of growth of real output, the price level is likely to remain stable. For this statement to be strictly true, of course, V must remain constant. On the other hand, if the Federal Reserve lets the money supply expand at a faster or slower rate than real income, the price level is likely to rise or fall.

How does the Federal Reserve work? How can the actions of any arm of the government influence the money supply to such an extent? Before these questions can be answered, we must resolve a more basic problem, that of defining what money itself is.

The components of the money supply

What are the components of a nation's money supply?

If money is defined as the community's store of liquid wealth, the money supply consists of a broad group of assets: currency, coin, demand and time deposits at commercial banks, savings accounts at savings and loan associations, short-term U. S. Treasury securities, perhaps stocks and bonds, and even life-insurance-policy reserves. This broad definition, encompassing a variety of financial instruments, is useful for some purposes. For example, empirical studies of the consumption function in which liquid assets were first excluded from consideration and then included as an independent variable have consistently found that changes in the level of liquid assets explain some of the variations in consumption outlays.

A second and widely used definition of money is as a medium of exchange. According to this definition, the components of the money supply are currency, coin, and demand deposits—only a few of the assets that can serve as a store of liquid wealth.

The distinction between the first and second definition of money is clear. Suppose an individual holds some of his savings in the form of securities that are traded on the New York Stock Exchange. Before he can spend these savings to buy, say, an automobile, he must first convert them into a medium of exchange. He must sell the securities and deposit the funds he receives in his checking account before he can begin to pay for the car.

When money is defined as a medium of exchange, a distinction must also be drawn between money and credit. Purchases can, of course, be made on credit. However, the debt that a buyer incurs by making a credit purchase must ultimately be repaid. The only instruments that lenders will accept in repayment of debt are the three assets which constitute a medium of exchange: currency, coin, and demand deposits.

The Federal Reserve uses the medium-of-exchange definition of money. It regularly publishes statistics on the money supply and related data, such as those in Table 22.1. These data show that, at the end of 1969,

TABLE 22.1

Money Supply and Related Data

(in billions of dollars)

Date	Money Supply			Time Deposits
	Total	Currency Component	Demand-Deposit Component	
December 1966	170.4	38.3	132.1	158.5
December 1967	181.7	40.4	141.3	183.7
December 1968	194.8	43.4	151.4	204.9
December 1969	199.6	46.1	153.7	194.1

SOURCE: *Federal Reserve Bulletin* (March 1970), p. A17.

the value of demand deposits in commercial banks exceeded $150 billion. This was about three and one-third times the value of the outstanding currency and coin. The volume of outstanding time deposits at the end of 1969, however, was approximately 25 percent greater than the volume of demand deposits.

A third definition of money is not based on any of its functions, but rather on its ability to forecast national income. Consider the theoretical relationship that was described in the opening paragraphs of this chapter: A change in the money value of national income is a function of a change in the money supply. The definition of the money supply is not specified in this relationship. As a result, statisticians testing this functional relationship can use different definitions of the money supply; they can alternately include or exclude different components in constructing the independent variable M_s. The particular set of components that contributes the most toward explaining variations in national income can then be defined as "money."

Statistical studies of this kind have been made, and they indicate that the definition of money which yields the best results over a long period of time includes the following components: currency, coin, demand deposits, and time deposits at commercial banks. Many economists therefore define the money supply of a country as the *sum* of these components.

To summarize, money can be defined in a number of ways: as liquid assets, as a medium of exchange, or as a variable with certain desirable statistical properties. In all three definitions, the money supply is intimately linked to the amount of deposits in commercial banks. As these deposits increase, the money supply rises; and as they contract, the money supply contracts. To explain how changes in the money supply come about, then, we must examine the activities of commercial banks in some detail.

Analyzing the money-creation process

The money supply of a country can be defined as the sum of the currency and coin in circulation and the volume of bank deposits. To understand how these deposits arise, suppose an individual living in an isolated community plans to open the first bank in the area. The first thing he does is sell $1,000 in equity to the community in exchange for cash. The balance sheet of the infant bank is then:

Balance Sheet of Newly Formed Bank			
Cash	$1,000	Equity	$1,000

A potential customer now approaches the banker and requests a $1,000 loan to build, say, a house. The bank, clearly, can grant the loan, since it has sufficient funds. The interest that the lender will pay on the borrowed funds will then be the bank's gross income. However, suppose that the banker, instead of giving the customer cash, explains to him the advantages of a checking account. For example, if he leaves the funds that are loaned to him on deposit, he can write checks for the precise amount of his expenditures. This will not only be convenient, but the cancelled checks that are returned to him will be a permanent record of each transaction. As long as the funds are on deposit, the borrower need have no fear of theft. Moreover, whenever he needs some ready spending money, he can always withdraw the amount he needs in the form of currency and coin. If the borrower recognizes the validity of these arguments and agrees to open the account, the balance sheet of the bank will become:

Balance Sheet After Granting First Loan			
Cash	$1,000	Equity	$1,000
Loan to builder	1,000	Builder's deposit account	1,000

As the home-builder purchases labor and materials, he pays with checks, and as the checks are presented for payment, the banker persuades each vendor to open an account at the bank. If a plumber receives a $250 payment from the builder and deposits the check in the bank, the balance sheet of the bank will be:

Balance Sheet After Opening Second Account

Cash	$1,000	Equity	$1,000
Loan to builder	1,000	Builder's deposit account	750
		Plumber's deposit account	250

A second borrower now approaches the bank for a loan. This potential borrower is a businessman who wants to borrow $1,000 to build up his inventory. Can the bank make the loan to him?

If the bank grants the loan, its income will rise, for it will receive interest on $2,000 in loans rather than on only $1,000. On the other hand, there is some risk attached to the transaction. If the bank makes the loan and all the deposits are withdrawn, its cash position will fall to zero. Then, if either the plumber or the builder decides to make a cash withdrawal as well, the bank will fail.

Let us assume that the banker is prepared to assume some risk to raise his income and grants the businessman's request for funds. However, he persuades him to hold a deposit, rather than cash. The balance sheet of the bank now reads:

Balance Sheet After Granting Second Loan

Cash	$1,000	Equity	$1,000
Loan to builder	1,000	Builder's deposit account	750
Loan to businessman	1,000	Plumber's deposit account	250
		Businessman's deposit account	1,000

Two questions now arise. First, how long can this process continue? How many loans can the bank extend? Second, as the bank expands its deposits, what happens to the money supply in the community?

The answer to both questions is straightforward. The bank can continue to expand its loans until the probability of cash withdrawals reaches the point where, in the opinion of the banker, it jeopardizes the safety of the institution. If the banker believes that the appropriate ratio of cash to deposits is 20 percent, then the $1,000 in cash that the bank has can support $5,000 in deposits. If he believes that the appropriate ratio is 10 percent, the $1,000 can support $10,000 in deposits. Once deposits have expanded to this level, the banker will refuse to grant additional credit.

The impact of the banker's loans will be felt throughout the community. More precisely, the national income of this isolated community will rise. This is because before the bank opened, the community's money supply consisted only of the currency and coin that the people held. As a result of the loans, deposits were created, increasing the money supply sharply. The rise in the money supply in turn will lead to a rise in the price level a rise in the level of output, or to some combination of the two.

A multibank economy

The actions of a single bank in an isolated community were described above. In practice, communities have more than one bank. Does the presence of other banks alter the major conclusion reached above, that the banking system can create money by extending credit?

To understand how the presence of one bank influences the actions of another, consider an economy in which there are two banks, A and B. Both banks have $100 in equity and $100 in cash, and their balance sheets are:

A				B			
Cash	$100	Equity	$100	Cash	$100	Equity	$100

Suppose a borrower comes to bank A for a $100 loan. Banker A must now consider the real possibility that if he extends the credit and gives the borrower a deposit account, the checks that are drawn on that account will be deposited in the bank B. Despite this possibility, he makes the loan. The balance sheets of the two banks are then:

A				B			
Cash	$100	Equity	$100	Cash	$100	Equity	$100
Loan	100	Deposit account	100				

Suppose that the worst does happen: The borrower writes a check and it is deposited in bank B. B sends the check to A for collection. A debits the depositor's account and sends the cash to B. The two balance sheets will now be:

A				B			
Loan	$100	Equity	$100	Cash	$200	Equity	$100
						Deposit account	100

Bank A cannot grant any further loans. Bank B, however, is highly liquid. If it estimates that it must maintain a maximum of 20 percent in cash for every dollar in a deposit account, it need hold only $20 in reserve. Since its cash position is $200, it can loan up to $180 to customers. Suppose B loans the entire $180 to its next customer. The balance sheet of the two banks then will be:

A				B			
Loan	$100	Equity	$100	Cash	$200	Equity	$100
				Loan	180	Deposit account	100
						Deposit account	180

If a check is written for the entire amount of this $180 deposit and placed in bank A, B will no longer be able to extend credit. Bank A's cash position, however, will rise to $180. If it also decides to hold 20 percent of its deposits in reserves ($36), it will have $144 dollars in excess reserves that it can use to make loans. Thus:

A			
Required reserves	$ 36	Equity	$100
Excess reserves	144	Deposit account	180
Total cash holdings	$180		
Loans	100		

B			
Required reserves	$ 20	Equity	$100
Excess reserves	0	Deposit account	100
Total cash holdings	$ 20		
Loans	180		

This process can now be repeated. If A extends a loan of $144 and the proceeds of that loan are eventually deposited in B, the balance sheet of the two banks will be:

A			
Required reserves	$ 36	Equity	$100
Excess reserves	0	Deposit account	180
Total cash holdings	$ 36		
Loans	$100		
	144		
	$244		

Money mechanics

B			
Required reserves	$ 48.80	Equity	$100
Excess reserves	115.20	Deposit account	100
Total cash holdings	$164	Deposit account	144
Loans	$180		

Thus after only three loans, the deposits of the two banks combined equals $424. Moreover, although bank A cannot make any more loans, bank B is in a position to loan an additional $115.20, which will lead to a further deposit expansion. The most important aspect of the process just described is that while each bank loaned only a portion of the funds that were deposited with it (or that it had in equity), the actions of the two banks taken together led to a rise in the total deposits of the community.

How long can this process of deposit creation last? How large will the total volume of deposits eventually be? Since the banks hold only 20 percent of their deposits in reserves, and since the cash reserves of the banking system are $200, the system can create $1,000 in deposits.

To summarize, a nation's banking system is a ready-made engine for creating money. Two things influence the maximum amount of money that the system as a whole can create: the amount of cash holdings, or reserves, that are available to it and the amount of required reserves that banks must hold. Thus, the potential size of the money supply can be found by solving the equation:

$$\text{Money supply} = \frac{\text{reserves}}{\text{required reserve ratio}} + \text{currency}$$

When reserves are fed into the banking system, a rise in deposits usually results. A banker's principal source of income is the revenue he receives from loans and investments. In the process of making these investments, however, deposits will be created.

The fact that the banking system can create money—and thus influence gross national product— raises a number of important policy questions. What instruments does the government have to control the behavior of banks? What is the relationship between the government's fiscal policy (its policy with respect to spending and taxing) and its monetary policy (its actions with respect to the money supply)?

Changes in the money supply will also influence interest rates. The effects of these changes are pervasive: A reduction in interest rates means that every stream of revenue generated by every asset will be valued at a higher rate than it would be otherwise, and the wealth position of individuals will improve. Similarly, a rise in interest rates means that the wealth position of individuals will fall. If assets that were purchased during a period when interest rates were low are sold during a period when they are high, capital losses will be sustained. If interest rates rise sharply over a short period, any institution holding a substantial amount of fixed-earning assets will sustain major capital losses. These losses may be large enough to wipe out the company's entire equity if its assets were revalued to reflect their market value.

The federal reserve system

One of the problems which plagued the American commercial-banking system from its inception was that the demand for credit differed in various parts of the country during the year. Banks in rural areas were confronted with a heavy demand for credit during the spring months as farmers tried to purchase fertilizer, equipment, and livestock. During the fall and winter, the rural banks encountered only a limited demand for credit, while banks in industrial areas were hard-pressed to meet the heavy demands for credit from retailers. The question therefore arose: How could banks borrow funds when they needed additional credit, and how could they invest their surplus funds when they had more than enough deposits than to meet the demand for loans?

To meet this problem, banks in rural areas developed relationships with banks in such major money-market centers as New York and Chicago. The money-market banks solicited the excess reserves of the rural banks when the latter had excess funds and invested them in highly liquid short-term instruments. Moreover, since the big-city banks pooled the funds from banks throughout the nation, they were in a position to sell credit to the rural banks during the critical months when their loan demand was at a peak.

From time to time, however, the system broke down. If the money-market banks faced a high demand for credit from their own commercial customers, they would not advance as much credit to the rural banks as they wanted. Moreover, whenever the total reserves available to the banking system contracted because people chose to increase the amount of currency and coin that they held, the money-market banks came under severe pressure to liquidate their loan portfolios rather than expand them.

During the recession of 1907, the problem of establishing an institution that could accommodate the disparate credit needs of banks came to a head. A plan was then proposed to establish "a banker's bank." Essentially, the plan was as follows:

(1) Commercial banks that affiliated with the institution, or became member banks, would hold their reserves in the form of deposits at the banker's bank.

(2) These deposits would constitute a pool, and the member commercial banks would be able to borrow funds from this pool as they needed them.

(3) The banker's bank would set from time to time the amount of deposits, or the reserve, that the affiliated commercial banks must maintain with it.

(4) The banker's bank could not make regular commercial loans. Rather, the assets it could hold would be limited to loans to affiliated banks and government bonds.

(5) In addition to holding the reserves of member banks, the banker's bank would also hold the working balances of the U. S. Treasury. The Treasury would use the bank in much the same way an individual uses an ordinary commercial bank.

(6) Finally, the banker's bank would be empowered to issue currency, and this currency would become the circulating medium of exchange of the country. Any member bank that needed currency to meet its customer's demands could buy the currency by drawing down its balances at the bank.

In 1914, twelve such banker's banks were formed, and we know them today as the Federal Reserve Banks. They are located in Boston, New York, Philadelphia, Cleveland, Richmond, Atlanta, Chicago, St. Louis, Minneapolis, Kansas City, Dallas, and San Francisco. The major activities of these banks are coordinated by a Board of Governors, appointed by the President of the United States. The Board submits its annual report, however, to Congress. The twelve Federal Reserve Banks, the Board of Governors, and the member commercial banks are known collectively as the Federal Reserve System.

The Federal Reserve Banks almost immediately became much more important as financial institutions than their founders had imagined they would be. It soon became evident that they could, virtually at will, make substantial changes in the nation's money supply. The Federal Reserve does this by altering the reserve base and by changing the required-reserve ratio. The two most important ways of altering the reserve base are through (1) open-market operations, i.e., the purchase and sale of government bonds and (2) loaning funds to commercial banks, i.e., discounting the securities that commercial banks hold.

To see how the Federal Reserve System operates, we shall examine in some detail the impact on bank reserves and the money supply when:

(1) a bank borrows money from the Federal Reserve,

(2) the Federal Reserve purchases bonds,

(3) the U. S. Treasury make disbursements,

(4) the public changes its holdings of cash,

(5) gold flows into the country, and

(6) reserve requirements change.

We shall assume that the initial condition of the Federal Reserve Banks and the commercial-banking system as a whole is as indicated by the balance sheets below:

Original Position
Federal Reserve Banks

Bonds	$150	Member-bank reserves	$100
		U. S. Treasury deposit	50

Commercial-Banking System

Reserves	$100	Equity	$100
Loans	300	Deposits	500
Bonds	200		

A BANK BORROWS FROM THE FEDERAL RESERVE

Say that a member bank borrows $10 from the Federal Reserve (i.e., from its district Federal Reserve Bank). When the Federal Reserve extends the loan, it credits the member bank's reserves, just as an individual's deposit is credited when he borrows from a commercial bank. The immediate effect of this loan is to raise excess reserves throughout the system by $10.

Balance Sheets Showing the Effect of Bank Borrowings
Federal Reserve Banks

Bonds	$150	Member-bank reserves	$110
Loans and discounts	10	U. S. Treasury deposit	50

Commercial-Banking System

Required reserves	$100	Equity	$100
Excess reserves	10	Deposits	500
Total reserves	$110	Borrowings from Federal Reserve	10
Loans	300		
Bonds	200		

The reserves that the borrowing bank receives will be quickly disseminated throughout the banking system as the borrowing bank makes loans to its customers and as checks are drawn against their accounts and deposited in other banks. If the commercial-banking system has a 20-percent reserve requirement, the $10 increment in reserves will result in a $50 expansion in deposits. When commercial banks repay their borrowings from the Federal Reserve, member-bank reserves will fall and the money supply will contract.

A FEDERAL RESERVE PURCHASE OF GOVERNMENT BONDS

Assume that the Federal Reserve purchases a government bond for $10 from a commercial bank. It will pay for the bond by crediting the reserve position of the selling bank. The effect of this purchase will be a change in the original balances of the Federal Reserve and the commercial-banking system as follows:

Balance Sheets Showing the Effect
of Federal Reserve Purchase of Bonds
Federal Reserve Banks

Bonds	$160	Member-bank reserves	$110
		U. S. Treasury deposit	50

Commercial-Banking System

Required reserves	$100	Equity	$100
Excess reserves	10	Deposits	500
Total reserves	$110		
Loans	300		
Investments	190		

The commercial-banking system now holds excess reserves. In an effort to raise their profits, banks will increase their loans and purchase other investments, thereby raising the level of demand deposits. The purchase of bonds by the Federal Reserve therefore leads to an increase in bank reserves and to an increase in bank deposits. Similarly, the sale of bonds by the Federal Reserve leads to a contraction of reserves and to a contraction of the money supply.

A DISBURSEMENT BY THE U. S. TREASURY

Assume that the U. S. Treasury makes a social-security payment to a retired worker of $10. The recipient will deposit the check in his commercial bank, and the bank will send the check to the Federal Reserve for collection.

Balance Sheets Showing the Effect
of a U. S. Treasury Disbursement
Federal Reserve Banks

Bonds	$150	Member-bank reserves	$110
		U. S. Treasury deposit	40

Commercial-Banking System

Required reserves	$102	Equity	$100
Excess reserves	8	Deposits	510
Total reserves	$110		
Loans	300		
Investment	200		

The commercial banking system now holds $8 in excess reserves. To increase their interest income, member banks will extend credit and ultimately raise deposits to $550.

A reduction of Treasury deposits at the Federal Reserve thus leads to an expansion of bank deposits; an increase in Treasury deposits (which could occur when people pay their tax bills) will lead to a contraction of member-bank reserves and to a reduction of the money supply.

A CHANGE IN THE PUBLIC'S HOLDINGS OF CURRENCY

Say that a depositor of a commercial bank decides to increase his holdings of currency by $10. A commercial bank can accommodate the depositor's request for currency by buying $10 in Federal Reserve notes from the Federal Reserve Bank. The commercial bank will pay for the $10 note by drawing down its reserve account by $10. As a result of the $10 reduction in reserves, the commercial-banking system incurs a deficit in its reserve position.

Balance Sheets Showing the Effect of a Cash Withdrawal
Federal Reserve Banks

Bonds	$150	Member-bank reserves	$ 90
		U. S. Treasury deposit	50
		Federal Reserve notes	
		outstanding	10

Commercial-Banking System

Required reserves	$ 98	Equity	$100
Reserve deficiency	8	Deposits	490
Total reserves	$ 90		
Loans	300		
Investments	200		

The reserve deficiency must, of course, be eliminated, for the banks are violating the law. They will correct it by calling in loans and investments until deposits are reduced to $450.

When the public increases its holdings of currency and coin, bank reserves are reduced, and demand deposits will contract. When the public lowers its holdings of currency and coin and deposits the funds in commercial banks, reserves are raised and the money supply will expand.

A CHANGE IN GOLD FLOWS

Suppose an exporter of goods and services receives gold from a foreign buyer in payment for a shipment. The exporter will sell the gold to the U.S. Treasury and receive a check drawn on the Treasury's account at the Federal Reserve. When he deposits the check in his commercial bank and it is sent to the Federal Reserve for payment, the Federal Reserve will credit the commercial bank's reserve account and debit the Treasury's balance. Member bank reserves will rise, and demand deposits can increase.

A CHANGE IN RESERVE REQUIREMENTS

Assume that the Federal Reserve changes the reserve requirement from 20 percent of all deposits to 25 percent. Since no change occurred in the total dollar amount of reserves available, the commercial-banking system will still hold $100 in reserves, its original position. These reserves, however, can now support only $400 in deposits, not $500. The commercial-banking system must reduce is outstanding loans and investments to that level.

An increase in bank reserve requirements will therefore lead to a contraction in the money supply; a reduction in required reserves will lead to an expansion of bank assets, bank deposits, and the money supply.

The minimum amount of reserves that a commercial bank which is a member of the Federal Reserve System must hold is set by the Board of Governors. The Board distinguishes between different kinds of banks (depending on their location) and between different kinds of deposits (time and demand). Banks located in "Reserve" cities (the largest cities in the country) are required to hold reserves equal to $17\frac{1}{2}$ percent of their demand deposits. Banks in all other cities are called country banks. Country banks with under $5 million in deposits need hold only 12½ percent of their deposits in reserves; all others must hold 13 percent. The reserve requirement for savings deposits in all banks is 3 percent.

The effect of these different required-reserve ratios is to increase the lending capacity of the banking system as a whole when deposits are shifted from demand to time or savings accounts, as long as the total reserves do not decrease. Similarly, as deposits shift from major cities to suburban areas, the lending capacity of the banking system will rise.

To summarize, the sample transactions traced above show that bank reserves can be raised or lowered in several ways. This does not mean, however, that the Federal Reserve cannot control the total amount of bank reserves in the system, and through this, the total stock of money in the nation. Rather, through its control over the purchase and sale of government bonds, and to a lesser extent, through its control over the extension of credit to member banks, the Federal Reserve can determine the level of bank reserves very precisely.

The relative contribution of different factors to the monetary base that lies behind the money supply—deposits plus currency—is indicated in Table 22.1. Note that while the base was $76.6 billion in May of 1970, Federal Reserve holdings of government bonds accounted for over 75 percent of this figure. Changes in bond holdings are wholly within the control of the Federal Reserve authorities and can be used to offset the effect on reserves of changes in other factors.

TABLE 22.1
Calculation of the Monetary Base—May 1970
(in millions of dollars)

Source of Monetary Base		Uses of Monetary Base	
Federal Reserve credit		Member-bank deposits	
Holdings of securities	+57,265	at Federal Reserve	+18,300
Discounts & advances	+ 1,066	Currency held by banks	+ 4,805
Float	+ 2,985	Currency held by the public	+53,490
Gold stock	+11,367		
Treasury currency outstanding	+ 6,967		
Treasury deposits at			
Federal Reserve	− 1,440		
Treasury cash holdings	− 544		
Other deposits and other			
Federal Reserve accounts	− 1,071		
Monetary base	+76,595		+76,595

SOURCE: Board of Governors of the Federal Reserve System, *Federal Reserve Bulletin.* The sources and uses of the base are a rearrangement of data contained in the Tables A4 and A5 in the Financial and Business Statistics section of the July 1970 *Bulletin.*

Money mechanics

The effect of a change in government expenditures
on the money supply

The analysis of how bank reserves are affected by various transactions provides a vehicle for analyzing some of the possible outcomes of a change in government expenditures and receipts. The income-expenditure framework presented in Chapter 21 can be used to derive the following set of equations:

(22–1) $Y = C + I + G$
(22–2) $C = a + bY$
(22–3) $I =$ exogenous factors
(22–4) $G =$ exogenous factors

where Y is national income, C is consumption outlays, I is investment outlays, and G is government outlays.

Substituting equation 22–2 for C in equation 22–1, we have:

$$Y = \frac{a + I + G}{1 - b}$$

If we consider only the effect of a change in government spending, the resulting change in income will be:

(22–5) $$\Delta Y = \frac{1}{1 - b} \Delta G$$

Thus if $b = .8$ and government expenditures increase by \$2, equation 22–5 indicates that national income can be expected to rise by \$10.

How is such a change in national income to be financed? Will the \$10 increase in income arise through an increase in the money supply, through an increase in the rate at which money is spent, or through some combination of the two? Or will the \$10 change not occur at all? This could happen if the \$2 rise in government spending were offset by a \$2 fall in investment outlays or foreign expenditures.

To explore these various possibilities, suppose that the rise in government expenditures is financed through the sale of government bonds by the U. S. Treasury to the Federal Reserve. The immediate effect of this sale on the Federal Reserve's balance sheet will be to raise both its hold-

Balance Sheet of Federal Reserve

Bonds +	(1)	Member-bank reserves +	(2)
		U. S. Treasury deposit +	(1)
		U. S. Treasury deposit −	(2)

ings of bonds and the Treasury deposit (step 1). When the funds are spent by the Treasury (step 2), an increase in bank reserves will occur, which will lead to a rise in the money supply. If a government expenditure is financed through the sale of bonds to the Federal Reserve, it is reasonable, therefore, to expect that national income will rise.

Now consider a second possibility; suppose that the rise in government outlays is financed through the sale of bonds to an individual who pays for the bonds with a check drawn on his bank deposit.

Federal Reserve

	Member-bank reserves −	(1)
	Member-bank reserves +	(2)
	U. S. Treasury deposit +	(1)
	U. S. Treasury deposit −	(2)

Commercial Banking System

Member-bank reserves −	(1)	Demand deposits −	(1)
Member-bank reserves +	(2)	Demand deposits +	(2)

Individual

Demand deposit −	(1)	
Government bond +	(1)	

The initial effect of the sale of bonds to an individual (step 1) will be to lower member-bank reserves and increase Treasury deposits. The sale of bonds to individuals, therefore, is deflationary. When the Treasury spends the money (step 2), bank reserves will rise.

If the increase in expenditures by the federal government exactly equals the revenues realized through the sale of bonds to individuals, no change will take place in bank reserves and the money supply will not expand. Under these conditions, it is possible that the added government expenditures will not lead to any increase in national income.

Suppose that bank reserves do not increase as a result of the government expenditures. National income could still rise if a change takes place in the rate at which the money supply is spent, i.e., if the velocity of money rises. Under what conditions will this occur?

A number of factors contribute to the velocity of money, or its reciprocal, the demand for money balances. First, velocity is sensitive to changes in income; as income rises, people prefer to hold larger money balances, for money is a superior good. Other things being equal, therefore, velocity will fall as income rises. Second, velocity is sensitive to the cost of holding money balances. This cost includes both the interest income forgone on the idle balance and any erosion of the value of the money that may be caused by inflation. The higher the interest rate, the less willing people will be to hold money balances, and the higher the velocity of money will be. Similarly, the faster prices are expected to rise, the more anxious people will be to draw down their money balances, and the higher the velocity of money will be. Whether the rise in government expenditures in our example will actually operate on income, interest rates, and prices so as to cause a rise in velocity, however, is debatable. Indeed, it is more likely that both prices and interest rates will rise faster when the money supply increases than when it remains constant. Thus a rise in government spending is more likely to cause an increase in velocity when it is accompanied by an increase in bank reserves.

To summarize, a rise in government spending may or may not lead to a rise in national income. What effect the added expenditure will have will depend on how it is financed. If the Federal Reserve does not permit government expenditures to raise reserves (if it takes an offsetting action, such as selling securities to banks) the added expenditures will not be inflationary. On the other hand, if the Federal Reserve stands by and lets the increase in expenditures cause a rise in bank reserves, the money supply will rise and demand pressure will build up. Under these conditions, it is likely that the government outlays will lead to a rise in national income.

An analysis of time-series data

The relationships that exist between the rate of change in the money supply, government spending, and national income can be traced empirically. In its monthly *Review,* the Federal Reserve Bank of St. Louis does just this. An excerpt from the April 1970 issue is presented below.

Excessive growth of total spending from 1964 to 1968, fostered by expansive monetary and fiscal actions, resulted in ever-mounting pressure on prices. The response of production to growth of demand for goods and services is limited by the productive capacity of the economy. Production can be expanded by employment of more resources, but as the economy approaches full employment, increasingly less efficient resources are employed, increases in production become more difficult and upward pressure on prices intensifies.

From 1964 to late 1968, total spending increased at an average 8 percent rate, while production capacity increased at about a 4 percent rate. During the early part of the period the economy had resources which could be tapped and consequently production could be increased to meet most of the sudden increase in demand, with little upward pressure on prices. As the unused resources were employed, however, growth of production was constrained and price increases accelerated. Prices rose at a 3 percent rate from 1965 to mid-1967, a 4 percent rate from mid-1967 through 1968, and a 5 percent rate in 1969.

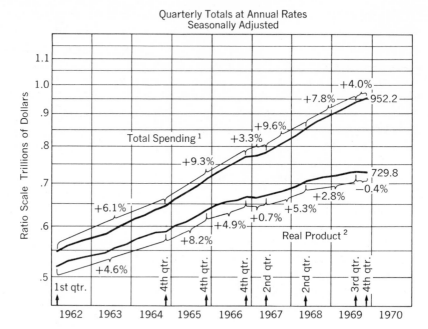

Quarterly Totals at Annual Rates
Seasonally Adjusted

¹ GNP in current dollars.
² GNP in 1958 dollars.

NOTE: Percentages are annual rates of change for periods indicated. Latest data plotted 4th quarter.

SOURCE: Federal Reserve Bank of St. Louis *Review* (April 1970), p. 3.

FIGURE 22.1

Demand and Production.

The accelerated growth of total spending was closely related to the rapid monetary expansion, which was apparently undertaken to counter the upward pressure on interest rates being generated by growing Federal government budget deficits and other large demands for credit. The stock of money in the economy was increased at a 5 percent average annual rate from 1964 to 1968, markedly faster than the 2 percent average rate of rise of money in the previous eight years. In the short run of a few months, increased monetary expansion did help to hold interest rates down by increasing the supply of loan funds. In the longer run, however, the faster rate of money growth stimulated total spending and price increases and thereby the demand for credit. The overall result was pronounced increases in interest rates.

The tax surcharge and the program of reduced Federal Government expenditure growth adopted in mid-1968 were designed to curb inflation but proved to have much less effect than had been intended. The growth of total spending was not slowed by the fiscal actions, and the rate of inflation continued to accelerate. The acceleration of price rises was fa-

492   Money mechanics

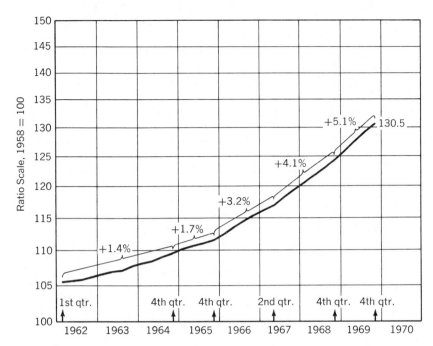

¹ As used in National Income Accounts

NOTE: Percentages are annual rates of change for periods indicated. Latest data plotted 4th quarter.

SOURCE: Federal Reserve Bank of St. Louis *Review* (April 1970), p. 4.

FIGURE 22.2

The General Price Index.¹

cilitated by stimulative monetary actions as the stock of money continued to grow at a 7 percent rate from June 1968 to January 1969, following a trend set in early 1967.

*   *   *

Monetary policy moved toward moderate restraint early in 1969, with money stock growth at a reduced 4 percent annual rate from January to June. Monetary influence became much more restrictive about mid-1969—the stock of money remained essentially unchanged through the last half of 1969. As yet, there has been no abatement of inflation, however, as the impact of the monetary restraint has fallen initially on real economic activity.

Once prices have risen in response to excess demand, actions taken to moderate total spending initially reduce production and have but a de-layed effect on prices. In the current situation, inflation was allowed to accelerate for four years before effective restraint was exercised. The longer inflation is allowed to continue, the more resistant it becomes to stabilization actions. Inflation becomes a major factor in expectations and planning, and is written into wages and other contracts, incorporated into interest rates, and considered in revenue forecasts of investors.

What is often called "cost-push" inflation in our economy today is more accurately the delayed effects of past excessive spending. For example the wage increases demanded by labor during recent years, cited as one of the primary factors in pushing up prices, actually reflect, in part, the increasing costs of living experienced in the past few years. Average hourly wages in manufacturing increased at a 6 percent annual rate during 1969 but, due to inflation, actual purchasing power of hourly wages was about unchanged. It is this experience which has caused labor to seek wage increases in excess of gains in productivity. These negotiated wage increases appear as increases in unit labor costs and consequently are assumed by some observers to be the cause of inflation. Unit labor costs in manufacturing have been increasing rapidly since mid-1965. However, these costs did not begin to rise sharply until more than a year after prices of industrial commodities began to increase. These "cost-push" factors are a part of the inflationary process and act to further inflation once it has begun. They are more a symptom of demand inflation than an independent influence.

The restrictive monetary action inaugurated early in 1969 and intensified at mid-year resulted in a slowdown of total spending late in the year. Total spending increased at a 4 percent annual rate from the third to the fourth quarter, down from an 8 percent rate of increase during the previous two years. The growth of total spending declined further in the first quarter of this year.

Virtually all of the recent moderation in total spending resulted in slowing of real product growth. Real output decreased slightly from the third to the fourth quarter and is expected to show a significant decline in the first quarter. Industrial production has decreased at a 5 percent annual rate since last July, compared with a 5.7 percent annual rate of increase over the previous two years.

Along with the moderation of production, growth of employment has declined. Payroll employment, which had expanded at a 3.4 percent annual rate from mid-1967 to mid-1969, increased at a 1.5 percent rate from June to October and since October it has increased at a 1.3 percent rate. Employment in manufacturing has declined sharply since last summer, and the average workweek of those employed has been reduced by almost one hour since late last year. Unemployment has risen since year-end, and reached 4.4 percent of the labor force in March, higher than the 3.7 percent average rate of the 1966–1969 period, but still well below the 5.5 percent average from 1961 to 1965.

Personal income grew at a 5.4 percent rate from August to February, after rising at a 9 percent rate in the previous year. Since the rate of increase of prices has not slowed, the reduced growth of income represents very little gain in purchasing power. Real personal income, which had increased at a 5 percent rate from late 1967 to the fall of last year, has since increased at about a 1 percent annual rate.

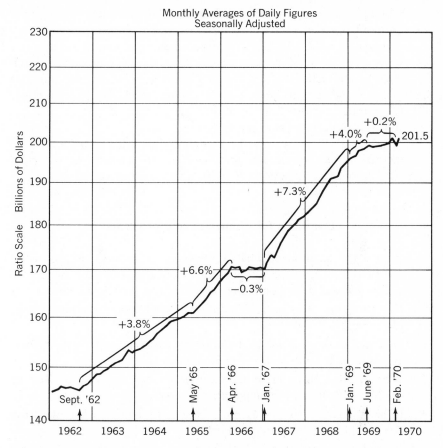

Monthly Averages of Daily Figures
Seasonally Adjusted

NOTE: Percentages are annual rates of change for periods indicated. Latest data plotted March 1970.

SOURCE: Federal Reserve Bank of St. Louis *Review* (April 1970), p. 5.

FIGURE 22.3
The Money Stock.

Summary

Large changes in the money supply can lead to changes in the money value of national income. While this statement is incontrovertible, there is some disagreement over how the money supply itself should be defined. All the definitions suggested, however, include currency, coin, and demand deposits of commercial banks. Some also include time deposits at commercial banks.

The banking system of the United States can create deposits. While no one bank can lend more than its excess reserves at any one time, the banking system as a whole can lend a multiple of the total reserves that are available to it.

A number of actions by the Treasury and the community at large can affect the level of total bank reserves. All these actions, however, can be offset by the actions of the Federal Reserve. Through the purchase and sale of bonds and through loans to commercial banks (discounting), the Federal Reserve can directly control the amount of reserves that are fed into the banking system at any time.

In recent years bank reserves have risen rapidly and the money supply has increased. As a result, the price level of the community has risen and the economy has experienced strong inflationary pressures.

Questions for discussion and problems

1. Why is the question of what components are included in the definition of the money supply significant? From the point of view of control, is a broad definition better or worse than a narrow one?

2. If a community had no required-reserve level, would the money supply expand indefinitely?

3. Why can a single bank in a multibank economy not create money, although all banks together can create money?

4. What are the three most important tools that the Federal Reserve has for controlling the amount of bank reserves?

5. If bank reserves rise as a result of a gold inflow, what offsetting action could the Federal Reserve take?

6. If the U. S. government collects more money in taxes than it spends, bank reserves will fall. What action could the Federal Reserve take to offset the actions of the Federal government?

7. Just because the Federal Reserve has the power to make the level of bank reserves any figure it wants, is it fair to blame them if money national income rises at an inflationary rate? Conversely, is it fair to blame the Federal Reserve if a drop in national income occurs?

   [*Answers to problems 8–11 follow references and suggested readings.*]

8. (a) If the banks of a community have $1,000 in reserves and are required to hold 20 percent in reserves, how large can the deposits in the community be?

   (b) If the reserve ratio falls to 10 percent, how large can the volume of deposits be?

   (c) If reserves rise to $2,000 and the reserve requirement is 10 percent, how large can the volume of deposits be?

9. A country's currency and coin can be used by banks as reserves. Sup-

pose that the required-reserve ratio is 10 percent, that banks hold $50 in reserves, and that $10 circulates as currency and coin. (a) What is the total money supply of the country? (b) During the summer months, many people go on vacation and withdraw money from the banking system, raising the currency and coin in circulation to $20. If nothing happens to replenish the lost reserves, what is the effect of the currency withdrawal on the money supply?

10. If the Federal Reserve wants to expand the money supply, should it
   (a) buy or sell government bonds?
   (b) raise or lower reserve requirements?
   (c) discount more bonds or fewer bonds?
   (d) encourage the Treasury to disburse funds faster or more slowly?
   (e) encourage people to hold more or less currency and coin?

11. What is the effect of a rise in government expenditures on bank reserves if the expenditures are financed entirely by
   (a) taxes?
   (b) printing new currency?
   (c) selling bonds to Federal Reserve Banks?

REFERENCES AND SUGGESTED READINGS

Articles

Ando, A., and Modigliani, Franco, "Velocity and the Investment Multiplier," *American Economic Review* (September 1965), pp. 693–728.

Chow, G., "On the Long Run and Short Run Demand Function for Money," *Journal of Political Economy* (April 1966), pp. 111–31.

Friedman, Milton, and Schwartz, Anna, "The Definition of Money: Net Wealth and Neutrality as Criteria," *Journal of Money, Credit and Banking,* vol. I (February 1969), pp. 1–14.

Goldfeld, S., and Kane, E., "The Determinants of Member Bank Borrowing," *Journal of Finance,* vol. XXI (September 1966), pp. 499–514.

Hester, Donald D., "Reflections on the Discount Window," *Journal of Money, Credit and Banking,* vol. XI (May 1970), pp. 151–58.

Johnson, Harry G., "Alternative Guiding Principles for the Use of Monetary Policy," *Essays in International Finance* (Princeton, N. J.: Princeton Univ. Press, November 1963), pp. 3–38.

Latane, H. A., "Income Velocity and Interest Rates—A Pragmatic Approach," *Review of Economics and Statistics,* vol. XLII (November 1960), pp. 445–49.

Meltzer, Allan H., "Public Policies as Causes of Fluctuations," *Journal of Money, Credit and Banking,* vol. II (February 1970), pp. 45–55.

Modigliani, Franco, Rasche, Robert, and Cooper, J. Philip, "Central Bank Policy, the Money Supply and the Short Term Rate of Interest," *Journal of Money, Credit and Banking,* vol. II (May 1970), pp. 166–218.

Polakoff, Murray, E., "Reluctance Elasticity, Least Cost, and Member Bank Borrowing: A Suggested Integration," *Journal of Finance,* vol. XV, no. 1 (1960), pp. 1–18.

Samuelson, Paul, "Reflections on Recent Federal Reserve Policy," *Journal of Money, Credit and Banking,* vol. II (February 1970), pp. 37–44.

Tobin, J., "A General Equilibrium Approach to Monetary Theory," *Journal of Money, Credit and Banking,* vol. I (February 1969), pp. 16–30.

————, "Towards Improving the Efficiency of the Monetary Mechanism," *Review of Economics and Statistics,* vol. XLII (August 1960), pp. 276–79.

Books

Anderson, Jay, *A Half Century of Federal Reserve Policymaking, 1914–1964,* (Federal Reserve Bank of Philadelphia, 1965).

Burgess, W. R., *The Reserve Banks and the Money Market* (New York: Harper, 1927).

Chandler, Lester, *Benjamin Strong, Central Banker* (Washington: Brookings Institute, 1958).

The Federal Reserve System After Fifty Years, vols. I and II, Hearings Before The Subcommittee on Domestic Finance of the Committee on Banking and Currency, House of Representatives, 88th Congress, 2nd Sess. (Washington, D. C.: Government Printing Office, 1964).

The Federal Reserve System: Purposes and Functions (Washington, D. C.: Board of Governors of the Federal Reserve System, 1963).

Friedman, Milton, and Schwartz, Anna, *A Monetary History of the United States, 1867–1960* (Princeton, N. J.: Princeton Univ. Press, 1963).

Goldfeld, S., *Commercial Bank Behavior and Economic Activity* (Amsterdam: North-Holland Publishing Co., 1966).

Gurley, J. G., and Shaw, E. S., *Money in a Theory of Finance* (Washington, D.C.: Brookings Institute, 1960).

Hardy, C. O., *Credit Policies of the Federal Reserve System* (Washington, D. C.: Brookings Institute, 1932).

Matthews, R. C. O., *The Business Cycle* (Chicago: Univ. of Chicago Press, 1959).

McKinney, G. W., *The Federal Reserve Discount Window: Administration in the Fifth District* (New Brunswick, N. J.: Rutgers Univ. Press, 1960).

Mints, Lloyd, *Monetary Policy for a Competitive Society* (New York: McGraw-Hill, 1950).

Patinkin, Don, *Money, Interest and Prices* (Evanston, Ill.: Row Peterson, 1956).

Riefler, Winfield, *Money Rates and Money Markets in the United States* (New York: Harper, 1930).

ANSWERS TO PROBLEMS 8–11

8. (a) $5,000
    (b) $10,000
    (c) $20,000
9. (a) The money supply is defined as deposits plus currency and coin. Since deposits are $500 and currency and coin are $10, the total stock of money is $510.
    (b) When currency and coin increase to $20, reserves fall from $50 to $40. The banking system will then have to contract the level of deposits to $400. The money supply will thus drop to $420.
10. (a) Buy.
    (b) Lower.
    (c) More.
    (d) Faster.
    (e) Less.
11. (a) There is no change.
    (b) Bank reserves will rise.
    (c) Bank reserves will rise.

The commercial bank in a
systems context

23

The last two chapters have stressed the important role of the commercial-banking system in our economy. We have seen how the banking system can create money and how, by changing the amount of reserves available to banks, the Federal Reserve can influence the level of national income, the price level, the interest rates that corporate borrowers must ultimately pay for borrowed funds, and other macroeconomic variables.

In this chapter, we shall adopt a different perspective. Here, we shall consider the individual commercial bank as a profit-maximizing institution. We shall deal with the following managerial and operating questions: To which potential borrowers should a bank lend money and to which should it refuse credit? How does an individual bank acquire the raw materials (i.e., deposits) that it needs to make loans? Can a bank borrow the funds that it needs to accommodate the loan demand of its customers? If it tries to borrow, what is likely to be the response of the Federal Reserve to its actions? The answers to these questions are important to a financial manager, for if a banking relationship is unprofitable or unsatisfactory to either the borrower or lender, it will soon be terminated.

The bank as a pool

To capture analytically the important characteristics of a commercial bank, imagine the following situation: Suppose a number of people are willing to pool their liquid resources in exchange for the right to withdraw an amount of money from the pool that is substantially greater than their original contribution to it. What considerations will guide the pool manager in determining which individuals or businesses should be allowed to join and which should be rejected?

One consideration is self-evident: The people or organizations who join should be able to repay the amount they borrow. The pool operator will want to take every reasonable precaution to ensure that they have this ability. For example, he may require collateral to be deposited with him when a withdrawal is made; he may insist that adequate financial records be maintained so that he can evaluate the borrower's financial status; and he may impose restrictions on the borrower's use of funds, on the sale of its assets, or on the amount of additional funds that can be acquired from other sources.

A second consideration is equally apparent and, for our purposes, more important. The pool operator must select the members so that not all of them will want to withdraw money from the pool simultaneously. An ideal pool, for example, would be one in which there were twelve members, each of whom deposited $100 dollars and only one of whom wanted the use of funds each month. Under these ideal conditions, each member could withdraw $1,200.

In practice, of course, it is unlikely that a pool operator could find such a perfect membership. It is much more likely that the members will deposit varying amounts of funds, that more than one member at a time will want to withdraw a multiple of what he deposited, and that the members will want to hold the funds for varying amounts of time.

The manager of a commercial bank is in much the same position as a pool operator. Many people are prepared to deposit their funds in a bank only if they are assured that when they need a loan, the bank will be able to accommodate them. Typically, no formal borrowing agreement is made when a customer first opens an account, and the banker is not obligated to honor every request made by his depositors. However, if a credit request is denied, the depositor is likely to withdraw his funds and join another, more accommodating pool—to close his account and open a new one at a competing bank.

Which customers, then, should a pool operator, or a bank, accept and grant loans to if it wishes to maximize its profits? To explore this question, assume that a pool operator is approached by ten people whose loan demand and potential deposit contribution to the pool are as shown in Table 23.1. This table is read as follows: Customer 1 wants a $100 loan for the next three periods. He can pay off half this loan in period 4 and will therefore want a $50 loan for periods 4, 5, and 6. At this time he will pay off the loan completely. Throughout the entire 7 periods, he will hold an average deposit of $25. Each of the borrowers is prepared to pay the rates indicated in Table 23.2 for the funds he wants to borrow.

Suppose, further, that if the pool operator accepts a deposit from the ith customer, his fixed costs for opening the account will be $1 and

The commercial bank in a systems context

TABLE 23.1
Loan Requirements for 7 Periods
and Expected Deposits by 10 Customers

Customer \ Period	1	2	3	4	5	6	7	Expected Deposits
1	$100	$100	$100	$50	$50	$50	0	$25
2	$100	0	0	$100	0	0	$100	$50
3	$50	$40	$30	$20	$10	0	0	$50
4	$400	$400	$400	$400	0	0	0	$50
5	0	$25	$50	$75	$100	$100	$100	$20
6	0	$50	$50	$50	0	0	0	$50
7	0	0	$10	$30	$40	$60	$90	$20
8	0	0	$30	$30	$30	0	0	$20
9	0	0	0	$100	$100	$100	$50	$20
10	0	0	0	0	$50	$50	$40	$50

his variable costs will be one half of 1 percent of the size of the deposit. Deposit costs, $_dC$, for the ith customer, then, are:

$$_dC_i = 1 + .005d_i$$

Let us assume that when the pool operator extends a loan his fixed costs for the loan are $4 and his variable costs are 4 percent of the size of the loan in the period in which it is made and 2 percent in each succeeding period. The cost of servicing the loan may be expected to be less than the cost of initiating it because a more intensive examination of the borrower's credit is made in the initial period than in subse-

TABLE 23.2
Interest Rates Customers
Are Prepared to Pay in
Each of the Next 7 Periods

Period	Rate	Period	Rate
1	.050	5	.060
2	.050	6	.060
3	.055	7	.060
4	.055		

quent periods. Loan costs for the ith customer, therefore, are:

$$_lC_i = 4 + .04a_{ij} + .02 \sum_{j=2}^{7} a_{ij}$$

where a is the amount of loan, i is the customer, and j is the period in which the loan is outstanding. The total costs associated with the ith customer are the sum of deposit costs and loan costs:

$$C_i = {}_dC_i + {}_lC_i$$

Suppose that the pool operator is, in fact, a bank. The profits, π, of the bank in any year will be the difference between the interest income it receives from its outstanding loans, rL, and the costs it incurs in servicing its customers, C. Which of the potential customers indicated in Table 23.1 should the bank accept to maximize its profits? How large will its total deposits be, and how much credit will it extend in each period?

Answers to these questions can be found by solving the following linear-programming problem:

$$\text{Maximize: } \sum_j (r_j L_j) - \sum_i C_i x_i$$

(1) $$\text{Subject to: } -\sum_i \sum_j a_{ij} x_i + L_j \leq 0$$

(2) $$0 \leq x_i \leq 1$$

(3) $$-\sum_i d_i x_i + M_j \leq 0$$

(4) $$-\sum_i \sum_j a_{ij} x_i + M_j - S_j \geq 0$$

(5) $$C_i = {}_dC_i + {}_lC_i$$

(6) $${}_dC_i = 1 + .005d_i$$

(7) $${}_lC_i = 4 + .04a_{ij} + .02 \sum_{j=2}^{7} a_{ij}$$

where L_j = the total amount loaned each period,
r_j = the rate of interest in the jth time period,
a_{ij} = the loan request of the ith customer in period j,
x_i = the percent of the ith customer loan and deposits accepted,
d_i = the deposit of the ith customer,
M_j = the total amount of deposits accepted in period j, and
S_j = the amount of cash that the bank keeps in its vault and does not loan out.

To see whether this particular problem has been captured by this formidable looking model, let us consider first the objective function and

The commercial bank in a systems context

then the constraints. The objective function states that the total profits of the banks are to be maximized. Profits are given by the difference between its total revenues (the interest rate it charges each period times the outstanding loan volume in each period) and the total costs associated with the customers it services. Actually, this model is a little unrealistic, since the bank can satisfy a fraction of the customer's needs without losing him completely. In practice, if a bank rejects a portion of a customer's request, i.e., if $x_i < 1$, it is likely to lose the account entirely, not just a portion of the customer's business.

The first constraint requires special attention because of the double-sigma sign. This notation means that in each period j the loan requests of the i potential borrowers are added together. Since the example has seven periods, seven summations must be performed to solve this problem. This constraint (or these seven constraints) defines the total volume of loans the bank makes each period, L_j. The total loans in period j will equal the sum of the loans that are extended to the i borrowers it chooses to serve in the period.

Since x_i is the percent of the ith customer's loan request that is honored and the percent of his deposit that is received, constraint 2 states that no customer can take on a negative value or be served more than once. The maximum amount that the bank can loan out in any period is limited by the amount of deposits it receives from each of its customers in each period. Note that in this model, the bank is not required to hold reserves against deposits. Including a more realistic reserve requirement of say, $17\frac{1}{2}$ percent, would not alter the basic structure of the problem. Constraint 4 states that the amount of loans granted in each period cannot exceed the amount of money that the bank has available to it. Constraint 5 identifies the total costs of servicing the ith customer as the sum of the deposit costs (6) and loan costs (7) associated with the ith customer.

If the bank uses the solution to this linear-programming problem as a guide, it will accept as customers applicants 1, 3, 6, 8 and 10 in full, but it will honor only 35 percent of 5's loan demands and only 31 percent of 2's requests. These customers will give the bank $237.65 in deposits. Its total profits will be $46.06, and it will allocate its funds over the next seven periods as in Table 23.3.

Customer 4 and customer 9 are rejected completely by the model. Had 4 been accepted, total profits would have fallen by $71.28, and had 9 been accepted, by $7.08, since the bank would then have had to reject other customers, whose requests for loans did not press against the constraint of available funds.

On the other hand if the bank had only one more dollar in deposits to loan out in period 3, its profits would have risen by 7.7 cents; if it had the dollar in period 4, its profits would have risen by 26.3 cents. An extra dollar in either of these periods would have enabled the bank

TABLE 23.3

The Period-by-Period Allocation
of Funds Recommended by
the Model

Period	Loans	Vault Cash
1	$181.17	$56.47
2	198.82	38.82
3	237.64	—
4	237.64	—
5	215.29	22.35
6	215.29	22.35
7	196.47	41.17

not only to make loans in that period, when it was short of funds, but to accommodate additional loan requests in other periods.

The implication of this example for commercial banking is twofold. First, the profitability of accepting a customer cannot be determined by evaluating the customer alone. The entire portfolio of opportunities before the bank must be considered in making the decision to accept or reject an account. Thus, a potential depositor may be a good customer to one bank and a poor one to another.

Second, the constraint that limits the ability of a bank to accept a customer is the amount of funds that it has to loan. Customers are prepared to contribute to the pool of deposits in a bank only as long as they can make withdrawals from the pool. If the bank cannot accommodate its customers' credit needs, they can be expected to take their business elsewhere.

In practice, of course, a bank can only estimate when a customer will ask for credit. To accommodate possible requests, therefore, it must keep a liquid reserve at all times. In the past many financial writers have argued that the reason a bank needs liquidity is to meet a potential deposit run-off, not as a reserve for potential loan expansion. It is true that if the customers of a bank draw down their deposits, the bank will have to liquidate its assets to meet the withdrawals. But when, and under what conditions, will a deposit run-off occur?

Bank deposits are now insured by the FDIC. Even if a bank fails, the first $20,000 of the deposit in any one account will be paid back by this government agency. In the 1950's and 1960's, there were some bank failures arising from embezzlement, fraud, and similar crimes. In none of these cases was there a massive panic and a sharp withdrawal of deposits, for the customers of the bank were assured that they would receive their funds.

A run-off, or, more accurately, a deposit contraction, may occur during a national depression. However, no individual bank can hold enough liquid assets in its own vaults to safeguard against this contingency. Moreover, it is the function of the Federal Reserve to be "the lender of the last resort," i.e., to supply liquidity to the banking system during a period of national crisis.

These considerations tend to support the conclusion reached above: that banks hold liquidity to accommodate the potential loan demand, much the same as a firm holds inventory to accommodate potential sales.

The money desk

Although a commercial banker resembles a pool operator in many ways, the analogy should not be extended too far. A banker has many options that a pool operator does not: He can secure funds from sources other than the people to whom he makes loans, and he can invest the funds that depositors do not withdraw in many ways.

A commercial bank, for example, can secure additional funds from savings deposits, by selling certificates of deposit, or CD's, or by borrowing from other banks. It can invest its excess funds in government bonds, mortgages, municipal bonds, or other assets. The purchase and sale of these money-market instruments is handled by the bank's *money desk*.

The fact that banks can secure funds from sources other than depositors and can make investments other than loans influences their choice of customers. Suppose that a bank is faced with the 10 customers described in Table 23.1 and can borrow money and invest funds at the rates indicated in Table 23.4. If the bank's cost factors are the same as in the first example, which customers will it select? How large will its profits be? How much will it borrow, and how much will it invest?

TABLE 23.4
Interest Rates Facing the Bank over
the Next 7 Periods

Period	Bank Borrowing Rate	Interest Rate on Bonds (Investment Rate)	Interest Rate on Loans to Customers
1	4.5%	4.0%	5.0
2	4.5	4.0	5.0
3	5.0	4.5	5.5
4	5.0	4.5	5.5
5	5.5	5.0	6.0
6	5.5	5.0	6.0
7	5.5	5.0	6.0

A linear-programming model similar to the one used earlier will provide the answers to these questions. The new model, however, will take into account the fact that the bank now has two sources of revenue (loan income and investment income), an additional expenditure (its interest outlays for borrowed money), and two sources of dollar inflows (deposits and borrowing). Now, the bank will maximize its profits if it accepts all customers except 4 and 7. It will receive $285 in deposits ($237.65 in the first example), and its profits ($46.06 in the first example) will be $63.61. Its deposits, borrowings, investments, and loans outstanding in each period are given in Table 23.5.

TABLE 23.5
Assets and Liabilities of the Bank When It Can Borrow and
Invest Funds in the Open Market

Period	Deposits	Borrow-ings	Total Funds Available	Loans	Investments
1	$285.00	—	$285	$250	$35
2	285.00	—	285	215	70
3	285.00	—	285	260	25
4	285.00	$140	425	425	—
5	285.00	55	340	340	—
6	285.00	35	320	320	—
7	285.00	5	290	290	—

Several comments about these data are in order. When a bank has more investment alternatives, i.e., when it can invest in other assets than loans to customers, it can take on new accounts and expand its deposits. Customers that were formerly unprofitable now become a source of earnings, for the funds they deposit can generate revenues during every period, not just during periods when the demand for loans is high. Thus, total deposits rise to $285, whereas before they were only $237.65. Because the bank has more deposits and because it borrows money to accommodate its customers, it can extend more credit than formerly. Outstanding loans in every period are higher than when the bank could not borrow in the money market. However, even though the borrowing rate is less than the loan rate, it does not pay for the bank to accept every potential customer. The increase in costs caused by accepting some customers will not be offset by the revenues they generate. For example, if the bank accepted customer 4, its profits would fall by $5.25; if it accepted customer 7, its profits would fall by $.40.

Incorporating both the opportunity to invest excess funds in bonds to raise funds from sources other than depositors does make the commercial-bank model presented above more realistic. However, it still has some severe limitations. For example, the model assumed that the bank could obtain unlimited funds from external sources. In practice, the supply schedule of funds of any one bank is not infinitely elastic.

A second limitation of the model is the assumption that the amount of money each customer holds on deposit is constant through time. In reality, the deposits of large business customers are likely to be drawn down during periods of high interest rates. This is because these periods coincide with prosperity throughout the nation and corporations have better alternatives for their money than demand deposits. The demands on the corporation for plant and equipment and trade credit, as well as for higher inventory, are also great. One way of financing the purchase of these assets is by drawing down bank deposits. On the other hand, when the economy is less prosperous, when interest rates are lower and when firms do not have attractive investment alternatives, they will build their deposits back up.

The deposits of individuals, in contrast to business deposits, are likely to move in the same direction as national income. As national income rises, individuals tend to be more prosperous and to hold more money in their bank accounts; conversely, as national income falls and unemployment spreads, personal deposits will decline.

This difference in the behavior of business and personal deposits has several implications. Many banks, especially large banks in major financial centers, tend to concentrate on serving business customers. At the peak of a business cycle, these banks may experience critical shortages of funds as the demand for business loans may be high and demand deposits may remain constant or decline moderately. Banks that service primarily individuals, on the other hand, will tend to grow and expand during the peak period of a business cycle. As the income of individuals rises, their bank accounts will grow, enabling these banks to expand their loans and to accommodate some of the customers who were refused credit by the business-oriented banks.

The problem of choosing an optimum mix of customers is, therefore, a difficult one. Not only does the loan demand of different customers differ over time, but their deposit practices vary as well.

To summarize, the examples given above show that a commercial bank, like any other firm, can be analyzed in terms of a systems framework. Specifying the linkages between the various activities of the bank, of course, is an important design problem. Perhaps the most difficult part of this problem is to specify the values of the coefficients of the equations that describe the firm. In practice, the bank's management will need both good judgment and an adequate information system to estimate these parameters precisely. Moreover, since their values will change over time, the bank must be constantly alert to new developments in both the money market and the economy as a whole.

In the examples here, an objective function, or goal, for the firm was first specified. The constraints that limited the firm's range of actions were then indicated. In the first example, the most important constraint on the bank's behavior was the availability of funds. In the second example, this constraint was relaxed by allowing the firm to obtain additional funds when it needed them and to invest excess funds whenever they arose. In each case, the optimum mix of customers was different.

Even when a bank has access to a money desk, however, the supply of funds is still a limiting factor as far as loan expansion is concerned. Banks cannot secure great quantities of funds in the money market without exposing themselves to extraordinary risks. Some of these risks will be documented below.

The chief problem of a commercial bank, then, is how to select the customers with whom it wants to build and maintain a long-run relationship. All banks would like to have customers that will grow and make more and more use of their services. And since they do not have the resources to accommodate all those who seek credit, they must decide which applicants to accept and which to reject. This decision is further complicated by the fact that once a bank refuses a customer's request for a loan, the customer can be expected to take both his present and his future business elsewhere.

Liability management

The inability of even the largest commercial banks to meet the loan demands of all their customers during a period of peak business activity was stressed in the last section. The limitation that inadequate funds imposes on the lending capacity of banks is obviously important to the financial managers of corporations, for it implies that they cannot rely on banks to satisfy all their needs for funds all the time. It is also obviously important to the managers of the country's commercial banks, for it means that much of their time is spent developing plans and strategies for securing the most important raw material in their production function, money.

The inability of banks to raise enough funds through their money desks during periods of prosperity to accommodate all their customers was the subject of an article by Robert E. Knight in the Kansas City Federal Reserve Bank's May 1970 *Monthly Review*. Portions of that article are reprinted below:

> Throughout most of the postwar period . . . banks have relied primarily on their holdings of U. S. Government securities as a reserve of

liquidity. A bank requiring funds to meet loan demands or deposit withdrawals could normally acquire them by selling securities. As a result, when the demand for loans rose, banks sold Government securities; when the demand subsided and loans were repaid, banks would acquire securities.

Within the last four or five years, this pattern has continued but banks have operated under severe constraints. Holdings of securities not pledged for public deposits were small, and many of these had suffered large capital losses which banks were reluctant to realize. Consequently, a number of money market banks which were particularly squeezed for loanable funds developed methods to improve the liquidity of their portfolios.

One way banks were able to improve their liquidity was by selling certificates of deposit. These instruments are negotiable time deposits, the interest rate on which is dictated by Regulation Q of the Federal Reserve.

From a very small base in 1961, large denomination CD's grew rapidly to become the second most important money market instrument by volume. Major banks soon learned that the supply of funds offered for CD's was very sensitive to changes in offering rates and that their ability to influence flows of time deposits could constitute an important source of liquidity. If additional funds were required to make loans or to meet deposit withdrawals, the rate of CD's could be raised; if fund inflows exceeded the bank's needs, the rate could be lowered.

The ability of banks to acquire funds by issuing CD's, however, is limited by Federal Reserve Regulation Q ceilings. When money market interest rates exceed the maximum rates payable, banks have difficulty attracting CD's and have generally experienced a runoff. During such periods, purchasers withdraw money to invest in higher yielding securities. Partly because the CD market cannot serve as a source of liquidity at all times and partly because rising interest rates have prompted banks to economize on their holdings of excess reserves, banks have developed alternative sources of liquidity.[1]

A second source of funds was borrowings from European banks or from the European branches of American-owned banks. These borrowings are called *Eurodollars*.

During 1969, Eurodollar borrowings constituted the most important non-deposit source of funds to banks. . . . Money market banks were also able to use Eurodollar sources to meet a significant share of their CD losses. However, during the fall of 1969, the Federal Reserve Board of Governors became convinced that large banks were using the Eurodollar market to deflect the impact of restrictive monetary policies to other banks.

[1] In July 1970, the Federal Reserve took off the interest-rate ceiling on large (over $100,000) CD's. The timing of this action by the Federal Reserve corresponded closely with the failure of the Penn Central Railroad that was discussed in Chapter 9.

Marginal reserve requirements on Eurodollar borrowings were imposed. By requiring banks to hold a 10 percent reserve against additional borrowings, the Board increased the cost of Eurodollar funds to banks, but did not prevent banks from seeking liquidity from this source.

The Federal funds market is still another source of funds for banks. This is a market in which banks with excess reserves sell them on an overnight basis to banks that are temporarily deficient in required reserves.

The Federal funds market has served both as a short- and long-run source of liquidity for banks. By borrowing and lending reserves, the banking system is able to adjust smoothly to differences in the flows of funds and to random shifts of deposits which are likely to be offsetting at different banks. The funds market has also allowed some money market banks to acquire funds for extended periods; these funds have been used to expand loans and to meet deposit withdrawals. However, since transactions in Federal funds do not affect the size of the reserve base of the banking system, they do not increase potential bank credit expansion.

The size of the Federal funds market is limited, and as other sources of borrowings became more and more restricted, banks developed a new approach for raising funds.

[They began] to sell loans or securities to bank holding companies or other bank affiliates which issue commercial paper. Another technique has been to sell loans or participations in pools of loans or securities to nonbank customers under agreements to repurchase. Sales of loans by large banks to their smaller correspondents has long been an established practice. Such transactions increase loanable funds for the selling bank and may provide a greater return than security investments to the smaller banks. Loans generally have been sold outright, but to maintain satisfactory correspondent relations the selling bank is normally prepared to buy back any loans experiencing difficulty in repayment. Since the selling bank probably would continue to service the loan, the original borrower might never know his loan had been sold. During 1969, however, several money market banks extended this practice by selling loans or participations in pools of various types of earning assets to nonbank customers under agreements to repurchase. (The extent of this market is documented in Table 23.6.)

In practice, a repurchase agreement (RP) involves the sale of paper with the condition that after a stated period of time the original seller will buy back the same paper at a predetermined price or yield. Since repurchase agreements during the early months of 1969 were not subject to Regulation Q, banks could offer them to holders of maturing CD's at interest rates competitive with money market rates. The maturities of the RP's did not necessarily bear any relation to the maturities of the underlying securities or loans and tended to vary from two months to a year. . . .

As banks became aware of the possibilities for acquiring loanable funds by selling paper under agreements the repurchase, to use of RP's increased sharply. Accurate figures are not available on the amount of funds obtained under such agreements, but estimates suggest that between May and August 1969, repurchase agreements involving loans or participations in pools of loans rose from about $1 billion to $2 billion. Most of these represented loans sold to unaffiliated bank customers; the fraction sold to bank holding companies or other bank related affiliates was relatively small.

By late July, the Board of Governors had concluded that banks were using RP's to raise funds in a manner which not only was inconsistent with the purposes and policies of Regulations D and Q but was also indistinguishable from deposit transactions, except on a formalistic basis. Accordingly, both regulations were amended to provide that any repurchase agreement entered into after July 25, 1969, with anyone other than a bank, on any asset other than U. S. Government or agency obligations, would be classified as a deposit for purposes of reserve requirements and interest rate ceilings. The provisions made the sale of loans under agreements to repurchase largely impossible during periods when money market interest rates exceed Regulation Q ceilings.

With one source of raising money after another being closed off to banks, they continued to search out still other methods to accommodate the credit needs of their customers.

TABLE 23.6
Bank Sales of Loans and Participations in Pools of Loans
(in millions of dollars)

| Date | Total | Sold to Nonbank Public | | Sold to Bank's Own Affiliates | |
		Sold Outright	Sold With Repurchase Agreements	Sold Outright	Sold With Repurchase Agreements
1969					
May 28	3,014	482	605	1,524	403
June 25	4,094	742	837	2,103	412
July 30	5,552	943	1,311	2,644	654
August 27	5,469	855	909	3,152	553
September 24	5,624	928	541	3,662	493
October 29	6,537	1,094	354	4,584	505
November 26	6,813	1,320	290	4,665	538
December 31	5,830	1,153	196	3,896	585
1970					
January 28	8,013	1,436	168	5,820	589
February 25	8,810	1,544	168	6,402	696
March 25	9,047	1,526	129	6,682	710
April 29	9,399	1,613	136	6,948	702

SOURCE: Robert E. Knight, "An Alternate Approach to Liquidity," Federal Reserve Bank of Kansas City, *Monthly Review* (May 1970), p. 13.

Liability management

During 1969, several large banks developed methods to satisfy loan demands without the necessity of supplying funds directly. These techniques basically involve the creation of ineligible acceptances and various forms of customer paper guarantees ("documented discount notes"). To a large extent these marketable securities have been created to serve customers who would normally be accommodated at banks were loanable funds more readily available.

Guaranteed customer paper has been used to aid bank customers which are not of prime standing in the commercial paper market. By attaching an irrevocable letter of credit, a bank may add its endorsement to an issue. The guarantee of payment at maturity in event of default by the issuer allows the commercial paper to be sold readily as a money market instrument, generally at rates of interest lower than the market would otherwise require. Since the letter of credit represents a contingent liability for the bank, it does not affect the bank's balance sheet.

Some banks have also experimented recently with ineligible acceptances as a means to finance unsecured loans. When a bank "accepts" paper drawn by a customer, the bank guarantees to redeem the paper at maturity. The use of the bank's name increases the marketability of the paper. For the service the bank charges a small fee and the customer agrees to provide the bank with funds for redemption in advance of the maturity of the acceptance. If a banker's acceptance grows out of transactions involving the export or import of goods, the shipment of goods in the United States, or the storage of readily marketable staples, it may serve as collateral for a loan at the Federal Reserve discount window. Since these newer acceptances have been used for other types of loans, however, they are "ineligible" to serve as collateral at the discount window.

The amount of funds acquired from these two sources has remained relatively small. [Table 23.7] indicates that weekly reporting banks have guaranteed about $270 million of customer paper and have created about $385 million in ineligible acceptances. The limited growth of these instruments is partly attributable to the fact that banks have generally been able to satisfy customers' requests for loans more directly by turning to alternative nondeposit sources of funds.

During the late 1960's, then, banks designed several new instruments to secure funds. Why did they not simply borrow money from the Federal Reserve? Why did they not take some of their securities, discount them, and use the funds they received to extend credit to their customers? The Kansas City Federal Reserve Bank discussed this possibility also.

The Federal Reserve System was initially created to serve as the lender of last resort to the banking system—an ultimate source of liquidity to help prevent the financial panics and banking crises which had characterized the National Banking System of the 19th century. Although the System has continued to function in this capacity, use of the discount window has provided a relatively small source of liquidity to banks throughout most of the postwar period. Federal Reserve policies have stressed that bank borrowing at the discount window should be under-

The commercial bank in a systems context

TABLE 23.7

Guaranteed Customer Paper and
Ineligible Acceptances
(in millions of dollars)

Date	Guaranteed Customer Paper	Ineligible Acceptances Created by Banks
1969		
May 28	122	38
June 25	138	64
July 30	126	108
August 27	180	137
September 24	184	150
October 29	211	159
November 26	224	198
December 31	269	138
1970		
January 28	278	223
February 25	282	283
March 25	289	361
April 29	272	385

SOURCE: Robert E. Knight, "An Alternative Approach to Liquidity," Federal Reserve Bank of Kansas City *Monthly Review* (May 1970), p. 14.

taken only when necessary and, except in unusual circumstances, be limited to short-term reserve needs. The Fed will not lend to banks to expand their loans and investments, but the discount window is generally open to banks suffering deposit losses or temporary reserve shortages. Close scrutiny is given to each application for credit and administrative pressures theoretically should assure that banks do not violate the basic guidelines.

Despite these policies, Chart 1 [Fig. 23.1] shows that total borrowings from the Federal Reserve have displayed a consistent cyclical pattern. Borrowings have risen during expansions as the demand for loans has increased and as money market interest rates have risen above the discount rate, and have fallen during recessions as the demand for loans has declined and interest rates have fallen relative to the discount rate. Nevertheless, the discount window has provided a relatively small fraction of total Federal Reserve credit. Between 1954 and 1968, borrowings fluctuated from negligible amounts to slightly over $1 billion. In 1969, however, borrowings rose temporarily to about $1.4 billion.

During the summer of 1968 . . . two new types of discounting were proposed. The "basic borrowing privilege" would enable a member bank to borrow up to a specified limit in as many as half of its weekly reserve periods. To prevent banks from borrowing to profit from short-term interest rate differentials, however, the discount rate would be changed more often to keep it closely in line with other short-term rates. Banks experiencing a large seasonal need for funds, persisting for a month or longer and which cannot be readily accommodated under the basic borrowing privilege, would be eligible for seasonal adjustment credit. Banks qualifying would be able to arrange in advance for loans from Reserve Banks to meet a portion of the anticipated seasonal need. It is believed that the seasonal borrowing privilege would primarily benefit small banks located in agricultural regions. These banks typically have an increase in loan demand during the summer months when deposits are declining or growing less rapidly.

Banks experiencing drains of funds which are not of a seasonal or emergency nature and are longer in duration or of larger amount would be allowed to apply for "other adjustment credit." The application would be subject to administrative review as is current borrowing. Credit would be given to banks only on a short-term basis pending an expected and timely reversal of their fund outflows or orderly adjustments in their assets and liabilities. This type of borrowing, therefore, would be very similar to the type permitted currently.

The likely effect of these provisions would be to expand greatly the magnitude of borrowing which occurs at the discount window. Borrowing at the Fed could become a much more important source of liquidity for banks. Nevertheless, under present arrangements the funds which banks have acquired from the discount window have satisfied a relatively small portion of their total liquidity needs. The modifications, moreover, are not likely to be introduced until the Fed wishes to achieve a significant easing of monetary policy.

To summarize, bankers have been inventive in designing new instruments to raise the funds that they require to meet their customers' needs. However, in an effort to control inflation by reducing the money supply and the lending capacity of banks, the Federal Reserve has actively restricted the use of the various instruments that were developed. As a result, bankers have found it more and more difficult to meet the demand for credit. Financial managers, in turn, have found it more and more troublesome to borrow money; and, to an increasing extent, have become more concerned with the operating problems of commercial banks. From a systems viewpoint, the constant changes in the environment within which banks operate mean that the parameters of the equations describing the money desk are subject to very wide variations. It is, therefore, extremely important for commercial bankers to constantly monitor the data on business conditions that become available and to revise their decision models as these conditions warrant.

Summary

The operations of a commercial bank were treated in this chapter from a systems point of view. The bank was assumed to have as an objective

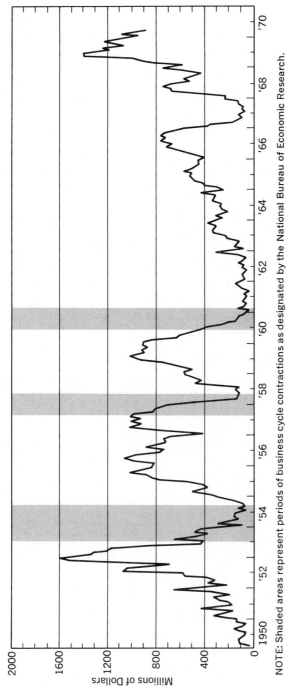

NOTE: Shaded areas represent periods of business cycle contractions as designated by the National Bureau of Economic Research.

SOURCE: Robert E. Knight, "An Alternative Approach to Liquidity," Federal Reserve Bank of Kansas City *Monthly Review* (May 1970), p. 15.

FIGURE 23.1

Borrowings by All Member Banks from the Federal Reserve System.

function the maximization of profits and to be faced with several constraints. The major constraints that were handled formally were the cash inflows and outflows associated with different customers and the prices at which funds could be borrowed and invested in money-market instruments. In addition to these constraints, banks also face physical-production and regulatory constraints.

It is a difficult task, of course, to forecast accurately what the interest rate on various assets will be at some future date. It is even harder to estimate what the future loan demand and deposit balances of various customers will be. Even so, the profits of a bank depend in large part on its ability to mobilize funds when customers need them.

The problems of bank managers and corporate financial managers are similar in many respects. The corporate financial manager must estimate his company's future cash flows, not only to know how to time his purchases, but to know whether he will be able to meet his bills as they fall due. A banker must also have some understanding of a customer's cash-flow position to estimate what loan demands it will make at a later date and what deposit balance he can reasonably expect it to hold. Moreover, just as a financial manager cannot judge the attractiveness of a project without knowing what its impact on other corporate activities will be, so a bank cannot judge the profitability of a potential corporate customer without first determining what the customer's impact on all the bank's resources will be.

The level of deposits is vitally important to commercial banks because their ability to secure funds from other sources is subject to a variety of government pressures and regulations. In the past, banks have tried to sell certificates of deposit, borrow in Europe, borrow excess reserves, sell commercial paper, and even sell their loans to persons and institutions that might have excess funds. The government has severely restricted the amount of funds that banks can raise from all these sources, and the net effect has been to make it more and more difficult for banks to serve their customers well.

Questions for discussion and problems

1. What implications would arise if a bank were thought of as a vault, rather than as a pool of funds?

2. Why does a money desk raise bank profits? If a bank had no money desk, how would its actions be affected?

3. Can linear-programming models be developed to help banks in their everyday decision making? In what areas might these models be most successful?

The commercial bank in a systems context

4. Why must bank planning models include the future cash requirements of customers? How can banks secure data on their customers' future needs?

5. What factors might explain the Federal Reserve's actions in restricting the range of alternatives open to the manager of a bank's money desk?

6. Why might the recent changes in discount policy make it easier for banks to borrow money from the Federal Reserve?

[*Answers to problems 7–9 follow references and suggested readings.*]

7. A bank has $100 in deposits and $10 in equity. It can hold four kinds of assets: (1) reserves, equal to 20 percent of its deposits; (2) consumer loans that yield a net return of 8 percent; (3) business loans that yield a net return of 3 percent; (4) and government bonds that yield a net return of 4 percent. The Federal Reserve also requires that the bank hold some equity to support these assets. The capital required is 5 percent of the outstanding government bonds and 10 percent of outstanding loans; no capital is required to back reserves. The bank also wants to maintain its position as a business bank and has established a policy that consumer loans must be less than 20 percent of its deposits plus equity. Design a linear-programming model that will let the bank maximize its profits subject to these constraints.

8. Banks A and B are the only two banks in the system. They have the following balance sheets:

A

Reserves	$ 20	Demand deposits	$100
Loans	100		

B

Reserves	$ 20	Demand deposits	$100
Loans	80		

The required reserve ratio for demand deposits is 20 percent and for time deposits, including CD's, 5 percent. If A sells a $10 CD to a depositor of B and B sells a $10 CD to a depositor of A, what happens to the lending capacity of the system?

9. (a) If a bank borrows $50 from the Federal Reserve, and reserve requirements are 20 percent, how much can deposits expand?

   (b) Examine Figure 23.1 on page 515. Would you say that bank borrowings from the Federal Reserve have aggravated or modified the business cycle?

REFERENCES AND SUGGESTED READINGS

Articles

Andersen, Leonall, and Burger, Albert E., "Asset Management and Commercial Bank Portfolio Behavior: Theory and Practice," *Journal of Finance,* vol. XXIV (May 1969), pp. 207–22.

Daellenbach, Hans G., and Archer, Stephen H., "The Optimal Bank Liquidity: A Multi-period Stochastic Model," *Journal of Financial and Quantitative Analysis,* vol. IV (September 1969), pp. 329–42.

Davis, R. G., and Guttentag, J. M., "Balance Requirements and Deposit Competition," *Journal of Political Economy,* vol. LXXXI (December 1963), pp. 581–85.

Greer, Carl C., "The Optimal Credit Acceptance Policy," *Journal of Financial and Quantitative Analysis,* vol. II (December 1967), pp. 399–417.

Hester, Donald, "An Empirical Examination of a Commercial Bank Loan Offer Function," *Yale Economic Essays* (Spring 1962), pp. 3–57.

Hodgman, Donald R., "The Deposit Relationship and Commercial Bank Investment Behavior," *Review of Economics and Statistics,* vol. XLIII (August 1961), pp. 257–68.

Jacobs, Donald P., "The Interaction Effects of Restrictions on Branching and Other Bank Regulations," *Journal of Finance,* vol. XX (May 1965), pp. 332–48.

Luttrell, Clifton B., "Member Bank Borrowing: Its Origin and Function," *Quarterly Review of Economics and Business,* Bureau of Economic and Business Research, Univ. of Illinois (Autumn 1968), pp. 55–65.

Maisel, Sherman J., "Some Relationships Between Assets and Liabilities of Thrift Institutions," *Journal of Finance,* vol. XXII (May 1968), pp. 367–78.

Meigs, James A., "The Changing Role of Banks in the Market for Equities," *Journal of Finance,* vol. XX (May 1965), pp. 368–78.

Mitchell, George W., "Interest Rates vs. Interest Ceilings in the Allocation of Credit Flows," *Journal of Finance,* vol. XXII (May 1967), pp. 265–73.

Murphy, Neil B., "A Test of the Deposit Relationship Hypothesis," *Journal of Financial and Quantitative Analysis,* vol. II (March 1967), pp. 51–57.

Smith, Paul F., "Pricing Policies on Consumer Loans at Commercial Banks," *Journal of Finance,* vol. XXV (May 1970), pp. 517–25.

Williams, Charles M., "Senior Securities—Boon for Banks," *Harvard Business Review* (July–August 1963), pp. 83–90.

Books

Cohen, Kalman J., and Hammer, Frederick S., *Analytical Methods in Banking,* (Homewood, Ill.: Irwin, 1966).

Goldsmith, Raymond W., *Financial Intermediaries in the American Economy Since 1900* (Princeton, N. J.: Princeton Univ. Press, 1958).

Hodgman, Donald R., *Commercial Bank Loan and Investment Policy* (Urbana, Ill.: Bureau of Economic and Business Research, 1963).

Jacobs, Donald P., *The Impact of Bank Examination Practices* (Committee on Banking and Currency, U. S. House of Representatives, 1964).

Jessup, Paul F., ed., *Innovations in Bank Management* (New York: Holt, Rinehart and Winston, 1969).

Robinson, Roland, *The Management of Bank Funds,* (New York: McGraw-Hill, 1962).

ANSWERS TO PROBLEMS 7–9

7. Maximize: $.08CL + .03BL + .04GB$ (objective function)
Subject to: $20 + CL + BL + GB \leq 110$ (deposit and equity constraint)
$.10CL + .10BL + .05GB \leq 10$ (capital constraint)
$CL \leq (.20)(110)$ (consumer-loan constraint)
$CL, BL, GB \geq 0$ (non-negativity constraints)

8. Since the two banks together now have $3 in excess reserves, loans can expand by $15 if demand deposits increase, or by $60 if additional CD's are purchased. The balance sheet of the two-bank system is then:

Balance Sheet of Banks A and B Combined

Required reserves against demand deposit	36	Demand deposits	$180
Required reserves against CD	1	Certificates of deposit	20
Total required reserves	$ 37		
Excess reserves	3		
Total Reserves	$ 40		
Loans	160		
	$200		$200

9. (a) Deposits can increase by $250. (b) Bank borrowings would appear to aggravate the business cycle since they rise during peak periods and fall during recessions.

Summary

SEVEN

Part One of this book was concerned with the finance function in a modern firm. The closing section returns to this theme. Chapter 24 briefly summarizes the central issues that were raised in the book—the problems that face the financial managers of firms today.

The finance function once again

24

The opening chapter of this book described the firm as a system capable of converting many different inputs into a wide variety of outputs. The model presented there, and reproduced as Figure 24.1, highlights the strategic relationships and feedback loops of the system.

A set of goals guide the organization. These goals are conditioned by information about both the external environment in which the firm operates and the skills and resources that management controls. They may be formally articulated, or they may exist only in the form of preferences that are shared by all the firm's top officers as to where the organization "ought to be" or what it "ought to look like" at some future date.

No organization can function effectively, however, unless the resources at its command and the goals it has established for itself are formally related. This linkage is supplied by the firm's global model, which performs several functions: It structures the information that the leaders of the organization will look for; i.e., it indicates what data is pertinent to the firm and what data is noise that can safely be ignored. The model also indicates the feasibility of certain investment programs; i.e., it will point out which resources are constrained, the probability of loss, the effect of the investment on other ventures, and so forth. Finally, the model gives rise to a set of decision rules about how the firm's physical inputs should be combined to produce the desired outputs. The global model, in short, is the firm's principal planning instrument.

Once the decisions indicated by the model are implemented, a second problem arises. Discrepancies inevitably arise between planned and actual outcomes. Thus the system must be consistently monitored to ensure that such problems are uncovered before they seriously interfere with the achievement of any of the corporate goals.

Sometimes the discrepancy between planned and actual results arises

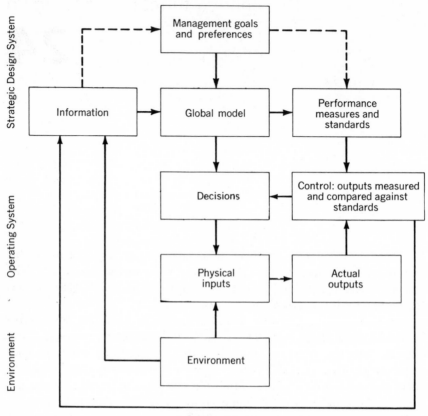

FIGURE 24.1

The Firm as a System

because the inputs did not perform as expected. Under these conditions, relatively minor corrective action may be sufficient. At other times, the plan itself may have been at fault. Important considerations may have been overlooked, or certain assumptions made in the global model may have been incorrect. Under these conditions, the corrective action may include revising the model itself.

The role of the financial officer in both the planning and control functions is critical. This is because many of the goals of the firm are financial. For example, the firm may want the price of its stock to appreciate; it may want the level of profits raised; it may want shareholder dividends to grow at a certain rate; and it may want the amount of debt in its capital structure kept to a reasonable minimum. The discrepancies between planned and actual results are also frequently stated in financial terms. Production will report that the outlays for a specific activity were higher than planned; divisional heads will report that profits were below the budgeted figures; sales managers will report that the dollars of revenues generated in a market were below the expected level; and so forth.

What tools, then, are available to the manager to help him read the environment, so that he can perform both the planning and control functions more effectively? How can these tools be used? What are their limitations? Answering these has been our chief concern in this book.

The financial statements of the firm are one of the most important control instruments available to financial managers. Thus, in Chapters 2, 3, and 4 stress was placed on the development and interpretation of these statements and the difficulties that arise in trying to capture the flows of revenues and outlays that occur. The measurement problems associated with these statements were also discussed. Finally, the utility to the owners of the enterprise of the various financial statements a firm prepares was questioned. Do the statements communicate relevant information about the firm's activities to its shareholders? Could another format for financial reports be more helpful? The new and provocative answers to these questions that are beginning to emerge were reviewed in this section.

Once new reporting formats are developed, new insights into corporate activities become possible. Moreover, these new corporate formats can be applied to macroeconomic entities such as the nation also. Chapter 5 described how the flow of funds data published by the Federal Reserve does this. The data generated by these reports show some of the supply and demand considerations that influence corporate financial decision making.

Reading, interpreting, and understanding financial statements, however, is just the beginning task of financial management. Decisions must be made and actions must be taken to achieve long- and short-term corporate goals. Chapters 6 through 9 focused on some of the tools corporate managers use in making short-term financial decisions. The characteristics of various short-term financial assets and liabilities were described; the models used to plan and control the size of these assets were discussed, and the economic consequences of decisions were examined.

Short-term financial planning is only one phase of the finance function. Decisions about which assets to purchase, how to finance them, and what dividends to pay shareholders also influence the vitality and growth potential of the firm. What target rate of return should a firm strive to achieve? How much do the funds that it uses cost? What is the impact of the decisions that are made with respect to one corporate activity on other corporate activities? These questions, discussed in Chapters 10 through 15, are the core concerns of financial planners.

The more one knows about financial management, the more apparent it becomes that the profitability of an investment project cannot be evaluated in isolation. Even so simple a question as, What is the cost of different financial instruments? cannot be answered without considering the effect of the use of the instrument on the firm's shareholders. Many models for testing the attractiveness of different projects were considered and discarded in Part Four, until finally a global model was developed that linked the supply schedule of a firm's inputs, the production function, and the demand for the firm's outputs. But this model in turn only opened the door to the problems that arise when the functions that describe the firm are not known with certainty. How is the problem of risk to be analyzed, and how can the phenomenon of uncertainty itself be incorporated in a framework for financial decisions? These are still the frontier areas of financial management.

The objective function of the global planning model—the maximization of shareholder welfare—is intimately linked to the factors that affect the price of the company's stock. Chapters 16 through 20 analyzed stock-valuation models, the institutional characteristics of the securities market, portfolio problems, investment trading strategies, and the theory of conglomerate mergers. Many of the factors discussed here lie outside the immediate control of the financial manager, yet he must understand and cope with them if he is to mobilize the resources of the firm effectively.

Two of the most important elements in the environment that affect a firm's investment opportunities and the price of its stock are the level of national income and the operations of the commercial-banking system. The treatment of these topics in Chapters 21, 22, and 23 was analytical rather than descriptive because, once again, the dominant concern of the financial manager is to develop a critical understanding of the forces that affect the firm.

In a profound sense, the material in these twenty-three chapters leaves much unsaid about the finance function. A firm is a social and political organization as well as an economic and technical one; the conflicts inevitable between members of an organization must be resolved, and a congruence must be achieved between the goals and aspirations of individuals and groups within the organization. These topics, although they are beyond the range of *Managerial Finance,* do not lie outside the field. They, too, must be considered by those who make decisions in the corporate system.

Glossary

Glossary

Accelerated depreciation. Writing off a larger portion of the value of an asset during the early years of its life.

Account payable. A debt that arises in the normal course of business and is not supported by negotiable paper. Credit extended by a supplier to a purchaser for goods shipped is considered an account payable by the purchaser.

Account receivable. A credit that arises in the normal course of business. Credit extended by a supplier to a purchaser for goods shipped is considered an account receivable by the supplier.

Accounts receivable turnover. The ratio of sales made on credit over a period to the average amount of receivables outstanding during that period.

Acid test ratio. The ratio of the sum of a firm's cash, marketable securities, and accounts receivable to its current liabilities.

Aging schedule. A report showing how long accounts receivable have been outstanding.

Amortize. To retire, or pay back, borrowings; thus a firm amortizes its bonds.

Ask price. In security trading, the price at which a seller of a stock is willing to sell.

Balloon payment. The last payment, which may be substantially larger than all the rest, on a bond that is not fully amortized over the life of the instrument.

Bank line. A line of credit; an arrangement to receive a loan from a bank.

Bankruptcy. A legal proceeding that frees a debtor from the financial obligation of meeting his debts as they fall due.

Basis point. A change of one-one hundredth of a percent in the price of a government security. Thus, if the price of a bond increases from $95.73 to $95.78, it increases by 5 basis points.

Bear market. A period during which stock prices fall sharply.

Bid price. In security trading, the price that a buyer is prepared to pay for a share of stock.

Bond. A long-term debt instrument.

Book value. The value of a share of stock, calculated by dividing the firm's net worth by the number of its outstanding shares; the value assigned to an asset on the company's financial statement.

Break-even point. The volume of output at which both profits and losses are zero. Break-even analysis expresses the relationship between fixed costs, variable costs, revenues, and output in a way that highlights unit profits.

Broker. In security transactions, an agent of the buyer or seller.

Bull market. A period during which stock prices rise rapidly.

Call. An option entitling holders to purchase a security at a fixed price; a notice by a corporation that it will redeem a bond at a given date.

Capital. A term used to refer to either the fixed plant and equipment of a corporation, its total assets, or its equity. See also working capital.

Capital budgeting. The process of evaluating the potential investments open to a firm and rationing the firm's investment resources among them.

Capital consumption. The deprecia- tion of a firm's capital assets during a period.

Capitalization of income. Division of a current flow (such as income) by an interest rate to convert the flow into an equivalent stock of wealth.

Capitalization rate. The rate of in- terest used to capitalize an income stream.

Capital market. The financial market for long-term funds.

Capital stock. The shares of a corporation.

Capital structure. The sum of a firm's long-term debt plus equity.

Cash budget. A schedule showing the cash receipts and disbursements of a firm.

Cash discount. A discount allowed by suppliers when payment is made prior to a specified date.

Cash flow. The increase in cash gen- erated through operations over a period; profits plus depreciation if other liability and asset accounts do not change.

Certainty equivalent. The certain return on an investment that would be as attractive as a higher but un- certain return.

Coefficient of variation. The stan- dard deviation divided by the mean.

Commercial paper. Unsecured short- term debt instruments.

Common stock. The ordinary shares of a corporation that carry no spe- cial dividend rights or preferred status.

Compensating balance. The amount of funds a firm is required to keep on deposit to compensate a bank for its services.

Compound interest. Interest paid not only on the original principal but on the interest earned in prior periods.

Conglomerate. A diversified firm that came into existence through the merger of two or more firms in unrelated industries.

Conversion price. The price at which stock can be obtained when a convertible bond is exchanged for shares.

Convertible bond. A bond that can be converted into shares at a fixed price.

Cost of capital. The discount rate used to convert the flow of revenues generated by a project into a stock of wealth.

Cumulative preferred stock. Pre- ferred stock issued with the under- standing that dividends will ac- cumulate if not paid.

Current assets. Assets that in the normal course of events will be con- verted into cash in a short period, usually within a year.

Current ratio. Current assets divided by current liabilities.

Dealer. In the securities industry, a person or firm that buys or sells securities for its own account rather than for another.

Debenture. A long-term bond not secured by specific property.

Debt service. The interest charges and principal due in a period.

Depreciation charge. The portion of the cost of an asset allocated to the company's expenses during a par- ticular year.

Discounted-cash-flow technique. A method of ranking projects in which the cash flows generated by the asset are discounted at some in- terest rate.

Dividend yield. The current dividend of a security divided by its market price.

Earnings multiplier. A ratio derived by dividing the price of a share of stock by the earnings per share.

Economic order quantity. The order size that will minimize the total cost of a firm's inventory.

Efficient frontier. The locus of points (i.e., the set of securities) that will minimize the variance of a portfolio.

Equity. The total funds invested in a business by its owners; total assets less total liabilities.

Excess present value. The difference between the present value and the purchase price of an asset.

External financing. Raising funds from sources outside the firm; e.g., by selling long-term bonds or issuing new shares of stock.

Factoring. Selling a firm's accounts receivables to another party at a discounted price.

FIFO (first-in-first-out). An inventory accounting system which assumes that the items received earliest by the firm are sold first.

Financial leverage. The ratio of a firm's total debt to its total assets.

Fixed assets. The long-term assets of a company, such as equipment, plant, and land.

Fixed costs. Costs that do not vary with output.

Float. The amount of funds that are tied up in the process of collection.

Fully diluted earnings. An accounting term for the earnings per share that would result if all options and conversion privileges on bonds and preferred shares were exercised.

Funded debt. The long-term debt of a corporation.

Goodwill. An intangible asset of the firm.

Gross profit margin. The ratio of revenues less the cost of goods sold to total revenues.

Holding company. A corporation that controls the voting stock of another corporation.

Hypothecate. To pledge something of value as collateral for a debt.

Income bond. A bond that pays interest only if sufficient funds are available from the company's earnings.

Indenture. The formal agreement between the issuer of a bond and the holder.

Index of profitability. The ratio of the present value of an asset to its purchase price.

Internal rate of return. The discount rate that makes the cash flows of a project equal to its purchase price.

Investment banking. Underwriting and selling newly issued securities to purchasers.

Lease. A contract entitling a person or company to use an asset owned by another party for a specified period in exchange for a stipulated payment.

Leveraging earnings. Altering the return on equity through the issuance of debt and preferred stock.

LIFO (last-in-first-out). An inventory accounting system which assumes that the items received last by the firm are sold first.

Line of credit. An arrangement to borrow a stipulated amount (the line) from a lender.

Liquidation. Terminating the existance of the firm by selling the assets to pay off debts or raise cash.

Liquidity. The ability of a company to meet its financial obligations as they fall due.

Liquidity trap. In economics, the point at which the demand for money is infinitely elastic with respect to the interest rate.

Listed security. A security that is listed for trading on one of the major stock exchanges.

Lock-box plan. A procedure that makes effective use of post office facilities to speed up the collection of checks and thereby reduce float.

Margin. In commercial transactions, the ratio of profits to sales; in securities transactions, the purchase of a security with partly borrowed funds.

Marginal cost. The cost associated with the production of one more unit.

Marginal revenue. The revenue associated with the sale of one more unit.

Market order. In securities transactions, an order to a broker to buy or sell securities at the current market price.

Materiality. An accounting term applied to any activity that contributes in a large, or material, way to the overall corporate activity being studied; such an activity has materiality.

Merger. The process whereby one corporation secures the voting stock of another.

Money desk. In a bank, the department responsible for buying and selling short-term funds.

Money market. The financial market for short-term funds.

Mortgage. A debt instrument secured by a specific piece of property.

Net present value. The difference between the present value of an asset and its purchase price; sometimes called excess present value.

Net worth. The total equity of a corporation.

Nominal interest rate. The rate of interest charged for funds, making no allowance for changes in the price level.

Objective function. In linear programming, the function that is maximized or minimized.

Open-market operations. The purchase and sale of government securities by the Federal Reserve.

Open order. In the securities market, an order to buy or sell securities at a stipulated price.

Opportunity cost. In economics, the alternatives that must be foregone to adopt a particular course of action.

Over-the-counter market. Securities markets other than the organized exchanges.

Paper profits. The profits that would be realized if a transaction were closed at a particular time.

Participating bond. A bond that has a variable return; the holder receives the normal interest on the bond and, in addition, shares to a specified extent in the profits of the enterprise.

Par value. The value stated on the face of a security.

Payable. A short-term liability.

Payback period. The length of time before the net revenue from a project will equal the purchase price of the asset.

Pay-out rate. The ratio of a firm's dividends to its total earnings.

Pension fund. A special purpose investment fund. The contributions to a pension fund may come from the management of a firm, the employees, or both.

Pooling of interest. An accounting term for the treatment of a merger that does not record the premium that is paid above the book value of an asset.

Present value. The current value of a future stream of revenues.

Price elasticity. In economics, the percentage change in the quantity of an item sold associated with the percentage change in price.

Primary earnings. In accounting, the earnings per share after taxes.

Prime rate. The interest rate that a commercial bank charges its largest and most desirable customers.

Profitability index. The ratio of the present value of a project to its purchase price.

Pro-forma statement. The financial statement that would result if an assumed series of events came to pass.

Prospectus. A statement, prepared by a company at the time it issues new securities, describing the state of its affairs.

Proxy. A document that gives one person the right to vote for another.

Put. In securities trading, an option to sell a security at a specified price.

Quantity theory of money. An economic theory that describes the relationship between money flows and national income.

Quick ratio. The ratio of a firm's cash, marketable securities, and accounts receivable to its current liabilities.

Red herring. In the securities market, an advance copy of a prospectus that contains all the data in the regular prospectus except the price at which the new securities are to be sold.

Refinancing. The process of replacing one set of debt instruments with another as the original instruments mature; also called refunding.

Reorganization. The lowering of a bankrupt company's debt and equity accounts to correspond to the new (and lower) value of its assets.

Residual value. The market value of an asset after some specified period, such as a lease period, has elapsed.

Retained earnings. The earnings remaining after the distribution of dividends by a firm.

Retention rate. The ratio of retained earnings to total earnings.

Risk. The probability of loss.

Risk premium. The difference between the expected rate of return on an asset that has a variable return and one with a certain return.

Round lot. In security transactions, a purchase or sell order of a standard size. On the New York Stock Exchange, a round lot is 100 shares.

Seasonal index. An index of the movement of a variable such as sales over a number of months or seasons.

Short covering. Purchasing a security to unwind a short sale; i.e., to be turned over to the person or firm that loaned the short seller the securities he needed to make delivery.

Short selling. In security analysis, selling shares not yet purchased. To make delivery to the buyer, the seller must borrow the securities that he sold.

Simple interest. Interest paid only on the original principal.

Simulation. The replication of a state of affairs under different assumptions. A firm's cash budget can be simulated by changing the rate at which payables are met or receivables are collected.

Specialist. A member of an exchange who is prepared to buy and sell securities for his own account, i.e., to act as a dealer.

Spread. The difference between the bid and ask price of a security.

Standard deviation. A measure of the dispersion of a random variable.

Stock dividend. A dividend in the form of stock rather than cash. This transaction reduces the firm's earned surplus account and increases its capital stock account.

Stock split. A method for increasing the number of outstanding shares; e.g., a 2-for-1 split occurs, each existing share is now counted as two shares. This transaction does not require a transfer of funds from the earned surplus account to the capital stock account.

Tangible assets. Assets such as machinery that have physical, material substance.

Tax-shield. In capital budgeting, some expenses (such as depreciation) lower taxes but do not adversely affect the cash flow of a corporation. The extent of the tax reduction is called the tax-shield.

Tender offer. A well publicized bid made by a corporation for all, or a prescribed number of, the securities of another corporation. Tender offers are frequently made when one company wants to merge with another.

Times interest earned. The ratio of a firm's earnings before interest and taxes to its total interest payments.

Transfer agent. The party (frequently a bank) charged with keeping a record of the ownership of the stocks and bonds of a corporation.

Uncollected funds. The dollar value of the checks that have been deposited in the firm's account but not yet collected by the bank from the drawee bank.

Undercapitalized. Having an inadequate amount of equity to carry on an operation of the scale that is undertaken.

Underwriting. The process of issuing new securities.

Utility schedule. A schedule showing the relationship between how well off a person is and another variable such as wealth.

Variance. The square of the standard deviation.

Warrant. A long-term option to purchase stock at a specified price.

Watered stock. A company's stock is said to be "watered" when the value of its assets, and hence the book value of its equity, is overstated.

Weighted average cost of capital. The average of the cost of debt and the cost of equity where each is weighted by the proportion of it in the firm's total capital structure.

Working capital. The difference between a firm's current assets and its current liabilities.

Appendixes

APPENDIX A

Present Value of $1

Periods Until Payment	2%	5%	8%	10%	13%	15%	18%	20%	23%
0	1.000	1.000	1.000	1.000	1.000	1.000	1.000	1.000	1.000
1	.980	.952	.926	.909	.885	.870	.847	.833	.813
2	.961	.907	.857	.826	.783	.756	.718	.694	.661
3	.942	.864	.794	.751	.693	.658	.609	.579	.537
4	.924	.823	.735	.683	.613	.572	.516	.482	.437
5	.906	.784	.681	.621	.543	.497	.437	.402	.355
6	.888	.746	.630	.564	.480	.432	.370	.335	.289
7	.871	.711	.583	.513	.425	.376	.314	.279	.235
8	.853	.677	.540	.467	.376	.327	.266	.233	.191
9	.837	.645	.500	.424	.333	.284	.225	.194	.155
10	.820	.614	.463	.386	.295	.247	.191	.162	.126
11	.804	.585	.429	.350	.261	.215	.162	.135	.103
12	.788	.557	.397	.319	.231	.187	.137	.112	.083
13	.773	.530	.368	.290	.204	.163	.116	.093	.068
14	.758	.505	.340	.263	.181	.141	.099	.078	.055
15	.743	.481	.315	.239	.160	.123	.084	.065	.045
16	.728	.458	.292	.218	.141	.107	.071	.054	.036
17	.714	.436	.270	.198	.125	.093	.060	.045	.030
18	.700	.416	.250	.180	.111	.081	.051	.038	.024
19	.686	.396	.232	.164	.098	.070	.043	.031	.020
20	.673	.377	.215	.149	.087	.061	.037	.026	.016
21	.660	.359	.199	.135	.077	.053	.031	.022	.013
22	.647	.342	.184	.123	.068	.046	.026	.018	.011
23	.634	.326	.170	.112	.060	.040	.022	.015	.009
24	.622	.310	.158	.102	.053	.035	.019	.013	.007
25	.610	.295	.146	.092	.047	.030	.016	.010	.006
26	.598	.281	.135	.084	.042	.026	.014	.009	.005
27	.586	.268	.125	.076	.037	.023	.011	.007	.004
28	.574	.255	.116	.069	.033	.020	.010	.006	.003
29	.563	.243	.107	.063	.029	.017	.008	.005	.002
30	.552	.231	.099	.057	.026	.015	.007	.004	.002

Periods Until Payment	25%	28%	30%	33%	35%	40%	45%	50%
0	1.000	1.000	1.000	1.000	1.000	1.000	1.000	1.000
1	.800	.781	.769	.752	.741	.714	.690	.667
2	.640	.610	.592	.565	.549	.510	.476	.444
3	.512	.477	.455	.425	.406	.364	.328	.296
4	.410	.373	.350	.320	.301	.260	.226	.198
5	.328	.291	.269	.240	.223	.186	.156	.132
6	.262	.227	.207	.181	.165	.133	.108	.088
7	.210	.178	.159	.136	.122	.095	.074	.059
8	.168	.139	.123	.102	.091	.068	.051	.039
9	.134	.108	.094	.077	.067	.048	.035	.026
10	.107	.085	.073	.058	.050	.035	.024	.017
11	.086	.066	.056	.043	.037	.025	.017	.012
12	.069	.052	.043	.033	.027	.018	.012	.008
13	.055	.040	.033	.025	.020	.013	.008	.005
14	.044	.032	.025	.018	.015	.009	.006	.003
15	.035	.025	.020	.014	.011	.006	.004	.002
16	.028	.019	.015	.010	.008	.005	.003	.002
17	.023	.015	.012	.008	.006	.003	.002	.001
18	.018	.012	.009	.006	.005	.002	.001	.001
19	.014	.009	.007	.004	.003	.002	.001	
20	.012	.007	.005	.003	.002	.001	.001	
21	.009	.006	.004	.003	.002	.001		
22	.007	.004	.003	.002	.001	.001		
23	.006	.003	.002	.001	.001			
24	.005	.003	.002	.001	.001			
25	.004	.002	.001	.001	.001			
26	.003	.002	.001	.001				
27	.002	.001	.001					
28	.002	.001	.001					
29	.002	.001						
30	.001	.001						

APPENDIX B

Present Value of $1 Received Annually

Periods Until Payment	2%	5%	8%	10%	13%	15%
1	1.02000	1.05000	1.08000	1.10000	1.13000	1.15000
2	1.04040	1.10250	1.16640	1.21000	1.27690	1.32250
3	1.06120	1.15762	1.25971	1.33100	1.44289	1.52087
4	1.08243	1.21550	1.36048	1.46410	1.63047	1.74900
5	1.10408	1.27628	1.46932	1.61051	1.84243	2.01135
6	1.12616	1.34009	1.58687	1.77156	2.08195	2.31305
7	1.14868	1.40709	1.71382	1.94871	2.35260	2.66001
8	1.17165	1.47745	1.85092	2.14358	2.65844	3.05901
9	1.19509	1.55132	1.99900	2.35794	3.00403	3.51787
10	1.21899	1.62889	2.15892	2.59374	3.39456	4.04555
11	1.24337	1.71033	2.33163	2.85311	3.83585	4.65238
12	1.26823	1.79585	2.51816	3.13842	4.33451	5.35024
13	1.29360	1.88564	2.71961	3.45226	4.89800	6.15277
14	1.31947	1.97992	2.93718	3.79749	5.53474	7.07569
15	1.34586	2.07892	3.17216	4.17724	6.25425	8.13704
16	1.37277	2.18286	3.42593	4.59496	7.06731	9.35760
17	1.40023	2.29201	3.70000	5.05446	7.98606	10.7612
18	1.42823	2.40661	3.99600	5.55990	9.02425	12.3754
19	1.45680	2.52694	4.31568	6.11589	10.1974	14.2317
20	1.48593	2.65328	4.66094	6.72748	11.5230	16.3664
21	1.51565	2.78595	5.03381	7.40023	13.0210	18.8214
22	1.54596	2.92524	5.43652	8.14025	14.7137	21.6446
23	1.57688	3.07151	5.87144	8.95428	16.6265	24.8913
24	1.60842	3.22508	6.34115	9.84971	18.7880	28.6250
25	1.64059	3.38633	6.84844	10.8346	21.2304	32.9188
26	1.67340	3.55565	7.39632	11.9181	23.9904	37.8566
27	1.70687	3.73343	7.98802	13.1099	27.1091	43.5351
28	1.74100	3.92010	8.62707	14.4209	30.6333	50.0653
29	1.77582	4.11611	9.31723	15.8630	34.6156	57.5751
30	1.81134	4.32191	10.0626	17.4493	39.1157	66.2114
31	1.84757	4.53801	10.8676	19.1942	44.2007	76.1431
32	1.88452	4.76491	11.7370	21.1136	49.9468	87.5646
33	1.92221	5.00315	12.6759	23.2250	56.4399	100.699
34	1.96065	5.25331	13.6900	25.5475	63.7771	115.804
35	1.99986	5.51598	14.7852	28.1022	72.0681	133.174
36	2.03986	5.79177	15.9680	30.9125	81.4369	153.150
37	2.08066	6.08136	17.2454	34.0037	92.0237	176.123
38	2.12227	6.38543	18.6251	37.4041	103.986	202.542
39	2.16472	6.70470	20.1151	41.1445	117.505	232.923
40	2.20801	7.03994	21.7243	45.2589	132.780	267.861
41	2.25217	7.39193	23.4622	49.7848	150.042	308.040
42	2.29721	7.76153	25.3392	54.7633	169.547	354.247
43	2.34316	8.14961	27.3663	60.2396	191.588	407.384
44	2.39002	8.55709	29.5556	66.2636	216.495	468.491
45	2.43782	8.98494	31.9201	72.8900	244.639	538.765
46	2.48658	9.43419	34.4737	80.1790	276.442	619.580
47	2.53631	9.90590	37.2316	88.1969	312.379	712.517
48	2.58703	10.4011	40.2101	97.0166	352.989	819.394
49	2.63877	10.9212	43.4269	106.718	398.877	942.303
50	2.69155	11.4673	46.9010	117.390	450.731	1083.64

Periods Until Payment	18%	20%	23%	25%	28%	30%
1	1.18000	1.20000	1.23000	1.25000	1.28000	1.30000
2	1.39240	1.44000	1.51290	1.56250	1.63840	1.69000
3	1.64303	1.72800	1.86086	1.95312	2.09715	2.19700
4	1.93877	2.07360	2.28886	2.44140	2.68435	2.85610
5	2.28775	2.48832	2.81530	3.05175	3.43597	3.71293
6	2.69955	2.98598	3.46282	3.81469	4.39804	4.82680
7	3.18547	3.58318	4.25927	4.76837	5.62949	6.27485
8	3.75885	4.29981	5.23890	5.96046	7.20575	8.15730
9	4.43544	5.15977	6.44385	7.45057	9.22336	10.6044
10	5.23382	6.19173	7.92594	9.31322	11.8059	13.7858
11	6.17591	7.43008	9.74890	11.6415	15.1115	17.9215
12	7.28758	8.91609	11.9911	14.5519	19.3427	23.2980
13	8.59934	10.6993	14.7491	18.1898	24.7587	30.2874
14	10.1472	12.8391	18.1414	22.7373	31.6912	39.3736
15	11.9737	15.4070	22.3139	28.4216	40.5647	51.1857
16	14.1289	18.4884	27.4461	35.5270	51.9228	66.5415
17	16.6721	22.1860	33.7587	44.4088	66.4612	86.5039
18	19.6731	26.6232	41.5232	55.5110	85.0703	112.455
19	23.2143	31.9479	51.0735	69.3887	108.890	146.191
20	27.3929	38.3375	62.8204	86.7359	139.379	190.049
21	32.3236	46.0050	77.2691	108.419	178.405	247.063
22	38.1418	55.2060	95.0410	135.524	228.358	321.182
23	45.0074	66.2472	116.900	169.406	292.299	417.537
24	53.1087	79.4966	143.787	211.757	374.142	542.798
25	62.6683	95.3959	176.858	264.696	478.902	705.638
26	73.9486	114.475	217.536	330.871	612.995	917.329
27	87.2593	137.370	267.569	413.588	784.634	1192.52
28	102.966	164.844	329.110	516.985	1004.33	1550.28
29	121.499	197.812	404.805	646.232	1285.54	2015.37
30	143.369	237.375	497.911	807.790	1645.49	2619.98
31	169.176	284.850	612.430	1009.73	2106.23	3405.97
32	199.627	341.820	753.289	1262.17	2695.97	4427.76
33	235.560	410.184	926.546	1577.71	3450.85	5756.09
34	277.961	492.221	1139.65	1972.14	4417.08	7482.92
35	327.994	590.665	1401.77	2465.17	5653.87	9727.80
36	387.033	708.798	1724.17	3081.47	7236.95	12646.1
37	456.700	850.558	2120.73	3851.83	9263.30	16439.9
38	538.906	1020.66	2608.50	4814.79	11857.0	21371.9
39	635.909	1224.80	3208.46	6018.49	15176.9	27783.5
40	750.372	1469.76	3946.40	7523.11	19426.5	36118.6
41	885.439	1763.71	4854.08	9403.89	24865.9	46954.2
42	1044.81	2116.45	5970.51	11754.8	31828.4	61040.4
43	1232.88	2539.74	7343.73	14693.5	40740.3	79352.5
44	1454.80	3047.69	9032.79	18366.9	52147.6	103158
45	1716.66	3657.23	11110.3	22958.7	66749.0	134105
46	2025.66	4388.68	13665.7	28698.3	85438.7	174337
47	2390.28	5266.41	16808.8	35872.9	109361	226638
48	2820.53	6319.70	20674.8	44841.2	139982	294630
49	3328.23	7583.64	25430.0	56051.5	179177	383019
50	3927.31	9100.36	31278.9	70064.3	229347	497924

Present Value of $1 Received Annually

Periods Until Payment	33%	35%	40%	45%	50%
1	1.33000	1.35000	1.40000	1.45000	1.50000
2	1.76890	1.82250	1.96000	2.10250	2.25000
3	2.35263	2.46037	2.74400	3.04862	3.37500
4	3.12900	3.32150	3.84160	4.42050	5.06250
5	4.16157	4.48403	5.37824	6.40973	7.59375
6	5.53490	6.05344	7.52953	9.29411	11.3906
7	7.36141	8.17214	10.5413	13.4764	17.0859
8	9.79068	11.0324	14.7578	19.5408	25.6288
9	13.0216	14.8937	20.6610	28.3342	38.4433
10	17.3187	20.1065	28.9254	41.0846	57.6649
11	23.0338	27.1438	40.4956	59.5727	86.4974
12	30.6350	36.6441	56.6938	86.3804	129.746
13	40.7446	49.4696	79.3714	125.251	194.619
14	54.1903	66.7839	111.120	181.614	291.928
15	72.0731	90.1583	155.568	263.341	437.893
16	95.8573	121.713	217.795	381.845	656.839
17	127.490	164.313	304.913	553.675	985.259
18	169.561	221.823	426.878	802.829	1477.88
19	225.517	299.461	597.629	1164.10	2216.83
20	299.938	404.272	836.681	1687.94	3325.24
21	398.917	545.767	1171.35	2447.52	4987.87
22	530.560	736.786	1639.89	3548.90	7481.80
23	705.645	994.661	2295.85	5145.91	11222.7
24	938.507	1342.79	3214.19	7461.57	16834.0
25	1248.21	1812.76	4499.87	10819.2	25251.0
26	1660.12	2447.23	6299.81	15687.9	37876.6
27	2207.96	3303.77	8819.74	22747.5	56814.9
28	2936.59	4460.09	12347.6	32983.9	85222.4
29	3905.67	6021.12	17286.6	47826.6	127833
30	5194.54	8128.51	24201.3	69348.6	191750
31	6908.73	10973.4	33881.9	100555	287625
32	9188.62	14814.2	47434.6	145805	431438
33	12220.8	19999.1	66408.5	211417	647157
34	16253.7	26998.8	92971.9	306555	970736
35	21617.4	36448.5	130160	444505	
36	28751.2	49205.4	182224	644533	
37	38239.1	66427.3	255114	934573	
38	50858.0	89676.9	357160		
39	67641.1	121063	500024		
40	89962.7	163436	700034		
41	119650	220638	980048		
42	159135	297862			
43	211649	402113			
44	281493	542853			
45	374386	732852			
46	497934	989350			
47	662252				
48	880795				

Appendix C

Areas Under the Standard Normal Probability Distribution Between the Mean and Successive Values of z.

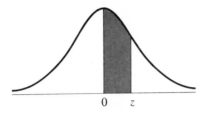

Example If $z = 1.00$, then the area between the mean and this value of z is 0.3413.

z	.00	.01	.02	.03	.04	.05	.06	.07	.08	.09
0.0	.0000	.0040	.0080	.0120	.0160	.0199	.0239	.0279	.0319	.0359
0.1	.0398	.0438	.0478	.0517	.0557	.0596	.0636	.0675	.0714	.0753
0.2	.0793	.0832	.0871	.0910	.0948	.0987	.1026	.1064	.1103	.1141
0.3	.1179	.1217	.1255	.1293	.1331	.1368	.1406	.1443	.1480	.1517
0.4	.1554	.1591	.1628	.1664	.1700	.1736	.1772	.1808	.1844	.1879
0.5	.1915	.1950	.1985	.2019	.2054	.2088	.2123	.2157	.2190	.2224
0.6	.2257	.2291	.2324	.2357	.2389	.2422	.2454	.2486	.2518	.2549
0.7	.2580	.2612	.2642	.2673	.2704	.2734	.2764	.2794	.2823	.2852
0.8	.2881	.2910	.2939	.2967	.2995	.3023	.3051	.3078	.3106	.3133
0.9	.3159	.3186	.3212	.3238	.3264	.3289	.3315	.3340	.3365	.3389
1.0	.3413	.3438	.3461	.3485	.3508	.3531	.3554	.3577	.3599	.3621
1.1	.3643	.3665	.3686	.3708	.3729	.3749	.3770	.3790	.3810	.3830
1.2	.3849	.3869	.3888	.3907	.3925	.3944	.3962	.3980	.3997	.4015
1.3	.4032	.4049	.4066	.4082	.4099	.4115	.4131	.4147	.4162	.4177
1.4	.4192	.4207	.4222	.4236	.4251	.4265	.4279	.4292	.4306	.4319
1.5	.4332	.4345	.4357	.4370	.4382	.4394	.4406	.4418	.4429	.4441
1.6	.4452	.4463	.4474	.4484	.4495	.4505	.4515	.4525	.4535	.4545
1.7	.4554	.4564	.4573	.4582	.4591	.4599	.4608	.4616	.4625	.4633
1.8	.4641	.4649	.4656	.4664	.4671	.4678	.4686	.4693	.4699	.4706
1.9	.4713	.4719	.4726	.4732	.4738	.4744	.4750	.4756	.4761	.4767
2.0	.4772	.4778	.4783	.4788	.4793	.4798	.4803	.4808	.4812	.4817
2.1	.4821	.4826	.4830	.4834	.4838	.4842	.4846	.4850	.4854	.4857
2.2	.4861	.4864	.4868	.4871	.4875	.4878	.4881	.4884	.4887	.4890
2.3	.4893	.4896	.4898	.4901	.4904	.4906	.4909	.4911	.4913	.4916
2.4	.4918	.4920	.4922	.4925	.4927	.4929	.4931	.4932	.4934	.4936
2.5	.4938	.4940	.4941	.4943	.4945	.4946	.4948	.4949	.4951	.4952
2.6	.4953	.4955	.4956	.4957	.4959	.4960	.4961	.4962	.4963	.4964
2.7	.4965	.4966	.4967	.4968	.4969	.4970	.4971	.4972	.4973	.4974
2.8	.4974	.4975	.4976	.4977	.4977	.4978	.4979	.4979	.4980	.4981
2.9	.4981	.4982	.4982	.4983	.4984	.4984	.4985	.4985	.4986	.4986
3.0	.49865	.4987	.4987	.4988	.4988	.4989	.4989	.4989	.4990	.4990
4.0	.49997									

From *Statistical Analysis for Decision Making* by Morris Hamburg,
© 1970 By Harcourt Brace Jovanovich, Inc. and reprinted with their permission.

Index

Index

Commercial bank (Continued)
    effects of changes in reserves on,
        484–85
    Federal Reserve membership, 483
    insurance of, 504
    management of liabilities, 508–16
    management styles, 500
    models of operations, 501–5
    operation of money desk, 505
    as a pool, 499
    role in money creation, 476
Commercial paper, 137, 184
Common stock, 339–401
    effect of corporate actions on price
        of, 361
    effect of purchases and sales on
        price of, 355
    price conformity to market move-
        ments, 390
    price movements over a business
        cycle, 347
    relationship to macroeconomic vari-
        ables, 348
    trading markets, 349
    use in mergers, 410
    valuation paradoxes, 361
    See also Valuation models
Comparative ratio analysis, 386–88
Compensating balance, 132, 181
Compound interest, 209
Computers in security analysis, 295
Conglomerates, 406
Constraints in capital budgeting,
        209–305
    economic functions, 298
    fixed capital, 270
    growth in earnings, 276
Consumption function, 461
Conversion premium, 413
Convertible bonds, 195, 413
Cooper, J. Philip, 497
Cooper, W. W., 286, 333
Cootner, Paul H., 359, 405
Copeland, Morris, 107
Corporate bonds, 55–58, 178
    demand for, 55
    distribution of ownership, 56
    supply of, 55
Corporate goals, 343
Corporate income taxes, effect on
    mergers, 409–17

Corporate income taxes (Continued)
    effect on segmented financial state-
        ments, 74
    effect on short term financial plan-
        ning, 114
    effect on working capital, 22
    relationship to financial variables,
        48–54
Cost of capital, 230–40
    capital structure proportions, 232
    computation of weighted average
        cost formula, 230
    cost of debt, 234
    cost of equity, 234
    cost of retained earnings, 235
    defined, 231
    in a dividend model, 252
    effect of different stock valuation
        models, 233, 247
    effect of variable income streams,
        239
    evaluation of weighted average cost
        formula, 236
    opportunity cost, 230
    in a public utility, 256–64
    relationship between return and
        cost, 229
    relationship to total wealth, 237
    target rate of return, 228
Costs, measurement of, 28
    timing of, 25
Council for Economic Advisors, 473
Cragg, John G., 403
Cramer, Joe, Jr., 86
Credit analysis policy, 4, 5
Crockett, Jean, 267
Crum, M. Colyer, 150, 404
Culbertson, John M., 200
Current assets, 59
Current liabilities, 59
Current ratio, 58
Customer profitability to a bank, 507

D

Daellenbach, Hans G., 518
Dalleck, Winston C., 173
Darling, Paul G., 381
Davidson, J. J., 150
Davidson, Sidney, 65
Davis, Richard G., 518
Dealers, 349
Dean, Joel, 226

Weston, J. Fred, 15, 129, 245, 422, 424
Whitmore, G. A., 359
Whitin, T. M., 173
Wiesenberger, Arthur, 446
Williams, Charles M., 518
Williamson, J. Peter, 200
Wippern, Ronald F., 245, 444
Wood, John H., 201
Woods, Donald H., 334
Working capital, 21, 22, 33

Working capital (Continued)
   calculation of, 21
   changes in, 24
Wright, F. K., 40

Y

Yield curves, 190

Z

Zeff, Stephen A., 424
Zinbarg, Edward D., 107, 359, 405

A 1
B 2
C 3
D 4
E 5
F 6
G 7
H 8
I 9
J 0

Index